A HANDBOOK FOR LIVING IN TURKEY

Pat Yale

Drawings by Trici Venola

Çitlembik Publications 109

© Çitlembik / Nettleberry Publications, 2006
© Pat Yale, 2006

Second printing, 2007

Library of Congress Cataloging-in-Publication Data

Yale, Pat
    A handbook for living in Turkey /Pat Yale.-2nd ed.-Istanbul:
Çitlembik Publications,2006.
    584 p.:ill.

ISBN: 978-9944-424-06-6
1. Turkey--Guidebooks.
I. Title.
LC:DR416 2006   DC:915.61

Editor: Nancy Öztürk
Illustrations: Trici Venola
Cover design: Devrim Gülşen

Printed at Ayhan Matbaası
Yüzyıl Mahallesi Matbaacılar Sitesi
5. Cad. No: 47 Bağcılar, İstanbul

In Turkey:
Şehbender Sokak 18/5
Asmalımescit - Tünel
34430 Istanbul
www.citlembik.com.tr

In the USA:
Nettleberry LLC
44030 123rd St.
Eden, South Dakota 57232
www.nettleberry.com

A HANDBOOK FOR LIVING IN TURKEY

Pat Yale

Drawings by Trici Venola

CONTENTS

APPENDICES

INTRODUCTION

In 1998 when I first came to live in Turkey there were still relatively few foreigners who had made the country their home, especially outside Istanbul
and Ankara. However, after 2002 that steady trickle of incomers swelled into
a flood and it quickly became apparent that although each of us knew scattered pieces of the jigsaw puzzle that made up life in Turkey, very little of this
information was stored in a permanent form so that everyone could share
it. These days websites like mymerhaba do a sterling job of keeping people
abreast of what is going on, as do monthly magazines like *Time Out* and *The
Guide*. However, I still felt that there was space for a book which would attempt to explain some aspects of Turkish culture at the same time as describ-
ing how different systems work and helping readers track down a few of the
more elusive retail desirables.

In the ideal world no doubt we would all speak perfect Turkish. However,
the reality is that when people first come to live in the country the Turkish
language often acts as a powerful barrier to getting things done, especially
as few officials speak foreign languages. Consequently I have assumed that
most readers of this book speak only limited Turkish. Apologies in advance to
those for whom my translations and word lists will seem superfluous.

Likewise in that ideal world we would all buy mainly Turkish products and
eat mainly Turkish food. However, most of us continue to crave the little luxuries we grew up with at home and, especially when times are hard, being able
to eat our favourite foods can be a source of great comfort, hence the inclu-
sion in this book of lists of shops selling foreign clothes, beauty products etc
and restaurants serving foreign foods.

As anyone who lives here quickly learns to their cost, accurate information
is often very hard to come by. This perennial problem has been compounded
by the fact that many of Turkey's laws are currently being revised to bring
them into line with EU requirements so that officialdom tends to be more
than usually confused about what is and isn't allowed. During the 18 months
that I have been researching this book it has sometimes felt as if I was shoot-

ing at a moving target as the laws changed almost as soon as I committed the details to paper. However, just as there was never going to be the perfect time to dig up the roads to build Istanbul's new Metro extension, so I decided that it was unlikely that waiting until some theoretically more stable time in the future came along would improve matters and decided to go ahead with the book anyway.

A quick note about currencies. At the time of writing many houses for sale or rent along the coast were being advertised in sterling or euros. Others in Istanbul were being advertised in US dollars. Elsewhere, their prices were being given in Turkish lira. For the sake of comparison I have opted to use euros for all but local and official prices except where the sum at issue is specific to another country when that country's currency has been used. Confused? Well, we probably are too!

Apologies for the clumsy usage of 'Westerners' to describe the amorphous group of settlers from more developed countries living in Turkey. Unfortunately there doesn't seem to be anything better.

I am profoundly grateful to the many friends who have helped me gather information and can almost hear them cheer as they realise they will finally be able to meet me without facing a barrage of questions about their lives. Particularly warm thanks are due to Ruth Lockwood of Tribal Collections in Göreme who read an early draft of the text and made innumerable helpful suggestions. Yvette and Şenol Koç, and Kylie Warner-Boyraz also answered many and varied questions on everything from building permits to health-care with great patience. Other people who have been especially helpful include Bron Barnacle, Chris and Mebrure Blom, Heather Brown, Faruk Çiftçi, Julie Dowdall, Andus Emge, Sheryl Entwhistle, Dawn Köse, Yılmaz Özlük, Lisa Raffonelli, Linda Robinson, Charlotte Tüzer, Mustafa Turgut, Mark Webster and Ali Yavuz. Esra Erdoğan of Garanti Bankası put me straight about many aspects of banking in Turkey while Corinne Parry of Hallmark Properties and the staff at Turyap and www.evbazar.com answered many questions about the new law for foreign home buyers. Özcan Söyer of Söyer Removals in Izmir was also kind enough to answer my questions about Customs. I am also indebted to the many users of the mymerhaba website who generously helped me fill in the gaps in my knowledge and to my Göreme neighbours who have, over the years, explained so much about their culture to me; I would also like to acknowledge with gratitude the teachers at Dilmer in Istanbul who ensured that I learnt enough Turkish to be able to understand their explanations. Warm thanks, too, to Ken Dakan and the staff of the Side Pension in Istanbul for providing the necessary homes from home on my many research trips. Also to Starbucks on İstiklal Caddesi for supplying the necessary office from office.

Of course without Nancy Öztürk at Çitlembik this project would never have seen the light of day. Without her help some of the more recent changes in the law might also have slipped by unnoticed – I owe a huge debt of thanks to her for all her encouragement and assistance. I would also like to thank Defne Orhun for taking on the vital task of tidying up my Turkish; and Zarife, Metin, Didem, Rachel and everyone else at Çitlembik who helped bring the book to fruition. Finally, the book has been greatly improved by Trici Venola's delightful drawings. Of course any errors and omissions that have crept into the text are entirely of my own making.

Because Turkey is changing so fast I cannot emphasise enough the need to check and recheck the latest news before embarking on costly undertakings, particularly property purchases. Although the author and publishers have done their best to ensure that the information in this book is as accurate as possible, they cannot take responsibility for any expense, damage or inconvenience caused to anyone using it. Should you find anything changed or feel that I have omitted something important I should be grateful if you could email me at pat@livinginturkey.info so that we can update the information as soon as possible.

Pat Yale
Istanbul, July 2006

CHAPTER 1

A NEW LIFE IN TURKEY

More and more people are moving to Turkey and making it their home for at least part of the year. Indeed, by 2004 there were believed to be at least 157,000 foreigners living in the country in addition to those who came and went on a regular basis. Until the mid-1990s most foreigners who were living in Turkey were either on short-term professional contracts (e.g. embassy staff), were English-language teachers or were the rare people who had married Turks. However, the coming of mass tourism has changed all that. Not only do lots of people who come to Turkey on holiday fall in love with Turks and decide to stay but others see what a wonderful country it is and decide to move here, either to retire or to start a new life. Many are Westerners taking advantage of sky-high property prices in their own countries which enable them either to re-mortgage their homes to finance a new life overseas or to sell up and use the proceeds of the sale to turn their dreams into reality.

So why should you think of moving to Turkey? There are many reasons but here are just a few of them:

- **The weather.** Of course it depends where you choose to settle but, if you move to the Turkish coast, chances are that you can give up the dismal northern European winter for the more inviting climate of Turkey.

- **Cheaper prices.** Like everywhere else, Turkey becomes more expensive by the year. However, for the time being it is still a considerably cheaper place to live than most of Western Europe, the USA, Australia or New Zealand.

- **Adventure.** Living in Turkey suits people of adventurous disposition who prefer not to know exactly what is going to happen every day. The only thing that is certain in Turkey is life's unpredictability.

- **The people.** Turkey's culture is famously welcoming and many visitors fall in love with the country because of the warmth and hospitality they experience here. Although there are always individuals who let the side down, in general most Turks are kindly, generous and trusting–even shopkeepers who have only just met you will usually extend short-term credit in a crisis without making a song and dance out of it.

- **Escaping the compensation culture.** Living in Turkey involves running all sorts of risks you probably wouldn't back home. But if you're the sort of person who prefers to take responsibility for your own behaviour then you'll probably find Turkey's relaxed atmosphere a breath of fresh air after the increasingly hamstrung Western world.

- **Escaping the worst excesses of modernisation.** Turkey may be as much in love with the mobile phone as anywhere else but so far you don't have to worry about identity theft here (which means no investing in the latest model of shredder!). And although some of the banks are starting to embrace the 'press one for your balance, press two to transfer cash' culture, so far it is in its infancy and can usually be circumvented.

- **Turkey is forging ahead.** Since the election of 2002 that brought Prime Minister Recep Tayyip Erdoğan to power, Turkey has been on something of a roll, with the infrastructure one of the main beneficiaries of IMF loans. There are still plenty of Cassandras who point to weaknesses underlying signs of apparent boom – huge external debt, locals living on credit, a tourism industry heavily slanted towards cheap package holidays whose chief beneficiaries are the international travel companies that organise them. But since the effective collapse of the economy in 2001 and the halving in value of the lira, the currency has remained stable for the last three years. The dodgiest banks have been weeded out, and Turkey has been working hard to adapt its systems to the European norms that would facilitate its entry to the European Union. It's a good feeling to live in a country where things seem to be improving rather than in one where they sometimes seem to be going backwards. And life gets easier every day.

Of course there are also reasons why a move to Turkey would not be right for everyone.

- Living in Turkey is unlikely to suit anyone who has to know exactly what is going to happen every day. Instead it's a country where the simplest trip to the supermarket can turn into an unexpected adventure.

- Nor would it suit anyone who hates the idea of learning another language. If you live in one of the coastal resorts where many people speak English you will be able to manage without Turkish but of course you will miss out on a lot of what makes the country tick.

- Although things are improving Turkey is still a tough country to live in if you are disabled or have mobility problems.

- Nor is Turkey particularly welcoming to gays and lesbians, although there are pockets of Istanbul where it is possible to lead an openly gay lifestyle.

- People who are fanatically opposed to smoking won't want to live in Turkey. Although public transport is largely smoke-free, few restaurants, let alone hotels, so much as acknowledge the existence of non-smokers.

- Inevitably a Middle-Eastern-shaped cloud hangs over Turkey's future. For all the promising work being done by the current government, the miasma of the Middle East casts a long shadow, periodically battering the tourism industry which is one of the mainstays of the economy. It probably doesn't pay to make too much of this but in the event that the chasm between the Islamic world and the West widens there can be no certainty over which side Turkey would take. The situation in the ex-Yugoslavia serves as a grim reminder that friends and neighbours can be persuaded to turn on each other under the influence of constant propaganda.

THE 'NEW' TURKEY

Turkey has changed enormously in the last five years, and particularly in the last three years. A rapid rise in the number of foreigners living in the country is just one aspect, albeit a particularly conspicuous one, of that change. In 2000 it is thought that around 300 British people owned properties in Turkey but by 2005 that figure had risen to an estimated 30,000 with many more waiting for permission for their sales to be completed. Since most of them settle in the same areas their presence can be very obvious especially around Marmaris, Dalyan and Fethiye. But it is not only the British who are settling. The number of Germans, Dutch, French and Belgians living in Turkey has also grown enormously while there are also plenty of Australians, New Zealanders, Americans and Japanese, as well as many Russians and East Europeans.

There are lots of reasons why there has been this sudden surge in settlement. Obviously the difference in house prices between Turkey and other countries kickstarted the boom which may well slow down again as Turkish prices rise in response to the demand. However, on their own house price differentials would not be enough to explain what has been happening since Turkish houses were much cheaper than those in Northern Europe long be-

WHAT YOU NEED TO KNOW ABOUT...

Atatürk

Mustafa Kemal was born in Thessaloniki (Salonica, then part of the Ottoman Empire) in 1881. He was the son of Zübeyde Hanım and Ali Rıza Bey – there were no surnames in those days. In 1909 he played a part in the events that brought the Young Turks to power but it wasn't until 1915 when he played a heroic part in the battle for Gallipoli that he really became a force to reckon with. When it became apparent that the victorious allies intended to partition Turkey amongst themselves Mustafa Kemal left Istanbul for Samsun on the Black Sea and started the ball rolling towards the Turkish War of Independence. There followed conventions in Amasya, Sivas, and Erzurum and eventually Mustafa Kemal became president of a new Grand National Assembly in Ankara. He took an active part in the battle of Sakarya which played a crucial role in turning the tide in favour of the Turkish nationalists against the invading Greeks. Mustafa Kemal went on to help negotiate the terms of the 1923 Treaty of Lausanne which put a final end to the war.

With the fighting behind him Mustafa Kemal moved fast to convert Turkey into the forward-looking secular state he wanted. He is best known for introducing the following reforms:

- Moving the capital from Constantinople (renamed Istanbul) to Ankara (1923)
- Abolishing the caliphate (1924) and the dervish orders (1925)
- Banning the wearing of the fez in favour of more European hats (1925)
- Replacing religious with civil marriage (1926)
- Replacing the Arabic alphabet with the Latin one (1928)
- Giving women the vote (1934)
- Introducing surnames – he took the surname 'Atatürk' (Father of the Turks) for himself (1935)
- Encouraging women to remove their veils

Mustafa Kemal Atatürk became the first president of the Turkish Republic in 1923 and has been a revered figure ever since; every schoolchild studies his life history and every square in the country boasts a bust or statue of him. Atatürk was undoubtedly a great man but he was also a flawed human being whose marriage lasted only a short time despite his fine words about women's rights. At 9.05 am on 10 November 1938, Atatürk died of cirrhosis in the Dolmabahçe Palace in Istanbul. The clocks there have stood still at that time ever since. Every year the country grinds to a halt for a minute's commemorative silence on the anniversary of his death.

Recommended reading: *Atatürk* by Patrick Kinross (1964), *Atatürk* by Andrew Mango (1999)

fore the start of the third millennium.

The boom could not have happened without the lifting of exchange controls which made it possible for people to move their money from one country to another and without the modernisation of international banking systems so that people living overseas could continue to have access to their cash at home. Nor could it have happened without the liberalisation of air fares which has led to cheaper fares to Turkey at least in summer.

But at the same time the speed at which Turkey itself was modernising started to accelerate as soon as there was a change of government in 2001. The Internet had already taken off very quickly which made it easier for people to communicate with friends and family even after a move overseas. In 1999 Digitürk also brought satellite television to Turkey which meant that foreigners could watch television in their own language and keep up with some of their favourite programmes from home. Globalisation has improved the range of foreign goods available in the supermarkets and foreign newspapers arrive in Turkey no more than one day late. In 1974 it was hard to find a bank in Istanbul that would change a travellers cheque; today it's often easier to find an ATM machine in Turkey than at home, the Turkish banking system has improved dramatically and Internet banking makes it possible to move your money around from the comfort of your Marmaris home. And of course there are now large expat communities all around Western Turkey so that newcomers have a built-in support network on which to rely.

The Turks, too, have changed. Twenty years ago a foreigner who chose to settle in a rural community was likely to have a tough time of it as villagers with little experience beyond their own community misinterpreted everything they did, sometimes in malicious ways. But by now even the villages have had time to get used to foreigners, and even communities that see few foreign visitors have satellite television to show them how differently life is lived elsewhere. The result is that most communities are more accepting of foreigners and their quirky ways than they used to be. In particular as the lot of young Turkish women has improved, so smaller communities are better able to accept the 'uncovered' foreign female without assuming that she is automatically immoral.

CULTURE SHOCK AND THE TURKISH CHARACTER

If you want to live in Turkey it pays to understand as much as you can about the society you are moving into. If your first experiences of Turkey have been on holiday in one of the resorts you may well have decided that the Turks are very similar to Westerners. However, with longer acquaintance you might come to discover that this isn't the whole picture and that the differences can be very important. The degree of culture shock may not be overwhelming but sometimes the country can seem more profoundly different with longer acquaintance rather than the other way round. That is one of the things that makes living here so endlessly intriguing.

Most people who have never visited the country think of Turkey as a Mus-

THE COST OF LIVING

It is difficult to say much that is meaningful about the cost of living in Turkey since so much depends on whether you are talking about Istanbul and the coast (the most expensive areas) or about remote inland areas (the cheapest).

Most people assume that Turkey is still a cheap place to live and it is certainly true that many locals manage to exist on very low wages (the minimum wage is around YTL700 per month). However, if you want to live a Western lifestyle, with your own well-heated home and car, then you may find that it is not quite as cheap as you had hoped. In general all imported foods (including pet food) are expensive. Electrical goods cost about the same in Turkey as in the UK. Clothes cost about the same or a little more than in the UK. Travelling by bus or train is considerably cheaper than it is in the UK. On the other hand buying a car (even a second-hand one) and petrol are much more expensive. House prices are rising at an astonishing speed and some houses along the coast now cost the same as the cheapest houses in the UK. Private schools and hospitals generally charge lower fees than in the UK (much lower than in the US). And unless you live in an area with natural gas or are prepared to heat your home with wood and coal, you may find heating fuels (electricity and bottled gas) surprisingly costly – you can easily spend more on heating a house through a Turkish winter than you would do in the UK unless you live on the coast.

On the other hand labour costs are still low by Western standards. This means that getting building work done is relatively cheap. It also means that having fittings and furniture hand-made can be a realistic option. Some building materials are also reasonably cheap; marble is much cheaper in Turkey than in the West, for example.

lim country and assume it will be difficult for a non-Muslim to fit in. However, Turkey is very different from the media images of Islamic countries like Iran and Syria. Certainly it *is* Islamic (98% of the population is Muslim). However, for historic reasons to do with its crossroads location and unique history, Turkey wears its Islam pretty lightly. For example the ban on drinking alcohol, which is taken so seriously in countries like Iran and Saudi Arabia, tends to be shrugged off in Turkey. That is not to say that everybody drinks alcohol or that it is always readily available. However, it is generally accepted that foreigners like their beer and wine and only rarely will that be a problem.

Likewise, although women in rural areas still tend to cover their heads and dress in many more layers of clothing than are strictly justified by the need to keep warm, in the big cities many women go bare-headed and many younger women wear clothing as skimpy and skin-tight as in the West. Very few Turks expect foreigners to put on a headscarf although most of them appreciate it if women keep their legs and shoulders covered and if men avoid Lycra-style, leave-nothing-to-the-imagination cycling shorts.

However, while Turkey can seem superficially pretty Westernised–especially if you restrict your travels to Istanbul and the coast–the reality is that the Turkish mindset is often very different from that of the West. Scrape below the surface and you will quickly come up with surprises.

It's never wise to generalise about big groups of people. That said, however, it is probably true to say that Turks are generally more gregarious than people from Western Europe and the USA. Individuality is not a prized virtue; rather, people are admired for fitting in with their family, friends and neighbours. Personal space is not much valued either (although this is changing in the big cities); friends expect to be able to drop in on you at any time of day or night, people will sit almost in your lap on buses, and it is not thought normal to want to eat alone, go to the pictures alone or do anything else alone.

Marriage and children are still hugely important in Turkey even if divorce is becoming more common. Because they are so important – and because a woman's status is still so dependent on her marital status – foreigners have to get used to being asked whether they are married almost in the same breath as they are asked their name; it is not meant to be nosiness or insulting although that is how it can come across to people used to having their private life treated with more circumspection.

Foreigners also have to get used to other unexpected questions and statements. Turks think nothing of enquiring the price of your every purchase (in the same way that they think it quite normal to announce to the assembled crowd exactly how much everyone has given as a wedding gift). Nor do they think it rude to comment on any weight gain or signs of exhaustion or ageing that you may show. This can take some getting used to, especially for women.

Turkish men and women did not traditionally touch each other in public, although this, too, is changing in the big cities. In rural areas, however, men and women are still generally segregated; people move around inside their houses as well as on buses to make sure that unrelated men and women are not seated beside each other. Elderly people are treated with respect; you greet them by kissing their hand and touching it briefly to your forehead. Women greet each other with an embrace and a kiss on each cheek; men are more likely to shake hands. It is still not unknown to come across devout men who would not shake hands with a woman even in a business situation; they may put their hands behind their backs if you reach out to them. Similarly, some men will place change on the counter rather than hand it directly to a woman.

In general Turks are more relaxed about alcohol than other Muslims. However what goes on the coast and in the cities doesn't necessarily go down as well in rural areas. In the country most women would never touch alcohol and even men may do so more rarely than in the West. Even men who drink in the week may opt not to do so on from Thursday night through to Saturday morning as a nod towards Islamic tradition. Rural weddings are often 'dry', at least on the surface.

The Turkish language contains a series of set phrases to deal with routine events such as sickness and death (see p. 438). It is also normal to spin out greetings and farewells, rather than rushing to get things over and done with, as in the West.

'Turkish time' is a jokey concept used to refer to the traditional tendency to treat appointments as approximations rather than fixed points in time. However, in areas visited by many foreigners, most Turks will respect exact appointments as far as they can.

Turks have a horror of draughts which means that houses are often horribly overheated by Western standards. Never offer a Turkish child an iced drink –their parents will have an apoplexy!

TURKEY TODAY

Many Westerners think of Turkey as a developing country, and it's true that when you glimpse mud roofs and women swathed in blankets, and when you trip on a broken pavement in gloomy lighting or sit interminably in someone's outer office waiting for something to happen you can feel that Turkey is still a long way behind Europe in its development. But then you see the up-to-the-minute Eskişehir tram or use your Akbil (electronic purse) to move around Istanbul by public transport or stop off in an Internet café equipped with an ADSL line and suddenly the picture becomes a lot more complicated.

It is probably fair to say that Western Turkey is considerably more developed than Eastern Turkey. But even within the west there will be pockets of under-development while in the east there will be pockets of modernisation. As a rule of thumb it's best to think of Turkish systems and choice of products as about twenty years behind the West. But it's a fast-changing situation–and some of what may register as under-development to economists can actually feel like a slower and more comfortable way of living to people interested in moving here.

EXPAT LIFE

For many people who come to live in Turkey the main attraction is the lively social life on offer in the coastal resorts. In places such as Hisarönü and Ovacık, near Fethiye, so many foreigners have settled that it is possible to have a party lifestyle right through the summer; some of it may involve Turks but much of it is entirely self-contained within the expat community.

WHAT YOU NEED TO KNOW ABOUT...

Islam

If you settle along the coast or in one of the big cities and limit your social life to mixing with foreigners then you can just about get by without knowing much about Islam. However, since most of the Turkish population is Muslim, it is as well to understand at least the basics of their religion.

Muslims believe that there is only one god *(Allah)* and that Mohammed, the last of a string of prophets, is his messenger. This is the essence of what is intoned during the call to prayer *(ezan)* that sounds from the minarets five times a day (see box p. 391), and saying and believing this is one of what are called the five pillars of Islam. The other four are: praying five times a day; fasting during the holy month of Ramadan *(Ramazan)*; giving alms to the poor; and making a pilgrimage to Mecca *(hac)* at least once during your lifetime if you can afford to.

Muslims take their faith from the holy book, the Koran, bestowed on them by Mohammed and regarded as the literal word of Allah. They revere as prophets most of those who appear in the Bible including Moses *(Musa)*, Abraham *(İbrahim)* and Jesus *(İsa)*. However, they do not believe that Jesus was the son of God or that he was crucified and rose from the dead.

There are several versions of the Islamic faith, but most Turks are Sunnis, unlike their Iranian neighbours who are Shiites. There is, however, a sizeable Alevi minority population whose beliefs are markedly different from those of the Sunni majority.

Despite the Koranic prohibition on drinking alcohol, most Turks are fairly relaxed about this (although in rural areas no self-respecting woman would ever touch alcohol). However, very few of them will eat pork. Away from the coast and the big cities most women still wear headscarves and cover themselves up from head to toe, although few of them wear anything like the *chador* or *burka* of Iran or Afghanistan. In rural areas many women wear scarves *(yemeni, yazma)* as much from tradition as profound religious faith.

However, in the last ten years there has been a revival of *hijab*-wearing and a surprising number of young women wear close-fitting scarves *(başörtüsü, türban)*, often with another headdress beneath them, that *do* reflect religious belief.

Recommended reading:

Teach Yourself Islam by Ruqaiyyah Maqsood, 1994. Unfortunately, like most books on Islam published in the West, this looks at Islam as practised in the Arab world which means that the names of festivals etc are given in Arabic rather than Turkish.

For other people, coming to live in Turkey is more about finding a peaceful lifestyle in a beautiful location, perhaps along the coast or in an interesting area like Cappadocia. Depending on where they choose to live they may also find it easy to socialise primarily with other foreigners. However, anyone moving to live in Western, Central or Eastern Anatolia is likely to find themselves either the sole *yabancı* (foreigner) in the area, or one of a very small social circle.

Unusually, away from Istanbul, Ankara and Izmir, the expat population is predominantly female. It also tends to be segregated along national lines, with the British, for example, making up the majority of expats around Fethiye and Altınkum, and the Germans dominating the community around Alanya.

Although there are many happy, well-adjusted foreigners living in Turkey, especially in Istanbul, it has to be said that there are also many oddball characters. It may well be true that you need to be slightly unusual to be able to fit happily into a completely different culture from your own. However, there are also foreigners who settle in other countries because they are unable to make a go of it in their own or because they are running away from drink, drug, marital or financial problems. With a relatively small pool of other foreigners to mix with, settlers are sometimes almost obliged to spend a lot of time with people who would not make natural friends at home. Such friendships can be cemented by shared experiences and the greater dependency on each other that comes from living in a developing country. However, they can also be fragile since they are not based on shared interests or similarity of personality.

FRIENDSHIP VERSUS HOSPITALITY

On short trips to Turkey most people are overwhelmed by the warmth of the welcome they receive. Unfortunately some of them make the mistake of assuming that if a Turk calls them a 'friend' then that is what they really mean even if they have only just met. This is to woefully misunderstand the tradition of hospitality (*misafirperverlik*) which plays such a big part in Turkish culture. Most Turkish women are able to whip up a meal for a seemingly unending stream of visitors; not to be able to do so would be seen as somehow failing in their duty as a housewife. Foreigners are readily incorporated into Turkish hospitality and Turks call strangers 'friends' as a way of making them feel at home. But of course true, meaningful friendship (*dostluk*) takes as long to develop here as anywhere else, so it is unwise to assume that everyone who claims you as a friend (*arkadaş*) will maintain their cordiality once you settle in the country. Nor would you always want all those 'friends' to hang around.

It's not an easy topic to raise but it also has to be said that some expat life, especially along the coast, is based on sexual promiscuity and particularly on relationships between older foreign women and younger Turkish men. Although there is nothing inherently wrong with that, it's worth noting that such relationships are rarely between equals – usually there is a vast disparity in wealth, education and worldly experience between the two people involved. It would be good to be able to report that these relationships were all a great success. In reality few of them last the test of time and during the course of them many foreign women part with large sums of money which could well have supported them through their retirement.

THE TURKS AND THE *YABANCILAR*

However long you stay in Turkey, life as a *yabancı* is never going to be exactly the same as life as a Turk. In general being a foreigner tends to work in your favour since most Turks are very hospitable and rush to help someone whom they perceive as being a guest in their country. Often you will be pushed to the front of queues, brought tea, given a better seat and generally made to feel that you are very special. On the other hand most people find the language hard to learn because the vocabulary is so different from the one they are used to. This can make wading through the bureaucracy involved in trying to live and work in Turkey very daunting.

On top of that Turkey remains fairly monocultural, a reality that tends to be concealed if you arrive on the coast and think all those tourists are typical. Even at its height the Ottoman Empire did not extend beyond the Middle East, North Africa and Southern Europe, which means that Turkey has none of the colonial ties that have so changed the complexion of most European countries. In addition, Turkey is only obliged to accept refugees from Western countries which means that it has not had to deal with the influx of foreigners from the poorer parts of the world that Europe, Australia and the USA have had to. The result is that foreigners still tend to stand out (except in the resorts, of course).

Political correctness has yet to rear its head in Turkey, so people do not feel the same wariness that many Westerners do about probing into people's backgrounds on the assumption that if they look different, then they must have come from somewhere else. What this means in practise is that you will have to get used to being asked over and again where you come from, even if you have lived in Turkey for decades. Since this is asked out of genuine curiosity most foreigners learn to live with it. However, for the children of foreigners born and brought up in Turkey it is likely to become increasingly galling. Only in Istanbul is this a relatively minor problem.

Most Turks have a fairly positive attitude towards foreigners although you can sense this wearing thin towards the end of the tourist season. These days few people still refer to foreigners as *gavur* (infidels), although you will hear the occasional casually anti-Semitic comment and the occasional grumble about 'Christian missionaries' (i.e. anyone who looks as if they come from a country that is nominally Christian).

WHAT YOU NEED TO KNOW ABOUT...

Turkish History I

This is not the place to delve into all the ins and outs of Turkish history - there are plenty of other excellent books that do that. However, there are some aspects of its past that you need to understand to make sense of what you see about you.

The Turks and the Greeks

That the Turks and the Greeks have long shared an antipathy is well-known. However, the reasons why this is so are not always so well-known.

Way back in history Greeks sailed from the mainland of what is modern Greece to establish city-states all around the Eastern Mediterranean. Many of those city-states were along the coast of what is now Turkey (then Asia Minor). In time most of them were absorbed into the Roman Empire as it took over everything that had once been Greece. That is why the coast of Turkey is so densely pockmarked with Graeco-Roman archaeological sites.

In time the Roman Empire outgrew its own strength and split into two. What is now Turkey became part of the Eastern - Byzantine - Roman Empire with its capital in Constantinople. Along the coast and well into the heart of Anatolia many people continued to be Christian and speak a version of Greek even as the Arabs started to penetrate the country from the south, bringing with them their new religion, Islam.

In 1453 Sultan Mehmet the Conqueror (Fatih Sultan Mehmet) seized Constantinople from the last of the Byzantine emperors, bringing to an end an empire that had existed for over a thousand years (an outpost around Trebizond/Trabzon continued to cling on for another 40 years). From then on all of what is modern-day Turkey became part of the rapidly growing Ottoman Empire.

In spite of that fact there continued to be a large population of 'Greeks' living deep in Anatolia well into the 20th century. Unfortunately they became pawns in the power struggle over the dying Ottoman Empire as Greek nationalists in mainland Greece nurtured the *Megali Idea*—the idea that everywhere that had once been Greek should become part of a Greater Greece all over again. At the end of the First World War, when the Ottoman Empire had been defeated, the victorious Allies planned to partition the country amongst themselves. The Greeks were encouraged to invade what is now Turkey, but in so doing they came up against Mustafa Kemal Atatürk and the Turkish nationalists who were determined to create a new Turkish Republic on the soil of Anatolia. The Greeks were defeated and forced out of Turkey. According to the terms of the Treaty of Lausanne which tied up the loose ends of the War of Turkish Independence in 1923, all those 'Greeks' still living in Turkey were forced to return to Greece while all those 'Turks' still living in Greece were forced to return to Turkey. Many more Greeks left Turkey than Turks returned which is why to this day there are so many 'Greek' houses standing empty all along the Turkish coast and into the heart of Cappadocia.

It is this history which underlies the tensions over Cyprus. When there was a coup d'état in Cyprus in 1974 and it appeared that the Greeks were on the verge of taking over the whole island, the Turkish Cypriots felt threatened and appealed for help to their Turkish compatriots in mainland Turkey. The result was the occupation of Northern Cyprus which led to the partition of the island, a division which has continued into the 21st century and was endorsed by referendum as recently as 2003.

Despite all this there is a still a sizeable Greek community, especially in Istanbul but also on Turkey's two Aegean islands, Gökçeada and Bozcaada. The celebrations for their Easter, which takes place on a later date than the Protestant/Catholic version, are still celebrated with gusto in many Istanbul churches.

NETWORKING

Turkey is still like many developing countries in the importance it places on family and personal ties. It would be hard to overemphasise the importance of who you know to easing your life in your new country. A foreigner who speaks no Turkish and has no friends in Turkey is going to find it very hard to get things done on their own. Few people who have spent enough time in Turkey to want to live there are likely to be entirely friendless. Some, however, have 'friends' who are not all they seem. If you think you may want to move to Turkey it is probably wise to be a little reticent at first and try and work out what other locals and resident foreigners think of people before throwing yourself whole-heartedly into new friendships. In particular it is not a good idea to listen to people who advise you not to talk to anyone else–often they are saying this because they know what bad references they will glean from other Turks.

IN CONCLUSION...

Turkey is an exciting country in which to live. The people are welcoming, the climate alluring and the history riveting. Moving here may not always go as smoothly as you might have hoped but, believe me, you are unlikely to regret the decision to do so.

WHAT YOU NEED TO KNOW ABOUT...

Turkish History II

The Ottoman Empire

The Ottoman Empire was one of the world's great superpowers from the 15th through until the early 20th century. What started out as a small Turkic sultanate based around Bursa became a power to reckon with in 1453 when Fatih Sultan Mehmet forced his way into Constantinople and drove out the Byzantine rulers. In so doing he consolidated the hold that the Ottomans had over most of what is now modern Turkey.

Over the next century or so the ascendant Ottomans grabbed large swathes of the Middle East, North Africa and the Balkans. During the reign of Süleyman the Magnificent (Kanuni Sultan Süleyman) they even battered on the gates of Vienna, leaving a legacy of Turkophobia that has lingered into modern times.

However, the Ottoman Empire eventually overreached itself and grew gradually weaker until it was widely derided as 'the Sick Man of Europe'. The fatal mistake came when the last Ottoman sultan took the wrong side in the First World War. Defeat led to the abolition of the sultanate and the founding of the Turkish Republic in 1923.

Perhaps because the Ottoman Empire was associated in most Turks' minds with defeat and because Atatürk regarded so many aspects of Ottoman life as backward-looking and old-fashioned, it has taken almost 80 years for all things Ottoman to come back into fashion. There was a time when no one wanted the many old Ottoman houses slowly rotting away in the city centres. Now, however, these are often properties of choice with people keen to create a boutique hotel or a private home with character. On the back of that revival has come a renewed interest in Ottoman textiles, smoking water pipes and many other aspects of a once reviled lifestyle.

CHAPTER 2

IN SEARCH OF THE PERFECT HOME

For many people the decision as to where to live is made for them. Either they are posted to the country for work - in which case, chances are that they will end up in Istanbul, Ankara, Izmir or Adana - or they fall in love with a Turk and decide to settle wherever they met them. But for a fortunate few - people in retirement, writers, artists, the independently wealthy - the entire country is their oyster and they can choose exactly where they want to live. For those lucky people this chapter outlines what each area of Turkey has to offer for a foreign settler. It also takes into account that some people may be considering buying properties in Turkey for investment purposes and may be interested in locations that are likely to become popular in the future.

It starts with a look at the big cities and then works round the western part of the coast, before moving inland to consider the prospects in Western, Central and Eastern Anatolia and along the Black Sea. It assumes that the reader has visited Turkey before and so does not describe the standard tourist attractions of the various towns, a job better left to conventional guidebooks. What it does do, however, is discuss access to the various regions and the sort of attractions (shops, schools, beaches etc) which are likely to be of most interest to long-term residents.

BEFORE YOU DECIDE:

Before you decide where you'd like to live you should ask yourself some searching questions. Being honest in your answers might help avoid much heartache later.

- What is most important to you – the location or the people?
- If it's the location, will you be able to find enough stimulation locally to keep you happy?
- Is your Turkish good enough to cope if most of your neighbours will be non-English-speaking?

- If the people are more important to you than the place, then do you actually need to buy? Maybe you would be better off renting. Bear in mind that expat communities tend to be very fluid and that friends come and go more than they do at home.

- Will you be able to handle the reduced choice of foods and other goods in Turkey? If choice is important to you, you should probably opt to live in or near to a city.

- Do you want to live in Turkey year-round? If so, have you considered what life will be like in winter when many of the coastal resorts effectively close down, and Central and Eastern Anatolia will be freezing cold and frequently blanketed with snow. Access also becomes trickier as most charter flights only operate in summer which means fewer visits from friends and family.

TOWN, VILLAGE OR COASTAL RESORT?

There are good and bad points to whatever decision you make about where to live, but it helps to be clear about the advantages and drawbacks of living in a town as opposed to a village or coastal resort.

The advantages of town-living are clear: in return for the additional noise, traffic, pollution and expense you are guaranteed a degree of anonymity that is impossible in smaller communities (an important consideration if you have an unconventional lifestyle, for example) as well as your pick of the theatres, cinemas, concert halls and decent shops. However, in Turkey only Istanbul really lives up to the promise of most Western cities. Ankara may be the capital but away from the small upmarket enclaves it is still conservative and inward-looking. Izmir is livelier and more relaxed, but elsewhere Turkish towns are not known for their exciting entertainment possibilities.

If, instead, you opt to live in a village you will have to adjust to goldfish-bowl conditions where your neighbours know what you are doing even before you do it. Entertainment and eating out options are likely to be very limited. Inland villages also suffer from harsh winters that take a lot of getting used to. Access, too, can be a problem except for car-owners. However, most Turkish villages still retain a real sense of community, with everyone taking part in the big events that mark people's lives and someone usually ready to help out in times of need.

In some ways the coastal resorts offer the perfect halfway house between towns and villages. Most have cinemas and good restaurants and shops to cater for their tourists. Their atmosphere also tends to be more relaxed and laid-back even than Istanbul's. On the other hand there may be little sense of being in the 'real' Turkey and most coastal resorts (with the exception of Antalya) turn into ghost towns in winter. People living in the resorts also have to cope with being treated as permanent tourists and charged tourist prices for many necessities.

ISTANBUL

Need to Know Info

Population: Between 12 and 16 million

Airports: Atatürk International Airport, Yeşilköy (Tel: 0212-663 6400, www.dhmiata.gov.tr); Sabiha Gökçen, Kurtköy, near Pendik (Tel: 0216-585 5850, www.sgairport.com)

Railway Stations: Sirkeci (Tel: 0212-527 0051); Haydarpaşa (Tel: 0216-336 0470) (www.tcdd.gov.tr)

Bus Stations: Esenler (Main Bus Terminal, Tel: 0212-658 0505); Harem (Tel: 0216-333 3673)

Climate: Hot (30°C max) in July and August, mild (3°C min) in winter, some snow but not usually long-lasting.

Nearest beaches: Kilyos and Şile on the Black Sea; Princes' Islands; Marmara and Avşa Islands in the Sea of Marmara.

Nearest ski resorts: Kartepe, near İzmit; Uludağ, near Bursa

For many people the most obviously inviting place to live in Turkey is Istanbul, the exotic cultural capital on the Bosphorus which straddles Europe and Asia. Istanbul is vast, vibrant and exciting. It has restaurants to suit all tastes, shops displaying the best that Turkey has to offer, language schools, cinemas, indeed almost all the trappings of Western life. It is here, most of all, that foreigners can live a life that approximates to the one they were used to at home.

In some ways that impression can be deceptive since there are some parts of the city which are extremely eastern in outlook, especially those suburbs which have been settled by recent migrants from the east of the country (e.g. Zeytinburnu). However, those are not the parts of the city where most foreigners choose to live.

People come to live in Istanbul because they are working for one of the consulates; because they work for large international companies with interests in Turkey; as teachers of English; as journalists; or because they are married to a Turk who lives there. However, there are also many foreigners in the city who arrived in Turkey and decided to stay but who relish the wider range of facilities and money-making opportunities in Istanbul. In particular, many English-speaking women find well-paid work nannying for the Istanbul elite who, in turn, prefer to live in the great city on the Bosphorus rather than in less inviting Ankara.

Why Choose Istanbul?

- Because the city with its Bosphorus location and Byzantine and Ottoman monuments is extremely beautiful and historically interesting.

- Because it offers the possibility of living a life as near to the one that you had at home as is possible in Turkey.

- Because the anonymity of a big city means that you need not make the adjustments that will be necessary if you live somewhere smaller.

- Because you are less likely to get bored in Istanbul than anywhere else in Turkey on account of the range of bookshops, cinemas, theatres, concert halls, restaurants etc.

- Because you will find the widest range of other expatriates with whom to socialise in Istanbul.

In 2006 easyJet started flying from London to Istanbul's Sabiha Gökçen airport, bringing air fares from the UK down. There are also many cheap flights to the city from France, Germany and the Netherlands. Competition between Turkish carriers is also hotting up so it is likely that air fares to Istanbul will start to fall, at least out of high season.

Where To Live

The Bosphorus is one of the city's most important features. Not only does it divide European from Asian Turkey but it also provides ready access from some parts of the city to others. Homes overlooking the Bosphorus are by far the most desirable; you'll pay an arm and a leg for a waterside property and even a small apartment with a Bosphorus view will come with the price marked up to reflect the value of what lies beyond its windows. These days it is rarely possible to demolish a waterfront building (which has not prevented sporadic suspicious fires taking out historic *yalı*s (wooden buildings) in prime locations). However, there are fewer truly lovely houses for sale or rent than you might hope.

Most foreigners choose to live in the European suburbs of Istanbul. Popular areas include Cihangir, Çukurcuma, Galatasaray, Şişli, Kurtuluş, Beşiktaş, Nişantaşı, Etiler, Levent, Ortaköy, Bebek, Arnavutköy and the new single family home subdivisions on the city's outskirts. On the Asian side they include: Üsküdar, Kadıköy, Suadiye, Moda, Göztepe and Çengelköy. All these suburbs have different things in their favour and you will have to visit and decide which set of assets most benefits you. Aside from cost, other important considerations might include:

- ease of access by public transport
- traffic and parking problems
- ease of access to shops
- whether there are schools and hospitals nearby
- whether there is work in the vicinity
- what cultural facilities are available locally
- whether there are other foreigners living nearby

These days it would be a fortunate foreigner who was able to live on the Princes' Islands, a group of largely traffic-free islands in the Sea of Marmara to which the well-heeled traditionally move for the summer months.

THE EUROPEAN SIDE

Old Istanbul

Most short-term visitors to Istanbul tend to stay in **Sultanahmet/Cankurtaran**, the area immediately around Sultanahmet Square, and close to Ayasofya, the Blue Mosque and the Topkapı Palace. But for all its beauty and proximity to the major historic landmarks, Sultanahmet is not necessarily a great place to live, not least because the battalions of carpet dealers take forever to distinguish 'local' foreigners from tourists and running the gauntlet of their sales spiel day after day quickly becomes irksome for women in particular. Twenty years ago this was an up-and-coming neighbourhood with many derelict properties but now even the flimsiest wooden property would be worth a small fortune. Although some local families still live in the area, most of it is given over to tourism businesses run by people from all over Turkey; intense competition means that it is increasingly hard for someone to make a go of a new business here. Rents in the area are generally high and such normal shops as there are charge tourist prices for everything. On the upside there is always someone around who speaks English. With the tramway and Cankurtaran station nearby, transport connections are also excellent.

A little away from the hectic activity of Sultanahmet is **Kumkapı** which is famed for its seafood restaurants. This is an area which retains a mixed residential population from many parts of Turkey. It has its own train station and boasts easy access to the shores of the Sea of Marmara. Apartments here tend to have large rooms and to be relatively cheap to rent (around €185 a month).

Fener and **Balat** stand side by side on the western shore of the Golden

Horn and are accessible from Eminönü by bus or ferry. Unusually for such a central location both suburbs are still residential areas with fine old houses crumbling away alongside reminders of the days when this was a Greek and Armenian neighbourhood – there are several churches here as well as the home of the Greek Patriarch who is still head of the Greek Orthodox Church. There are lots of local shops and several inviting restaurants, either inland or overlooking the shores of the Golden Horn. Parts of Fener and Balat are very hilly which means good views but steep hauls home with the shopping. For the time being both Fener and Balat are very run-down. However, UNESCO has big plans for the twin suburbs which might make them attractive to someone looking for a place to buy in central Istanbul as a long-term investment. You would certainly need to learn Turkish to be able to communicate with your neighbours.

Central Istanbul

Most permanent residents of Istanbul prefer to live either across the Golden Horn in Beyoğlu or along the shores of the Bosphorus. For single people and childless couples **Cihangir** is a particularly popular part of the city. It lies south-east of Taksim Square, the heart of modern Turkey, in close proximity to İstiklal Caddesi, a hectic pedestrianised thoroughfare. Many Cihangir apartment blocks date back to the 19th century when this area was very popular with European settlers. In recent years Cihangir has gained a reputation as a popular place for gay people to live. However, it is also popular with writers, artists and professionals. Sıraselviler Caddesi, the main drag, is a narrow, busy thoroughfare where traffic noise would be a constant intrusion. However, it is very much the heart of the neighbourhood with shops, supermarkets, several good delicatessens selling European foods and wines, and a pleasant tea garden in the lee of the local mosque. There are popular bars and nightclubs at the Taksim end of Sıraselviler Caddesi which is also the location of both the Taksim İlkyardım Hastanesi (State First Aid Hospital) and the Alman Hastanesi (German Hospital). Many Cihangir apartment blocks have Bosphorus views, which inevitably inflate their price. However, some have been blighted by noise blaring from nightclubs across the Bosphorus and from İstiklal Caddesi on summer nights. This is also an area with very steep streets, some of them stepped, making it suitable only for the reasonably fit.

Çukurcuma, near Cihangir, is an increasingly popular neighbourhood famed for its antique shops. The Ali Paşa Hamamı has a gay and straight clientele, and offers separate sessions for women. The area has its own local shops and offers easy access both to Sıraselviler Caddesi and Istiklal Caddesi.

As prices in Cihangir and Çukurcuma have soared, so **Galatasaray**, the area directly east of Istiklal Caddesi, has grown in popularity. Galatasaray has much the same appeal as Cihangir although there are fewer shops. Recently one entire street was rebranded as 'Fransız Sokağı (French St)', a stepped area of restaurants and bars given a superficially French makeover; local property prices have soared in expectation that other streets will get a similar treatment. However, the apartments around French St are likely to be noisier as a result of what has been done to make them more attractive. Like Cihangir, Galatasaray has a lot of very steep and/or stepped streets which limit its appeal for older or less able residents and mothers with young children. Lucky buyers have found apartments in the area with original frescoed ceilings, albeit usually in need of restoration.

Until recently the southern end of Istiklal Caddesi was run-down and neglected. Now, however, as the Beyoğlu beautification project has got into its stride and buyers have been priced out of the northern end, some of the buzziest parts of Istanbul are around **Tepebaşı** and **Galata**, the district around the Galata Tower. These areas have all the same pluses as the Cihangir-Galatasaray neighbourhood - fine old apartment blocks, decent local shops, proximity to an exciting nightlife, good transport links etc - although the back streets can still feel pretty heavy at night.

Property buyers in search of a bargain have been scouring the fringes of Beyoğlu for bargains, and **Tarlabaşı, Kasımpaşa, Karaköy,** even **Hasköy,** have been identified as possible future hot spots. Most contain interesting old buildings just crying out for restoration. However, in the short-term they also tend to have either high crime rates or very conservative local populations.

Harbiye is an upmarket neighbourhood within easy walking distance of Taksim Square but without the steep hills of Cihangir and Galatasaray. Cumhuriyet Caddesi, the main thoroughfare, boasts some luxurious shops as well as many airline offices and classy hotels. A little further from the buzz of Istiklal Caddesi are the suburbs of **Şişli, Osmanbey, Feriköy** and **Kurtuluş,** four of Istanbul's more upmarket and family-friendly central suburbs, with some attractive and expensive shops on their doorsteps. All four are within easy reach of Taksim and Istiklal Caddesi and close to the metro. They are also handy for the vast new Cevahir Shopping Mall. Şisli is increasingly popular with foreigners and some local shops sell foreign foodstuffs, but rents have soared recently - you are unlikely to find anything for less than €290 a month.

However, street parking is virtually impossible in the narrow streets so if you have a car you will need to factor in the cost of garaging. Rents start to come down when you get to Dolapdere, an adjacent area with a poor reputation.

The Downside of Living In Istanbul

- The traffic can be horrific especially if you need to cross over one of the two Bosphorus bridges during rush hour or to drive along the European shore of the Bosphorus over the weekend.

- In a big city noise and crowding are inevitable problems.

- Unfortunately in the last few years the crime rate in Istanbul has soared with street theft burglary and car crime blighting people's lives in the same way that they do in other big cities.

- Geologists all agree that it is only time before a huge earthquake hits Istanbul. Some parts of the city are thought to be more at risk than others. However no one doubts that many of the flimsy apartment blocks thrown up over the last 20 years will come down. Properties thought to be at particular risk often look invitingly cheap but compulsory earthquake insurance is likely to prove small comfort if the worst comes to the worst.

Nişantaşı and **Teşvikiye** are particularly swanky parts of town, clean, leafy and with wonderful shops if you can afford their price tags. Rents are generally high although some flats can be found in Nişantaşı for about €620 a month. The area is within walking distance of the metro to Taksim and has lots of good cafes and several cinemas but parking is usually a problem.

Etiler/Ulus is a particularly wealthy area of Istanbul near to the vast Akmerkez Shopping Mall. It has wide tree-lined streets with good pavements and is full of wealthy people and expensive clubs and restaurants.

Just north of the centre and connected to Taksim Square by metro **Levent** is an important banking and financial district divided into two parts : 1. Levent and 4. Levent. Rents and apartment prices tend to be higher on the Akmerkez side of Levent but there are cheaper places in adjoining Gültepe and Çeliktepe. The Tuesday market in 4. Levent is a great place to come for upmarket clothes and other pricey goods.

Bosphorus Suburbs

For people who prefer a waterside location **Beşiktaş** is a pleasant, if rather run-down, waterside suburb with easy access to shops, supermarkets, a market, restaurants and an excellent cultural centre. Lots of university students live here which means that there is plenty of cheap, if sometimes noisy, accommodation. It has good connections by ferry to other parts of the city and frequent dolmuşes to Taksim. The extension to the tramway should eventually ease the heavy flow of traffic through the area.

Ortaköy is another popular waterside suburb with a lively bar scene and a great Sunday handicrafts market. It has reasonable access by ferry to the other side of the Bosphorus during commuting hours, and hopefully the extended tramway will ease the traffic congestion that used to plague it. It would be tough finding anywhere to rent near the popular waterfront square where most buildings now house restaurants. Ortaköy is convenient for Kabataş High School and Galatasaray University.

Arnavutköy is an upmarket suburb with some gorgeous wooden houses still lining the waterfront. Since 1979 it has been part of a conservation area where buildings cannot be demolished. Many of the houses in the area are narrow-fronted and attached to the neighbouring properties on both sides. The Migros and Macro supermarkets in Kuruçeşme are good for the weekly shop.

Bebek is another pleasant waterside suburb in the shadow of Bosphorus University. It is more upmarket than Beşiktaş or Ortaköy and has a good English-language bookshop and some pleasant cafes and restaurants. Again, nearby Kuruçeşme is handy for the weekly shop and the area is convenient for the Yeni Yıldız College and Bebek primary school. Parking can be a nightmare.

If you're hoping to live in a traditional waterfront home, or *yalı*, **Rumelihisarı**, in the shadow of the great medieval castle that gave it its name, is a good place to start hunting. Should you find something, it is likely to cost between €2,900,000 and €4,250,000 to buy; a mere €8,250 per month to rent. There are also a few *yalı*s that have been divided into flats; to buy one of those is likely to cost you between €410,000 and €750,000; to rent between €1,650 and €2,500 per month. However, there are several significant drawbacks to living in this neighbourhood: parking is a nightmare, and there is no access to cable TV or natural gas.

Centred on the inviting Çınaraltı Meydanı, **Emirgan** is another attractive waterside suburb with some fine old wooden houses. Emirgan wood, a landscaped park just inland from the Bosphorus, makes a fine place for family picnics. Inland Emirgan also has spacious, modern apartments in lovely settings, some with great views.

If you don't mind the sky-high prices, **Yeniköy** is a particularly pleasing, upmarket suburb where a lot of wealthy individuals live behind hefty security fences. Apartments here rent for between €500 and €2,500 a month; you'll pay between €82,500 and €660,000 to buy one. When the odd wooden *yalı* comes on the market it goes for between €3,250,000 and; €5,000,000; apartments in them go for between €825,000 and €1,250,000. As usual, there are problems with parking and weekend traffic but commuter ferries ease the path to work.

People coming to work for NATO or the US Embassy sometimes find themselves living inland from Yeniköy in **Maslak,** a family-oriented modern suburb with little oriental character. The big drawback to living here is distance from anything interesting other than work which can mean hours spent stuck in traffic jams at weekends. However, it is handy for the big Parkorman entertainment centre, the Belgrade Forest and the Black Sea beaches. A metro extension should eventually make access to central Istanbul much easier.

Back on the waterfront, **Tarabya** is a sleepy, upmarket residential neighbourhood popular with foreigners despite being plagued by noise and traffic problems. A few *yalı*s here fetch slightly lower prices than in Yeniköy – between €825,000 and €3,300,000 to buy and from €2,500 to €5,750 per month to rent. The best shops are in nearby Yeniköy, Sarıyer and Maslak. Many people working for Adidas and Nike live here.

With one of the most attractive waterside settings along the Bosphorus, **Sarıyer** is further from the town centre than other waterside suburbs but has a less congested location, with a wider variety of shops close at hand. This is one of the better suburbs for access by public transport, with ferries to back up the buses and dolmuşes.

Outlying Surburbs

Past Sarıyer and hidden away beyond the Belgrade Forest is **Zekeriyaköy,** a secluded, upmarket suburb which has become especially popular with British families because of its proximity to the British International School. Even the shops and cafes have a British feel to them. Of course it's very long way from the town centre which is also true of **Kemerburgaz (Kemer County)**, another upmarket, family-friendly suburb way inland from Tarabya. The huge free-standing houses here are vaguely reminiscent of those around Boston (hence the area's nickname – 'Little America') and residents are free to use a range of facilities including a swimming pool and children's play area (although they must pay to join the local golf club).

Still on the European side although far from the historic town centre is **Bakırköy** which has lots of cheap accommodation and is popular with students. It is near the airport and within easy reach of the tram into town. Many businesses are based in this area where there are also several English-language schools. A big draw for music fans would be proximity to the large Mydonose Showland concert venue near the airport.

THE ASIAN SIDE

Üsküdar is a pleasant waterside suburb with several interesting historic mosques, an excellent hamam and a fine promenade that overlooks the pretty Maiden's Tower (*Kız Kulesi*). It's close to the Harem bus station for buses to Anatolia and has a major transport intersection for travelling around the rest of the city. The frequent public and private ferries to Eminönü and Beşiktaş run until late at night. Üsküdar is rather conservative, so would not suit anyone for whom a wild nightlife was vital. It has a wide range of cafes and restaurants (including floating restaurants by the pier) but few bars. The nearest large shopping malls are the Capitol and Carrefour Shopping Centres.

Like Üsküdar, **Çengelköy** is rather conservative. However, it does have access to the waterfront with the predictable pleasing tea garden for soaking up the views. It has a hilly location with many apartment blocks on slopes too steep for everybody's comfort and the through traffic can be a nightmare.

Kadıköy, too, has an inviting waterside location, with tea gardens lined up to take in the view of Sarayburnu across the Bosphorus. However, it is livelier than Üsküdar and has one street, Karanfil Sokak, so full of bars that it is known familiarly as Barlar Sokağı/Bar St. Instead of historic mosques it boasts one cinema (the Rexx) that showcases films during the annual Istanbul Film Festival and a great range of small shops, including the Greenhouse bookshop. It also has a renowned Salı Pazarı (Tuesday market) that spreads across a huge area; this, and the less well-known Pazar Pazarı (Sunday Market), are great places to come in search of cheap clothes. There are frequent public ferries to Eminönü, and Kadıköy is near to both Haydarpaşa railway station and Harem bus station for transport to Anatolia.

Inland from Kadıköy is the middle-class suburb of **Acıbadem** which is convenient both for people who need to commute to work elsewhere in the city or who have a car to park. It's a quiet district, offering spacious apartments in tree-lined streets, and has good shops within easy walking distance.

As a place to live **Suadiye** is less obviously appealing than Kadıköy although it too has a pleasant waterside promenade. However, it is a more upmarket neighbourhood with more substantial housing. Its big selling point is proximity to Bağdat Caddesi, one of Istanbul's major shopping streets with branches of Mothercare, Marks & Spencer, Remzi Kitabevi etc.

✓ Cinema(s)
✓ Supermarket(s)
✓ English-language bookshop(s)
✓ Foreign-language school(s)
✓ Church(es)
✓ Synagogue(s)

Göztepe is one of Istanbul's leafier suburbs where rents regularly exceed €500 a month. It has the advantage of proximity to the Bağdat Caddesi shops and Carrefour, and to the shores of the Bosphorus. However, it has been plagued by car crime recently, and since it lacks much buzz of its own residents tend to rack up big bills getting to livelier parts of town. Fortunately the transport connections are good.

Inland from Üsküdar is Ümraniye and, beyond that, **Atakent,** one of the longer established modern housing areas which has become increasingly popular with families. Rents tend to be lower than in Üsküdar. However, for anyone working on the European side of the city the journey to work can take up to an hour and a half at busy times of day.

ANKARA

Need to Know Info

Population: 4 million
Airport: Esenboğa International Airport (Tel: 0312-398 0348)
Railway Station: Ankara Train Station (Tel: 0312-311 0620)
Bus Station: AŞTI (Tel: 0312-224 1000, www.asti.com.tr)
Climate: Extremely hot in July and August (35°C max), extremely cold in winter (-5°C min) with regular snow
Nearest Ski Resort: Kartalkaya, near Bolu

Ankara is the city in the heart of Anatolia that Atatürk turned into the capital of the new Turkish Republic. Since it had been little more than a village until then, Ankara has none of the beauty and glamour of Istanbul. Instead it is a big, brash, superficially modern city with many of the drawbacks (traffic congestion, crowds, noise) of Istanbul but with few of the compensating attractions. Consequently most of the foreigners who are living in Ankara are there because of their work rather than because they have chosen to settle there. Since foreigners are so much less common in Ankara (away from the diplomatic enclave of Çankaya) those few who do settle there stand out more which can make life rather uncomfortable, especially for women. Away from the city centre Ankara is also far more conservative and less cosmopolitan than Istanbul which can make it harder to maintain a foreign lifestyle.

On the plus side Ankara has good connections with everywhere else in Turkey. Its bus station (AŞTI) is the second busiest in the country and the airport offers direct flights to many other parts of the world. Ankara also has a decent selection of cinemas, English-language bookshops, classy restaurants, supermarkets and foreign-language schools. The large student population breathes life into areas such as Kızılay, an excellent place to go for restaurants, Internet cafes, bookshops etc.

Some of the inner suburbs have pleasant tree-lined streets. However, with the exception of the Kale and Ulus areas Ankara's architecture is almost uniformly mundane. Most foreigners tend to live in the more upmarket districts of Çankaya and Gaziosmanpaşa.

✓	Cinema(s)
✓	Supermarket(s)
✓	English-language bookshop(s)
✓	Foreign-language school(s)
X	Church(es)
X	Synagogue(s)

Çankaya is a leafy district with good infrastructure close to the centre of town and within walking district of the Tunalı Hilmi Caddesi shopping area and Arjantin Caddesi cafes. The Botanical Gardens at the foot of the Atakule are another plus as are the supermarket and cinema inside the tower. Nearby **Gaziosmanpaşa** shares many of the advantages of Çankaya. Both are within easy reach of most of the embassies and upmarket hotels.

More traditionally Turkish is **Dikmen**, which is just five minutes' walk from the hubbub of Kızılay. It is a long-established, quiet residential neighbourhood with decent pavements and good dolmuş connections to other parts of town. To live here happily it probably helps to speak at least some Turkish.

The most historically interesting and architecturally appealing part of Ankara is the **Kale**, the ancient fortified area on top of a hill where the Archaeological Museum and the new Çengelhan Rahmi Koç Museum jostle for space alongside a growing number of cafes and restaurants. Until recently no one was much interested in the Kale and most of the old Ottoman houses that lined the cobbled streets were occupied by poor village Turks. Recently, however, there has been a boom in enthusiasm and houses there now change hands for extraordinary sums of money. The rise in value mainly reflects increased business interest since the Kale would not be an easy area in which to live: the hill is steep, the houses decaying, the winter weather harsh and the noise from the bars and restaurants intrusive.

Ulus is the area below the Kale which centres on the Heykel, with its dramatic statue of Atatürk. The main streets are lined with shops, and there are a small covered market and several banks nearby. However, tucked away in the back streets there are still some old wooden houses dating back to Ottoman times. Most are in need of extensive restoration. So far, though, there has been little interest in buying them.

Pros: Work opportunities; access to central Anatolia; reasonable shopping facilities; diplomatic expat community	**Cons:** Conservative atmosphere; ugly architecture; traffic problems; pollution

IZMIR

Need To Know Info

Population: 2,250,000

Airport: Adnan Menderes Airport (Tel: 0232-274 2424)

Railway Station: Basmane (Tel: 0232-484 8638); Alsancak (Tel: 0232-464 7795)

Bus Station: IZOTAS (Tel: 0232-472 1010, www.izotas.com.tr)

Ferry Connection to Greece: Çeşme to Chios (Sakız)

Climate: Hot and dry in July and August (33°C max), mild in winter (4°C min) with rare snow

Nearest beaches: Çeşme peninsula; Kuşadası; Foça

Nearest ski resort: Davraz (Isparta); Uludağ (Bursa)

On the surface, Izmir, like Ankara, is a concrete jungle which was robbed of most of its historic centre first by a great fire in 1922 and then by an earthquake. However, unlike Ankara, Izmir has a waterfront location which has been greatly improved over the last few years so that going out for a meal on the bay-facing Kordon is now one of the joys of living in the city.

Few foreigners choose to settle in Izmir. Instead they usually come there for work (Izmir attracts a lot of English teachers), and rent rather than buy during their stay. People who intend to stay longer usually buy in the surrounding area instead of in the town centre because Izmir offers easy access to the Çeşme Peninsula and to some inviting smaller resorts to the north, such as Foça and Yeni Foça.

If you do choose to live in Izmir, the city is renowned for its laid-back atmosphere; where Ankara tends to the conservative, Izmir has a large student population and a sense of its own unique identity that is partly derived from its long history as a foreign trading settlement. You will find bookshops, Internet cafes and great restaurants all over town, and although transport used to be a nightmare it has steadily improved with the creation of a new metro and the rearrangement of bus stops and services. You can also get about parts of the city in summer by using the coastal ferries. The weekend ferry between Izmir and Istanbul was recently resurrected to offer a luxury boat trip. The fare exceeds the cost of a plane ticket but this has always been a very pleasant and relaxing way to get between the two cities. Izmir is also a short hop to Çeşme and the ferries to Chios for the visa-hop.

✓	Cinema(s)
✓	Supermarket(s)
✓	English-language bookshop(s)
X	Foreign-language school(s)
✓	Church(es)
X	Synagogue(s)

Alsancak is the one part of central Izmir which still retains some fine old Chios-style housing. In recent years many of these properties have been restored and turned into bars, restaurants and nightclubs. The end result is to make this a less attractive area to live in because of the constant noise although it is one of the most enjoyable parts of town in which to socialise. If you do choose to live here you will probably find that parking is a real problem.

Once the residential area of choice of wealthy Levantine merchants, **Bornova** still retains some fine old mansions. However, most of them have been colonised by university departments and other businesses. The suburb is on Izmir's metro line which means that it offers easy access to the city centre.

Across the bay from the centre of Izmir is **Karşıyaka** which boasts a long pedestrianised shopping street with plentiful cheap places to eat. The suburb still retains some old Chios-style houses which the government plans to restore, so it is likely to become steadily more inviting. The fact that you can get to and from work in the city centre by ferry is a considerable plus.

Pros: Reasonable range of urban amenities but easier to get around than Ankara or Istanbul; less conservative than Ankara; coastal location with easy access to beaches and historic sites	**Cons:** Ugly architecture and no great sights; traffic congestion; fairly small expat community

ADANA

Need To Know Info

Population: 1 million
Airport: Adana Şakirpaşa Airport (Tel: 0322-435 0380)
Railway Station: Adana Railway Station (Tel: 0322-453 3172)
Bus Station: Adana Bus Terminal (Tel: 0322-428 2047)

Climate: Hot and humid in summer (34°C max), mild in winter (6°C min), rarely snow

Nearest Beaches: Karataş; Yumurtalık; Kızkalesi

Famous for its spicy kebabs, Adana is Turkey's fourth biggest city and on a map its location, on the Eastern Mediterranean coast, looks very appealing. In reality, however, Adana is a big, noisy modern city which suffers badly from humidity in summer. Nevertheless some foreigners have settled there, not least because there is a large American air base on the outskirts of town at Incirlik.

✓	Cinema(s):
✓	Supermarket(s):
X	English-language bookshop(s):
X	Foreign-language school(s):
X	Church(es):
X	Synagogue(s):

Adana has several reasonably-priced Turkish baths and some excellent shopping opportunities – with few tourists coming to town prices are refreshingly moderate. The new Sabancı mosque and the adjacent park have greatly improved the riverside ambience.

Pros: Close to beaches; good shopping opportunities; busy airport; American expat community at nearby Incirlik	**Cons**: Humidity; largely ugly town with no major sights; small expat community apart from Incirlik

BURSA

Need To Know Info

Population: 1 million

Airport: Bursa Yenişehir Airport (Tel: 0224-247 7701)

Bus Station: Bursa Bus Terminal (Tel: 0242-261 5400)

IDO Fast Ferries to Istanbul: From Yalova and Bandırma Terminal (Tel: 0224-444 4436, www.ido.com.tr)

Climate: Temperate climate without extremes

Nearest beaches: Marmara Islands

Nearest Ski Resort: Uludağ

Bursa is Turkey's fifth largest city and it, too, has become a much more appealing place in which to live over the last few years. It is an industrial town, known for its textiles and car factories, which means that few foreigners have chosen to settle there except as teachers or spouses. However, Bursa lies in the lee of Uludağ, the mountain which boasts Turkey's most sophisticated ski resort, and there is some lovely countryside in the vicinity. At the same time it is only a short hop away from Istanbul across the Sea of Marmara and is within easy reach of the beach resorts of the Marmara Islands, so its location could hardly be bettered.

Bursa offers a wide range of restaurants and some decent bars and cafes. Shopping here is also good, with the sprawling bazaar proving a great place to pick up towels in particular, while the Zafer Plaza Shopping Centre offers brand-name labels (as well as a decent cinema). However, with no big expat community living in Bursa, you would need to learn to speak Turkish and would have to cope without the little Western luxuries that crop up from time to time in places where lots of foreigners shop.

✓	Cinema(s)
✓	Supermarket(s)
X	English-language bookshop(s)
X	Foreign-language school(s)
X	Church(es)
X	Synagogue(s)

Although it would be possible to live in the heart of Bursa, the more pleasant neighbourhoods are away from the centre. In particular Çekirge is an airy spa district 1.5 kilometres from the city centre. Regular bus and dolmuş connections mean that it is easy to get in and out of town. Although the main road through Çekirge is extremely busy, it is nothing like as alarming as Atatürk Caddesi which slices through the city centre. Çekirge Caddesi is lined with inviting modern apartment blocks that look as if a great deal more care went into their design than is the case in most Turkish suburbs. Many boast balconies with splendid views over the hills and downtown Bursa. There are several fine old spa baths in the area although prices are inevitably slanted towards tourists.

Pros: Attractively green and hilly location with many hamams; historic buildings; authentically Turkish feel; excellent range of normal shops.	**Cons:** Little expat life; limited flights; distressingly busy main road through centre.

ESCAPING THE CITIES

By far the majority of foreigners settling in Turkey choose to live along the coast where the climate is mild even in winter and where the amenities provided for tourists are available to settlers too. Most foreigners have bought houses along the South Aegean and the Western Mediterranean, although there are pockets of settlement along the North Aegean and Eastern Mediterranean coasts too. Only the Black Sea remains largely virgin territory and that is probably because its notoriously damp climate makes it less appealing to Northern European sun-seekers.

THE NORTH AEGEAN

Need To Know Info

Airports: Istanbul (Atatürk International), Izmir (Adnan Menderes), Bursa (Yenişehir)

IDO Fast Ferries: From Istanbul to Yalova and Bandırma (Tel: 0212 444 4436, www.ido.com.tr)

Ferry Connections to Greece: Ayvalık to Lesbos (Midilli); Çeşme to Chios (Sakız)

Best Beaches: Gelibolu Peninsula (Kum Limanı, Seddülbahir); Bozcaada (Ayazma, Ayana, Habbele); Ayvalık (Sarımsaklı); Assos (Kadırga); Foça/Yeni Foça (linking coastline); Çeşme Peninsula (Ilıca, Altınkum, Dalyan, Alaçatı)

Nearest Ski Resorts: Uludağ (Bursa), Davraz (Isparta)

Climate: Hot and dry in summer (33°C max), mild in winter (4°C min), snow rare

The North Aegean region of Turkey consists of parts of the provinces of Çanakkale and Balıkesir, as well as most of the province of Izmir. It's an area of attractive, if sometimes overdeveloped, coastline which is very popular with holidaying Turks. Greek islands are often visible from the shore; their proximity is handy if you will need to go in and out of Turkey on regular visa-hops.

Moving down the coast from the Dardanelles, the first big town you come to is **Çanakkale** (pop. 60,000) which has a beautiful location overlooking the straits. Çanakkale is a busy port for ferries across the Dardanelles and also to Turkey's two inhabited Aegean islands: Gökçeada and Bozcaada. Most of old Çanakkale disappeared during earthquakes in the 20th century, so the modern city largely consists of ugly concrete buildings. However, the superb setting does much to soften their appearance and the city has a wide, attractive main street and a pleasant waterside promenade. There are a few trendy bars, many simple restaurants, a cinema and a supermarket. For the time being foreigners cannot buy here, although were this to change, the nearby small resort of **Güzelyalı** is quieter than central Çanakkale and offers wonderful views over the Straits. An English teacher who lived in the town for a year reported finding it a strain since she was never able to go anywhere without attracting attention.

Foreigners are also prohibited from buying on Gökçeada and Bozcaada, although refugees from Istanbul and Izmir are rapidly moving in. Until 1923 both these islands had large Greek populations. **Gökçeada** (pop. 8,000) is the rockier and more remote of the two islands; in winter ferry services to the mainland can be severely disrupted by bad weather. The island consists of a series of scattered settlements of which Kaleköy is the most developed for tourism. Inland, Tepeköy and Zeytinli have upmarket tourist developments aimed at Turkish and Greek visitors. Gökçeada town has very little going for it, beyond a bank and a couple of basic restaurants.

It is more of a shame that foreigners can't buy on **Bozcaada** (pop. 2,500), a delightful island with sandy beaches, a massive castle, a restaurant-ringed harbour and a settlement that has so far escaped the worst of modern development. Turks from elsewhere are moving here to open pensions and restore old Greek houses but there is only one foreign resident (Australian), so no expat life. Nor is there a cinema or foreign-language bookshop – for such luxuries you would need to travel to Çanakkale or beyond.

Moving south along the North Aegean coast you come eventually to gorgeous **Assos/Behramkale,** a pair of villages that do have a few foreign residents (Dutch and American) drawn there by their beauty rather than their amenities. Assos itself is a cluster of half-a-dozen stone-built hotels facing a harbour. Behind them a road zigzags uphill past crumbling ruins to the modern village of Behramkale where most of the houses have been built from local stone. Views from here are stupendous and most of the resident foreigners run pensions catering to tourists who come here for the serenity. But there are very few properties still available which gives them premium value. Even if you could find something to buy you would have to be ready to restore in accordance with strict conservation-area regulations. The reward, however, would be a dream home.

Assos is fairly cut off and for most amenities you would have to travel to Çanakkale, Bergama or beyond. There is a lively weekly market in nearby Ayvacık for stocking up on fruit, vegetables and other fresh produce.

From Assos the coast road is heavily built-up with holiday homes for Turks until you reach **Ayvalık** (pop. 32,000), a resort town which had a large Greek population until 1923. More Greeks left Ayvalık than Turks moved in which means that the narrow back streets are full of fine old Ottoman houses, many of them standing empty. Slowly these are being bought by a mixture of foreigners (Dutch, British, German) and Turks from the big cities, although most need a lot of work done to them and planning regulations restrict what changes can be made. Some have been turned into tasteful small boutique hotels although the market for this must be nearing saturation.

Ayvalık is a real town with several supermarkets and assorted other shops, particularly specialising in selling olive-oil products. Facing it across the bay, and connected to it by a causeway, is Cunda (Alibey Adası) which has yet more abandoned Ottoman houses and a fine range of seafood restaurants plus the odd disco. Some old warehouses on the mainland are also being done up as small but trendy cafes. South of Ayvalık there are stretches of sandy beach in and around the overblown resort of Sarımsaklı. The road linking Ayvalık to the beaches is lined with sturdy mansions, most of them set in their own gardens.

For the time being house prices in Ayvalık remain reasonable by Western standards and few locals seem to have set themselves up as estate agents as yet. But the town is a long way from the nearest airport and, despite the attractive properties available, it would not be easy to make money from renting out a property here. The expat community seems to get on well together although it is too small to have much impact on the town's atmosphere.

South from Ayvalık and inland from the coast is **Bergama** (pop. 50,000) which has some of Turkey's most striking archaeological sites but which has missed out on big-time tourism. Unfortunately that does not mean that it is a particularly pretty place. Instead it mainly consists of one long highway lined with modern apartment blocks. The one attractive old Ottoman quarter, to the north, has some inviting old stone houses and one French resident although rumour has it that it may soon be redeveloped. Bergama has a lively market and a few indifferent restaurants. Otherwise it is short of the sort of amenities that usually appeal to foreign settlers. The town's atmosphere also tends to the conservative - the hamam, for example, is for men only.

Not far from Bergama is the small seaside resort of **Dikili** (pop. 20,000). It is not an especially exciting town. However, it is one of the few places along the North Aegean coast where house prices have yet to take off dramatically.

Continuing down the coast from Bergama you need to detour from the highway to reach **Foça** (pop. 15,000), an inviting small town set round a double bay. Foça lives for tourism and has several good fish restaurants as well as a small harbourside supermarket. There are a couple of pleasant bars but not much else in the way of amenities. On the other hand it is only one and a half hours by bus from the bright lights of Izmir which means that it would be possible to work there and live in Foça, at least at weekends. Facing the bay there are many old Ottoman houses waiting for restoration. Because of its tourism industry Foça is less conservative than Bergama although it has a very small expat community.

Surprisingly, in the last two years it is really nearby **Yeni Foça** (pop. 3,000) that has become the property hotspot. Yeni Foça faces onto a thin strip of sand but its back streets are chock-a-block with abandoned Ottoman houses. Four years ago most of these were semi-derelict but recently there has been a flurry of activity and now many of them have been bought either by Izmir residents or by Germans in particular. As a result the place is now awash with 'estate agencies' although most of the people running them are extremely new to the business. Restoration is speeding ahead but in piecemeal fashion so that while some houses are being returned to their original appearance, others are being given stone-cladding or other aberrations. If you fancy living here the advice would be to buy now while you still have the chance. Bear in mind, though, that Yeni Foça has very limited amenities and that access to Izmir is less easy than from Foça itself (this could always change, of course).

West of the Izmir conurbation a new motorway runs out to **Çeşme** and the ferries to Chios. Çeşme itself is a lively holiday resort, particularly popular with Turks, and it has a full range of restaurants and cafes, as well as a big supermarket and cinema on the outskirts. However, a far nicer place to live would be nearby **Alaçatı** which is famous in Turkey for its windsurfing beaches. Like Yeni Foça, Alaçatı is full of old Ottoman houses but whereas the restoration of Yeni Foça is being carried out in haphazard fashion, in Alaçatı it has been far more methodical and alarmingly upmarket. Slowly the centre is filling up with classy hotels and restaurants catering to the monied elite of Istanbul and Izmir; would-be incomers might want to bear in mind the sort of exclusive atmosphere that that is creating. The fact remains, though, that Alaçatı is gorgeous and within easy reach of pleasant beaches (Dalyan, Altınkum, Ilıca) and the amenities of both Çeşme and Izmir.

THE SOUTH AEGEAN

Need To Know Info

Airports: Izmir (Adnan Menderes); Dalaman; Milas-Bodrum

Ferry Connections to Greece: Kuşadası to Samos; Bodrum to Kos and Rhodes (Rodos); Marmaris to Rhodes; Datça to Rhodes and Symi.

Best Beaches: Selçuk (Pamucak, Yoncaköy, Dilek Peninsula); Kuşadası (Kadınlar Denizi, Kuştur); Altınkum; Ören; Bodrum peninsula (Akyarlar, Bitez, Gümüşlük, Karaincir, Mazı, Ortakent); Datça; Marmaris (Cleopatra's Beach, Selimiye, Bozburun)

Nearest ski resort: Davraz (Isparta)

Climate: Hot and dry in summer (35°C max), mild in winter (5°C min), snow rare

The South Aegean consists of parts of the provinces of Izmir, Aydın and Muğla. This stretch of the Turkish coast is especially popular with foreign tourists who pour into Kuşadası, Altınkum, Bodrum and Marmaris in their thousands every summer. There are also several popular backpacker resorts along this stretch of coast, including Selçuk, the most common base for visiting the magnificent ruins at Ephesus (Efes). As with the North Aegean, the islands of the Dodecanese are frequently visible just off shore which means that it is easy for foreign settlers to hop across to Greece to renew their visas.

Just an hour by bus south of Izmir is **Selçuk** (pop.23,000), a surprisingly inviting small town set on and around a hill and surrounded by orchards. Tourist development here has been on a smaller scale than in Kuşadası and Bodrum and the innumerable pensions are far less visually scarring than the package-holiday hotels further south. Selçuk has a decent range of restaurants and shops (although prices reflect the largely tourist clientele) and there are wonderful beaches at nearby Pamucak and Yoncaköy. It also has good transport links; the regular bus service to Izmir aside, it also has a railway station right in the centre of town. There is also a decent hamam with Friday set aside for women.

What Selçuk doesn't have is much interesting old housing. There are a few places hidden away down back streets, especially in the area near St John's Basilica, but mostly people live in apartment blocks and housing cooperative schemes. Some foreigners have bought in the surrounding countryside where some stone-built houses still await restoration. However, doing this can involve all sorts of hassle with installing utilities.

Selçuk has a small expat community (Australian, British, Japanese) but since most of the foreigners are working in pensions they tend to be in competition with each other which hardly encourages socialising. On the other hand many Turks here speak good English. The town is also regarded as relatively user-friendly for people with mobility problems.

Kuşadası (pop. 50,000) is the antithesis of Selçuk, a big, brash port town which heaves with tourists in summer and attracts the sort of holidaymakers for whom Bar Street (an alley of British, German and Dutch pubs) was designed. Its waterfront location is potentially appealing, although most of it is now backed with high-rise hotels, and there are decent beaches nearby. Kuşadası has restaurants and cafes to suit all tastes and pockets as well as two hamams, a cinema, several supermarkets and all sorts of shops with stock and prices aimed straight at tourists.

Most of the housing in Kuşadası was thrown up over the last 20 years.

✓	Cinema(s)
✓	Supermarket(s)
✓	English-language bookshop(s)
✓	Private hospital
X	Foreign-language school(s)
X	Church(es)
X	Synagogue(s)

However, in the centre there are still many old Ottoman houses, some of them turned into pensions and restaurants. This would be the nicest place to buy a house, although it is unlikely to be quiet and the steep hills take some getting used to.

Kuşadası has a resident expat community not all of whom are working in tourism which encourages more socialising. It seems to appeal particularly to the British and Irish. Daily ferries to Samos are perfect for visa-hopping.

Pros: Lively expat lifestyle; easy access to ferries and airport; lots of shops and amenities; ferry to Samos for visa-hop	**Cons:** Tourist prices; raucous party lifestyle; ugly development; little work except in tourism

Between Kuşadası and Izmir the small settlement of **Özdere** is popular with the Dutch but turns into a ghost town in winter.

Not far from Selçuk and Kuşadası is **Altınkum,** a small resort with a fine beach completely overlooked by hotels. There is seasonal work to be found here but not much in the way of interesting accommodation; for that you would need to look a little further inland around Yenişehir/Didim where there are still some old Ottoman houses available. Altınkum is especially popular with the British and is far more affordable than resorts like Bodrum. It is within an hour's drive of Bodrum airport which should help if you are buying a property with a view to renting it to holidaymakers.

Just before Bodrum you come to the small resort of **Ören**, which has a long strip of beach. Unfortunately, emissions from the Kemerköy power station have attracted some worrying publicity, so that this is probably not the best place to think of settling. Similarly **Güllük** is rendered less attractive by the bauxite trucks that rumble through town on a regular basis. More inviting than either of these places is tiny **Kıyıkışlacık/Iassos** which boasts a pretty, hilly location with a few apartment blocks looking down on a pleasant harbour. There are a few fish restaurants near the harbour but little else. This is a place that would suit the type of settler who wants to keep away from the tourist crowds.

Continuing south you come eventually to **Bodrum** (pop. 25,000) which is just as popular a tourist resort as Kuşadası but which has managed to hold on to more of its aesthetic appeal through conservation laws that restrict

the building of new high-rises within the town centre and its immediate surroundings. The result is that Bodrum consists of a pile of pretty cuboid white
buildings with blue trim rising gently from the seashore. Out of the high season it is still a wonderful place to live; in high season it would be many people's idea of hell. These days properties in Bodrum tend to go for between
€70,000 and €100,000, the prices nudged up not just by expat buyers but
also by well-heeled Istanbullus who have always favoured Bodrum as their
seaside retreat of choice.

✓	Cinema(s)
✓	Supermarket(s)
✓	English-language bookshop(s)
✓	Private hospital
X	Foreign-language school(s)
X	Church(es)
X	Synagogue(s)

Bodrum is renowned for its nightlife
which even manages to encompass some
gay bars as well as pounding discos like the
famous Halikarnas. It has some wonderful
restaurants, *meyhanes* and cafes, and the
harbour, with wooden yachts bobbing up
and down in front of a promenade lined
with palm trees and children's play areas,
is simply delightful. Inevitably the town-centre shops reflect the tourist clientele but Bodrum also has supermarkets where prices are more reasonable
and cinemas showing films in the original language. Unfortunately it is some
way from Izmir which means that major shopping trips require quite an expe-
dition. Although it has an international airport, that is also some way out of
town near Milas and is not as busy as you might expect.

There is already a thriving expat community in Bodrum (an estimated
4,000 foreigners have settled there in the last five years) which swells in summer when the tour operator reps arrive. Many resident Turks speak excellent
English. Regular ferries to Kos and Rhodes ensure that renewing a visa is usually plain sailing.

Pros: Attractive location and town centre; lively expat lifestyle; excellent shops and restaurants; ferry to Kos for visa-hop.	**Cons:** Extremely noisy in summer; high prices; distance from major urban centre; flights relatively limited; growing urban sprawl.

Beyond Bodrum itself lies the **Bodrum Peninsula** which becomes more
built-up with every passing year. Some of the development is pretty crass
(Gümbet springs to mind) but in the north around Göltürkbükü there is also
some of the most exclusive coastal development in Turkey, all designer hotels
and restaurants to match. Yalıkavak is also attractive and already has a number
of German residents. Turgutreis has a lovely new marina but is a designated
military zone which means it is difficult for foreigners to buy property there.

It is increasingly hard to find a place on the peninsula to buy a house that will not have its view threatened by new development; indeed, if thinking of buying here you need to think hard about how the area is likely to develop over the next 10 years. Take Gümüşlük, for example. A picture-postcard bay, it has a preservation order to prevent any new building. However, that has not been enough to prevent its peerless views being marred by new housing developments that are marching steadily over the hills. Elsewhere on the peninsula other people have built new properties with three stories and huge windows that completely ignore the small-scale character of traditional Bodrum properties. Despite this, bargain properties are few and far between; to buy a property in posh Göltürkbükü, for example, is likely to cost between €250,000 and €1,250,000; in Gümüşlük €100,000 is more normal.

South of Bodrum, **Marmaris** (pop. 23,000) was once a gorgeous fishing village at the bottom of a steep hill looking out over azure seas. However the last 20 years have not been kind to the town which has been developed at pell-mell rate to suit the needs of the bottom end of the British package-holiday market. The harbour is still pretty, with its line-up of wooden yachts, and the bazaar grows yearly bigger and more varied. At one time Marmaris was believed to have 3,000 restaurants, and the nightlife along Barlar Sokağı (Bar St) is famously raucous. There are supermarkets (MMM Migros, Gima and Maxi Tansaş), a sprawling bazaar, cinemas and plenty of shops with an eye to the tourist dollar. To the west Marmaris sprawls seamlessly into İçmiler which was developed for the package-holiday market but has some attractive residential streets.

To get to Marmaris you either have to fly into Bodrum (Milas) airport or Dalaman airport and then endure a long transfer along the coast. The town is also remote from big centres of population which means you are likely to pay more for your shopping than elsewhere. However, it is easy to pop across to Rhodes to renew your visa throughout the year.

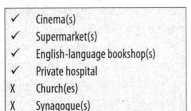

✓	Cinema(s)
✓	Supermarket(s)
✓	English-language bookshop(s)
✓	Private hospital
X	Church(es)
X	Synagogue(s)

Marmaris has a resident expat community which swells in summer when the tour company reps hit town. In fact the population figure given for the town is effectively meaningless as in summer the tourists push it up to more like 75,000. At that time, all the amenities come under considerable strain. However, in winter Marmaris can feel like a ghost town.

These days there are few interesting properties to buy in Marmaris although there are still some old Ottoman houses on the hill round the castle and backing onto the harbour; some of these might have made very attractive homes were it not for the noise from nearby bars and clubs. Prices also reflect the fact that those properties that do come on the market are usually snapped up by tourism enterprises.

Inland from the harbour is the sprawling suburb of Armutlan where there are plenty of rental properties available. Since this is a long-established residential area with decent infrastructure it might make a good area to buy in.

Pros: Harbourside location with mountain backdrop; lively expat lifestyle; good amenities; ferry to Rhodes for visa-hop.	**Cons:** No airport nearby; low-budget package tourism in summer; ugly development and inadequate infrastructure away from centre.

Northeast of Marmaris is **Muğla** (pop. 40,000), a provincial capital and a surprisingly pretty little town with some of the appeal of Bodrum, especially in its back streets which nurture the same little white houses with blue trim. Because Muğla is inland it has attracted far less attention from foreigners; its backwater status also means that it lacks most of the amenities foreigners crave. However, for people interested in traditional architecture it would certainly repay a look. In any case, Muğla is where many foreign residents of Bodrum, Marmaris and Fethiye have to come to sort out their paperwork.

West of Marmaris, the land stretches out into two fingers along the Reşadiye Peninsula. This is a delightful and so far largely unspoilt part of the coastline because, until recently, there was no major highway linking it to Marmaris. Several foreigners have bought old houses on the peninsula and turned them into classy boutique hotels. Otherwise the obvious place of interest here is **Datça** (pop. 6,500), way out at the western end of the peninsula and very popular with holidaying Turks. Datça remains fairly sleepy – a reminder of what Marmaris must once have been like – although in high summer the tourists bring inevitable noise and disruption. There are few amenities out here, beyond a string of restaurants and an outdoor cinema overlooking the bay. Anyone looking for a more picturesque place to buy a house might want to drop into tiny **Eski Datça (Old Datça)**, a few miles back on the road towards Marmaris where some lovely old stone cottages have been turned into attractive bougainvillea-draped pensions. In summer regular ferries from Datça to Rhodes and Symi make it easy to renew a visa.

The one place on the peninsula that has been heavily developed is **Turunç**. A number of foreigners have settled there because of the successful tourism businesses there. However, there are few attractive old properties in town. Far more inviting are smaller settlements like **Söğut, Selimiye** and **Bozburun.**

THE WESTERN MEDITERRANEAN

Need To Know Info

Airports: Dalaman International Airport; Antalya International Airport

Ferry Connections to Greece: Kaş to Kastellorizo (Meis)

Best Beaches: Iztuzu (Dalyan); Çalış; Belcekız and Ölüdeniz Lagoon; Gemiler; Günlüklü; Kabak; Kelebek Vadisi (Butterfly Valley); Patara; Kaputaş; Olimpos/Çıralı; Topçam; Lara Beach (Antalya)

Climate: Hot and dry in summer (35°C max - high humidity around Antalya), mild in winter (6°C min), snow rare

The Western Mediterranean coast of Turkey consists of parts of the provinces of Muğla and Antalya. It's a beautiful part of Turkey and very popular with British tourists in particular; indeed, this is the part of Turkey that is being most rapidly snapped up by foreigners. However, access to some parts of it is not particularly easy; the Taurus Mountains press in on the coast meaning that there is just a narrow, winding coast road from Fethiye to Antalya. Depending on your viewpoint this is either a blessing because it has meant that resorts like Kaş and Kalkan could not grow into sprawling monsters like Kuşadası and Marmaris, or a curse because it slows journeys down and inflicts motion sickness on the weak-stomached.

Heading along the coast from Marmaris you come first to the small but increasingly popular resort of **Köyceğiz** (pop. 8,000), set on the shores of an exquisite lake. Although it is a potentially inviting spot it has very few amenities; for serious shopping you would need to travel into Marmaris, one hour away by bus. At one time the village boasted many fine old traditional houses but these days few remain to catch the eye of would-be restorers. Livelier is **Dalyan** which started out as a backpacker resort but has metamorphosed into a package-holiday destination. Dalyan has an idyllic riverside setting, with a rock face pitted with pretty Lycian tombs immediately facing it (the downside of the river is that it attracts hordes of mosquitoes). Boats ferry visitors to and from Iztuzu beach, a fine stretch of sand used by nesting loggerhead turtles, a short distance away.

Dalyan is a conservation area which means that all the recent development is at least low-rise and relatively spread out; most properties boast sizeable gardens. The village centre has had its pavements and kerbs levelled, making it more manageable for people with mobility problems. The village also has a selection of restaurants and bars, a small Migros and a growing number of pensions. Otherwise it has few amenities. However, it is close to the international airport at Dalaman which makes coming and going from Europe fairly simple, at least in summer, and the small town of Ortaca nearby (pop. 16,000) has a better selection of shops. The growing expat community even has its own newspaper, *Evet*. Not far away **Sarıgerme** has a pleasant beach that is being developed as an alternative to Dalyan but for the time being there are only hotels there. Recently Dalaman was designated a Tourism Development Area and there are plans for a golf course and new marina. Prices in the area are therefore likely to rise in the short-term.

Continuing east towards Fethiye, the small yachting resort of **Göcek** could one day grow into a place where foreigners would want to settle en masse – it certainly has the picture-postcard harbour in its favour. But it is the area around Fethiye itself that is currently most popular with British settlers in particular.

Fethiye (pop. 50,000) is an inviting medium-sized resort with a picturesque harbour backed by soaring mountains and overlooking a bay which is dotted with rocky islands. The town centre has a lively bazaar (although most of the shops are aimed at tourists) with a decent (mixed) hamam and lots of restaurants. There are also several supermarkets (Gima, MM Migros, Bim), two cinemas and a large Tuesday market and a second-hand bookstall. Fethiye itself lacks a beach but there are decent stretches of sand in nearby Ölüdeniz. In summer the centre is bustling and noisy although normal Turkish life resumes at the end of the season. Although there is flat land along the shoreline, much of Fethiye is extremely hilly, making it a doubtful choice of home for elderly people or anyone with mobility problems.

✓	Cinema(s)
✓	Supermarket(s)
✓	English-language bookshop(s)
✓	Private hospital
X	Church(es)
X	Synagogue(s)

Recent years have seen every man and his dog turn property dealer and now Fethiye boasts around 400 estate agencies, an extraordinary number for a town of its size. In the town itself the residential area of choice is 2. Karagözler to the east, where waterfront houses sell for around €215,000. There are still a few old houses in the town centre, especially around the Telmessos excavations. However, some are slated for destruction and others would be extremely pricy both to buy and to restore. Some parts of the city centre are also very noisy at night.

For people looking to rent rather than buy prices are highest in 2. Karagözler where the hills offer the prospect of sea views (although beware of solar panels blocking them). To rent a three-bed apartment here might cost around €400 a month, with hefty heating prices in winter because the hillside makes it very damp. Prices are more reasonable across town in suburbs like Tuzla and Babataş where for €180-275 you can rent a pleasant house with garden.

Pros: Real town with range of amenities; lively expat lifestyle; beautiful location; close to Hisarönü/Ovacık for wider choice of restaurants and bars	**Cons:** Little cheap accommodation; no big mall for clothes shopping; some areas with poor infrastructure; steep hills

However, it is not really Fethiye itself that has become the main property hotspot. Instead that accolade belongs to **Hisarönü/Ovacık** up in the hills above Ölüdeniz. Hisarönü is a wholly new construction, built in an effort to protect beautiful **Ölüdeniz** from overdevelopment. It became very popular with British and Irish holidaymakers and soon spawned all sorts of cafes and restaurants aimed straight at them. Before long a lively expat community had developed and soon people started to buy plots of land to build their own houses in and around the settlement. Unfortunately there has been little centralised planning for this expansion which means that people have built in wildly disparate styles. The resulting mish-mash would not suit everybody although there's no doubt that the British in particular can't get enough of Hisarönü, widely dubbed 'Little England' by the locals and resembling Blackpool during the Illuminations on summer nights.

It's not difficult to see the appeal. A short walk or dolmuş ride away, Ölüdeniz itself has a gorgeous unspoilt lagoon and a long strip of sandy beach. Hisarönü is also within easy reach (half an hour by dolmuş) of Fethiye, with its shops and amenities. The surrounding countryside is also absolutely stunning with wonderful possibilities for walking (the popular Lycian Way long-distance trekking route starts here), swimming, paragliding, golf and other water sports. At the same time because it is not actually a town Hisarönü has none of the snags of traffic jams, noise and general aggro that are associated with living in an urban area.

Estate agents also love Hisarönü but it pays to take some of their 'guarantees' of soaring property values with a shovel of salt. It's true that prices are likely to rise, especially if Turkey goes into the EU. However, there is still plenty of fresh land for building in the area so for some time to come it may be that people will prefer to start afresh rather than pay the premium cost of second-hand properties. At the time of writing properties in Hisarönü and Ovacık were selling for between €100,000 and €180,000.

A few foreigners live in Ölüdeniz itself but although that means they are even closer to the beach they are also subjected to noise from the many bars and restaurants. The difficulty of piping water down to the settlement has also meant that some have ended up with unexpectedly high water bills.

Pros: Full-on expat lifestyle; great location with easy access to Fethiye beaches and country-side.	**Cons:** Little Turkish culture; ugly over-development; expensive shops.

Down the hill from Hisarönü is the abandoned Greek village of Kayaköy where no new building has been permitted, despite several tries by would-be developers. However, a few pensions and restaurants have been built on the fringes and some are run by foreigners.

As prices have skyrocketed in Hisarönü/Ovacık property developers have started looking inland for places to sell. Some people have bought in the small town of Kemer, others in Üzümlü, while at the time of writing some agents were pushing homes in Seki, close to Turkey's newest ski resort. A few people have also started to buy and build on the mountainside near Tlos/Yaka. Before buying in any of these places you would need to check whether the seller actually has a *tapu* (title deed) for the property since not all the land in the Fethiye hinterland has been surveyed and registered.

Continuing east along the coast you will come to **Gelemiş**, a small inland settlement behind the spectacular stretch of coast that is Patara Beach. Before setting your heart on living here you need to be aware that much of the development at Gelemiş is illegal and may eventually be demolished.

Further east along the coast is **Kalkan** (pop. 3,500), an attractive small settlement of two-storied stone houses with red-tiled roofs tripping down a hill to the sea. Over the last five years it, too, has acquired a sizeable expat community, much of it British. Since space is at a premium here prices have been soaring - at the time of writing the restored 150-year-old Custom House was on the market for a cool €575,000. However, Kalkan has almost no amenities and in winter the town effectively closes down.

In the last few years Kalkan's popularity has lead to frantic development of the surrounding area and the infrastructure has yet to keep pace. You may get more for your money in terms of space in the suburbs of Kalamar Bay and Kışla. However, they lack the atmosphere of the town centre. There is also some development in the mountains backing Kalkan where prices sometimes reach UK levels.

Even further east is **Kaş** (pop. 8,000), one of Turkey's most popular small resorts despite the absence of a beach actually in town. An increasing number of foreigners (mainly British) are settling in Kaş and some of them work in the tourism industry. There are restaurants and bars aplenty, and some very upmarket shops aimed at tourists (although there is also a Migros). The harbour makes an attractive backdrop to daily life and ferries to the Greek island of Meis (Kastellorizo) offer the possibility of visa-hopping without a long journey.

Unfortunately (or fortunately, depending on how you look at it) the number of properties available in old Kaş is strictly limited. As a result many foreigners are now having properties purpose built for them on the adjacent Çukurbağ peninsula, leading to a kind of coastal sprawl. Villas here fetch prices well into six figures and there is virtually no land left for new building. You really need a car to live on the peninsula as the dolmuşes are infrequent and only run in summer.

There is also some development behind Kaş in the Çerçiler area. Some of it is illegal so you would need to be particularly careful before going ahead with a purchase.

One of the biggest drawbacks to living in Kaş is reaching it in the first place. Although there is often talk of a new airport, for the time being getting there involves flying into either Antalya or Dalaman airport and then enduring a long transfer journey along a beautiful but sickeningly winding road.

Pros: Attractive harbourside location and town centre; small expat community; reasonable choice of shops and restaurants; close to Kastellorizo for visa-hops.	**Cons:** Distance from nearest airport; cost of housing; few work opportunities apart from tourism

Close to Kaş and most readily accessible by boat from Üçağız is exquisite little **Kaleköy (Kekova)** where a few stone houses tumble down a hillside dotted with small cafes and pensions. The views are to die for but unfortunately that means that so are the prices - even the tiniest cottage there now comes with a €300,000 price tag in spite of water supply problems and the fact that the island has no amenities and virtually closes down for five months of the year. The Koç family have a summer home here and although they visit only rarely their presence has probably helped ensure that the village is completely protected from unsightly development.

Just before you reach Antalya you come to **Olimpos**, the small, hugely popular backpacker resort built up around a collection of treehouses and chalets overlooking a river and backed by the half-hidden ruins of the Olympos archaeological site. The beach at Olimpos and the soaring Bey Mountains behind it are undoubted attractions but few foreigners would want to settle actually in the valley except to work there in summer. Instead, the places of choice nearby are **Çıralı**, a fast-growing beach community where some foreigners have opened pensions and hotels, and **Adrasan** which is not dissimilar.

The Olimpos area is relatively peaceful and cut-off but once past it you soon come to the Greater Antalya sprawl, a long sequence of newly-built resorts and golf courses, few of them with anything much to offer beyond sun and sand. **Kemer** is a purpose-built resort which lacks much that is authentically Turkish although the surrounding countryside is beautiful, some of it falling within the Bey Mountains National Park. It has proved popular with Russian and German buyers, although British settlers seem to prefer nearby **Çamyuva** where prices are usually higher.

Antalya (pop. 500,000), on the other hand, makes a great place to live. It's a town that appears to have everything going for it - beaches, restaurants, cinemas, decent shops, an excellent English-language bookshop, some lovely old stone houses in the historic centre and an international airport for easy access. Antalya's setting is splendid, set as it is around a picturesque harbour ringed with bars and restaurants and with a backdrop of rocky islands. If there is anywhere on the coast where you could live a fairly normal Western-style urban life, then Antalya fits the bill perfectly. Not surprisingly lots of foreigners have already settled there, living in everything from new-built apartments to restored Ottoman houses.

✓ Cinema(s)
✓ Supermarket(s)
✓ English-language bookshop(s)
✓ Private hospital
✓ Church
X Synagogue

If your tastes run to older properties then the best place to start looking would be the historic Kaleiçi (Inner Castle) area of Antalya, parts of which overlook the harbour, and adjacent Haşim İşcan. In this part of town there are still many old wattle-and-daub Ottoman houses in a poor state of repair and awaiting a buyer. However, this is also an area with a thriving tourist industry based on small pensions and boutique hotels. It is therefore unlikely that you would be able to pick up a bargain property. The cost of restoring the houses is also likely to be very high – the standard set by the best of the existing hotels is exceptional and conservation laws dictate what can and cannot be done. If you do want to buy in Kaleiçi you would also need to take into account the drawbacks of mass tourism throughout the summer with the accompanying noise from bars that boom out music into the early hours. There is also prostitute activity associated with some of the bars and nightclubs.

Although Antalya is officially a resort, the Konyaaltı beach is only a strip of pebbles which gets jampacked in summer; Lara beach is better but 12km east of the town centre. Such is the allure of the sea, however, that these are the most popular areas in which to buy, with some of the highest prices.

Pros: Real town with great range of amenities; beautiful harbourside location; lively expat life; year-round airport.	**Cons:** Usual urban problems of noise and traffic congestion; high costs.

THE EASTERN MEDITERRANEAN
Need To Know Info

Airports: Antalya International Airport; Adana Şakirpaşa Airport

Ferry Connections to Northern Cyprus: Taşucu, Mersin

Best Beaches: Side; Alanya; Kızkalesi; Anamur; Arsuz (Hatay)

Climate: Hot and humid in summer (35°C max), mild in winter (6°C min), snow rare

Nearest Ski Resorts: Saklıkent; Davraz (Isparta)

The Eastern Mediterranean consists of parts of the provinces of Antalya, İçel, Adana and Hatay. However, east of Adana foreign settlement effectively dries up.

West of Antalya the main foreign language spoken along the coast is English, but east of Antalya this gives way abruptly to German. Heading east you come quickly to **Manavgat**, a compact town set astride a river. A few foreigners have bought properties in and around Manavgat. However, most interest focuses on smaller **Side** (pop. 18,000), a fishing village turned overblown resort but which boasts a fine stretch of beach and some impressive Roman ruins. The old part of Side is almost entirely given over to tourism, with shops catering exclusively to foreign buyers; for normal shopping you have to go to Manavgat, a short dolmuş ride away. In summer the nightlife is lively and the restaurants inviting although most people would find the tourist hustlers an aggravation; because there is a steady turnover of staff you have to re-establish the fact that you live in Side at the start of every season.

Further east from Side is **Alanya** (pop. 110,000), where the Seljuk remains astride a steep hill are all but lost above the full-on tourism development. Alanya caters almost exclusively to package-holidaymakers which means that it has large numbers of hotels and apartments together with a lot of very similar restaurants and shops catering exclusively to foreigners. There's a lively nightlife focused on discos where anything goes, and several supermarkets and cinemas. Alanya is most popular with German, Dutch and Scandinavian settlers and there are currently an estimated 6,000 foreign homeowners there.

In central Alanya some of the most expensive apartments are on the slopes of the hill where they benefit from cool breezes and wonderful sea views. The hillside is very quiet and green - rather like a vertical park - but living in the town centre could be very noisy; the suburbs of Oba and Cikcikli are likelier to be quieter. Cheaper apartments are available east of Alanya in Mahmutlar although the infrastructure is currently very poor.

Pros: Easy access to beaches; lively expat lifestyle; reasonable amenities.	**Cons:** No local airport; original town swamped by tourist development; high costs.

Beyond Alanya foreign tourism falls off dramatically although there is a lot of coastal development aimed at domestic tourists. The town of **Anamur** (pop. 50,000) is theoretically inviting, with a fine beach and some striking ruins, but as yet it has not attracted much attention from Westerners. Even further east you come to **Silifke** (pop. 85,000) and **Taşucu**. Silifke may be the bigger town but it is still a pretty sleepy place, tripping out along the banks of a river, with its own supermarket and cinema but few foreign settlers to take advantage of them. Foreigners have been known to buy in Taşucu which is Turkey's main port for travel to Northern Cyprus and so extremely handy for visa-hopping trips. However, although it has an easy-going atmosphere there are few amenities and no expat life to speak of.

Past Silifke the coast becomes increasingly industrialised and unappealing. **Kızkalesi** is growing rapidly as a resort overlooking a lovely beach but offers virtually nothing in the way of non-tourist life. **Mersin/İcel** (pop. 750,000) is a big port town. It is more attractive as a place to live than Adana, simply because it is smaller and more manageable but it has little to draw outsiders, despite a full range of supermarkets, restaurants, shops and cinemas. **Tarsus** (pop. 192,000) has a famous name but is too far inland to hold much appeal to foreign settlers although there is an American school there.

East of Adana the coastline takes an abrupt turn southwards towards Syria, passing through the industrial town of Iskenderun. This part of the coast is likely to become even more heavily industrialised as the oil terminal at Ceyhan gets into its stride. The only town in the area that is likely to appeal to outsiders is **Antakya** (pop. 140,000) which has had the odd English teacher put down temporary roots there. However, there is no expat community, so although the bazaar is alluringly exotic, and there are decent restaurants, a cinema, supermarkets and a few historic monuments, it is unlikely that many foreigners will be moving in in the foreseeable future. At the time of writing foreigners were no longer allowed to buy in Hatay province. Should the situation change, Antakya is well placed for visa-hops to Syria – always assuming you hold a passport that doesn't make obtaining a Syrian visa prohibitively expensive.

CAPPADOCIA (KAPADOKYA)
Need To Know Info

Airports: Ankara Esenboğa Airport; Kayseri Airport
Climate: Very hot and dry in summer (42°C max); very cold and snowy in winter (-10°C min); perfect in spring and autumn
Nearest Ski Resort: Mt Erciyes (Kayseri)

For the time being hardly any foreigners are buying in the Turkish heartland of Anatolia. The one exception to this general rule is Cappadocia, the spectacularly beautiful region at the heart of the country which was created by the action of wind and rain beating down on volcanic tuff. The landscape is utterly extraordinary - a mass of gorges interspersed with fantastic rock formations (*peribacaları* - 'fairy chimneys') - and since time immemorial people have been carving caves out of the soft rock to serve as wineries, storerooms, stables, churches and homes.

In the 1960s it looked as if cave living might be on its way out as villagers were moved away from potentially dangerous rock formations into more modern homes. However, not all the houses were judged unsafe and some people still continued to live a troglodyte lifestyle. Then in the 1980s mass tourism brought a sudden influx of foreign visitors to the area. A handful chose to stay, usually after meeting and marrying Cappadocian Turks. In the 1990s a few foreigners started to settle out of love for the landscape. Most of them were keen to buy and restore the old cave houses, many by then abandoned and in very poor condition. This tendency has accelerated in the 2000s with ever more foreigners (mostly Europeans but with a smattering of Australians, Americans, etc) settling in Cappadocia. These days it is a rare (and very small) Cappadocian village that doesn't have at least one foreign settler.

Before deciding to buy in Cappadocia you need to bear a few things in mind. One is the harsh Anatolian winter which regularly brings metres of snow. In a bad year this can start in November and drag through until April although a more usual winter sees snow lasting from late December until March. The cold aside, this makes for great difficulty in getting around, and burst water pipes, leaks from the thaw and other weather-related problems are routine.

Secondly, most of the old cave properties lie in conservation areas where what you can do to them is regulated by the Nevşehir authorities. Since most people who buy here love the old houses this isn't usually a problem. However, it does lead to additional costs and may prevent you making changes that would make life easier and more comfortable. Threats of court action and jail sentences constantly float in the Cappadocian air. However, although some Turks have been jailed for breaking the conservation laws, so far no foreigners have been sent to join them.

Thirdly, access is always going to be a pain. Although the airport at Kayseri offers daily flights to Istanbul, it is an eleven-hour bus ride to Istanbul or Antalya. Even Ankara is six hours away by bus (although much less by car, foregoing the lunch stop). Should Nevşehir airport ever reopen, it would speed access by about half an hour. However, air fares remain high unless you travel at very unsocial hours.

Nevşehir Amenities	
✓	Cinema(s)
✓	Supermarket(s)
✓	Private Hospital
X	English-language bookshop
X	Church
X	Synagogue

Finally you need to make sure that you are not buying an *afet ev* (disaster house – i.e. a house that was declared unsafe back in the 1950s and '60s). Some of these houses are now being reoccupied but to be on the safe side you would need to have a geological survey carried out to make sure that your chosen property was stable.

As yet Cappadocia has no official estate agents with handy shop windows. Finding something to buy comes down to taking the time to look, getting to know locals and discovering what is available. It pays to be a little wary – fingers have been badly burnt as a result of a too trusting approach.

Although it is easy to find new apartments to rent in Avanos and Ürgüp, rental accommodation is in short supply in Göreme and Uçhisar, especially if you are hoping to find something old and in decent repair.

Pros: Spectacular landscape; authentic Turkish village life; varied expat lifestyle; relatively cheap housing and rents.	**Cons:** Lack of amenities; poor transport links; harsh winters; few work alternatives to tourism; dust - everywhere!

You won't find 'Cappadocia' marked on a map since it is a marketing term which reuses the evocative old Roman provincial name to describe an area that takes in parts of the provinces of Aksaray, Nevşehir, Kayseri and Niğde. The following is a summary of what the different Cappadocian villages have to offer:

Uçhisar (pop. 3,850) is one of the prettiest villages, set as it is around a striking *kale* (castle) visible for miles around and a cluster of fairy chimneys. Traditionally Uçhisar has been particularly popular with French visitors which means that many of the Turkish residents speak good French. Perhaps inevitably, therefore, most of the people who have bought properties in Uçhisar recently are French (or German). There is also a small community of Turks who have moved here from elsewhere in Turkey to restore old cave properties, usually as hotels.

Uçhisar is very close to Nevşehir, the provincial centre, which is handy for shopping as Uçhisar itself has little other than carpet and souvenir shops. There are a few restaurants, including one good, if pricey, French restaurant. However, there is little of the expat camaraderie to be found in nearby Göreme and in winter Uçhisar virtually closes down. Most locals have vacated the old part of town too which means that it can feel unnervingly deserted except at the height of summer.

House prices in Uçhisar have been rising steeply as outside buyers move in. At the moment there is a great deal of building work going on there, most of it quite tastefully carried out under the supervision of the Nevşehir authorities. However, it remains to be seen whether there is actually a market for the new hotels, all of them aiming for the same well-heeled clientele, and that could affect future development in the village.

The backpacker destination of choice for many years, **Göreme** (pop. 2,000) manages to generate some tourism business even in the depths of winter which makes it a livelier place to live than Uçhisar. Like Uçhisar, Göreme boasts some spectacular rock formations. It also has many cave houses although it is becoming increasingly hard to find any for sale. This is partly because the housing stock was always pretty limited, partly because any houses that are halfway habitable are already inhabited and partly because one entire *mahalle* (neighbourhood) has been turned over to tourism, putting yet more pressure on the remaining housing stock. These days the only residential areas with cave houses left are the Orta and Aydınlı *mahalle*s which means that most settlers are buying there. Not surprisingly, house prices in Göreme have skyrocketed over the last five years and it takes a lot of hard looking and determination to find anything at a reasonable price. Usually the starting price for properties that require a complete makeover is at least €50,000.

Most of the shops in Göreme are aimed at a tourist clientele and have higher prices as a consequence; for anything more than basics residents are dependent on shopping trips to Nevşehir, 10 minutes away by dolmuş. However, Göreme does boast its own music and book shop and several book exchanges which resident foreigners can dip into. There are several lively bars and plenty of restaurants, two of them exceptionally good.

What really makes Göreme stand out is the expat life that has developed there. Even in winter there will be at least 10 foreigners living in Göreme, a number that shoots up in summer when foreigners with Turkish partners return to run tourism businesses alongside a handful of 'regulars' who come to stay for a multitude of different reasons. Many of the younger Göremelis have also been working in tourism for a long time and are well used to the strange ways of foreigners. To fit in with the locals it pays to tone down any extremes of behaviour and remember that local women don't drink, and wear excessive quantities of clothes. That aside, however, you should be able to live quite comfortably in the village without having to make many changes to your lifestyle.

Not far from Göreme is the small village of **Çavuşin** where fewer foreigners have settled. As a result house prices tend to be lower and you may be able to buy a bigger piece of land than in Göreme or Avanos for the same money. However, there are few amenities in the village; nor is there much of an expat life.

Avanos (pop. 16,000) feels like a real town compared with Uçhisar and Göreme, so it is likely to suit people who prefer to have a little more anonymity alongside urban conveniences. It is not as pretty as the two smaller villages although the Kızılırmak River running through the middle is a definite plus in summer. At first sight it doesn't look as if much remains of old Avanos. However, if you poke around in the back streets you will soon realise that many of the old cave houses still survive, albeit often in ruinous condition. The houses are often grander than those in Uçhisar and Göreme, with fine carvings that evoke their lost Greek owners. Until recently demand for old houses in Avanos had been relatively low which kept prices reasonable. However, as more people become interested, so they are likely to rise, if not quite to Göreme levels.

Avanos has plenty of shops selling furniture and household goods as well as groceries. It also has lots of pottery shops. The Friday market is bigger than Göreme's and metamorphoses into a plant centre in spring. There are also lots of banks in Avanos as well as a branch of UPS for urgent deliveries.

At the time of writing sleepy **Ortahisar** (pop. 4,000) seemed to be becoming the settlement area of choice with foreigners. This is partly because of the quality of its wonderful old Ottoman houses and partly because Ortahisar managed to miss the big-time tourism boat and so feels more 'authentically' Turkish. There are very few amenities here, beyond basic village cafes, although there are several antique shops and a carpenter who specialises in restoring old furniture (albeit at snail's pace).

Ortahisar is home to a mixed bag of foreigners, including Americans and Germans. Most have bought their own houses, and it's worth knowing that you will get more for your money here than in Göreme or Uçhisar; houses are bigger, sturdier and altogether more elegant (town houses rather than village homes) - which is not to suggest that they don't need just as much money spent on them as anywhere else.

One or two foreigners have also settled in tiny **İbrahimpaşa**, an out-of-the-way village with a pretty location overlooking a ravine. There are some interesting cave houses in need of restoration, and one antique dealer selling artefacts with which to furnish them, but you would need to be a very self-sufficient person to be happy living here. There are virtually no amenities and even public transport is less frequent than elsewhere in Cappadocia.

Like Avanos, **Ürgüp** (pop. 13,500) is a real small town with a useful range of amenities and shops that cater for more than the tourists. The centre of Ürgüp looks thoroughly modern although it is dominated by a chunk of rock as pierced with holes as a slice of Swiss cheese. That western side of town still has fine old cave houses, many of them once the property of Greeks. In the last 10 years many of these have been restored and turned into boutique hotels. A few have also been turned into delightful private homes. Prices in Ürgüp vary widely; although some houses are cheaper than in Avanos, others are phenomenally expensive, reflecting their splendour.

Ürgüp has several good restaurants and bars, a local winery and a big Saturday market. There is also a small cinema-cum-concert hall. It also has an extensive and useful industrial estate (*sanayi sitesi*) where it is possible to find carpenters, ironworkers, marble workers, upholsterers etc.

South of Ürgüp lies beautiful **Mustafapaşa** (pop. 2,500), the old Greek Sinasos, which has a range of fine cave houses. As elsewhere in Cappadocia, some of these have been restored as boutique hotels, but there are still many awaiting similar treatment, sometimes in surprisingly prominent positions. Recently a *medrese* was turned into a university department which should bring new life to the village.

Mustafapaşa has never been a big tourist destination which means that it has a limited range of amenities; for almost all shopping you would have to travel to Ürgüp, a half-hour bus ride away. However, Mustafapaşa has one big claim to fame and that was that the hit TV series *Asmalı Konak* was originally filmed in the Old Greek House here. This went on to garner great popularity, sprouting a feature-film-length version as well as a follow-on series that was filmed in Ürgüp. The consequent attention has tended to push up prices in Mustafapaşa, although as yet only one or two foreigners have settled here.

Far away from central Cappadocia, near Aksaray, is **Güzelyurt** (pop. 4,000), a lovely village with old cave houses set on a bluff. Tourism has barely brushed Güzelyurt, which means that it feels more authentically Turkish to outsiders; it would certainly be desirable to be able to speak the language if you were going to live here. There is a limited range of amenities; for serious shopping you would need to head for Aksaray. However, Güzelyurt is close to Mt Hasan and makes a good base for trekking, horse-riding and other outdoor activities. It is also close to the popular Ihlara Gorge. A few foreigners have bought and renovated grand old Greek houses with spectacular views as homes or pensions.

A couple of foreigners have also ended up living in **Kayseri** (pop. 550,000), a big, bustling town which has been booming lately but which would still strike an outsider as very conservative. The shops are better than average, and a couple of cinemas provide Hollywood entertainment. But after the bazaar closes in the evening the city centre reverts to its origins and a lone foreign female can feel very conspicuous. Most of the fine old Greek, Armenian and Turkish houses that foreigners might have itched to restore have been pulled down to make way for a new highway. Some still survive in nearby **Talas** but that is not a village which is likely to attract foreign settlers for years to come.

Kayseri has the best local airport offering twice-daily flights from Cappadocia to Istanbul all year round.

THE REST OF TURKEY

At the time of writing few other areas of Turkey had attracted foreign settlers. However, with an eye to the future this section offers a quick round-up of what is available in less popular areas.

THRACE (TRAKYA)

Need To Know Info

Airports: Istanbul Atatürk International Airport; İstanbul Sabiha Gökçen International Airport.

Ferry Connections: Eceabat to Çanakkale; Gelibolu to Lapseki

Best Beaches: Erikli; Hamzakoy (Gelibolu); Kum Limanı (Seddülbahir)

Climate: Hot in July and August (28°C max), mild in winter (6°C min).

Border Crossings: Uzunköprü (Greece by train); Ipsala and Pazarkule (Greece by road); Kapıkule (Bulgaria by road)

Thrace is the small part of western Turkey that is geographically part of Europe. It consists of the provinces of Edirne, Kırklareli and Tekirdağ, as well as parts of the provinces of Istanbul and Çanakkale, is hemmed in between the Black Sea to the north and the Sea of Marmara to the south, and has borders with both Greece and Bulgaria. Its location means that it provides a crucial link between Europe and Istanbul, and by Turkish standards the roads in Thrace are extremely busy.

The most attractive town in Thrace is **Edirne** (pop. 115,000) which is tucked into the border area between Turkey, Greece and Bulgaria. Edirne has some stunning early Ottoman mosques and unlike so many Turkish towns does not sprawl into ugly concrete suburbs. Instead it is ringed with meadows offering pleasant weekend walking opportunities. Two rivers run through the southern part of town and every June the meadows host the largest oil-wrestling competition in Turkey.

Edirne, with its rural suburbs, might make a pleasant place to live; the Karaağaç suburb is particularly inviting with some lovely old wooden houses. The town centre has inviting restaurants and street cafes, a cinema and a supermarket. However, there is no foreign community – nor even much foreign tourism - in the town and you would need to speak Turkish to fit in here. If you needed to spend a lot of time in Greek Thrace it would almost certainly be cheaper to live in Edirne. However, the military might be reluctant to allow houses close to the borders to be sold to foreigners.

Edirne aside, the other large population centre in Thrace is **Tekirdağ** (pop. 108,000), a graceless town on the main road to Istanbul. In its favour Tekirdağ faces the sea and has a pleasant seafront promenade. However, it has little to offer foreign settlers for the time being.

To the south-west of Thrace a strip of land threads between the Dardanelles and the Aegean. The biggest settlement on this peninsula is **Gelibolu** (pop. 23,000), a port town linked to Lapseki on the far side of the Dardanelles by a ferry. Gelibolu harbour has some inviting fish restaurants, and the suburb of Hamzaköy has a strip of beach. However, this is a sleepy place which would not be attractive to many foreign settlers.

At the far end of the peninsula is the tiny settlement of **Eceabat** (pop. 4,500) which has a lively tourist industry, especially around ANZAC Day (25 April). At least one Australian has settled in Eceabat. However, most English-speakers are transient tourists or people running hotels, pensions, bars and restaurants about town.

WESTERN ANATOLIA

Need To Know Info

Airports: Istanbul Atatürk International Airport; İstanbul Sabiha Gökçen International Airport; Ankara Esenboğa Airport; Izmir Adnan Menderes Airport; Denizli Çardak Airport

Climate: Hot and dry in summer (32°C max), very cold in winter (-8°C min), snow possible

Nearest Ski Resort: Davraz (Isparta); Uludağ (Bursa)

So far foreigners have shown little interest in settling in Western Anatolia, with its extreme climate and often problematic transport issues. This section merely outlines the major settlements and suggests places where attractive properties are available for adventurous purchasers. It might also interest people looking for somewhere to buy as a long-term investment.

Heading east from Istanbul towards Ankara you pass first through **Kocaeli/İzmit** (pop.181,000), one of Turkey's biggest industrial centres. Although the town is pleasantly situated on the shores of the Sea of Marmara, it is an ugly modern conurbation which was terribly damaged by the earthquake of 1999. Few foreigners would choose to live here.

South of Kocaeli is pretty little **İznik** (pop. 20,000) which still retains its medieval walls and many traces of its illustrious past. Iznik might make a pleasant place to live since it is surrounded by greenery and has a reasonable range of amenities. It is also within easy reach of Bursa and Istanbul. The British writer Azize Ethem settled in a village near Iznik. However, since there are no resident expats in town its atmosphere is likely to be conservative; you would need to be able to speak Turkish to fit in.

East of Kocaeli the road to Ankara skirts **Bolu**, an uninspiring provincial capital with only a lively market in its favour. South-west of Bolu is **Mudurnu**, a small town close to beautiful Lake Abant, which boasts some delightful old Ottoman wooden houses. One or two have been restored as boutique hotels, but others still await the architect's hand. Mudurnu has an interesting old bazaar and a fine hamam to make up for a shortage of supermarkets, cinemas and other amenities. So far it has not attracted foreign attention but it could well do so in the future.

North-east of Bolu is the ugly industrial town of **Karabük** and far prettier **Safranbolu** (pop. 32,000). Safranbolu has been designated a World Heritage Site because of the quality and quantity of its surviving Ottoman housing and it's a delightful place to visit. However, a few Japanese wives aside, few foreigners have chosen to settle there, although Turks from elsewhere in the country have moved in to buy up old properties and turn them into hotels. Nowadays it is unlikely that anyone could find a bargain-priced house in Safranbolu. Even finding somewhere reasonable to rent is becoming tricky.

If you were interested in buying a Safranbolu-style house these days you might be better off looking further afield, say in nearby **Yörükköy,** which is full of splendid old wooden houses, most of them abandoned. The biggest problem is likely to be finding the owners and getting them to agree to sell. However, Yörükköy is starting to be discovered by Istanbullus which means that prices will probably rise rapidly in the near future.

South of Izmit is the large town of **Eskişehir** (pop 500,000), a rapidly developing university town which boasts a host of new cafes and restaurants. It also recently acquired a flashy new tramway which makes getting around town very easy. There are a number of hot springs in the vicinity. However, since Eskişehir looks just like a modern town anywhere else in the world it has not proved popular with foreign tourists, let alone settlers. The occasional English teacher who has spent time there reports that life is unexciting and that they stood out like a sore thumb. The same is also true of the pottery town of **Kütahya** (pop. 175,000) and of conservative **Afyon** (pop. 130,000), further to the south. Neither has attracted settlers although were they to come, they would find prices pleasingly low and that there are many old wooden and stone Ottoman houses crying out for restoration. **Uşak** (pop. 140,000) also has a few old Ottoman houses but is even more off-the-beaten-track as far as foreigners are concerned.

Western Anatolia has two tourism honeypots where it would be easier for foreigners to settle. The World Heritage Site of **Pamukkale** (pop. 2,500) is just outside the big textile-manufacturing town of **Denizli** (pop. 275,000). Denizli itself is a nothingy sort of town whereas Pamukkale is a prettyish village at the foot of the famous 'Cotton Castle' – a terrace of cascading white rock formations in which pools of warm water gather. But life there is likely to prove pretty dull, with all the shops and restaurants focused on tourists and little cultural life or even expat community spirit.

Similarly, **Eğirdir** (pop.17,000), on the lake of the same name, makes a great base for people with a love of the outdoor life, with plentiful trekking and mountaineering opportunities in the vicinity. However, it is a fairly conservative place, as is **Isparta**, the nearest big town. A foreigner who recently tried to set up a business in the surrounding countryside found that suspicion of outsiders rendered it virtually impossible.

THE BLACK SEA

Need To Know Info

Airports: Trabzon Airport; Samsun Çarşamba Airport

Best Beaches: Amasra; Çaka

Nearest Ski Resort: Mt Palandöken (Erzurum)

Climate: Mild and wet in winter (7°C min), warm and wet in summer (26°C max). Snow in Kaçkar Mountains from October to May.

The one part of the Turkish coast that foreign settlers have virtually ignored is the Black Sea which is notorious for its damp weather all year round – good for tea-growing perhaps, but not so great if you're looking to escape the dodgy northern European climate.

The Black Sea coastline stretches all the way from Istanbul via Samsun and Trabzon to the Georgian border, near Hopa. Road access to this part of Turkey used to be slow but although that is still true of the western end, the road at the eastern end is being upgraded to speed the flow of traffic. The summer ferry that used to link Istanbul with Samsun and Trabzon has died a death but new cheap flights to Trabzon have made access to the eastern end of the Black Sea much easier.

Heading east along the coast you arrive in **Amasra** (pop. 7,000), a pleasant small seaside resort in the province of Bolu with a reasonable range of amenities. Next up is **Sinop** (pop. 100,000), the provincial capital, then **Samsun** (pop. 635,000), an ugly port town with little to offer foreigners. Beyond Samsun the provincial capitals of **Ordu** (pop. 415,000) and **Giresun** (pop. 280,000) are pleasant, if sleepy places. Then you arrive in Trabzon.

Trabzon (pop. 485,000) is a lively port town which has grown fat on the proceeds of trade with the ex-Soviet republics of Georgia and Azerbaijan. It's a modern town with excellent shops, supermarkets, cinemas, hamams and an English-language bookshop as well as a decent bazaar area and several historic monuments. The football team (Trabzonspor) is also one of Turkey's most popular. The two flies in the ointment are the relentless city-centre traffic and the equally relentless prostitute activity to the north-east of Atatürk Alanı, the main square. Most of the housing in Trabzon is in new tower blocks. However the Ortahisar *mahalle* does have some pleasant old housing.

So far Westerners have not shown much interest in settling in Trabzon although there is a Russian expat community there as well as the Georgian and Azeri ones. Theoretically anyone settling in Trabzon would be able to visa-hop either to Georgia or across the Black Sea to Russia or the Ukraine. In practise, however, while it's easy to pick up a Georgian visa, the journey there and the corruption at the border don't make this a particularly attractive option. Getting visas for Russia is likely to prove tricky although the Ukraine recently lifted visa requirements for citizens of many Western countries including the USA and the EU states. To live in Trabzon happily you would certainly need to learn Turkish.

Beyond Trabzon the only other settlement of minor interest is **Rize** (pop. 200,000) which might suit someone wanting to settle and do business with Georgia (it is far more appealing than Hopa which, while closer to the border, is a dreary pit-stop of a place). Rize is known for its tea-growing industry but is otherwise a fairly unexciting modern town. There is a reasonable selection of local shops and the odd decent restaurant but beyond that few amenities to attract foreigners.

The area around **Yusufeli** on the Çoruh River used to be very popular with white-water rafters. However, the town was blighted by plans for a dam which have now come to fruition so few foreigners wanted to live there. Keen outdoor types might still be interested in the small mountain village of **Ayder** in the Kaçkar Mountains although it is only comfortably habitable from May through to October. **Artvin** is a small town with a theoretically idyllic lofty location. Unfortunately, it has been completely wrecked by insensitive development.

CENTRAL ANATOLIA

Need To Know Info

Airports: Ankara Esenboğa Airport; Konya Airport; Kayseri Erkilet Airport

Climate: Hot and dry in summer (40°C max), very cold and snowy in winter (-10°C min).

Nearest Ski Resort: Mt Erciyes (Kayseri); Mt Palandöken (Erzurum)

To the north-east of Ankara lie several old towns which are waiting to be discovered by outside buyers with an interest in the 'real' Turkey. **Kastamonu** (pop. 70,000) is perhaps the least developed even though it has an inviting town centre with many huge Ottoman houses awaiting restoration, but any foreigner choosing to settle here would be a real trailblazer and would have to learn Turkish to have any chance of fitting in. There is a cinema but little else in the way of formal entertainment.

Tokat (pop. 115,000) is not immediately inviting and is extremely conservative. It boasts one of Turkey's finest hamams and some stunning Ottoman houses, one of them restored and open to the public. But it is unlikely that a foreigner would want to buy here for the foreseeable future. More immediately inviting is **Amasya** (pop. 75,000) which grew up along the banks of the Yeşilırmak River and in the shadow of some graceful, rock-cut Pontic tombs. Turks themselves have been discovering Amasya's lovely old wooden houses, which means that prices here are likely to be higher than in Tokat or Kastamonu. However, people with an interest in restoring old buildings would at least be guaranteed the company of other like-minded souls.

Sivas (pop. 250,000) is a much bigger town with a reputation, once again, for conservatism. Although the historic centre has some attractive old Seljuk structures, there are not so many old Ottoman houses here and the town would make an unlikely base for foreign settlers – unless, perhaps, they were psoriasis-sufferers wanting regular access to the 'magic' fish in the pools at Balıklı Kaplıca, about an hour away by car.

Further south, **Konya** (pop.750,000) is a thriving metropolis – one of Turkey's so-called 'Anatolian tigers'. However, it is an extremely conservative town, birthplace of Necmettin Erbakan, one of Turkey's more religious political leaders, as well as to the famous Mevlana, founding father of the Whirling Dervishes. Few foreigners have tried to make a life here and those that have report that its attractions quickly pall. There are plenty of shops, although not even the supermarkets stock much foreign produce. Cultural opportunities

tend to revolve quite literally around the cult of the Whirling Dervishes although there are also a couple of local cinemas. Although it is not impossible
to buy alcohol in Konya, this is not somewhere where you would want to be
seen making a fetish out of drinking.

There are a few old wooden houses crumbling away in the city centre but
generally concrete apartment blocks reign supreme in Konya.

EASTERN ANATOLIA

Need To Know Info

Airports: Diyarbakır Airport; Gaziantep Oğuzeli Airport; Şanlıurfa Airport;
Mardin Airport; Van Ferit Melen Airport; Erzurum Airport.

Climate: Extremely hot in summer (round Şanlıurfa temperatures up to
45°C are common), extremely cold and snowy in winter (around Erzurum
temperatures as low as -30°C are possible)

Throughout the 1990s Eastern Turkey was effectively off-limits to all but
the hardier kind of traveller as the PKK (Kurdistan Workers Party) and the Turkish army fought a low-level civil war. However, since the capture and imprisonment of the PKK leader Abdullah Öcalan in 1999 the situation in the east
had been steadily improved, at least in terms of security. Unfortunately, in
2006 there was a resurgence of PKK activity in the east and it remains to be
seen whether this will continue. This is still the poorest, least developed part
of the country. It goes without saying that it is also the part of Turkey which
has the smallest number of foreign settlers.

In spite of that there are a couple of areas which have the potential to become attractive to outside buyers. Foremost among them is the area around
Şanlıurfa (Urfa, pop. 850,000), the beautiful old town where the Prophet
İbrahim (Abraham) is believed to have been born in a cave. Urfa is a popular
pilgrim centre, which makes for an extremely conservative atmosphere. However, there are some huge and stunning properties tucked away down its back
streets which have great potential to be turned into boutique hotels. Anyone
wishing to take one on would need to be fluent in Turkish and well-versed
in the local cultural norms. Otherwise their life here would quickly become
unhappy. Foreign women are likely to face a particularly tough time here.

East of Urfa are two small towns whose day is about to come in terms of
tourism. **Mardin** (pop. 55,000) has a gorgeous town centre in spite of the offputting outskirts. Had it not been for the troubles of the past two decades it
would have had a flourishing tourism industry. However, it has finally started

to make up for lost time. For a foreigner to buy a property here would probably prove tricky, and as a place to live, unless they were fluent in Turkish and/
or Kurdish, Mardin would probably be tough. But it is one of the few really
inviting places in Turkey where tourism is still in its infancy and the business
potential is incredible.

Midyat (pop. 65,000) is like Mardin in spades. It has the same glorious old
honey-coloured houses with a distinctly Arabic look to them but if Mardin
was off the tourist map in the 1990s, Midyat didn't even make the index. Once
again it would be a tough place for a foreigner to make a life for themselves
– but the potential for new tourism businesses is almost limitless.

Hasankeyf (pop. 5,000) is another delightfully overlooked settlement
hugging the banks of the Tigris (Dicle) River with a cliff-face soaring over it.
Unfortunately, it still has the threat of a dam project hanging over it. Were
that to be removed, then this too would be a place where tourism could flour-
ish in the future – and where there are, as yet, no boutique hotels!

Elsewhere in the east potential residents will find slim pickings. In the
north-east, the town of **Erzincan** was all but destroyed by an earthquake in
1939 and is an ugly modern town. **Erzurum** (pop. 350,000) has a university
which gives it a certain kind of student liveliness. However, that barely papers
over a deeply conservative town which holds an unenviable reputation for
some of the coldest temperatures in winter.

Doğubeyazıt (pop. 35,000), close to the Iranian border, has a pleasant setting, in the shadow of Mt Ararat (Ağrı), but it is a dreary modern town where
foreigners would struggle to fit in.

Van (pop. 450,000), however, has a certain laid-back appeal which means
that some visitors have been able to imagine living there. If they did so, they
would have easy access to Turkey's largest (but partially polluted) lake, Lake
Van, and to a reasonable selection of shops, cinemas and other facilities. Even
so, it would be a delusion to imagine society in Van to be anything other than
traditional and conservative.

Few foreigners would want to settle in **Diyarbakır** (pop.350,000) at the
moment. This town, on the banks of the Tigris River and ringed by brooding
basalt walls, was – and still is – the heartland of Kurdish separatism. It has
swollen phenomenally in size since the 1980s and has many social problems
to contend with. The atmosphere here is more relaxed than it was a decade
ago but can still be tense.

There is a flourishing tourism industry attached to Mt Nemrut, near
Adıyaman (pop. 180,000) and **Kahta** (pop. 60,000). However, neither place

has much to offer outsiders. Like Batman, Adıyaman is primarily an oil town, big, ugly and inward-looking. Kahta should be more inviting but in reality the locals have been slow to recognise how tourism could be used to make life more appealing for everyone. The town consists of a long canyon of ugly modern buildings. There's nothing for a restorer to get their teeth into.

Both **Malatya** (pop. 370,000) and **Gaziantep** (pop. 1 million) grew enormously during the 1990s and both are considerably more appealing than they used to be. However, at the moment they are not places many foreigners would plump to live in; the odd one who did so would no doubt feel like a fish out of water but would learn Turkish and/or Kurdish extremely quickly!

CHAPTER 3

THE RENTING GAME

Most foreigners who live and work in Turkey rent their accommodation rather than buying it, particularly if they live in one of the big cities where there is plenty of choice. In particular people who are coming to work in Ankara or Izmir for a relatively short period of time usually opt to rent rather than buy. If you only want to stay in Turkey for a year or so, it is almost certainly easier, and cheaper, to rent property than to buy one (although see Chapter 2 for suggestions about property as an investment). Unless you have a particularly well-paid job, you should assume that you will be going to rent an apartment rather than a house since this is currently the most common unit of housing in Turkish towns.

Even if you know that you eventually want to buy a property in Turkey it is still a good idea to rent somewhere first. This will give you a chance to make sure that you really do want to settle in the place you have chosen; living somewhere is, after all, a very different matter from just holidaying there. By renting first you give yourself a chance to see how well you cope with the changing seasons, especially winter when the tourists have all gone home. While you rent you will also have a chance to assess the actual value of properties in the area without any pressure to buy. You will also be on hand to hear when something good comes on the market.

FINDING SOMEWHERE TO RENT

These days most big Turkish towns, especially in the west, have efficient systems to enable people to find somewhere to rent. However, in more rural areas things may still be more casual, and often dependent on whom you know.

In Town:

A fortunate few people work for companies which have apartments that they rent out to their short-term staff. However, most people have to find their own homes in which case good places to start looking are the property pages of the *Turkish Daily News* or *The New Anatolian*. Several reputable estate agents advertise there, although most of the properties they handle are in the more upmarket suburbs of Istanbul and Ankara. Many of the estate agents listed on pp. 457-463 also handle rental properties. The monthly property magazine *Emlak Pazarı* also carries adverts for rental properties.

Alternatively, if you know where you would like to live you can visit the area and find a local estate agent (*emlakçı*). Cards in estate agency windows usually list little more than the square metreage of each property, how many rooms they have and how much the monthly rent is. As a consequence you will probably have to visit several apartments before finding one that suits your requirements. Bear in mind that top flats tend to command the highest rents because they have the best views (Bosphorus views command the highest prices of all). The exception will be in a block of flats which lacks a lift (*asansör*) in which case the ground-floor flats command the premium rents. It is unusual to find lifts in any but the most modern apartment blocks so if you want to rent one of the flats with character in the centre of Istanbul you may well have to get used to climbing many flights of stairs several times every day.

If an *emlakçı* finds you a flat you must expect to pay them one month's rent for their services. Since most landlords also want one month's rent upfront as well as another month's rent as a deposit, moving into a flat can prove an expensive proposition.

If you are looking for a flat-share, it's a good idea to inspect the noticeboards in Internet cafes, hostels and language schools where people with rooms to let advertise. Alternatively, look out for signs in windows reading *Kıralık Daire* (Flat for Rent). These usually carry a phone number for you to contact the owner. However, it is not very likely that someone English-speaking will answer the phone so unless your Turkish is good you may need to ask a Turkish friend to help make the initial contact.

You can also look in local magazines aimed at expats such as Fethiye's *Land of Lights* since these contain ads placed by foreign property owners. Most of these ads are really for holiday rentals but owners may be prepared to consider normal rentals too.

In the Country:

In rural areas you are unlikely to find rental agents or any other formal system for finding rooms to let. Instead you will need to ask around to find out what is available. Rents in rural areas are dramatically lower than those in town (often no more than €75 a month). However, there may be very little rental accommodation since most families build and live in their own homes. What accommodation is available may need a great deal of work done before you can move in; in particular the bathroom and kitchen may need a lot of modernisation. On the bright side, foreigners are usually seen as potentially good tenants who will not run away without paying the rent or leave the property in ruins when they go. On the downside it is likely that they will be asked for a higher rent than a local on the assumption that most foreigners are wealthy. Occasionally unmarried couples may find landlords reluctant to rent to them.

In rural areas it is common to be asked to pay several months' or even a year's rent upfront. There's not much point in expecting a rebate should you decide to move out early.

TYPICAL MONTHLY RENTS IN TURKEY, WINTER 2004		
Province	District	Monthly Rent (YTL)
ADANA	Reşatbey	220-660
ADANA	Turgut Özal	275-550
ADANA	Yüzevle	530-850
ADANA	Toros	230-450
ALANYA	Centre	200-700
ANKARA	Aydınlıkevler	370-530
ANKARA	Çankaya	350-800
ANKARA	Kavaklıdere	470-720
ANKARA	Kızılay	550-800
ANKARA	Yıldız	400-500
ANTALYA	Mahmutlar	220-420
ANTALYA	Konyaaltı	650-1,100
ANTALYA	Yeşilbahçe	850-1,100
BOLU	Bahçelievler Mahallesi	230-340
BOLU	Beşkavaklar Mahallesi	320-430

BURSA	Yıldırım	170-220
BURSA	Osmangazi	330-550
BURSA	Nilüfer	550-1,100
CAPPADOCIA	Avanos	150-200
CAPPADOCIA	Göreme	130-200
CAPPADOCIA	Ürgüp	150-200
DENİZLİ	Çamlık	430-1,500
DENİZLİ	Severgazi	280-550
ESKİŞEHİR	Hoşnudiye	450-1,100
ESKİŞEHİR	Hasan Polatkan	550-1,100
ESKİŞEHİR	Vişnelik	350-650
GAZİANTEP	İbrahimli Mahallesi	270-380
GAZİANTEP	Değirmiçem	350-450
GAZİANTEP	Ordu Caddesi	220-400
HATAY	Ormancılar	120-230
HATAY	Mete Aslan	120-550
İZMİR	Alsancak	550-1,100
İZMİR	Bornova	330-850
İZMİR	Buca	220-650
İZMİR	Girne	440-700
İZMİR	Karşıyaka	300-500
KAYSERİ	Melikgazi	250-300
KAYSERİ	Kocasinan	250-300
KOCAELİ	Central İzmit	450-550
KOCAELİ	Yahya Kaptan	330-650
KONYA	Centre	350-800
KONYA	Meram	350-800
MUĞLA	Central Bodrum	500-1,200
MUĞLA	Bodrum Yalıkavak	450-1,100
MUĞLA	Bodrum Turgutreis	350-800
SAMSUN	Atakum	230-800
SAMSUN	Ellialtılar	350-800
SİVAS	İstasyon Caddesi	650-1,600
SİVAS	Mehmet Paşa Mahallesi	280-550

ŞANLIURFA	Bahçelievler	300-450
ŞANLIURFA	Yenişehir	450-550
TEKİRDAĞ	Çorlu	300-450
TEKİRDAĞ	Centre	200-300
TRABZON	Beşirli	340-550
TRABZON	Erdoğdu	200-350
TRABZON	Kalkınma	300-600

(Source: Turyap, October 2005 - for updates see www.turyap.com.tr)

WHAT TO EXPECT

In Turkey the terms 'furnished' and 'unfurnished' don't always mean what you might expect. A 'furnished' property will probably have kitchen and bathroom fittings but may not have beds, tables, chairs or light fittings; an 'unfurnished' property may not even have basic kitchen and bathroom fittings.

If you come from a country where landlords are expected to have every gas and electrical appliance checked for safety every year, it may come as a surprise to discover just how unsafe some rental properties in Turkey can be. Particularly if you're renting an old property it's not unusual to find the sockets sparking dangerously or the gas water heater installed without sufficient ventilation. So the first thing you need to do is have an electrician and/or plumber check everything thoroughly for you. At the very least you should get a Turkish friend who knows something about building to look the property over for you.

It is also common to find that you need to do quite a lot of modernising yourself. The kitchens in old Turkish properties are usually very basic, without proper work surfaces or fitted cupboards. Bathrooms may have only squat toilets and elementary showers. It is quite normal to find that there are no floor coverings or curtains. There may not be any fitted central heating appliances either. And all that is before you look at the décor which may be absolutely hideous.

If you need to do a lot of work to make a flat habitable it is normal to negotiate a discounted rent with the landlord. You might, for example, ask them to agree to forego the rent until you have paid for the kitchen cupboards. In that way the landlord gets the work done without any trouble on their part and when you leave the property is more attractive to a new tenant.

RENTS

Rents in Istanbul in particular have been rising steeply but what you'll pay very much depends on where you want to live and what facilities you require. For a villa in upmarket Yeniköy with a garden, swimming pool and Bosphorus views, for example, you might have to pay as much as €5,000 a month. For a three-bedroom flat in Cihangir with Bosphorus views you might pay €2,000 a month. However, for a standard two-bedroom flat in Şişli without exciting views you might pay more like €525 a month.

Rents tend to be lower even in the upmarket parts of Ankara; for example, you might expect to pay €525 a month for a three-bedroom furnished or unfurnished flat in Gaziosmanpaşa (GOP), rising to €1,250 for a three-bedroom furnished flat in Çankaya. If you want to rent an entire house in an area like Konutkent or Beysukent, your rent can be anything from €650 to €4,000.

In rural areas rents remain lower than in towns. For example, in Göreme in Cappadocia you are more likely to pay around €90-125 per month.

Rents are usually set for a year at a time, and at the end of the year landlords often used to hike the rent by much more than the rate of inflation. In 2005, the law was amended so that it became illegal to raise rents by more than the rate of inflation. If the tenant failed to make a payment the landlord used to be within their rights to demand upfront payment of the rest of the year's rent. However, that is also no longer legal.

Deposits: In 2005 a new law decreed that landlords could only ask for up to three months' rent as a deposit. This is supposed to be placed in a separate bank account which should not be accessed without the tenant's permission. However, since people have sometimes had trouble getting their deposit back, some tenants fail to pay their last month's rent without asking their landlord's permission. Alternatively, they ask the incoming tenant to pay the new deposit to them rather than to the landlord.

TENANCY AGREEMENTS

As in other countries, the most secure tenancies are those where you have a written agreement with the landlord or letting agent. In Turkey you may well be able to secure such an agreement in the big towns or along the coast. In rural areas, however, private unwritten agreements are still normal. If you do have a written agreement you should ensure that everything on it is typed; if anything is hand-written both parties to the agreement should counter-sign the writing to authenticate it. Ideally every page of the contract should be signed by both parties. It is a good idea to have a clause built into the contract that allows you to give two month's notice if you need to move before the lease is up. (See pages 579-582 for a sample rental contract.)

In Town: If you are renting through an estate agent, you should get a written agreement which sets out such basics as the monthly rent. You may agree on a fixed length of time for the rental. However, if no time scale has been agreed, it is usually assumed that the rental period will be extended at the end of the year unless the landlord has asked for the property back. Rents in Turkey are normally fixed for a year at a time and can be paid in Turkish lira or any other currency specified by the landlord. As long as inflation was high, many of them asked for foreign currency. Now that it is more stable they may be happier to take Turkish lira. Occasionally disagreements erupt when landlords try to renegotiate the rent retrospectively to compensate for losses made on exchange rates.

A landlord is entitled to ask for the property back with no notice if they, their spouse or their children want to occupy it. The rental agreement also becomes null and void if the tenant fails to make two payments within the year. If the landlord decides to sell the property the new owner is entitled to give the tenants notice. If they do not leave willingly, the new owner can go to court to have them evicted although this is likely to be a long-winded process. A tenant who does not want to leave when the property is sold can ask the Land Registration Office to register their rent. The new owner is then unable to raise it arbitrarily in an effort to force them out.

Theoretically the landlord is supposed to maintain the property in a safe condition while the tenant has the duty not to damage it. However, if either side reneges on their side of the bargain there is not likely to be much the other side can do about it.

Before you move in it is perfectly reasonable to ask the landlord to have the property cleaned and any cracks or other damage repaired. To avoid disputes later always get them to sign a document setting out what they have agreed to do.

The landlord is expected to pay any taxes due on the property except for the environment cleaning tax (*çevre temizlik vergisi*) which the tenant normally pays along with their water bill. The tenant is also responsible for all the utility bills. You should make sure none of these are shared with any adjoining property and that, if they are, that you have come to an agreement on how they are to be shared. Should you be fortunate enough to be living in property paid for by a consulate you are exempt from paying the environment cleaning tax.

TYPICAL ISTANBUL RENTS, SUMMER 2006			
District	Monthly Rent (YTL)	District	Monthly Rent (YTL)
Ataşehir	500-750	Koşuyolu	450-650
Avcılar	300-450	Kozyatağı	650-850
Bakırköy	800-1,200	Kurtköy	250-400
Beşiktaş	900-1,500	Küçükçekmece	300-450
Beylikdüzü	300-600	Maçka	1,500-2,250
Bostancı	850-1,100	Maltepe	350-500
Büyükçekmece	300-450	Nişantaşı	1,500-2,250
Cihangir	900-1,200	Pendik	300-450
Çekmeköy	450-800	Salacak	750-1,000
Erenköy	650-900	Şişli	800-1,200
Fatih	900-1,200	Teşvikiye	1,000-1,700
Florya	1,000-1,500	Ümraniye	600-700
Göztepe	900-1,200	Üsküdar	900-1,400
Kadıköy	750-1,000	Yeşilköy	750-950
Kartal	650-900	Zeytinburnu	350-600
(Source: Turyap, 2006)			

In the Country: In rural areas the idea of a tenancy agreement is, as yet, barely understood which means that you may have no formal rights at all. Your landlord may decide to do building work on the property without warning you. S/he may also decide to evict you at a moment's notice. On the other hand you, too, can quit without giving any notice should you wish to do so. Theoretically, normal state rental law applies. In practise trying to insist on your rights is unlikely to get you anywhere.

Before signing any agreement you should make sure you know the answer to the following questions:

- How much are the monthly rent and deposit? Will you be charged extra if you are late with the rent?
- Will the lease be renewable and will the rent increase if you renew it?
- Are there any service charges (apartments)?

- Who pays the utility bills?
- Who is responsible for maintenance and running repairs?
- Are the kitchen appliances, the light fittings etc included in the rent?
- Who is responsible for shared areas such as the garden?
- Can you keep a dog or cat?
- Will you be able to install a phone line in your own name?
- On what conditions will the landlord/lady have the right to enter the property?
- If you want to make improvements to the property will you be able to get a rent rebate?
- When was the wiring last checked for safety?
- How much notice do you have to give if you want to leave before your lease is up? Will you have to pay extra if you leave early?

APARTMENT LIVING

As anywhere else in the world, living in a block of flats can involve tensions brought about by enforced proximity. It is not uncommon, for example, for flats to have balconies on which some tenants may want to hold barbecues, regardless of the result in terms of smell and smoke for their neighbours up-stairs. Noise and partying can drive other tenants mad.

These problems are common to flat-living everywhere in the world. Some Westerners, however, also find it hard to come to terms with the omnipres-ence of their neighbours who may think it perfectly normal to drop in when-ever they like. Western women, in particular, sometimes find it difficult to cope with their neighbours' incessant interest in who they are having to visit them and what they are doing in their flats. Turkish neighbours may think this reflects on their honour - Westerners are inclined to think it is none of their business. Since more women stay at home all day than is usual in the West, women who work at home may find it hard to persuade their neighbours to allow them to get on in peace.

On the other hand if you are away a lot apartment living may feel more secure than living in a house since it will be harder for a burglar to get in un-observed. What's more, neighbours may be happy to look after the flat while you're away and to get it ready for your return.

COMMON SERVICES

Apartment living also involves coming to terms with arrangements for common services.

Heating: You should try to get an approximate idea of heating bills before you agree to move into a property since sometimes these can be higher than the rent.

Very often the heating in a block of flats is centrally controlled. Even if you can control the temperature of the radiators in your own flat you may have no say over when the heating comes on and goes off at the start and end of winter which may lead to higher bills than you might like (since most Turks like the heating on higher and for longer than most Europeans).

The *kapıcı*: If you rent an apartment in a block of flats you will usually find that there is a *kapıcı* (caretaker, concierge) whose job it is to keep a set of spare keys, look after the payment of certain bills, deliver bread and news-papers to the flats, and keep the shared parts of the block clean. By law the kapaci must be paid the minimum wage plus social security. These costs are divided between the occupants of the flats. If there are a lot of tenants the charge may be as little as YTL15-20 but where there are only a few tenants the sum could come to more than you might expect.

Gated communities: In many parts of Istanbul and Ankara people rent apartments in complexes which have a lockable front gate, usually guarded by a watchman. Not only is this good for security but it also ensures that only local residents are able to park in the complex grounds.

Postal services: Most blocks of flats have mailboxes in the hall where post is left for the individual flats; post is never delivered to individual flats. In rural areas you usually have to go to the post office to collect your mail.

Garbage collection: Tenants usually put their garbage in bags outside their doors ready for collection on a specified day of the week.

WHAT TO DO BEFORE MOVING IN

Whether you choose a house or an apartment there are certain things you should always do before agreeing to take on a rented property.

- Get the meters read. If you don't you could find yourself liable for any out-standing debts.
- Check all the plugs and sockets for safety.
- Check that all gas appliances are in safe locations (e.g. not in bathrooms) and that they are adequately vented.
- Run all the taps to make sure that none of the pipes are blocked. You

should do this even if the property is brand new as builders often leave rubble in the pipes which then leads to flooding.

- Take an inventory of what is in the flat. You may find that a previous tenant has removed everything down to the lightbulbs but by doing this you guard against having the landlord blame you for anything missing.

MOVING FROM ONE HOUSE TO ANOTHER

If you are moving from one town property to another, you will be able to move your belongings just as you would at home in a hired truck. In a rural area, however, it is just as usual to make use of someone's tractor and trailer for moving.

WHAT TO SAY			
bathroom	*banyo*	long-term	*uzun vade*
bathtub	*küvet*	mailbox	*posta kutusu*
bedroom	*yatak odası*	more central	*daha merkezi*
bigger	*daha büyük*	new	*yeni*
central heating	*kalorifer tesisatı*	noisy	*gürültülü*
cheaper	*daha ucuz*	old	*eski*
clean	*temiz*	quiet	*sessiz*
concierge	*kapıcı*	removals	*nakliyat*
contract	*kontrat/sözleşme*	rent	*kira*
counter/work surface	*tezgâh*	security	*güvenlik*
dirty	*kirli*	short-term	*kısa vade*
estate agent	*emlakçı*	shower	*duş*
furnished	*mobilyalı*	sink	*lavabo*
house/apartment for rent	*kiralık ev/daire*	smaller	*daha küçük*
inventory	*envanter*	smelly	*pis kokulu*
key/s	*anahtar/lar*	tenant	*kiracı*
kitchen	*mutfak*	the water heater is dangerous	*şofben tehlikeli*
landlord	*ev sahibi*	to rent	*kiralamak*
lift	*asansör*	toilet	*tuvalet*
living room/lounge	*salon*	too expensive	*çok pahalı*
top floor/ground floor	*üst kat/zemin katı*	with a stove	*sobalı*
weekly/monthly/yearly	*haftalık/aylık/yıllık*	I want a sea/Bosphorus view	*deniz/Boğaz manzarası istiyorum*

CHAPTER 4

BUYING YOUR OWN PIECE OF TURKEY

Not long ago it was a rare foreigner who owned a property in Turkey. However, in the last five years the number of foreign property owners has soared
with the inevitable consequence of rising prices in the most popular areas.
That said, property in Turkey remains cheap by the standards of the UK, USA
or Australia/New Zealand and recent changes to the law have made it easier
for foreigners to buy in Turkey.

In general, the law relating to who can buy a house in Turkey is based on
reciprocity. This means that if a Turk can buy in your home country, then you
will be able to buy in Turkey. It used to be the case that foreigners could only
buy properties outright in settlements large enough to have a Belediye (Town
Hall). This meant that if you wanted to buy in a village of less than 2000 residents
you would have had to do so with a Turkish partner. However, in July 2003 that
stipulation was removed. For two years foreigners were allowed to buy outright anywhere in Turkey except in areas subject to military restrictions (which,
unfortunately, rules out buying on the islands of Bozcaada or Gökçeada). Amid
fears that the Syrians were buying up the area around Antakya, the Israelis were
snapping up the newly-irrigated land around Harran and the British and Germans were buying up the south coast, the law was suspended in 2005. In 2006
it was reinstated with a stipulation that foreigners should not be allowed to
buy more than 2.5 hectares of land without special permission from Parliament.
However, the law is nothing like as clear as it used to be since foreigners are
now only able to buy on the same terms as Turks in areas with a Belediye or
'contiguous areas'; if they want to buy in rural areas they must now set up a
limited company to do so. Foreigners are still forbidden to buy land in military,
strategic and security zones and the Council of Ministers is also authorised to
designate zones which will be declared off-limits to foreign buyers because of
their importance in terms of agriculture, mining, energy, history, culture or flo-

ra. Ultimately the responsibility for confirming that it is legal to sell a particular piece of land lies with the Tapu (deed) Office whose searches should throw up any problems. An upper limit of 0.5% has also been placed on how much land in each province can be owned by foreigners but there is nothing to prevent them buying more than one property.

Foreign companies can now own property in Turkey which means that they can accept property as collateral for a loan. Associations and religious groups are, however, forbidden to buy land. The government reserves the right to compulsorily purchase for the price the buyers paid for it any land which is used for non-authorised purposes.

WHO CAN BUY PROPERTY IN TURKEY		
Citizens of the following countries are allowed to buy property in Turkey:		
Andorra	Finland	New Zealand
Argentina	France	North Cyprus
Australia	Germany	Norway
Austria	Greece	Poland
Belgium	Hungary	Portugal
Bosnia-Herzegovina	Ireland	Serbia
Brazil	Israel	Singapore
Canada	Italy	South Africa
Chile	Luxembourg	Spain
Colombia	Mexico	Sweden
Croatia	Monaco	Switzerland
Denmark	Montenegro	UK
Estonia	Netherlands	USA
For other nationalities see the list provided on: www.turkisheconomy.org.uk/buyingproperty/property.html		

Buying a property in Turkey is subject to many quirks and can seem a far more casual process than in, for example, the UK. However, as Turkey gears up for EU membership it is likely that many of these quirks will be ironed out and procedures will become more formal and bureaucratic.

Note that in some parts of the country, especially near the coast, laws prohibit property developers from building on more than 5% of their land. How that 5% is defined appears to be the subject of some uncertainty, however, with some authorities claiming that the square metreage of every floor counts towards the total and others saying that it is only the size of the ground floor that matters.

THE DECISION TO BUY

Before making up your mind to buy a property you should feel sure that you have spent enough time in the country to know that you will be happy here. In particular, this means making sure that you have visited out of season as well as in the height of summer since many of the coast resorts can resemble ghost towns in winter.

It is also worth asking yourself whether you need to buy. While it is certainly true that most Turkish house prices are still lower than those in northern Europe, prices are rising rapidly in many areas so that bargains are becoming harder to find. At the same time away from Istanbul rents can sometimes be pleasingly low. It is worth considering whether you might be just as happy renting without the potential expenses and complications that come with buying.

WHAT TO BUY

There are several different categories of property for sale:

Buying Off-Plan: Some people buy properties that haven't yet been built on the basis of the plans and architectural drawings. If you do want to do that you need to make particularly sure that the company you are using is reputable, which means spending time asking around locally (or getting a lawyer to do this) and inspecting other properties that it has developed. Sometimes discounts are available for buying off-plan and in the overheated condition of the recent Turkish market some properties have actually risen in value before they were even completed, but bear in mind that architectural drawings have a tendency to look more attractive than the finished items. Be sure to check that the location already has adequate infrastructure in place and that the development is legal (i.e. that the developer owns the land or has a legal agreement to build on it with the owner).

One advantage of buying off-plan is that you can sometimes (but not always) have a say in the design and finish of your new property. Another is that you normally pay in instalments, either on fixed dates or as each phase of the work is completed. Never hand over the final payment without checking that the completed work is as you wanted as it may be hard to persuade the developer to return once they have all the money. Bear in mind that building an entire complex can take up to 18 months, making this an unsuitable method of purchase for people who want to move into their new home speedily.

New-build Properties: The recent boom in house sales has mainly come from properties that have already been completed and whose design and finish the buyers have been unable to influence.

A new-build property should come with a guarantee valid for at least five years (doors and windows should also be guaranteed for at least five years and all the other internal fittings such as the taps and lights for one). However, that is no substitute for visiting it and checking everything thoroughly before handing over the final instalment of your payment; if you take a surveyor with you they should be someone appointed by you to give an independent analysis. When the property is completed it should be issued with an *iskân raporu* (habitation certificate) that confirms it is fit to live in and complies with building regulations. Without this certificate you may find it impossible to get the utilities connected.

Before buying a new-build property you should inspect its location very carefully. In Turkey infrastructural development tends to lag behind house construction which means you can end up living in what resembles a building site with no local amenities for many years after the completion of a property. If you are buying your property for its view you should also consider what could be built close to or in front of it to mar that view.

Designing Your Own Home: If you have more money and time you may want to ask an estate agent to find you a piece of land and then put you in touch with an architect who can design a house to suit your specific needs. Before agreeing to employ an architect you should always try to see other projects they have worked on. Ideally, you should also meet them to establish if you have similar views about buildings. Not all Turkish architects are especially sympathetic to the environment or particularly imaginative so you may need to talk to several before making a decision.

Resale Properties: As the Turkish property market has developed, so properties are starting to be resold. Some were built relatively recently while others are older properties.

'New' Resale Properties: There has been so much new building over the last decade that some properties are starting to return to the market as their owners either decide they want to move elsewhere or leave Turkey. Unfortunately with so much building still going on owners may find it harder to sell, especially at a profit, than they had hoped. This is particularly the case because since the dual earthquakes of 1999 building standards have improved, a tendency that has been reinforced as foreigners started to buy en masse and expected better, particularly in terms of bathrooms, kitchens and general finish. Nowadays it may not be much more expensive for someone to buy

a brand-new building, with its guarantees intact, than to buy second-hand. 'New' resale properties may not meet the latest anti-earthquake measures and may also have been built before the boom in foreign ownership which means that they may have been designed to suit Turkish rather than Western tastes, in particular with smaller rooms than Westerners tend to like; many buyers have decided to knock out internal walls to make rooms bigger which pushes up the real price of their purchase.

A further problem for people hoping to resell their property is that new-build properties can usually be paid for in instalments (see p. 105) whereas second-hand properties usually have to be paid for in one lump sum.

On the plus side 'new' resale properties are often cheaper than new-built ones, and because they were built first they are sometimes closest to the sea, with the best views. Certainly it's always worth looking at older houses before deciding to pay more for something brand-new.

Old Resale Properties: Looking in the windows of the south-coast estate agencies you could be forgiven for thinking there are no properties to be had that are more than two or three years old. But of course it is perfectly possible to find truly old properties for sale in most parts of Turkey although you may have to look harder to find the right estate agent to help you or do most of the legwork yourself.

If you do opt to buy an old property you must be prepared to do a lot of modernising at the very least.

TYPES OF PROPERTY

As in any country, there are many different types of accommodation available in Turkey. In towns most people live in high-rise apartment blocks, often in high-density *siteler* (housing estates). However, in more upmarket parts of town there will also be some detached houses with gardens available. Along the coast there are innumerable developments of duplexes – two-storey houses, usually with their own garden. There are also many purpose-built villas, often in complexes with their own swimming pools and other shared facilities. The most individual properties tend to be in rural areas where old wood-and-stone Ottoman houses still survive, sometimes with their own plots of land. In Cappadocia many people still live in houses partially carved out of the rockface, while in the area around Urfa and Mardin in the south-east extended families live in huge, stone-built houses with enclosed courtyards.

What you want to buy will depend on your personal needs. Some people want a property that they can move straight into without having to do any work on it, whereas for others finding a property with character that they can restore is half the fun of moving to Turkey.

This section describes some of the types of property available and the pros and cons of choosing them.

Apartments: Traditionally Turks tended to live in extended families in houses that were expanded as their families grew. These days, however, younger Turks prefer to live in their own homes, usually apartments in blocks of six or more storeys, sometimes with other family members on other floors. As a result most Turkish towns now contain hundreds of blocks of flats, some of them built above shops, some of them stand-alone blocks.

Similar residential blocks can be found in most of the larger coastal resorts and many foreigners have bought apartments which they either live in all year round or let out for part of it. These apartments vary enormously in size and quality. The smallest and cheapest will have just one or two bedrooms. Others will be huge, with four or five bedrooms and balconies; some may even have shared access to gardens and swimming pools. In Istanbul there are some truly stunning apartments overlooking the Bosphorus in the suburbs to the south of the centre. Lovely as they are, these apartments tend to make very expensive purchases.

For people who only intend to live in Turkey for part of the year, apartments can be perfect because neighbours can usually be relied on to keep an eye on them and perhaps go in just before their return to turn on the heating, air the flat etc. For people concerned with security apartments have the obvious plus that they are harder to break into unnoticed than detached properties.

On the downside apartment-living inevitably involves a certain amount of compromising to fit in with other residents. Noise, nosy neighbours and lack of control over central heating are just some of the problems that can occur. If you have a car parking can be a problem and smaller apartments may lack storage space. It is also important to bear in mind that many of Turkey's apartment blocks have been thrown up in a hurry and not to the highest of standards. In the aftermath of the terrible earthquakes of 1999 it became clear that shoddy workmanship had contributed to the collapse of many blocks. Before buying an apartment you should do your best to have an independent surveyor look the building over – an unusually low price could be an indication that the block has not been constructed as carefully as it should have been.

Town Houses: In general Turkish towns are short of the detached family houses with gardens that British people take for granted, although there are a few towns which still boast considerable quantities of historic wood or stone houses (see Special Properties below). Two adjacent residential neighbour-hoods of Istanbul that do have a number of old town houses are Fener and Balat on the west side of the Golden Horn. For the time being these are both very down-at-heel but they are due to be renovated courtesy of UNESCO grants and have many stone houses on steep slopes overlooking the Golden Horn.

Villas: Increasingly, foreign buyers are homing in on new-built villas – stand-alone houses of two storeys which may or may not be grouped with others. They may have their own private pools and gardens or may share these facilities with adjacent villas. Villas are usually to be found in smaller coastal resorts or on the outskirts of the larger resorts. Foreign buyers may plan to live in them all year round or they may buy them intending to let them as holiday homes for part of the year. However, Turkey has a limited winter season which means that unless they plan to live in their villa themselves in the winter, owners may find their property standing empty for several months of the year.

A modern villa may be very attractive in itself. However, many of them have been built in isolation from other facilities which means that owners without cars may feel cut-off from the rest of the community. Even with a car, they may find themselves leading an American-style, car-oriented life and having to drive everywhere, whether to shop or be entertained. The cost of maintaining common facilities like swimming pools can also be surprisingly high. Security may be a worry if you are planning to leave a villa empty for part of the year.

Some of the most popular properties tend to be in complexes because the added security tends to outweigh any problems caused by having neigh-bours nearby. Buying into a complex also tends to reduce problems over connecting and maintaining the utilities.

Co-operative Housing Complexes (*Siteler*): Because Turkey has had up to now only a vestigial mortgage system and bank loans have tended to be very expensive, many people who wanted a house have not been able to afford to buy one. One answer has been to buy into a co-operative housing development. With such a project a group of people get together and put up enough money for work to start on an apartment block or group of houses. Every year they pay in more money until eventually the complex is finished and they can move in. Sometimes they even do some of the building work themselves.

There are risks attached to such projects because of the time span involved.

It has been known, for example, for the builder to go bust or even vanish with the funds before the properties were completed, leaving the investors with just the shell of a potential home. What's more some co-operative developers get permission for a set number of units, then build more than was agreed. When that happens it becomes impossible to give each person in the co-operative a legal *tapu* (title deed) when the complex is completed. The co-operative as a whole will continue to own the entire complex which can make reselling individual units tricky, especially if by the time you come to sell they have been used, for example, as security against a debt.

On the plus side the people involved in building the complex often have some say in its development. This means that the end product usually meets their personal needs more closely than if they had bought on off-the-peg property. Certainly they will have a say over the final fittings, tiles and paintwork which makes this a cheap way to acquire an individual interior. The complex may also have facilities that would not be available to individual house owners (e.g. shops or a swimming pool).

Because of the long gestation period, few foreigners buy into such projects unless they are married to Turks. However, arguably a share in a co-operative project might prove a worthwhile long-term investment.

If you do decide to take part in a co-operative housing scheme you will find that living in one is much like living in an apartment complex in the UK. Although you may own your own house you will have to share the cost of maintaining common areas and there will be a management committee (*yönetim planı*) to look after such matters. Most of your neighbours are likely to be Turks which means you will need to learn to speak the language and get to grips with the quirks of Turkish culture.

Timeshare: Due to the hard-sell antics of some Spanish sellers in particular, timeshare does not have a particularly good image and Turkey has few timeshare developments. See p. 463 for a couple of possibilities.

Special Properties:

Ottoman Houses: For people who love old buildings some of Turkey's finest properties are the surviving old wooden houses dating back to the late Ottoman period. Most are at least one hundred years old. These houses are usually built on two or three storeys, with the upper stories jutting out over the lower ones and windows angled to soak up the sun. Often they have stone courtyards on the ground floor and many built-in features on the upper floors. Some even have frescoed walls and stained glass, wooden fretwork across the windows and fine carved wooden ceilings. Most of these houses were built of wattle and daub which can be in a very poor state of repair. Inevitably, therefore, restoration costs can be very high and some seemingly 'Ottoman' houses are actually exact replicas of the houses that once stood on the spot.

If you are especially interested in old wooden houses, towns to explore would include Safranbolu (likely to be the most expensive), Kastamonu, Amasya, Mudurnu, Beypazarı and the Kaleiçi area of Antalya.

Cave Houses: Cappadocia, in the heart of Anatolia, has innumerable old troglodyte dwellings in varying states of repair. Most of these houses have seemingly normal stone facades which may be only 50 to 80 years old but behind them lie networks of cave rooms, some of which may have been used as living quarters, some of which may have been stables, wineries or storerooms. It is hard to know how old the cave parts of these houses are as there are few surviving written records but some may be up to 1000 years old.

Some of the cave houses are still in a reasonable state of repair but others are ruinous and restoration costs often match or outstrip the cost of buying the property. In every case they are in need of modernisation; few, for example, have modern bathrooms even if they have electricity and running water.

If you are especially interested in cave houses, places to explore would include Uçhisar, Göreme, Avanos, Ürgüp, Ortahisar, İbrahimpaşa and Mustafapaşa.

Greek Town Houses: In some areas where there were large Greek communities before 1923 there are still many fine old stone houses, usually on two storeys and built to house individual families. Although these may have stood empty for many years and need restoration and modernisation, they are often still habitable. Living in a house like this would probably seem very like living in a terraced house in Britain.

If you are especially interested in old Greek houses, places to look in would include Ayvalık and Cunda, Yeni Foça, Alaçatı and Bozcaada Town (although foreigners cannot currently buy on Bozcaada). Some of the cave houses in Avanos, Ürgüp, Ortahisar and Mustafapaşa also used to belong to 'Greeks'.

Mardin-Style Houses: Although foreigners have not so far shown much interest in buying properties east of Cappadocia, one obvious area that has houses with enormous potential is the part of Turkey that extends east from Şanlıurfa through Mardin to Midyat. All three of these towns boast stunning properties built out of honey-coloured stone and set around vast courtyards. The facades of the houses are usually attractively decorated and internally they usually have fine stone-built porches as well. These houses are usually huge since they were intended to accommodate extended families, so theoretically, as tourism picks up in the east, they would make excellent pensions.

Mud-Brick Houses: In rural areas many houses were traditionally made from mud-brick strengthened with straw and roofed with tree trunks. The area between the trunks was covered with plant-based flat mats and then the whole roof was caked with mud which was rolled flat with a stone roller. Families used to sleep out on these flat roofs during hot times of year but they were also useful for storing items, and for drying apricots, tomatoes and the washing.

Potentially some of these mud-brick houses could make very attractive homes although they usually require extensive modernisation or virtual re-building.

Timber Houses: If you find contemporary Turkish building styles depressing you might want to consider buying a modern timber house. These are being produced for prices starting at around €80,000 although some of the cheaper standard models are uninspiring (see p. 143). One idea might be to buy a plot of land, construct a timber house to live in while a more solid stone house is built, then rent out the timber house as a holiday let when the other house is finished. Timber houses usually take three to six months to build.

WHAT YOU NEED TO KNOW ABOUT TURKEY AND THE EUROPEAN UNION

Turkey first applied to join the European Union in 1989 although it had been expressing interest since 1963. In 1999 the EU finally agreed to start accession discussions with Turkey provided it agreed to a long list of improvements on human rights, democracy and administrative and economic competence. Many of these changes have been made and in 2005 the EU duly began accession talks. However even the most optimistic of commentators assumes that it will be another 5 to 10 years before the country is actually accepted and there is still no absolute certainty that it will be.

That has not stopped some unscrupulous estate agents and property developers selling land to prospective buyers on the basis that it is 'guaranteed' to rise in value when Turkey joins the EU.

Of course these profits may well materialise. Eventually EU citizens may also be freed from the need to buy visas to enter the country. However for the time being it would probably be unwise to buy solely on the assumption that Turkey will be admitted to the EU.

To find out the latest progress on Turkey's EU negotiations look at www.abhaber.com.

FINDING A SUITABLE PROPERTY

There are many different sources of information for people thinking of buying a property in Turkey. However, there can be no substitute for your own on-the-ground research. Although buying a property in Turkey can be perfectly safe and straightforward, the people who tend to have the most problems are those who spend very little time looking and who too readily trust other people to do the work for them. Ideally you should put aside plenty of time to look around to make sure that you have considered all your options and not just the first suitable property that becomes available. Only by taking your time can you be sure that you have a feel for how much you should be paying for what. Ideally you should consider renting in your chosen area or at least taking a long-stay holiday there before making up your mind to buy. Short inspection visits are useful if you already know the area well but on their own are unlikely to be an adequate basis on which to make a decision.

Turkish Estate Agents: For many people deciding to a buy a property in Turkey is a casual matter, the result of an enjoyable holiday during which they noticed how much lower house prices were in Turkey than at home. For others, however, there will have been a more considered decision to buy in Turkey. These people will be pleased to discover that in the big cities of the west and along the coast there are now plenty of estate agents ready to help them find a property.

However, a few words of caution are in order. At the moment anyone can set up in business as an estate agent which means that many of the agencies that have opened in the last few years are staffed by people with little or no experience behind them. What's more the information provided in the windows of Turkish estate agents doesn't always match that available in the most suspect agency in the UK (this is less true on the south coast). Nor is it subject to the legal protections provided by Western consumer law. Many estate agencies are really construction companies which build and then sell new properties. Normally they also handle rental properties and will manage buy-to-let properties for their owners. Other agents double as travel agents, jewellers, etc. The only national chain of Turkish agencies is Turyap (www.turyap.com.tr) which has been in business for 20 years.

Where possible you should use an estate agent recommended by someone else who has used their services. Where that is not possible you should make enquiries with several agencies before deciding which one to use; the same property may be handled by several agents who may offer it for very different prices.

Turkish estate agents normally charge both the buyer and the seller a commission of around 3% on all sales, but this amount is sometimes negotiable on high figure sales.

Foreign Estate Agents: As the property market has taken off, so some overseas estate agents have expanded their portfolios to take in Turkish properties. Some of these estate agencies are large and well-established but may deal only in more expensive properties. Others have been set up by people with strong links to Turkey (they may offer some of the cheaper properties). The US estate agency chains Century 21 (www.century21.com.tr) and Remax (www.remax.com.tr) also have offices in some of the larger Turkish cities.

Buying through an overseas agent may end up costing you more if they are using a Turkish agent as an intermediary. However, you may find it easier and more comfortable to deal with agents who understand your mind-set and speak your language perfectly.

Of course some Turkish estate agents make life easier for their clients by employing expat staff or foreign partners who can speak English and other languages perfectly.

For a list of estate agents specialising in Turkish properties see Appendix I.

UNDERSTANDING TURKISH ADDRESSES

As with so many other things in Turkey addresses can seem topsy-turvy to Western minds. So, for example, an address may start by giving the neighbourhood (*mahalle(si)*) in which the building is situated, followed by the street name (*cadde(si)* or *sokak/sokağı*) and number (always after the street name). If the street is a side turning off a main road, the name of the main road may come before the name of the actual street. Details of the block (in a complex) and the floor (*kat*) on which an apartment (*daire*) is situated go AFTER the street name and not before as is conventional in the West. When two numbers are separated by a slash the first indicates the street number and the second the apartment number. If a number and a letter are separated by a slash the letter indicates the unit number. Some Turkish streets are numbered which can lead to especially confusing addresses; 3. Sokak No: 3 for example, means house number 3 on 3rd (3.) Street.

arka(sı)	behind	*karşı(sı)*	opposite
mevkii locality		*üzeri*	on
yanı	next to	*yol(u)*	road

Turkish Newspapers and Magazines: Some of the better and longer established agencies in Istanbul and Ankara advertise in the *Turkish Daily News* or *The New Anatolian* which therefore make good places to start your research. Most of these agencies specialise in selling (and renting) properties in the more upmarket parts of the cities. They are likely to have English-speaking staff on hand to help.

Provided you can read Turkish (or have a friend who can), you can also look in the Turkish daily newspapers such as *Hürriyet* and *Sabah* for properties for sale. Chances are that prices will be cheaper in these papers than in the English-language ones. The monthly property magazine *Emlak Pazarı* also advertises properties for sale around the country.

You can also look in local newspapers aimed at expats such as *Land of Lights* (Fethiye area) or *Evet* (Dalyan area). These carry private and commercial advertisements offering properties for sale.

Foreign Newspapers and Property Magazines: As the Turkish property market has expanded so magazines and newspapers have started to run articles about buying homes there. Some of the best places to start looking include the British *Homes Overseas, Escape, A Place in the Sun* and *Exclusive Holidays* magazines. However, you may also find advertisements for some properties in weekend editions of *The Times, Daily Telegraph* and *Mail on Sunday*.

The Internet: It is also possible to search the Internet for properties for sale since many agents with offices in the cities or the resorts place ads there. However, some sites may not be linked to a specific office and some websites have even shown images of properties that were not for sale. Again, you MUST exercise caution. It never makes sense to buy without having visited the office of the estate agent to check that they are genuine. Use the Internet to get a general picture of what may be on offer but don't use it to the exclusion of everything else. Bear in mind, too, that most of the websites offering property in Turkey are aimed at foreigners with prices generally pitched higher as a consequence.

Property Shows: Until recently property shows didn't usually carry information about properties in Turkey. However, as the market has grown, so has what you can learn from a visit to such shows. Those organised by the *Homes Overseas* (www.homesoverseas.co.uk) and *A Place in the Sun* (www.aplaceinthesunlive.com) magazines may be the most useful. Property shows usually take place in spring and autumn.

Word of Mouth: Away from the big cities and coastal areas finding a property is more likely to be the result of word-of-mouth recommendation. If you have found somewhere where you think you would like to buy, you will need to ask around to find out what is available. Bear in mind that if the owners know that the potential buyer is a foreigner, the price is likely to rise accordingly, so if you have a friend you can trust to do the negotiating for you, then that might be advisable. However, you will need to establish some ground rules first. Some people have been very disappointed to find that 'friends' who were negotiating on their behalf also negotiated themselves a large commission – up to 10% of the sale price rather than the 1-3% that might be the norm in the West. Others have seen money handed over as a deposit simply disappear into a 'friend's' pocket.

Auctions (*Müzayedeler*): Serious property developers with good Turkish might also want to consider buying at auctions. Often such properties are being sold in order to pay off debts, either because the owner has chosen to sell or because the court has ordered him/her to do so. Sometimes it is possible to find a bargain property at an auction but since most foreigners would have to pay a lawyer to do their bidding for them (and there is a small bidding fee), the cost is usually higher than they might assume.

If you do want to try the auctions you will probably need local help to find out when they are on. The courts will advertise forced sales in local papers about two months before they take place. Turyap (www.turyap.com.tr) and Eskidji (www.eskidji.com) deal with property auctions. Otherwise you will need to look out for local notices.

Unlike normal property sales, those made at auction are liable to KDV (Turkish VAT, see p. 296).

Inspection Trips

Some estate agents will arrange inspection trips to enable potential buyers to look at specific properties, with flights, airport transfers, accommodation and sometimes even meals thrown in with a tour of properties in which you might be interested. If you take up such an offer don't let yourself be rushed into a decision and ignore advice to bring a banker's draft to pay a deposit with you. It is probably wiser to come on an independent trip and do your own thorough research before contemplating buying. However, if you do take up the offer of an inspection trip and then buy from the agent organising it they may deduct the cost of the trip from their eventual fee.

THE DÖNÜM

The dönüm is an old Ottoman land measurement that is still in use in modern Turkey. It is the rough equivalent of 1000 square metres or half an acre.

POTENTIAL PROBLEMS

Multiple Ownership: The Turkish system of inheritance has an important bearing on how easy it may be to buy a property. When somebody dies their property is normally divided between all their children, and when any of them dies their share of the property is then subdivided again between all *their* children. The result can be that within a couple of generations a single house becomes the property of 10 or more owners, not all of them necessarily still living in the same location or even in Turkey. Before the property can be sold all the owners have to agree to sell which can be a nightmare, especially where some of the owners live in Istanbul or Ankara and think in terms of big-city prices or where some of them live in northern Europe and think in terms of northern European prices. As a result of this system houses that might otherwise look attractive to a foreign buyer fall into disrepair and even collapse without the owners being able to agree a sale.

In general, the fewer the owners, the lower the price of a property is likely to be.

In theory, if only one person holds out against selling a property in multiple ownership it is possible to go to court and force them to sell. However, this is likely to be a protracted and stressful procedure.

State-owned Land: The Turkish state owns the seashore as well as most forests, mountains, marshy areas and other areas unsuitable for agriculture, as well as land used for roads, cemeteries, town squares and other public amenities. From time to time some of this land is sold to private individuals or leased to them for up to 60 years. As the value of land has been rising just when the government needs to find more money, there have been more sales of state land recently. Anyone buying such land needs to make sure that all the paperwork to legitimise the transfer has been completed correctly.

Historic monuments also belong to the state. In most cases this has no bearing on private purchasers. However, in Cappadocia all the fairy chimneys that dot the landscape technically continue to belong to the state even if they are privately 'owned' and inhabited. Usually this is no cause for concern although there are occasional fears that the state may choose to evict chimney residents or slap a steep tax on them.

***Hazine* (Treasury) Land:** Some more land is reserved for the state in case they need to build access roads or other amenities. Unlike other land, *hazine* land can never be rezoned (although there are occasional auctions at which it is sold off), so you need to check local maps carefully to ensure that there is no such land positioned in a way that might, for example, block access to your property.

***Orman* (Forestry) Land:** Similarly difficult to buy is forestry land and so-called '2B' land. Should you buy land designated in this way you risk having to buy it again from the government at some point in the future.

WHO IS IN CHARGE HERE?

Muhtarlık – The smallest settlements are in the care of a *muhtar* (headman) who may 'authorise' land sales, etc. In bigger settlements the *muhtar* will be headman of a particular neighbourhood and may have to sign official documents, for example, to confirm your residence in his area.

Belediye - Settlements of more than 2000 people will have a *Belediye* (town hall) run by a *reis* or *başkan* (mayor) and *meclis* (council). The *Belediye* can usually approve building works except in conservation zones.

Kaymakamlık - Larger areas are under the control of a *kaymakam* (head official of a district).

Valilik - Provinces are governed by a *vali* (governor) who may have to counter-sign your residency permit.

Buying with a Partner: In the past when foreigners couldn't buy land in rural areas one way to circumvent the rule was to buy together with a Turk. However, this often led to problems later, especially when a restored property soared in value or when one of the partners had invested more money than the other. These days it is rarely necessary to buy with Turkish partner simply to be able to own the land. However, some people do still buy with friends, either Turkish or foreign. If you do decide to buy with a friend you need to be sure that the relationship is likely to stand the test of time and is between two people of equal financial standing. If you buy a piece of land with a friend or partner and it is not subdivided between you, then you need to be aware that you could become liable for any debt the other partner has secured against the property.

AGREEING A FAIR PRICE

If you are buying a property in Istanbul, Ankara, Izmir or along the coast and you are using an estate agency, chances are that the price will have been decided in advance and your scope for bartering will be about the same as if you were buying in the UK or elsewhere in the West. If you are buying privately, however (which is in the norm in rural areas), then you will have to negotiate a price directly with the seller.

The Turkish property market is still in its infancy which means that there are not always established norms against which you can measure prices. Locals may have an approximate idea of the value of a particular plot of land, but even they can come up against intransigent owners who won't budge from an unrealistic price tag. In towns it is still relatively easy to find out what other apartments or houses in an area have sold for and therefore what the 'value' of a particular property is. However, in rural areas where the properties are scattered about and where each is very different, the owners may just work out what they want to do with the sale price (buy an apartment or two in a neighbouring town, buy a car, set up a business) and then charge whatever they think that will cost them. The result can be some completely fantastic asking prices from which the owners are extremely reluctant to budge.

It doesn't help that house-price inflation in many areas of Turkey has been steep over the last few years. As a result a price that may have seemed reasonable one year ago can have become completely unrealistic a year later. Knowing this tends to put pressure on potential buyers to agree a quick purchase. However, unless you are absolutely certain that the property is for you, you should not let yourself be rushed into buying something just because the price is likely to rise in the future.

It cannot be stressed highly enough that the only way to get a feel for the 'real' value of property in a specific area is to go there and spend long enough there (i.e. longer than a short holiday visit) to carry out your own comprehensive research. You should not trust an intermediary to do the legwork for you. If at all possible you should find other foreigners who have bought in the same area and ask them what they paid, in which year and for what square metreage of land. Try and ask more than one person in case the one you pick on was also the one who paid over the odds!

Because of the problem of multiple ownership, agreeing on a price may take some time as all the owners of the property will have to accept it. However, once the price has been agreed you may be surprised at how fast the sale moves to closure compared with experience in the West.

The golden rules for avoiding an over-expensive purchase are:

- Take your time and look at lots of properties.

- Ask a variety of foreigners and local people what they paid for their properties.

- Don't allow yourself to be rushed into a decision with dire predictions of price rises to come.

- Try and get a Turk you know really well to act as an intermediary so that the owners don't increase the price just because the would-be buyer is a foreigner.

- Avoid properties with more than four or five owners.

TYPICAL HOUSE PRICES FOR TURKISH PROVINCES, SUMMER 2005

Province	District	Price in YTL (000s)
ADANA	Reşatbey	70-80
ADANA	Turgut Özal	90-160
ADANA	Yüzevler	90-200
ADANA	Toros	45-95
ANKARA	Aydınevler	55-80
ANKARA	Çankaya	80-135
ANKARA	Kavaklıdere	90-155
ANKARA	Kızılay	80-110
ANKARA	Yıldız	80-120
ANTALYA	Alanya Atatürk Cd.	110-150
ANTALYA	Alanya Keykubat	150-360
ANTALYA	Mahmutlar	110-230
ANTALYA	Konyaaltı	200-430
ANTALYA	Yeşilbahçe	230-420
BOLU	Bahçelievler Mahallesi	60-130
BOLU	Beşkavaklar Mahallesi	45-125
BURSA	Yıldırım	30-50
BURSA	Osmangazi	60-80
BURSA	Nilüfer	60-220
KAPADOKYA	Avanos	50-150
KAPADOKYA	Göreme	50-150
KAPADOKYA	Ürgüp	50-200
DENİZLİ	Çamlık	170-320
DENİZLİ	Severgazi	75-130
ESKİŞEHİR	Hoşnudiye	75-160
ESKİŞEHİR	Hasan Polatkan	90-270
ESKİŞEHİR	Vişnelik	70-110
GAZİANTEP	İbrahimli Mahallesi	65-85
GAZİANTEP	Değirmiçem	55-75

GAZİANTEP	Ordu Caddesi	47-95
HATAY	Ormancılar	27-33
HATAY	Mete Aslan	27-45
IZMIR	Alsancak	120-230
IZMIR	Bornova	55-190
IZMIR	Buca	45-120
IZMIR	Girne	85-125
IZMIR	Karşıyaka	55-100
KAYSERİ	Melikgazi	120-200
KAYSERİ	Kocasinan	110-200
KOCAELİ	Merkez	55-85
KOCAELİ	Yahya Kaptan	65-90
KONYA	Merkez	80-230
KONYA	Meram	60-400
KONYA	Selçuklu	30-70
KONYA	Karatay	17-52
MUĞLA	Bodrum Merkez	80-160
MUĞLA	Bodrum Yalıkavak	70-120
MUĞLA	Bodrum Turgutreis	85-160
SAMSUN	Atakum	35-270
SAMSUN	Ellialtılar	80-300
SİVAS	Istasyon Caddesi	110-270
SİVAS	Mehmet Paşa Mahallesi	70-130
ŞANLIURFA	Bahçelievler	43-65
ŞANLIURFA	Yenişehir	75-110
TEKİRDAĞ	Çorlu	43-65
TEKİRDAĞ	Merkez	27-48
TRABZON	Beşirli	60-110
TRABZON	Erdoğdu	35-90
TRABZON	Kalkınma	45-110

(Source: Turyap, October 2005 - for updates, see www.turyap.com.tr)

WHAT YOU CAN EXPECT TO PAY

It is difficult to say what you will have to pay for a property in Turkey since it entirely depends on what you want to buy and where. However, it was probably true at the time of writing that properties in Cappadocia were cheap in comparison with those on the coast, even allowing for recent house price inflation. On the coast your money will stretch further in overdeveloped resorts like Kuşadası and Altınkum than in more upmarket ones such as Kaş, Kalkan and Bodrum; it is still just about possible to buy small apartments for around the equivalent of £30,000 in some of the resorts but in most places you are looking at paying more like £100,000 for even the smallest villa. In Istanbul even the smallest apartment is likely to cost in excess of £50,000. Unless Turkey suffers another economic setback, these prices can only continue to rise.

BUYING IN A CONSERVATION AREA *(KORUMA BÖLGESİ)*

In certain parts of the country historic buildings are subject to protection orders as they would be at home. If you want to buy in a conservation area you will need to make enquiries about what can and cannot be done to a property before deciding to part with your money. Otherwise you could be in for some expensive shocks. The department dealing with conservation areas is called the *Anıtlar Kurulu Müdürlüğü* (Monument Protection Management).

Istanbul: Properties along the shores of the Bosphorus are normally subject to strict controls, especially if they are old. You will not be allowed to pull your property down to rebuild it. Nor will you be able to make significant changes to the façades of older properties.

The Coast: Although there has been a great deal of unsightly development along the Turkish coast, you may find that you need to obtain special permission to alter properties that are close to the waterfront. There may also be restrictions on how high you can build, how close to the water, how much of the land you can build on and which months you can build in. Normally you will not be allowed to build within 100 metres of the sea.

Cappadocia: Most of Cappadocia's old stone houses are now covered by protection orders supervised by Nevşehir, the provincial capital. To find out what degree of protection is attached to a specific house you will need to visit the local Belediye to see the town plan which will indicate into which zone the property you want to buy falls. The most basic village houses are usually subject only to restrictions on what can be done to their exterior in an attempt to retain a homogenous appearance. That this law is not uniformly applied will be obvious on even the most casual visit to the region. However, it is most forcefully applied against Turks with local businesses and foreign buyers, the people whom the authorities presumably believe have the money to do things properly. Someone from Nevşehir Museum will visit and photograph the house and discuss whatever changes you want to make. Unless you want to alter the appearance of the external windows and doors, this is unlikely to be a big problem.

If the house you are interested in is attached to a fairy chimney, things immediately become more complicated. In the first place you will probably have to pay for a geological survey to assess how stable the chimney is. Then you will have to pay an architect to drawn up a *proje* (project) showing exactly what will be done to the house. This will have to be approved by the Anıtlar Kurulu (Monuments Committee) behind the museum in Nevşehir before you can start work.

It is sometimes possible to have an awkward zoning designation altered. However, this is likely to be a time-consuming (think years rather than months) process.

Areas of Archaeological Interest: If the property you are interested in is in an area of archaeological importance you may need permission from the local museum authorities to buy or restore it.

Military Bases: If the property you are interested in is close to a military base you will need special permission from the military to buy it. Sometimes this will be forthcoming, at other times it will not.

WHAT TO ASK BEFORE AGREEING TO BUY

Just as you would when buying a property at home you need to visit any property that interests you with a list of your minimum requirements. For example, how many bedrooms do you want? Do the rooms all need to be on one floor? Must that be the ground floor? Are you prepared to buy a property in need of modernisation or do you want something you can move into immediately?

Other questions to ask include:

- Which direction does the house face? Will there be enough/too much sun?
- How close to the property is the nearest mosque (especially important if you are a light sleeper)?

- Is there undeveloped land nearby? If so, what effect would it have on your property if someone built on it?
- Is the local infrastructure adequate? For example, are there already sewerage lines in place?
- If the infrastructure is *not* already in place, how easy/expensive will it be to organise suitable utilities?
- Is the local water supply adequate?
- Does a *tapu* (title deed) for the site exist?
- (In Cappadocia) Who owns the caves under your property?
- Is a foreigner likely to be welcomed by the locals?

TYPICAL HOUSE PRICES FOR ISTANBUL, SUMMER 2006		
	Price in YTL (000s)	
ISTANBUL	Avcılar	85-125
ISTANBUL	Bakırköy	125-180
ISTANBUL	Beşiktaş	150-225
ISTANBUL	Bostancı	150-200
ISTANBUL	Cihangir	120-200
ISTANBUL	Fatih	120-150
ISTANBUL	Florya	135-200
ISTANBUL	Göztepe	150-190
ISTANBUL	Kadıköy	75-135
ISTANBUL	Kartal	110-140
ISTANBUL	Nişantaşı	185-275
ISTANBUL	Şişli	100-150
ISTANBUL	Teşvikiye	170-330
ISTANBUL	Ümraniye	110-150
ISTANBUL	Üsküdar	150-250

FINDING A LAWYER *(AVUKAT)*

In Turkey it is not necessarily the norm to appoint a solicitor to handle conveyancing. Ideally, of course, foreigners would be well advised to use a solicitor because they understand the sales process so much less well than the Turks themselves. However, it is not always easy to find a solicitor who speaks

English. Nor are many solicitors particularly well-informed about property law. You could, perhaps, use a specialist UK lawyer to help out. However, it will not be easy to find someone who understands British and Turkish law well. In any case this might result in additional costs.

In rural areas where it is common to make a private arrangement with the seller you may decide not to use a lawyer. However, in urban areas it is normal to do so. Although you could find a solicitor simply by looking in a phone book or looking for a business sign, it is wise to find a Turk or resident foreigner whose advice you trust and make arrangements with a lawyer they recommend. If you are buying a property through an estate agent they should be able to put you in touch with a lawyer to handle the conveyancing. However, you may prefer to appoint an independent lawyer. The websites of overseas embassies often list lawyers who speak the appropriate language.

If you want to buy a house but you can't stay in the country long enough to see the process through, then it is possible to give a *vekâletname* (power of attorney) to a solicitor who can complete the sale for you. It is not advisable to let a friend do this for you unless you know them extremely well. It is possible to get a British solicitor to draw up a power-of-attorney but to be accepted in Turkey this has to be counter-signed by the Foreign & Commonwealth Office, adding to the expense and time the process takes.

When appointing a Turkish lawyer you should bear in mind that you are unlikely to have any legal redress against them if anything goes wrong. Few lawyers have professional indemnity insurance; nor do many of them keep their client's money in a separate bank account.

WHO TO CONTACT

The British Embassy has a list of English-speaking lawyers on its website (www.britishembassy.org.tr)

Turkey

Denton Wilde Sapte: Tel: 0212-284 6091, www.dentonwildesapte.com, Alt Zeren Sokak No: 7, Daire: 1, Levent, Istanbul

TAPO (Turkish Attorneys & Paralegals Online): Tel: 0252-645 2313, www.tapo.co.uk

UK

Acacia International: Tel: 07000-565710, www.acacia-int.com, 61 Walham Green Court, Fulham Rd, London SW6 2DQ

John Howell & Co: Tel 0207-420 0400, www.tapu.co.uk, The Old Glassworks, 22 Endell St, London WC2H 9AD

Mazars: Tel: 0207-377 1000, www.mazars.co.uk, 24 Bevis Marks, London EC3A 7NR

Ireland

Mazars: Tel: 0353-1-449 4400, www.mazars.ie, Harcourt Centre, Block 3, Harcourt Rd, Dublin 2

SURVEYING THE PROPERTY

One problem with buying a house in Turkey is that is not normal to have a survey done and might be hard to find a qualified surveyor (*kadastro mühendisi)* to do the work. Instead you are likely to be dependent on what you notice about the property yourself. In lieu of a surveyor it is wise to take a trusted builder to look at the property and tell you what work will need doing to it and any problems that they can detect.

The following improvements will probably have to be made to anything but the newest property:

- Rewiring – Istanbul apartment blocks often have wiring that is very dangerous.
- Replacing an *a la turca* (squat) toilet with an *a la franca* (pedestal) version.
- Installing a modern bath and/or shower.
- Installing kitchen cupboards and work surfaces/wholly remodelling the kitchen.

Foreigners who are buying in towns are usually buying houses or apartments in need of modernisation but which are at least structurally sound. In rural areas, however, they may be buying the shell of a property with the intention of turning it into a modern house. It is important not to underestimate the cost of the work involved. Although building costs are much lower in Turkey than in the West, it is likely that you will have to pay as much again (possibly even more) to restore the shell of a house as what you paid to purchase it. To restore a simple stone house in Cappadocia, for example, is likely to cost at least €22,000-30,000.

For a fee, the estate agency Türyap (www.turyap.com.tr) will prepare a report on a specific property which will include such details as:

- The exact address on the *tapu*
- Whether there are any impediments to purchase

- Whether there are any outstanding utility bills
- The condition of each room and its fittings

At the very least you should go to the local town planning office (probably in the Belediye building) and find out the number of the *tapu* for the land you are hoping to buy. Armed with this information you can then visit the *tapu* office and look at a map which will show you the extents of the land and who owns it. Back at the town planning office you can also check whether there are any plans in the pipeline that might affect the property; the local plan, for example, should be able to show you if the land has been designated for a purpose other than residency.

CONTRACTS *(SÖZLEŞMELER)*

When agreeing to buy a piece of land you need to be sure that the person you are buying it from is legally capable of signing a contract. This means that they must be:

- over 18 years old
- of sound mind

If you are buying from a married couple then both partners need to sign the contract. If the seller is elderly (defined as over 65) then in some cases you may need to get a medical certificate stating that they were in sound mind at the time of the sale. If the land is owned by someone who has been certified as having mental problems then the courts, as their guardian, may refuse to allow the sale to proceed.

If you are buying in a big town or one of the coastal resorts you may find you have to sign three contracts before completing your sale. The first will be a reservation contract which is intended to show that you are serious and should mean that the owner stops trying to sell the property to anyone else. Once this is signed you usually hand over a small holding deposit. Your lawyer should then carry out a title search to make sure the seller legally owns the land and a planning search to check that it has proper planning permission and no outstanding charges secured against it. Although other searches are also possible none of them will give you much information about the wider picture - to know what plans the local authority may have for new roads etc you will be dependent on what can be found out by asking around. These searches can usually be completed in less than a week.

About a month later you will sign a preliminary contract which means that the military checks (see below) can start. You normally pay around 30% of the agreed selling price at this point. Once the checks are complete you will sign a final purchase contract and pay the balance (*bakiye)* of the purchase price (*alış bedeli)* in exchange for the *tapu.*

MILITARY CHECKS

The slowest part of the sales process is likely to be waiting for the Turkish military to approve your application to buy. Military checks are initiated by the seller rather than the buyer and come in two parts. The military will want to be sure that you do not have a criminal record, that you don't have any outstanding debts and that you are not in any other way 'undesirable' but they will also want to decide if the piece of land you want to buy lies within a militarily sensitive area (and this can mean parts of the coast, especially where they overlook the Greek islands). These checks can take up to three months to complete and the process is being slowed down by the sheer quantity of applications currently being pushed through the system. If you can't stay in the country until the checks are finished you can give a solicitor power of attorney to complete the purchase for you once the military checks are complete. Normally the checks are more of an inconvenience than a problem and there is reason to hope that they may eventually be scrapped, at least for EU citizens.

To avoid having to submit to the military checks you could set up a **Turkish limited company** (see p. 242) to buy the property. You will probably have to use a lawyer to do this and the fee is likely to amount to around €2,200. Once the company has been set up it will have to prepare accounts every year at an additional cost. If you want to rent the property out you will be able to offset some of your costs against annual corporation tax of 30%. However, you might find yourself liable to pay tax for your own use of the property as a benefit in kind. If you resell the property within two years the sale would also qualify for Turkish **capital gains tax** although the first YTL10,000 of inflation-adjusted profit is not liable for tax.

THE *KADASTRO* & *TAPU* OFFICES (LAND REGISTRY OFFICES)

The Kadastro is the department charged with allocating all the land in Turkey and assessing it for tax purposes. This is an ongoing task since not all land in Turkey has been legally allocated to date. The Kadastro department is usually situated in the provincial capital.

The Kadastro is distinct from the Tapu Office (also called the Land Registry) which has a record of all locally existing title deeds and mortgages. When you pay for your new property you usually do so in front of an official from the Tapu Office.

THE TITLE DEED *(TAPU)*

Once the sale has been agreed, the purchaser will have to give the seller the agreed price in exchange for the title deed, or *tapu*. This exchange normally takes place in the Land Registry Office of the provincial government office (*Valilik*). All the owners of the property are expected to attend this exchange so that they can sign the paperwork. If the buyer is a foreigner they are also expected to bring along a translator (*tercüman*) who will require a small payment for their services (this is not obligatory where the foreign buyer is the spouse of a Turk). Although the translator is supposed to translate the entire document, chances are that they will only actually translate anything that looks mildly contentious (i.e. they may well ask you some questions rather than provide what we would think of as a translation).

The *tapu* is an extremely important legal document because it is the proof that a property exchange has taken place. It would be extremely unwise to to proceed without one and it is NEVER advisable to agree to a purchase in which the name on the *tapu* will be anything other than your own. If, for example, you permit a friend to buy a property for you in their name, the property is legally theirs for as long as their name remains on the *tapu*. Even if you trust the friend you should bear in mind that, were they to meet with an accident while the deed was still in their name, the house would probably become the property of their children because of Turkey's inheritance laws (see p. 441).

There is still a lot of land in Turkey which has not been surveyed and issued with title deeds. This means that many Turks in rural areas have built houses on property that is not officially theirs. If you buy a property in such a situation, you could conceivably lose everything. As a result the received wisdom is that you should never buy a property which doesn't have a *tapu*. Some land that does not have a *tapu* is nevertheless covered by a village deed which will not be recorded at the land registry office. Since there is disagreement about the legal validity of these deeds you should not buy land with only a village deed if you are at all risk-averse.

Occasionally you may hear of land which has been measured for a *tapu* but which may be relatively cheap because of its uncertain status. It is up to you whether you want to buy in such circumstances.

Note that there are several types of *tapu*. If you want to borrow money to buy an old building you will need to find out whether there is a *tapu* for the building as well as for the land it stands on (*kat irtifakı/mülkiyeti)*; without that a bank is unlikely to lend you money to buy.

Having a *tapu* in your own name is likely to make it easier to gain Turkish residency.

WHO TO CONTACT
Fethiye & Around

Barış Insurance: Tel: 0252-612 9856, Fax: 0252-612 9857, Atatürk Caddesi, Gökçe Apt. No: 51, Kat: 1, Fethiye. Help with most aspects of house purchase, will writing etc.

Fethiye Translation Office: Tel: 0252-612 3520, www.fethiyetranslation.com, Post Office arkası, Atatürk Caddesi, Fethiye.

PAYING FOR THE PROPERTY

In the booming south and south-west areas of Turkey estate agents are starting to accept normal British cheques issued in sterling. However, away from there that is unlikely to be possible. It may seem strange to pay for a house in cash. However, that is perfectly normal in Turkey where cheques are rarely used. Sometimes you can pay for your property in a mixture of currencies. While the Turkish lira was weak sellers usually wanted foreigners to pay them in hard currency but as the lira has strengthened they have become happier to accept liras.

Unless you have a large amount of cash with you, the best procedure is to open a Turkish bank account in sterling, dollars or euros (see Chapter 11). Once you have done that you can arrange for your bank at home to transfer the money to the Turkish bank account. Then you can withdraw it to pay for your property or arrange to have it transferred direct to the seller's bank account. A bank transfer from abroad usually takes less than a week and shouldn't cost much more than €40. In the past Turkish banks sometimes postponed acknowledging that they had received a transfer so that they could keep the interest. As interest rates have fallen in line with inflation, so their incentive to do this has fallen accordingly.

Bear in mind that if you agree to a sale price in a currency other than the one in which you have your bank account (e.g. Turkish lira or euros) you will be exposed to any fluctuations in the exchange rates - and even a seemingly small move can make a big difference when you're talking about the price of a house. One way to deal with this is to try to insist that the conversion rate on the day of the sale will apply regardless of what actually happens, although not all sellers will agree to that. Alternatively you can ask a currency dealer for advice on forward buying etc (see p. 254).

If you are buying a new-build property from a construction company you do not usually have to pay the entire purchase price upfront. Usually you pay a deposit of 5%, with a further payment of 5% expected one month later. You then pay a further 50% of the price in two-monthly stages until the completion date when the final 40% becomes due. Sometimes you will need to put down a deposit of 10%.

WHO TO CONTACT

Istanbul Tapu ve Kadastro: İstanbul Bölge Müdürlüğü, At Meydanı, Sultanahmet, Istanbul.

Muğla Tapu ve Kadastro: Tel: 0252-214 1345, Özel Idare Binası Kat: 2, Koca Mustafa Efendi Caddesi, Muğla.

THE COST OF PROPERTY PURCHASES

Aside from the cost of the property itself you should budget for:

- 3% commission to the estate agent
- 3% property purchase tax (theoretically shared with the seller)
- Registration fee of up to €375 for recording the sale at the Land Registry
- Small fee to translator
- Solicitor's fee
- Cost of building and/or electricity projects (see p. 169) if required

---

PROPERTY PURCHASE TAX *(EMLAK VERGİSİ)*

The Turkish government levies a property purchase tax on all property exchanges. Since this is 3% of the sale price it is customary (although obviously illegal) to understate the purchase price to reduce this obligation. In theory the buyer pays half this tax and the seller the other half; in practise you may find yourself paying the entire sum. As Turkey moves towards EU membership it is likely to become harder to understate the cost which means that the amount you have to pay is likely to increase. If you understate the value of the house this can have tax consequences if you want to sell it later; if it appears that you made a bigger profit than you really did you will be liable for a higher capital gains tax bill.

ENVIRONMENT CLEANING TAX *(ÇEVRE TEMİZLİK VERGİSİ)*

All property owners are liable to pay an environment cleaning tax *(çevre temizlik vergisi)*. The tax, which usually amounts to about 10% of your annual water bill and is paid twice a year in May and November, covers garbage collection and other clean-up services.

FIRST DAY IN YOUR NEW HOME

When someone has just moved into a new house it is just as customary for neighbours to visit and introduce themselves as it would be at home. Visitors are likely to bring either a small token gift or a sample of their home cooking – when you return the bowl you should reciprocate with a sample of your own cooking.

Turks do not normally have house-warming parties as recognised in the West. However in some parts of the country new homeowners are still expected to slaughter a sheep and share the meat with their friends and neighbours in recognition of their good fortune.

WORDS YOU NEED TO KNOW

apartment block	*apartman*
approximately	*yaklaşık*
building	*imar*
building regulations	*imar durumu*
buyer	*alıcı*
cave house	*kaya ev*
contract	*sözleşme/kontrat*
deposit	*depozito*
discount	*indirim*
duplex	*dubleks*
estate agent	*emlakçı*
farm	*çiftlik*
farmland	*tarla*
flat/apartment	*daire/apartman dairesi*
freehold property	*kat mülkiyeti*
house/apartment/land for sale	*satılık ev/daire/arsa*
housing estate	*site(si)*
immovable property/real estate	*gayrimenkul*
instalment	*taksit*
luxury apartment	*lüks daire*
mountain(s)	*dağ(lar)*
orchard	*meyve bahçesi*
Ottoman house	*Osmanlı evi*

power-of-attorney	vekâlet(name)
price	fiyat
price rise	zam
project	proje
'promise to transfer' document	kat irtifakı
river	ırmak
sea view	deniz manzarası
seller	satıcı
shared but undivided land	iştirak halinde mülkiyet
tree(s)	ağaç(lar)
view	manzara
with central heating	kombili/kaloriferli
witness	tanık
wooden house	ahşap ev

See also p. 101.

FURTHER INFORMATION

- *Buying a Property in Turkey* by John Howell and Tim Locke (Cadogan). More details on the legal side of buying a property and on tax planning.
- *Buying in Turkey* by Dominic Whiting (Apogee Publishing). Information on what to buy in most popular parts of Turkey, together with case studies.
- *www.evbazar.com* Useful website with good, clear explanation of buying process.
- *www.tapu.co.uk* John Howell's website with information for potential property buyers.

CHAPTER 5

THE BUILDING BUSINESS

Whatever sort of property you decide to buy, the chances are that you will have to do some work either to modernise it or to decorate it according to your own taste. In some areas, however, it is likely that you will have to do a great deal more than that – buying a house in Cappadocia, for example, often means buying the shell of a house which needs virtual rebuilding. Sometimes the building on the land that you want to buy will be beyond restoration, in which case you will be looking at tearing it down and starting all over again.

Unlike in the UK some Turkish estate agents, especially in the coastal resorts, double as property developers. If you want a house built from scratch you may therefore find their services useful.

> **BEWARE!**
>
> It is rarely possible to contract a team of workers and then leave them to get on with their work unsupervised; do that and chances are that you will return to find that things have come adrift. Turkish workers love to make their own decisions about colour schemes and other details and their tastes may not remotely resemble yours. So if you don't want to come back and find a line of baby-pink finish running around your kitchen cupboards, the solution is to stay on site and watch what is happening at all times.

TRADITIONAL TURKISH HOUSES

If you have bought either an old Ottoman wooden house or a Cappadocian cave house you will have to choose between restoring it in keeping with Turkish or Western house style. If the house is a listed building this choice may not be yours to make. However, quite often the only limitations are on what you can do to the external appearance of a property.

Ottoman Wooden Houses: In a traditional Ottoman house the kitchen was usually on the ground floor. On the first floor there would be two main reception rooms: a men's room (*selamlık*) and a women's room (*haremlik*). These rooms were used both for socialising and for sleeping and eating. Traditionally they had bench seating (*sedir*) running round the walls. During the day family members sat on the *sedir* but at night it also doubled up as beds; blankets were folded up and stored in alcoves in the wall during the day. Meals were taken sitting on the floor around a low wooden table; this, too, was stored away in an alcove during the day.

Consequently, most old Ottoman houses, even when they have lost their *sedir*, tend to have many alcoves and niches in the walls. There was little standing furniture and Westerners are sometimes surprised to find how few places there are in a largish house to place items like wardrobes and chests-of-drawers that we regard as essentials. Unfortunately except in the largest of rooms the placing of a conventional bed in a room with a *sedir* tends to spoil its proportions.

Occasionally you may be able to buy a property with original frescoes that require meticulous conservation. Some apartments in the centre of Istanbul, for example, have fine painted ceilings and/or walls. Often these have been painted over so it's always worth checking a discreet corner carefully before peeling off old paintwork. If you buy an old Ottoman property in any of the central Anatolian towns you would be well advised to check for frescoes on the walls and ceilings before repainting.

Old wooden houses often retain some of their wooden interior decoration (look out especially for *dönme dolaplar* - revolving cupboards for serving food from the kitchen to the dining room; original *sedirs;* and wooden railings that marked the ends of *sedirs* and effectively divided up the room). Such features are just as worthy of preservation as ceiling roses and stained-glass doors in Victorian houses in the UK and as their value is increasingly recognised so the likelihood that they will be stolen from empty houses is also growing. In the centre of Istanbul there are also some fine rooms with wood-and-glass partitions and wood panelling on the walls. Once again these features may be obscured by coats of paint added years later when wood became unfashionable. In some Cappadocian houses beautiful old linenfold panelling still lines the walls while the ceilings are made of flat wood often with a sunburst (*göbek*) in the centre and fine carving around the edge. Unfortunately all too often such woodwork has either been stripped out long ago for firewood or, more recently, for sale to hoteliers and the owners of fine newly-restored properties.

Ottoman houses often had big fireplaces with large hoods (*şömine*) which may still be usable. However, fireplaces these days have a resale value and it is not unusual to find that they have been removed from properties that have been left empty.

Cave Houses: In Ottoman times people lived in Cappadocian cave houses in a very similar way, so often these houses also had *sedirs* running round the wall and innumerable niches and alcoves cut into them. They too tended to have fireplaces for use in the cold winters. However, on top of these traditional Turkish features, cave houses often have many other holes cut into them. Sometimes these were mangers for animals but other interesting holes in the walls may have served as wineries (one large square hole for treading the grapes with a drain in one side leading to a smaller hole where the juice would be stored) or for making grape molasses (*pekmez*). Circular holes in the ground with a channel running away from them used to serve as *tandır* ovens for making bread or stews.

If your newly-bought property incorporates any of these features, you may well want to conserve them and turn them into special features. Your Turkish builder, more used to the demands of modern Turks, may baulk at your requirements but if you hold your ground you may end up with a more interesting home as a result, as well as with a property that may fetch a premium when it comes to resale.

WHERE TO FIND INFORMATION

If you want to see what the old wooden houses looked like in their heyday so that you know how to restore yours in keeping with its original appearance several properties around the country are open to the public. These include:

- Latifoğlu Konağı, Tokat
- Güpgüpoğlu Konağı, Kayseri
- Çakıroğlu Konağı, Birgi
- Kaymakamlar Müzesi, Safranbolu
- Mümtazlar Konağı, Safranbolu
- Kileciler Evi, Safranbolu
- Liva Paşa Konağı, Kastamonu
- Hasan Süzer Etnografi Müzesi, Gaziantep

At the time of writing none of the Cappadocian cave houses was open to the public. However, several have been turned into hotels, pensions and restaurants so you can visit them to soak up general ideas about restoration.

Most bookshops stock books about Turkish houses. It's also worth visiting the specialist architectural bookshop *Yapı Kitabevi* in Istanbul (for details, see Appendix VII).

BUILDING SEASON

In prime tourist areas along the coast and in the historic heart of Istanbul you will not be allowed to undertake any building work from the start of May until the end of October (if you spot men hard at work by flashlights after 10 pm you can be pretty sure they are working illegally). In Cappadocia, the harsh winter means that the building season usually only runs from April through to November.

QUOTES FOR BUILDING WORK

Before taking on a house which needs significant work done to it you need to get an estimate of the likely cost (obviously if you can do some of it yourself that will reduce the price). You also need to consider how long it is likely to take to do the work. Depending on your circumstances you may have to add on the cost of renting somewhere to live either in Turkey or abroad while the work is completed.

As always, it is advisable to get several builders to give you an estimate for the work that needs doing. This is likely to be possible in big towns. However, in rural areas there may be only one electrician or plumber available. Even for carpentry, where there may be several possible contenders for the job, chances are that one will be the craftsman of choice. In such circumstances your only guarantee that the price you are being offered is reasonable will be to find out where else the men have worked and then compare the price you are quoted with what other people have paid. If the property you are restoring is historically interesting you should assume that you will have to pay slightly more for skilled craftsmen who know how to do good restoration work.

It's an unpalatable fact that foreigners are likely to be quoted more for any job than locals. This is most likely to be a significant problem if you don't have trusted friends in the locality; if you do you are unlikely to be overcharged significantly. Lone women, especially in rural areas, should bear in mind that Turkish workmen are not used to taking orders (or advice) from females; being female can also lead to a higher quote than normal.

It is sometimes worth employing an overseer who can get the necessary quotes for you. However, you need to be sure that you can trust the overseer not to take an overly large commission. You should also accept that most workmen will still know that the work is being done for a foreigner - and adjust their quotes upwards anyway.

Some foreigners become obsessed with the danger of being 'ripped off'. Somehow you have to walk the fine line between letting yourself be taken for a fool and becoming unrealistically convinced that every deviation from a quotation is a trick rather than simple miscalculation.

When getting quotes you should bear in mind some of the idiosyncrasies of Turkish building work. If you ask a carpenter (*marangoz*) to make you a set of windows, for example, you should not assume that the price includes glass – for that you need a separate quote from a glazier (*camcı*). Likewise, a plumber (*sucu*) may quote you for the labour without the parts, as may an electrician (*elektrikçi*). In general, quotes for woodwork do not include the cost of varnishing (*vernik*) which must be obtained separately.

Never let yourself get talked into paying all the money upfront. Either pay a deposit and arrange to pay in instalments as the work is completed or pay half upfront and agree to pay the rest when the work is finished.

TURKISH TOOLBOX *(ALET ÇANTASI)*			
axe	*balta*	plaster	*alçı*
bolt	*cıvata*	plasterer	*sıvacı*
hacksaw	*demir testeresi*	pliers	*pense/kerpeten*
hammer	*çekiç*	putty	*silikon*
hosepipe	*hortum*	rawlplug	*dübel*
ladder	*merdiven*	sandpaper	*zımpara kâğıdı*
monkey wrench	*İngiliz anahtarı*	saw	*testere*
nail	*çivi*	screw	*vida*
nut	*somun*	screwdriver	*tornavida*
pick	*kazma*	shovel	*kürek*
pincers	*kerpeten*	spanner	*somun anahtar*
pipe	*boru*	wheelbarrow	*el arabası*

CHOOSING YOUR WORKMEN

In the big cities there may be a large pool of workers to choose from (and labour can be cheaper in expensive Istanbul because of the ferocious competition for work), but in rural areas you may have little choice about which workers to use. Even where that is the case, it is essential to take local advice over who to employ – there are very few places left where you won't be able to find someone to recommend builders to you. Visit properties that you know have been beautifully restored and ask their owners which builders they used and what they paid them.

If you have no idea where to start looking for workers it's usually worth visiting the industrial estate (*sanayi sitesi*) of the nearest town where many craftsmen have offices.

Many Turkish workers operate in teams under a foreman (*usta*). Where that is the case you discuss your needs with the *usta* who organises his team accordingly. Normally you pay the *usta* all the money for the job and he then pays his team for what they have done. The *usta* is always going to be male for the foreseeable future and he may not be accustomed to taking instructions from a woman; if you don't have a male partner, it may be as well to rope in a friend to help. Away from Istanbul and parts of the coast you are unlikely to find an English-speaking *usta*.

Despite the jokes about Turkish time, many Turkish workers put in a very good day's work, taking only short breaks for tea and lunch. Often they will arrive on site with a little gas stove to brew their own tea; if not, you might like to supply tea for them. Likewise, they will probably appreciate it if you occasionally treat them to a *pide* (Turkish pizza) lunch. Sometimes their building quote will include the cost of food and drink. Sometimes an out-of-town team of workers may even expect you to pay for overnight accommodation for them as well.

Sometimes the *usta* will have all the tools needed for the job but often you will be expected to supply spades, wheelbarrows, hoses and other necessities. Big DIY stores such as Bauhaus, Koçtaş and Praktiker in the larger towns sell a complete range of imported power tools such as Black & Deckers at similar prices to what you would pay at home. Slowly a market in hired tools is also developing, especially in the south-west.

For a list of places to buy tools, see Appendix VII.

BUILDING PERMITS (YAPI RUHSATI)

You should never assume that you can just start work where and when you please. In towns you may well need a building permit before you can make any significant changes to a property, and if you are working on an Ottoman stone or wooden house or a Cappadocian cave house you will almost certainly need permission from the conservation authorities BEFORE you start work. If you don't get the necessary permissions and someone spots what you are doing and reports you, the authorities will have the right to make you stop work immediately and maybe even reverse what you have already done (in practise this rarely seems to happen).

Restoration: Before starting work on restoring a property in a conservation area you will need to visit the Çevre Koruma Müdürlüğü (Environmental Protection Management) in the provincial capital and apply for permission to carry out the work. Someone from the department will visit the property and take photographs of its condition. Then they will explain what can and cannot be done to it. In many cases they will insist that you employ an architect (*mimar*) to draw up a project (*proje)* for the work to be done. Since this can add several thousand pounds to the cost of the work, you should try to get someone from the Koruma Müdürlüğü to inspect the property BEFORE you commit yourself to buying.

Unfortunately the people in charge of supervising conservation areas are often civil servants with no great sympathy for architecture. The result is that the rules are often applied either randomly or too rigorously. One person will get off scot-free despite slapping concrete all over a stone house while another will be jailed for building wooden access stairs to a fairy chimney. Turks do actually go to jail for infringements of the building code, so you should never ignore the need to get the right permissions before starting work. However, although one or two foreign buyers have had problems with the authorities, so far none has been imprisoned. Doubtless the authorities know what bad publicity this would lead to – especially if what the foreigner was accused of doing wrong actually turned out to be much nicer than what their neighbour, who was not in any trouble, had done to their property! But as more foreigners settle in Turkey the time may come when this changes.

If someone is helping you to organise the paperwork it is a sensible precaution to ask to see all the permits. Then you can take them to a public notary (*noter*) and have them translated to avoid misunderstandings later.

It may be easier to get permission to build something relatively simple and add to it later rather than to start out with a very complex design which the authorities may be reluctant to approve.

Rebuilding: If you want to completely rebuild a property on your land you need a different set of permits. Before you start work you will need to get a construction permit (*imar planı*) from the Fen Memuru in the Belediye. If there is any doubt about the extents of the property someone from the Belediye will come and measure the site, inserting markers to indicate the edges of the land. Then you give the permit to an architect who will draw up a plan for you. If you think you may want to extend the property later (e.g. to build a third floor) you can keep costs down by getting them to draw up the entire project from the start. Once the plan is complete you show it to the Belediye. If they approve it they will give you a licence (*ruhsat*) valid for five years to complete the work. When it is completed the Belediye will check that the work complies with the plan. If it does they will give you a residence permit (*oturma izni*) which means that you can start applying to have the utilities connected. You will need to take out insurance (*inşaat sigortası*) to cover your workers against injury while building is in progress.

Building from Scratch: If you have bought a piece of land to build on you need to be clear about how much of it can be developed; in rural and coastal areas you may only be able to build on 5% of the land while in urban areas 25-30% is usually the norm. Then you will have to get an architect to draw up a building plan which will be submitted to the local authorities to obtain planning permission. The architect should also supply you with a list of the materials that will be required to build according to their specification.

Once the plan has been approved you should put a notice on your property identifying yourself as the owner and indicating who will be doing the work and when it is due for completion. It is also normal to affix a sign reading '*İnşaata girmek tehlikeli ve yasaktır*' (Entering this building site is dangerous and forbidden).

When the work is complete you should get a habitation report (*iskân raporu*) which will confirm that the house is completed according to the regulations and that all necessary taxes have been paid.

THINKING AHEAD

If you have a team of workers on site it is vital that you think through all your likely requirements for the future to avoid having to call them back again later on. You may think you only need one telephone line but it might be better to install two or three to allow for separate fax and Internet lines in the future. You may think you only need one television socket but it might be better to have several installed in case you buy a second or third television set later. Rarely will builders make any suggestions themselves; conversely you may find you have to specifically ask them to do things you would think could be taken for granted (e.g. insulating water pipes in areas with harsh winters).

SPECIAL CASES

Cappadocian Stone Houses: If you are restoring or rebuilding a property in Cappadocia you will have to decide whether you are going to do the work using new or old stones (taş). There are many quarries (taş ocakları) around Nevşehir and Ürgüp that sell new stones in a variety of colours and strengths. However, if you want your new work to blend in with what already exists you will need to find a supply of old stones which is much trickier. At the time of writing it was possible to buy large quantities of old stones in Nevşehir as entire old neighbourhoods were demolished to make way for modern housing. However, eventually this source of stones will dry up. It might be possible to buy old stones in other local villages. However, chances are that these are being cannibalised from buildings as in need of protection and restoration as the one you are working on.

Because of the harsh Anatolian winter you will need to buy strong (sağlam) stones to build external features like stairs. It is normal to protect the stonework from frost damage by lining the tops of walls with vine twigs (çubuk) which double as a handy source of kindling wood.

A FEW HINTS ON BUILDING MATERIALS

- **Concrete (Beton):** Wherever you are building you should have a choice as to whether to use ready-made concrete (hazır beton) or the type that is mixed on the spot. Ready-made is cheaper but it is not always possible for the large delivery lorries to access cramped building sites. Nor is it always advisable to opt for the cheapest available concrete; following the dreadful earthquakes of 1999 it was discovered that some of the collapsed buildings had been erected using weak concrete mixed with sand and shells.
- **Cement (Çimento):** Cement comes in different colours - if you are building in a conservation area with stone buildings you may find that white cement looks better than more normal grey. You will probably need to point this out to your builder.
- **Scaffolding (İskele):** Scaffolding used in Turkey would not be given the time of day in most Western countries. Usually it is made from wooden poles; only rarely do you see metal scaffolding poles.

Timber Houses: If you are thinking of erecting a timber house on your property it's worth knowing that cedar (sedir) is stronger and longer-lasting than pine (çam). However, cedar is both more expensive and harder to find than pine. It is easy to find floor plans for timber houses on the Internet although it may be trickier to find builders able to translate the plans into finished masterpieces in Turkey. The average wooden house is expected to last for 30 years and will need to be treated against fungal and insect attack and with fire-retardant material. It can be stained to a colour of your choice and the stain should last for up to five years.

IT'S MADE FROM...

brass	*pirinç*	plastic (as in sheeting)	*plastik/naylon*
brick	*tuğla*	sand	*kum*
copper	*bakır*	stone	*taş*
glass	*cam*	tile	*fayans*
iron	*demir*	tin	*teneke*
marble	*mermer*	wood	*ahşap/tahta*
material	*madde*	wrought iron	*ferforje*

INSTALLING THE UTILITIES

Electricity (Elektrik)

Good electricians (*elektrikçi*) are as scarce in Turkey as anywhere else and wiring a property can be both costly and time-consuming; if you are able to do some of this work yourself you will save yourself many headaches. Many electricians miss appointments and turn up without all the tools required to do the necessary work. Some of the work is also likely to be farmed out to apprentices who may or may not put in a good day's work if their boss is out of sight. Normally you pay for the necessary electrical parts separately from the labour involved, so make sure that any quote you get takes that into account. In towns there may be many electricians to choose from but in rural areas there may be only one or two, ensuring that they can charge more or less what they like and work more or less when they please.

Plumbing (*Su tesisatı*)

The standard of much Turkish plumbing is lamentable. For some reason, Turks don't install U-bend pipes to sinks and toilets which can lead to unpleasant smells. Sinks that readily block up are also tediously common. Things may be slowly improving but you need to pay particularly close attention whenever plumbing is in progress. Once the work is finished try and persuade the plumber (*sucu/tesisatçı*) to send water through the pipes at high pressure to ensure that there are no hairline cracks that will start leaking. Also, try to ensure that no building rubble is carelessly dropped into overflow drains. If you have installed underfloor heating watch carefully when it is first turned on in case nails have been punched through any of the pipes when the flooring was being installed and make sure that the pipes have been insulated as they can burst during a cold snap, causing considerable upheaval and expense.

WHAT TO SAY	
13-amp fuse	*on üç amperlik sigorta*
adapter	*adaptör*
double/triple socket	*ikilik/üçlük*
earth wire	*topraklama kablosu*
electric socket/power point	*priz*
extension lead	*uzatma kablosu*
fuse	*sigorta*
fuse box	*sigorta kutusu*
generator	*jeneratör*
light bulb	*ampul*
light socket	*lamba duyu*
light switch	*lamba anahtarı/düğmesi*
mains switch	*şalter*
plug	*fiş*
shaving point	*tıraş makinesi prizi*
switch	*elektrik düğmesi*
wall socket	*duvar prizi*
wire	*kablo*
wiring	*elektrik tesisatı*

Insulation (*İzolasyon*): Burst pipes may be a fact of winter life in many parts of Turkey but you can give yourself a better chance of surviving the cold by making sure that your pipes are insulated before they are laid. This is not something that all plumbers think of automatically, so you may need to be very firm that you want it done. Insulating materials are cheap and readily available so it is a very false economy to go without.

WHAT TO SAY	
burst pipe	*patlamış boru*
drain (sink)	*pis su borusu*
leak	*sızıntı*
sink	*lavabo*
stopcock	*su vanası*
tap/faucet	*musluk*
washer	*rondela*
water pipe	*su borusu*

Sewerage (*Kanalizasyon*)

If your property is not already connected to the public sewerage system you may have to pay between €180 and €450 to have it connected. The price will depend on the size of your property.

Septic Tanks *(Foseptik):* If you have bought a property in a rural area it may have a septic tank to dispose of bathroom and/or kitchen waste. You should always have the tank inspected because you will probably want to replace it with a more modern model. If so, you may need special planning permission. Make sure you install a tank big enough to cope with the heaviest use you can envisage in order to reduce the number of costly trips to empty it that will be needed.

A FEW HINTS ON STRUCTURAL WORK

Walls (*Duvarlar*)

If you are restoring a property in Cappadocia building work usually starts with someone scraping down (*tıraşlamak*) the walls of the house both inside and out with a double-sided implement called a comb (*tarak*). Local stone is soft but hardens on exposure to air. However over the years the surface may start to crumble; scraping takes the surface back to harder stone. It also removes the accumulated stains of the centuries (e.g. smoke-blackening from fires).

Roofs (*Çatılar*)

Access: If you are laying a new roof remember to build in external access so that when someone comes to install a solar panel and/or satellite dish they will be able to get onto the roof easily. Don't assume that insulation will be included unless you specifically ask for it.

Flat Roofs: In some parts of Central Anatolia flat roofs were traditionally covered with grass which was regularly smoothed down with large stone rollers. A few people have started to copy this tradition since it helps improve insulation.

Rain Chains: In Cappadocia it was traditional to hang chains a foot or so out from the roof to encourage water to run off the roof without running down the walls, an idea worth copying even today.

Courtyards (*Avlular/Hayatlar*)

Many Turkish houses have courtyards rather than proper gardens. If repairing a courtyard you should make sure that all necessary pipes and cables have been installed BEFORE the paving stones are laid and that the ground slopes slightly away from the house to allow for proper drainage. If you are planning to have plants in pots then make sure there is an outdoor tap for easy watering.

WINDOWS *(PENCERE)* AND DOUBLE-GLAZING *(İSO CAM)*

Life in most Turkish towns can be noisy for all sorts of reasons, not least the minarets from which the call to prayer is broadcast five times a day, starting at dawn. One way to deaden the noise is to invest in double-glazing which can reduce the volume, although at the price of raising the temperature inside the house. However, in summer you will need the windows open in many parts of the country which will render this improvement null and void.

You might also want to consider double-glazing if you own a property in Central or Eastern Anatolia where winter temperatures are harsh enough to make any investment that can raise the heating level worth considering. It may also help keep the heating costs down, however marginally.

These days many people opt for PVC windows because these are sturdier than wooden window frames. It is possible to reduce the damaging impact on the visual environment by buying wood-stained PVC windows although these are more expensive than standard white ones. If you do want PVC, reputable firms include Adopen, Egepen, Fıratpen, Pakpen, Pimapen and Winhouse, among others. If, however, you are restoring an old house you might prefer to get a carpenter to make traditional wooden frames for you. Remember that you will need to order the glass for the windows separately from the frames.

AIR CONDITIONING *(KLİMA)*

No matter where you live in Turkey the July and August temperatures can be stupefying. Along the coast sea breezes help keep the heat down but in Central and Eastern Anatolia you are looking at temperatures in the high 30s and low 40s as a matter of routine. In such circumstances installing air conditioning can be a worthwhile investment despite the initial cost. These days many units on sale serve as air conditioning in summer and central heating in winter; typically, a combined unit like this will cost around €200. Costs have been coming down recently as manufacturers started outsourcing parts to China.

In a house restored to 'period' appearance a ceiling fan (*vantilatör*) can look more appropriate. At the very least consider installing windows that open in such a way as to allow a through breeze. In older Cappadocian houses, for example, the lower panels of wooden windows open separately from the rest of the window which makes it easier to regulate the temperature.

WHAT SHAPE DO YOU WANT? (*HANGİ ŞEKİL İSTİYORSUNUZ?*)	
octagonal	*sekizgen biçiminde*
oval	*oval*
rectangular	*dikdörtgen şeklinde*
round	*yuvarlak şekil*
square	*kare*
triangular	*üçgen biçiminde*

CENTRAL HEATING (*KALORİFER TESİSATI*)

The majority of Turkey's older housing blocks are heated using coal to fire the central heating. Outside the major cities, using any other kind of fuel is still fairly uncommon and usually expensive. When installing central heating you will need to pay close attention to where builders are putting the radiators (*radyatör/petekler*). Turks usually like to place radiators under windows, on the assumption that the rising heat will counteract the incoming cold. Westerners tend to think that much of the heat goes straight out of the window and prefer the radiators elsewhere. You may need to be very insistent to get them where you want.

Central heating can be run off coal, oil, gas or electricity; an expensive form of synthetic coal is also available. Normal coal is the cheapest and most commonly used fuel, and fine if you have someone to shovel it for you (in apartment blocks this is usually done centrally). Oil (*fueloil*) is cheaper than gas or electricity but is messy and requires a large storage tank. LPG and electricity are both very expensive. If you are in an area connected to natural gas, this is the most efficient and cleanest form of heating as well as being fairly inexpensive. Elsewhere, however, you will have to use large LPG gas bottles which may last only a short period and run out at unpredictable times; many think them potentially dangerous as well. Electrically-fired central heating is probably safer. However, electricity takes longer to warm the radiators and cools down whenever there is a power cut. It is also very expensive.

DO IT YOURSELF

In Turkey every man sees himself as a DIY expert, which is hardly surprising since people often build their own homes and do their own plumbing and electricity - whether they know how to or not – in order to save money. The standard of most DIY is not very high. However, these days it is increasingly easy to buy the equipment needed to do a good job, especially in the big towns.

Even if you don't do the work yourself it is helpful to have a basic idea about DIY in order to be able to advise your builders on what you want, so you may want to sign up for a course to learn the basics before you leave your home country.

For a list of DIY material stockists, see Appendix VII.

GARDENS *(BAHÇE)*

Because so many Turks live in apartments, gardening *(bahçıvanlık)* is not such a common pastime as it is in countries such as the UK. Most village women pride themselves on their windowbox-style floral displays (often planted in old white-cheese or sunflower-oil cans) but they are usually grown from cuttings passed from one to another. As a result a market in garden produce has been slow to develop in Turkey.

These days, however, there are nurseries *(fidanlık)* in the outskirts of most of the big towns. In rural areas stalls selling plants and garden produce usually show up at the local markets every spring; itinerant plant sellers also visit each sizeable community in turn. Big DIY stores such as Bauhaus, Koçtaş and Praktiker (see p. 495) sell all sorts of garden tools as well as garden furniture.

It is easy to buy hoses, shovels and wheelbarrows in the industrial estates attached to most towns. You can also buy small shovels. However, small forks as used by British gardeners are hard to come by; most people prefer gadgets that resemble miniature rakes. Plastic plant pots are also easy to find, although not always in the sizes you want. A good place to buy proper terracotta pots is Avanos in Cappadocia; the pottery on sale in the town centre may be touristy but back-street shops sell more prosaic plant pots. In and around Avanos there are also large warehouses which export pots to Europe; the seconds are sold very cheaply.

For a list of places to buy gardening equipment see Appendix VII.

SWIMMING POOLS *(YÜZME HAVUZU)*

People who buy houses along the coast often find that it already has a pool. However, if you are building a house in a coastal or rural area you may want to factor in the cost of installing one (usually between €14,800-30,000). At the moment Turkey has few regulations about the design of pools although in some areas (e.g. Cappadocia) where water is in short supply it may be difficult to get the local Belediye to grant planning permission.

It is possible to save money on your pool by, for example, foregoing a good filter and circulation system. Painting over concrete rather than using blue lining tiles can also save you money. However, in the long term you are likely to regret such economies because they increase both the cost and the ease of maintaining your pool. Ideally you want to invest in the best overflow system you can afford to reduce the amount of time spent fishing out leaves, dead insects and other debris.

Provided you choose your pool design carefully maintaining it shouldn't be difficult. You will need regular supplies of acid and alkaline materials to maintain the correct Ph balance of the water (these materials can be dangerous) as well as a supply of chlorine and algicide; the people who install your pool will either be able to keep you supplied with these or will be able to put you in touch with a firm that can. Obviously if your pool is intended as part of a business (e.g. in the grounds of a pension) it will cost more to maintain than if it is merely being used by a family.

For a list of swimming pool contractors, see Appendix VI.

IN THE GARDEN CENTRE			
branch	*dal*	oleander	*zakkum*
bulb	*soğan*	plant	*fidan*
bush	*çalılık*	rose	*gül*
crocus	*çiğdem*	seed	*tohum*
flower	*çiçek*	shovel	*kürek*
flowerpot	*saksı*	spade	*bahçıvan beli*
fountain	*çeşme*	sundial	*güneş saati*
geranium	*sardunya*	sunflower	*ayçiçeği*
honeysuckle	*hanımeli*	sweet-smelling	*güzel kokulu*
hose	*hortum*	to prune	*budamak*
iris	*süsen*	tree	*ağaç*
leaf	*yaprak*	tulip	*lale*
lily	*zambak*	violet	*menekşe*
manure	*gübre*	wallflower	*sarı şebboy*
marigold	*kadifeçiçeği*	wheelbarrow	*el arabası*
narcissus	*nergis*		

WHAT BUILDERS CAN AND CANNOT DO

According to the Turkish Civil Code no one is allowed to cause harm to other people unjustly. This is generally interpreted as meaning, for example, that people building a house cannot do so in a way that impinges on other people's rights to a view. However, as anyone who has ever spent any time in Turkey will know this legal provision is more honoured in the breach than the observance. If you wanted to go to court to prevent someone building something that would spoil your own view it would be up to you to prove that the damage you were complaining about would actually occur. Expect the case to drag on for years.

USEFUL VOCABULARY

basement/cellar	*bodrum*	internal (wall) tile	*fayans*
battery	*pil/akü*	light shaft/conservatory	*aydınlık*
bay window	*cumba*	loft/attic	*çatı katı*
building site	*inşaat yeri/alanı*	loose	*gevşek*
builder	*müteahhit/inşaatcı*	low	*alçak*
cement mixer	*çimento karıştırıcı*	permit	*izin/ruhsat*
cupboard	*dolap*	plank	*tahta/kereste*
deep	*derin*	planning permission	*yapı ruhsatı*
door	*kapı*	restoration	*restorasyon/onarım*
doorbell	*zil*	to carve	*oymak*
doorhandle	*kapı kolu*	to restore	*restore etmek/onarmak*
engineer	*mühendis*	shutters	*kepenk*
external (roof) tile	*tuğla/kiremit*	square metre	*metre kare*
fence	*parmaklık*	stairs/ladder	*merdiven*
floor covering	*yer döşemesi*	strong	*sağlam*
foreman	*usta/kalfa*	suction fan/small window fan	*aspiratör*
foundations	*temel*	support column	*kiriş/sütun/direk*
ground floor	*giriş kat/zemin kat*	too weak	*çok zayıf*
gutter	*çatı oluğu*	wall	*duvar*
hall	*hol/koridor*	wide	*geniş*
handle	*kol*	window	*pencere*
high	*yüksek*	workman	*işçi*
hinge	*menteşe*	It will be expensive.	*Pahalı olacak.*
hole	*delik/boşluk*		

CHAPTER 6

INTERIORS

Although wealthy Istanbullus will always have had beautiful homes with luxurious fixtures and fittings, the average Turkish home tends to be very simple, with unadorned white walls and only the most functional of furniture. Until recently that meant that it was not easy to buy attractive furnishings or even decorating materials away from the big cities. However, as income levels have risen and the housing market has taken off, so has the market in home furnishings - most towns now boast shops selling enticing furniture, tiles and fabrics and there are many magazines devoted to interior decoration (*iç mimarlık*). Some people now earn a good living as interior designers, especially in trendier areas of Istanbul and Ankara.

Browsing the Turkish versions of magazines like *House Beautiful, Country Homes, Home Art* and *Wallpaper* should give you plenty of ideas as well as supplying contact details for many stockists of household furnishings. Lavishly illustrated coffee-table books such as *Living in Istanbul* by Lale Apa (Flammarion) and *Living in Turkey* by Stephanie Yerasmos (Thames and Hudson) should also act as great sources of ideas.

PAINTING AND DECORATING

These days you can buy a decent range of paint colours in most city centres. Major paint manufacturers include:
- Dewelux
- Dyo (www.dyo.com.tr)
- Filli Boya (www.filliboya.com.tr)
- Marshall

Although normal paintbrushes are readily available, house-painters often use a machine that sprays paint onto walls and ceilings. Unless you insist that they do so they are unlikely to cover doors, windows or the edges of floors or walls, so that you end up with paint sprayed all over everything.

One quirk to be aware of if you live in Cappadocia is the use of a special whitewash called *badana*. This comes as a powder which has to be mixed with water. It is extremely messy to use but adheres to the walls of caves in a way which normal paint does not. However, *badana* needs frequent renewal and if you repaint over old paint the new layer peels away more quickly than the original one did.

COLOUR SCHEMES			
black	*siyah/kara*	lilac	*eflatun*
blue	*mavi*	matt	*mat*
brown	*kahverengi*	orange	*turuncu*
cream	*krem*	pink	*pembe*
dark (as in *koyu yeşil* - dark green)	*koyu*	purple	*mor*
darker	*daha koyu*	red	*kırmızı*
gold	*altın*	satin	*saten*
green	*yeşil*	silver	*gümüş*
grey	*gri*	white	*beyaz*
light (as in *açık yeşil* – light green)	*açık*	yellow	*sarı*
lighter	*daha açık*		

FLOORS *(YERLER)*

If you are occupying a ready-built house or apartment it should already have suitable floor covering. If, however, you have built or restored your own property you will have to decide whether to lay a wooden floor or opt for concrete covered with lino, tiles or some other material.

Carpets and Kilims: Turkey is famous for its carpet (*halı*) trade although these days much of what is on sale in the shops has been imported from Iran, the Caucasus, Pakistan, Afghanistan or even China. You may want to buy carpets or kilims to cover wooden floorboards. A cheaper option is to buy a type of thin corded carpet sold on rolls up to two metres wide and cut to meet your requirements, the most popular brand of which is called *halıfleks*. It comes in a variety of colours.

These days wall-to-wall carpeting (*duvardan duvara halı*) is not very fashionable in the West. However, you might want to install it in an inner-city apartment in which case extensive choices and qualities are available.

WHAT TO READ

- *Carpets from the Tents, Cottages and Workshops of Asia* by Jon Thompson (Laurence Kin). A good run through the basics of oriental carpet know-how.
- *Living With Kilims* by Alastair Hull, Nicholas Barnard & James Merrell (Thames & Hudson). Inspirational photographs of contemporary homes with kilims.

Tiles: Attractive floor tiles are readily available for reasonable prices in most big towns. Good tiling companies include:

- Çanakkale Seramik (www.canakkaleseramik.com.tr)
- Ege Seramik (www.egeseramik.com)
- Toprak Seramik (www.toprakseramik.com.tr)
- Vitra (www.vitra.com.tr)

All of them produce catalogues and you can usually order from them in even the smallest local shops.

Wooden Floors: Fashionable wooden floors are a little trickier. Most readily available, inexpensive wood is pine or poplar; if you want hardwood it is likely to be both harder to find and pricier. Although old houses were built using wide floorboards, it is no longer easy to find wide boards (*ahşap*) - usually they cost at least twice the normal price. Whichever wood you choose it is important to ensure that it has been properly treated; if it has not been allowed to dry for long enough it will quickly warp so that you end up with a floor that looks rougher than the sea.

Carpenters usually leave sanded floorboards a natural pine colour unless you ask to have them darkened – having this done at a later stage is likely to involve a lot of disruption and additional expense. Traditionally people have thought that oriental carpets looked best against plain pine boards. However, increasingly tastes are tending towards darker ones.

Parquet (*parke*) flooring is also readily available but doesn't stand up to hard wear as well as real wood.

WHICH WOOD IS WHICH			
cedar	*sedir*	poplar	*kavak*
hornbeam	*gürgen*	rosewood	*gül*
oak	*meşe*	walnut	*ceviz*
pine	*çam*		

WALLS *(DUVAR)*

Turks rarely use wallpaper to cover their walls. Most people simply paint them, although historically some walls in central Anatolia were clad with wood which resembled the linenfold panelling common in 16th and 17th-century English mansions. Cappadocian cave walls are often left plain with the hatching of the tools used to create them the only decoration.

For a list of wallpaper stockists see Appendix II.

CEILINGS *(TAVAN)*

In most houses ceilings are simply painted white. Sometimes there will be a central feature rather like a ceiling rose in a Victorian house in the UK. It is even possible to find Cappadocian cave houses with 'ceiling roses' carved out of the rock.

Grand old Ottoman houses with wood-panelled walls often had wooden ceilings as well. These were usually flat, with a wooden sunburst, sometimes coloured, in the centre and fine carvings round the edge. It is sometimes possible to buy complete sets of old wood panelling taken out of houses that have been demolished or left to rot. However, these are not only increasingly hard to find but also expensive. Modern carpenters can often make good reproductions and it is possible to buy replica sunbursts in towns such as Kayseri.

Village houses often have plain, flat wooden ceilings supported by complete poplar trunks, sometimes left plain, sometimes varnished. Occasionally you still find houses with a form of matting laid between the trunks.

WHAT TO ASK FOR	
paint	*boya*
paintbrush	*boya fırçası*
paper borders	*bordür*
pattern	*desen*
wallpaper	*duvar kâğıdı*

KITCHENS *(MUTFAK)*

In ready-built Turkish houses and apartments, especially older ones, the kitchens are often small and lacking in work surfaces or cupboard space. It is therefore very likely that you will need to refit your kitchen. There are reputable companies that can supply complete fitted kitchens for you. Alternatively, you may want to commission a carpenter to make cupboards to your own design.

Plumbing and Wiring: Pay attention when your kitchen is being plumbed and wired or you will find too few electricity sockets installed in positions that are not at all convenient. Since few Turkish men spend much time in the kitchen, your workmen will probably have little idea what should go where. You may need to be very insistent to get what you want done as you want it done.

Water Heaters: Turkish water heaters (*şofben*) are not always installed sufficiently carefully, and you will need to check that yours is properly vented for safety. Before deciding which model to buy make sure that it comes with a timer - astonishingly some Turkish *kombis* (combination heaters) don't have timers even when they will be fuelling expensive central heating as well as hot water. Among the reputable firms that supply water heaters all over Turkey are DemirDöküm (www.demirdokum.com.tr) and Baymak (www.baymak.com.tr). It is difficult to buy electric *kombis* and those that are available seem to be less reliable than their gas-operated equivalents.

There is a market in second-hand water heaters but if you buy an old model you should check that it is not missing any crucial parts (e.g. the knobs that enable you to control the flow of water).

Work Surfaces: Marble, much of it from around Afyon, is much cheaper in Turkey than in Europe or the USA which means that installing a marble work surface may cost little more than installing a plastic or concrete one. Often sinks come ready-built into marble work surfaces, which is a shame since they are usually too small and shallow for convenience; if you want a deep sink or a double drainer set into a marble work surface you may have to order it separately and expect to pay more for the privilege. Marble work surfaces scratch and discolour relatively easily. It is also easy to break a lot of glasses in a marble sink. One solution is a plastic washing-up bowl. However ready-made sinks are usually only big enough for a very small bowl.

White and Electrical Goods: White goods cost virtually the same in Turkey as in the UK and are normally made to high standards which means that it makes little sense to have your old fridges and cookers shipped from home. Turkey has three major home-grown manufacturers of white goods: Arçelik, Vestel and Beko. In all three cases service is good and professional and you will not have to wait long for someone to come and repair something that has broken down. These firms also have efficient delivery services even in rural areas; you rarely pay extra for this. You can also buy white and electrical goods from Bosch, Moulinex and Siemens but their prices tend to be considerably higher.

Electrical goods can almost always be bought for one lump sum payment or in installments (*taksit*). Surprisingly, bargaining still takes place even over the latest model of plasma television.

Most normal electrical gadgets (toasters, microwave ovens, irons, vacuum cleaners) are available in Turkey, although away from the big towns choice may be limited. Before buying anything - especially from unknown labels - check it over carefully since sometimes features that you take for granted may be missing. You can, for example, buy hair-driers that have only one setting - too hot!

If you agree to forego a guarantee (*garanti*) you may be able to buy some items for almost half the normal price. In theory you could cut your costs by buying international products over the Internet. However, on arrival they attract such hefty Customs dues that the savings are virtually wiped out.

IN THE WHITE GOODS SHOP *(BEYAZ EŞYA DÜKKÂNINDA)*	
freezer	*derin dondurucu*
fridge	*buzdolabı*
hair-drier	*saç kurutma makinesi*
iron	*ütü*
microwave	*mikrodalga fırın*
music centre	*müzik sistemi*
oven	*fırın/ocak*
spin drier	*kurutma makinesi*
television	*televizyon*
toaster	*ekmek kızartma makinesi*
vacuum cleaner	*elektrik süpürgesi*
washing machine	*çamaşır makinası*

Useful Contacts

Arçelik: Tel: 444 0888, www.arcelik.com.tr
Beko: Tel: 444 1404, www.beko.com.tr
Bosch: Tel: 444 6333, www.boschevaletleri.com
Vestel: Tel: 0800-219 0112, www.vestel.com.tr

HOUSEHOLD GOODS

All over Turkey *zücaciyeci* shops sell glass, kitchenwares, crockery, cutlery, pots, pans, and everything else you need to equip a house. Some are like the Pound Stores in the UK where everything is dirt cheap; others charge higher prices for better quality goods. For example, shops selling genuine Teflon products will have prices similar to those in the West, while those selling locally-made Tefal (www.tefal.com.tr) will be cheaper.

There are many quirks to this sort of shopping. You will discover, for example, the broom without a handle, the brush without a pan, even the mirror without glass. Worst still, you will discover the blight of the family. Since Turkish families are so large and take their entertainment obligations so seriously, almost all the attractive dinner services and cutlery sets come with servings for a dozen or more people and prices to match.

In Istanbul a good place to start shopping for cheap household goods is the area immediately behind the Spice Bazaar (*Mısır Çarşısı*) in Eminönü where there are lots of kitchenware stores. For more upmarket crockery and cutlery head for Nişantaşı and Etiler.

KITCHEN UTENSILS *(MUTFAK ALETLERİ)*			
bottle opener	*şişe açacağı*	knife	*bıçak*
can opener	*konserve açacağı*	lid	*kapak*
coffee cup/mug	*fincan*	pepper shaker	*biberlik*
cooking pot	*tencere*	plate	*tabak*
corkscrew	*tirbuşon*	salt cellar	*tuzluk*
crockery	*tabak takımı*	saucer	*çay tabağı*
cutlery	*çatal-bıçak*	spoon	*kaşık*
earthenware jug	*testi*	sugar bowl	*şekerlik*
fork	*çatal*	tea glass	*çay bardağı*
frying pan	*tava*	teaspoon	*çay kaşığı*
glass	*bardak*	wine glass	*kadeh*

BATHROOMS *(BANYOLAR)*

Traditionally Turks used squat toilets and had very rudimentary shower facilities, often tucked inside a cupboard with a high step. As a result most foreign buyers want to improve their bathrooms. Until recently this was a recipe for disaster. Not only was it difficult to find decent bathroom fittings but plumbers and tilers were notorious for slapdash work. Nowadays, however, several companies specialise in producing very attractive bathroom fittings (sometimes imported) and companies like Çanakkale Seramik, Vitra and Ege Seramik (see p. 155) produce extremely pleasing tiles and bathroom fittings in a variety of modern designs.

You must still keep a close eye on work in progress; plumbers think nothing of bashing through tiles to install taps and other fittings without making good the damage afterwards. You should also keep an eye on the positioning of items like towel rails and toilet-paper holders since workers often attach them to the wall in random locations that turn out to be very inconvenient (too low down and on the wrong side of the pedestal in the case of toilet-roll holders, nowhere near the bath or sink in the case of towel rails).

The existence of hamams meant that Turks traditionally had no use for bathtubs although these are now readily available (make sure the one you choose is long enough to lie down in). If you would like to have your own hamam, there may be a marble-worker at the *sanayi sitesi* who can manufacture the necessary basin. These days it is also easy to buy Jacuzzis and power-showers, albeit at a hefty price.

Islam requires its adherents to wash in flowing water which means that Turkish baths and sinks are never fitted with plugs. These are hard to find in Turkey so you might want to bring some of the multi-fit variety from home.

WHAT TO ASK FOR			
bathtub	*küvet*	tap	*musluk*
cistern	*su deposu*	toilet	*tuvalet*
plug	*tıkaç*	toilet bowl	*klozet*
shower	*duş*	toilet seat	*klozet kapağı*
sink	*lavabo*	towel rail	*havluluk*

BEDROOMS *(YATAK ODASI)*

Beds: Traditionally Turks slept on a bed on the floor or on a *sedir* (bench seat) running round the walls of their sitting room and stored their bedding away in niches in the walls during the day. As a result the idea of a free-standing bed was not a familiar one. In big towns, however, the wealthy often slept in fine metal-framed ornamental beds; scour the antique shops to find one for yourself.

Modern companies like Yataş and İstikbal make and sell reasonably-priced orthopedic mattresses.

Bedding: In the past many Turks slept under wool or horsehair quilts which they sometimes made themselves. Shops selling quilts covered in traditional bright-coloured satin are easy to find in all the big towns. You may want to have yours stuffed with a synthetic material instead of wool or horsehair since these are both heavy and can harbour mites.

Although major mattress-makers like Yataş and İstikbal sell sheets and duvets to fit their products, other ready-made sheets often turn out to be too short or narrow for standard mattresses. Luckily, it is easy to have plain sheets run up to your measurements at the weekly markets. However, there are also shops that sell more luxurious bedding, sometimes in handy packs complete with pillowcases. If you're buying a duvet check that the cover is completely removable since some are stitched to the duvet along one side which makes washing them tricky.

You'll soon tire of the standard mustard and brown Turkish blanket (*battaniye*) but finding more attractive designs is not always easy. On the other hand ordinary blankets can be bought by weight and are very reasonably priced.

Bedside Lights: You may think that nothing can go wrong with the design of a bedroom. However, Turks are not big readers and the idea of reading in bed is a novelty. If you want bedside lights you will need to make sure that the sockets are put in sensible places to make that possible – your Turkish electrician is likely to be far more interested in where you want to put the compulsory bedroom television!

BUYING TOWELS & BEDDING			
blanket	*battaniye*	pillow	*yastık*
cushion	*minder*	pillowcase	*yastık yüzü/kılıfı*
duvet/doona	*tüy yorgan*	quilt	*yorgan*
flannel/hand towel	*el havlusu*	sheet	*çarşaf*
horsehair quilt	*yün yorgan*	towel	*havlu*
mattress	*yatak*	under-mattress	*şilte*

FURNISHING YOUR HOME

Furnishing a house in Turkey can be almost as expensive as furnishing a house at home. These days there are many stores specialising in furniture (*mobilya*) and some of what they sell is perfectly attractive. However, traditional Turkish taste in furnishing was very different from Western taste so that away from the big cities you may have to look hard to find, for example, a three-piece suite that you like. Of course in the big cities there are now branches of international companies such as Laura Ashley provided you are prepared to pay the same prices as at home.

Chain stores specialising in selling household furniture include:

- Bellona   (www.bellona.com.tr)
- İdaş   (www.idas.com.tr)
- Istikbal   (www.istikbal.com.tr)
- Kelebek   (www.kelebek.com.tr)
- Seray   (www.seray.com)
- Yataş   (www.yatas.com.tr)

Prices are reasonable and you may be lucky and find exactly what you want. However, if you don't you shouldn't despair since there are also shops selling more individual items in the more upmarket parts of the big towns. Larger branches of supermarkets such as Yimpaş also sell some furniture. It is particularly difficult to find good ready-made cupboards, chests-of-drawers and wardrobes.

The Swedish company IKEA sells its popular, stylish furniture out of its two stores in Istanbul and Izmir (see p. 465). The Turkish firm Tepe Home (www.tepehome.com.tr) also sells lovely household furnishings. It has branches in Istanbul, Ankara, Izmir, Adana, Bursa and Konya.

IN THE FURNITURE SHOP *(MOBİLYA)*			
armchair	*koltuk*	drawer	*çekmece*
bed	*karyola/yatak*	footstool	*tabure*
bedside table/ nightstand	*tuvalet masası*	glass-fronted display cabinet	*vitrin*
bracket	*ayak**	mirror	*ayna*
chair	*sandalye/iskemle*	shelf	*raf*
chest-of-drawers/ dresser	*komodin*	single bed	*tek kişilik yatak*
cupboard	*dolap*	sofa/couch	*kanepe*
desk	*yazı masası*	table	*masa*
double bed	*iki kişilik yatak*	wardrobe	*gardırop*
dowrybox	*sandık*		

* Usually needs explanation, as in *raf ayağı* –bracket for a shelf; *şömine ayakları* - supports for a chimneybreast, etc.

The good news is that because it is much cheaper to get things made in Turkey than in Western Europe, if you can't find furniture that you like it is possible to have it ready-made to your own specifications. In general the workmanship will be good and the fabrics very attractive. However, you may not always know how long you are going to have to wait for the finished product.

Second-Hand Furniture (*İkinci El Mobilya*): In general Turks tend to be unenthusiastic about second-hand goods although most towns will have a few outlets for used goods. Expats, however, are often well placed to hear about second-hand furniture that is going for a song since departing foreigners rarely want to take all their belongings away with them. It's always worth looking on the noticeboards at Taksim Dilmer to see if anyone is selling anything you need. Alternatively, check the back pages of *Lale*, the magazine of the International Women of Istanbul group, or the classified ads in local expat magazines such as Fethiye's *Land of Lights*. You could also place your own advert asking if anyone wants to sell second-hand household artefacts. It is particularly easy to pick up electrical goods second-hand although they will not have been checked for safety.

Antiques (*Antika*): If you want to furnish your house in traditional style, you will need to comb Turkey's antique shops for suitable items. Unfortunately you will find yourself in competition with hotel and pension owners trying to find things to improve their properties and high-society types for whom everything Ottoman is suddenly *très chic*. In Istanbul the Çukurcuma area east of İstiklal Caddesi is renowned for its antique shops. Its fame, however, means that bargains are likely to be few and far between. The same is increasingly true of the Horhor Bit Pazarı in Fatih. Üsküdar is also known for its antique shops and there are also some good antique shops inside the Grand Bazaar (*Kapalı Çarşı*).

Elsewhere in Turkey there are a few places which are renowned for their antique sellers. One of the less likely places is **Tokat** where several antique dealers work together in a *han* off Sulu Sokak. In **Ankara** antique dealers congregate near the Parmak Kapısı entrance to the citadel and along Gözcü Sokak. You're unlikely to find many bargains but the quality of items on sale tends to be high.

For addresses of antique shops see Appendix II. Note that Arçelik sells a range of modern fridges designed to look as if they are old.

Reclamation Yards: Gone are the old days when anyone wanting to decorate their house in traditional style could pick up antique woodwork by weight rather than design. These days there are many dealers who buy up (or simply remove) old fixtures and fittings from derelict houses and sell them on for prices little different from those in traditional antique shops. **Kayseri** has several reclamation yards and there is another large one near **Uçhisar** in Cappadocia. Several of the antique dealers in Istanbul's **Grand Bazaar** also have large depots elsewhere where you can buy things like old marble fountains.

Auction Houses (*Müzayedeciler*): Istanbul also has several auction houses which sell antiques and paintings. For addresses see Appendix II.

CURTAINS *(PERDE)* AND UPHOLSTERY *(DÖŞEMELİK KUMAŞ)*

Turkey sells some wonderful curtain materials at very reasonable prices. Fabric roller blinds (*jaluzi*) are also available but cost more and may have to be ordered from Istanbul. Zorlu Tekstil produces a particularly fine range of materials in its Taç Collection; to find the nearest stockist go to www.tac.com.tr.

The cost of upholstery is a snip which means that you can buy a battered old chair and re-cover it without it costing an arm and a leg. If no one can recommend a good upholsterer to you head for the industrial estate (*sanayi sitesi*) where you are almost guaranteed to find one.

For a list of fabric suppliers see Appendix II.

IN THE CURTAIN SHOP			
cotton	*pamuk*	silk	*ipek*
curtain hook	*perde düğmesi*	thick	*kalın*
curtain rail	*korniş*	thin	*ince*
fabric	*kumaş*	velvet	*kadife*
gauze	*tül*	wool	*yün*
linen	*keten*		

LIGHTS *(LAMBA)*

At an early stage in any project you will have to decide where the lights and light switches are to go. Finding a good electrician is often one of the toughest tasks and finding one who will do the wiring neatly and discreetly is even harder. You may have to watch very carefully where they are about to place the sockets and how they intend to place them. The worker may also be poor at lining up sockets so that they are straight.

Finding attractive light fittings away from the big towns is fairly difficult and it's rarely possible to buy a lampshade (*abajur*) separately from the lamp (except in IKEA, of course); you may have to travel to one of the out-of-town shopping malls to ensure a decent choice. Alternatively in rural areas it is possible to improvise with a range of ethnographic artefacts, such as old wooden yoghurt churns or metal hamam bowls. It is also possible to have spotlights fitted into all sorts of old artefacts. However, if they are made of wood you should be careful as the spotlights can set fire to it very quickly.

Branches of Bauhaus, Carrefour, IKEA and Praktiker sell standard lamps as well as a full range of wall and ceiling lights.

PICTURE FRAMES (ÇERÇEVE) AND MIRRORS (AYNA)

Although you can buy ready-made picture frames it's also easy and relatively cheap to get them purpose-designed, especially if you are planning to frame things like embroidery or original prints.

It is sometimes possible to buy mirrors with glass already in them but often you have to buy the frame and then have glass cut to fit it. Look in antique shops for large Ottoman mirrors with elaborate gilt frames but don't expect to find many bargains; even newly made replicas are quite pricey although branches of Dösim (see p. 499) often sell reasonably priced 'antique' mirrors.

DOMESTIC HELP

You can usually find a maid, nanny, babysitter, cook or driver by asking around; if you live in an apartment the *kapıcı* is a good place to start. In Istanbul you can also try Domestic Employment Services (Tel: 0216-308 6404, www.personnel-turkey.com) which employs a lot of Filipinos. In Fethiye ring 0252-612 1872 to find a cleaner.

It is possible to employ a live-in maid but that can sometimes be problematic because, as her employer, you become responsible for the safeguarding of her honour. Generally, it is easier to employ people who have their own accommodation.

Household Pests: As anywhere in the world you may have to cope with infestations of insects, mice, rats and other pests. Especially in summer flies can make life miserable; if building a house from scratch you might want to consider incorporating fly-screens into windows and doors although this will be a novel idea to most Turkish carpenters. If you live near water (e.g. in Dalyan) mosquitoes can be a torment; only in the south-east are they a serious

CLEANING EQUIPMENT (TEMİZLİK MALZEMELERİ)

bleach	çamaşır suyu	ironing board	ütü tahtası/masası
broom	süpürge	soap powder	çamaşır tozu
brush	fırça	sponge	sünger
bucket	kova	tea towel	kurulama bezi
clean	temiz	to clean	temizlemek
cloth	bez	to iron	ütülemek
clothes peg	çamaşır mandalı	to mop	bezle silmek
dirt	kir/pislik	to sweep	süpürmek
dirty	kirli	to wash	yıkamak
dishcloth	bulaşık bezi	vacuum cleaner	elektrik süpürgesi
dust	toz	very clean	tertemiz
duster	tozbezi	washing line	çamaşır ipi
dustpan	faraş	washing up	bulaşık deterjanı
iron	ütü		

risk to health but you might want to avoid encouraging them with ponds near your house. Even in Istanbul scorpions can be a nuisance, especially in spring and autumn. Although they normally cause pain rather than anything more serious, parents will want to keep them well clear of their offspring.

These days some of the big international companies sell their sprays and other pest deterrents in Turkey. However, there are also many home remedies that you may want to ask your neighbours about.

WHAT TO SAY

ant	karınca	mouse	fare
cockroach	hamamböceği	pellet	pelet
fly	sinek	rat	iri fare/sıçan
fly swatter	sineklik	scentless spray	kokusuz spreyi
fly-paper	sinek kağıdı	scorpion	akrep
insect	böcek	snake	yılan
insecticide	böcek ilacı	spider	örümcek
mosquito	sivrisinek	trap	kapan

CHAPTER 7

GETTING CONNECTED

Whether you are buying or renting a property in Turkey you will need to get to grips with the utility companies. At present these are all state-owned which may mean that prices are higher than they might be if there was competition but also means that you waste less time on the complex price comparisons that are one of the banes of modern Western life.

> **BEWARE!**
>
> If you come from the safety-conscious West you need to be aware of the potential dangers lurking in many Turkish homes. Wiring may be so ancient as to be a fire hazard with sockets that routinely flash when you try to plug anything into them. Gas water heaters may be installed with inadequate or no ventilation. The concept of annual gas and electricity safety checks is unknown in Turkey. It is your responsibility to check that all appliances in a property you are thinking to buy or rent have been made safe.

ELECTRICITY *(ELEKTRİK)*

In Turkey electricity is provided by TEDAŞ although you pay your bills to MEDAŞ (in Istanbul it is BEDAŞ and AYEDAŞ, depending on which side of the Bosphorus you live on; in Ankara it is BEDAŞ). If you are taking over a new property you will have to visit the nearest TEDAŞ/ MEDAŞ office and ask to open a new account *(abonelik, elektrik aboneliği)*. Before you can do so you will be expected to pay any outstanding bill attached to the property so before buying it may be wise to visit the office and check whether there are any such bills. If you are only renting any outstanding charge is technically the landlord's responsibility.

Electricity usage is metered and someone from TEDAŞ calls round every two months to read the meter *(saat/sayaç)*. If you are out they will be unable to do this and the bill will simply be rolled over until they can call again. If you are at work all day this can be problematic and can result in your meter going unread for many months, so it may be as well to leave a key with a neighbour who can let the meter reader in. There are automatic fines for late payment of your bill. However, increasingly the meter reader may leave a blank bill if you're out. You can then read your own meter and take the bill to TEDAŞ, BEDAŞ or whoever or to the Belediye for them to calculate the amount owed. Some companies (including BEDAŞ in Ankara) are also moving towards a pre-paid card system of payment.

The meter readers have machines which print out your bill on the spot although no legitimate meter-reader ever asks for payment on the spot. The bill will indicate a time frame within which it should be paid. Increasingly you are expected to pay the money into an account at one of the banks specified on the bill although in rural areas you may still be able to pay at the Belediye, post office or other government office.

Before buying a resale property you need to find out if it has an electricity supply. If it does, then you will need to take the meter to the TEDAŞ office to be read and pay any outstanding bill. You may need to buy a new, more modern electricity meter (*elektrik saati/sayacı*) and have it in installed at the property; digital meters give the most accurate, and usually lowest, readings.

Provided there was an existing electricity supply to the house that is the most complicated it gets, even if the house has to be completely rewired. However, if there was no electricity supply to the property, you will have to pay TEDAŞ to prepare an *elektrik projesi* before you can open a new account, an additional expense to build into your costing.

ELECTRICITY – THE FACTS

Turkey's electricity voltage is 220v as in Europe. However, to use some heavy-duty appliances (e.g. a combined electric water heater and central heating system) you may have to get permission from the Belediye to raise the voltage to the industrial level of 380v and pay a fee accordingly.

Most sockets *(lamba duyu)* are round and two-pinned as in France. The earth wire *(topraklama kablosu)* is usually yellow.

Many Turks try to use as little electricity as possible because of the price and so low-level light bulbs (25 amp, 60 amp) are common. If you are having lighting installed and the electrician is supplying the bulbs, make sure that s/he provides sensible 75 amp/100 amp bulbs *(elektrik ampulü)* unless you want to have to replace them all with a new set.

For information about plugs, sockets, adaptors etc go to www.kropla.com.

Solar Panels (*Güneş Enerjisi*): These days many Turkish rooftops sprout a selection of solar panels to take advantage of the ferocious summer sun. Solar panels provide cheap, abundant and very hot water in summer. They are also regarded as environmentally friendly despite their damaging impact on the visual landscape. If you opt for a panel you need to remember that they can freeze and crack in winter unless you put anti-freeze (*antifriz*) into them. You will also need to have a back-up system in place that automatically switches on when the water temperature falls too low, as it will probably do in winter.

To make your panels slightly less obtrusive opt for lying the tank on its side rather than pointing upright. It is also possible to have them painted so that they blend in better with their surroundings. Alternatively you can conceal the system behind a parapet on a flat roof or behind bushes on the ground.

Home Electricity Generators (*Jeneratör*): To protect yourself against the inconvenience of power cuts you can buy a home generator. A smallish manually-operated generator is likely to cost around €1,200.

POWER CUTS (*ELEKTRİK KESİNTİSİ*)

Wherever you live in Turkey you need to bear in mind the likelihood of power cuts. Although these are relatively rare in the big cities and along the coast they are still fairly common in rural areas, and tend to occur most frequently at those coldest, busiest times when pressure on the supply reaches its highest. Power cuts are also common whenever work is taking place on the power supply. Sometimes you will be given advance warning; more commonly you will not.

Several things follow from this:

- Firstly, you need to ensure that your most important appliances are attached to surge protectors – every year many electrical appliances are written off by the power surges that accompany the return of the supply and so far the power company is under no obligation to replace the damaged items. You should also connect your computer and anything equally important to a UPS (uninterruptible power supply) device; this will kick in when the lights go off and give you time to save your work and close the system down properly.
- Secondly, it pays to have some methods of lighting/heating/cooking that are not dependent on electricity so that you are not left helpless when the supply cuts out. Supermarkets and electrical shops sell neon lighting strips that can be charged up ready to come on automatically when the electricity goes off but it's as well to have a torch and a supply of matches ready to hand as well. Having a cooker that operates on both gas and electricity is also a good idea.
- Buying a private back-up generator (*jeneratör*) is possible but expensive.
- You should consider household insurance that covers against damage to your appliances following a power surge as well as for the loss of the contents of your fridge-freezer after a prolonged power outage.

GAS (GAZ)

Most of Turkey's big cities are either already connected to natural gas (*doğalgaz*) or are in the process of being connected. In Istanbul natural gas is supplied by İGDAŞ (Tel; 444 3636, www.igdas.com.tr), in Ankara by EGO (Tel: 0312-231 7180, www.ego.gov.tr). However, many rural areas remain dependent on bottled LPG gas supplies.

Provided the property you are renting or buying is already connected to natural gas, you will only need to visit the local office of the gas company and open a new account (*abonelik, gaz aboneliği*). As with electricity, you will be expected to pay any outstanding bill first so it pays to try and find out before you buy or move in whether such a bill exists. However, if you are merely renting, the onus is on the landlord/lady to pay any outstanding bills.

If the property is not connected to natural gas you can arrange to pay to have it connected (provided there is a local supply). If you are living in an apartment block, you can then recoup some of the cost from other tenants who also want to sign up to the supply. Gas usage is metered and the meter-man calls round to read the meters; if you are out at work most of the day it may be wise to have the meter placed outside where he will be able to read it. Increasingly the big towns (including Ankara) are moving towards a pre-paid card system for gas payments.

Where there is no natural gas you may have to rely on bottled liquid propane gas (*tüp gaz*) which comes in a variety of sizes suitable for a range of purposes. Mostly people use small or medium-sized bottles to operate cookers and gas water heaters. One medium-sized bottle usually supplies a family with cooking fuel for six to eight weeks or with water for four weeks (YTL32 per bottle). There are also industrial-sized bottles (*sanayi tüpü*) which can be used to generate central heating and hot water. However, these are unwieldy and rather impractical as they usually stop generating enough power to do the job properly well before the gas actually runs out. One large *tüp* will only supply heating and water for a house for one week to 10 days, so it is also very expensive (YTL100 per bottle).

Gas bottles are delivered to houses on a regular basis. In big towns you will hear the delivery lorries doing their rounds, playing theme tunes reminiscent of those used by ice cream vendors to alert users to their presence – you call out if you want a bottle delivered to your property. You pay on the spot and the delivery man will probably connect the bottle and remove the empty one for you. Alternatively, you can phone the shop that sells the bottles and ask them to visit on their next round; you either pay immediately or when you next visit the shop. The industrial-sized bottles usually have to be ordered separately.

When a new bottle is delivered make sure its plastic seal is intact; unscrupulous salespeople have been known to sell bottles which have already been partially used. If you are going to connect the bottles yourself you need to be sure that you know what you are doing as they are potentially dangerous. Turks sometimes run a lighted match round the connection to check that it is sealed; it's more sensible to apply sudsy water to the connection and watch for bubbles to rise through it to indicate leaking gas. Keep a supply of rubber washers handy for the mechanism that links the bottle to the pipes since these wear out very quickly.

When buying a gas-operated cooker it's worth considering a model that has one ring that operates off electricity. Then when the gas bottle runs out you will be able to continue cooking until the new one is delivered.

WHO TO CALL WHEN THE GAS RUNS OUT

Istanbul

- *Aygaz:* tel 0800-211 4070, www.aygaz.com.tr
- *Ipragaz:* tel 0212-249 0408
- *Likidgaz:* tel 0212-252 2730

HEATING *(ISITMA TESİSATI)*

No matter where you live in Turkey how you decide to heat your home will have important consequences in terms of comfort and cost. On the coast this may not be a big issue but inland making the wrong decision can leave you cold and out of pocket.

Stoves (*Soba*): Traditionally most Turkish houses were heated by stoves which burnt wood (*odun*) and coal (*kömür*). In rural areas these remain the favoured means of heating, being by far the cheapest. A judiciously-placed stove can be used to heat most of the rooms on one floor of a house. What's more a stove can also be used to maintain a constant supply of hot water; the most modern models can also be used for baking potatoes and other simple foods. With a nifty gadget attached to their up-pipe they can also be used to dry clothes in wet weather. On the downside, however, it is hard to regulate the precise temperature of a room with a stove so that many Turkish homes are stiflingly hot and uncomfortable in all but the coldest weather.

Stoves can also be dangerous - even lethal - should wind cause the smoke to blow back inside the house during the night. What's more, to operate a stove you need plenty of storage space for the wood, coal and kindling wood, and stoking up the stove can be dirty and occasionally dangerous. In particular wind can cause carbon monoxide fumes to flow back down the pipes into the house with potentially lethal consequences. Despite this, smoke alarms are extremely hard to find in Turkey, let alone gadgets to test for carbon monoxide fumes - bring these from home if you can. Even with a metal tray under your stove you may also want to place a piece of insulating material there as well since a hot stove can scorch or burn right through floorboards.

Stoves are usually for sale in one particular part of town where you will also be able to buy all the things you need to go with them: straight and curved pipes, a fire-resistant metal tray to stand the stove on, metal coal buckets, handles for lifting the coal buckets and natty pieces of hooked metal for lifting the top lid of a stove.

If your rented property has a wood and coal-burning stove but you would prefer an alternative means of heating it may be worth discussing this with your landlord/lady. The installation cost may be high but they may be prepared to let you stop paying the rent until it has been recouped.

What Type of Coal? There are many different types of coal on sale in Turkey. American coke burns best but unfortunately it is officially banned from sale because of the pollution it causes - this hangs like a cloud over some towns in winter. Coal imported (*ithal*) from Russia and Africa is generally thought to be best although it is more expensive than locally-produced fuel.

People start organising their wood and coal supplies in August and September; if you leave it much later you may find the best stuff already gone. Coal merchants usually deliver coal to individual houses although they may dump it in the street outside for you to bring in. This is hard enough when it is in sacks but sometimes they just dump it in big piles outside your door. In Turkey people commonly bag up coal in plastic bags and then toss the whole bag into the stove - convenient and clean if hardly good for the environment.

Tiled Stoves: The stoves commonly used in Turkish homes are ugly and functional. However, in the 19th century the town houses of the wealthy were often heated using beautiful tile-covered stoves (*çini soba*). These are now hard to find except in pricy antique shops. For some suggested stockists, see Appendix II.

Bottled Gas Heaters (*Tüp Gaz Soba*)

One alternative to a stove is a gas heater operating off a small gas bottle. These are usually clean, effective and relatively cheap to operate. However, they can be smelly and only heat the room in which they are located. They also tend to soak up the oxygen from the atmosphere so people hang little tubs of water in front of them to refresh the air.

Electric Fires (*Elektrik Sobası*)

You can also buy a range of electric fires, usually on wheels for easy mobility. These, too, are clean, although operating them is more expensive than using a gas heater. The best electric fires have thermostat controls so that they turn off and on according to the ambient temperature. Some cheaper models quickly fall apart while others have significant design faults (e.g. burning the floorboards underneath them.). Whatever other forms of heating you have in the house you may want to have an electric fire available for immediate heat on those colder evenings.

Central Heating (*Kalorifer Tesisatı*)

In towns most apartment blocks have some form of central heating. Usually this is centrally controlled which means you cannot decide for yourself when it will be turned on and off at the start and end of winter. Usually you can turn individual radiators on and off, although in older apartment blocks this, too, may be centrally controlled which may mean that the apartment is too hot for much of the time.

If you are installing a private central heating system this is likely to prove expensive. You will also have to weigh up the relative merits and costs of the different fuels available to fire the system and decide whether you want the same system (*kombi*) to operate the central heating and the hot water or just the central heating.

- The cheapest fuel is coal. However, this has the same drawbacks as using a coal stove: you need somewhere to store the coal and handling it will always be dusty and dirty.

- Slightly more expensive is some form of oil but this also requires that you have somewhere spacious to store it. Some forms of oil are also very dirty to handle.

- In towns where there is natural gas this likely to be the cheapest option other than coal. However, using bottled gas is incredibly expensive. The bottles for the gas will be large and unwieldy and always run out at the most inconvenient times.

- Electricity has the virtues of cleanliness and consistency although if there is a power cut you will be left in the cold. However, this is often the case anyway since even if you are using some other form of fuel there may well be an electric connection to the central heating radiators. Electricity is, inevitably, very expensive.

Underfloor Heating (*Döşeme Altından Isıtma*)

Underfloor heating is a fairly novel concept in Turkey (see p. 144). It is most suitable for warmer parts of the country because it takes time to warm up and can freeze in winter, resulting in costly disruption.

Fireplaces (*Şömine*)

Grander homes in Istanbul are sometimes fitted with English-style fireplaces, either set around a real solid-fuel fire or around an artificial fire using natural gas, liquid gas or electricity. Sometimes these fireplaces front a convection, conduction or radiation heating system that will work in the same way as central heating. It will be expensive but very effective. It is also possible to buy French-style wood-burning stoves that circulate heat through the house via vents in the walls. On their own they will not provide enough warmth in very cold weather. However, they do provide a useful, and attractive, top-up.

For some suggested stove stockists, see Appendix II.

AIR CONDITIONING (*KLİMA*)

No matter where you choose to live it is likely to be very hot in July and August. Luxury modern apartments and houses may come with in-built air conditioning. However, older houses and apartments will never have such a system and you will need to weigh up whether the comfort it offers outweighs the cost of installation.

The obvious – and cheaper! - alternative is a fan or series of them. You can also buy plug-in air conditioning units that can be attached to the wall.

Opting for neither air conditioning nor fans is likely to leave you hot and bothered for several months of every year but you can bring air conditioning costs down by keeping windows closed and curtains drawn during the hottest parts of the day and by designing your home to maximise on any through breezes.

WATER *(SU)*

Provided you are renting or buying a property that already has a water supply you will only need to visit the water company (ASKİ in Ankara or İSKİ in Istanbul) or the Belediye to open a new account (*abonelik, su aboneliği*) and pay any outstanding bill. However, if there is no existing supply you will have to open a new account and then find a plumber (*sıhhi tesisatçı*) to do the necessary work. In big towns there may be specialist plumbers; elsewhere you may find that the electrician doubles up as the plumber in which case you can get one quotation for having all the wiring and plumbing done at the same time. It will probably cost you around €165 to have your property connected to the water supply plus whatever charges the plumber levies for his work.

Since water shortages are a fact of life in many parts of rural Anatolia you may want to install a back-up tank with pump (*su pompası/hidrafor*) which will kick in when the mains supply cuts off. Alternatively you may want to keep stocks of bottled water in the house to use in an emergency. It's as well to know where the nearest fountain/spring (*çeşme*) is so that you can fetch water from there too. However, bear in mind that some spring water may not be entirely safe for drinking; there is unlikely to be a warning sign unless the water is completely undrinkable. It is vital to make sure you have turned off all taps following a cut - if you go out with one still left on you could come back to find your house flooded.

In the big towns tap water is theoretically safe to drink, although it has an unpleasantly chlorinated flavour. In rural areas it is unwise to drink the water straight from the tap since giardia and other water-borne illnesses are common, especially in summer. Bottled water is cheap and ubiquitous but if you can't find any make sure you boil your local supply for at least 15 minutes.

WASTE DISPOSAL

Most parts of Turkey have efficient rubbish disposal systems, often using exactly the same huge lorries that chew everything up in the back as are seen in Europe. Householders pay a small biannual tax (*çevre temizlik vergisi* - environment cleaning tax) which covers the cost of waste disposal. Normally you will have to take your rubbish to the nearest rubbish bin (*çöp kutusu/bidonu*) to be collected but there are none of the petty limitations on what you can put in them that are the bane of life in, for example, the UK.

Unfortunately although rubbish is removed from homes and streets effectively it is often dumped in uncovered sites which become hideous eyesores. Inevitably rubbish blows into surrounding areas, compounding a general problem of littering that mars many roadsides. The problem is made worse in rural areas by a tradition that everything purchased, even a newspaper or bar of chocolate, should be put into a plastic bag so that neighbours can't see what you have bought.

Some local councils have introduced recycling schemes for glass and paper but this is by no means universal. However, in Turkey there is also a small army of poor people who earn money by sorting through garbage, and removing paper, glass, metals and any recyclables of resale value. They take these to various collection centres (usually co-ordinated by a 'gypsy king' who then resells everything to appropriate factories). You will sometimes see these people dragging huge canvas carts for paper, or pushing handcarts for everything else. One reason why many towns have been reluctant to establish recycling programmes is that these people will lose their primary source of income.

TELEPHONE *(TELEFON)*, FAX *(FAKS)* AND INTERNET

Telephone

In Turkey land telephone lines are provided by the monopoly supplier Türk Telekom. Although the government is trying to find a buyer, there is as yet little competition in the telephone market which means that prices are high by international standards, especially for international calls. The situation is not helped by the fact that heavy taxes are levied on phone bills.

If you are buying a property that already has a phone you should check before going ahead that there is no outstanding phone bill. If there is you will be expected to pay it and if you don't the phone company will prevent you using the phone to make outgoing calls.

Opening an Account: If you have Turkish residency you should be able to open a normal telephone account at a main post office on production of your passport, proof of your address and bank account details. Some branches will require non-resident foreigners to find a Turkish friend who is prepared to provide them with a line in their name; however this is getting less common. Phone bills must be paid monthly either in person at the post office (expect long queues on the last day for payment) or through a standing order from your bank account.

NO MATTER WHERE YOU ARE...

Turkey has some phone numbers that can be dialled without a local dialling code wherever you are in the country. They always start with '444' and are very popular with transport companies.

Tariffs: Türk Telekom has five different tariffs including one for small users (*hesaplı hat*) and another for heavy users (*konuşkan hat*). There is also a summer tariff (*yazlık hat*) for people who move house during the hotter months. However, their website is confusing; to get the best deal you will probably need to ask advice. Unless you ask for one of the alternatives it will be assumed that you want a standard line rental.

Mobile Phones: If you can't get a landline you can fall back on a mobile phone (*cep telefonu*). Mobile phone services are offered by Turkcell, Telsim and Avea. If you have residency you can open an account with one of these companies and arrange to pay the bills monthly; they will want to see your passport and bank account details. Non-residents can either ask a friend to open an account for them or sign up to a counter system. This means buying counters (*kontörler*) which can be topped up as required. Counter cards are sold by most grocer's shops and newsagent's. Calls are cheaper with a proper mobile phone account than using a counter card although the cards are protection against unexpectedly high bills.

Calling from a mobile phone is more expensive than calling from a landline (unless you are phoning from one mobile to another) so this could be a pricey alternative if you need to make many long-distance or international calls. Motel sells boxes that can be attached to conventional phones and which automatically reduce the cost of long-distance and international calls. There are also phonecards which offer reduced-price calls if you punch in a special number before dialling.

Phone Services: Although phone bills are automatically itemised you need to contact Türk Telekom and register for call forwarding, call waiting, automatic redialling, conference call and phone locking services. It is surprisingly difficult to buy an answer phone in Turkey, although some top-range Panasonic phones have them. Some cheap phones have small protruding screens which indicate the last number that called the line.

IT'S FREE

As in the UK numbers prefaced with 0800 are free in Turkey.

Wiring: Don't be surprised if your telephone is wired by pushing a line through the wall rather than by using a proper junction box. This won't be much of a problem until the time comes to plug something else into the line when you may find yourself wishing it had been done properly in the first place.

Almost unbelievably the state still sometimes taps the phone-lines of people who register them with a foreign name.

FINDING A TELEPHONE NUMBER

Although the mymerhaba website has some Yellow Pages-style information there was at the time of writing no true Yellow Pages directory for Turkey. Türk Telekom has an online directory service (www.ttrehber.gov.tr) although it is only in Turkish. You can make one or two free enquiries but then you will be asked to subscribe. Call 118 for normal directory enquiries.

Beyaz Sayfalar	White Pages (home phone numbers)		
Sarı Sayfalar	Yellow Pages (business phone numbers)		
ad	name	*soyad*	surname
il	province	*mahalle*	neighbourhood
bul	find	*temizle*	wipe clean
hata	error	*abonelik*	subscription

WHO TO CALL FOR A PHONE LINE

Avea: Tel: 444 1500, www.avea.com.tr

Telsim: Tel: 444 0542, www.teslim.com.tr

Türkcell: Tel 444 0532, www.turkcell.com.tr

Türk Telekom: Tel 444 1444, www.telekom.gov.tr

Internet Telephony: Recently people have started using the Internet to make calls for no more than the cost of the connection. To use these services you need a computer with the necessary software downloaded, a microphone and speakers. Free services usually only work for phoning people who have also signed up to the same system although for a small fee you can also phone from your computer to normal landlines abroad. Popular services include Skype (www.skype.com) and Googletalk (www.google.com/talk/).

Using Mobile Phones Abroad: If you want to use your Turkcell card overseas you will need to phone 2222. If you use the counter system you need to dial *111 and then press YES on arrival overseas. This system supposedly works in 170 countries around the world.

It is possible to bring your old handset from overseas and then buy a Turkish SIM card. However, before doing this you should check whether the existing SIM card has been locked to prevent you doing this. If it has you will need to contact your network supplier and see if it can be unlocked first.

TELEPHONE ETIQUETTE

Most Turks answer the phone by saying either '*Alo*' or '*Efendim*'. So far, so familiar. What is more unexpected is that they don't always say good-bye at the end of the call; instead conversations tend to trail off until one or other party puts the receiver down. The rule of thumb seems to be that the person making the call should end it, but you can always drop in hints that you're ready to hang up: 'thank you for calling,' 'it was nice hearing from you again,' or 'give my greetings to your...' should do it.

dialling tone	*çevir sesi*
dialling code	*telefon kodu*
engaged	*meşgul*
number	*rakam*
operator	*operatör/santral*
telephone card	*telefon kartı*
telephone directory	*telefon rehberi*
switchboard	*telefon santralı*
All our lines are busy.	*Bütün hatlarımız doludur.*
Can I leave a message?	*Mesaj bırakabilir miyim?*
Can I speak to Ali?	*Ali ile görüşebilir miyim?*
Do you want to hold?	*Bekler misiniz?*
Hello	*Alo/efendim*
I'll call again later.	*Daha sonra yeniden arayacağım.*
Is Ayşe there?	*Ayşe orada mı?*
It's Pat.	*Ben Pat.*
One minute/second please	*Bir dakika/saniye lütfen.*
Please check/wait and try again.	*Lütfen control edip/bekleyip tekrar arayınız.*
She's not here at the moment.	*Şu anda burada değil.*
The number has changed.	*Bu numara değişmiştir.*
The number you called is wrong.	*Yanlış numarayı aradınız.*
There's no reply	*Cevap yok.*
When will she be back?	*Ne zaman geri döner?*
Who's calling?	*Kim arıyor?*
Wrong number.	*Yanlış numara.*

Fax

It is easy to buy a fax or fax/phone in Turkey and this may still be a worthwhile investment given the charges made by the post office or private suppliers for sending a fax. Although the Internet is widely used in Turkey many businesses still use faxes more often than email; in particular most government departments still rely on phones and faxes rather than email to conduct their business.

Internet

Although Turkey took to the Internet like a duck to water that does not mean that connections are always either good or reliable, although they are generally cheap. In the big cities and along the coast it is increasingly possible to hook-up to an ADSL line (although even these can be slower and clunkier than in the West). However, in smaller rural areas connections can be so slow that it sometimes feels like wading through mud to get your emails onto the screen.

If you don't want to install an ADSL line it is perfectly easy either to download a server or to buy an Internet package for around €18 for three months. Internet phone usage is very cheap and appears as a separate item on phone bills.

Where ADSL services are available you have to apply for them at a main post office. You will then receive a separate monthly ADSL bill alongside your normal telephone bill; a restricted monthly package costs around YTL29, a limitless monthly package YTL49. A fee of around YTL70 for the connection comes with your first bill. When the bill arrives you have less time to pay than with a normal telephone bill although the service is usually reconnected speedily once you do pay. Paying by standing order reduces the risk of being cut off.

If you don't have a Turkish server it is still possible to access the Türk Telekom Internet service on an ad hoc basis by dialling 146. However, this is a premium-rate line to be used very sparingly.

The main Turkish servers are:

- E-Kolay (www.e-kolay.net)
- Kaynet (www.kaynet.net)
- Superonline (www.superonline.com)
- Ttnet (www.telekom.gov.tr)

TELEVISION, VIDEO AND DVD

Television (*Televizyon*)

Turkish television services are only of interest to foreigners with good Turkish-language skills although most news broadcasts come with written summaries in Turkish that even the less linguistically gifted may be able to understand. However, these days it is easy to sign up for satellite television services that provide channels in several languages, including English, French, German, Italian and Russian. The main supplier of such services is Digitürk which offers hundreds of channels, including BBC World, BBC Prime, CNN International, Euro News, CNBC-e, National Geographic, Moviemax and the History Channel for a monthly fee of around YTL30 (family packet). For around YTL35 a month it is possible to view a wider range of film channels (cinema packet) but it costs at least YTL60 to access the main sports channel. There is also a pay-per-view system for films. Parents are able to block channels they think unsuitable for their children including the soft-porn channels for which there is a higher subscription fee.

To access Digitürk you will need to buy a black box (*Digikutu/Digibox*) and decoder card (*Digitürk kartı*) as well as a satellite dish (*çanak anten*). Installing these (always done by Digitürk technicians) is not usually problematic although the dish has to be put in a location where the signal is detectable. This can occasionally be difficult - the fairy chimneys in Göreme have been known to block the signal as have summer leaves on Istanbul trees.

In theory you are not supposed to transfer satellite dishes or black decoder boxes between users. However, if you don't mind pretending to be the person in whose name the system was originally installed you may be able to save some money by buying a second-hand system left behind by someone who is leaving the country. If you move to another address you are expected to resubscribe to Digitürk rather than take your dish with you. If you are caught breaking the rules the company will send someone to take your black box away.

Digitürk offers a professional back-up service although you need to be able to speak basic Turkish. However, their bills often arrive late and there are fines for late payment. If you set up a standing order at your bank you should be able to avoid problems (see p. 251). Note that Digitürk often offers special offers to existing subscribers, so keep an eye out for possible savings.

In Istanbul and Ankara Türk Telekom provides a cable television service which screens BBC, CNN, TV5 and RTL programmes. You can also sign up to Cine5 or buy a dish that picks up digital television services free. However, one of Digitürk's big pluses is that you can watch films on it in either Turkish or their original language. This is not possible with the other services.

WHAT'S ON TONIGHT

If you don't subscribe to one of the satellite service you will have to get used to a diet of Turkish soaps, quiz programmes and elderly films, many dating to the 1950s, '60s and '70s when *Yeşilçam* was the Turkish equivalent of Hollywood and most of them starring the late toothy actor, Kemal Sunal. There are also Turkish versions of worldwide hit series like *The Weakest Link*, *Who Wants to be a Millionaire?* and *Pop Idol*, as well as classy serials *(diziler)* which attract a fanatical following; recent examples included *Asmalı Konak* and *Kurtlar Vadisi*. Information about what's on appears in all the main daily newspapers.

All this is, of course, excellent for improving your grasp on contemporary Turkish usage. However, the reality is that most foreigners stop watching Turkish television as soon as they have access to satellite television. If you have Digitürk, the company publishes a monthly magazine listing the main schedules. Most of the channels you are likely to want to use also post their timetables on the Internet and publish them in *The New Anatolian* and *Turkish Daily News*. You can also check the day's schedule through the e-information button on your Digitürk hand controller *(kumanda)*.

WHO TO CONTACT

Cine5: tel 0212-340 5555, www.cine5.com.tr

Digitürk: tel 0212-473 7373, www.digitürk.gen.tr

WHAT IT MEANS

Sinyal seviyesinde azalma var.	The signal reception has weakened.
Sinyal seviyesini iyileştirmek için bağlantıları kontrol ediniz.	To improve the signal check your connections.
Kanal değiştirmek için 'Yukarı' ya da 'Aşağı' tuşlarını kullanınız.	To change channels use the up *(yukarı)* and down *(aşağı)* keys

Video

Turkey uses the PAL video system (as in the UK but not in the USA). However, video recorders are increasingly hard to find as DVD players sweep the board. Even if you can find a recorder to buy you need to be aware that not all of them allow you to record one programme while watching another. There is a steep tax on imported video recorders (see p. 431).

VCD and DVD Players

VCD players are cheaper and more common than the DVD versions. However, as the price of the latter has fallen, so more people are investing in DVD players and their even higher quality DVX cousins. Some films on VCD and DVD are in English with Turkish subtitles so check when you buy. Pirated DVDs are ubiquitous and extremely cheap but usually of low quality. The country is trying to put an end to pirating, and is prosecuting producers, sellers and buyers as they are caught.

RADIO (RADYO)

You can pick up the BBC World Service on shortwave radio on 12095kHz, 15070kHz and 15400kHz and the Voice of America on1260kHz and 15205kHz. It is also possible to receive some foreign radio stations over the Internet; try www.bbc.co.uk/radio/ or www.radio-locator.com.

There are many national and local radio stations in Turkey, some of them with foreign-language programmes (a few of these stations can be picked up on Digitürk as well as on conventional radios). Some can only be received in Istanbul. However, others can be picked up online at www.creatonic.com/tronline/.

POSTAL SERVICES (POSTA HİZMETLERİ)

In general the Turkish postal service is very efficient. Every sizeable settlement will have a post office (postane, PTT; www.ptt.gov.tr) where you can post mail and collect it. Even though the telephone service is now separate from the postal one there will usually be public phoneboxes in or near the post office. Larger post offices also have poste restante services which may be useful while you are in the process of moving. You can also send faxes from some (but not all) post offices. Some also have Internet services and phones offering metered calls on the counter – handy for the months before you get your own line. Although post offices don't sell stationery, in towns there are sometimes stalls selling envelopes and postcards outside.

Opening Hours: Most post offices open from 8.30am to noon and from 1.30pm to 5pm although in the big cities there will be no lunch-time closure. They are usually closed on Saturday afternoon and all day Sunday.

Delivery Service: In towns postmen usually deliver mail to houses and the postboxes in the halls of apartment blocks. Parcels must be collected from the parcel office. In rural areas the postman may deliver to some central properties but you may be expected to collect your mail from the post office yourself. Usually the local postman becomes expert at recognising post addressed to foreigners and will keep it all until you collect it.

Bill Payments: Phone bills are still paid at post offices and there can be very long queues on the last dates for payment. You can also pay your tel-

ephone, ADSL and electricity bills at computerised post offices and buy OTS
cards for use on toll roads. Computerisation means that you can pay your bills
at any post office in the country, not just at the one closest to home.

AT THE POST OFFICE *(POSTANEDE)*			
airmail	*uçak ile/uçakla*	parcel	*koli*
bubble wrap	*balon naylonu*	payments & receipts	*havale-posta çeki (kabul) tahsilat*
bureau de change	*döviz bürosu*	phonecard	*telefon kartı*
express	*ekspres*	postbox	*posta kutusu (PK)*
fragile	*kırılgan/kırılacak eşya*	postcard	*kartpostal*
glue	*tutkal*	registered mail	*kayıtlı/taahhütlü*
inter-city mail	*şehirlerarası*	scissors	*makas*
letter	*mektup*	small parcel	*paket*
local mail	*şehiriçi*	special delivery	*APS*
overseas mail	*uluslararası*	stamp	*pul*
packaging	*ambalaj*	string	*ip*

Parcels: Parcel services are more erratic than the regular postal services.
Sometimes you will be expected to let the postman inspect the contents of
the parcel and sometimes you won't, so it makes sense to leave parcels un-
sealed and take along string and parcel tape to close them in the post office.

Some parcels arrive from abroad unopened and with no customs due on
them. Others will arrive opened and with payment expected - there seems
to be no rhyme or reason behind this. You should not send anything that can
be construed as a medicine through the post – if you do and the parcel is
opened the outcome is likely to be expensive and time-consuming. Note that
vitamins are sometimes regarded as 'medicine' – even Vegemite delivery has
been held up because a Customs officer spotted the word 'vitamin' on the
label. If you send more than three of any one item there is also a danger that
Customs will decide you intend to sell them and levy tax accordingly.

Since the advent of the Internet Customs officers seem to have become
more interested in the content of parcels. Small packets with a value of more
than €100 now attract tax. However, special conditions apply for one month
before and after the New Year, Kurban Bayramı and Ramazan Bayramı. During
these months you are allowed to receive gifts worth up to €300 free of duty.

To qualify the items should still have their tags on. You should also ask your friends and relatives to write *'hediyelik'* (gift) on the customs declaration.

Main Post Offices
Istanbul
Tel: 0212-513 3407, Büyük Postane, Büyük Postane Caddesi, Sirkeci
Tel: 0212-292 4085, Cumhuriyet Caddesi 2, Taksim
For parcels: Davutpaşa Caddesi 99, Cevizlibağ. Opposite the Ülker factory.

Ankara
Tel: 0312-327 1755, Atatürk Bulvarı, Ulus
For parcels: Eşref Bitlis Caddesi 8, Yenimahalle

Izmir
Tel: 0232-247 7979, Cumhuriyet Meydanı

PAYING THE BILLS

If you have a Turkish bank account you can arrange to make automatic bill payments direct from your account which is particularly useful if you are away from home a lot. Internet banking also makes it easier to pay your bills (*fatura*) from home.

All bills come with a final payment date (*son ödeme tarihi*). Generally speaking, you have least time to pay before being disconnected with ADSL Internet access (just one week). With phone bills you usually get up to 10 days to pay before you are cut off. If you don't pay your electricity bill on time you will find a fine added to the next bill. If the meter reader is unable to gain access to you property you can go a long time before the power is cut off (the same is true with water bills). However, if you simply don't pay your bill you are only likely to get about one month's leeway. State utility companies don't send reminder bills so you need to be watchful.

Digitürk will cut you off if you leave a bill unpaid for a month. However, they are fairly persistent in chasing you to pay or reconnect.

WHAT TO SAY WHEN THINGS GO WRONG			
guarantee	*garanti*	The system isn't working	*Sistem çalışmıyor.*
repairman	*tamirci*	The toilet/sink is blocked	*Tuvalet/lavabo tıkalı*
The gas is leaking	*Gaz kaçırıyor.*	user's manual	*kullanma kılavuzu*
The guarantee has expired	*Garantisi bitti.*	When can you repair it?	*Ne zaman tamir edebilirsiniz?*

CHAPTER 8

TYING THE KNOT

On even the briefest of visits to Turkey it will be obvious how many relationships there are between foreigners and Turks. The majority are between Western women and Turkish men although in the big cities there are also plenty of relationships in which the male is the foreigner. Some such partnerships end in marriage but unfortunately many flounder as the harsher realities of cross-cultural living become apparent.

COURTSHIP AND DATING

In traditional Turkish society there was no such thing as dating. A woman's honour was of enormous consequence to her family who took responsibility for finding her a suitable husband, sometimes as soon as she reached puberty. When tourism first came to Turkey people were taken aback at the casual way that Westerners organised their love lives. However, as the years passed, so many Turks came to accept Western ways and certainly in the holiday resorts young men often work their way through a string of foreign girlfriends before finally settling down either with one of them or, almost as frequently, with a Turk deemed more 'suitable' by their family.

Many of the holiday romances that blossom into something deeper are between couples of roughly similar age and background. However, there are also many relationships between men in their twenties and women in their forties and fifties. Of course some of these are genuine love matches. Others, however, appear to be last-ditch tries at romance on the woman's part, while on the man's hope of pecuniary gain or of an escape route to the West seem to play a considerable part. Too many women end up handing over money that would have seen them through their retirement in return for their fling.

WHAT YOU NEED TO KNOW ABOUT WOMEN'S STATUS IN TURKEY

Despite the fact that Turkey is a Muslim country where, traditionally, women had fewer rights than men, many Western women who have been brought up expecting to be treated as the equal of men are choosing to settle here. Some, although by no means all, of them have Turkish partners.

Although there are small fs of Turkey, particularly in the east, where women are still covered from head to toe and where they rarely venture from the house even in daylight without their husband's permission, in general women in Turkey have much greater freedom than women anywhere else in the Islamic world. This greater freedom has been enshrined in law as recently as 2002 when the new Civil Code (*Medeni Kanun*) decreed that men and women were equal partners in marriage and that women had a right to a half share in all property acquired during the marriage following a divorce. Men are no longer required by law to be the family bread-winner and women do not need their husband's permission to work outside the home.

However, there is often a big gap between what the law says and the reality on the ground. So in the east maybe one in 10 women still lives in a polygamous marriage and many women are forced to marry before they reach the age of consent. Legally adultery may not be a crime but every year many women are still killed by their families in so-called 'honour killings' and the law still permits lighter penalties in such cases.

According to the current Civil Code women can buy and sell goods on the same basis as men and can make their own independent income tax declarations. In theory women must be paid the same wage as men if their work takes place in the same workplace and is of equal productivity. However, since few jobs have been properly evaluated it is difficult for women to prove that they are being discriminated against on the grounds of their sex.

Women are entitled to eight weeks statutory paid maternity leave before and after the birth of each child. They are also entitled to take six months' leave without pay after the birth of their children and employers are not allowed to sack them until that period has come to an end. There are some jobs that are still barred to women (e.g. in mines).

Useful Addresses

- *Foundation for the Support of Women's Work (Kadın Emeğini Değerlendirme Vakfı - KEDV): Tel: 0212-292 2672*, www.kedv.org.tr, Bekar Sokak No: 17, Beyoğlu, Istanbul
- *Flying Broom (Uçan Süpürge):* Tel: 0312-427 0020, www.ucansupurge.org.index, Büyükelçi Sokağı No: 20/4, Kavaklıdere, Ankara
- *National Council of Turkish Women:* Tel: 0312-419 4591, Fax: 0312-419 4591, PK No: 44, Yenişehir, Ankara
- *Women for Women's Human Rights - New Ways Foundation:* Tel: 0212-251 0029, www.wwhr.org. İnönü Caddesi No: 37/6, Saadet Apt, Gümüşsuyu, Istanbul

Japanese women seem to be relatively good at making a go of relationships with Turkish men. This could be in part because their language is grammatically similar to Turkish which means that they often learn Turkish quite easily. Traditional Japanese culture also expected women to play a subservient role which may mean that Japanese women do not have quite the same expectations of equality that young Westerners usually bring to their relationships.

Conversely women from Russia and the ex-Soviet republics struggle with their public image as 'Natashas' (prostitutes). Even women who are trying hard to live a respectable life in Turkey can find men responding very negatively as soon as they announce their names or where they come from.

As yet AIDS is not a major problem. However, Turkish men are rarely keen to use condoms. It pays to be a little cautious, especially in resort areas where promiscuity is common.

ENGAGEMENT (NİŞAN)

There are no specific requirements before you can get engaged in Turkey. While some couples like to keep things low-key, others put on a big party for their friends and family. The couple may bring gold rings (yüzük) with their names inscribed inside them to the ceremony. These are tied together with red ribbon. Once they put them on the oldest man in the family cuts the ribbon and says a few words of congratulation.

If there is a party the guests may bring the same sort of gifts as they would to the actual wedding (see below). The couple will also dress up as formally as they would do for the wedding, although the bride won't wear white (red is quite normal). The bride's family are expected to pick up the expense of the engagement party, whereas the groom's family traditionally pays for the wedding.

MARRIAGE (EVLİLİK)

Turkish men and women must be 18 before they can marry except in exceptional circumstances when a court can permit marriage at 16 (the woman has to be willing and consent will not necessarily be given just because she is pregnant). People who are registered as mentally ill can only get married if they have a doctor's report that says that there is no impediment to their wedding.

Weddings are as big a deal in Turkey as in any Western country and in the towns people are spending an increasing amount of money on them. Specialist wedding planners have even started putting in an appearance at hotels such as Istanbul's Four Seasons, although most people still rely on family and friends to help organise everything.

THE WAY THINGS WERE

In traditional Turkish society marriages were arranged between families rather than between the couple concerned. It was not unknown for the bride and groom to see each other for the first time on their wedding day; indeed some couples were effectively betrothed at birth. Sometimes families would know a girl they wanted to marry their son or vice versa. Otherwise older women might visit the local hamam with an eye to finding a suitable bride for their son.

Once a family heard about a girl they thought appropriate they would send a couple of women to visit the family in question. The potential bride would serve coffee to the guests, giving them an opportunity to size her up. This occasion was called the *görücü usulü* ('time for seeing'). If all went well after a couple of these meetings the two families would conduct discreet research into each other's affairs and morals. If no problems emerged the two families would then discuss a suitable dowry, without which the betrothal could not go ahead.

Once the marriage had been agreed, the wedding ceremony was organised. Traditionally it was spread out over five days. On Monday the bride's trousseau was moved from her parents' house to that of her bridegroom in her dowry box *(çeyiz sandığı)*. Then on Tuesday the bride *(gelin)* would go to the hamam with her friends for a party. In the meantime her groom-to-be *(damat)* would raise a Turkish flag *(bayrak)* over his family home and serve a meal to as many friends and family as possible. He would also march through town with a group of friends holding the *bayrak* aloft.

On Wednesday the bride held her henna night *(kına gecesi)*. Her mother-in-law-to-be unrolled a silk runner in front of her and then her friends would approach holding candles and place coins on her head (this was thought to encourage fertility). Then the bride walked along the runner to her new mother-in-law and kissed her hand as a gesture of respect. Once the rituals were out of the way the women would sing and dance, and tuck into fruit and nuts. It was customary to include sad songs in the repertoire to encourage suitable gloom in the bride at the thought of leaving her family.

On Thursday the bride had her hair and make-up done before moving to her groom's house. The wedding ceremony took place on Friday, the holiest day of the week. Wealthy brides went to their wedding dressed in a purple velvet robe heavily embroidered in gold (although regional variations included something made out of heavy grey school uniform material in Cappadocia). Over their faces they wore red veils decorated with gold coins.

Afterwards the couple's friends and family attended the Trotter Day *(Paça Günü)* and drank bowls of sheep's trotter soup. They would then wait to hear that the marriage had been consummated. Proof was sometimes required in the form of a bloody sheet *(murat çarşafı)*. A gun was sometimes fired into the air to let the town know that the marriage had been consummated.

Marriages between Turks and Foreigners: Not so long ago it was a very rare foreigner who actually tied the knot in Turkey. These days, however, it is becoming more and more common, especially in Istanbul, Cappadocia and along the coast. When one of the couple is Turkish the marriage can only take place under Turkish law and be conducted by Turkish wedding officials.

Marriages between Two Foreigners: Where both of a couple are foreign they can be married by Turkish officials or officials from their own country. If both come from the same country they can be married by representatives of their country; where they are from different countries they can only be married by Turkish wedding officials.

THE WEDDING DAY(S)

For many Turks a wedding (*düğün)* comes in two stages: the civil ceremony followed by the religious one or vice versa.

> Traditionally it was believed that whichever one of the couple managed to stand on the other's foot first immediately after the wedding would wear the trousers in the marriage.

The Civil Ceremony (*Nikah*):

Since Turkey is a secular society the only weddings acknowledged by the state are civil weddings. Many couples still undergo a religious ceremony as well, but unless they have previously attended a civil ceremony (*resmî nikah)* their marriage will not be valid under Turkish law. The *nikah* ceremony must take place in the presence of a marriage officer (*nikah memuru)* employed by the local Belediye.

If you thought civil marriage ceremonies were short at home, prepare yourself to discover that Turkey does it even faster. It's still normal for the couple's family and friends to gather in large numbers at the wedding venue (which is never a place of worship). However, there will barely be time for them all to be seated before the ceremony - which is conducted entirely in Turkish - will be over. The couple will need two witnesses (*şahit*), preferably including one who speaks Turkish. There is some uncertainty over whether a foreigner can act as a witness. However, a foreign-born Turkish citizen is certainly acceptable.

Venues: Many couples get married in a *nikah/düğün salonu* (wedding room) which is usually attached to or run by the Belediye. Often these are spartan, unromantic buildings where men and women may be expected to sit separately. However, you can get married wherever you like and some couples have chosen to tie the knot in their favourite coastal resorts. Luxury hotels are often the favourite settings for wealthier urban couples but the latest fashion is for outdoor weddings in a country setting, with dinner catered and music brought in. In Cappadocia couples have married in restaurants with romantic fairy chimneys or even in the exotic surrounds of a restored caravanserai. Some foreigners are even allowed - or required - to get married in their embassy or consulate.

Istanbul

See p. 523 for a list of outside caterers and p. 467 for a list of some of the more popular romantic venues. Note that the most popular venues get booked up months ahead, especially over weekends.

The Religious Ceremony (İmam Nikahı):

Not all Turks bother with a religious ceremony but the more traditional and religious families still like to have an *imam* bless their relationships. Although the religious ceremony should take place after the civil version since the state does not recognise it as true marriage, some families still opt to put the religious ceremony first with the civil version following, sometimes days later. If there is no civil ceremony the law does not regard the couple as married, with all that means for women in terms of lost honour and financial insecurity.

THE FESTIVITIES

Traditionally Turkish weddings went on for up to five days but these days most last no more than three days, sometimes even less in the big towns.

***Bayrak* Ceremony:** On the first day of a rural wedding the groom's family hold a flag (*bayrak*) gathering. The Turkish flag is raised over their house and food is provided for as many of their friends and family as they can afford to feed (the invitation may be extended to the whole community by means of an announcement over the loudspeaker system).

Preparing the Wedding Chamber: In the days leading up to a rural wedding the bride's family will prepare the wedding chamber. This will be decorated with all the embroidery that the bride has worked in her youth so that guests will be able to visit and admire. Normally the bed is given an extra mattress so that layers of embroidered sheets can be displayed down the side of the bed. In rural areas it is still sometimes the case that a special sheet (*çarşaf*) will be provided that can be inspected for blood after the consummation of the marriage to ensure that the bride was a virgin. Luckily this is increasingly rare.

Kına Gecesi: The night before the wedding the bride-to-be (*gelin*) holds a *kına gecesi* (henna night), a women-only gathering which may involve only her friends and family (usual in towns) or the whole community (still common in rural areas). If it is a small, private affair, the mother-in-law-to-be may lay on simple drinks and refreshments before daubing her daughter-in-law-to-be's hand with henna. In rural areas, it is less common to provide food and the only drink available may be water or soft drinks. The bride's family will hire seats for as many guests as they expect, and music will be laid on for dancing. Towards the end of the evening the bride will sit amongst her guests with a red veil concealing her face. Her mother-in-law will bring a bowl of henna and daub her hands and feet with it. These will then be bound with cloth so that the henna can take effect overnight. Sometimes coins are pressed into the henna before the hand-binding. Because it is difficult for a woman to undress once her hands have been bound the mother-in-law often pretends to henna her new daughter-in-law's hand and then puts a special mitten (kına eldiveni) on it. When it is time to go to bed, the bride gets undressed and undergoes the real hennaing.

Although many Middle Eastern countries still trace pretty patterns on the hands and feet of brides-to-be, Turkish hennaing mostly consists of placing a ball of henna in the middle of the hand and then wrapping the fingers over it and binding them. This leaves a circular stain in the middle of the palm and a red tinge on the fingertips and nails. Since this is not particularly attractive, young women in the big cities are rarely keen to have this done. Foreign brides are often similarly reluctant, especially as they know that urbanites will look down on them if their hands are orange. Traditionally, the bride's female friends and family also had their hands and feet hennaed but this, too, is becoming less common. Even when women have their hands hennaed, they rarely have their feet coloured as well.

Note that the henna is often twisted into silver foil and placed in a basket (kına sepeti) to be handed round the guests. The packets look disconcertingly like wrapped toffees. Don't be fooled!

In many urban families the henna party is still held but it is transformed into a hen (bachelorette) party attended by close family members and young friends.

Pre-Wedding Visiting: In some places, on the day before the wedding the groom will visit the home of his bride-to-be with his closest male friends. Draped in a flag (bayrak) he will dance to celebrate his coming nuptials before retreating again.

The Convoy: Depending on where the wedding is to take place guests often assemble in their vehicles at the bridegroom's house and then set off in a flag-waving, horn-blaring convoy behind the car carrying the couple to the venue. If you have never been in one of these convoys before you may find the experience quite scary; the return trip, when some of the drivers have been drinking, can be even worse. After the ceremony the happy couple often careen around town in a car with their initials embossed on the back window and a number plate reading 'We're Marrying' ('*Evleniyoruz*'). People often block the path of the wedding car and demand tips (*bahşiş*) to let it pass, so make sure you set out with plenty of loose change.

The *Gala*: In rural central Anatolia the bride may hold an afternoon *gala* (party) on the day after the wedding and invite female friends and family. At this party the bride often wears a hired traditional costume. Friends arrive with presents of sweets and chocolates. As on the henna night, there will be music and dancing.

Alcohol: Alcohol played no part in traditional weddings although these days the men (if not necessarily the women) will almost always have a drink to celebrate a friend's wedding.

THE DETAILS

Invitations (*Davetiye*): Formal wedding invitations are a relatively new innovation and in rural areas people are still often invited to weddings by word of mouth combined with an announcement from the local loudspeaker system. In the big towns there are whole shops devoted to preparing lavish wedding invitation cards; in rural areas normal printers will do the job. The same shops also prepare *bonbonniéres* (takeaway gifts for guests), typically a few sugared almonds prettily tied up with ribbon.

Wedding Dresses (*Gelinlik*): People are sometimes surprised to find that Muslim Turkish brides get married in the same flowing white dresses as their Western counterparts. The only difference is that it is customary for the bride's father to tie a red sash (*bekâret*) symbolising virginity around her waist. But just as Western women who have been living with their partners for years still wear white to their church weddings, so Turkish women who are not actually virgins will still wear the sash – and no one sees anything wrong with Western brides (who are not normally assumed to be virgins) wearing their sash with pride.

Every town has shops full of wedding dresses in all shapes and sizes; the Fatih district of Istanbul is positively awash with them. The price tends to rise in summer, which is peak wedding season, so it pays to buy out of season; expect to pay around YTL700 for a dress, veil and tiara. If you don't want to splash out for your own gown, you can usually hire one for about YTL100 less than the cost of buying in the big towns. Alternatively you can get a dress specially made. If you go for this option, make sure to allow plenty of time for fittings since it is quite common for first and even second tries to prove unsuitable. White evening dresses from more upmarket shops sometimes prove cheaper and more appealing to Western tastes.

Grooms also dress up for their big day in morning suits (*damatlık elbisesi*) or something similar (these can also be hired). In towns wedding guests may also put on a show for the occasion although in rural areas even the couple's immediate family may turn up for the ceremony in their everyday clothes.

For suggestions as to where to buy wedding dresses, see Appendix III.

Wedding Rings (*Nikah Yüzüğü*): Turks wear gold wedding bands just as in the West. Traditionally these were worn on the third finger of the right hand as the left hand was reserved for actions regarded as dirty. However, these days it is just as usual for them to wear their rings on the third finger of the left hand.

Hairdressers (*Kuaför*): Most Turkish brides have their hair twisted into a pile of loops and knots for their big day. Hairdressers charge a lot – and I mean a lot! – to do this, so if you want your hair done for your wedding but don't want to pay through the nose for it, it is better to say that you need something special for a party or other special occasion.

Flowers (*Çiçek*): Although Turkish brides usually carry a bouquet, the groom and his party do not usually bother with buttonholes. It is normal to have flowers on the bridal table and at the reception, if there is one. Some friends of the family, especially if they have their own business, will send large oval bouquets criss-crossed with advertising banners for display. The choice of flowers available is more limited than in the West and you will need to shop around for a good price.

Wedding Cakes (*Düğün Pastası*): Turks go in for towering affairs made out of sponge that can be brought into the reception with great ceremony. It is normal to tip the people who carry the cake in and those who help cut it.

Photography (*Fotoğraf*): Even if you have a photographer friend you may find it very hard to persuade the venue to allow anyone other than their official photographer to take the wedding photos. Usually they do a perfectly good job. The problems tend to arise with the developing since Turks tend to favour heavily airbrushed portraits set in front of wholly artificial backgrounds of sunsets, mountains and oceans. Do yourself a favour and have some photographs taken privately away from the marriage venue before or after the ceremony.

Wedding Planners: As Turkey becomes more sophisticated so companies offering to handle all the arrangements have started to appear. For obvious reasons they are mostly to be found in the more upmarket areas of Istanbul.

Most of the four and five-star hotels will be able to direct you to someone suitable. For some suggested addresses, see Appendix III.

SORTING OUT THE PAPERWORK

If you are British the first thing you will have to do before getting married is post the banns of your marriage at the British Embassy or Consulate for one month preceding the planned wedding date. You will have to have been in Turkey for three weeks before you can do this. The Embassy charges YTL100 for posting banns. Other nationalities do not have to post banns or stay for a fixed period of time before marrying.

Everyone planning to get married in Turkey, whether Turkish or foreign, has to have a health check and get a health report (*sağlık raporu*) which certifies that they are free of serious illness. To get this you will need to take blood and hepatitis tests, and have a chest X-ray to check for TB. Although it's easier to get all the checks done in one place you can save money by shopping around and perhaps having different things done in different places. The tests are likely to cost around YTL100 for a couple.

Once you have had your health checks done you will need to take your report to a Clinic Health Inspector (*Sağlık Müdürü*) who will sign it. You will have to pay for the report and to have it signed, a sum amounting to around YTL12.

All foreigners have to have their passports translated, which is likely to cost around YTL20. When having this done you should take great care that your name is written with the correct 'i' since it is easy for confusion to arise between the two different 'i's in Turkish (be especially careful where a foreigner's name is written in capital letters in their passport since this can lead to particular confusion over the 'i's). A *noter* will have to approve the translation which will cost another YTL30 or so.

You will have to get your embassy or consulate to issue you with a Certificate of No Impediment to Marriage (*Evlenmeye Engel Gösterilmediği Hususunda Şehadetname);* some countries will only allow their home embassies or consulates to provide this. Embassies charge around YTL80 for administering an oath that there is no impediment and then another YTL95 for the paperwork.

The certificate of no impediment has to be taken to the Marriage Department (*Evlendirme Dairesi*) in big towns or the Belediye in smaller towns along with the bride or groom's *aile nüfus kayıt örneği* (family registration document) which shows the marital status of every family member; a copy of this can be obtained from the *Nüfus* department of the local Valilik. At the same time the Evlenme Dairesi or Belediye will need to see the identity papers of both partners, together with their health reports.

Evlenme Dairesi or Belediye officials will then prepare the marriage registration document, charging around YTL120 for the process. At the *nikah* ceremony the couple both sign a marriage ledger with photographs of each of them. Afterwards they are given a marriage book (*aile cüzdanı*) which confirms their new marital status. Where one of the couple is foreign they will have to sign a paper stating that they can read and write Turkish and understand what they are undertaking. They will also be asked if they wish to take out Turkish citizenship. For many people this is now possible after three years of marriage. However, it may well delay things if they do not say at once that they intend to opt for Turkish citizenship.

You can marry free of charge in the local *nikah salonu* but if you choose to marry elsewhere you may have to pay YTL100 to the wedding official together with the cost of their transport to the venue.

After their marriage women can now choose to keep their maiden name, adopt their husband's surname or opt for a double-barrelled surname. If they wish to keep their own name they will need to fill out a special form in the Evlenme Dairesi or Belediye. You need to be quite sure what you are asking for since it is time-consuming and expensive to change your name again if there is any mistake.

At the time of writing pre-nuptial agreements were not legally valid under Turkish law.

THE ROLE OF THE *GELİN*

If as a Western woman you marry a Turk from a well-educated family in one of the big cities you shouldn't find settling into married life any harder than it would be at home. If however you marry into a smaller community especially in the east you may be surprised to discover the rigid role still assigned to the *gelin* (the daughter-in-law). In traditional families, particularly poorer ones, it is still the norm for the daughter-in-law to move into her husband's family home where she will be subordinate in status to her mother-in-law. She will be expected to take on much of the housework together with such duties as waiting on guests, serving tea etc. In the most traditional households the behaviour and demeanour of the *gelin* will be taken as a reflection of the family which means that what she can and cannot do outside her new home is likely to be severely curtailed.

Things are certainly changing but some women have been surprised to discover their seemingly Westernised husbands expecting them to adapt to Turkish norms as soon as they have a ring on their finger. Even if they met their husbands in bars or discos they sometimes find such places completely out of bounds to them once they become the *gelin*.

WEDDING PRESENTS *(DÜĞÜN HEDİYESİ)*

In the big towns and coastal resorts modern Turkish couples often receive the same sort of wedding presents as their counterparts in the West - they may even prepare lists of desirable gifts as in the West. In the country, however, it is still more usual to give the couple money or gold *(altın)*. All jewellery shops sell gold coins specifically intended for weddings (as well as births and circumcisions). They come in a variety of sizes – quarter *(çeyrek)*, half *(yarım)* or whole *(tam)* coin - and with a little red ribbon *(kırmızı kurdele)* attached to a clasp so that you can pin the coin to a special red sash worn by the bride or groom during the *takı töreni* (wedding present ceremony). If you are giving cash, the notes should also be pinned to the sash. In the big cities the happy couple may walk from table to table carrying a velvet pouch into which their guests can place their donations. The worst shock for foreigners is to discover that what they are giving may be announced to the assembled crowd. What's more a note will be made so that in due course the couple can give an equivalent gift when it comes to the donor's turn.

Traditionally the groom's family bought most of the furniture for the new couple's house as part of the dowry. However, these days it is quite common for the bride's family to fit out the bedroom and kitchen and the groom's the sitting and dining rooms.

For a list of shops selling suitable presents for weddings, see Appendix VII.

The Trousseau *(Çeyiz)*

In traditional households a young women and her mother would hand-make items for her trousseau throughout her youth. In rural areas this custom still continues and most brides take ample stocks of embroidered sheets, towels and pillowcases to their new homes, often conveyed there in a special dowrybox *(çeyiz sandığı)*. In towns, this is more rarely the case.

THE HONEYMOON *(BALAYI)*

In traditional Turkish society there were no honeymoons and this continues to be the case in rural areas. However, more modern Turkish and mixed couples will be as keen to take a holiday after their nuptials as Westerners are.

RIGHTS AND RESPONSIBILITIES FOLLOWING MARRIAGE

Provided neither one of a couple who marry in Turkey is Turkish, their rights and responsibilities after marriage continue to be dictated by the laws of their country of origin. If, however, one of the couple is Turkish, then the couple's rights and duties after marriage are dictated by Turkish law.

MARRIAGE GUIDANCE

When a couple are having marital difficulties it is normal for their Turkish family to intervene and act as mediators with the aim of keeping them together whenever possible. Marriage guidance as it is understood in the West is rarely available, especially to foreigners because of the language difficulty. However, in Istanbul there are some psychiatrists and psychologists who work as marriage or family counsellors. See Miscellaneous Health Contacts in Appendix VIII for one suggested address.

Marriage in Turkey – Myth and Reality

- Although Islam allows men to have up to four wives polygamy has not been legal in Turkey since 1926. However perhaps one in 10 women in Eastern Turkey still lives in a polygamous household.
- Both partners in a marriage must be 18 except in exceptional circumstances (although many women may be engaged at 16).
- Religious marriages are not legally valid unless the couple have also undertaken a civil ceremony. However perhaps one couple in 10 in Eastern Turkey has only undergone a religious ceremony which offers the women no legal safeguards should the union fail.
- Arranged marriages are still very common in rural Turkey although women usually have the chance to refuse a groom they don't like.
- Where parents have refused a couple their permission to marry they may choose to elope in the hope that their parents will then accept their choice. However in parts of Eastern Turkey this could be very risky since women are still sometimes killed for 'dishonouring' their families.

DIVORCE (BOŞANMA)

Forget all that 'I divorce you, I divorce you, I divorce you' business. Under Turkish law divorce is only possible in the following circumstances:
- non-consummation of the marriage
- adultery
- criminality
- desertion (after at least six months)
- insanity
- domestic violence
- attempted murder of spouse
- dishonourable lifestyle of spouse

- irretrievable breakdown of marriage (e.g. refusal to have sex)
- incurable insanity
- homosexuality

To apply for a divorce you file suit with the Family Court (*Aile Mahkemesi*). Turkish law recognises the idea of greater fault in the breakdown of a marriage. This means that the partner regarded as least at fault can claim damages from the other, regardless of the sex of the more guilty party. Damages can be paid either in a lump sum or in instalments. The less guilty party can also claim alimony if divorce leaves them in a financially precarious position. Alimony will cease as soon as they remarry.

A couple who have been married for one year can agree to divorce provided the arrangements they have made for their children and property are acceptable to the court. If the initial application for divorce is rejected by the court, the couple must wait another three years before applying again. If they continue to claim 'domestic disturbance', a divorce must be granted.

While grounds for a divorce, adultery (*zina*) is no longer a crime despite an attempt to reinstate it as such as recently as 2005. This is probably just as well since marital fidelity is not, generally speaking, the Turkish male's strongest suit.

Legal Separation

It is possible to apply to the courts for a legal separation provided you can prove that at least one of the grounds for divorce exists. Legal separations can last for up to three years. If the couple have not been reconciled at the end of that period they can then apply for a divorce. On rare occasions people who have applied for divorce have been given only a legal separation because the judge believed their marriage could be repaired.

Child Custody and Support Following Divorce

When parents decide to divorce a court will want to hear what arrangements have been made for custody (*velayet*) of the children. A judge will then make the final decision about who should have custody and when and where the non-custodial parent will be able to visit. There is no concept of joint custody, only sole custody. The non-custodial parent is supposed to contribute towards their child's upbringing. If the circumstances of the parent with custody change (e.g. if they remarry), either parent can apply to the court to have the terms of the settlement altered.

This is the theory. In practise, at least in rural areas, men still assume that it is their right to keep their children since they are normally the family bread-winners. The courts will not necessarily object to this since the man will give the child to his mother to rear - there are few true single dads in Turkey. In the past women were often sent back to their families in disgrace after a divorce. However, this situation is changing and some women even manage to survive more than one divorce quite happily.

A new husband or wife has no automatic right of custody over a child from a previous marriage. When someone remarries the new partner is not always happy to take on children from a previous relationship. These children sometimes end up virtually abandoned or in the custody of elderly grand-parents.

If a foreign partner wants to leave Turkey with their children they need their Turkish partner or ex-partner's consent to do so. If the Turkish partner contests their right to take the child out of the country there is a fair chance that the courts will rule in favour of the Turk even if they are the non-custodial parent.

Turkey has signed most international conventions on child maintenance which means in theory that a court order against a Turk taken out in another country should be upheld by the Turkish courts. In practise this is likely to be a protracted and unpleasant battle.

Turkey has also signed the European Convention on Returning Children to Their Homeland and the International Convention Concerning the Prevention of International Child Kidnapping. Both these treaties exist to prevent parents removing their children from their country of residence without the consent of their (usually ex) partner.

Property Arrangements Following Divorce

Under the latest version of the Civil Code men and women have equal rights to any property acquired after their marriage, although each spouse continues to have sole right to property that they owned before the marriage. In parts of Turkey where dowry payments are still made, the dowry would be regarded as part of the women's property before the marriage which means that she has a right to retain it after a divorce.

REMARRIAGE

Since polygamy is illegal anyone wishing to remarry will have to prove that they have legally terminated any previous marriage. A woman cannot remarry for 300 days after the termination of her previous marriage. The idea behind this is that a new husband can be sure she is not pregnant by her previous husband. However, women's rights groups oppose this requirement as discriminatory.

DE FACTO PARTNERSHIPS

At the time of writing Turkey did not recognise the existence of *de facto* partnerships whether between couples of the same or different sexes. What this means is that the death of one half of an unmarried couple can leave the other in an uncertain position. Turkish inheritance law dictates that the dead partner's property will pass to their children, parents and other close relatives unless specific arrangements to the contrary have been made.

There is no longer any concept of illegitimacy in Turkey. The children of *de facto* partners will be regarded as the children of the mother and will carry her surname. The mother will have a legal right to claim alimony for their maintenance if the couple are not living together permanently. Provided the children's paternity has been established beyond doubt they will have exactly the same rights to a share in their father's assets on his death as the children of a married couple.

GAY AND LESBIAN RELATIONSHIPS

Although there is no law forbidding male or female homosexuality (*eşcinsellik*) Turks usually frown on the idea of gay sex which makes it difficult for Turks to live an openly gay life except in parts of Istanbul, Izmir and the coast. Turks usually regard only the passive partner in a male homosexual relationship as truly gay which allows many men to persuade themselves that they are actually heterosexual while still being involved in partnerships the West would regard as gay.

Because of the stigma attached to being gay many homosexual Turks still marry and have children, just as they did in 1950s' Britain. However, homosexuality is regarded as grounds for a divorce and the homosexual spouse would be treated as the partner at fault when it came to assessing rights to compensation or alimony.

Most foreign homosexuals manage to live quite comfortably in Turkey without harassment. However, some have found their Turkish partners reluctant to admit the relationship in public and occasionally someone's homosexuality has been used in quite crude blackmail attempts.

WHAT TO SAY	
alimony	*nafaka*
couple	*çift*
custody	*velayet*
honour	*namus*
husband	*koca*
husband & wife	*karı koca*
single	*bekar*
spouse	*eş*
to get divorced	*boşanmak*
to get engaged	*nişanlanmak*
to get married	*evlenmek*
virginity	*bekaret*
wedding anniversary	*evlenme yıldönümü*
wife	*karı/hanım*

CHAPTER 9

BRINGING UP CHILDREN IN TURKEY

Although Turkey is not very child-friendly in the practical sense that it is understood in the West (i.e. not every service station and department store will have baby-changing facilities), it is extremely child-friendly in the more important sense of actually liking children. So your restaurant may not be able to rise to a high-chair for your baby. However, that does not mean they will be greeted with scowls as is so often the case in some Western countries. On the contrary, the waiters are likely to crowd around, beaming and reaching out to pinch its cheeks – this being a favoured Turkish way of showing appreciation of young children.

Having children in Turkey brings its own special set of problems. However, most parents will feel far less anxious about their children's well-being in a society which still tends to treasure children's innocence and where paedophilia is not, apparently, a big issue. Westerners who marry Turks will find that the extended family still plays a big part in child-rearing, with grandmothers often happy to look after children during the day while their mother works.

Some couples who marry in Turkey will have babies and rear them in Turkey. Other couples will arrive in Turkey with their children in tow. Although the needs of the two groups may overlap, there are also important differences especially when it comes to schooling.

PREGNANCY *(HAMİLELİK)*

These days working women are entitled to eight weeks' paid maternity leave *(doğum izni)* before and after the birth of their children.

Turkey does not have a formal system of ante-natal care which means you will struggle to find classes to prepare both men and women for the changes about to occur in their lives. If you live in Istanbul it may be worth checking the ads in *Lale,* the magazine of the International Women of Istanbul group, to see if anyone is advertising classes. However, most women who can afford to will find a gynaecologist and visit them regularly during their pregnancy. Even in rural areas it is possible for women to have regular scans to check on the baby's progress, especially if they can afford to pay for the service. Monthly check-ups cost around YTL60, including the cost of the scans. You can also get an amniocentesis if you want to check for the risk of Down's Syndrome (*Down Sendromu*).

Purpose-designed maternity clothes that are likely to appeal to Western tastes are not easy to find. The child-centred department store Mothercare sells a limited range of Western-style maternity clothes but they are expensive by Turkish standards.

For a list of shops stocking maternity clothes, see under clothes in Appendix VII.

GIVING BIRTH (*DOĞUM YAPMA*)

Istanbul, Izmir and Ankara all have excellent maternity hospitals where you will probably find the procedures fairly similar to how they would be at home. However, you are unlikely to find much awareness of alternative approaches to childbirth. Even in the big cities it is still usual for women to be urged to stay in bed during labour. Water births, aromatic candles, squatting or any of the other developments that have given women more control over their birth experience in the West are very new concepts and mothers will have to do a lot of shopping and asking around to find such services; start your search at Memorial Hospital in Istanbul which is said to be in the process of establishing a birthing unit that includes these kinds of alternatives. Women are expected to do as they are told rather than be active participants in decisions over the birth. On the upside, however, even the smallest Turkish village will have a midwife (*ebe)* who is able to carry out medical examinations.

Elsewhere state maternity hospitals suffer from the same failings as other state hospitals. They are often forbidding places which practise old-fashioned methods of childbirth. Fathers are not encouraged to play a part in the birth although some hospitals may allow them to be present if their wife (usually foreign) insists. Caesareans are common and often seem to be performed as much to suit the hospital's timetable as because of actual medical need; if you really don't want one you may have to be very insistent. In the big cities you can be sure of being given adequate pain relief, whether you are having a natural birth or a Caesarean. In rural areas, however, epidurals are rarely provided, so some women have woken up after Caesareans in extreme pain which only eases when drugs administered after the event have had time to take effect. If you want to be sure of avoiding such an unpleasant experience you will need to check carefully what services are available at your chosen hospital and may have to travel to take advantage of the better facilities in the big cities. A natural birth is likely to cost between YTL350 and YTL750, a Caesarean up to YTL1,500.

Many state maternity hospitals lack facilities to deal with premature babies, so in an emergency a woman may have to be taken some way away from home to give her baby its best chance. In the worst of circumstances it is not unknown for mothers to be sent home from hospital with severely disabled babies that are not expected to live because the hospital has no facilities to care for them.

It is still normal for mothers to stay in hospital for a few days after the birth. If you don't have public or private insurance you will be charged for this time. However, new mothers are given little help or assistance even with things like bathing their baby. Members of the extended family can visit at any time and some stay overnight in the hospital to help out.

Despite the general modesty of Turkish society, Western women have sometimes been surprised at how little attention is paid to their privacy while they are in hospital.

On the day that the child is born it will be given a vitamin K jab; its heel will also be pricked to check its blood group. Three days later it will be given a vaccination against hepatitis B. After it falls off, it is customary for the baby's umbilical cord to be ritually buried.

For a list of maternity hospitals see Appendix VIII.

Although several foreign women have given birth safely in the maternity hospital in Nevşehir, this is not an experience to be recommended; if you can afford it you would be better off going to Ankara or Istanbul. Turkey has a relatively high infant mortality rate compared to the UK and most other Western countries so it isn't worth taking unnecessary risks.

WHAT TO SAY			
amniocentesis	*amniyosentez*	infertility	*kısırlık*
breech birth	*ters doğum*	pregnant	*hamile/gebe*
Caesarean	*Sezaryen*	Rhesus negative	*RH negatif*
eclampsia	*eklamsi*	Rhesus positive	*RH pozitif*
ectopic pregnancy	*dış gebelik*	ultrasound	*ultrason*

THE FIRST FEW DAYS

In traditional Turkish society it was normal for a mother to stay indoors with her baby for the first 40 days of its life. In the cities this is no longer the norm. However, in rural areas the idea of a mother's lying-in still continues and those who get up and go out early must expect to have their effrontery commented on by all and sundry.

The parents' families will expect to play a big part in the infant's first few days of life, and friends will visit en masse, often expecting the mother to be ready to entertain them with food and drink. Guests bring gold coins to pin to the baby's clothes. Alternatively they may bring a *nazar boncuğu,* one of the small blue-eye beads which are believed to ward off the evil eye. This will be pinned to the baby's clothes along with an extract from the Koran in a little leather pouch. In a further attempt to ward off the evil eye, visitors try not to be too openly admiring: *Maşallah* (May God protect you), they will say, after any compliment. This also results in what Westerners would regard as a very perverse situation in which, for example, some people will say 'what a naughty girl' to a child that is behaving perfectly well.

Westerners accustomed to getting a helping hand from state-paid nurses and health advisors may be very disappointed to discover just how little post-natal assistance is offered to new mothers. Instead many new mothers with Turkish mothers-in-law find the all-encompassing 'assistance' given by them in the first few days rather overwhelming. They may also find it difficult to cope with the many old wives' tales which fill the air. In particular the Turkish fear of draughts means that mothers-in-law may insist on swaddling the baby in a way that Westerners might fear would cause them to overheat. Women with their own ideas about child-rearing may have to be very assertive to get their own way. On the positive side women exhausted from giving birth will probably find that they can rely on an extensive family support network, ready to help out at all hours with babysitting and home-cooked meals.

Breast-feeding is strongly encouraged and mothers who intend to return to work may need to express milk for their babies. Unfortunately effective breast pumps are both hard to find and expensive – around YTL140 for one that will do the job effectively.

SORTING OUT THE PAPERWORK

The hospital will provide the new parents with a birth certificate (*doğum kaydı*). This has to be taken to the Nüfus Department at the Valilik together with the identity cards of both parents so that the baby's birth can be registered. The registrars will ask the new baby's name; although it is no longer essential to give the child a Turkish name, they can only have two given names in addition to the father's surname. The child's birth must be registered within a month; any delay will result in a fine in an effort to deter people from holding back registration to postpone their child's admission to school and/or the army.

Once the baby's birth has been registered, he or she will be issued with their own *kimlik* card (see p. 401). This does not have to have a photo until the child reaches the age of 15 although you can ask to add one at a younger age if you want.

WHAT TO SAY			
baby	*bebek*	dummy	*emzik*
baby/child minder	*bebek/çocuk bakıcısı*	high chair	*yüksek mama iskemlesi*
bib	*mama önlüğü*	nappy/diaper	*çocuk bezi*
bottle	*biberon*	nursery	*anaokulu*
child	*çocuk*	potty	*lazımlık*
child seat for car	*çocuk koltuğu*	powdered milk	*süt tozu*
clothes	*giysi*	pram	*çocuk arabası*
cot	*çocuk yatağı*	pushchair	*puset*
cottonwool	*hidrofil pamuk*	teat	*meme*
cradle	*beşik*	tinned baby food	*konserve bebek maması*
disposable nappy	*hazır çocuk bezi*	toy	*oyuncak*
doll	*oyuncak bebek*	toyshop	*oyuncakçı*

Registering a Birth with an Overseas Embassy

The parents of children from mixed marriages (or de facto relationships) may also want to register the birth at the embassy of the foreign parent in order to guarantee their right to dual and/or foreign citizenship. To do this you will normally need to take the originals of the baby's birth certificate together with the parents' birth certificates and marriage certificate to the relevant embassy and pay a fee to register the birth. Often this necessitates a trip to Ankara.

To find out exactly what papers are required by individual embassies you should first try consulting their websites since most embassies now operate touch-tone telephone enquiry systems that quickly run up big bills.

HOW OLD IS THIS CHILD?

Obvious you might think. But rural Turks count a child's age differently from most Westerners so that a baby is regarded as being one and what we think of as a one-year-old child is regarded as being two etc. Which can lead to some confusion...

COST OF REARING A BABY

You shouldn't assume that rearing a baby in Turkey is cheap. The following are just some of the inevitable costs:

- baby formula   average cost for 300gr packet YTL6.25
- nappies   YTL20-25 cheapest packet
- baby wipes   YTL2.5 (240)
- nappy rash cream   YTL7 per tube
- baby shampoo   YTL7-8 per bottle
- bottle   YTL8-10
- teat   YTL5
- Capol   YTL4-3 per bottle
- baby vitamins   YTL4 for three-week supply

Bebelac, Milupa, Hero, Ülker and Nestle manufacture small jars of baby food but they are very expensive – YTL2.75 for the cheapest 130gr jar. Most people will find it cheaper to invest in a food processor and make their own blends of fruit and vegetables.

Additional costs you might not think of include the charge for some non-compulsory vaccinations, including MMR. A course of anti-meningitis jabs is likely to come to around YTL125. Routine medical check-ups are not free either; you will usually pay around YTL60 per visit.

Also quite pricey are the Bebe D'Or range of dummies, bottles, teething rings and other baby accoutrements imported from Switzerland.

NAMES AND NAMING CEREMONIES

Some mixed Turkish-foreign couples give their children Turkish names, while others give them foreign names, usually chosen so that their Turkish relatives will be able to pronounce them. When choosing a name it is wise to remember the differences between the Turkish and Latin alphabets to avoid problems later; for example if you give your child the Turkish name Ceyda but spell it 'Jeyda' so foreign relatives will know how to pronounce it you are likely to bestow on your child a lifetime of hassle with Turkish paperwork.

Like foreign names, most Turkish names have a meaning. The chosen name may have something to do with when the child was born (e.g. Ramazan for a boy or Bahar [spring] for a girl) or with the weather that was taking place at the time of birth (e.g. Yağmur [rain] for a girl or Tufan [storm] for a boy). However, it is also common to name children after other family members living or dead. In rural areas conservatism reigns when it comes to children's names, with most boys called Mehmet, Mustafa, Mahmut or Ali and most girls called Fatma or Ayşe, but in the cities there is the same craving for originality that results in British children being named after their place of conception. Turkish names are often abbreviated so that Abdullah becomes Apo, İbrahim İbo and Fatma Fatoş. Parents often opt to give their children similar-sounding names: Can and Cem, for example, or Sinan and Selim.

If you'd like to choose a Turkish name visit www.learningpracticalturkish.com for a list of girls' and boys' given names together with their meanings.

Families often hold a naming ceremony for their babies. Either a local imam or an older male member of the family will hold the baby in the direction of Mecca and whisper words from the Koran into its left ear. He will then whisper the baby's name into its right ear three times. This is usually followed by an informal family party.

If you decide to give your child a foreign name you will need to check that it is not written in Turkish spelling on their *kimlik* card which could lead to confusion later on.

ADOPTION *(EVLAT EDİNME)*

A couple both need to be at least 30 before they can adopt a child and they can only do so jointly. They must also have been married for at least five years.

A single person can also adopt a child provided they are over 30. However, it is unlikely that a single foreigner would be able to adopt a Turkish child without considerable difficulty.

BABYSITTERS *(ÇOCUK BAKICISI)*

Turks tend to depend on their extended families for things like babysitting. However, in the big cities and coastal resorts there are some organised babysitting services. If you do require paid childcare you will probably find it much cheaper than in your native country. It is also readily available – ask around and you are sure to find someone willing to help out in return for a small salary.

For one suggested address, see under babysitting services in Appendix X.

VACCINATIONS (AŞI)

Turkey has an efficient system for vaccinating young children; in rural areas it is common to hear the loudspeaker systems spewing out the names of infants that are expected at the Sağlık Ocağı for their vaccinations. Children are given a BCG against TB as well as free jabs against Hepatitis B, polio, measles, diphtheria and tetanus. However, parents must pay for an MMR against measles, mumps and rubella and for a jab against chickenpox. Fees for vaccinations that must be paid for are surprisingly steep - between YTL 30 and YTL 75 a time.

CHILDHOOD ILLNESSES			
chickenpox	*su çiçeği*	jaundice	*sarılık*
colic	*kolik*	measles	*kızamık*
diphtheria	*difteri*	mumps	*kabakulak*
earache	*kulak ağrısı*	polio	*çocuk felci*
fever	*ateş*	TB	*verem*
fits	*havale*	tetanus	*tetanoz*
German measles	*kızamıkçık*	thrush	*pamukçuk*

SAFETY (GÜVENLİK)

Safety is rarely at the top of the Turkish agenda and accordingly it is not easy to find the sort of safety devices (cupboard locks, stairwell gates etc) that might be considered routine at home. You will also need to inspect items marketed for children very carefully to make sure that they really are safe – this applies as much to rocking cradle-beds as to toys with ill-fitting eyes.

Small items like fridge and cupboard locks are sometimes available at branches of Migros. Alternatively, try Mothercare (for addresses see Appendix VII). IKEA and branches of Joker sell papooses, safety gates to fit to stairs and expensive baby listening devices (for addresses see Appendix VII). Mothercare also sells children's car seats. If you can't find what you want it's worth trying the website of *Anne Bebek* (Mother and Baby) magazine (Tel: 0212-324 9347, www.annebebek.com.tr).

THE GROWING CHILD

As your child starts to grow up you may find many facilities that you take for granted in the West in short supply in Turkey. Although restaurants in the big cities and holiday resorts will increasingly be able to provide a high chair for a baby, such a thing is still rare elsewhere, as are purpose-designed baby-changing facilities. Pushchairs and prams are not as normal as in the West, no doubt in part because the state of most pavements and kerbs would make using them extremely difficult. So many mothers carry their babies around either in blankets or soft cradles.

In urban areas it is now possible to find playgroups and mother-and-toddler groups, some of them organised according to nationality; to find out what is available in your area contact any of the groups listed in Chapter 19. In Istanbul there is also a branch of Gymboree (see p. 471) which provides structured play and early learning for under-fives. In rural areas some local governments have also started to organise playgroups and parenting classes although you would probably need confident Turkish to be able to join them.

Rearing a Bilingual Child

The best way to ensure that your child will grow up able to speak two languages effortlessly is for you and your partner only to speak to it in your native tongue (i.e. if the mother is British and the father Turkish, the mother should speak to the child only in English while the father speaks to it only in Turkish).

FOR MORE INFORMATION

- www.buy.edu/~bilingual/faq - Straightforward answers to frequently answered questions on bilingualism
- *A Parents' and Teachers' Guide to Bilingualism* by Colin Baker

---

BOY OR GIRL?

Although Turks place particular emphasis on the importance of boy babies few families still make problems for a woman who gives birth to a girl. However in rural areas you may still encounter elderly people who express commiserations that a mother did not have that all-important son.

Although it is normal for couples to be told the sex of their baby-to-be unless they specifically ask not to be this does not seem to lead to female foetuses being aborted as happens in other male-dominated societies.

In rural areas however some couples whose first children are girls will keep on trying until they get a boy even when they can barely afford to maintain their existing children.

CLOTHING YOUR CHILDREN

Most big towns have shops that sell baby clothes, although items sized for newborns are hard to find except in the more expensive shops. You may also find that the clothes available don't suit your personal tastes, although the situation is steadily improving. In rural areas it is still normal for family members to knit vast quantities of baby clothes ready for a birth. To avoid sartorial disaster you might want to suggest your preference in terms of colour, wool type and design.

All the big shopping centres have stores selling clothes for children. Turkey also manufactures clothes for many foreign brand names - you can find end-of-line items or slightly damaged clothes at very low prices in discount stores.

Many of the shopping malls have supervised children's play areas to enable mothers to shop in peace.

TREES FOR CHILDREN

In traditional society it was common for families to plant poplar or pine trees to celebrate the birth of a boy and apple, mulberry or chestnut trees to celebrate the birth of a girl. The trees were later cut and the wood sold to pay for a daughter's wedding. In these environmentally sensitive times this is a custom many mixed couples might like to consider perpetuating.

THE TURKISH EDUCATION SYSTEM

In Turkey children generally start school when they are six (they need to be at least 72 months). They attend primary school (*ilköğretim*) until they are 14 when they leave with a primary school certificate (*ilkokul diploması*). This first eight years of schooling is compulsory and free for all children, boys and girls, although parents have to pay for pens and school uniforms. Schools are normally co-educational and uniforms compulsory.

The Turkish education system is rigidly secular. Neither children nor their teachers are allowed to wear headscarves in school and instead of a daily act of worship, children start and end the week watching the raising of the Turkish flag and singing the national anthem, the İstiklal Marşı (see p. 578). In other words, nationalism takes the place traditionally filled by religion in many Western schools. However, from the fourth grade upwards, there are formal religious studies' classes centred on Islam and the Koran rather than comparative religions. The parents of non-Turkish children are usually asked if they want their children to attend but you should check before enrolling your child if this would be important to you.

Private Nurseries

The standard Turkish state education system does not automatically encompass nursery-age children. However, there are many private nurseries (*çocuk odası*) and creches (*kreş*) aimed primarily at the children of the Istanbul elite or of expats and mixed marriages. Many offer a curriculum to match those of Britain. Most cater for children aged two to six.

State Kindergartens (*Anaokulu*)

These days many schools have an *anaokulu* attached to them. These kindergartens take children for the year preceding the start of primary school so that they can get used to going to school more gently. Many are attached to private schools but there are also some in the villages. *Anaokulu* pupils usually wear a red uniform with white collar. To send a child to *anaokulu* for year can cost parents around YTL800 in costs for school drinks and food, notebooks, uniform etc.

Primary School (*İlköğretim*)

Schools are usually open from 8.15 am to 3 pm, with an hour off for lunch. Most state schools don't have cafeterias so that their pupils often go home for lunch or eat the packed lunch they bring with them.

Up to Grade 6 children have one teacher for all subjects, but from Grade 6 upwards there are individual subject teachers.

School Year: The school year starts in mid-September and runs through until mid-June with a three-month summer break. Other school holidays are dictated by the moving feasts of Ramazan and Kurban Bayramı, with additional days off for other public holidays. In winter many schools have to close for days on end because of snow.

Uniforms (Okul Kıyafeti): Younger students wear a standard blue uniform with white collar; from 11 onwards they wear a uniform specific to their area. School uniforms are can be usually be bought at the local *pazar*.

The Curriculum: Turkey has a centralised national curriculum, studied in all schools. By Western standards, the Turkish education system has always been very conservative. Children were encouraged to learn by rote and questioning was not encouraged. Even writing was learnt by memorising certain set sentences. Youngsters would laboriously copy out pages of information (for example, about the life of Atatürk), an exercise that appeared to Westerners to have little educational value. However, in 2006 a new curriculum aimed at encouraging more independent thought was introduced. It remains to be seen how effective it will be in changing engrained traditions.

The range of subjects taught is fairly limited, although the basics are usually well covered. English is the most commonly taught foreign language. Children start studying it in middle school, with between two and four hours a week devoted to the subject. Unfortunately few state schools employ native English-speakers to teach English, although some private schools do.

Class Size: As elsewhere in the world, private schools tend to have much smaller classes than state schools. In state schools in Istanbul it is not unusual to find classes of more than 60 pupils, and in such circumstances a child has to be very determined to learn anything at all. Sometimes school buildings are not big enough to cope with all the children so that classes take place in two wholly separate sessions, before and after lunch.

Secondary School (*Lise*)

Children are allowed to leave school at 14. However, increasingly many of them are continuing into secondary education with another three years at a high school (*lise*). High schools fall into two broad categories: those offering a general education to prepare students for higher education; and *meslek liseleri* which offer a vocational or technical education to prepare students for the world of work. Which type of *lise* a student attends depends on their choice and what grade they obtain in their OKS (*Ortaöğretim Kurumları Sınavı*), the high school entry exam at the end of primary school. Students leave secondary school at 17 or 18.

There are several different kinds of general high schools: for example, in an Anadolu Lisesi pupils study their major subjects in a foreign language, while in a Fen Lisesi they specialise in science. At some Meslek Liseleri (trade schools) pupils study computer science, electronics, chemistry, building or mechanics as if undertaking a traditional apprenticeship. At others they study more professional subjects such as tourism, commerce, journalism, textiles, printing, librarianship or health sciences (nursing and midwifery). In an Anadolu Teknik Lisesi they study technical subjects such as computer science and journalism in a foreign language.

Secondary school uniforms are not standard throughout Turkey and each school will tell parents where they can buy the appropriate clothing. A complete new school uniform can cost around YTL120.

Private Schools (*Kolej/Özel Lise*)

Many Turkish and foreign parents are suspicious of standards in state schools. As a result, as per capita incomes have risen, so more and more private schools have opened. Standards at these schools are not uniformly good. However, facilities are usually infinitely better than those available at the local state school, with smaller class sizes and better qualified teachers. Private schools may have swimming pools, well-stocked libraries, lunchtime clubs for students, cafeterias and any number of other extras that justify their high fees: commonly at least €1,500 a year (although famous private schools like Istanbul's Robert College charge considerably more).

On top of the school fees parents usually have to pay for buses to ferry their children to and from school. Often they pay much higher charges for books, etc than state school parents. They also need to budget for the cost of school trips and other extras. Private schools usually have on-site cafeterias, for the use of which there is another charge.

Most private schools offer options that are not available to state-school students. For example, students can sit Cambridge University English-language exams, or SAT (Scholastic Assessment Test) and TOEFL (Test of English as a Foreign Language) exams which facilitate entry to overseas universities. However, parents need to be aware that other countries may not recognise qualifications obtained from Turkish private schools that are *not* accredited international schools (see below). This can make it hard to have your child enrolled in an overseas university. This is not a problem in Istanbul, Ankara and Izmir where parents have a choice of international schools to which to send their children; however, in Cappadocia there are no officially recognised international schools.

International Schools

The children of mixed Turkish-foreign parents who were born in Turkey often grow up bilingual which means that they can attend either the local state school or its private equivalent, depending on their parents' wishes. However, the children of parents who move to Turkey for work usually know no Turkish and so could not realistically go to the local school. Instead there are several international schools in both Istanbul and Ankara which teach students in languages other than Turkish.

There are two types of foreign-language school to choose from. Some follow the curriculum of another country and accept only children with foreign passports. Others follow Turkish school guidelines but provide more foreign-language teaching than normal.

Fees at international schools are high although many students have their fees paid by the companies their parents are working for or even by an overseas government.

Many international schools prepare 16 to 19-year-old students to take the *International Baccalaureate (IB)*, an academically challenging set of exams. Acquiring an IB gives a student a better than average chance of getting into an overseas university. However, to get into a Turkish university they still need to sit the normal Turkish university exam.

The best international schools are members of the European Council of International Schools (ECIS) and/or the Near East South Asia Council of Schools (NESA).

For a list of international and other schools, see Appendix IV.

WHAT TO SAY			
class	*sınıf*	registration/ enrolment	*kayıt*
exam	*sınav*	school	*okul*
high school	*lise*	teacher	*öğretmen*
private school	*özel okul*	university	*üniversite*

Registering a Child at a State School

If you live in a small town with only one school then registering your child there should be very straightforward once they reach six or seven. If you live in Istanbul or Ankara, however, it can be trickier. However, if you go to http://ilsis.meb.gov.tr and then to the *e-kayıt* section you will be able to fill out a form to have your child assigned to a local school. You will need your child's *kimlik* (ID) card to complete some of the details. You should fill out this form before mid-July of the year in which you want your child to begin school. Expect to have had a school place assigned to you by mid-August.

School Discipline

Although children are no longer beaten in Turkish schools, there is still more physical chastisement than would be expected in, for example, a British school; a common punishment is to pull the ear of a child who is misbehaving. Some private schools, especially in Istanbul, where they may have a lot of foreign students, prohibit all physical punishment. Others, however, allow it unless the parents have specifically forbidden it.

Until recently schoolgirls who were thought to be 'unchaste' could be forced to submit to a virginity test. Since 1999, however, that is no longer permitted. However, children can still be expelled from school for behaviour which 'contradicts commonly accepted social values and influences the educational atmosphere in a negative way' and this can be used against girls who are seen as wayward. In general, however, peer pressure tends to encourage conformity rather than its opposite as is so often the case in the West.

Alternative Schooling

Once they finish primary school some Turkish children are sent to boarding schools in different towns, depending on their grades in their exams. These schools are free and may offer greater opportunities to poorer children than would be possible in their home area.

Some parents prefer not to send their children either to Turkey's state schools or to their conventional private counterparts. The few alternatives such as Montessori schools are listed in Appendix IV.

The *İmam Hatip Lisesi*. Turkish children with very religious parents are often sent to private *imam hatip* high schools. Originally set up to train government-employed *imam*s (Muslim religious leaders), these schools accept both boy and girl students and teach the conventional curriculum but with a heavy emphasis on religion and Arabic. Until recently graduates of *imam hatip liseleri* could not go to university, but the government has now passed a hotly contested decree to reverse this discrimination. It is unlikely that non-Muslims would want their children to attend such schools.

TURKISH UNIVERSITIES

These days there are universities in almost all of Turkey's large towns. Some Turkish students also go to university in Northern Cyprus. All the older universities are state-owned but there are an increasing number of private universities as well.

To get a place at a Turkish university, students need to have passed exams in maths, literature, Turkish history, philosophy and geography. They must pay a small annual fee to attend even a state university.

At the time of writing female students at Turkish universities were not allowed to wear headscarves in the interests of upholding Turkey's secular-state status. Male students were also forbidden to grow beards. The European Court of Human Rights upheld Turkey's right to impose these restrictions as recently as 2003 so it is unlikely that they will be lifted any day soon.

University Entrance Exams: In their last year of school all students can take the national university entrance exam (*ÖSS - Öğrenci Seçme Sınavı*; Student Selection Exam) which is based on two multiple-choice exam papers (the logic of the scoring system will seem strange to many Westerners, with three wrong answers cancelling out one correct one). Students are then assigned to universities and subjects, based on their test scores and the list of schools and faculties they have selected. To study medicine or law at the best universities in Istanbul and Ankara, students need to get very high grades.

If they fail to get the scores they want at their first attempt students can try again a year later. Before doing so they usually attend classes at a private school (*dershane*) in an attempt to improve their grade. If they do badly again, they can have another try. And another. And another.

The results of exams, whether for university or high school placement, are publicly displayed and published in the newspapers.

Foreign Students: To study at a Turkish university you will usually need a good level of Turkish even if some (or most) of the teaching is in English. To enrol, you must achieve a score of 45 or more in the *YÖS (Yabancı Öğrenciler Sınavı*; Foreign Students Exam), a pair of tests given in Ankara and several other foreign countries every June. To take the YÖS you must first register with the Öğrenci Seçme ve Yerleştirme Merkezi (ÖSYM, Student Selection and Placement Centre; www.osym.gov.tr) in Ankara. If you pass you will have a year to get your Turkish up to scratch. Courses offered by TÖMER in particular (see p. 543) are aimed at preparing foreign students to cope with a Turkish university course.

Alternatively, you must have received a minimum of 1200 points (with at least 650 points in maths) in the SAT (Scholastic Aptitude Test). The SAT can be taken at various locations in Turkey and in almost every country around the globe. If you achieve the desired test results you can then apply directly to the university of your choice.

Some overseas students find it hard to adapt to a tertiary education system which still prefers the regurgitation of old information to the development of new ideas. They are often surprised at how little students expect to participate in class, even at universities with a good reputation like METU (the Middle East Technical University in Ankara).

If you want to study in Turkey but your parents are neither diplomats nor living in Turkey with a legal work visa then you will need to apply for a student visa. This can be a time-consuming and frustrating procedure and it is not unknown for a course to have finished before the visa materialises!

For a list of Turkish universities see Appendix IV.

OVERSEAS UNIVERSITIES

If you want your child to study at an overseas university it is best to enrol them at one of the international schools which base their teaching on the assumption that many of their pupils will want to study abroad. There are also some schools that specialise in preparing pupils to study at an American University for which they will have to have passed the SAT and TOEFL exams (see above).

CORRESPONDENCE COURSES

Turkey has an open-learning school (*Açıköğretim Lisesi;* Tel: 0312-296 9400) to help people who did not stay at school catch up on their education later in life.

ENTERTAINING YOUR CHILDREN

Although there are lots of toys on sale in Turkey, few are educational. Nor would many of the soft toys be regarded as safe in the West because of insecurely stitched on eyes etc. There are some attractive Turkish-language books for pre-school-age children, although finding English-language books is a taller order.

Increasingly new children's playgrounds are pleasingly designed with plastic apparatus standing on grass or sand. However, older facilities are often potentially lethal, rusting and neglected. Most parents won't need advising not to let their children play on them without checking carefully first.

Hollywood films are usually shown in cinemas with Turkish subtitles, but those aimed specifically at children are often dubbed - unfortunate if you have a child who doesn't understand Turkish.

Courses: Slowly but surely activity centres for children are being set up, primarily in Istanbul but also in some other big towns. In Izmir the Elma Book House doubles as an activity centre offering courses in arts and crafts, pottery and music for children; for contact details, see under bookshops in Appendix VII.

Scouts and Guides: The International Women of Istanbul group organises Cub Scout (6-10), Boy Scout (11-18), Brownie (6-8) and Girl Scout (8 and up) groups. For most up-to-date contact details, see *Lale,* the magazine of the IWI. There are also scout groups in Ankara: for cub scouts (Tel: 0312-235 0239, for boy scouts (Tel:: 0312-235 8402 and for girl scouts (Tel: 0312-447 4144).

Summer Camps: Turkish schools close in mid-June and don't open again until early September. This three-month break can be trying for both children and parents and, not surprisingly, there are some summer camps that exist to keep the kids amused until classes start again. These are mostly in the resort areas and are expensive enough to deter all but the most well-heeled of parents, although there are also a few state summer schools like the one at Kefken, near İzmit, which is run by Beyoğlu Belediyesi. Most of them focus on improving children's language skills or artistic and sports abilities. To find out what's on offer you should check the websites of the private schools long before the summer - the Robert College summer schools sell out well ahead of time.

Toyshops: Branches of Toys 'R' Us usually open from 10 am to 10 pm daily. For addresses see Appendix VII.

FAMILY OUTINGS

Turkey has few attractions aimed specifically at children, so that it can be harder to organise family outings than in the West. However, most of the big resorts have vast water parks and other distractions to suit both Turkish and English-speaking children. Most big cities also boast Lunapark funfairs of varying quality. From June through to September the Istanbul bus company İETT organises weekend picnic excursions to the Belgrade Forest, as well as to Istanbul Zoo. These are advertised on the buses near to the relevant dates.

For water park, zoo and other addresses see Appendix X.

Zoos and Theme Parks: Turkish zoos do not offer the same standards of animal welfare as would be expected in the UK, USA or Australia. You might want to visit the zoo (*hayvanat bahçesi*) yourself before taking your child there.

BOOKS FOR CHILDREN

If your child was born in Turkey and speaks Turkish or is bilingual, the good news is that there are an ever-increasing number of good quality books for children available even in quite small rural towns. If, however, you are after books for your children in another language then you may well have to import most of them yourself (or use an Internet bookshop like Amazon).

Recently a few children's books about Turkey have been published in English. These include:

- *Zeynep - The Seagull of Galata Tower,* Julia Townsend (Çitlembik Publications)

- *Purple Butterflies,* Debra Menase (Çitlembik Publications)
- *The Rainbow,* Debra Menase (Çitlembik Publications)
- *Exploring Turkey,* Amy Chaple (Çitlembik Publications)
- *Folk Costumes of Turkey,* Amy Chaple (Çitlembik Publications)

Mira Publishing in Istanbul also produces useful books, including educational books in English; for contact details see under bookshops in Appendix VII.

RESTAURANTS CATERING FOR CHILDREN

Although Turks are very fond of children and will usually make them welcome in restaurants, that doesn't mean that many restaurants have either special facilities or special menus for kids. For that you will usually have to frequent one of the foreign-owned chain restaurants; addresses are listed in Appendix IX.

WHAT IT MEANS	
aileye mahsustur	reserved for families
aile salonu	family room

SECOND-GENERATION KIDS

The children of mixed Turkish-foreign parents have one huge advantage over their peers which is that they usually grow up speaking two languages fluently. They may also feel at home in two very different cultures.

However, it is also likely that children of mixed parentage may grow up feeling torn in two directions. Foreign parents who chose to settle in Turkey may accept that they are condemned to be eternal outsiders, forever *yabancıs*, if not 'tourists'. They may feel that this is a price worth paying and justified by, for example, their own poor Turkish. For their bilingual children born in the country, however, it can be a great pain to be endlessly asked about their parentage, to be endlessly complimented on their lovely Turkish and generally treated as if they are outsiders. There is no easy answer to this but it is something to bear in mind before deciding to bring up your children in Turkey.

The worst problems may affect adolescent girls growing up in more conservative/rural parts of Turkey where their behaviour may still be regarded as reflecting on their entire family. If their own mothers have led 'liberated' lives, it may be especially hard for their daughters to accept the need to trim their own sails in order to avoid provoking the dreaded *dedikodu* (gossip).

TO CIRCUMCISE OR NOT TO CIRCUMCISE?

Every Muslim boy is circumcised at around the age of eight or nine although the *sünnet* (circumcision) can take place at any age between two and 14. Circumcision marks a form of transition to manhood and is a big day in any boy's life and you will see special circumcision suits on sale in shops all over the country. They consist of a satin suit usually in blue and white with a feathery trim together with a sceptre and a matching crown bearing the word *Maşallah* to ward off the evil eye. In the past the boy would have been dressed in this outfit and then paraded around town on a horse. These days the horses have mostly vanished but the outfits live on.

On the day of a circumcision the parents of the boy will usually throw a party for family and friends who will come with gifts (often of gold coins) for the boy in question. These days most boys are circumcised under local anaesthetic in the local hospital. However there are still some itinerant *sünnetçi* (circumcisers) who will come and carry out the procedure in the boy's home. While he is doing his work the boy is held by a *kirve,* usually a close friend of the family who then takes on a role not unlike that of a godparent to the child. Afterwards the boy rests on his bed beneath decorations reminiscent of Christmas paper-chains. Friends and family visit and compliment him on his bravery. Graphic photos are often taken and shown to all and sundry.

For some Western mothers the idea of having their son circumcised at such a relatively late age can be problematic. However sometimes their husbands will insist on the tradition. Some mothers also decide that if they don't go along with it they will be depriving their son of what is seen as a rite of passage for all Turkish boys and the gifts that go with it. Others agree a compromise whereby their son is circumcised in hospital shortly after birth. If you want to do this be sure to make arrangments well in advance.

Where there is more than one boy in a household the family may wait and have all their sons circumcised at the same time. In areas where there are many poor families the local authority may make arrangements and pay for mass circumcision ceremonies some of which are televised. Turks of Jewish faith circumcise their sons immediately after birth and many Istanbul hospitals have special rooms to accommodate mother, infant and the guests who have come to view the ceremony.

Girls are never circumcised in Turkey.

MILITARY SERVICE *(ASKERLİK)*

All young Turkish men are required to undertake military service at some time between the ages of 20 and 46. The fact that one of their parents is a foreigner makes no difference to this requirement; if a foreign man takes on Turkish citizenship between these ages he also becomes eligible for military service. After a three-month training period, men are usually sent to serve in the army in an area other than the one in which they grew up since this is seen as a way of helping people think of the sprawling area of Anatolia as one country. Men who speak English or another foreign language are often sent to resort areas although there is no guarantee of this.

During their military service men are paid an extremely nominal sum of money which varies according to location (those serving in Northern Cyprus are paid slightly more than those in Turkey itself). They also receive two months' holiday split up into one and two-week blocks at the discretion of their commanding officer.

Leaving for military service is the second big rite of passage for most young men. The night before they are due to depart their family will lay on a meal for all their friends who then escort them to the local bus or train station. There groups of friends perform a farewell dance to the sound of pipe and drum.

Despite all this encouragement some men are still not keen to go into the army. Students can defer their military service until they have received their degree which has led to some people taking a very long time to complete obscure courses such as Latin. Men with university degrees can either do six months' service as a non-enlisted soldier with the same low pay, or 15 months' service as an officer with higher pay. It is also sometimes possible to pay your way out of doing part of your military service. Turks who have been living and working outside the country for three consecutive years can do just one month's service if they agree to pay a sum equalling approximately €5,750. When there are too many men available, the military occasionally allows some of them to pay to be excused from the bulk of their military service; the last such 'military pardon' cost €9,750.

Many Turkish families are reluctant to let their daughters marry men who have not completed their military service. Some employers are also reluctant to give them jobs since they might have to allow them time off to perform their obligations.

Women do not take part in military service in Turkey. Nor are they expected to do anything in its place.

CHAPTER 10

WORKING LIFE

Some people, especially those employed in the embassies and consulates, by multinational companies or in the foreign-language schools, come to live in Turkey because their work brings them here. Others decide to stay in Turkey and then set about looking for work which will enable them to live a normal lifestyle. Yet others come to Turkey on holiday and pick up casual work that pays their bed and board, albeit illegally.

If you want to work in Turkey there are not as many options as you might hope, especially if you don't speak Turkish, and many of them pay very poorly. One obvious possibility is to work as an English teacher, a type of employment that is available in many parts of the country. Other openings lie in tourism where there are usually plenty of casual summer jobs. A few people manage to find work on the *The New Anatolian*, the *Turkish Daily News* or other English-language publications. For women one of the best paid options is to take up a post as a nanny to a wealthy family in one of the big cities.

Some professional posts (as doctors, dentists, midwives, pharmacists, vets and tour guides, or in the civil service and the law) are still barred to foreigners, despite ongoing efforts to get this changed. Foreigners are also forbidden to own newspapers or sell the dwindling number of state monopoly products. However, foreigners who have married Turks and become Turkish citizens have a right to practise these occupations as well as any others. It is common to come across foreigners who have opened pensions or restaurants alone or with their Turkish partners. A few have also made the grade as carpet-sellers or retailers of other local produce.

Finding Work: Most expats who work professionally in Turkey find their jobs before they arrive in the country. However, teachers sometimes land employment after arrival even if this does sometimes mean leaving Turkey to organise the paperwork and/or acquire the necessary qualifications before starting work. Most jobs in tourism are picked up casually or by word of mouth, particularly because most people know where they would like to work.

If you are looking for casual work you could try the noticeboard at the Orient Hostel in Istanbul. For anything more serious try the noticeboards at the Taksim Dilmer and Tömer language schools or at Marmara and Boğaziçi universities. It's also worth looking in the classified ads of expat magazines such as Fethiye's *Land of Lights*. To find work as a teacher you will need to approach each school directly, although teachers who are moving on often let other expats know of impending vacancies.

For information about work permits and visas, see p. 402.

Working Conditions: A lucky few people who work for the embassies, consulates and large international companies work a standard 8.30am to 5pm week, with Saturday and Sunday off. However, foreigners who are working in tourism have to cope with a far longer working week: in effect all day every day at the height of the season. Nannies and teachers in language schools may have to work erratic hours to suit their employers. You should not assume that you will be able to take Christmas off as a holiday - more usually you will be expected to take the same holidays as Turks (Şeker Bayramı and Kurban Bayramı - see p. 322), although those working in tourism will have to take their holidays during the winter when business is quiet. Usually you have to have been working for a company for many years before you are eligible for more than two weeks' annual holiday.

Free accommodation may be a perk of the job for those working in tourism, or as nannies or teachers.

In general unless you have a contract written in Turkish you should not assume a written agreement has much validity. Many employers tacitly expect their foreign staff to work illegally, leaving the country to renew their tourist visa every three months at their own expense.

TEACHING ENGLISH OR ANOTHER FOREIGN LANGUAGE (ÖĞRETMENLİK)

There is a great hunger for English-language teaching in Turkey which means that this sort of work is easy to find. However, the best paid jobs with the best conditions go to people with a degree and proper TESOL, TEFL, CELTA or PGCE qualifications; to give yourself the best opportunity it pays to take a course and obtain a certificate to wave at employers before leaving home.

Intensive one-month teaching courses may be hard work and cost around €900 but can be a great investment.

Finding Work: The lucky few teachers find work in Turkish schools or universities before they leave home, perhaps through programmes run by the British Council and its peers or through adverts in newspapers like *The Guardian* and the *Times Education Supplement (TES)*. However, if you want to teach in private language schools (*dershane)* you can often find a job after arriving in Turkey, either by visiting the schools, checking the noticeboards or through word-of-mouth referral.

You should expect to have to show:

- cv/resumé
- degree/diploma
- teaching certificate
- passport
- photograph

WHO TO CONTACT

Turkeng: Tel: 0242 445 1356, www.angelfire.com/biz/turkeng. Teacher placement agency recruiting teachers for private language schools, universities and private high schools in Turkey.

State and Private Schools: Foreigners cannot teach in Turkish state schools, which means that unless you have acquired Turkish citizenship you can forget enquiring at the local primary. A few fortunate people find secure teaching work in private schools. These posts are relatively well paid and have the advantage of long holidays, especially over the summer (almost two months). However, these days the schools are almost as bureaucratic as those in the UK, with teachers expected to prepare lesson plans a year ahead and take part in many out of school activities. They may also have to abide by the school's dress code and other regulations. On the upside, teachers are still highly respected in Turkey; 'öğretmenim (my teacher)' still plays an important part in many children's lives and teachers can expect to be bombarded with tokens of esteem on the annual Teachers' Day (*Öğretmenler Günü*, 24 November).

Dershanes: Without a TEFL certificate you may still be able to find work in some *dershanes*, which are private schools that supplement the state system, particularly in helping students pass the university entrance exam. However, the most reputable *dershanes* will also want to see formal teaching qualifications.

Private Language Schools: There are many specialist language schools in Turkey; Istanbul alone has around 200 of them. The more reputable schools will want to see your qualifications and will offer you a formal teaching contract; others may be more casual. Usually teachers work for between 24 and 30 hours a week, although their shifts may be split, with, perhaps, work in the morning and evening and time off in the afternoon particularly if they are teaching adults. You may not be guaranteed two consecutive days off per week. Depending on how exchange rates are moving you may be paid in lira or foreign currency or a combination of the two but pay is not normally high.

Some schools promise to get their teachers a work permit. However, more commonly they expect them to work illegally on a tourist visa and leave the country to get a new visa every three months. Accommodation is often provided free although it may not be of a very high quality or in an especially desirable location. You may also be expected to share it with other teachers. You should always check the room before accepting a post.

Some schools try to prevent their teachers taking on private work to supplement their wages; others have no problem with this.

Before accepting a teaching post you should ask the following questions:
- How much will you be paid per hour? When will you be paid?
- Will the school provide accommodation? Where? Will you have to share?
- If they will not provide accommodation, how much do you need to earn to make a realistic living?
- Will the school get you a work permit? If not, will they pay the cost of going in and out of Turkey to renew your visa every three months?
- What hours will you have to work? Will your shifts be split so that they leave you with little free time?
- Will you have two consecutive days' leave each week?
- Can you have Christmas Day off?

For more information about teaching English in Turkey visit the teacher forums on Dave's ESL Café website (www.eslcafe.com) or try www.teflturkey. com. For a list of language schools in Turkey see Appendix XI.

Private Tuition

Such is the demand for English teaching that it is always possible to find work as a private English tutor for a minimum of €30 an hour. Sometimes this work can be found through word-of-mouth recommendation. However, if you want to be sure of finding employment your best bet is to place an advertisement either in *The New Anatolian, Turkish Daily News* or *Time Out* or in the sort of places where people seeking tutors may think to look (Internet cafes, hostels, gyms, consulates, private schools, etc). You can also advertise on *mymerhaba* (www.mymerhaba.com) or in *Lale,* the magazine of the International Women of Istanbul group. Before accepting a student you should make sure that you agree about payment if they cancel at short notice or go away on holiday.

TOURISM *(TURİZM)*

Tourism is one of Turkey's biggest industries and English-speakers are vital to its smooth operation. Consequently most employment opportunities for foreigners outside Istanbul tend to be in tourism. Restaurants, carpet shops, jewellery shops and pensions are usually crying out for summer staff who are prepared to work for little more than their bed and board and, if they're lucky, commission on their sales.

If you know where you want to work, your best bet is to arrive there very early in the season (late March or April) and ask around. The more people you ask, the better your chance of landing a job. You should expect to have to put in very long hours, seven days a week, since this is the norm for Turks who work in tourism.

Note that foreigners are not allowed to work as tour guides in Turkey. Even if the tour company has provided an English-speaking escort they are expected to give way to a local Turkish guide whenever they visit an officially-recognised historic site.

With all the more casual openings in tourism you should be wary of promises of anything more than bed and board. Try and arrange to be paid daily at first and leave at the first sign that the promised wages are not going to materialise. It is almost always a mistake to work on in the hope that they will appear later.

Bar Work

Bar owners are often keen to employ foreigners who they hope will help to generate a suitably sociable atmosphere, thereby encouraging sales. This work is rarely legal and you may find you get paid in alcohol and board rather than in hard cash.

Pensions & Hotels

Many foreigners work in pensions and hotels, either with their Turkish partners or on their own. Unless they own the property this work is also likely to be illegal and the wages are likely to amount to little more than bed and board. If they own the property, however, this line of business can be very lucrative. In the past most foreigners tended to own small backpacker pensions but these days just as many own the sort of boutique hotels that grace the pages of *The Little Hotel Book*.

Although there is no guarantee that a pension or hotel run by a foreigner will be a success, foreigners do bring a number of advantages to the business which predispose it to success. In the first place they speak the language of their guests (and this is a plus whether that language is English, French or Japanese). In the second, they tend to have a wider world view as a result of their travels which means that they may have a more realistic understanding of what foreign tourists expect from their accommodation. They are also more likely to have been brought up in a culture in which the guest is always right so that they may be more inclined to be flexible and less defensive when something goes wrong.

A word of warning is needed here. For every foreigner who owns their own hotel and is making a good living from it, there will be one who has invested in a property with a Turkish partner, then lost their entire investment when the relationship went sour. You should bear in mind that, as with buying a house, a hotel or pension will only belong to the person whose name is on the title deed. If you are not married to the owner you are likely to have few rights if things go wrong. It is possible to go to court and attempt to obtain redress if you think you have lost out, but this is likely to prove an expensive and protracted battle. In other words if you meet and fall in love with a Turk, you should still be very wary before agreeing to an arrangement in which a joint venture is to be largely financed by you, the foreign partner.

Opening a Pension: Not surprisingly there are a lot of bureaucratic hoops to jump through before you can open a pension. You are not allowed to open a pension right beside a school, a mosque or the Belediye, and before you can start work you will have to obtain a licence from the police and from the Belediye. The local police will want to see the following documentation before giving you a licence:

- A photocopy of the title deed (*tapu*) for the property

- Planning permission for a new building
- A fire safety certificate
- Proof that you have a clean police record
- Proof that you are not carrying any infectious diseases, which involves a trip to hospital for a full medical (this has to be renewed annually)
- A statement from the local headman (*muhtar*) confirming your identity and address

In most parts of Turkey the local authorities set maximum price levels for all except private (*özel*) hotels and pensions; you can charge less than these prices but not more. Whether you charge in Turkish lira or another currency is up to you. Businesses have to pay higher prices for electricity and water, so you must expect bills to be steeper than at home.

Starting a Small Tour Operation or Travel Agency

Tour Operation (Gezi İşletmecisi): Some people who have enjoyed holidays in Turkey or have lived here for some time proceed to set up their own small tour operation, sometimes visiting the usual sites in smaller groups, sometimes specialising in bringing together a group of like-minded people (e.g. potters). If you want to do something like this you will need to study the law relating to tour operations in your own country. Everyone offering package tours out of European Union countries, for example, is bound by the terms of the European Union Package Holiday Directive (http://europa.eu.int/comm./consumers). Usually the law has been designed to protect clients' money if the tour operator ceases to trade, so you may have to have enough capital to be able to pay for all the services you need upfront without touching your clients' money until after the tour is completed.

Travel Agency (Seyahat Ajansı): An alternative is to set up a travel agency offering tailor-made tours of Turkey. If you are selling all the components of the trip (i.e. the flights, hotels, car hire etc) separately you may not need to comply with the law relating to tour operations. However, you would need to check the legal position carefully before assuming this. Legal travel agencies in Turkey need to belong to TURSAB (see Appendix V) and buying a TURSAB licence is expensive.

Working for an Overseas Tour Operator: If you want something more reliable and a bit better paid, you could approach tour operators in your home country that include Turkey in their programmes. They may need resort reps or even guides, although there are fewer such openings than you might hope. You don't necessarily have to speak Turkish although it may help. If you are accepted you will need to apply for a special tour company rep visa which is valid for six months in a period of 12 months.

Some overland tour companies pass through Turkey and employ staff as drivers and cooks, and to accompany their passengers. However, their staff are often expected to pay for their own training and are then paid very little for their work, leaving them dependent on commission from sales of carpets, alcohol and meals to their groups.

For a list of some British and Australian tour operators who feature Turkey in their programmes see Appendix XIX. The UK website www.abta.com/destinations/turkey.html also lists many smaller tour operators.

NANNYING (ÇOCUK BAKICISI)

In the West nannying tends to have a very poor image with only professionally-qualified nannies able to attract decent salaries. Many 'nannies' are little more than badly paid au pairs. However, this is not the case in Turkey where wealthy families are often ready to pay good money to have their children cared for by a native English-speaking nanny who doubles as a teacher. You can earn at least €150 a week for this sort of work in Istanbul although in Ankara and Izmir the wages are lower. Many nanny jobs in Istanbul are on the Asian side of the city so you can often make life easier for yourself by living over there too.

There are often considerable perks attached to nannying. You may, for example, get your bed and board paid for. You may be ferried to and from work by the parents' chauffeur. You may get taken on holidays with the family or to concerts, etc for which they have the best tickets. Sometimes it is possible to find nannying work which only covers weekends or the summer holidays.

On the downside, however, many monied families are demanding, if not downright dysfunctional, so you shouldn't expect an easy ride. Your working hours may also be erratic and some families think nothing of going away on holiday, leaving their nanny unpaid, at a moment's notice. Others are depressingly reluctant payers.

Before accepting a nannying position you should ask the following questions:

- How much will you be paid per hour?
- Will you be paid in Turkish lira or foreign currency? When will you be paid?

- Will you still be paid if the family go on holiday without you or cancel a visit at short notice?
- What hours will you have to work? (It is better to agree specific hours rather than commit to staying, for example, 'until the children are in bed' – this could lead to much longer hours than anticipated.)
- What time will you be able to have off? Will it have to be at the same time as the family holiday? Can you have Christmas Day off?
- What duties will you have to perform?
- Will the family provide you with accommodation? Do they want you to live in? If you have to find your own accommodation, how much will you need to earn to make a realistic living?
- Will the family provide you with transport to and from work? If not, how much will you have to spend on fares to get to work?

Many people find their work through word of mouth. However, there are also several agencies which may be able to find you a placement.

WHO TO CONTACT

- *Anglo-Nannies*: Tel: 0212-287 6898, www.anglonannies.com, Bebek Yolu Sokak, Ebru Apart No: 25/2, Etiler, Istanbul; Tel: 0208-944 6677, 2 St Marks Place, Wimbledon, London SW19 7ND, UK; Tel: 0033-4 42 71 99 18, 3 Lotissement du Revestin, 13600 La Ciotat, Marseille, France
- *Great Au Pair:* Tel: 925-478 4100, www.greataupair.com, Intelimark Enterprises, 1329 Highway 395 North, Suite 10-333, Gardnerville, North Virginia 89410, USA
- *Total Nannies:* Tel: 0208-542 3067, Fax: 0208-762 1387, 37 Leamington Avenue, Morden, Surrey SM4 4DQ, UK

EXPORTING TURKISH PRODUCTS

A few foreigners make a living out of exporting produce from Turkey. Usually they opt for typically Turkish arts and crafts for which they see a market in their home country. However, a few people have also chosen to export more prosaic goods (such as children's shoes) where they have noticed that the price of the product is cheap enough in Turkey to make it possible to add on the export cost and still make a profit at home. The key to success with that sort of selling is to track down the wholesale (*toptan*) outlets that sell to Turkish retail (*perakende*) shops. The strengthening of the Turkish lira over the last few years had made it harder to do this profitably. However, at the time of writing the value of the lira had dropped again which might help make Turkish exports more competitive.

Increasingly people are also using the Internet as a means of selling Turkish products to the overseas market.

Few of the people involved in export (*ihracat*) live in Turkey all year round but this is work that suits people who want to be able to come and go regularly.

INVESTING IN PROPERTY

Property Development

Until recently few foreigners would have thought of earning a living in Turkey as a property developer. However, the gradual evolution of a property market alongside the explosive growth in the number of foreigners wanting to live in Turkey has turned this into a more appealing prospect for people with enough capital to get started.

The most promising areas for property developers are Istanbul, and the Aegean and Western Mediterranean coastlines. However, the two areas are very different. In Istanbul most foreign property developers are buying up old properties in the town centre, restoring and modernising them and then selling them on, either immediately or after a period of renting them out. In the last couple of years prices in Istanbul have risen so sharply that some people have been able to make big money out of their purchase; in some parts of the city prices are thought to have risen by 80% in 2005 alone. If you are interested in trying your hand at this you should know that prices in Cihangir, Çukurçuma and Galata have already risen steeply. It is thought that adjacent areas like Tarlabaşı and Karaköy are likely to follow suit in the near future while properties along both shores of the Golden Horn (Fener, Balat, Hasköy) are worth considering as longer-term investments. As elsewhere, the would-be developer's mantra should be location, location, location: properties near to tram and Metro stops, and good shopping facilities attract the same premium prices as they would in London or New York.

Along the coast property developers are more likely to buy up plots of land and then build on them, either on their own or in partnership with a Turk. Once again, some people are hoping to make a quick return on their investment by selling immediately while others are hoping to rent out their property in the short term and then sell later. Over the last three years some people have been able to make huge profits on their investment as prices soared (by around 30-40% in some cases in 2004-5). However, it is possible that they will level out eventually in which case it may become harder to dip in and out of the market quickly.

If you have owned a property for more than five years your profit on its sale should be free of Turkish tax. However, if you sell it before then it is subject to capital gains tax. If you under-declared the value of the property when you first bought it that could mean having to pay more capital gains tax when you come to sell it. You should also take advice as to the tax implications in your home country.

Rental

Holiday Lets: If you own a property in Turkey but don't want to live in it all year round you can always try and let it as a holiday home. The arrival of the Internet has made this a realistic option since it is now easier to make contact with potential holidaymakers. However, you should remember that the Turkish holiday season is very short – really only from May through to the end of October. Although there is no reason why you should not try to let your property for a longer period, the reality is that most of the resorts slump into ghost towns at the start of November which makes them fairly unattractive propositions. Most charter flights also stop operating in October although there are currently efforts to extend the season, especially in south-west Turkey.

Before buying somewhere with renting it out as your primary motive you should always ask yourself the following questions:

- How far is the property from the nearest airport? Most people dislike transfers that take more than an hour and Turkey's winding coastline is notoriously tough on people who suffer from motion sickness.
- How many weeks of the year are you likely to be able to rent out the property and for how much money?
- How many weeks would you be able to stay in it yourself?
- How much will you need to pay to a letting agent, cleaners etc?
- What attractions and amenities are nearby?
- Will your property look attractive to someone surfing the web? Properties with sea views are always going to attract premium rents.
- Does the property have all the amenities needed to rent it out? If not, how much will it cost to install them?

Along Turkey's south coast you can expect to let a villa for between €740 and €1,000 a week. However, if you use a Turkish agent to let the property for you they will probably take 15-20% commission on the rent. It is also possible to hire a manager who will look after the property for you while you are away, and make sure that the bills are paid and running repairs undertaken. Along the coast many estate agents offer a cleaning and garbage-removal service for as little as €15 a week. However, once you have taken into account tax payments and the inevitable costs of wear and tear, these costs could make the rental income seem less attractive. Should you want someone to manage your property for you it's worth looking in a local expat magazine such as Fethiye's *Land of Lights* (www.landoflights.net) for suitable companies.

If you want to rent out your property privately a website on the Internet is obviously a good place to advertise. You could also place an ad in the British *The Lady* magazine (www.lady.co.uk) or in a local English-language magazine such as Fethiye's *Land of Lights*.

If you do rent out your property, you should declare the income for tax either in Turkey or in your home country. Until recently many people didn't do this and managed to get away with it. However, as Turkey moves towards EU accession this is likely to get harder to do.

Normal Rentals: Until recently rents, even in the big cities, were very low which made letting a property out an unattractive proposition for most foreigners. However, the economic crash of 2001 brought a temporary halt to new building work, although not to the flow of migrants into the towns. With more people chasing fewer flats, prices started to rise quite dramatically. They have continued to do so ever since.

If you own a property in Istanbul it is increasingly possible to let it for a decent monthly income. The highest rents are for properties overlooking the Bosphorus which cost a fortune to buy in the first place. However, it is still possible to pick up flats in the centre of Istanbul for a reasonable price. Once restored these should also bring in a sensible monthly income. You can also make a profit on rental properties in Ankara, Izmir, Fethiye and Antalya.

Elsewhere letting out a property is unlikely to be lucrative because of the low level of rents. Considering how much you would have to invest to make a property attractive to a tenant in the first place, the rent would never be enough to bring in a profit.

JOURNALISM *(GAZETECİLİK)*

Most foreigners working as journalists (*gazeteci*) in Turkey are employed by foreign newspapers, magazines and radio/TV channels. This work is almost always organised before they arrive in the country. Some freelance journalists have also found work as stringers for overseas media outlets. However, this work is not easy to obtain since the Western media doesn't usually devote much space to Turkey. Editors may become interested when a big story develops but as soon as it dies down again they are liable to lose interest just as quickly. Experienced Turkey hands are frequently upset to find that newspapers prefer to send a home journalist to cover a Turkey story rather than rely on people on the ground; often the best that the local journo can expect is to be paid to set up interviews and act as general minder for the incoming foreign journalist.

Before you can work as a journalist in Turkey you need to obtain **accreditation**. If you plan to be in the country for less than three months you can sort out the paperwork through the press office of the Turkish Embassy in your own country. It is also possible to arrange temporary accreditation from inside Turkey although it is a bit of a palaver. If you plan to stay in the country for longer than three months you will need permanent accreditation. This, too, is easier sorted out from abroad. Permanent accreditation has to be renewed annually.

There are occasional vacancies on the *The New Anatolian* and *Turkish Daily News* for English-speaking journalists, editors (*editör*), copy editors (*düzeltmen/redactör*) or proofreaders (*düzeltmen*). Most of these posts are based in Ankara which could be a drawback. They also tend to be poorly paid.

WHO TO CONTACT
Ankara
- *Agence France-Presse:* Tel: 0312-468 9680
- *Associated Press:* Tel: 0312-428 2709
- *BBC:* Tel: 0312-438 2101
- *Reuters:* Tel: 0312-446 2940
- *The New Anatolian:* Tel: 0312-447 5647, Fax: 0312-446 8374, Hülya Sokak No: 45, Gaziosmanpaşa
- *Turkish Daily News:* Tel: 0312-468 9178, www.turkishdailynews.com.tr, İran Caddesi, Karum İş Merkezi No: 21/443, Kat: 6, Gaziosmanpaşa

Freelance journalists (*serbest gazeteci*) can also pick up work on magazines which focus on Turkey. None of them pays its staff particularly well. However, if you already have one source of income they can provide a useful supplement – especially if you live near enough to chase up slow payments! Note that *Cornucopia* tends to use known writers and that *Skylife* prefers to use Turkish journalists and have their articles translated into English.

- *Cornucopia:* Tel: 0212-248 3607, www.cornucopia.net, PK. 191, Teşvikiye, Istanbul. Thrice-yearly glossy features magazine on all aspects of Turkish life.

- *On Air:* Tel: 0212-288 7970, Fax: 0212-288 6236, Kasap Sokak, Kat 6, No: 22 Hilmi Hak Han, Esentepe, Istanbul. Onur Air's in-flight magazine with articles on all aspects of life in Turkey.

- *Skylife:* Tel: 0212-269 4527, www.cordisgroup.com.tr, Levent Mahallesi, 4. Gazeteciler Sitesi, Ebulula Mardin Caddesi, Ülgen Sokak No: 18/A, Akatlar, Istanbul. Turkish Airlines' excellent in-flight magazine covering all aspects of Turkish life.

- *The Guide:* Tel: 0212-274 6262, www.apa.com.tr, Doktor Orhan Birman İş Merkezi, Barbaros Bulvarı, Kat: 10, No: 121, Balmumcu, Istanbul; Ankara; Bodrum. Monthly what's on magazine.

- *Time Out Istanbul:* Tel: 0212-287 1990, www.timeoutistanbul.com, Yoğurtçu Zülfü Sokak No: 6, Bebek, Istanbul. Monthly entertainment magazine.

SELF-EMPLOYMENT *(SERBEST ÇALIŞMA)*

Quite a lot of people live in Turkey and work in the sort of occupations that the authorities barely regard as work: writing, painting, photography etc. In theory you need a work permit to carry out even these trades and in theory you also need to pay tax on the proceeds. However, many people seem to live in Turkey for years without doing either of these things.

Setting up a Business

If you want to start a business in Turkey things become much more complicated. In theory the government has made it easier to start your own business. However, the paperwork involved in setting up a company, combined with the difficulty involved in obtaining work permits and visas (see p. 402), still act as a considerable disincentive to all but the most determined.

If you do want to set up your own business you must first decide how you would like to register it. Turkey offers several possible business structures, the most common of which are:

- **Limited Liability Companies (Limited Şirket):** To start a limited liability company in Turkey you need two people and a minimum capital of

YTL5000. One person has to act as the company director. Since your liability to loss is limited to the sum of the share capital in the company this is usually the safest option.

- **Joint Stock Companies (Anonim Şirket, A.Ş.)**: To start a joint stock company in Turkey you need five people and a minimum capital of YTL50,000. There has to be a Board of Directors consisting of five people and the company is obliged to appoint an auditor.

What foreign-owned business can and cannot do is dictated by the terms of the Foreign Direct Investment Act. It is beyond the scope of this book to delve into the detail of company formation but the complete law can be accessed via www.treasury.gov.tr.

Doing Business in Turkey

Until June 2003 investing in Turkey was extremely difficult, particularly for small businesses. Would-be foreign investors were required to transfer at least US$50,000 to Turkey before they could set up their own business. In 2003, however, this requirement was scrapped and foreigners no longer need to invest a specific sum before starting a business. What is more they are now free to export their capital and profits without hindrance. Under the Direct Investment Law foreign investors are only required to inform the Undersecretary of the Treasury that they are starting up a business, whereas before they had to seek active permission. The intension behind these changes was to encourage foreign investment and help meet the criteria for EU membership.

In 2006 Turkey is an interesting place in which to do business. It can be very stimulating because for the time being its slight 'backwardness' means that not every idea has already been tried. So one couple can decide to set up a clay-pigeon shooting farm, while someone else can establish a website aimed at expats and have no initial competition. On the other hand in smaller towns and villages it can be very difficult to make a new idea work, with the depressing result that ever more pensions and restaurants end up chasing a static pool of potential clients. Turks excel at copying which means that if you do have a good idea that works you should assume that someone else will quickly emulate it - right down to copying your brochures, name and business cards!

For the last few years most people had regarded the Turkish lira as overvalued against the dollar, euro and pound; it had held its value consistently between 2002 and early 2006, regardless of inflation. That meant that much of the benefit that exporters gained from the weak lira had been lost just as China was expanding its export markets dramatically. In 2006 the lira dropped in value again which should work in favour of business. However, at the time of writing it remained to be seen whether this was a lasting 'correction' or not.

Recommended reading:

- *Doing Business in Turkey* IBS Group, Tel: 0212-252 2480, www.ibsresearch. com, Neşehan, İstiklal Caddesi, Turnacıbaşı Sokak No: 19, Kat: 3, Beyoğlu, Istanbul
- *Emerging Turkey 2005* Oxford Business Group, Tel: 0207-403 7213, www. oxfordbusinessgroup.com, 33 St James's Square, London SW1Y 4JS, UK
- *Executive's Handbook Turkey 2005* Intermedia Group, Tel: 0212-287 2803, www.intermedia.com.tr, İnşirah Sokak No: 13, Anadolu Apt, Blok A, Daire: 2, Bebek, Istanbul

---

KINGS OF INDUSTRY - KOÇ AND SABANCI

No one can live in Turkey for long without noticing the ubiquitous names, Koç and Sabancı. They crop up everywhere - on banks, supermarkets, cement mixers, schools, universities, art galleries and museums - and they are the family names of Turkey's two most successful industrialists who developed their enormous business empires as the Turkish republic grew up.

Vehbi Koç started his working life as an Ankara grocer but by the time of his death Koç Holding, a grouping of more than 100 companies, appeared in *Fortune* magazine's list of the world's 500 largest companies and Vehbi Koç was Turkey's wealthiest man. His industrial empire encompassed food, retailing, banking and insurance, energy, cars, tourism and education. Arçelik is part of the Koç empire as are Migros and the American Hospital in Istanbul. Vehbi Koç set up charitable foundations to benefit education, health and social services, a tradition continued by his descendants. Vebhi Koç died in 1996.

Sakıp Sabancı started life as the son of a cotton trader and rose to become one of Turkey's greatest industrialists, with fingers in the textiles, food, tourism, packaging, cars, chemicals, cement, insurance and banking pies. An art collector himself, he went on to become a notable philanthropist. Sakıp Sabancı died in 2004.

WHO TO CONTACT

- *Turkish-British Chamber of Commerce & Industry (Türk İngiliz Ticaret ve Sanayi Odası):* Tel: 0207-321 0999, www.tbcci.org/Tur/, Bury House, 33 Bury St, London SW1W 6AU, UK
- *Undersecretariat to Treasury Ministry (T.C. Başbakanlık Hazine Müsteşarlığı):* Tel: 0312-204 6000, www.treasury.gov.tr, İnönü Bulvarı No: 36, Ankara

SEX WORK

Perhaps surprisingly, sex work is legal in Turkey and owners of brothels have to pay social security premiums for their workers as well as normal income tax. They are also responsible for ensuring that their workers are free of venereal diseases. It is illegal to force anyone to work as a prostitute (*fahişe*) and there are also legal penalties for physical assaults on prostitutes. Some foreign sex workers have married Turks and set up families in the country. However, society as a whole is as critical of prostitution as a career as anywhere else in the world.

Even on the briefest of visits to Turkey it will be apparent that many women from Eastern Europe and the ex-Soviet states have come here to work as prostitutes (hence the pejorative use of the name 'Natasha' to mean a prostitute). Some of the women working in this way are supporting families back home; others are saving up to start businesses or buy homes in their own countries. Few of these women work in the official brothels (*genelev*) which are usually on the outskirts of town and have been condemned by the anti-slavery movement as operating a form of modern-day servitude.

SHOP WORK

In the tourist resorts English-speakers are often required to serve in shops. This work is rarely legal and every now and then there will be a scare when the local *jandarma* come round to check on everyone's credentials. However, shop work rarely requires prior experience, so it can be one of the few options available to non-Turkish speakers.

Occasionally foreigners have been successful in setting up their own shops in Turkey. For example, one American woman has set up a shop in the most upmarket quarter of Istanbul's Grand Bazaar to sell unusual souvenirs.

A few foreigners have also made a success out of selling carpets or other valuable items. Their foreignness has worked in their favour since, for good or bad, many tourists prefer to buy from people who not only speak their own language but are also used to their own way of shopping. As more and more dubious characters have moved into the carpet business, so many tourists have become wary of falling for suspect sales ploys – a foreign face can make them feel far more comfortable. However, if someone offers you a job in a carpet shop you should be aware that it may well be on a commission-only basis (i.e. no sale, no fee). Occasionally tourists are asked to 'recommend' specific carpet shops to fellow tourists. This 'work' too will be on a commission-only basis and is unlikely to win you many friends amongst your fellow foreigners if they cotton on to what you are doing.

TRANSLATING *(TERCÜMANLIK)*

If you can speak Turkish fluently it is sometimes possible to find work as a translator, work which can be very varied (subtitling films, translating books, summarising newspaper content, translating song lyrics etc) but can materialise at short notice. This means that you will need to have a mobile phone and be ready to rush home whenever a call comes.

Translation Agencies:

- *Çitlembik:* Tel: 0212-292 3032, Şehbender Sokak No: 18/4, Asmalımescit, Beyoğlu, Istanbul
- *Wordsmith:* Tel: 0212-287 3971, Beyazgül Sokak No: 58, Arnavutköy, Istanbul
- *Net Centre:* Tel: 0242-248 0338, İsmet Paşa Caddesi, İkizhan B Blok No: 15, Antalya

WORKING FOR EMBASSIES, CONSULATES AND NGOs

Some of the best paid and most professional work to be had in Turkey is in the various embassies, consulates and non-governmental organisations. Unfortunately most of these jobs have to be organised before you come to Turkey and the competition will always be intense.

For a list of embassies and consulates, see p. 568.

WHAT TO SAY			
apprentice	*stajyer*	partner	*ortak*
business card	*kartvizit*	partnership	*ortaklık*
casual work	*devamlı olmayan iş*	part-time	*yarı zamanlı iş*
company	*şirket/firma*	pension-owner	*pansiyoncu*
consultant	*danışman*	product(s)	*ürün(ler)*
customer/client	*müşteri*	profit/earnings	*kâr/kazanç*
distributor/supplier	*dağıtımcı/bayi*	proposal	*teklif/öneri*
employee	*memur/işçi/görevli*	resume/cv	*özgeçmiş*
employer	*patron*	retail	*perakende*
exhibition	*sergi*	salary	*maaş*

experienced	tecrübeli	self-employed	serbest çalışan
export	ihraç	to sack	kovulmak
full time work	tam zamanlı iş	to work	çalışmak
hard-working	çalışkan	trade fair	ticaret fuarı
import	ithal	trade/business	ticaret
income tax	gelir vergisi	translator	tercüman/çevirmen
interview	görüşme	wholesale	toptan
job advert	iş ilanı	work	iş
manager	müdür	work colleague	iş arkadaşı
meeting	toplantı	workplace	işyeri
office	büro/ofis		

CHAPTER 11

FINANCIAL KNOW-HOW

Once you have settled in Turkey you will want to organise your finances as well as you would do at home. Until recently this was not particularly easy. However, since the banking crisis of 2001 those banks that survived have been modernising their systems and nowadays some are at least as efficient as their counterparts in the West.

WHICH BANK TO CHOOSE

In 2001 Turkey was brought to its knees by an economic crisis sparked off by a banking crisis. Several banks collapsed in the ensuing period and for a year or so it was hard to have confidence in any of them. Now, however, the situation is much improved. Those banks that survived seem fairly robust and, as Turkey moves to meet the requirements for EU membership, most of them are modernising fast. It has helped that inflation has been brought down to manageable proportions and that the old currency, with its cumbersome six zeroes, has been replaced with a new, more manageable one. But many people had their fingers badly burnt in 2001 and it is impossible to recommend putting your money in any other than the best known banks.

The largest banks in Turkey are the last three state-owned banks (Halk Bankası, Ziraat Bankası and Şekerbank), and, in order of size, Yapı Kredi Bankası-Koçbank (Koçbank bought Yapı Kredi in 2005), Türkiye İş Bankası, Akbank and Garanti Bankası, all of them privately owned. Akbank has won awards for its customer service while Garanti Bankası actively courts expat customers with promises of English-speaking staff in all its branches (not always fulfilled). Oyakbank is owned by the Turkish armed forces pension fund which means that is unlikely to run out of funds any day soon.

Most of the main banks have branches in all the Turkish towns. Some also have stand-alone cash-machines in useful locations. All the machines have multilingual instructions for use.

For a list of Turkish banks see Appendix VI.

Security: Whichever bank you choose to use the government only guarantees to refund up to YTL50,000 of your money in the event of another crisis. For that reason it is probably sensible to put your money in more than one bank if you have a lot of it.

Foreign Banks

Of the well-known foreign banks only HSBC has a branch network inside Turkey although there doesn't seem to be as much advantage as you might assume to be gained from opening an account there. However, some other foreign banks do have representation in Istanbul.

For a list of foreign banks with representation in Turkey see Appendix VI.

Opening a Bank Account

Officially, to open a Turkish lira bank account you need to have a residency permit (*ikamet*). However, depending on whom you know and how much money you want to invest, you may find some banks allowing you to open a current account (*vadesiz hesap)* without one. In theory you also need to have a tax number (see p. 405) before you can open a bank account. However, if the interest being earned on the account is low, the bank may also be prepared to overlook this requirement. Tax is automatically deducted from interest-bearing accounts at a rate appropriate to unearned income.

You do not need a residency permit to open an account in US dollars, pounds or euros although these accounts pay low or no interest.

Operating a Bank Account

Once you have opened a Turkish lira account you will be able to apply for an ATM card that will allow you to operate your account and make cash withdrawals (*para çekme)* from a cash-machine as you would at home. Normally you must collect the card from the bank and then phone a special number to get a pin number to use it. In theory if the card has a Switch/Maestro/Cirrus number you will be able to use it to draw out money from other banks as you would with your home card (normally you will be charged commission for this service as in the US). You should also be able to use it as a debit card when you go shopping and see the correct symbols displayed. However, it is not safe to assume that your card will work in the machines of banks other than those of the issuer – sometimes it will, sometimes it won't.

Turkey does not permit unauthorised overdrafts, so if there is no money in your account you will not be able to withdraw cash from an ATM regardless as you might be able to in the UK.

WHAT TO SAY			
account	*hesap*	account number	*hesap numarası*
account book	*hesap defteri*	bank transfer	*havale*

Internet Banking

The advent of Internet banking has made it easier to manage your home bank account from Turkey (although bear in mind that power outages and slow Internet connections can still be a problem). However, most Turkish banks also have Internet banking systems, so once you have established a local bank account you should be able to manage it from home. As elsewhere you often earn slightly higher rates of interest on Internet accounts than on bank-based ones. However, you should try to find out how secure the site is before putting your money into an Internet account.

Television Banking

You can access your Yapı Kredi and Halk Bankası accounts via Digitürk.

Setting Up Standing Orders (*Otomatik Fatura Ödeme*)

You can pay for your natural gas, electricity, water, telephone, mobile phone, ADSL line, Digitürk, credit card bill and other services by getting the bank to set up a standing order from your current account. In theory this is a good idea since bills sometimes arrive late. However, it has been known for the standing orders to fail resulting in a service being cut off, so you need to keep an eye on what is happening to your account.

Arranging to make a regular payment from one private bank account to another private bank account is usually too expensive to be worthwhile.

The Cheque-Free Society

Although Turkey does have cheques (*çek*), you can live in the country for a very long time without ever seeing one. Instead, if you are buying something that would have been paid for by cheque in the UK you will often be given a bank account number into which you pay the sum owed. Once the vendor has checked that the funds have arrived in the account they should release the goods. Unfortunately most banks levy hefty flat-rate charges for processing such transfers (*havale*): YTL 18-25 is normal. Cheques are only normally used for sizeable sums of money or in commercial transactions where the company writing the cheque does not actually have the cash at the time it is issued.

MINOR DETAILS

If you do need to write a cheque it helps to know that:
- Turkey uses dots rather than commas when writing large numbers e.g. 2.500.000
- The percentage sign appears before rather than after numbers e.g. %75
- Dates are written with the specific date first, then the month, then the day, then the year e.g. 29 December Thursday 2005.
- Turkey writes the number 7 with a line slashed through the upright

---

ISLAMIC BANKING (*FAİZSİZ BANKACILIK*)

Islam prohibits the taking of interest (*faiz*) which means that conventional bank accounts are unacceptable to devout Muslims. Instead Turkey has a number of finance houses which offer more acceptable arrangements. Normally these operate by, for example, buying houses or cars and then selling them to would-be owners at a higher price than was originally paid. The would-be owner then pays the bank this higher price in instalments and does not technically 'own' the car or house until the entire debt has been paid. Islamic banks also refuse to invest in companies that deal in *haram* (forbidden) products such as pork, alcohol or anything to do with gambling.

Turkey has two Islamic banks - Turkish Bank and Türk Arap Bankası - and three Islamic finance houses - Kuveyt Türk, Asya Finans amd Family Finans Kurumu. In 2006 the government started offering the same kind of financial guarantees (see above) to people who invest in Islamic finance houses as they do to people who invest in a bank. By 2015 it has been estimated that Islamic banks could be accounting for up to 10% of the assets held by Turkish banks.

Because of the prohibition on taking interest, some Turks invest their money in completely different ways; for example, many put their money into companies such as Yimpaş and Kombasan that actively market themselves as Islamic. This alternative approach to business is sometimes called 'green capitalism' because green is the favoured colour of Islam.

FOREIGN EXCHANGE *(DÖVİZ)*

Foreigners working in Turkey are often paid in hard currency, sometimes in cash, which means that they have a particular interest in the many foreign exchange bureaux that change foreign currencies more quickly and often for better rates than the banks. Most foreign exchange bureaux are only really interested in dollars, euros and pounds although in Istanbul you may be able to get them to accept other currencies.

In rural areas people often depend on gold shops to exchange foreign currencies for them. These shops sometimes offer better rates than the banks and foreign exchange bureaux.

Exchange Rates: Many foreign workers are paid in foreign currencies. To find out the latest exchange rates tune into TRT Telegün, the Turkish teletext service, which is available through some satellite television services. Alternatively go to www.xe.com, www.oanda.com or look at the website of your own bank.

The 'Free' Market: Turkey has no black market. However, if you wander up to Altın Sokak, an alleyway near the Mahmutpaşa gate of the Grand Bazaar, you will find a flourishing free currency market, with hundreds of men exchanging dollars and euros at the keenest rates.

Not Quite Like Banking at Home

- When you acquire a Turkish ATM card you will be told to keep your password secret. However, it is quite common to stand in line behind individuals who are blithely accessing the accounts of two or more friends or relatives.
- Often you will see an elderly Turk standing pathetically in front of an ATM machine. They can't read and are waiting for someone to come along and help them.
- Forget the Data Protection Act – in Turkish banks it's common for people to crowd around a computer and look at everybody else's business. They will also butt into transactions with 'helpful' comments.
- On the other hand in rural Turkey at least it's still not unknown to be given the private phone number of whoever is handling your account so that you can call them to discuss it at any time.

SECURITY *(GÜVENLİK)*

Although Turkey is not as plagued with ATM problems as some Western countries, you still need to be careful when using them, especially in popular tourist areas. Make sure no one is standing close enough to read your pin number and be on your guard if anyone offers to 'help' you at the machine unless you have specifically asked them to - often it can be an excuse for sleight-of-hand that leaves you with a fake card in place of the real one. When you have just taken money out of an ATM check that no one is watching or following you. Put the money away as quickly and securely as you can.

Although they have the names of the main banks displayed on them, many ATM machines, especially in the bigger towns, are operated as franchises. This can lead to delays in recovering your card should the machine swallow it.

TRANSFERRING MONEY TO TURKEY

If you have opened a foreign currency Turkish bank account, your home bank should have no trouble transferring money into it in less than a week (this is usually more easily organised FROM the other country to Turkey than FROM Turkey). Most banks will charge around €040 for the service; the Turkish bank will also make a charge for processing the transfer.

To make a transfer you need to know:

- The name of the bank to which the money is to be sent
- The account number and name to which the money is to be sent
- The Swift code of the bank to which the money is to be sent
- The IBAN number of the bank to which the money is to be sent

Unfortunately tighter regulations to prevent money laundering and to try and stem the flow of money to terrorists mean that you may have to answer many more questions than hitherto. Some overseas banks will be happier to transfer money for you if you have already made previous transfers which suggest to them that you have a regular relationship with Turkey.

Western Union Money Transfers: If you need to transfer money from abroad to Turkey and don't have a Turkish bank account you can use a branch of Western Union instead. Western Union works with the following banks in Turkey:

- Denizbank   444 0800 (www.denizbank.com.tr)
- Dışbank   444 0144 (www.disbank.com.tr)
- Finansbank   444 0900 (www.finansbank.com.tr)
- MNGBank   444 0664 (www.mngbank.com.tr)
- Oyakbank   444 0600 (www.oyakbank.com.tr)

Moneygrams: You can also use a moneygram to send money to a branch of the Koçbank (Tel: 4440555, wwww.kocbank.com.tr) from around 150 countries. Your remittance should reach Turkey in around 10 minutes.

Foreign Exchange Brokers: Most people use their banks to transfer funds from one country to another. However, specialist currency brokers can also make the transfer for you, and often their exchange rates are better. They should also be able to advise on whether it is to your advantage to involve yourself in such financial complexities as spot or forward transactions or limit orders. Some may also be able to advise on offshore banking possibilities.

For a list of foreign exchange brokers, see Appendix VI.

INSURANCE *(SİGORTA)*

Many people live in Turkey for years without any kind of insurance. However, it is worth considering taking out some policies, particularly to cover the cost of private medical treatment. Since power failures and surges are a regular occurrence you might also want to look for a household policy that covers you against losing your appliances to a surge or the contents of your deep-freeze to a prolonged failure. Water problems are also rife in apartment buildings, so make sure your policy covers water damage too. As the crime rate in Istanbul rises, so insurance against theft is starting to look more sensible.

Policies can be bought from banks or from specialised insurance offices. The following types of insurance are available:

- *DASK (Doğal Afet Sigortaları Kurumu* - Natural Disasters Insurance Board). Since the disastrous earthquakes of 1999 it has been obligatory for all householders to take out insurance against *deprem* (earthquake*)* damage
- *Ferdi Kaza* (Personal Accident). Covers you against damaging a third party during an accident.
- *Hırsızlık* (Theft). Covers you against theft in the home. Remember to check for exclusions, maximum payouts on single items and excess payments.
- *İşyeri Güvencesi* (Workplace). Covers your workplace against fire, theft and other hazards.
- *Kapkaç* (Theft). Covers you against pickpocketing, including the loss of your mobile phone.
- *Kasko* (Automobile). Covers you against fire and theft of your car, as well as providing a breakdown service.
- *Kedi Köpek Sağlık* (Pet Health). Covers your pets against veterinary costs.
- *Nakliyat* (Removals). Covers property in transit.
- *Sağlık* (Health). Covers you for treatment in a private hospital. Before buying a policy check which private hospitals it covers and how long you must have been paying the premiums before you can take advantage of it. You normally need to be under 55 to apply for health cover.

- *Seyahat* (Travel). Covers you against theft and sickness while travelling overseas.

- *Yangın* (Fire). Covers you against fire in your home.

- *Yuvam* (Household). Covers your home and belongings against theft and damage as a result of heavy snow, flooding etc. Look out for the usual excess charges and other clauses that mean you will not be paid what you expected.

Insurance Companies: The main insurance companies have branches in all the big towns.

- Ak Sigorta (www.aksigorta.com.tr)
- Anadolu Sigorta (www.anadolusigorta.com.tr)
- Axaoyak (www.axaoyak.com.tr)
- Başak Sigorta (www.basak.com.tr)
- Finans Sigorta (www.finanssigorta.com.tr)
- Güneş Sigorta (www.gunessigorta.com.tr)
- İhlas Sigorta (www.ihlassigorta.com.tr)
- İsviçre Sigorta (www.isvicre-sigorta.com.tr)
- Yapı Kredi Sigorta (www.yksigorta.com.tr)

WHAT IT MEANS	
ilişki(ler)	contact(s)
bilgi	information
online hizmetler	online services
yatırım	payment; deposit; investment
işlem	procedure
destek hizmetleri	support services
hasar ihbarlarınız için	to report damage

SSK: If you are legally employed in Turkey your employer is required to pay for state social security (*sosyal sigorta*) for you. This then covers your medical costs (see p. 299) and retirement benefits (see p. 436). Because it is quite expensive many employers try not to pay the instalments. When agreeing a wage you should check whether it covers social security payments.

Expat Insurance Policies: It is also possible to use an overseas company to insure yourself, especially for medical treatment, while you are living abroad.

For a list of expat insurance companies, see Appendix VI.

CREDIT CARDS *(KREDİ KARTI)*

To apply for a Turkish credit card you need to be a Turkish citizen. However, if you have a large enough sum of money in the bank it may agree to an arrangement whereby a sum of money equal to your credit limit will be blocked in your account. This will not stop you earning interest on the money. However, you will not be able to withdraw the money as long as you keep the card or have a debt outstanding against it. Special permission will be needed for any such arrangement so don't expect the card to materialise in a hurry.

At the time of writing Turkey was starting to use the Chip and Pin system for credit card identification. To get a pin number for your card you usually have to phone a call centre which means that you need enough Turkish to be able to understand the options available; even if the bank advertises assistance in English you may find that this is an automated message system which is not always easy to use. It is often easier to set up a pin number through your Internet banking system than over the phone.

Although credit cards are generally used in the same way as in the West there are a few oddities. It is rarely possible to use a credit card to pay for a transaction over the phone in Turkey. Away from the big cities if you pay for something with a credit card and then decide that it is not what you wanted you will be unable to obtain a refund to the card unless you take it back on the same day that you bought it.

On the positive side you can sometimes use a credit card to pay for something in instalments but without incurring interest (*faizsiz*) which can be a considerable benefit.

There are several different kinds of credit card available and all offer different benefits:

Shop and Miles Cards: The Shop and Miles cards issued by Garanti Bankası (www.shopandmiles.com) allow you to accumulate points towards the purchase of tickets on Turkish Airlines' flights. You will get one point for every three lira that you spend on the card. However, only a few seats on each flight are reserved for card-holders and in summer there may be too few spaces available to meet demand. If you don't use your points within a certain time limit you will lose them.

Sea and Miles Card: Deniz Bank operates a similar scheme that allows you to accumulate points and redeem them for tickets on İDO ferries.

Bonus/Maximum/Axess/World/İdeal Cards: Most banks have credit cards that allow you to accumulate points that can be redeemed for money-off purchases in shops which display the relevant decal.

- Bonus Card (www.bonus.com.tr) Garanti Bankası
- Maximum Card (www.maximum.com.tr) Türkiye İş Bankası
- Axess (www.akbank.com.tr/axess) Akbank
- CardFinans (www.cardfinans.com.tr) Finansbank
- World Card (www.worldcard.com.tr) Yapı Kredi
- İdeal Card (www.disbank.com.tr/en/products/retail_ideal_card.jsp) Fortis.

MORTGAGES (*İPOTEK*)

Turkey has only a vestigial mortgage system. Until recently exorbitant bank interest rates meant that no one could afford to borrow the money to buy a house. At the same time, families traditionally built their own homes – there was no real housing market and so no need for mortgages. This is slowly changing as Turkey brings inflation under control and refines its systems in line with the rest of Europe. However, foreigners are unlikely to be able to borrow the money to buy a house in Turkey from a Turkish bank in the foreseeable future unless they are Turkish citizens.

Turkish Mortgages: For the last couple of years banks have been lending money to enable people to buy a house - look for signs saying something like '*20 yıl vadeyle konut kredisi*' (20-year fixed-term building loan). However, while a 25-year mortgage would be the norm in the UK, in Turkey the banks are likely to suggest that you borrow the money for five or 10 years at the most (20-year loans are available but not much favoured). Interest rates, while fixed, are currently around 20% but you don't have to pay tax on the money borrowed. Normally you will be expected to pay a deposit of around 30% of the value of the property. At the time of writing Turkish banks would only give mortgages to Turkish citizens. There is nothing to stop you pairing up with a Turkish citizen who is in a position to take out a mortgage. However, you should only do this if you know the person well enough to be sure that they are trustworthy. Some estate agents are even taking out loans on behalf of their clients which may or may not be a good thing.

It is expected that a proper mortgage system which will permit people to borrow for up to 25 years will be introduced in 2007.

Building Loans: If you want to start building from scratch instead of buying a house from a previous owner you can apply to the bank for a *konut kredisi* (building loan). This is marginally more expensive than a mortgage, especially considering that you must pay 5% tax on the money borrowed. Again, such loans are only currently available to Turkish citizens.

Re-mortgaging a Property at Home: It is unlikely that a foreign bank would lend you the entire purchase price of a property in Turkey if that was what you said you wanted the money for. But if you can't take out a mortgage in Turkey, there is nothing to stop you re-mortgaging your house overseas in order to raise the money to buy a house in Turkey provided there is adequate equity in it. Nor is there anything to stop you selling your house overseas and using the proceeds of the sale to buy a house in Turkey.

For many people it will be less stressful to deal with a foreign bank, if only because it removes the language difficulties. Despite rumours that some British banks have started lending towards the purchase of properties in Turkey, it is not likely to be easy to persuade an overseas lender to part with money for such a purpose.

OTHER BANK LOANS

Increasingly Turks buy big-ticket items like cars on bank loans. People also have a tendency to take out one big bank loan to consolidate existing smaller loans because the amount of interest to be paid is fixed. As a foreigner you will probably have trouble taking out any kind of loan. However, if you are a Turkish citizen it should not be too difficult. As in the West the bank may want to value any assets you have as security against the loan in which case you will have to complete a property evaluation report.

TAXATION *(VERGİ)*

Once you start working in Turkey you must pay tax on whatever you earn. Most Western countries have double-taxation agreements which ensure that you don't have to pay tax twice on the same amount of money (once in Turkey and once in your native country) but this is something you should always double-check before starting work.

In order to pay tax, you must first get a tax number to identify you (see p. 405) - this is the case even if you only put your money in an interest-generating Turkish bank account. To get a tax number you must go to the Maliye Bakanlığı (tax department), often but not always in the local Valilik.

Double-Taxation Agreements

In theory someone living in Turkey for part of the year and somewhere else for the rest of the year could find themselves subject to taxation on the same income in two separate countries. To avoid this happening Turkey has double-taxation agreements with the following countries:

Albania	Israel	Saudi Arabia
Algeria	Italy	Singapore
Austria	Japan	Slovakia
Azerbaijan	Jordan	Slovenia
Belarus	Kazakhstan	South Korea
Bangladesh	Kyrgzstan	Spain
Belgium	Kuwait	Sudan
Bulgaria	Latvia	Sweden
Czech Republic	Lithuania	Tajikistan
Croatia	Macedonia	TR of Northern Cyprus
China	Malaysia	Tunisia
Denmark	Moldova	Turkmenistan
Egypt	Mongolia	Ukraine
Finland	Netherlands	United Arab Emirates
France	Norway	UK
Germany	Pakistan	USA
Hungary	Poland	Uzbekistan
India	Romania	
Indonesia	Russia	

In 2005 Turkey and New Zealand were discussing a double-taxation agreement. There is currently no such agreement between Turkey and Australia.

Income Tax (*Gelir Vergisi*)

Before moving permanently to Turkey you would be well advised to contact the tax authorities in your home country who should be able to explain the rules on tax residency to you. Turkey regards anyone who spends six months in the country as tax resident, regardless of whether they have legal residency or not. Most countries will also claim you as tax resident if you stay in them for more than a set number of days (183 days in the UK). In theory this could mean you become liable to tax in two countries on the same income. In practise, though, Turkey has double-taxation agreements with many countries to prevent this happening.

In Turkey people earning up to YTL7,000 pay 15% tax, those earning up to YTL16,000 20%, those earning up to YTL40,000 27% and those earning over YTL40,000 35%. If you are letting out your property as a holiday home you could be liable for tax on the entire rental income unless you have bought the house through a company (see p. 103).

It is beyond the scope of this book to describe the Turkish taxation system in detail and anyone who has an income here is strongly advised to take legal advice about their liabilities. There are many exemptions which means that how much you have to pay may not be as much as you might at first fear; you do not, for example, usually have to pay tax on the first YTL600 or so of monthly income as this is regarded as the minimum needed to live on. Nor do you pay tax on your social security contributions. Some workers are exempt from income tax. Such lucky people include journalists and academics who are in Turkey on fixed contracts.

The Turkish tax year runs from 1 January to 31 December and tax is calculated and paid on what was earned during that period in February-March of the following year (i.e. you pay tax on money earned between January and December 2006 in February/March 2007). Tax is then paid in four instalments; late payment attracts a 4% penalty. Employers are usually responsible for deducting tax payments for their staff who do not have to fill out an individual tax form.

WHERE TO FIND MORE INFORMATION

- *www.pwcglobal.com* Website of the PriceWaterhouseCoopers accountancy firm with a number of useful tax guides
- *www.needanadviser.com* Financial experts on hand to give you personal advice

Britain: The UK has a double-taxation agreement with Turkey which means you should not have to pay tax in both countries. If you don't want to continue paying tax in the UK you will have to prove to the Inland Revenue that you are no longer resident there. Before leaving you should contact the Inspector of Taxes at your local tax office. In order to accept that you are no longer liable for UK taxes they will probably want to see proof that you have disposed of your home in the UK and have either bought or are renting a property in Turkey. Even if you still own a house in the UK you may be able to prove that you are no longer resident although if you rent out that house you will have to pay tax on the income.

If you only intend to stay in Turkey temporarily you will need to be careful not to return to Britain for more than 183 days in any one year (or 91 days a year averaged out for four years). If you exceed that time period, you will once again become liable to UK income tax. The Inland Revenue sets out the answer to other frequently answered questions at www.inlandrevenue.gov.uk/international/faqs.htm. It also has a questionnaire which it uses to establish whether someone is or is not tax-resident in the UK.

WHO TO CONTACT

The Centre for Non-Residents (CNR): Tel: 0151-472 6196, www.inlandrevenue.gov.uk/cnr, St John's House, Merton Rd, Bootle, Merseyside L69 9BB, UK

INVESTING IN TURKEY *(TÜRKİYE'DE YATIRIM YAPMAK)*

Until recently few people would have considered investing in Turkey because of its shaky economic history and astronomic inflation rates. However, as the government has got to grips with inflation and the economy has started to recover from the 2001 crisis, so Turkey, like other emerging markets, has started to look like quite a good bet for careful investment.

Bank Accounts: At the time of writing fixed-term Turkish lira bank accounts were paying considerably more interest than those in the West; rates of around 16% for large investments were not uncommon. This reflected the fact that inflation still stood at between 10% and 12%, and that taking out a loan in Turkey was still costing around 20% per annum. It therefore makes sense to invest capital in a Turkish bank provided that you choose the bank carefully and remember that you are only guaranteed to get up to YTL50,000 back should the bank collapse.

Money can be invested on what is called '*repo*', a system of time depositing whereby the rate of interest you are paid depends on how long you leave the money in the bank. Although you earn daily interest on your money, you get a higher rate of interest if you guarantee to leave it untouched for one or three months. You can still withdraw the money if you need to although you would lose the extra interest.

Istanbul Stock Exchange (*Borsa*): Since 2002 the Turkish Stock Exchange (www.ise.org) has been booming, with some stocks rising by up to 50%. However, these rises came after a period in which many people saw their investments plummet in value; there is no guarantee that such returns will continue. Blue-chip companies like Turkish Airlines, the Sabancı companies and those producing concrete probably remain some of the safest bets.

Most banks have advisors on hand to help you decide which companies to invest in.

WHO TO CONTACT

Istanbul Stock Exchange (İMKB): Tel: 0212-298 2100, www.ise.org, Reşitpaşa Mahallesi, Tuncay Artun Caddesi, Emirgan, Istanbul

GETTING INTO DEBT

Over the last 10 years the use of credit cards has become commonplace in Turkey, with the familiar consequence that some people have run up unpayable bills. However, Turkish banks will not normally give credit cards to non-Turkish citizens (see p. 257).

If you borrow money from someone to cover a debt (*borç*) you will be asked to sign one or more *senet*s (promissory notes) which commit you to repaying the money. When you repay the money you must retrieve the *senet*, sign it and tear through the official stamp on it as proof that the debt has been paid. If you cannot produce the signed and torn *senet* it would be possible for someone to claim that the debt was still outstanding. If someone fails to honour an outstanding *senet* the person to whom the money is owed can go to court to have debt payment enforced. This can result in the courts ordering the seizure of the debtor's assets, including their home.

WHAT TO SAY			
accountant	*muhasebe*	personal banking	*bireysel bankacılık*
addition	*toplama*	plus	*artı*
bank loan	*kredi*	price	*fiyat*
bill/invoice	*fatura*	quantity/amount	*miktar*
branch	*şube(si)*	rate of exchange	*kur*
capital	*sermaye*	receipt	*makbuz/fiş*
cash deposit	*para yatırma*	receipt form	*tahsilat belgesi*
charge	*masraf*	remainder	*bakiye*
commission	*komisyon*	sender	*gönderici*
date	*tarih*	subtraction	*çıkarma*
division	*bölme*	tax	*tahsilat/vergi*
fixed term	*vade*	to borrow	*borç/ödünç almak*
guarantor	*kefil*	to lend	*borç/ödünç vermek*
investment	*yatırım*	to multiply	*çoğaltmak*
loose change	*bozuk para*	total	*tutar/toplam*
minus	*eksi*	useable amount	*kullanılabilir bakiye*
paper money	*kâğıt para*	value	*değer*
percent (e.g. *yüzde seksen* – 80%)	*yüzde*		

CHAPTER 12

SHOPPING TRIPS

Increasingly, Turkey seems like two completely different countries when it comes to shopping. These days there is almost nothing that can't be found with a bit of hunting about in Istanbul, Ankara or Izmir. This is partly the result of globalisation which means that more overseas produce is now available in the shops and partly a response to increasing affluence in some parts of the country, which means that there is a growing market for better quality household goods, clothes etc.

However, away from the big cities, shopping in the average Turkish super-market will still come as a shock to people from Western countries who are used to being spoilt for choice. If you see something you like - especially if it's an imported item - buy it immediately. It may not grace the shelves again.

SHOPPING HOURS (*MESAİ/ÇALIŞMA SAATLERİ*)

In Turkey it is a rare shop that is only open from 9am to 5pm five or six days a week; more usual is the shop that opens at 7.30am and is still open at 8pm or 9pm daily, even if it is only selling groceries. In tourist areas general stores and shops selling items specifically aimed at tourists will often stay open until midnight. Supermarkets are often open from 10am until 10pm.

However, if you are going to shop for white goods or furniture in a big town it is probably wise to assume the shop may be shut on Sunday; always phone to check before setting out. Even if a shop would normally be closed, phoning to say that you are coming to buy something specific may result in it being opened again specially for you.

One quirk of shopping in Turkey is arriving to find that the shop is closed for half-an-hour or so while the *patron* (shopkeeper) goes to the mosque. This is particularly likely to be the case on Fridays around lunchtime when even men who don't bother at other times in the week shut up shop to pray.

For details of public holidays when shops may be closed, see p. 321.

> **'Buyurun'**
>
> The single most irritating word in Turkish, *'buyurun'* can mean 'after you', 'here's the money', 'can I help you?' and many other things. The problem arises when your Turkish is not very robust. *'Buyurun?'* the cheery shopkeeper says and stands right beside you waiting for <u>you</u> to reply. Except that you can't.

THE SHOPPING EXPERIENCE

Many shops in Turkey are exactly like those in the West; these days supermarkets have bar codes on all their products and these are scanned at the checkout where you are given exactly the same itemised receipt as you would be at home. However, some aspects of shopping in Turkey will still seem strange to a foreigner. For example, if you come from a country where it is very hard to catch a shop assistant's eye, it may feel uncomfortable to find Turkish shop assistants following you around the store as if you were a potential shoplifter. Tempting as it is to turn tail and run, you'd be well advised to learn to turn this enthusiasm to help to your advantage so that the shopping experience becomes more pleasant and companionable.

WHERE TO SHOP			
alcohol retailer	*tekel bayii*	gift shop	*hediyelik eşya dükkânı*
bakery	*fırın*	greengrocer	*manav*
bookshop	*kitabevi*	haberdashery	*tuhafiyeci*
butcher	*kasap*	hardware store	*nalburiye/hırdavatçı*
cakeshop	*pastane*	jeweller	*kuyumcu/mücevherci*
camera shop	*fotoğrafçı*	kitchen shop	*zücaciyeci*
carpet shop	*halıcı*	large store	*mağaza*
delicatessen	*şarküteri*	newsagent's	*gazete bayii*
draper's shop	*kumaşçı*	perfumery	*parfümeri*
dried fruit and nuts shop	*kuruyemişçi*	record shop	*plakçı*
fishmonger's	*balıkçı*	shopping centre	*alışveriş merkezi (AVM)*
florist	*çiçekçi*	stationery shop	*kırtasiye*
general store	*bakkal/market/dükkân*	toyshop	*oyuncakçı*

There are also many quirks to shopping in Turkey. In rural areas you will still be sold eggs without boxes, brooms without handles and pans without brushes. You will find it extremely difficult to buy six place settings for a table since most Turks buy for huge extended families and want at least 12 of everything (forget buying just one of anything!). Curious assortments of things may also be on sale in the same shop: keys with tombstones, for example, or Korans with foam to stuff pillows.

Turkish shopkeepers may also observe unfamiliar customs. Some will, for example, roll out their prayer mats and pray in the shop right in front of you (don't interrupt lest they have to start the ritual all over again). Often tea will be summoned from a nearby tea-house to lubricate the sales patter. If you arrive when the staff are eating, more food may be ordered so that you can join them. And if you are the first customer of the day don't be surprised if the shopkeeper throws your money (*siftah*) on the floor, then picks it up again and touches it to his chin for good luck.

BEWARE!

Even supermarkets sometimes leave items on their shelves when they are long past their sell-by date - this is most likely to happen in small, out-of-the-way locations and in winter. Items left in a freezer during a prolonged power cut often go bad but are still left on sale - this includes such seemingly innocuous items as ice cream.

HOW MANY DO YOU WANT?

bir	one	*on iki*	twelve
iki	two	*yirmi*	twenty
üç	three	*otuz*	thirty
dört	four	*kırk*	forty
beş	five	*elli*	fifty
altı	six	*altmış*	sixty
yedi	seven	*yetmiş*	seventy
sekiz	eight	*seksen*	eighty
dokuz	nine	*doksan*	ninety
on	ten	*yüz*	one hundred
on bir	eleven	*bin*	one thousand

Theoretically Turks believe that the customer is always right. However, the compensation culture is yet to take root here so you should not assume that this will always translate into speedy redress if something you bought proves defective. Shopkeepers are often reluctant to admit that they don't have what you want and may persist in trying to sell you something in a different colour or size or even a completely different item, no matter how much you protest.

I'd like to buy...	...almak istiyorum
I'll take it.	Alıyorum
Do you want anything else?	Başka bir arzunuz var mı?
Do you have another one?	Başka var mı?
Could you keep it for me?	Benim için ayırır mısınız?
I want to return this.	Bunu geri vermek istiyorum
Can you give me a receipt?	Fiş alabilir miyim?
How much is that altogether?	Hepsi ne kadar?
I don't want it.	İstemiyorum
There are none left	Kalmadı
Can I have my money back?	Paramı geri alabilir miym?
I'm just looking.	Sadece bakıyorum
Can I look at that?	Şuna bakabilir miyim?
We have/we stock...	Var/bulunur
There's one in the window	Vitrinde bir tane var
That's enough, thanks	Yeterli, teşekkür ederim

Bargaining (*Pazarlık Yapmak*): Most people assume that Middle Eastern-style bargaining is still routine in Turkey. In reality, however, fixed prices are becoming the norm except in rural areas, in markets, in small family-run businesses and in the poorer south-east generally.

When is bargaining still appropriate? Well, if you are shopping somewhere touristy like the Grand Bazaar (Kapalı Çarşı), then you *must* continue to bargain if you don't want to pay over the odds – shopkeepers in places like that know that tourists expect to bargain and adjust their prices upwards accordingly. Elsewhere, however, even some carpet shops have fixed prices although they are rarely displayed.

It is still worth bargaining if you are buying several of a particular item or if you will be spending a lot of money in a single shop; for example, if you intend to buy all your light fitments in one shop you might want to 'discuss' the price with the owner to get a decent discount (*indirim/tenzilat*) and perhaps another small item thrown in free (*bedava/ücretsiz*).

In general you don't bargain for groceries or other household goods, and supermarkets display the prices of all items on the shelves. On the other hand if you are buying white goods from a shop such as Arçelik where you might assume the price would be fixed, it may be possible to get a discount, especially if you – or your friend – knows the shopkeeper, or if you are buying several items at the same time. Many clothes shops are also receptive to bargaining. An offer to pay in cash (*nakit*), rather than with your credit card, often acts as an incentive for the shop owner to give you a discount.

Tourists often haggle over the price of bus tickets. If you live in a town with a big tourist trade the bus company is likely to volunteer a reduction if they know you. Elsewhere you should assume bus fares are fixed, as are dolmuş and train fares.

If you are travelling around Turkey for business you may want to negotiate a reduction in the price of your hotel room, especially if you are staying for several days. It is not the norm to walk into a business-class hotel and immediately pay the amount listed behind the reception desk – often you can get away with half or two-thirds of that price.

The most important thing is to try and get a feel for the value of the lira and what things are actually worth so that you will come to know when a vendor probably expects you to barter. Unfortunately this takes time. But even Westerners who are uncomfortable with bargaining should be able to round prices down without feeling awkward.

Virtually unobtainable	
Ground nutmeg	Vegemite/Marmite
Condensed/evaporated milk	Indian curry pastes
Vanilla essence	Self-raising flour
Non-cube brown sugar	Caster sugar
Treacle/golden syrup	Blueberries
Salt & vinegar crisps	All Bran
Limes/lime juice	Pecan nuts
Marshmallows	Custard powder
Cranberry sauce	Mince pies
White vinegar	Creamed corn
Gelatine	Popadums
Couscous	Weetabix

Very expensive and/or hard to find	
Foreign cheeses (Edam, Parmesan, etc)	Ready-made baby food
Imported mustard	Prawn crackers
Pet food/pet toys	Basil
Canned fruit	Fresh pineapple
Veal	Wine/imported alcohol
Coconuts/coconut milk	Haircare products
Kidney beans	Pasteurised milk
Hermesetas	Sensodyne toothpaste
Taco shells	Maple syrup
Pork products	Fresh coriander

What's Cheap and What's Not: In general it is safe to assume that any items wanted only by foreigners will be expensive, especially where they have to be imported. So you must expect to pay more for Kellogg's Cornflakes, real Cheddar cheese, fruit-flavoured yoghurts etc. Cat and dog food is also horribly expensive by Western standards since it is all imported.

SPOTTING A BARGAIN	
The following signs all indicate price reductions:	
1 alana, 1 bedava	Buy one, get one free
2 al, 1 öde	Buy two, pay for one
Bitiriyoruz	Closing down sale
Etiketin yarısı	Half marked price
Havale indirimi	Discount for payment direct into bank account – benefit often cancelled out by bank transfer (*havale*) fee
İndirim/tenzilat	Discount
Nakit indirimi	Discount for cash payment
Tüm ürünlerde %... indirim	...% discount on all products
Yazlık ürünlerde %60 indirim	Summer items 60% off

Peşin or Taksit? When you are buying big-ticket items you will usually see two prices displayed: one for paying in full (*peşin*) and another for paying in instalments (*taksit*). As ever, you pay extra for the convenience of paying in instalments. You are also likely to be able to negotiate a discount for paying in full in cash (*nakit*).

HOW MUCH IS THAT?	
bargain-priced	*indirimli*
cheap	*ucuz*
expensive	*pahalı*
How much is a kilo/one?	*Kilosu/tanesi ne kadar?*
How much?	*Ne kadar? Kaç para?*

Surprisingly, it is sometimes possible to use your credit card to pay by instalments without incurring extra interest payments. However, some shops won't accept credit-card payments at all because of the commission (*komisyon*) charged to the vendor.

I'D LIKE TO PAY WITH...	
cash	*nakit*
credit card	*kredi kartı*

FOOD *(YİYECEK)* AND DRINK *(İÇECEK)*

Shopping Baskets

Turkey is a great place to shop for food, provided you don't expect too much variety. Even supermarkets usually stock only larger quantities of a similar range of goods to those found at your neighbourhood *bakkal*. However, the quality of the fruit, vegetables, eggs, cheese, meat and fish available at the various markets (*pazar*) is usually extremely high.

For information about shopping for babies see p. 212.

Milk *(Süt)* and Milk Products *(Süt Ürünleri)*

Supermarkets usually sell one type of milk as a loss-leader but away from Istanbul, Ankara and Izmir you will look in vain for pasteurised fresh milk (*günlük pastörize süt*). Instead the norm is packeted long-life milk (*uzun ömürlü süt*). The Pınar Company sells organic milk for a third as much again as a litre of the non-organic variety. You can also buy low-fat (*yarım yağlı*) milk and milk fortified with vitamins or calcium in most big supermarkets.

Yoghurt (*yoğurt*) is available everywhere although the fruit-flavoured versions are not so easy to find except in towns and tourist areas.

Butter *(Tereyağı)* & Margarine *(Margarin)*: Turks eat more margarine than butter and consequently butter is considerably more expensive. You can find margarine made from olive oil and mixed plant oils.

The Weekly Shop	YTL		YTL
Eggs (yumurta)	1.25 (12)	White cheese (beyaz peynir)	4.20 (500gr)
Milk(süt)	1.20 (litre)	Bread (ekmek)	0.25 (loaf)
Yoghurt (yoğurt)	1.20 (500gr)	Rice (pirinç)	2.75 (1kg)
Tomatoes (domates)	1.35 (1kg)	Cucumber (salatalık/hıyar)	0.50 (one)
Potatoes (patates)	1.20 (1kg)	Onions (soğan)	0.75 (1kg)
Green pepper (yeşil biber)	1.00 (1kg)	Tomato paste (salça)	2.00 (litre)
Pasta (makarna)	0.80 (500gr)	Margarine/butter (margarin/ tereyağı)	1.00 (250gr)/3.00 (250gr)
Lettuce (yeşil salata)	1.00 (1kg)	Chicken (tavuk)	3.80 (1kg)
Herbs (şifalı otlar)	0.75 (1kg)	Mince (kıyma)	2.50 (250gr)
Apples (elma)	0.90 (1kg)	Oranges (portakal)	1.00 (1kg)
Garlic (sarımsak)	2.50 (1kg)	Olives (zeytin)	3.20 (500gr)
Coffee (kahve)	8.75 (100gr)	Tea (çay)	8.80 (100 bags)
Sugar (şeker)	1.60 (900gr)	Biscuits (bisküvi)	0.75 (packet)
Cereal/muesli (müsli)	3.25 (250gr)	Fruit juice (meyve suyu)	1.50 (litre)
Honey (bal)	3.40 (225gr)	Jam (reçel)	1.00 (650gr)

Cheese (Peynir): Turkey has many different regional cheeses. However, the most commonly available cheeses are *beyaz peynir* (white cheese), a soft sheep's or cow's cheese, and *kaşar peyniri* (yellow cheese), which looks rather like Cheddar. Like Cheddar, *kaşar* can be bought in different strengths - if you like your cheese strong look for *eski kaşar*. White cheeses have usually been matured either in a metal drum (*teneke)* or in a goat or sheepskin (*tulum).* Goat's cheese is *keçi peyniri.*

Eggs (Yumurta)

Eggs are very cheap but are not sold by size as in the West; supermarkets often sell smaller eggs than local shops or street traders. Although eggs bought from local shops may have come from free-range chickens, those on sale in supermarkets are likely to have come from factory-farmed birds. Not all eggs come in boxes so it's wise to hold onto at least one box when you find one. Often they are sold in huge trays, which make things hard for solo shoppers.

The Monthly Shop	YTL		YTL
Cooking oil *(sıvıyağ)*	3.50 (litre, corn)	Batteries *(pil)*	4.90 (4 x AAA)
Toothpaste *(diş macunu)*	1.00 (50ml)	Soap *(sabun)*	0.20 (bar)
Shampoo/conditioner *(şampuan/saç kremi)*	4.60 (400ml)/ 6.00 (200ml)	Washing powder *(çamaşır tozu)*	7.50 (2.5kg)
Fabric conditioner *(yumuşatıcı)*	1.60 (1kg)	Bleach *(çamaşır suyu)*	0.90 (1kg)
Water/soda water *(su/ maden suyu)*	0.45 (1.5 litres)/ 0.20 (small bottle)	Toilet paper *(tuvalet kâğıdı)*	3.45 (12 rolls)
Paper towels *(kâğıt havlu)*	2.50 (2 rolls)	Deodorant *(deodorant)*	3.50 (bottle
Aluminium foil *(alüminyum folyo)*	2.00 (roll)	Washing-up liquid *(bulaşık deterjanı)*	1.60 (750gr)
Flour *(un)*	0.65 (500gr)		

Bread *(Ekmek)*

Wherever you go in Turkey, there is likely to be a bakery *(fırın)*, and unsliced white loaves *(beyaz ekmek)* are readily available and very cheap (YTL0.25). In towns you will be able to buy a wider range of breads, including some brown breads *(siyah ekmek)* and soft, flat *pide* bread. However, in the villages you can usually buy only standard white loaves. The supermarkets often have their own bakeries which turn out a more interesting range of breads and rolls, including wholemeal *(kepekli)* and rye *(çavdar)* bread. Packeted sliced bread for toast is also available in the supermarkets.

Particularly tasty breads to look out for include thick rounds of *Trabzon ekmeği; taş odun ekmeği* which has been baked over wood in a stone oven; and *bazlama*, a heavy white bread which is tasty toasted.

Meat (*Et*) & Fish (*Balık*)

Most Turkish meat is of high quality although the best cuts can be expensive. Mince *(kıyma)* is usually prepared in front of you and you can choose to have more expensive cuts minced if you prefer it fat-free *(yağsız)*. Reputable suppliers of fresh chickens include Banvit, Erpiliç, Mudurnu and Ömur.

Unless you have been told otherwise you should assume that all meat has been prepared using the *helal* method decreed by Islam. This involves slitting the animal's throat and hanging it to ensure that all the blood has been drained from the meat.

Away from the coast fishmongers' shops are not as common as butcher's shops. Where they do exist you can ask them to remove the head and bones for you - a small tip is expected for doing this.

At the Butcher *(Kasapta)*

beef	*sığır eti*	pork	*domuz eti*
brain	*beyin*	rabbit	*tavşan*
breast	*göğüs*	rump	*but*
chicken	*tavuk/piliç*	salami	*salam*
duck	*ördek*	sausage	*sosis*
garlic sausage	*sucuk*	sirloin steak	*bonfile*
ham	*jambon*	skinless sausage	*soyulmuş sosis*
heart	*yürek*	sliced meat	*kuşbaşı et*
kidneys	*böbrek*	steak	*biftek*
lamb	*kuzu eti*	tongue	*dil*
lamb chop/cutlet	*pirzola*	trotters	*paça*
liver	*ciğer*	turkey	*hindi*
mince	*kıyma*	wing	*kanat*
offal	*sakatat*	Please trim off the fat	*Lütfen yağını çıkartınız*
pastrami	*pastırma*		

At the Fishmonger *(Balıkçıda)*

anchovy	*hamsi*	red coralfish	*mercan*
black bream	*karagöz*	red mullet	*barbunya*
bluefish	*lüfer*	salmon	*somon*
bonito	*palamut*	sardine	*sardalya*
crab	*yengeç*	sea bass	*levrek*
gilt-head bream	*çipura*	shrimps	*karides*
grey mullet	*kefal*	sole	*dil balığı*
lobster	*istakoz*	squid	*kalamar*
mackerel	*uskumru/istavrit*	swordfish	*kılıç balığı*
mussels	*midye*	trout	*alabalık*
octopus	*ahtapot*	tuna fish	*ton balığı*
prawns	*karides*	turbot	*kalkan*
Please take the head off		*Lütfen kafasını çıkartınız*	
Please clean this		*Lütfen temizleyiniz*	

Fruit (*Meyve*) & Vegetables (*Sebze*)

In general the quality of fruit and vegetables on sale in Turkey is extremely high; for those used to pre-packaged Western products it can come as a pleasant surprise to discover just how tasty, for example, tomatoes can be when they have not been forced. Some fruit and vegetables also grow to proportions that would not be normal in the West; Diyarbakır, in particular, is renowned for its outsize watermelons.

Seasonality is still very important, with fruits like melons and apricots in abundant supply in summer, and grapes and apples commonplace in autumn. Citrus fruits are cheap and ubiquitous in spring. These days some fruits such as strawberries are forced in greenhouses in order to get them into the shops out of season, but, as in the West, the end results tend to lack the flavour of fruits allowed to mature at their own pace.

Of course you cannot buy the same range of fruit and veg as you could in a city such as London or New York. Kiwi fruits (*kivi*) are becoming more common, and pineapples (*ananas*) are starting to put in an appearance but it is hard to find fresh blackberries (*böğürtlen*) or raspberries (*frambuaz*). Seedless grapes (*çekirdeksiz üzüm*) from the Izmir region are also much harder to find than the seeded variety. Bananas (*muz*) from around Manavgat and Anamur are regarded as particularly tasty and are cheaper than the imported variety. Avocados (*avokado*) are sometimes available but usually expensive. Most herbs are easy to find, with rocket (*roka*) especially tasty.

Supermarkets usually stock fruit and vegetables although the smaller chains often sell poor quality, overpriced produce - you are usually better off with a specialist greengrocer. In supermarkets and large greengrocer's don't forget to bag up your produce and take it to be weighed before proceeding to the checkout counter.

Rice (*Pirinç*) & Pasta (*Makarna*)

Turks eat a lot of rice and pasta. They also often cook bulgur wheat (*bulgur*) into various pilafs to give them a more interesting texture. Supermarkets are always well-stocked with rice and pasta in a variety of shapes; the best ordinary rice is the *baldo* variety. Increasingly you can also find brown rice and pasta, as well as jasmine rice, albeit at marked-up prices.

At the Greengrocer *(Manavda)*

Fruit *(Meyve)*

apple	elma	peach	şeftali
apricot	kayısı	pear	armut
banana	muz	persimmon	hurma
cherry	kiraz	pineapple	ananas
date	hurma	plum	erik
fig	incir	pomegranate	nar
grape	üzüm	quince	ayva
grapefruit	greyfurt	raspberry	ahududu
mandarin	mandalina	sour cherry	vişne
melon	kavun	strawberry	çilek
mulberry	dut	watermelon	karpuz
orange	portakal		

Vegetables *(Sebze)*

artichoke	enginar	leek	pırasa
asparagus	kuşkonmaz	lettuce	yeşil salata
aubergine/eggplant	patlıcan	mushroom	mantar
avocado	avokado	okra	bamya
beans	fasulye	onion	soğan
beetroot	pancar	peas	bezelye
Brussels sprout	brüksel lahanası	potato	patates
cabbage	lahana	pumpkin	balkabağı
carrot	havuç	radish	kırmızı turp
cauliflower	karnıbahar	red cabbage	kırmızı lahana
celery	kereviz sapı	red pepper	kırmızı biber
celery root	kereviz	rocket	roka
chickpeas	nohut	spinach	ıspanak
cucumber	salatalık	tomato	domates
garlic	sarımsak	zucchini/courgette	kabak
green pepper	yeşil biber		

Coffee (*Kahve*) & Tea (*Çay*)

While you can find a full range of leaf and bag teas, including herbal and fruit teas, in all the supermarkets, finding fresh coffee (or even Jacobs instant coffee) is a much taller order in a country where Nescafe has been king for many years. Caffeine-free (*kafeinsiz*) instant coffee and ground (*filtre*) coffee can also be found in major supermarkets now. Otherwise, head for your nearest branch of Starbucks to stock up.

WHAT'S FOR TEA?			
apple tea	*elma çayı*	linden tea	*ıhlamur çayı*
camomile tea	*papatya çayı*	mint tea	*nane çayı*
fennel tea	*rezene çayı*	rosehip tea	*kuşburnu çayı*
green tea	*yeşil çay*	sage tea	*adaçayı*
instant orange tea	*oralet*	teabag	*poşet çay*
lemon tea	*limon çayı*		

Alcohol (*Alkol*)

Because of the Islamic prohibition on the sale of alcohol not all shops will stock it. In particular supermarkets run by religious foundations and families such as Yimpaş, Beğendik and Alfa do not sell alcohol. On the other hand, large and small supermarkets owned by major or foreign companies (such as Migros, Gima, Dia, Şok and others) carry a decent ranges of wines and beers, and sometimes even hard liquor.

Compared with most Western countries there are few other alcohol retailers - look out for signs saying 'Tekel Bayii' (Tekel distributor) when you want to buy alcohol, although many small groceries in the major cities will carry beer and wine.

WHAT TO ASK FOR			
beer	*bira*	red	*kırmızı*
bottle of wine	*bir şişe şarap*	sparkling	*köpüklü*
brandy	*konyak*	vodka	*votka*
draught beer	*fıçı bira*	whisky	*viski*
dry	*sek*	white	*beyaz*
gin	*cin*	wine	*şarap*
medium dry	*demi sek*	with ice	*buzlu*

If it is important to you that a product should be completely alcohol-free, look for labels reading *alkolsuz*.

Sweets (*Şekerleme*) & Chocolate (*Çikolata*)

Turkey may be best known for its chewy Turkish delight but this appears to be more popular with tourists than locals. Turks themselves seem to prefer wrapped chocolate fondants and hard sugary sweets called *akide*. They are also fond of incredibly sugary *pişmaniye* from Konya and chocolate-coated horse chestnuts (*kestane*) from Bursa. *Helva* is eaten in a wide variety of forms; *yaş helva* (wet helva) is more like marzipan than what Westerners normally think of as helva.

The Turkish chocolate-making company Ülker/Alpella specialises in producing local versions of familiar Western products; its Balmond brand, for example, is distinguishable from a Toblerone only by its shape, while its Kranç is like a Nestle Crunch bar.

In Istanbul, along İstiklal Caddesi, you will see shops selling big blocks of (often nutty) chocolate wrapped in silver paper. It's easy to assume that this is a smuggled product. Instead it is Meşhur Beyoğlu Çikolata, a brand popular as a reminder of Istanbul childhoods.

SPICES (BAHARAT)...			
allspice	*yenibahar*	nutmeg	*muskat*
black pepper	*karabiber*	paprika	*tatlı kırmızı biber*
caraway seeds	*keraviye*	peppercorns	*tane biber*
cardamom	*kakule*	pine nut	*çamfıstığı*
cayenne/chilli pepper	*acı biber*	poppy seed	*haşhaş tohumu*
cinnamon	*tarçın*	saffron	*safran*
cloves	*karanfil*	salt	*tuz*
coconut	*hindistan cevizi*	sesame	*susam*
cumin	*kimyon*	sumac	*sumak*
curry powder	*köri*	turmeric	*zerdeçal*
ginger	*zencefil*	vanilla	*vanilya*

Ice cream (*Dondurma*)

Turkey is renowned for a particular type of ice cream so thick that it can be eaten with a knife and fork. It hails from Kahramanmaraş in the east, but these days is sold with great ceremony by costumed ice cream vendors all around

Turkey. That doesn't mean that you can't buy the usual range of packeted ice creams, some of which are produced by Algida (in collaboration with Walls) and Ülker/Alpella. You can also buy the sort of ice cream that comes in scoops and cones in most big towns. The biggest name in local ice cream sales is Mado which has 66 branches in Istanbul alone.

...AND HERBS *(ŞİFALI OTLAR)*			
basil	*fesleğen*	mint	*nane*
bay leaves	*defne yaprağı*	oregano	*yabani mercanköşk*
capers	*kapari*	parsley	*maydanoz*
chicory	*radika*	rosemary	*biberiye*
coriander seeds	*kişniş*	sage	*adaçayı*
dill	*dereotu*	sorrel	*kuzukulağı*
fennel seed	*rezene*	tarragon	*tarhun*
marjoram	*mercanköşk*	thyme	*kekik*

LOCAL SHOPS

Most shopping is done at local *'markets'* (also known as *dükkâns* or *bakkals*) which are simply grocery shops rather like the corner shops in the UK or convenience stores in the USA. These shops usually sell basic foodstuffs as well as standard household cleaning materials, cigarettes, newspapers, phonecards, etc. If you go out without your money a neighbourhood shop may let you run up a tab for later payment. However, prices at local stores are often higher than in the supermarkets, especially in tourist areas.

SUPERMARKETS & HYPERMARKETS

Given that Turkey has had Western-style supermarkets for less than 20 years it is astonishing to discover that they have already captured one-third of the grocery market; already there are signs that they will drive out the small grocery shops and street markets in the same way that they already have done in the UK and USA.

The experience of shopping in a Turkish supermarket will be familiar, with prices clearly displayed on the shelves and machines to check the prices of any items that have been overlooked. At the checkout you will be presented with an itemised receipt and will be able to pay with a Turkish credit or debit card. The main difference manifests itself in the more limited range of goods on sale and the greater emphasis on service - you may, for example, be helped to load your shopping into your car (for complex reasons the person who does this may appreciate being 'tipped' with your receipt).

IN THE SUPERMARKET *(SÜPERMARKETTE)*	
frozen food	*dondurulmuş yiyecekler*
free customer transport	*müşteri servisi*
ready-prepared meals	*hazır yemek*
tinned	*konserve*
use before (date)	*son kullanma tarihi (SKT)/tarihinden önce tüketilmelidir*

The major supermarket chains are:

- Alfa
- Beğendik (www.begendik.com.tr)
- Bim (www.bim.com.tr)
- Carrefour (www.carrefour.com.tr)
- Dia
- Gima (www.gima.com.tr)
- Kipa (www.kipa.com.tr)
- Macro
- Metro
- Migros (www.migros.com.tr)
- REAL
- Şok (www.migros.com.tr/magazalar_sok_bul.asp)
- Tansaş (www.tansas.com.tr)
- Tespo
- Yimpaş (www.yimpas.com.tr)

Although most supermarkets sell a similar range of products there are a few things that distinguish them. Alfa, Yimpaş and Beğendik, for example, are owned by religious companies, which translates into headscarfed women at the check-out and no alcohol for sale. Carrefour, however, is partially French-owned, Makro is German-owned and Kipa is part-owned by the British retail giant Tesco. Once Swiss-owned, Migros is now part of the vast Koç group and offers an online shopping service and a range of own-brand products. Bim sells a more limited selection of goods but advertises that it sells retail goods at wholesale prices. Şok (part of the Migros group) and Dia sell a smaller range of goods but at discounted prices. Tespo and Makro are cash-and-carry wholesale outlets - you need a membership card to use them.

Increasingly the supermarkets have large out-of-town and shopping-mall stores as well as smaller city-centre branches. Migros, for example, designates its stores with between one and three Ms to indicate their size and the range of goods available: a one-M Migros sells roughly the same items as a corner *bakkal*, a two-M Migros has a wider range of goods and a three-M Migros sells everything from clothes and stationery to food and electrical goods (there are also Migros hypermarkets in Istanbul, Ankara, Antalya, Gaziantep and Ordu).

Most of the big supermarket chains offer customer-loyalty schemes; you hand your card over at the check-out desk to be credited with points. To find out how many points have been credited to your card you usually go to the customer services desk (*müşteri hizmetleri*). The points can then be offset against purchases in the store or against special offers. You don't have to be a Turkish citizen to have one of these cards - just ask on your next visit to the store and the cashier will fill out the necessary paperwork and issue the card on the spot. Migros and Gima charge YTL1 for their cards but you can easily earn that back buying a single item that is on special offer. The Carrefour card is free but you only earn points on one day a week (which varies with the store); on other days the card entitles you to discounts on certain items.

Look out, too, for two-for-the-price-of-one offers and other marketing wheezes familiar from the West. Just before Ramazan there are often many special offers, including money-back coupons that have to be used within a certain time frame.

STREET MARKETS *(HALK PAZARI)*

The best places to shop for fruit and vegetables remain the street markets which take place almost everywhere in Turkey on a weekly basis. Usually the same stallholders visit a sequence of towns in one area one after another. For example, in Cappadocia it is market day in Nevşehir on Monday; in Göreme on Wednesday; in Avanos on Friday; and in Ürgüp on Saturday. On the Bodrum Peninsula it is market day in Türkbükü on Monday; in Gölköy on Tuesday; in Bitez, Gümüşlük, Gündoğ and Ortakent on Wednesday; in Bitez and Yalıkavak on Thursday; in Turgutreis on Saturday; and in Gümbet on Sunday. Except for along the coast, most street markets are aimed at locals rather than visitors. However, coastal markets may also sell items such as fake branded jeans, handbags and souvenirs for tourists.

As well as fruit and veg, most street markets sell a range of fresh cheeses, eggs, some meat, dry biscuits, cleaning materials, some clothes and some fabrics. There will also be a range of plastic goods: washing baskets, washing-up bowls etc. Usually you will be able to choose material for curtains or sheets and arrange to have it made up during the week and delivered to you at the market when the stallholder calls again. Likewise you may be able to organise alterations to clothes which can be brought back to you, adjusted according to specification, a week later. In spring some markets also sell plants, flowers and soil.

Depending on where you are you may also be able to buy local specialities at the market. For example, the Bolu market sells locally-grown mushrooms, while the Uzunköprü market sells fine baskets made by Thracian gypsies.

WHERE TO GO

Istanbul

- *Balıkpazarı:* Covered fish market opposite Galatasaray Lisesi on İstiklal Caddesi. Stalls selling freshly fried mussels. Also fruit and vegetables.
- *Beşiktaş Çarşısı:* Across road from Beşiktaş ferry terminal, small covered market selling fruit and veg.
- *Eminönü Pazarı:* Stalls aimed at locals on both sides of *Mısır Çarşısı*. On one side plants, pets, pet food - and leeches; on the other meat, cheeses, preserves, fruit and veg.
- *Karaköy Balıkpazarı:* Near Galata Bridge. Fresh fish.
- *Mısır Çarşısı (Spice Bazaar):* Touristy covered bazaar selling spices, herbs, fruit and nuts etc.

Ankara

- *Sıhhiye:* Wednesday and Saturday markets
- *Çankaya:* Saturday market

Itinerant Traders

Turkey still has many street traders who travel around selling their produce from mobile stalls or out of the back of lorries and cars. In particular there are still many itinerant fruit and vegetable vendors, as well as itinerant sellers of plants in spring. In rural areas some of these traders drive around the streets calling out their wares. Elsewhere they park in a central location and set up an ad hoc market. Often the Belediye will broadcast what is on sale and for what price over their loudspeaker system (Turkish only). You can expect to find everything from fresh honeycomb to tasty special breads and fat-tailed sheep being sold in this informal fashion.

Other itinerant traders include knife-grinders (*bileyci*), people with laminating machines for covering ID cards, tinsmiths who will tin the insides of copper pots (*kalaycı*), and old-fashioned scrap-metal traders (*hurdacı/eskici*) who call round for people's old stove buckets and other paraphernalia. It is sometimes worth inspecting the contents of their trucks in case what someone else regards as rubbish is of interest to you as a foreigner.

Occasionally people from out of town also arrive to sell bric-a-brac and old furniture. Many of these traders know who is most likely to buy their produce and go straight to them but there is nothing to stop you putting in a bid for anything interesting.

From time to time you will also see men walking around with carpets slung over their shoulders (*sırtçı*). In theory there is nothing to stop you asking to see their wares. However, they are usually heading straight for the nearest carpet shop.

SPECIALITY FOOD AND DRINK SHOPS

Most speciality food and drink shops are in Istanbul, although there are a few aimed at foreigners in the resorts. For a list see Appendix VII.

FOOD SUBSTITUTES

Where specific food items are not available in Turkey it is sometimes possible to use locally available items as substitutes. For example, golden syrup is unavailable but many recipes will work just as well if you substitute locally made grape syrup (*pekmez*) for it. You can also add a few drops of *pekmez* to granulated sugar as a substitute for brown sugar. In the same way you can use fine *bulgur* for recipes which ask for couscous. Vanilla essence is not available but instead you can use vanilla powder (*vanilya tozu*).

ORGANIC FOODS (*ORGANİK YİYECEK*)

There is a growing interest in organic products, if only in the wealthier parts of Turkey because, as in the West, almost all organic products come with a significant price mark-up. The area around Bolu is particularly known for its organic produce; if you are driving from Istanbul to Ankara along the old road over Mt Bolu it's worth stopping at Gökdemir Dinlenme Tesisleri which stocks a wide range of organic produce in its shop. English Gardens in Istanbul (see under garden suppliers in Appendix VII for contact details) recently began supplying organic vegetable boxes to customers who request the service, and a new organic foods street market has just started up in Kurtuluş/Şişli.

SHOPPING MALLS *(ALIŞVERİŞ MERKEZİ)*

Turkey has a growing number of town-centre and out-of-town shopping malls which resemble the giant malls to be found all over the Western world, right down to the same brand-name stores inside them (Marks & Spencer, Body Shop, Zara et al) and the vast car parks outside. These are great places to shop for clothes, furniture and household goods under one roof. Some also contain branches of the larger supermarkets such as Migros and Carrefour. Most also have a bookshop with some foreign-language titles as well as food halls similar to those found in UK shopping centres and US shopping malls. Often there is a children's play area. A few even offer wireless *(kablosuz)* Internet services. Most have banks and/or cash machines, as well as cinemas.

For a list of shopping malls see Appendix VII.

CLOTHES *(GİYSİ)*

Clothing can cost as little or as much as you want it to although if you come from the UK you may decide that basic cheap clothing (for example, T-shirts, socks, tights etc) may actually cost less at home. If you want to keep to a budget, your best bet is to frequent the various street markets (see above) which always carry a range of T-shirts, jumpers, trousers, underwear etc. In Istanbul the most famous of these markets is the Salı Pazarı that takes place in Kadıköy every Tuesday; literally hundreds of stalls fill an enormous area – just follow the crowds to find it.

WHAT TO SAY	
Başka renk var mı?	Do you have any other colours?
Bedenim...	I'm size...
Çok büyük	It's too big
Çok küçük	It's too small
Daha büyüğü var mı?	Do you have a bigger size?
Daha küçüğü var mı?	Do you have a smaller size?
Soyunma/deneme odası	Changing room

Elsewhere in Istanbul you can find some fashionable clothes shops along İstiklal Caddesi in Beyoğlu but for a better choice you should head for Bağdat Caddesi in Suadiye. If you want to shop for the upmarket brand names (Versace, Gucci, Louis Vuitton etc) you should head straight for Teşvikiye and

Nişantaşı (or the airport). All over Turkey you will also be able to pick up cheap imitations of famous brand names; start looking in Istanbul's Grand Bazaar, but be careful about taking some of the knock-offs through Custom controls in your home country.

Turkey has an important home-grown textile industry. Although much of what is made is exported good Turkish labels to look out for include Mavi (www.mavi.com) and Little Big (for jeans), and Yargıcı, Mudo, Beymen, Abbate, Kiğılı, YKM and Koton for a wider range of clothes.

Increasingly you can shop at exactly the same clothes shops as at home, especially in Istanbul where there are branches of Marks & Spencer, Debenhams, Dorothy Perkins, Top Shop/Top Man, Zara, Mango, Rodi, Quiksilver etc. Expect prices to be slightly higher than at home though.

Women often complain that they can't find larger sizes of clothing. Faik Sönmez (www.faiksonmez.com) specialises in larger sizes; the website lists its shops in Istanbul, Ankara, Izmir, Bursa, Konya, Adana, Trabzon and Gaziantep. New large-size shops, and corners in other shops, are also beginning to spring up (look for *büyük beden* signs in shop windows). There are also branches of the UK outsize clothes specialist Evans in Istanbul shopping malls.

TURKISH WARDROBE			
belt	*kemer*	pyjamas	*pijama*
blouse	*bluz*	raincoat	*yağmurluk*
bra	*sütyen*	shirt	*gömlek*
collar	*yaka*	shorts	*şort*
dress	*elbise*	skirt	*etek*
dressing gown	*bornoz*	socks	*çorap*
gloves	*eldiven*	suit	*takım elbise*
hat	*şapka*	sweater	*kazak*
headscarf	*eşarp*	swimsuit	*mayo*
jacket	*ceket*	tie	*kravat*
jeans	*kot*	tights/pantyhose	*külotlu çorap*
knickers/underpants	*külot*	trousers/pants	*pantolon*
men's coat	*palto*	T-shirt	*tişört*
neckscarf	*atkı*	underwear	*iç çamaşır*
nightdress	*gecelik*	woman's coat	*manto*

CLOTHES SIZES FOR WOMEN

BLOUSES			DRESSES			SHOES		
USA	EU	UK	USA	EU	UK	USA	EU	UK
8	36	30	4	36	8	4	35	2.5
10	38	32	6	38	10	5	36	3.5
12	40	34	8	40	12	6	37	4.5
14	42	36	10	42	14	7	38	5.5
16	44	38	12	44	16	8	39	6.5
18	46	40	14	46	18	9	40	7.5
	16	48	20	10	41	8.5		

CLOTHES SIZES FOR MEN

SHIRTS			SUITS			SHOES		
USA	EU	UK	USA	EU	UK	USA	EU	UK
14.5	37	30	34	44	8	7.5	40	7
15	38	32	36	46	10	8.5	41	8
15.5	39	34	38	48	12	9.5	42	9
15.75	40	36	40	50	14	10.5	43	10
16	41	38	42	52	16	11.5	44	11
16.5	42	40	44	54	18	12.5	45	12
	46	56	20	13.5	46	13		

Turkish Labels

The textile industry is one of Turkey's main sources of income and although much of what is produced is exported there are several stores selling excellent home-manufactured clothes. Many of the longer-established stores started life selling men's clothing and have since expanded into clothes for women and children; the newer ones generally catered for the whole family from the outset.

Mainstream, youth-oriented labels include Collezione (www.collezione. com.tr), Tiffany Tomato, YKM, LC Waikiki/LCW, Koton and Boyner/Çarşı. Abbate (www.abbate.com.tr), Kiğılı, Gömlekci Hüseyin and Bil's produce classy men's shirts. Beymen also started out as a top-end men's fashion shop although it now caters for all the family; it is renowned for its tailor-made clothes and promise of life-long free alterations. Beymen Megastores incorporate other equally luxurious brand-name shops. Mavi Jeans (www.mavijeans.com.tr) are Turkey's answer to Levi's. Vakko is known for its luxurious rich textiles, although these days it also sells a range of household goods etc; Vakkorama is its young, trendier sister.

Factory Outlets

Istanbul is factory outlet heaven. You can find many of them by looking them up on the Internet or by exploring the back streets of Merter. The Export Shopping Mall in the Alkent Compound in Etiler sells brand-name labels such as Gap, Banana Republic and Naf Naf at reduced prices. There are also an increasing number of outlet shops on the outskirts of the larger cities that sell big-name labels at discount prices.

For a list of factory outlet centres see Appendix VII.

UNDERWEAR *(İÇ ÇAMAŞIR)*

One of the most unnerving discoveries for newly-arrived foreign females is that women's underwear is often sold by men. This is not the case in flashy Istanbul stores or Marks & Spencer, of course, but if you prefer to buy cheap knickers from the market you will almost certainly find yourself being served by a man. That's fine if you know your size and can make off in a hurry but it's distinctly unsettling if you need to ask questions.

Interestingly, you can buy just as much sexy lingerie in Turkey as in the West.

WHAT TO SAY			
boots	*botlar*	shoe polish	*ayakkabı cilası*
cobbler	*ayakkabıcı*	shoelaces	*ayakkabı bağcığı*
pair of shoes	*bir çift ayakkabı*	slippers	*terlik*
sandals	*sandalet*		

SHOES *(AYAKKABI)*

Turkey uses the same shoe sizes as the rest of Europe (for conversion chart, see box p. 286), Since removing your shoes before entering people's houses is de rigueur, do yourself a favour and cultivate a taste for slip-ons. Popular brands include Beta, Ceyo, Greyder and Polaris (www.polaris.gen.tr). Nike and Adidas outlets are also ubiquitous.

It is not easy to get your children's feet properly measured for shoes. Kifidis sells orthopaedic shoes for adults and children and makes sure it gets your child's size right; their products are, of course, more expensive than regular shoes.

NON-FOOD STREET MARKETS

Many of Turkey's markets sell food alongside other goods. However, there are also markets that specialise in selling non-food items. Some of them are craft markets (*el sanatı pazarı*), others are flea markets (*bitpazarı*).

TAHTAKALE

Tahtakale/ Mahmutpaşa is the wonderful part of Istanbul that spreads out west from Mısır Çarşısı (the Egyptian Bazaar). Unlike the Grand Bazaar, the Mahmutpaşa and Tahtakale shopping streets are frequented almost entirely by Turks and so retain an atmosphere akin to an authentic oriental bazaar. It sometimes seems as if you can buy anything here, from feather dusters to wooden chopping boards, from cocktail cherries to freshly-ground coffee, and from cheap T-shirts to Monopoly boards in Turkish. Tahtakale is particularly good for wrapping paper and party decorations, for plastic glasses and straws, for hardware and cheap children's games. Interspersed among the tiny shops are small kebab restaurants and the fine Café Istanbul in what was once the local hamam.

In **Istanbul** the *Ortaköy Crafts Market* sells jewellery, handbags, paintings by local artists etc in the streets running back from the waterfront every Saturday and Sunday. The following clothes markets are also worth visiting:

- *Çarşamba:* Darüşşafaka Caddesi, Fatih. Bustling Wednesday market.
- *Kadıköy:* Sprawling Tuesday market.
- *Salıpazarı:* Kuşdili Sokak, Fenerbahçe. Busy Tuesday and Sunday markets.

You might also want to visit the following flea markets:

- *Çukurcuma Bit Pazarı:* Beyoğlu Caddesi. Every Sunday from 9am to 8pm.
- *Horhor Bit Pazarı:* Horhor Caddesi, Kırk Tulumba Sokak No: 13, Fatih. Six floors of antiques.
- *Kasımpaşa Bit Pazarı:* Kulaksız Caddesi No: 5, Büyük Çarşı, Kasımpaşa

The **Izmir** *Bit Pazarı* on the first weekend of every month is another fun place to browse.

DVDs

In Istanbul the Sinanpaşa Pasajı above McDonald's in Beşiktaş stocks good quality, if pirated, DVDs. Check that they are in English before parting with your cash.

FOREIGN-LANGUAGE BOOKS

Istanbul has several excellent English-language bookshops, as well as one or two selling books in French and German. Ankara and Izmir also have a handful of English-language bookshops, as do most of the major coastal resorts. Elsewhere there are few foreign-language bookshops although pensions in popular tourist areas run second-hand book exchanges. You can always order books over the Internet from www.amazon.co.uk or www.amazon.com, both of which have a good record on deliveries even to rural Turkey (club together with friends to place an order and reduce postage costs). You can also order English books from Pandora (www.pandora.com.tr) in Istanbul.

For a list of bookshops, see Appendix VII.

Second-Hand Books

In Istanbul try looking for second-hand books in the **Sahaflar Çarşısı** (Old Book Bazaar), next to the Grand Bazaar in Beyazıt. However, most of the stalls concentrate on university textbooks rather than dog-eared Western paperbacks. A better bet is the **Aslıhan Pasajı**, an arcade off the western side of the Balık Pazarı in Beyoğlu where several dealers stock old paperbacks in assorted languages.

In Ankara head straight for **Olgunlar Sokak** where rows of second-hand bookstalls line a pedestrianised street. Most of the books are in Turkish but you can pick up old magazines and a few books in English and German.

For other suggestions see Appendix VII.

IN THE STATIONER'S *(KIRTASİYEDE)*			
brown paper	*kahverengi kâğıt*	paper clip	*raptiye*
calculator	*hesap makinesi*	pen	*kalem*
coloured pencil	*boya kalemi*	pencil	*kurşunkalem*
compass	*pusula*	pencil sharpener	*kalemtıraş*
envelope	*zarf*	ruler	*cetvel*
eraser	*silgi*	scissors	*makas*
folder	*dosya*	staple	*tel zımba*
glue	*tutkal/zamk*	stapler	*zımba*
lined paper	*çizgili kâğıt*	string	*ip/sicim*
notebook	*defter*	writing pad	*bloknot*
paper	*kâğıt*		

STATIONERY (KIRTASİYE)

Big towns usually have a specific area with lots of stationery shops. In addition the US chain Office 1 Stationery (www.office1.com.tr) is opening a growing number of stores in all the main towns. Big supermarkets such as Migros and Carrefour also carry stocks of reasonably-priced stationery.

If you want box files that don't have covers designed for children you will need to look a bit harder or import them - not such a problem if you use them as packaging for other items.

For a list of stationers, see Appendix VII.

COMPUTERS (BİLGİSAYAR)

Turkish-made computers such as the Casper range (www.casper.com.tr for sales outlets countrywide) are considerably cheaper than imported ones and not necessarily any less reliable. Of course they come with Turkish keyboards but these can usually be changed for an English one without too much difficulty. All programming will be in Turkish unless you specifically request – and pay – for English. For more information about the layout of Turkish keyboards, see p. 566.

WHAT TO SAY	
desktop computer	masaüstü bilgisayar
ink cartridge refills	kartuş dolumu yapılır
keyboard	klavye
laptop computer	taşınabilir bilgisayar
mouse	fare
printer	yazıcı
scanner	tarayıcı
screen	ekran

SPECIAL OCCASIONS

Birthdays

Traditionally Turks did not celebrate birthdays which means that real birthday cards are hard to find, even in the big cities - bring supplies from home. It is fairly easy to find candles (mum) although they sometimes come without holders and are stuck directly into the cake.

Presents (*Doğum Günü Hediyesi*)

Plenty of shops all over the country sell perfect gift items. Branches of Dösim sell wonderful replicas of historic items at surprisingly reasonable prices. The İznik Vakfı sells magnificent copies of ancient İznik pottery and tiles. Branches of Mudo sell luxurious items for decorating homes, as do branches of Tepe Home. Branches of Paşabahçe sell stunning glassware, both practical and decorative, with designs changing frequently.

When you buy an item that could be a present the shopkeeper will probably ask you *'Hediye mi?'* (Is it a present?) If you say yes they will wrap it for you at no extra cost.

For a list of suggested places to buy presents, see Appendix VII.

GRAND/COVERED BAZAAR (*KAPALI ÇARŞI*)

The Grand Bazaar, with its 4000-plus shops, is a great place to come if you're feeling strong and are good at bargaining. Much of the merchandise is pretty touristy, with inflated prices to match. However, many dealers still buy some of their produce in the shops and *hans* around and above the bazaar, so it doesn't pay to write it off altogether. The bazaar is also a good place to shop for different kinds of hand-woven fabrics and embroideries. If you need gold coins to give as wedding or circumcision gifts, it should certainly be your first port of call.

Recently a few more unusual shops have opened inside the bazaar. If your wallet is feeling +y you might want to look at:

- *Deli Kızın Yeri*: Tel: 0212-511 1914, www.delikiz.com, Halıcılar Caddesi No: 42. Novelty gifts and cards.
- *Deli Kızın Yeri Junior*: Tel: 0212-511 1915, Halıcılar Caddesi No: 42. Children's games etc.
- *Abdulla Natural Products*: Tel: 0212-522 9078, www.abdulla.com, Halıcılar Caddesi No: 53. Luxury bathroom items from all over Turkey.

Christmas (*Noel*)

Now that Turkey has absorbed all the trappings of Christmas for its New Year (*Yılbaşı*) celebrations (see p. 325) you can buy paper-chains, tinsel and Christmas tree decorations fairly easily in the cities. Since most have been imported from China they are not always of the highest quality but prices are pleasingly low by European standards (around YTL0.50 per bauble, YTL1 per paper chain). Plastic Christmas trees (*Noel ağacı*) can be picked up cheaply in Tahtakale (or more expensively in Akmerkez Shopping Mall). In Bahçeköy you can buy real fir trees from the Belgrade Forest; in general, though, real Christmas trees are very expensive. Although mistletoe grows on Turkish trees no one has yet cottoned on to the idea of selling it to foreigners but in Istanbul gypsy flower-sellers tout pricy branches of *yılbaşı çiçeği* (New Year flowers) with red berries which make a good alternative to holly.

Because the decorations are really aimed at the Turkish New Year they appear in the shops a bit late for relaxed Christmas shopping. Most of Istanbul's special present fairs (*hediye fuarı*) also only get into their stride in late December, although those organised by foreigners start earlier.

Christmas Dinner Ingredients

Gone are the days when it was virtually impossible to find ready-prepared turkeys; nowadays companies like Banvit sell their turkeys packaged together with a bag to cook them in, a thermometer and a book of suitable recipes. If you'd prefer a fresh bird they can usually be found in Beyoğlu Fish Market (*Balık Pazarı*) off İstiklal Caddesi; Şütte, in the same market, sells bacon, cocktail sausages and other pork products. You still can't find ready-made mince pies, Christmas cake or Christmas pudding in the shops; bring the ready-made versions from home or make your own mincemeat etc – all the necessary ingredients are available.

Decorations (*Süsleme*)

In Istanbul the first place to start looking for Christmas decorations is Tahtakale (see box p. 288), the bustling market that spreads west from the Spice Bazaar area of Eminönü. In the weeks leading up to the New Year, all the shops that normally sell wrapping paper, etc fill up with Christmas decorations and fierce competition ensures that prices are very reasonable unless you're after an outsize inflatable Father Christmas. Elsewhere your best bets are the general-purpose cheapie markets (often with names like Salı Pazarı or Pazarıstan) which roll out the decorations from mid-December onwards.

Presents (*Hediye*)

All the shops listed on p. 291 stock items suitable for Christmas presents. However, the special present fairs (*hediye fuarı*) that run in December are also excellent (and untouristy) places to shop. Note that those run by non-Westerners start operating very close to Christmas as they are really aimed at the Turkish New Year market.

Istanbul

Beşiktaş Hediye Fuarı: Tel: 0212-267 3626, www.hediyefuari.com, Dolmabahçe Kültür Merkezi, Beşiktaş. 22-31 December. Range of handicrafts (particularly candles) and other gift items. Open 11 am to 9.30 pm daily.

CNR Hediye Fuarı: Tel: 0212-465 7474, www.cnr-hediyelikesya, Yeşilköy. 23-31 December. In large exhibition centre near Atatürk Airport.

IWI Christmas Bazaar: In Hilton International Convention and Exhibition Centre, usually last weekend of November. Proceeds support IWI charities.

Mövenpick Hotel: Tel: 0212-319 2929, Büyükdere Caddesi, 4. Levent. 'Christmas Street' in hotel lobby sells sweets, handicrafts, Christmas cakes, *glühwein* mixes and gift items. Open throughout December 10 am to 10 pm daily.

Portobello: Tel: 0212-244 1759, Casa d'Italia, Circolo Roma, Meşrutiyet Caddesi No: 161, Beyoğlu. Christmas bazaar combined with Italian food market in early December.

Ankara

American Women's: Last week of November/first week of December
Ankara Charities: Last week of November/first week of December
British Women's Bazaar: Usually first Sunday in December

Easter (*Paskalya*)

Easter celebrations have yet to take off even in Istanbul, so it is hard to find cards, let alone Easter eggs. However, Armenian-owned Hobby Dekorasyon sells a selection of imported Easter decorations (see under Christmas decorations in Appendix VII for details). You can also buy animal and egg shaped chocolates in several Istanbul sweetshops; for some suggestions see Appendix VII.

SECOND-HAND GOODS (İKİNCİ EL / 2. EL EŞYALAR)

In general Turks are not keen on buying second-hand items. As a result the country lacks the chains of charity shops that can make shopping for clothes relatively cheap, especially in the UK. However, each large town usually has an *'eskici'* shop or a street of these shops that sell a range of used items; although most of it is junk sometimes there are real finds to be had if you're willing to dig through it all. Most towns also have shops selling second-hand electrical goods although you should not assume that items on sale have been tested to ensure that they are safe.

TAILORS (*TERZİ*)

Most Turkish towns will have several tailors who can run up new clothes for much less than they would cost at home. It is probably best to assume you will need more than one fitting to get the garments right though.

WHAT TO SAY

bust	*bust*	leg	*bacak*
chest	*göğüs*	measurements	*ölçü*
collar	*yaka*	pin	*toplu iğne*
hip	*kalça*	waist	*bel*

REPAIR SHOPS *(TAMİRCİ)*

Turkey is not yet a throwaway society, and many things can still be repaired here surprisingly cheaply. For example, there are still many shoe-repairers who charge very little for their work. Look out, too, for hand weavers (*örücü*) who can repair a rip in an expensive suit or dress using threads delicately pulled from a concealed hem, thus rendering the damage invisible. Clocks and watches can be repaired without hassle, and it goes without saying that there are many people who can make an old carpet look like new again. Even the retailers of white goods usually offer a reliable repairs services. The downside to all this is that companies may persist in trying to repair an item that has never worked rather than simply replacing it as you, the purchaser, might prefer.

WHAT TO SAY

Can you repair this clock/watch?	*Bu saati tamir edebilir misiniz?*
Can you mend this?	*Bunu tamir edebilir misiniz?*
Could you reheel/resole this for me?	*Bunun topuğını/tabanını yapar mısınız?*

HANDICRAFTS *(EL SANATI)*

In Turkey women continue to make many household items that are commonly bought in the West. Knitting (*örme),* sewing *(dikme),* embroidery (*nakış)* and now jewellery-making (*takı tasarım)* are common occupations for women across the social strata, which means that there are still many shops selling the materials needed to practise these handicrafts. There are also many shops selling trays, boxes and other objects that can be decorated to make them more individual and attractive.

I'D LIKE... *(...İSTİYORUM)*

bead	*boncuk*	pin	*toplu iğne*
button	*düğme*	ribbon	*kurdele*

fabric	kumaş	scissors	makas
knitting needle	örgü şişi/şiş	sewing machine	dikiş makinesi
lace	dantel	tape measure	metre
needle	iğne	thread	iplik
paint	boya	zip	fermuar
paintbrush	boya fırçası		

INTERNET SHOPPING

If you live a long way from a big town shopping on the Internet can be extremely useful; try www.hepsiburada.com, www.estore.com etc for a wide range of items. Cargo costs can push prices up, as can bank charges for transferring funds to the retailer. However, some things, such as pet food, are cheaper bought this way than in conventional shops, and a choice of cargo companies means that you can pick the cheapest.

If you live in town but have little time for shopping you may also want to use the Migros Internet shopping service to save time.

The Turkish equivalent of ebay is www.gittigidiyor.com although at the time of the writing the site was in Turkish only and most of the advertisers were retailers rather than private individuals.

WHAT IT MEANS			
adet	quantity	kampanya	special offer
alışverişi tamamla	complete sale	satın alma işlemine devam	continue with sale
ara	search	sepet(im)	shopping basket
at sepete	put in basket	sepete ekle	add to basket
güncelle	update	sipariş sorgulama	queries about order
hesap/hesabım	bill	tüm ürünler	all products
istek listesi	wish list	yeni ürün	new product

Shopping Magazines: The Turkish equivalent of the British *Exchange & Mart* is the weekly *Tüketici* (The Consumer) which carries adverts for houses, cars, furniture etc.

DISCOUNT CARDS (*İNDİRİM KARTI*)

Tired of being charged tourist prices for everything, a group of Fethiye residents have banded together to develop the **Elite Card,** which, for YTL75 per year, entitles the holder to discounts at listed shops. Holders also get a year's free subscription to *Land of Lights* and free text messages translating the most important local announcements. Staff in the Elite Card office will also be prepared to help with explanations when the holder's Turkish lets them down in a shop.

DUTY-FREE SHOPPING (*GÜMRÜKSÜZ ALIŞVERİŞ*)

Most shopping in Turkey is subject to the Turkish equivalent of VAT (KDV – *Katma Değer Vergisi*), levied at between 8% and 18%. People who are leaving Turkey are entitled to claim back the tax levied on big-ticket items (i.e. things costing more than around $100) which were paid for in Turkish lira. Clearly people who are living permanently in Turkey are not really eligible for this refund. However, some foreigners who go in and out of the country regularly to renew their visas claim back the tax paid on their shopping at the same time.

If you want to reclaim the tax you must obtain a Global Refund Cheque and present it at a cash refund point within three months of the purchase. Shops participating in the scheme should display a 'Tax Free Shopping' logo. When you go to leave the country you should show the Customs officials your purchases and receipts as well as your passport. They will stamp the Global Refund Cheque for you. Then you take the Cheque to the nearest Cash Refund Office to reclaim your cash. You may only do this for up to three months after making the purchase.

Alternatively you can post the stamped Cheques back to the Global Refund Turkey office provided you do this within 30 days of leaving the country. You should send details of the bank account you want credited or the address to which you want a refund cheque sent. That's the theory. In practise, of course, the cheque may never arrive.

The system also works in reverse which means that if you have Turkish residency you can claim VAT back on goods bought on a visit of less than three months to your home country. Normally you get a Customs officer at the port or airport to stamp your Global Refund Form and then present it to the VAT refund desk which is usually in the departure lounge.

And when the craving for home food gets too much…

WHO TO CONTACT

- *expatdirect.co.uk* - They'll post your Heinz baked beans and Cadbury's Dairy Milk, although with postage costs starting at more than £20 for one kilo you'll need to be feeling pretty ravenous!

WHAT TO SAY	
cash desk/cashier	*kasa*
consumer	*tüketici*
customer	*müşteri*
customer services information line	*müşteri hizmetleri danışma hattı*
free consumer information line	*ücretsiz tüketici danışma hattı*
guarantee	*garanti*
not for sale	*satış dışı/satılmaz*
order for goods	*sipariş*
receipt	*fiş*
refund	*iade*
shopping	*alışveriş*

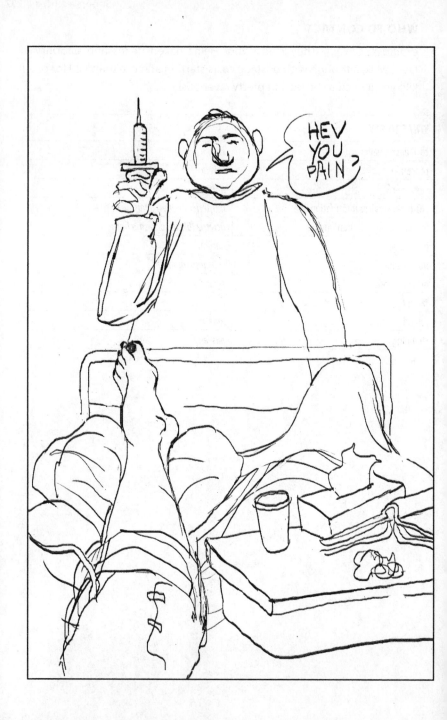

CHAPTER 13

HEALTH MATTERS

On the whole people who move to Turkey don't need to worry too much about serious illnesses specific to the country. However, every expat needs to think about what will happen if they do fall ill or have an accident, and this is especially the case for people who are retiring to Turkey at a time in life when health problems tend to increase. Although every Turkish town has its quota of doctors, dentists and hospitals, the standard of diagnosis and treatment is not always as high as it could be. Prices for treatment in state facilities are low by Western standards. However, many foreigners prefer to opt for private medical treatment and the better care that it buys. For any serious illness it is certainly wise to head straight for a hospital in one of the big cities - your embassy should be able to advise on which is best. Inevitably treatment at these hospitals can be expensive unless you have arranged suitable insurance cover well in advance of falling ill.

Since Turkey is not yet part of the EU, European citizens cannot depend on free reciprocal healthcare as elsewhere in Europe.

Government Health and Pension Plan: If you are legally employed in Turkey your employer is required to pay for state health insurance and a pension plan for you. While there were until very recently three rather cumbersome and different state-run plans (Bağ-Kur, SSK and Emekli Sandık) these are now being merged into one 'social security' plan that includes both healthcare and pensions. This coverage allows insured employees and their families to receive free healthcare in government-owned and run hospitals and clinics, and/or partial or full payment of fees in selected private hospitals which have opted to participate in the system. A small percentage of the cost of medicines must be paid by the patient. This new system is also intended to provide all children with free healthcare at government hospitals up to the age of 18.

The government is also phasing out the old prescription pads that people used to have to show to get their price reductions in favour of a social security card with a bar code that incorporates details of their eligibility. This is simply swiped into the computers in hospitals and pharmacies just as a credit card would be in a supermarket.

Yeşil Kart: People who are completely destitute (defined as being without a house, car or income) are eligible for a green card (*yeşil kart*) which entitles them to free healthcare. Fortunately few foreigners living in Turkey are likely to be hard-up enough to qualify.

WHAT YOU MIGHT CATCH

Although Turkey is a fairly healthy country, most foreigners who are new to it succumb to a stomach bug. Usually this is minor and clears up within a few days. However, more persistent problems should be checked out with a doctor since giardia is common.

Also common, although not much talked about, is hepatitis A, which some people seem to pick up while they are in hospital. Hepatitis B is also common in Turkey. It is wise to have yourself vaccinated before you arrive in Turkey although jabs are also available in the country.

There are occasional typhoid outbreaks in eastern Turkey and some areas of the south-east also suffer from a malaria problem. TB is also fairly common (treatment is provided free).

Fortunately AIDS is not yet a big problem, although it is only likely to remain that way if everybody abides by the safe-sex message, especially in the resort areas where promiscuity is commonplace.

WHERE TO GET MORE DETAILS

www.who-int/en

COMMON HEALTH HAZARDS
Smoking (*Sigara İçmek*)

If you are someone who finds it hard to deal with cigarette smoke then Turkey will not be the country for you. Although the government is trying to raise awareness of the health risks associated with smoking, with publicity campaigns in schools and poster campaigns elsewhere, most adult men still smoke – and smoke a lot. Local-brand cigarettes are absurdly cheap by Western standards, which does nothing to curb people's enthusiasm for them. More than 150,000 Turks die every year from smoking-related illnesses.

Thankfully buses are now smoke-free zones and the rules are rigorously applied except to the driver and his mate (which means non-smoking women get a raw deal since they are usually assigned the seats immediately behind the driver). Trains have smoke-free compartments although the rule is not as conscientiously applied as on the buses. Few hotels have smoke-free floors or even rooms. Government offices have 'no smoking' signs up – but nobody pays them any attention.

Curiously, some expats who come from countries with rigorous anti-smoking policies are amongst the worst offenders when it comes to lighting up in Turkey, even in restaurants and in people's homes.

Obesity (*Obezite*)

Turkey is officially one of the fattest countries in the world – or so reported *National Geographic* in 2004. The most likely culprit is bread which Turks eat in vast quantities every day and with every meal. Another likely contributor is sugar which is piled into tea glasses in frightening quantities – three cubes per small glass is common and most people down at least three glasses per tea-drinking session. People also drink a lot of canned soft drinks which also contain more sugar than most of them realise.

Diabetes (*Şeker Hastası*)

For the same reasons that Turkey has so many overweight people it also has a disproportionately high number of people with diabetes (*şeker hastası*). Late diagnosis and inadequate treatment mean that some of these people end up losing limbs to their illness. Foreigners who have eaten a balanced diet prior to arriving in Turkey should not need to worry unduly about this. However, it is as well to be aware of the danger of a high sugar intake.

Most supermarkets sell a range of low-sugar foods for diabetics but they are not particularly cheap.

High/Low Blood Pressure (*Yüksek/Düşük Tansiyon*)

Large numbers of Turks also suffer from high or low blood pressure which has led to rocketing sales of devices for measuring one's own blood pressure. Once again, foreigners should not have to worry about this unless they already had a problem before arriving in Turkey.

SYMPTOMS (BELİRTİLER)

blood	kan	rash	deride kızarıklık/şişlik
bruise	çürük/bere/ezik	sneeze	hapşırık
burn	yanık	sore throat	boğaz ağrısı
constipation	kabızlık	spots	sivilce
cough	öksürük	swelling	şiş(lik)
cut	kesik	to faint	bayılmak
diarrhoea	ishal	to vomit	kusmak
earache	kulak ağrısı	Where does it hurt?	Neresi acıyor?
fever	ateş	Does it hurt now/here?	Şimdi/burası acıyor mu?
fit	nöbet	slight pain	hafif ağrı
inflammation	iltihap	sharp pain	şiddetli ağrı
insomnia	uykusuzluk	It hurts a lot	Çok ağrıyor
itchy	kaşıntı	It doesn't hurt much	Çok ağrımıyor
lump	yumru	My head is spinning	Başım dönüyor
nausea	mide bulantısı	I feel sick	Midem bulanıyor
pain	ağrı		

Allergies (Alerji)

Turkey has all the normal allergens - dust, cat fur, grass pollen, etc - but hay-fever sufferers need to know that the pollen of the iğde (white olive) tree can also make people feel ill. It flowers in late April through to late June.

Common Cold (Nezle)

You are just as likely to succumb to a cold in Turkey as anywhere else. The local remedy of choice is Gripin which is available in every pharmacy. As elsewhere flu (grip) is more serious. Flu jabs are available in pharmacies from October onwards - look for signs reading 'Grip aşısı gelmiştir' (flu jabs have arrived) or something similar.

Hypochondria (Hastalık Hastası)

Many Turks are hypochondriacs, alert to every ache and pain and with an obsessive interest in potential health risks that most Westerners take in their stride. Fear of draughts is one such concern that results in rooms being heated to stupifying temperatures. Another is fear of swallowing cat hair which means that most Turks refuse to let cats inside their homes. Such health worries are primarily part of the life of rural women, many of whom have had little education and little access to good healthcare. Many have also spent long years working in their fields which probably accounts for most of the aches and pains.

YOU HAVE GOT...			
abscess	*apse*	heart attack	*kalp krizi*
Aids	*Aids*	hepatitis	*kara sarılık*
allergy	*alerji*	indigestion	*mide fesadı/ hazımsızlık*
anaemia	*kansızlık*	infection	*enfeksiyon*
angina	*anjin*	insect bite	*böcek sokması*
appendicitis	*apandisit*	jaundice	*sarılık*
arthritis	*artrit*	malaria	*sıtma*
asthma	*astım*	migraine	*migren*
bite	*ısırık*	pneumonia	*zatürre*
broken	*kırık*	rabies	*kuduz*
bronchitis	*bronşit*	rheumatism	*romatizma*
burn	*yanık*	scorpion bite	*akrep sokması*
cancer	*kanser*	sea sickness	*deniz tutması*
cholera	*kolera*	sprain	*burkulma*
cold	*nezle*	stroke	*felç*
concussion	*beyin sarsıntısı*	sunburn	*güneş yanığı*
constipation	*kabızlık*	TB	*tüberküloz/verem*
cystitis	*sistit*	thrush	*mantar hastalığı/ pamukçuk*
diabetes	*şeker hastası*	tonsillitis	*bademcik iltihabı*
diarrhoea	*ishal*	travel sickness	*araba tutması*
epilepsy	*sara*	ulcer	*ülser*
flu	*grip*	urinary infection	*idraryolu enfeksyonu*
food poisoning	*gıda zehirlenmesi*	VD	*zührevi hastalık*
gastroenteritis	*gastrit*	wound/injury	*yara*
hangover	*içki sonrası baş ağrısı*		

For example, *Grip olmuşsunuz* - you have got a cold; *Romatizmanız var* - you have got rheumatism.

DOCTORS *(DOKTOR)*

Unlike in the UK, Turks do not register with a local general practitioner. Instead they can visit any doctor they like, provided they can pay for the treatment. Most Turkish doctors specialise in a particular area of medicine so if you have a good idea what is wrong with you then you can look for a doctor whose sign advertises that speciality. Many doctors choose to practise close to the local hospital, so that is a good place to start looking. You should not assume a Turkish doctor will be able to speak a foreign language unless they work in a private hospital in Istanbul, Ankara, Izmir, Adana or one of the coastal resorts. However, they are usually happy if you bring along a friend to help with translating. A basic consultation with a doctor usually costs around €35 but the amount can rise considerably depending on the doctor's fame and practice speciality; in Istanbul you would probably except to pay more like €100 to see a good doctor.

Turks who are covered by the government-sponsored insurance policy (see p. 306) will go to see a hospital doctor for any health problem, not just in an emergency. As a result hospitals are very overstretched and you must expect to queue for everything.

For a list of English-speaking doctors in Istanbul go to www.usconsulate-Istanbul.org.tr.

LOOK FOR...	
cardiology/heart problems	*kardiyoloji*
gynaecology	*jinekoloji*
internal illness specialist	*dahiliye/ iç hastalıkları uzmanı*
neurology/nerve problems	*nöroloji*
oncology/cancer specialist	*onkoloji*
orthopedics/bone problems	*ortopedi*
paediatry/children's illnesses	*pediatri*
pathology	*patoloji*
plastic surgery	*plastik cerrahi*
psychiatry	*psikiyatri*
skin problems	*dermatoloji*
specialist	*uzman*
surgeon	*cerrah*
urology	*üroloji*

PHARMACIES *(ECZANE)*

Many drugs that can only be obtained on prescription in the UK (e.g. antibiotics, Viagra) are available over the counter in a Turkish pharmacy. Pharmacists can also offer some basic health advice, administer injections, take your blood pressure and treat minor injuries. Some pharmacies can even order medicines from abroad.

There are plenty of pharmacies in all Turkey's big towns and most sizeable villages will have one too. In the towns there is always a duty pharmacist *(nöbetçi eczane)* who provides a 24-hour service; other pharmacies will have details of whose turn it is to be the *nöbetçi* displayed in the window.

IN THE PHARMACY *(ECZANEDE)*			
after meals	*yemeklerden sonra*	IUD	*spiral*
antibiotic	*antibiyotik*	laxative	*mushil*
antidote	*panzehir*	lip salve	*dudak kremi*
antihistamine	*antihistamin*	lotion	*losyon*
antiseptic	*antiseptik*	medicine	*ilaç*
Aspirin	*Aspirin*	mosquito repellent	*sivrisinek kovucu*
bandage	*sargı*	painkillers	*ağrı kesici*
before meals	*yemeklerden önce*	penicillin	*penisilin*
codeine	*kodein*	pill(s)	*hap(lar)*
cotton wool	*pamuk*	plaster	*yara bandı/yakı*
directions for use	*kullanım şekli*	prescription	*reçete*
enema	*lavman*	sedative	*sakinleştirici*
eye/nose drops	*göz/burun damlası*	sleeping pill	*uyku hapı*
for external use	*haricen kullanılır*	syrup	*şurup*
for internal use	*dahilen kullanılır*	throat pastilles	*boğaz pastili*
insect repellent	*böcek ilacı*	twice a day	*günde iki kere*

If you go to a Turkish doctor it is almost unheard of to leave without a prescription for three or four separate items even if there has been no clear diagnosis of your illness. Partly this is a cultural problem – people don't expect to get better unless they have taken pills – but partly it is because some drug companies are rumoured to give doctors money for selling their products. Local doctors are poorly paid by international standards, so over-prescribing acts as a handy boost to their income.

In general medicines are cheap by international standards although the cost can mount up when you are always buying multiple items. People with state health insurance usually pay only 10% to 20% of the cost of any medication. There can be some surprises over price. For example, although a conventional Ventolin inhaler to treat an asthma attack costs less than the UK prescription charge, it is more expensive to buy a preventative Becotide inhaler in Turkey than in the UK; nor are they always readily available. Some doctors try and sell the most expensive medicines to foreigners - always ask if there is a cheaper generic equivalent.

Where To Find More Information

www.eczanemonline.com.tr (Turkish only)
www.turkeycentral.com/Health

HOSPITALS *(HASTANE)*

Turkey has two separate hospital systems, one run by the state, the other run privately. In general the highest standards of care, cleanliness etc are to be found in private hospitals. However, misdiagnosis of illnesses can still occur even in a private hospital. Sometimes patients are also given too large a dose of medicine - you should be especially careful to check the dose of any drug offered to a child although the information for most medicaments is only provided in Turkish. For the time being doctors don't expect to provide their patients with much information - even people with obvious problems such as unexplained lumps may be told 'it's nothing'. In such circumstances the Internet can be an invaluable source of additional information-see p. 515 for some suggestions.

State & SSK Hospitals (*Devlet Hastanesi*)

Unless you have private insurance you are likely to be treated for any serious illness or accident in the nearest state hospital *(devlet hastanesi)*. Standards in these hospitals vary considerably but many are under-resourced and pretty grim. There may be no doctors on duty overnight, leaving ancillary staff to help out in an emergency. Friends and relatives are expected to bring in food and anything else a patient may need. They often provide some basic care as well - a problem if you are living alone and don't have someone to help you. In comparison with the norm in the West nurses are sometimes poorly trained and do relatively little to help their patients. Privacy is not a priority - there are unlikely to be curtains around beds. Some basic equipment may not be working due to shortages of parts. You may struggle to find English-speaking staff to help you.

Teaching hospitals usually have higher standards than normal state hospitals although levels of cleanliness can still be disappointingly low; since their physicians are generally considered to be the most knowledgeable, you often have to trade off inadequate nursing against better medical care.

Hospitals are frequently short of blood (you sometimes hear requests for blood delivered over the public address system) so you may need to bring along your own donors. For that reason it is a good idea to find out your blood group and then see which of your friends has the same.

For a list of state hospitals see Appendix VIII.

IN HOSPITAL *(HASTANEDE)*			
anaesthetic	*narkoz*	patient	*hasta*
artery	*atardamar*	plaster cast	*alçı*
blood group	*kan grubu*	pulse	*nabız*
blood test	*kan tahlili*	side effects	*yan etkiler*
emergency service	*acil servis*	specialist	*uzman*
examination	*muayene*	stitches	*dikiş*
ill	*hasta*	surgeon	*cerrah*
illness	*hastalık*	treatment	*tedavi*
injection(s)	*iğne(ler)*	urine test	*idrar tahlili*
nurse	*hemşire*	vein	*damar*
operation	*ameliyat*	X-ray	*film/röntgen*

Private Hospitals (*Özel Hastane*) & Clinics

Because of the failings of the state hospital system most people who can afford to prefer to use private hospitals. The best private hospitals in Istanbul and Ankara have standards of treatment and cleanliness to match anything anywhere else in the world. Normally they will have staff who speak English and other foreign languages as well.

If you just need an X-ray or some other minor treatment and don't have medical insurance it may be cheaper to visit a state hospital for advice and only go to a private hospital when you know that you need specific treatment.

It may come as a surprise to find that some private hospitals (e.g. the Yimpaş hospitals) operate a dual pricing system, with foreigners charged more on the assumption that they will be 'tourists' with health insurance. If possible you should go to such hospitals with your residency permit and with a friendly Turk who can convince them that you live locally and so should be charged the local price.

Since 2006, patients have been able to use their government-sponsored insurance policies as a contribution towards the cost of care at private hospitals.

For a list of private hospitals see Appendix VIII.

WHERE DOES IT HURT? *(NERESİ AĞRIYOR?)*			
ankle	*ayak bileği*	liver	*karaciğer*
appendix	*apandisit*	lung(s)	*akciğer(ler)*
arm	*kol*	mouth	*ağız*
back	*sırt*	muscle	*kas*
bladder	*idrar torbası/mesane*	neck	*boyun*
bone	*kemik*	nerve	*sinir*
breast	*meme*	nose	*burun*
cheek	*yanak*	pancreas	*pankreas*
chest	*göğüs*	penis	*erkeklik uzvu/penis*
chin/jaw	*çene*	rib	*kaburga*
ear(s)	*kulak(lar)*	shoulder	*omuz*
elbow	*dirsek*	skin	*cilt*
eye(s)	*göz(ler)*	spine	*belkemiği*
finger	*parmak*	stomach	*mide/karın*
fingernail	*tırnak*	tendon	*tendon*
foot	*ayak*	testicles	*erbezi*
genitals	*cinsel organlar*	thigh	*baldır*
hand	*el*	throat	*boğaz*
head	*baş/kafa*	thumb	*başparmak*
heart	*kalp*	thyroid	*tiroit*
heel	*topuk*	toe	*ayak parmağı*
hip	*kalça*	toenail	*ayak tırnağı*
intestine	*bağırsak*	tongue	*dil*
joint	*eklem*	tonsils	*bademcik*
kidney(s)	*böbrek(ler)*	tooth/teeth	*diş(ler)*
knee	*diz*	vagina	*vajina*
leg	*bacak*	waist	*bel*
ligament	*lif*	wrist	*bilek*
lip(s)	*dudak(lar)*		
For example, *Başım ağrıyor* - my head hurts/I have a headache; *Karnım ağrıyor* - my stomach aches.			

LOCAL HEALTH CLINICS *(SAĞLIK OCAĞI)*

In rural areas there may be no private doctors available. Instead there may be a health clinic where you can get simple medical advice, vaccinations, baby check-ups etc. The clinics are usually staffed by a doctor and nurse who will be able to advise on what you should do if they don't have the facilities to help you. Their services are free to local social insurance holders; others pay only a nominal sum for a check-up and any treatment or medicines.

AMBULANCE *(AMBULANS)* SERVICE

In an emergency you can call 112 for an ambulance. However, it is sometimes quicker just to call a taxi to get to hospital. Most private hospitals have their own ambulances with modern life-saving equipment on board. If it's not on the list in the appendix, you should make sure you have recorded the telephone number of the ambulance service for your local hospital to use in an emergency.

For a list of companies supplying ambulances and air ambulances see Appendix VIII.

WOMEN'S HEALTH *(KADIN SAĞLIĞI)*

Periods (*Aybaşı/âdet*) & Sanitary Products

While it is easy to find sanitary towels (*hijyenik kadın bağı*), usually made by the local companies Orkid (www.orkid.com.tr), Carefree, Evy Lady (www.evylady.com) and Libresse (www.libresse.com.tr), it is far harder to find tampons (*tampon*) since Islam's emphasis on virginity until marriage undermines the potential market for such intrusive protection. When you can find tampons they usually come in one size only and are relatively expensive.

Contraception (*Doğum Kontrolü*)

You can buy condoms over the counter in pharmacies and they are usually very cheap. Durex products are readily available. The pill is also readily obtainable in pharmacies, although the morning-after pill may not be so obviously available - look for signs saying '*ertesi gün hapı*' in pharmacy windows and expect to pay around YTL18. You can also buy the birth control patch over the counter at pharmacies.

Married Turks needs their spouse's consent before they can be sterilised.

WHERE TO GET MORE INFORMATION

Istanbul

Women & Children's Health, Education & Research Unit (Kadın ve Çocuk Sağlığı Eğitim ve Araştırma Birimi): Tel: 0212-631 9831, Cerrahi Monoblok Karşısı, Millet Caddesi, Çapa. Smear tests. Pregnancy tests. Abortions. HIV tests.

Ankara

Turkish Family Planning Association (Türkiye Aile Planlaması Derneği): Tel: 0312-441 7800, www.tapd.org.tr, Cemal Nadır Sokak No: 11, Çankaya, Ankara

WHAT TO SAY			
birth control patch	*doğum control bantı*	condom	*prezervatif*
birth control pills	*doğum kontrol hapı*	diaphragm	*diyafram*
coil/IUD	*spiral*	morning-after pill	*ertesi gün hapı*

Maternity Hospitals (*Doğum Hastanesi ve Doğumevi*)

For information about giving birth in Turkey, see Chapter 9.
For a list of maternity hospitals see Appendix VIII.

Abortion (*Kürtaj*)

Abortion is legal during the first 10 weeks' of the foetus' life and most hospitals will be able to carry out a termination. Provided the mother and her husband have government insurance this will cover the cost of the abortion.

After 10 weeks abortion is only permitted to save the life or protect the health of the mother or if the foetus is damaged. Unless there is an immediate risk to the mother's life, an obstetrician or gynaecologist will have to confirm the need for the abortion before it can be carried out. It is illegal for anyone other than a qualified gynaecologist or obstetrician to carry out an abortion. Unless there is an immediate risk to the woman her husband will also have to give his consent to the procedure.

Women talk about abortions in a way that suggests that there is little social stigma attached to them. However, there is little in the way of pre- or post-abortion counselling.

Miscarriage (*Düşük*)

Miscarriages are as common in Turkey as anywhere else and most hospitals are able to provide women with a D&C (*küretaj*) afterwards.

Menopause (*Menopoz*)

Going through the menopause is exactly the same in Turkey as it would be anywhere else. However, the tendency to overheat houses can be a problem for people experiencing hot flushes - the best thing to do is wear removable layers, bearing in mind that the bottom layers need to be as modest as the top ones. You might also want to invest in a cheap fan (*yelpaze*). Turkish physicians are apt to insist that their menopausal patients use hormone supplements; you may have to be just as insistent if you decide you don't want to.

WHAT TO SAY	
HRT	*hormon replasman tedavisi*
mammogram	*mammogram*
period	*âdet / regli*
period pain	*âdet ağrısı*
PMS	*âdet öncesi sendromu*
smear test	*PAP smear*

Emergency:	
Ambulance	112
To find a hospital in an emergency	Tel: 444 0911
Cankurtaran/doktor çağırın	Call an ambulance/the doctor.

DENTISTS (*DİŞ HEKİMİ/DİŞÇİ*)

There are all sorts of dentists, ranging from thoroughly professional physician dentists whose surgeries resemble those in the West to other 'dental technicians' who learnt by watching and are good for little more than making dentures. Dental treatment in Turkey is much cheaper than in the UK or the USA, so if you need a lot of work done you might want to consider a trip to Ankara or Istanbul for excellent treatment at very reasonable prices.

You can buy Oral-B toothbrushes in Turkey. Alongside İpana, the local brand of toothpaste, you can also buy Signal and Colgate. It is not always so easy to find special brands like Sensodyne and they are expensive. Flossing materials are also hard to come by.

The US Embassy website (http://turkey.usembassy.gov) has a list of English-speaking dentists in Istanbul, Ankara, Izmir and Antalya. For a list of foreign-language-speaking dentists see Appendix VIII. Many of the private hospitals are now opening dental care and surgical units and some of these are top quality.

WHAT TO SAY

abscess	*apse*	lower tooth	*alt diş*
back tooth	*arka/yan diş*	mouth ulcer	*aft/pamukçuk*
bridge	*köprü*	root canal treatment	*kanal tedavisi*
cavity	*çürük*	to extract	*çektirmek*
crown	*kron*	to fill	*doldurmak*
dental floss	*diş ipi*	tooth/teeth	*diş(ler)*
enamel	*diş minesi*	toothache	*diş ağrısı*
false teeth	*takma diş*	toothbrush	*diş fırçası*
filling	*dolgu*	toothpaste	*diş macunu*
front tooth	*ön diş*	upper tooth	*üst diş*
gum	*dişeti*	X-ray	*film/röntgen*

OPTICIANS *(GÖZLÜKÇÜ)* AND EYE HOSPITALS *(GÖZ HASTANESİ)*

Most Turkish opticians and opthamalogists are just as good as those in the West and prices are comparatively low unless you choose to frequent one of the high-profile shops in Istanbul that sell only designer specs. If your Turkish is not good enough to cope with an eye examination it's worth bringing your prescription from home and having it made up in Turkey. Varifocals can sometimes cost less in Turkey than in the UK and can usually be made up at shorter notice; opticians in and around Fethiye where many British people have retired sometimes specialise in varifocals.

Turkey is gaining a reputation for expertise in laser eye surgery, and patients have started coming here from abroad for treatment. Some Turkish surgeons have even started training visiting doctors in the latest methods.

For a list of opticians and eye hospitals, see Appendix VIII.

WHAT TO SAY

astigmatism	*astigmat*	long sight	*hipermetrop*
contact lenses	*kontakt lensler*	short sight	*miyop*
eye test	*göz muayenesi*	soaking solution	*koruyucu sıvı*
eyedrops	*göz damlası*	soft contact lenses	*yumuşak kontakt lensler*
gas-permeable lenses	*gaz geçirgen lensler*	sunglasses	*güneş gözlüğü*
glasses	*gözlük*	varifocals	*variluks*

MENTAL HEALTH *(RUH SAĞLIĞI)*

Thankfully few foreigners living in Turkey have serious mental health problems. However, some struggle with depression brought on by isolation from friends, family and the familiarity of their own culture. This is less of a problem in big cities like Istanbul, Izmir and Ankara with sizeable expat populations. Nor is it likely to be much of a problem in big coastal resorts like Alanya and Ölüdeniz. However, in some of the smaller resorts foreigners can feel very alone, especially if they or their partner works in the cut-throat conditions of the tourism industry which hardly encourages socialising with other expats in a similar situation. For some Western women it can also be difficult coming to terms with more sharply defined gender roles in Turkey. This can show itself in arguments over a male partner's failure to take any part in domestic arrangements or in misery at being expected to play the endlessly *çay*-serving good *gelin* by their Turkish families. Women whose partners work in the tourism industry can also find themselves worn down by the expectation that they will work without break from April to November, especially when their language skills are seen as crucial to the success of the business.

There are some tried and tested ways to minimalise the stresses and strains:

- Establish realistic working hours from the beginning.
- Consider setting up a local newspaper or, better still, a yahoo group (www. yahoo.com) where expats can exchange thoughts and experiences. You'd be surprised how cheering it can be when someone points you in the direction of some newly imported foodstuff such as Emmenthal cheese.
- Try and learn enough Turkish to talk to your neighbours.
- Buy a webcam and sign up to an Internet phone service such as Skype so that you can keep in touch with home without bankrupting yourself.

Unfortunately if you do succumb to more serious mental illness Turkey may not be the best place for you. Istanbul has several excellent psychiatrists who speak English and some of the hospitals provide good in-hospital mental healthcare. However, the language barrier means that most state-offered therapeutic services will be off-limits to all but the most fluent linguists.

VACCINATIONS *(AŞI)*

Although rabies is present in Turkey not all hospitals stock anti-rabies vaccine to be administered after a bite - you may want to have a course of anti-rabies jabs before moving here.

For information about childhood vaccinations see Appendix VIII.

For the address of the Istanbul health centre which offers pre-travel vaccinations, see under miscellaneous health contacts in Appendix VIII.

WHAT TO SAY			
flu jab	*grip aşısı*	injection under the skin	*deri altına iğne*
injection into a vein	*damardan iğne*	syringe	*şırınga*

SPECIALIST MEDICAL SERVICES

Physiotherapy (*Fizyoterapi)*

It is possible to get physiotherapy in the big private hospitals although it is very expensive, not least because you will have to pay both for the actual therapist and for a doctor to supervise them.

Alcoholics Anonymous

Alcohol is readily available in most parts of Turkey and, sadly, some people, both Turks and foreigners, gradually succumb to alcoholism. If you think you might need help it's worth knowing that there are branches of Alcoholics Anonymous in Turkey; to find the nearest go to www.adsizalkolikler.com.

SELF-DIAGNOSIS

It is never wise to rely on self-diagnosis of medical problems. However, if your Turkish is not very good you may sometimes feel the need to do some research of your own to give you an idea what is wrong before you approach a doctor. If so, the following websites make good places to start:

www.nhsdirect.nhs.uk Website of the British National Health Service with dictionary of medical conditions.

www.healthfinder.gov US medical site with more limited dictionary of medical conditions.

ALTERNATIVE MEDICINE PRACTITIONERS

To find private individuals offering massage, aromatherapy or other alternative medicines, check the classified ads pages of *Lale*, the magazine of the International Women of Istanbul group. For a list of alternative therapists in Istanbul, Ankara and Izmir, see Appendix VIII.

Hamams

Before paying a fortune for a private masseur/se it's worth remembering the Turkish baths (*hamam*). Traditionally, Turkish houses didn't have private bathrooms. Instead people went to the local *hamam* for a thorough scrub and massage (*masaj*). Most hamams either had separate sections for men and women (*çift hamamı*) or set aside separate times in the day/week for the two sexes. Men were washed and massaged by men, and women by women.

Unfortunately as people have acquired private bathrooms the need for hamams has faded. Although some men still go to them for the sheer pleasure of the pampering, fewer Turkish women continue to use hamams, so in many places there are no longer facilities for women. Hamams for men will usually accept foreign females as bathers, but women who are living in Turkey quickly come to feel uncomfortable with such an arrangement as they realise how outrageous it would seem to local women. Hamams catering for tourists usually charge extortionate prices, meaning that visits must remain a rare treat. In contrast local hamams are often extremely cheap; if you can find one you should get a good massage for a fraction of the price charged by private practitioners. Even in tourist areas a visit to a hamam won't always cost more than going to a private masseur/se.

If you are renting a flat with dubious washing facilities you may want to find out where the nearest hamam is as a matter of necessity. Some are used as gay meeting places. The only way to be sure about a particular hamam is to ask around locally.

WHAT TO SAY			
bowl	*tas*	mirror	*ayna*
clogs	*takunya/nalın*	'navel stone' (central slab)	*göbektaşı*
cold water	*soğuk su*	normal towel	*havlu*
comb	*tarak*	shampoo	*şampuan*
hair-dryer	*saç kurutma makinesi*	shower	*duş*
hot water	*sıcak su*	soap	*sabun*
masseur	*masör*	special rough scrubbing mitten	*kese*
masseuse	*masöz*	wrap towel	*peştamal*

Special Diets (*Özel Rejimler*)

If you are on a special diet it is not always easy to find the foods you need and when you do the price is likely to be relatively high. Most of the big food-producers now make calorie-conscious 'light' versions of their products but these usually cost more than the higher-calorie versions.

Vegetarians: Vegetarians need to be aware that many seemingly meat-free dishes will have been prepared using meat stock. It is possible to buy soya mince and chunks in most supermarkets but vegans are likely to struggle when it comes to eating out.

Diabetics: Diabetics can buy a range of sugar-free products in the big supermarkets, although artificial sweeteners (*tatlandırıcı*) may be hard to find and expensive. Try looking in pharmacies as well as in supermarkets.

WHAT TO SAY			
acupuncture	*akupunktur*	massage	*masaj*
diabetic	*diyabetik*	meditation	*meditasyon*
flour	*ün*	vegetarian	*vejetaryen*
herbalist	*şifalı ot satıcısı*	wheat	*buğday*
homeopathy	*homeopati*	without sugar	*şekersiz*

DISABILITY

Until recently Turkey was a terrible place in which to be disabled (*engelli, özürlü*) since the obstacles encountered on a typical excursion out of doors were a problem to everyone let alone anyone with a mobility problem. Slowly, things are starting to improve and the Istanbul *tramvay* was recently upgraded to provide the disabled access which had been built into the plans for its Metro extension. However, it's not much use a wheelchair-user being able to access the tram if the pavement leading to the platforms is too broken to be useable.

Some roadside service stations have disabled toilet facilities but this is by no mean routine, and even when public buildings have lifts these are often far too small for wheelchair users. Increasingly towns are providing sloped kerbs to make moving around easier and a few towns such as Selçuk near Izmir have level pavements and kerbs in the town centre. But there are still too many newly installed access ramps so steeply angled that they would guarantee an accident should anyone actually try to use them.

If things are tough for people with mobility problems, they are even tougher for those who are blind with almost no signs in Braille (except at Istanbul airport). Nor do banks have hearing loops to help the hard of hearing.

For useful contacts, look under miscellaneous health contacts in Appendix VIII.

WHAT TO SAY

blind	*kör*	to lipread	*dudak okumak*
crutches	*koltuk değnekleri*	wheelchair	*tekerlekli sandalye*
deaf	*sağır*	wheelchair entrance	*tekerlekli sandalye giriş*
deaf mute	*sağır-dilsiz*	I need help	*Yardıma ihtiyacım var*
hearing aid	*işitme cihazı*	I'm blind	*Ben körüm*
mute	*dilsiz*	I'm deaf	*Ben sağırım*
sign language	*işaret dili*		

WHAT TO SAY

addiction	*bağımlılık*	scan	*tomografi/MR*
appointment	*randevu*	septic	*mikroplu*
blister	*su toplaması*	splinter	*kıymık*
blood pressure	*tansiyon*	sunburn	*güneş yanığı*
consulting room	*muayenehane*	thermometer	*termometre/derece*
degree	*derece*	to break	*kırmak*
first aid	*ilkyardım*	to breathe	*nefes almak*
infectious	*bulaşıcı*	to sprain	*burkmak*
medical	*tıp*	to sting	*sokmak*
pollen	*polen/çiçektozu*		

CHAPTER 14

THE SOCIAL WHIRL

It is difficult to generalise about socialising in Turkey since so much will depend on where you choose to live and what sort of social life you are seeking. If, for example, you settle in Istanbul you can anticipate a social life not so very different from the one you had at home, especially if you mix mainly with other expatriates and professional Turks. Istanbul has wonderful restaurants, lively nightclubs, cinemas showing films in their original languages, art galleries with changing exhibitions, a full range of concert venues and festivals catering for almost every taste. There are also opportunities to study all sorts of subjects and practise all manner of crafts. If you settle on the coast you will not have access to the same range of cultural activities (except perhaps in Antalya). You will, on the other hand, be able to have a wild nightlife, at least over the summer months. But if you settle inland you may find your opportunities for socialising in a Western way far more constrained. Village-style socialising tends to be family-oriented and centres on visiting, tea parties, engagements, weddings and circumcisions. If you can't speak Turkish you may be thrown back on a small pool of fellow expats, not all of whom would have made natural friends at home.

CULTURE SHOCK

How much culture shock you will feel in Turkey depends on where you live. If you settle in one of the coastal resorts or in Istanbul or Izmir, life can seem comfortingly familiar, especially if you choose to restrict most of your socialising to other expats and mixed Turkish-foreign couples. Elsewhere in Turkey you may feel that you have moved to a country where life is very different from what you were used to. This can even be the case in Ankara, the capital city, which is, for the most part, a conservative place which clings to traditional values.

Alcohol: Along the coast and in Istanbul and Izmir many Turks drink beer, wine and *rakı* and you won't feel that you are doing anything wrong in emulating them (except during the holy month of Ramazan). Move inland, however, and you won't find it easy even to buy alcohol except in tourist areas such as Cappadocia or towns with a sizeable tourist industry. In rural areas respectable women never drink alcohol and nor do more conservative men; the typical rural wedding is therefore likely to be dry. Even Turks who happily knock back a drink most of the time may refrain from doing so on Thursday evening and all day Friday as a nod of recognition to the Koranic prohibition on alcohol.

Clothes: When it comes to clothing Turkey gives off a very mixed message. Once again, in the coastal resorts and in certain parts of Istanbul (especially around Beyoğlu) and Izmir it can seem that women can get away with wearing anything. You will see young Turkish women in skin-tight jeans and skimpy tops who would no more think of wearing a headscarf than any Westerner. But once again you only have to move inland (even to parts of Ankara) and you will find most women completely covered in baggy clothing and clad in scarves of one sort or another. Should you want to go visiting in such areas it would be inappropriate to do so in short shorts and a singlet. Instead you will need to find a compromise way of dressing that suits you and fits in with your particular community.

Sexual Segregation: In Istanbul, Izmir and along the coast men and women socialise together except in the most conservative neighbourhoods. However, in rural areas life is still sexually segregated. This will be obvious to anyone who has ever travelled by bus or dolmuş and either been assigned to a men's (*bay*) or women's (*bayan*) seat, or asked to move so that a woman isn't seated next to an unrelated man. However, what comes as more of a surprise is to find that same segregation applying in homes too, with family members moving around the available seating automatically as new guests arrive so that unrelated men and women don't sit beside each other.

In rural areas men and women spend much of their spare time in separate activities. The men pass their evenings in the local tea-house (*kahvehane/ kıraathane)* while their wives sit at home with their friends and knit, sew and watch TV. A foreign woman can go into a tea-house without anyone criticising her. However, it is not regarded as appropriate behaviour and most foreign women who live in Turkey soon learn to give tea-houses a wide berth.

The problem for outsiders is that the two systems can be running in parallel. In Cappadocia, for example, many newcomers mix with young Turks in the bars and restaurants and don't realise that such behaviour would not be regarded as respectable in their family homes. This makes it very easy to make mistakes. It is also easy to misunderstand the bending of the rules that allows valuable 'tourists' to do much as they please. Once you choose to settle somewhere you may find that leeway being withdrawn. This is even more likely to be the case once you marry and start a family which may explain why many young couples who meet in rural Turkey ultimately move back to the woman's home country where she will not be so restricted. Turkish women who marry Western men, however, tend to gain greater freedom in the process.

THE TURKISH YEAR

Although Turkish businesses follow the Gregorian calendar, Turkish social life revolves around the main events of the Islamic calendar in which Ramazan and Kurban Bayramı are the highlights. *Bayram* is the general Turkish word for a festival-type holiday and you should greet your friends and neighbours with the expression *iyi bayramlar* (happy holidays).

Note that rural Turks often describe months not by their proper names but by their place in the calendar; so they will refer to the third month (*üçüncü ay*) instead of March or the sixth month (*altıncı ay*) instead of June.

Ramazan: During the holy month of Ramazan, Muslims are supposed to fast from dawn to dusk for 30 days. Not only are they supposed to refrain from eating and drinking, but they are also expected to avoid smoking or having sex during daylight hours. Observant Muslims will not even take a headache tablet during the fasting hours.

In the past the fast (*oruç*) was supposed to start as soon as an imam holding one piece of white and one piece of black thread could tell the two apart in the daylight. These days, of course, the times are calculated more scientifically and televisions indicate the exact moment that the fast can be broken in every town around the country. In order to prepare for going without food all day, people are woken by drummers before dawn so that they can eat a large breakfast (*sahur*). When the call to prayer announces the end of the fasting period, everyone sits down with their family for a special meal (*iftar*) which often starts with dates and olives and proceeds to soup and then a main meal. Since families often have a second, bigger meal before going to bed some people actually manage to put on weight during Ramazan.

Not everybody has to fast. Children are exempt as are pregnant and feeding mothers, the sick, the elderly and travellers. Menstruating women are not supposed to fast during Ramazan but have to make up the missed days later. Foreigners are not expected to take part in the fast although many Turks appreciate it if they do (others view it as hypocrisy); however, it is thought bad manners to eat, drink or smoke in front of people who are fasting. In cities such as Istanbul perhaps only a quarter of the population fasts and most restaurants stay open. In rural areas, however, perhaps 85% of people fast and most restaurants close during the day unless they anticipate a tourist clientele (a few continue to serve food discreetly behind curtained windows).

During Ramazan special meals are prepared for *iftar*, the break-of-fast meal. At this time of year it is regarded as particularly worthy to invite outsiders to share the meal, so there is a good chance you will be invited to eat *iftar* with a family to whom you are close. It's a great opportunity not just to share in the sense of camaraderie but also to try out dishes like *güllaç* (a rosewater-flavoured pudding) that are rarely served at other times of year. All sorts of interesting breads also put in an appearance over Ramazan. Even if the food is already on the table you should never start eating until the *ezan* (call to prayer) indicates that the day's fast has ended and the family have offered a swift prayer of thanks.

In Istanbul in particular Ramazan can seem like a time of celebration, with crowds pouring into the Hippodrome every evening to enjoy special titbits on sale from small wooden houses set up there temporarily. Elsewhere, however, the month can seem more like an endurance test, with tempers short and time dragging. In many parts of the country tents reminiscent of circus ones (*Ramazan çadırı*) are set up; poorer members of the community can go to these tents for free *iftar* meals.

Since the date of Ramazan is dictated by the lunar calendar it happens 11 days earlier each year. It is not a public holiday.

WHAT TO SAY	
Are you fasting?/Have you vowed to fast?	*Oruç tutuyor musun?/Niyetli misin?*
May your Ramazan be blessed.	(more polite) *Ramazanınız kutlu/mübarek olsun.*
date	*hurma*
olive	*zeytin*
drummer	*davulcu*

Şeker Bayramı

When Ramazan ends, people celebrate with a three-day holiday called Ramazan or Şeker Bayramı (Sweets Holiday), during which everybody visits everybody else. Children go from door to door kissing the hands of their elders and collecting sweets and gifts of loose change (*bayram harçlığı/ bayram parası*). Adults drop in on friends and relatives and nibble fruit and nuts. Wherever possible they buy and wear new clothes for the occasion.

As a foreigner you are likely to be invited to join in the round of visiting. And of course the children will appreciate your gifts of sweets and money as much as anybody else's. If you have a Turkish family you should take a gift like a box of chocolates or buy clothes for the children when you go visiting.

WHAT'S ON THE TRAY *(TEPSİDE NE VAR?)*			
apple	*elma*	mandarin orange	*mandalina*
biscuit(s)/cookie(s)	*kurabiye(ler)*	orange	*portakal*
cake	*pasta*	peanuts	*fıstık*
chickpeas	*leblebi/nohut*	popcorn	*patlamış mısır*
crisps	*cips*	sunflower seeds	*ayçekirdeği*
hazelnuts	*fındık*	walnuts	*ceviz*
honey-soaked pastry	*baklava*		

Kurban Bayramı

The other major religious holiday in the Turkish social calendar is Kurban Bayramı (the Sacrifice Holiday) when every head of household who can afford to do so slaughters a sheep or cow in memory of İbrahim's near sacrifice of his son İsmael. The meat is then divided into seven parts; some of it is given to friends and family and some to the poor. The sheepskins are later collected and sold for charity.

This is another time of great socialising and communal dining. Children's foreheads are sometimes daubed with a spot of blood for good luck. You may be invited to eat some of the meat at a morning feast; this is regarded as an honour and if you have objections to meat-eating it would be better to find a reason not to attend rather than show up and not eat. Afterwards the children call round once again for *bayram harçlığı* and once again everyone eats their fill of fruit and nuts.

This is the year's longest public holiday, with banks and businesses closing for up to nine days depending on which calendar day the four-day festival falls on.

Some foreigners dislike Kurban Bayramı because they regard the ritualistic slaughter of animals as unnecessary, particularly since it is often done by men with no knowledge of how to kill swiftly and cleanly (until recently the killing was often carried out in public but these days the government is doing its best to ensure that it is done in special slaughterhouses in the cities at least). Others accept the idea behind the slaughter: namely that we should remember and appreciate the source of our food, and share our good fortune with the poor. But these days even some Turks prefer to make a donation to charity instead of killing an animal, and every year the television channels conduct a lively debate over the rights and wrongs of the sacrifice.

WHAT TO SAY	
butcher	*kasap*
cow	*inek*
Did you make a sacrifice? (literally 'did you cut?')	*Kurban kestin(iz) mi?*
first/second/third/fourth day of bayram	*bayramın birinci/ikinci/üçüncü /dördüncü günü*
goat	*keçi*
May your holidays be blessed.	*Bayramınız kutlu/mübarek olsun.*
prayer	*dua*
sacrificial animal	*kurbanlık*
sheep	*koyun*

Other Holidays

The Turkish calendar has a few other fixtures which are celebrated with varying degrees of pomp and ceremony; children bang drums and march, and much homage is paid to statues and busts of Atatürk countrywide. The most traditional holidays are National Sovereignty & Children's Day, Youth & Sports Day, Victory Day, Republic Day and the anniversary of Atatürk's death. Many people travel to visit friends and family over all the *bayrams* and public transport can be very overcrowded.

23 April - National Sovereignty & Children's Day (Ulusal Egemenlik ve Çocuk Bayramı): This national holiday commemorates the first meeting of the Turkish Grand National Assembly (the republican parliament) in 1920. This may be significant to the politicians but for most people the fact that it is also Children's Day tends to be more important, with schools the length and breadth of the country organising festivals, parades etc to entertain the locals. Children and overseas students are invited to visit Turkey at this time and some foreigners have one or two to stay just like Turkish parents.

19 May - Youth & Sports Day (Gençlik ve Spor Bayramı): On 19 May the country commemorates Atatürk's birth in 1881. Schools arrange for their pupils to entertain their elders in much the same way as they did on National Sovereignty and Children's Day. Sports activities take place all over the country and there are often special concerts and other activities aimed at young people.

29 May. Istanbul celebrates Fatih Mehmet's (Mehmet the Conqueror) capture of the city from the Byzantines in 1453.

30 August - Victory Day (Zafer Bayramı): On 30 August Turkey remembers its victory over the Greeks at Dumlupınar during the Turkish War of Independence. There are celebrations in Ankara and Izmir but otherwise this is a fairly low-key holiday.

29 October - Republic Day (Cumhuriyet Bayramı): On 29 October Turkey celebrates the founding of the Turkish Republic in 1923. This, too, is a fairly low-key holiday.

10 November - Anniversary of Atatürk's Death: At 9.05am Turkey grinds to a halt for one minute to remember the exact time of Atatürk's death in Istanbul's Dolmabahçe Palace in 1938.

These traditional holidays aside, there are a few other dates which are becoming important to the Turkish calendar. Even Hallowe'en is slowly creeping up on the Turks.

1 January - New Year's Day (Yılbaşı): Many foreigners are surprised to arrive in Muslim Turkey for the New Year and discover many of the trappings of Christmas in evidence, right down to Christmas dinners in restaurants and Christmas carols being played over supermarket tannoys. This is because the Turks have co-opted most of our Christmas traditions (except the story of the Nativity) and attached them instead to their celebrations for 1 January. Increasingly Noel Baba (Father Christmas) pops up all over the place and Turks find it hard to understand that their foreign friends are celebrating Christmas rather than the New Year.

14 February – Valentine's Day (Sevgililer Günü): Lovers' Day (our Valentine's Day) is also becoming a fixture in the calendar as shops and restaurants in the big cities rush to cash in on a commercial opportunity. Don't expect anyone to celebrate it in downtown Kangal though.

21 March - Nevruz: Until recently it was illegal to celebrate the Middle Eastern spring festival because it was associated with the Kurds and the separatist cause. These days, however, the government actually organises events to celebrate Nevruz. This can be a lively occasion, especially since one traditional way of celebrating was to jump over bonfires. However, in the recent past Nevruz celebrations were often the trigger for violence and it still pays to be careful in towns such as Diyarbakır.

2nd Sunday of May – Mother's Day (Anneler Günü): The Turkish Mother's Day is also increasingly popular, with luxury hotels in the big cities providing celebratory lunches and increased gift and flower-giving in the villages.

3rd Sunday of June – Father's Day (Babalar Günü): The Turkish Father's Day is also an increasingly popular fixture in the social calendar, celebrated with much agonising over what to buy dad.

WHAT TO SAY WHEN

The Turkish language contains a number of useful set phrases to deal with life's routine eventualities. Knowing when to use them can make you seem more of an insider than you really are.

Hoş geldiniz	Welcome!
Hoş bulduk	Set response to *hoş geldiniz*.
Güle güle	Goodbye (said by the person staying). It means literally, 'go with a smile'.
Allahaısmarladık	Goodbye (said by the person leaving). It means literally, 'may Allah be with you.'
Selâmaleyküm	'Peace be with you' in Arabic. Said by traditional men when arriving somewhere or boarding a bus.
Aleykümselâm	Set response to *selâmaleyküm*. Both these phrases are generally said only by men to other men.
Afiyet olsun	Bon appetit! Said when sitting down to eat, when finishing a meal, or to someone else who is eating.
Şerefe/Şerefinize	Cheers! It means literally, 'to your good honour'.
Elinize sağlık	Health to your hands. Said to your host/ess to compliment them on their cooking at the end of the meal. Also said to compliment someone on their handwork.
Geçmiş olsun	May it be in your past. Said to someone who is ill or has suffered some misfortune.
Kolay gelsin	May it go easily for you. Said to someone who is working.
Çok yaşa	Long life! Said to someone who has just sneezed.
Sen de gör	Set response to *çok yaşa*.
Kusura bakma/özür dilerim	I'm sorry.
İnşallah	God willing. Said whenever there is room for doubt about something.
Maşallah	Wonderful! or Praise be! Said to a young child to ward off bad luck, or to someone who has had a stroke of good fortune .
Hayırlı olsun/iyi şanslar/bol şans	Good luck.
Darısı başına	May your turn come next. Said by someone who has had good fortune.

İyi/hayırlı yolculuklar	Bon voyage.
Kutlu olsun/tebrikler	Congratulations.
İyi bayramlar	Happy holidays
Mutlu yıllar	Happy birthday
Nice senelere	Many happy returns.
Estağfurullah	I'm sorry but what can I do? Said in reply to a compliment.
Gözün(üz) aydın	May your eyes shine. Said to someone who receives good news or is reconciled with a loved one.
Güle güle kullan(ın)	May it give you pleasure. Said to someone who receives something new.
Güle güle otur(un)	May you live there happily. Said to someone who moves to a new house.
Güle güle giy(in)	May you wear it happily. Said to someone who gets new clothes.
Allah mesut etsin	May Allah make you happy. Said to newlyweds.
Allah analı babalı büyütsün	May Allah allow it to be raised by its parents. Said to a newborn baby.
Allah kavuştursun	May Allah reunite you. Said to someone whose loved one is departing.
Allah bereket versin	May Allah give you abundance. Said to someone opening a new business.
Zahmet olacak	It will be a trouble for you. Said when asking a favour.

SEEING IN THE NEW YEAR

With every passing year, New Year (Yılbaşı) becomes a bigger deal in Turkey and there are now several street party-style celebratory events to choose from. The longest-lived is the one in Taksim Square but there are also street parties along Valikonağı and Abdi İpekçi Caddesis and in Şişli.

Many luxury hotels offer special New Year menus which differ little from traditional Christmas and Thanksgiving dinners (i.e. turkey and all the trimmings). If you want to dine out on New Year's Eve you should book well ahead and expect to pay considerably over the odds. Be sure to check what's on the menu in case it turns out to be something Turkish instead of turkey!

For a list of places offering New Year's Eve dinners in Istanbul, see Appendix IX.

THE RELATIVES (AKRABA)

In Turkey the family (*aile*) is the foundation of everything. For people from Western societies where family ties have become more tenuous it can be a surprise to discover just how important it is to know exactly who is related to whom in a Turkish village in particular. Such is the importance of family that non-family members are often co-opted into the family by means of honorary titles – see How to Address People below.

How to Address People

aunt's husband	*enişte*	mother	*anne*
brother	*erkek kardeş*	mother-in-law	*kayınvalide/kaynana*
brother-in-law (husband's/wife's brother)	*kayınbirader*	nephew/niece	*yeğen*
brother-in-law (sister's husband)	*enişte*	older brother	*abi/ağabey*
daughter-in-law	*gelin*	older sister	*abla*
father	*baba*	paternal aunt	*hala*
father-in-law	*kayınpeder*	paternal grandmother	*babaanne*
granddaughter	*kız torun*	paternal uncle	*amca*
grandson	*erkek torun*	sister	*kız kardeş*
great grandfather	*büyükdede*	sister-in-law (brother's wife)	*yenge*
great grandmother	*nine*	sister-in-law (husband's sister)	*görümce*
maternal aunt	*teyze*	sister-in-law (wife's sister)	*baldız*
maternal grandmother	*anneanne*	son-in-law	*damat*
maternal uncle	*dayı*	uncle's wife	*yenge*
maternal/paternal grandfather	*dede*		

BIRTHDAYS

These days most Turks know when their birthday (*doğum günü* or *yaş günü*) is and have some idea about celebrating it. Traditionally, however, birthdays were not important and many older Turks, especially in rural areas, don't even know the exact date on which they were born. Because birthdays were not important you shouldn't expect friends in rural areas to give you birthday presents. Nor will they expect any from you, although they'll probably be pleased with anything you do give. You will have trouble finding any birthday card to send, let alone one you actually like.

Of course in the towns it is now quite normal to celebrate birthdays with parties and presents. Not surprisingly the custom is slowly infiltrating the rest of the country, especially the areas where there are a lot of foreign settlers.

VISITING *(ZİYARET)*

Visiting plays a huge role in traditional Turkish social life. Although distance and transport difficulties mean that city-dwellers ring their friends before dropping in on them, in rural areas it is still quite normal for visitors to arrive unannounced at any time of day or night, and, magically, most hostesses appear to be able to rustle up a meal to order. Although whole families visit each other, rural women spend even more of their time in this kind of socialising because they are not encouraged to be out on the streets otherwise.

WHAT TO SAY			
calendar	*takvim*	invitation	*davet*
diary	*günlük*	to invite	*davet etmek*
guest	*misafir*	to visit	*ziyaret etmek*

How to Address Turks

In Turkish it is not normal to refer to someone by only their given name (*ad*). If you don't know the person very well or you have a formal relationship with them you should address them as *Bey* (Mr) or *Hanım* (Ms), words which follow the given name, as in Ali Bey and Ayşe Hanım. Interestingly, husbands and wives may sometimes use these forms of address as a way of indicating respect.

If you know someone very well, you may just call them by their given name. Alternatively you tag onto that a word indicating some familial relationship, even where that doesn't really exist (rather like calling older female friends of your parents 'aunt' even when they aren't really related). If someone is a bit older than you you call them *abla* (big sister) or *abi* (big brother); if they are considerably older you call them *teyze* (aunt) or *amca* (uncle). These titles also follow the given name, as in Fatma Teyze and Mehmet Amca.

In writing you use the terms *Bay* (Mr) and *Bayan* (Ms) instead. These terms precede the surname (*soyadı*), as in Bay Korkmaz and Bayan Koç. Letters can also be addressed to both sexes as Sayın (respected) Mehmet Korkmaz or Sayın Ayşe Koç

Turkish women habitually greet each other with a kiss on each cheek and a hug. Men are more inclined to shake hands. Younger members of the family often greet their elders by kissing their hand and touching it briefly to their forehead as a sign of respect. This is especially the case during bayrams.

Taking Tea

Although people normally associate the idea of a tea ceremony with Japan, the Turkish rituals attached to serving tea (*çay*) to guests are almost as elaborate. Except in the cities, few people have kettles (*su ısıtıcısı*). Instead tea is brewed in a double-burner (*çaydanlık*), often over the stove. This can be a slow process, so an invitation to tea does not always mean the quick encounter you might anticipate.

Once the tea is brewed the youngest woman in the household (often the daughter-in-law) serves it to guests in tiny tulip-shaped tea glasses placed on saucers. She also hands round the sugar bowl, before retreating to sit by the stove and wait for each glass to be emptied before offering refills. It is the norm to drink at least three glasses of tea and almost an affront to refuse a second. If you want weak tea ask for it *açık;* stronger tea is *demli* or *koyu*. Once you have drunk your fill place your teaspoon across the top of the glass to indicate that you have had enough.

ONLY JOKING *(ŞAKA YAPIYORUM)*

You might expect the Turkish sense of humour to be very different from its Western equivalent. However, some Turks are as good at irony and sarcasm as the British. Slapstick is also a staple of Turkish television.

A popular butt of jokes are the Laz people of the Black Sea coast as personified by a man called Temel about whom bookloads of jokes have been written. Some of the traditional stories told about Nasreddin Hoca (the turban-clad man you see sitting backwards on a donkey) are also funny although there is usually a point to their humour.

Turks often worry that they will have overstepped the mark with a foreigner and will rush to reassure you that they were only joking. The few topics completely off-limits to humour include Atatürk, Turkishness, anything to do with the Kurds or Armenians, and anything to do with the Koran.

Turkish hostesses normally serve nibbles with the tea. Usually these consist of a plate of salty (crackers, tiny pizzas etc) and sweet (biscuits or plain cake) snacks. In the countryside you may be offered a bowl of sunflower or pumpkin seeds (which you crack open with your front teeth), a bowl of salted popcorn, or fruit which is usually peeled before being eaten. It is regarded as impolite to decline to eat anything, although once you get to know people they will be sympathetic to individual likes and dislikes.

If you bring a cake or biscuits, don't be surprised to find them placed on a shelf rather than being handed around with the tea. This is so that other guests can't judge you on the quality of your gift and so that the hostess won't lose face if she doesn't like what you've brought.

In many parts of Turkey women organise monthly tea parties which take place in each of their homes in turn. Sometimes the women invited all chip in a set sum of money to pay for the refreshments. Sometimes they club together and buy the hostess a gold coin or bracelet as a way of helping each other build up some savings. If you're invited to one of these gatherings you may or may not be expected to contribute. In Istanbul if you are invited to a tea party it is much more likely that the hostess will provide all the refreshments free.

IN THE TEAHOUSE (KAHVEHANEDE)

Especially in rural or working-class neighbourhoods it is still common for men to spend their evenings in tea-houses (called 'coffee-houses' in rural areas even though coffee is rarely served). Here they while away the hours over games of Okey and cards, the conversation liberally lubricated with glasses of çay. Until recently the traditional nargile (water-pipe) seemed in danger of dying out. However, recently it has undergone a revival and is now a staple not just of touristy tea-houses but also of those frequented by Turkish students.

Although foreign women can go into most tea-houses without inviting adverse comment, most women who have settled in Turkey soon learn to give them the same wide berth as their local sisters.

Gift-Giving: If you are visiting someone for the first time you will be expected to bring some token gift. Appropriate gifts might include baklava, dry biscuits (kuru pasta) or chocolates although in rural areas don't be surprised if someone offers you something as mundane as a box of sugar lumps. In towns it might be appropriate to give flowers but think carefully before bringing a bottle of wine since not everyone drinks alcohol. Turks rarely open gifts in front of the giver which can come as a surprise (and disappointment) to Westerners. This is intended to save everybody's face and certainly avoids the usual litany of platitudes about how the item was just what was wanted.

Reading the Coffee Grains: Just as some people in the UK gaze into the tea leaves in the hope of seeing the future, so Turks stare into their coffee grains in the same expectation. Until recently this was a dying rural tradition.

However, in the last few years reading the coffee grains (*fal*) has come back into fashion and in Istanbul, Izmir, Ankara and other big towns there are now people making a decent living out of the fortune-telling.

MY STAR SIGN IS...			
Capricorn	*Oğlak*	Cancer	*Yengeç*
Aquarius	*Kova*	Leo	*Aslan*
Pisces	*Balık*	Virgo	*Başak*
Aries	*Koç*	Libra	*Terazi*
Taurus	*Boğa*	Scorpio	*Akrep*
Gemini	*İkizler*	Sagittarius	*Yay*

SHARING MEALS AT HOME AND AWAY

Turkish cuisine is widely regarded as one of the finest in the world and eating out is one of the great pleasures of living in the country. However, you will probably eat at home or in the homes of friends much more frequently than in restaurants.

Eating at Home

If you are invited to a friend's house in one of the big cities, chances are that meals will be eaten in very much the same way as they are in the West (i.e. sitting at a table and with everybody having their own separate plate and cutlery). If, however, you are invited to eat in a home in a rural area you may find that the family still sit on the floor to eat around a low table with a cloth spread across their laps to catch the crumbs. Sometimes everyone will have their own plate but often there will be communal dishes to pick from; where that is the case you should help yourself only to the food nearest to yourself, resisting the temptation to reach across the table and grab a tasty morsel on the far side. Rural Turks usually eat using a spoon and fork but if you ask for one, a knife can usually be found. At the end of the meal it is common for a single glass of drinking water to be passed round the assembled throng.

All Turks tend to press their guests to eat more; perversely, it's also considered polite for a guest to refuse more when first offered. But don't let these customs worry you - most Turks know that foreigners can't be expected to understand the minutiae of local etiquette and make the appropriate allowances. When you really have had enough place your knife and fork or fork and spoon on the plate so that they form an open triangle rather than side by side as is normal in the West.

READ THAT RECIPE *(TARİFE/REÇETE)*

afterwards	*sonra*	olive oil	*zeytinyağı*
artificial cream	*krem şanti*	on top	*üzeri*
bicarbonate of soda	*karbonat*	piece/portion	*adet (1 adet yumarta = 1 egg)*
butter	*tereyağı*	preparation	*hazırlanışı*
cake tin	*kek kalıbı*	rolled oats	*yulaf ezmesi*
consistency	*kıvam*	salt	*tuz*
cornstarch	*mısır nişastası*	slice	*dilim*
dessertspoon	*tatlı kaşığı*	small-sized	*küçük boy*
egg	*yumurta*	sugar	*şeker*
egg white	*yumurta akı*	tablespoon	*yemek kaşığı*
egg yolk	*yumurta sarısı*	tea-glassful	*çay bardağı*
first	*önce*	teaspoon	*çay kaşığı*
flour	*un*	thicker	*daha koyu*
food mixer	*mikser*	to add	*eklemek*
fried	*tava*	to bake	*fırında pişirmek*
granulated sugar	*toz şeker*	to beat/whisk	*çırpmak*
grated	*rendelenmiş*	to boil	*kaynatmak*
grated chocolate	*çikolata rendesi*	to stew	*haşlamak*
high speed	*yüksek devir*	to cook	*pişirmek*
ingredients	*malzemeler*	to empty	*boşaltmak*
large-sized	*büyük boy*	to grill	*ızgara yapmak*
lemon juice	*limon suyu*	to increase	*artırmak*
lighter	*daha yumuşak*	to leave	*bekletmek*
liquid	*sıvı*	to roast	*kavurmak*
low speed	*düşük devir*	to sprinkle	*serpmek*
margarine	*margarin*	to turn upside down	*ters çevirmek*
middle-sized	*orta boy*	vanilla powder	*vanilya*
mixture	*karışım*	water-glassful	*su bardağı*

If you are asked to dinner in Istanbul, Izmir or Ankara you can expect to be offered a fairly wide range of dishes, including meat, fish or chicken. In rural areas, however, you are more likely to be served mainly vegetable dishes, perhaps perked up with the odd small piece of meat. Soups are a mainstay of meals, along with rice, bulgur, chickpeas and beans. If you are a special guest a dessert may be provided; otherwise dessert is not always part of an everyday meal.

DO's AND DON'TS FOR VISITORS

Do:

- Remove your shoes at the front door. Your host/ess will usually give you slippers (*terlik*) to wear indoors.
- Always eat something of what is offered, even if it is only a mouthful.
- Use your left hand to cover your mouth when using a toothpick (*kürdan*).
- Wear the plastic shoes provided to go into the toilet. Your host/ess may hang a guest towel on the outside doorknob for you.
- Put all toilet paper into the bin provided to avoid flooding the house.
- Always say '*maşallah*' after praising anything, especially a small child.
- Uncross your legs if someone is speaking to you.

Don't:

- Sit down beside a member of the opposite sex unless invited to do so by the host/ess.
- Point the soles of your feet at anyone - this is seen as insulting.
- Sprawl on a settee - this is seen as impolite.
- Blow your nose loudly in public. Either retreat to the toilet or blow gently and discreetly.
- Throw away any bread. Bread is seen as a sacred gift from Allah – if a piece is dropped some people will pick it up, kiss it and touch it to their forehead.
- Enter a house when only women are present if you are a man on your own - however innocently intended, this could be construed as damaging the honour (*namus*) of the women present.

Takeaway Food

Turkey has a few pizza delivery services similar to those in the West. Most *lokanta*s will also rush round with soup and kebabs as and when. If you live in Istanbul, Ankara or Izmir and can't be bothered cooking it's also worth trying www.yemeksepeti.com, a website which lists many more upmarket restaurants with home-delivery services.

Cooking at Home

Once you have a home of your own you will be able to prepare your own meals. However, although what is available in the shops is steadily improving you may not be able to find all the ingredients you have been used to. This may mean amending or abandoning some of your favourite recipes. For example, self-raising flour is not available in Turkey and it may take a few tries before you discover how much baking powder you need to add to Turkish flour to get the result you are anticipating.

There are several excellent Turkish cookery books available although unless you can read Turkish you may find them difficult to use. Particularly mouth-watering are the books by Emine Beder (published by İnkilap).

WHAT TO LOOK FOR

- *Secrets of the Turkish Kitchen* by Angie Mitchell (Çitlembik)
- *Classic Turkish Cookery* by Ghillie & Jonathan Basan (St Martin's Press)

Eating in a Restaurant

Chances are if you eat out in a restaurant it will be with Turks who are used to this. Almost all Turkish restaurants have normal tables and chairs, except in a few tourist areas where people are trying to revive the traditional ways of eating. Everyone will have their own plate, cutlery and glass in a conventional restaurant.

WHAT TO SAY			
bill	*hesap*	napkin	*peçete*
breakfast	*kahvaltı*	restaurant	*lokanta/restoran*
child's portion	*çocuk porsiyonu*	service charge	*servis*
dessert	*tatlı*	tip	*bahşiş*
dinner	*akşam yemeği*	waiter	*garson*
family area	*aile salonu*	without meat	*etsiz*
lunch	*öğle yemeği*	without oil	*yağsız*
menu	*menü*	without salt	*tuzsuz*
Can I see the menu please?		*Menüye bakabilir miyim?*	
Can you bring the bill please?		*Lütfen, hesabı getirebilir misiniz?*	

A standard restaurant meal might consist of a soup followed by a main course and then either a milk pudding or a plate of seasonal fruits. It is normally followed by a glass of tea unless you specifically ask for coffee. You won't always be offered alcohol except in tourist areas or in *meyhane*s which are like Greek tavernas. In a *meyhane* a meal usually starts with a range of hot and cold *meze*s which include assorted salads, small fish dishes, cheese and perhaps *humus* or *cacık*. The *meze*s alone can be enough to fill you up but if they don't, then you can order fish or grilled meat as a main course. The meal will be rounded off with fruit and a glass of tea, but along the way it will have been well lubricated with wine or *rakı*. Since you usually pay for *meze*s by the dish it's wise to resist over-ordering.

One Turkish custom that Westerners take a while to get used to is that it is normal for the host to pay for the entire meal for everybody, especially when foreign guests are present. Westernised Turks are coming round to the idea of going Dutch (or going German, as they call it) but generally this is still seen as rather strange. You should bear this in mind before inviting a Turkish friend to a pricey restaurant, since it can be very embarrassing if they refuse to let you contribute to the cost of a large bill. You should also remember the obligation it places upon you to reciprocate the generosity from time to time. It is not yet common for a female to pay for an entire meal and before insisting you should consider whether your host could feel humiliated if he is not seen to foot the bill; if you, as a female, are planning to pay, you should give the waiter a small but meaningful nod to make sure he will discreetly hand you the bill. The one exception to this is in tourist resorts where the exact opposite may apply, with young Turkish males taking it for granted that their 'rich' foreign partner will pick up the tab for their meals. As prices rise it may be that the custom of one person paying for everyone will die a death as it has done in the West.

PLEASE PASS THE... (LÜTFEN...VEREBİLİR MİSİNİZ?)			
ketchup	ketçap	pepper	biber
mayonnaise	mayonez	salt	tuz
mustard	hardal	vinegar	sirke

Tipping: It is normal to leave around 10% of the bill as a tip in restaurants, although in more basic *lokanta*s it is acceptable just to round the bill up a little. Before leaving the 10% you should check the bill to make sure the tip has not already been added. Bills are often totted up, then folded over with the total scrawled on the back. Just occasionally this may prevent you seeing some fiddling or that the service charge has already been included.

Foreign Restaurants

For people coming to Turkey from the big multicultural cities of the West such as London, Paris, New York and Melbourne, it can be a shock to discover how few 'ethnic' restaurants there are even in Istanbul. In particular newcomers often bemoan the dearth of restaurants selling Asian food anywhere except in Istanbul, Ankara and the coastal resorts. Turkish food may be wonderful but for people used to being able to pick and choose from all the world's great cuisines it can quickly come to be seen as rather limited, especially as most Turks hate to tamper with tried and tested recipes. A 'New Turkish' cuisine is slowly evolving but mainly consists of restaurants offering a range of

Western dishes alongside the Turkish ones; rarely are the old recipes altered although they may be presented with more flair.

For those times when you feel that you really need the taste of home, Appendix IX has a list of ethnic restaurants, most of them inevitably in Istanbul. In the coastal resorts it is easy to find the few 'ethnic' restaurants although how authentic they are when most serve a mix of Indian, Chinese and Mexican dishes remains to be verified.

Vegetarian Restaurants

For the time being, there are few vegetarians in Turkey. However, in big tourist areas and in the trendier districts of Istanbul there are a few purely vegetarian restaurants and other eating places that offer some dishes to suit non-meat-eaters. However, you need to be aware that meat stock may have been used in the creation of even such supposedly vegetarian-friendly dishes as lentil soup (*mercimek çorbası*).

To be sure there is no meat in your dish, say '*et yemiyorum*' (I don't eat any meat) to the waiter, but prepare to be surprised anyway.

Vegans will have a hard time of it in Turkey. However, you can always try saying '*yalnız meyve sebze yiyorum*' (I only eat fruit and vegetables).

For a list of vegetarian restaurants see Appendix IX.

Kosher Restaurants

Since Turkey only has a small Jewish population these days there are few kosher restaurants. However, Muslims, like Jews, avoid eating pork which means that many restaurants may have suitable dishes available. They will not, of course, have been certified by a rabbi.

Kosher restaurants are listed in Appendix IX.

FORMAL CATERING

In the biggest cities it is possible to arrange for outside caterers to organise your parties for you. This is seen as prestigious because of the inevitable associated cost. Most of the caterers listed below can provide chairs, tables, cutlery and crockery as well as food, drink and music for a party. Some catering companies also hire out private venues if you don't want your guests to dine in your own house. There is a list of professional catering firms in Appendix IX.

FURTHER READING

- *Culture Shock! Turkey* by Arın Bayraktaroğlu (Kuperard)
- *Culture Smart! Turkey – A Quick Guide to Customs & Etiquette* by Charlotte McPherson (Greenhouse)

CHAPTER 15

HAVING FUN

If you are a sports lover then to live happily in Turkey you are going to need to find ways both to play sports and watch them. Unfortunately although most of the male population is football-crazy there are not many facilities for other sports once you get away from the big cities and the coast where a wide range of water sports are available to residents alongside the tourists. In particular Turkey lacks the network of state-funded leisure centres that liven up most Western cities, although Istanbul has a few new sports complexes. More are likely to open over the next few years.

As income levels rise so there are a growing number of facilities for keeping fit and indulging in pastimes like yoga. Often these are in upmarket hotels or areas with large resident foreign populations or big tourist markets.

In the last five years multiplex cinemas, often attached to supermarkets, have opened in most urban centres. There are fewer theatres and concert halls and, as so often, the best high culture tends to take place in the capital city, Ankara, as well as in Istanbul and Izmir. Exceptions to this would be the summer performances that are staged in the amphitheatres at Ephesus and Aspendos.

SPORTS

Sports facilities are improving rapidly, especially along the coast as adventure tourism gets into its stride in Turkey. Of course, you, as a resident, can use these facilities as well and will have the opportunity to use them during the quieter times of year when prices are sometimes lower.

For a list of shops stocking sports equipment, see Appendix VII. Note that there are a lot of stores selling equipment for hunting and fishing clustered around the Karaköy/Tophane district of Istanbul.

GOLF

Most of Turkey's golf courses are concentrated around Antalya in the Belek area. However, there are also some golf clubs within easy reach of Istanbul and along the south-west coast. In general the Istanbul clubs tend to be for members only; those along the coast are not so exclusive.

There is a list of golf courses in Appendix X.

GYMS

Turks generally see keeping fit as a male activity which means that most of the cheaper gyms are the preserve of preening males. Women will probably feel more relaxed in the more expensive and exclusive gyms unless they can find a cheaper one with a ladies-only day.

There is a list of gyms in Appendix X.

HUNTING *(AVCILIK)* AND FISHING *(BALIK TUTMAK)*

In rural areas hunting is still a popular activity between September and December. People usually hunt pheasants, partridges and quail although professional hunters also go after brown bears, ibexes, deer and wolves. Foreigners need to hunt in groups organised by an authorised travel agency which will be able to advise on which animals and birds can and cannot be hunted. For a complete list of hunting and gun clubs go to http://goturkey. kultur.gov.tr. There are gun shops all over the country although you need a police licence to own a gun.

You don't need permission to fish in Turkey's rivers and seas.

WHAT IT MEANS	
Av yasak	Hunting forbidden
Av kısıtlı	Hunting restricted
Av serbest	Hunting permitted

MOUNTAINEERING *(DAĞCILIK)*

Mountaineering is an increasingly popular Turkish hobby. Foreign tourists are usually most interested in climbing Turkey's highest mountain, Ağrı Dağı (Mt Ararat, 5137m) in the east near Doğubeyazıt, but mountaineering is also possible in the Toros-Aladağlar, Cilo-Sat and Kaçkar ranges. Some people also climb Hasan Dağı (Mt Hasan, 3268m), near Aksaray and Erciyes Dağı (Mt Erciyes, 3916m) overlooking Kayseri.

TO FIND OUT MORE

- *Department of Youth & Sports Turkish Mountaineering Federation:* Tel: 0312-310 1518, Ulus, Ankara
- *www.allaboutturkey.com/mountain.htm* Information on all the climbable mountains plus a list of university mountaineering clubs
- *www.akut.org.tr* Akut - Turkish Search & Rescue Organisation

RUNNING *(KOŞMA)*

There are **Hash House Harrier** groups in Istanbul, Ankara, Izmir, Antalya, İncirlik and Fethiye; for more information go to www.ih3.org.

Istanbul

The **Intercontinental Istanbul-Eurasia Marathon** takes place annually in mid-October (Tel: 0212-234 4200, www.istanbulmarathon.org). The route starts on the Asian shore, crosses the Bosphorus Bridge, winds round town and finishes outside the BJK Stadium, opposite the Dolmabahçe Palace. It grows more popular every year.

SWIMMING *(YÜZME)*

Few Turks know how to swim since swimming lessons are not part of school curricula (the better private schools sometimes have their own pools). There are very few Olympic-length swimming pools *(yüzme havuzu)* open to the public. Normally if there is no pool in your accommodation complex, your choices will come down to those available in local hotels which are often open to outsiders in return for payment. Even in the big cities the idea of the sports centre with a pool available to everyone is a novelty. Instead you will be dependent on the facilities in the upmarket hotels which issue day passes to non-residents, albeit for a steep fee. It's slightly cheaper to use their pools midweek rather than at the weekend.

For a list of swimming pools open to the public see Appendix X.

TENNIS *(TENİS)*

If you want to play tennis in Turkey you will almost certainly have to join one of the private tennis clubs – most admit only members and their guests. A list of clubs appears in Appendix X.

WATER SPORTS

Turkey's thriving tourist industry ensures that all sorts of water sports are on offer in the resorts. You can go water-skiing, kayaking and canoeing in all of them; scuba diving is also routinely available. White-water rafting is possible in the Aladağ National Park; at Yusufeli; near Dalaman; and just outside Antalya in the Köprülü Kanyon. If you'd rather just laze on a beach, www.blue-flag.org lists those beaches in Turkey that have been awarded blue-flag status for their cleaniness.

Turkey's main marinas are listed in Appendix X.

Sailers and yachties will certainly want to be in Bodrum for the **International Wooden Yacht Regatta** which takes place every October. Programme details are available from ERA Bodrum Yacht Club (Tel: 0252-316 2310, www.bodrumcup.com, Neyzen Tevfk Caddesi No: 160/A)

WINTER SPORTS

One of the pleasures of living in Turkey is that the country's vast size and varied climate means that you can be sunbathing near Antalya one day, then skiing in Saklıkent the next. Here are details of the various ski resorts although when the season starts and ends each year depends on when snow falls:

- *Davras Dağı*: 25km from Isparta. Two hotels. Skiing from mid-December to end of March. Snowboarding.

- *Erciyes Dağı*: 25km from Kayseri. Skiing at 2200m-3100m from mid-November to mid-April. Two chairlifts, two T-bars. Equipment hire. Two hotels.

- *Ilgaz*: 40km from Kastamonu. Skiing from 1765m-2587m from mid-December to end of March. Three hotels.

- *Kartalkaya*: 38km from Bolu, 200km from Ankara airport, 275km from Istanbul airport. Skiing in the Köroğlu Mountains at 1880m-2220m from mid-December to late March. Three chairlifts, seven T-bars. Equipment hire. Three hotels. Cross-country and Alpine skiing possible.

- *Kartepe*: 115km from Istanbul. Three chairlifts, one T-bar. One hotel.

- *Palandöken*: 5km from Erzurum. Skiing at 2200m-3100m from mid-December to mid-May. Three chairlifts, one T-bar. Equipment hire. Three hotels.

- *Saklıkent*: 51km from Antalya. Skiing at 1850m-2200m from mid-December to April. Two T-bars. Two hotels. Snowboarding and paintballing.

- *Sarıkamış:* 60km from Kars. Skiing at 2200m-2650m from late December to late March. Two chairlifts, one T-bar. Equipment hire. Two hotels.

- *Uludağ:* 270km from Istanbul, near Bursa. Skiing at 2450m in Uludağ National Park from mid-December to late March. One cable car, five chairlifts, seven T-bars. Equipment hire. Nine hotels. Cross-country and Alpine skiing possible.

TO FIND OUT MORE

- *Dept of Youth & Sports Turkish Skiing Federation:* Tel: 0312-311 0764, Ulus, Ankara

- *Istanbul Municipality Sports Association (Istanbul Büyükşehir Belediyesi Spor Etkinlikleri):* Tel: 0212-234 4200, www.ibbsporetkin.com, Libadiye Caddesi, Küçükçiftlik, Lunapark karşısı, Dolmabahçe. Website offers lots of information about sporting activities in Istanbul but only in Turkish.

YOGA *(YOGA)*

In the last few years yoga has been taking off in a big way, with a few top-notch yoga centres in Istanbul and several yoga retreats along the coast, especially around Bodrum, Marmaris and Fethiye. There are, of course, many types of yoga. For venues offering Sahaja yoga in Turkey go to www.sahajayogaturkey.f2s.com. Otherwise, there is a list of yoga venues in Appendix X.

WHAT TO SAY			
active	*dinç*	to hunt	*avlanmak*
healthy	*sağlıklı*	to run	*koşmak*
to exercise	*egzersiz yapmak*	to swim	*yüzmek*
to fish	*balık tutmak*	to walk	*yürümek*
to go skiing	*kayak kaymak*		

Spectator Sports

FOOTBALL (*FUTBOL*)

All big Turkish towns have professional football teams, many of them attracting a fanatical following. Every summer weekend you will be able to attend a football match and usually this will offer an enjoyable insight into male culture. Unfortunately Turkey is no longer immune to the sort of football violence that blights many European matches; competition is stiffest between Turkey's top four teams (Galatasaray, Fenerbahçe, Beşiktaş and Trabzon) but fights have broken out during and after the games of other teams as well.

Even if you don't want to attend live matches the coming of satellite TV means that you can watch football virtually every night of the week. Many bars and clubs host big-screen TVs; sometimes they show the most popular matches free of charge, sometimes they levy a fee. If you want to bet on the results look for a shop displaying the 'İddaa' crossed-fingers logo.

Details of Turkey's most popular football clubs appear in Appendix X.

BASKETBALL (*BASKETBOL*)

Basketball is an increasingly popular sport in Turkey and all three of the big Istanbul football outfits (Galatasaray, Fenerbahçe and Beşiktaş) also have basketball teams. Other hugely popular teams include the Efes Pilsen and Ülker teams. Men and women's teams play a couple of times a week from October through to June.

TO FIND OUT MORE

- *Turkish Basketball Federation:* Tel: 0212-679 7420, www.tbf.org.tr

HORSE RACING (*AT YARIŞI*)

Turks are keen horse racing fans and there are tracks in Istanbul, Izmir, Adana, Bursa, Urfa and Elazığ. Betting is co-ordinated by the Turkish Jockey Club (*Türkiye Jokey Kulübü* - www.tjk.org).

FORMULA ONE GRAND PRIX RACING

Istanbul recently started hosting Formula One Grand Prix racing every August. It takes place at the brand-new Istanbul Parkı circuit at Tuzla/Kurtköy, way out from the city centre near the Sahiba Gökçen airport. Tickets for the three-day event sell out quickly but are available from www.biletix.com.

OIL WRESTLING (*YAĞLI GÜREŞ*)

Even if you're not usually keen on wrestling, while in Turkey you should certainly try to watch a bout of the oily version. The most famous contests take place each June in the Kırkpınar area of Edirne, but if you keep an eye out you should spot posters advertising local events, especially along the coast.

TO FIND OUT MORE

- *Turkish Traditional Sports Federation:* Tel: 0312-311 6193, Ankara
- *www.allaboutturkey.com/yagligures.htm*: Detailed description of the sport.

CAMEL WRESTLING (*DEVE GÜREŞİ*)

Another very colourful Turkish sport that is well worth watching is camel wrestling which takes place along the Aegean coast in winter when the male camels come into heat. The best known bout is the one that takes place in Selçuk around the third week of January but you should be able to spot posters advertising other contests right through until April.

TO FIND OUT MORE

- *Turkish Traditional Sports Federation:* Tel: 0312-311 6193, Ankara
- *www.allaboutturkey.com/camel.htm*: Detailed description of the sport.

CİRİT

Cirit is a Turkish equestrian sport with its roots in Central Asia. During a typical bout, contestants compete to dehorse each other using javelins. Most events take place in early summer, although there is usually one in Uşak to commemorate Cumhuriyet Bayramı on 29 October. As *cirit* has gained in popularity recently some contestants have toured their sport round Central Anatolia, so it's always worth keeping a look out for posters.

TO FIND OUT MORE

- *Turkish Traditional Sports Federation:* Tel: 0312-311 6193, Ankara
- *www.turkishculture.org*: Detailed description of the sport.

HAIR (*SAÇ*) AND BEAUTY (*GÜZELLİK*)

Urban women have always been as keen as their counterparts elsewhere in the world on making themselves look good. In rural areas wearing make-up (*makyaj*) is still frowned on. Elsewhere, though, some younger Turkish women favour a more heavily made-up look than is popular in the West. Even in the remotest towns there will always be a hairdressing salon which sometimes doubles as a general beauty parlour. Of course there are barber's shops everywhere as well.

Hairdressers (*Kuaför*): In Western Turkey a trip to the hairdresser is very similar to a trip to the hairdresser at home. These days most salons use the same hair-care products as in the West and even organic products are starting to put in an appearance, albeit at a high price. The biggest problem is likely to be explaining what you want in Turkish - if you don't think your Turkish is up to it and you can't find a Turkish-speaking friend to go with you try taking a photo from a magazine that shows what you would like done.

It is not always necessary to make an appointment (*randevu)* for a haircut although salons are increasingly busy as living standards and incomes rise. Try and avoid going to the hairdresser's on a Friday or Saturday since these are the days when women have their hair done ready for weekend weddings and other social events - you might end up waiting hours to be served. It's wise to tip your coiffeur to ensure good service when you return.

As in the West, many hairdressers also offer manicures (*manikür*), pedicures (*pedikür)* and waxing (*ağda*) services (these are especially important in Turkey since Islam requires women to remove all their body hair) at prices much lower than those you pay in the West. In the richer parts of the big cities you can also find beauty centres offering a range of services, including cellulite reduction, Botox etc; look in the back of the Turkish version of *Cosmopolitan* for addresses.

Only in Eastern Turkey does a visit to the hairdresser become more exotic. Once you get inside the salon everything will seem perfectly normal. However, since sexual segregation is still taken very seriously in most parts of the east you may have some trouble finding a women's hairdresser and when you do its entrance may be inconspicuous, with the windows covered to prevent anyone peeping in.

Barbers (*Berber*): Men find a trip to the Turkish barber more of an adventure since many still offer a full shaving service using cut-throat razors (*ustura*) as well as the normal hair-cutting. It is also usual for barbers to tweak out ear hair and burn off any surplus facial hair. Barbers also offer head and shoulder massages as part of their service which can cause some misunderstanding in tourist areas where foreign women go into what is basically a barber's shop and don't know exactly when the 'massage' should stop.

Hair and Beauty Products

There are a number of beauty products which are popular in Turkey but not much known, or used, elsewhere. For example, henna (*kına*) is frequently used to colour hair anything from deep brown to a rather lurid orange.

Both Avon (www.avon.com.tr) and Oriflame (www.oriflame.com) have a large and devoted clientele, especially in rural areas where women are still not expected to go out shopping more than necessary. Buying from a catalogue makes life easier for them.

Clarin's beauty products are available from Debenham's and Douglas in Istanbul, albeit at a mark-up on British prices. For a list of other shops selling beauty products see Appendix VII.

I'D LIKE...			
aftershave	tıraş losyonu	hairspray	saç spreyi
bald	kel	highlights	röfle
beard	sakal	laser hair removal	lazer epilasyon
bikini wax	bikini ağdası	leg wax	bacak ağdası
blow-dry	fön	lighter (weight)	daha hafif
centre parting	ortadan ayrılmak	moustache	bıyık
colouring	boya	my hair	saçlarım
comb	tarak	perm	perma
conditioner	saç kremi	razorblade	jilet
cosmetics	makyaj malzemesi	scissors	makas
curly	kıvırcık	shampoo	şampuan
cut & blow-dry please	kesip fönleyin lütfen	shave	tıraş
eyebrow	kaş	shaver	tıraş makinesi
hair gel	jel	shaving foam	tıraş köpüğü
hair grips	saç tokaları	shorter	daha kısa
dyeing hair roots	dip boyası	side parting	yandan ayrilmak
hairbrush	saç fırçası	straight	düz
haircut (man – includes shave)	saç tıraşı	straightening	düzleştirme
haircut (woman)	saç kesimi	thinner	daha ince
hair-drier	saç kurutma makinesi		

HEALTH CENTRES

Many of the big hotels have glistening new health centres that sometimes double as more upmarket gyms. A list appears in Appendix X.

SPAS AND THERMAL RESORTS

Earthquakes may be the downside of Turkey's geographical location but the upside is that the country is liberally dotted with hot springs (*kaplıca)* that shoot out of the earth at temperatures varying from cool to boiling hot. Most have simple resorts built around them and advertise the health benefits of bathing in their waters. However, they are usually disappointingly unattractive to Western eyes, with little attempt made to prettify what are very utilitarian buildings. A list of some of the best appears in Appendix X.

Day Spas: Increasingly hotels and resorts are including purpose-built day spas into their plans to cater for an upmarket and often foreign clientele who require something more visually inviting than the old-style thermal resorts. Most are also open to day visitors on payment of a fee. A list of possibilities appears in Appendix X.

CINEMAS *(SİNEMA)*

These days you don't have to wait long for the latest Hollywood blockbuster to hit Turkish cinema screens and foreigners have a distinct advantage over the locals since most new films are shown in their original language with Turkish subtitles (children's films are usually dubbed).

Cinema-going used to be restricted to the biggest cities, but recently multiplex cinemas have opened in most urban areas. Some are flashier than others, and prices are often high by Turkish standards (though not by London or New York ones). One quirk to be aware of is that you are expected to tip the usher some loose change for showing you to your seat. You may also have to pay to use the toilets. As in the West, drinks and sweets on sale at cinemas are extortionately expensive.

The *Turkish Daily News* and *The New Anatolian* give listings for what is on in Istanbul, Ankara and Izmir, but they are not always accurate; nor are they comprehensive. Otherwise you will have to wait to find out what's on. *Time Out Istanbul* (English edition) reviews new films as they come out. The mymerhaba website (www.mymerhaba.com) also highlights new films in its events calendar as they go on release in Istanbul and Ankara, while the Biletix website (see below) indicates which movies are selling best - unfortunately its write-ups are in Turkish only for the time being.

Some cinemas offer discounts for afternoon showings and on certain days, as well as giving discounts to students. Prices at cinemas in the flashy shopping centres are often particularly steep (around YTL15) whereas in rural areas they can be blissfully low (around YTL2.5).

If you can't find anything that you want to watch and can get a group of friends together you can book a small private cinema at Kafika and choose from their collection of films on DVD (for details, see under Beyoğlu cinemas in Appendix X).

A list of cinemas appears in Appendix X.

Open-air cinemas: In summer it's great to be able to head for an open-air cinema. In Istanbul most open at the weekend or on one or two weekday evenings only; in the resorts they open most nights. A list of open-air cinemas appears in Appendix X.

COURSES *(KURS)* AND LECTURES *(SEMİNER)*

Apart from studying Turkish you can take many other courses in English, especially if you live in Istanbul or one of the coastal resorts. Many are advertised in *Lale* and *Land of Lights*; dance and Turkish cookery classes are listed in Appendix X. Of course if your Turkish is good enough to study alongside native Turkish-speakers it will open up many more opportunities; there are, for example, many photography and art classes on offer in Istanbul and many of the embassies offer classes in their own languages, primarily aimed at Turks but open to anyone who can keep up.

Especially if you live in Istanbul you will also be able to attend regular seminars and lectures on all sorts of subjects, Turkish and otherwise. *Time Out* lists many such events. The Greenhouse bookshop in Kadıköy offers a monthly programme of events which are advertised on the door several months ahead. Bonjour Ankara (Tel: 0312-446 5076) also organises lectures in French on the first Wednesday of the month at the Sheraton Hotel at 11am.

TICKETS FOR EVERYTHING

If you want to go to a concert or other organised event but don't want to risk missing a ticket or having to wait in a long queue, then the answer is Biletix (Tel: 0216-454 1555, www.biletix.com.tr), the Istanbul-based ticket agency. Contact Biletix between 8.30am and 9pm Monday to Friday or between 10am and 9pm on Saturday and Sunday. Many book and music shops are also Biletix outlets. Part of the website is in English.

CONCERTS *(KONSER)* & OTHER CULTURAL EVENTS

Particularly if you live in Istanbul you will have ample opportunity to attend concerts featuring every kind of music from pop to classical. Going to the theatre (*tiyatro*) will be a taller order unless you speak fluent Turkish, although you might want to catch a performance of Karagöz shadow puppetry (because these performances are usually in Turkish they are not as child-friendly for non-Turkish-speaking offspring as you might expect). Tickets are usually reasonably priced but popular events sell out quickly.

Istanbul is also the best place for art-lovers, with many changing exhibitions (*sergi*) to supplement the permanent ones in the Museum of Modern Art, and Pera and Sabancı museums. Many of these exhibitions take place in the small galleries along İstiklal Caddesi and around Taksim Square.

To find out what's on where consult *Time Out Istanbul* or the mymerhaba website's events calendar. Alternatively the Biletix website (www.biletix.com) has information about current events. You can also book tickets through this site.

Even if you no longer see yourself as a tourist you might want to visit either Ephesus or Aspendos to listen to concerts or watch plays in such superb settings; mymerhaba and Biletix have all the details.

GAMES PEOPLE PLAY			
ace	*as*	diamonds	*karo*
backgammon	*tavla*	hearts	*kalp*
billiards/pool	*bilardo*	jack/knave	*vale/oğlan*
cards	*kâğıt oyunu*	king	*papaz*
chess	*satranç*	OK	*okey*
clubs	*sinek*	queen	*kız*
crossword	*bulmaca*	spades	*maça*

THE CULTURAL FESTIVAL CALENDAR

If you live in Istanbul in particular you will be able to take advantage of a never-ending sequence of festivals which bring big name artistes to town. Antalya, too, has several festivals, although Ankara and Izmir are not so lively.

Istanbul

Istanbul Foundation for Culture & Art (Istanbul Kültür Sanat Vakfı): Tel: 0212-334 0700, www.iksv.org, İstiklal Caddesi No:146, Luvr Apt D: 10, Beyoğlu. Sells tickets for most of the festivals listed below.

April/May: Istanbul International Film Festival hosted by the Atlas, Beyoğlu, Emek, Sinepop and Rexx cinemas. Turkish films are given subtitles, so if your

Turkish is rusty this is a chance to get to see some of the big-name indigenous movies you might have missed on their normal runs. Book early for most popular events; see Appendix X for contact details.

May: International Istanbul Theatre Festival. Rare opportunity to watch international theatre (i.e. not in Turkish), usually at the Atatürk and Aksanat cultural centres and other central venues. See under classical music venues in Appendix X for addresses.

May: International Istanbul Puppet Festival. Held at the Kenter Theatre, Halaskargazi Caddesi No: 36, Harbiye (Tel: 0212-246 3589, www.tiyatronline. com).

June: International Istanbul Music Festival (tickets: 0216-454 1555) Book particularly early if you want to attend performances of Mozart's *Abduction from the Seraglio* in Topkapı Palace.

July: International Istanbul Jazz Festival.

September: Rock'n' Coke Festival. Pop music festival (www.rockncoke.com) at Hezarfen Havaalanı, Büyükçekmece

September-November: International Istanbul Biennale Arts Festival

In the Fall: Istanbul Book Fair. Held at the Tüyap Centre, Tepebaşı (Tel: 0212-212 3100)

November/December: Efes Pilsen Blues Festival (www.efespilsen.com). Mobile festival using locations in Adana, Antalya, Ankara, Bursa, Diyarbakır, Eskişehir, Gaziantep, Istanbul, Izmir, Kayseri, Konya, Northern Cyprus, Samsun, Tekirdağ and Trabzon.

Ankara

April-May: International Ankara Music Festival (www.ankarafestival.com)

April-May: Ankara International Film Festival (www.filmfestankara.org.tr)

May: International Women's Film Festival (http://festival.ucansupurge. org)

August: Bilkent International Anatolia Music Festival

Izmir

June-July: International Izmir Festival (www.iksev.org). Performances in the ruined theatre at Ephesus.

Adana

June: Golden Cocoon Film Festival (*Altın Koza*)

Antalya

June-July: Aspendos Opera and Ballet Festival. Performances in the restored theatre at Aspendos.

October-November: Golden Orange Film Festival (*Altın Portakal*, www.altınportakal.org.tr)

Bodrum

August: International Bodrum Ballet Festival (Tel: 0252-316 2516)

Eskişehir

May: Eskişehir Film Days (Tel: 0222-335 0580)

LIBRARIES *(KÜTÜPHANE)*

Most Belediyes maintain a small local library which is useful for school-age children who often use it as a quiet place to do their homework. Although most libraries offer a public borrowing system like those in the West, almost all the books will be in Turkish. They also tend to be pretty ancient. The foreign-language and specialist libraries are more likely to be of interest although it would be wise to phone first to ensure that you will be allowed in (security worries recently led to the closure of the British Council library in Istanbul).

For a list of specialist libraries, see Appendix X.

MAGAZINES *(DERGİ)*

If you can read Turkish you will have as wide a range of magazines to choose from as at home, but even if you can't there are some local magazines on the newsstand which you will probably want to buy. You can usually pick up the latest editions of *Time, Newsweek* and *The Economist* as well.

English-language Magazines

Time Out Istanbul: www.timeoutistanbul.com. Monthly mag which provides quirky local news alongside listings for cinemas, theatres, restaurants etc.

The Guide: www.theguideistanbul.com. More permanent listings for shops, airlines, travel agencies etc alongside topical articles and essays on aspects of Turkish life. *The Guide* also publishes Ankara, Antalya and Bodrum editions. The Antalya edition is translated into Russian.

Cornucopia: www.cornucopia.net/. Triennial glossy magazine which describes itself as catering for Turkey connoisseurs. It contains articles on all sorts of aspects of Turkish life, history and culture.

Skylife: www.thy.com/skylife. Monthly magazine of the Turkish national carrier. Has carved out a distinctive niche, with articles on all sorts of idiosyncratic bits and pieces. Great place to find out about small, off-the-beaten-track places to visit.

On Air: Similarly interesting Onur Air in-flight magazine, probing into all sorts of unexpected aspects of living in Turkey.

Turkish-language Magazines

There are Turkish versions of many familiar glossy titles such as *Cosmopolitan, Esquire* and *Marie Claire*. If you can read Turkish these are excellent sources of contemporary information but even if you can't their adverts are often illuminating.

Atlas: www.kesfetmekicinbak.com. Glossy monthly with articles about off-the-beaten-track corners of Turkey.

Gezi: Glossy monthly with articles about off-the-beaten-track corners of Turkey.

National Geographic Türkiye: www.nationalgeographic.com.tr. Local version of the venerable geographic magazine with some articles about Turkey.

NEWSPAPERS *(GAZETE)*

English-language newspapers

In Istanbul, Ankara, Izmir and the coastal resorts you can buy day-old copies of many international newspapers (*The Guardian, The Times, Le Monde, Le Soir, Le Figaro, La Stampa, El Pais, Il Giornale, Die Zeit, Bild, Frankfurter Allgemeine, Süddeutsche Zeitung, De Telegraaf, International Herald Tribune, USA Today* etc.) all year round. In Cappadocia you can also get most of these newspapers and magazines during the summer (April to October). Elsewhere and at other times of year you will be thrown back on the local English-language press unless you can read Turkish. Of course you can always go on online and read the cyber version of your favourite papers for much less money than if you bought the printed version.

Turkish Daily News: Turkey's longest-lived English-language daily newspaper is the staid *Turkish Daily News* (TDN; www.turkishdailynews.com), which provides a round-up of international events alongside overly detailed information about Turkish politics. The Sunday *Probe* edition summarises the week's news. It's cheap and can be found on sale in at least one outlet in most big towns but it hardly makes a riveting read.

The New Anatolian: *TDN* has competition from *The New Anatolian*, set up by the *TDN's* owners after the Doğan Media Group bought a stake in the original. Unfortunately this means that there is little to choose between the two in terms of content.

Executive News Digest: Subscriber service provided by Intermedia (Tel: 0212-287 2803, www.intermedia.com.tr). Summary of contents of Turkey's main newspapers can be faxed or emailed to you daily.

Expat Publications

In the big tourist resorts there are also locally-produced newspapers and magazines, usually in English. Examples include the *Fethiye Times* (www.fethiyetimes.com) and *Land of Lights* (www.landoflights.net), and Dalyan's *Evet*. These make useful starting points for finding out about everything from property prices to how to get involved in local projects.

Turkish-language newspapers

If you can read Turkish your options expand considerably. Turkey has a flourishing newspaper industry with the newsstands groaning beneath the weight of competing titles - over 30 at the last count. Not all of them produce quality journalism, and few show much interest in the wider world. Still, they will keep you posted with what is going on in the country – and they cost a fraction of the price of imported newspapers.

Cumhuriyet: The broadsheet newspaper founded by Atatürk is still going strong although your Turkish will need to be robust to make much headway with it. Its politics are broadly left-wing which doesn't necessarily mean exactly the same in Turkish as it does in English. In other words, don't expect *Cumhuriyet* to be the Turkish version of *The Guardian*.

Hürriyet/Milliyet/Sabah (www.hurriyet.com.tr/English/): Middle-of-the-road publications and more manageable in their use of language. They serve up a modicum of news alongside a diet of lifestyle pieces, some of it interesting once you are living in Turkey. In particular, *Hürriyet*'s *Cuma* section on Fridays has run a highly successful series of features highlighting the 10 best representatives of different categories of restaurant, club etc. Some of these pages have even been published in book form (*En İyi On*).

Radikal: Paper of choice for those who like a left-leaning paper but can't cope with *Cumhuriyet*.

Zaman (www.zaman.com)/Yeni Şafak: These two papers take a broadly Islamic look at the news.

Akşam: Left-of-centre newspaper with politics rather like those of the British *Mirror*.

Vatan/Posta: Cheaper, simpler newspapers with politics similar to *Milliyet*, *Sabah*, etc.

Dünya (www.dunyagazetesi.com): Pink-page paper focusing on politics and economics – Turkish equivalent of *Financial Times*.

Bulvar: Turkish equivalent of the notorious British *Sun*. You won't need much Turkish to 'read' it since it mostly consists of pin-ups and celebrity mug-shots.

Star: Bland centrist newspaper currently in receivership and in search of a new identity.

CHAPTER 16

LEARNING THE LANGUAGE

Many foreigners live in Turkey for years without ever learning the language. However, if you do take the trouble to learn Turkish it is likely to pay enormous dividends in terms of understanding the society into which you have chosen to move.

So how should you set about learning?

The lucky linguistically gifted will pick up the basics of Turkish from listening to Turks and trying to talk to them. However, most people will find that they make only limited progress by this method, particularly when it comes to using correct grammatical forms.

These are the primary difficulties for English-speaking students of Turkish:

- The sentence structure is the reverse of the one to which we are accustomed, with the verb at the end of the sentence.

- Turkish uses a series of suffixes (word endings) to indicate not just the tense of the sentence but also the person who is speaking. For example, *geliyorum* means 'I am coming' while *geldin* means 'you came'. The result of adding suffix to suffix can be the creation of some scarily lengthy words. The Guinness Book of World Records gives *'Çekoslavakyalılaştırabilemedik lerimizdenmisiniz?'* (50 letters) as the longest ever single word. However, since this means 'are you one of that group of people that we couldn't Czechoslovakianise?' you are hardly likely to come across it in daily life. On the other hand you might see such stunners as *gerçekleştirmektedir* (21 letters – 'it is being put into process') or *yayınlanamamaktadır* (19 – 'it cannot be published') as a matter of routine.

- Much of the Turkish vocabulary is derived from Arabic and Farsi rather than Latin. Although words used to refer to modern phenomena may have been taken from French, German or English, it is rarely easy to guess the meaning of words in the way that an English speaker can with, for example, French or Spanish.

There are four main methods of studying Turkish more methodically. You can:

- Buy a teach yourself package and study at home
- Attend a formal Turkish course either at home or in Turkey
- Hire a private tutor
- Study on the Internet

TEACH YOURSELF BOOKS AND TAPES

There are several teach yourself Turkish packages on the market. The best is *Teach Yourself Turkish* by Asuman Celen and David Pollard which can be bought as a stand-alone book or as a book-and-cassette package. *Teach Yourself Turkish* consists of a series of chapters, each of which contains a dialogue, followed by questions, which segue into specific grammatical explanations, more questions and then a final dialogue. It builds up from basics to fairly advanced Turkish and concentrates on the vocabulary you are likely to need in daily life.

Another option is Hugo's *Turkish in Three Months*. This also concentrates on day-to-day vocabulary but is not as imaginative as *Teach Yourself Turkish*. For most people its three-month promise is also likely to prove wildly over-optimistic.

Linguaphone (www.linguaphone.co.uk) has been teaching foreign languages to students for many years. It offers a book and tape package for learning Turkish, as do the American Foreign Service Institute (FSI, www.learn-how-to-speak-turkish.com), Fono (Tel: 0212-422 7760, www.fono.com.tr) and *Colloquial Turkish* (Routledge). If you'd rather opt for Turkish-published books there is also the *Türkçe Öğrenelim* series, as well as a set of books produced by the Dilmer language school.

The Ada, Greenhouse and Pandora bookshops in İstanbul (see p. 484) stock a wide choice of teach yourself Turkish titles.

TURKISH COURSES

Before Arriving In Turkey

Many British local authorities provide summer courses aimed at enabling students to get by on a Turkish holiday. Details of such courses are usually available at the local library and on the Internet.

A few overseas universities also offer Turkish courses.

For a list of Turkish courses overseas see Appendix XI.

Learning Turkish in Turkey

The most popular place to learn Turkish in Turkey is Istanbul where several companies provide courses all year round. Typically, the language schools offer morning, afternoon, evening and weekend courses targeted at differing levels of ability. Most courses are spread out over two months, with 12 hours of classes per week. However there are also more intensive courses which involve 20 hours of classes per week. When calculating how much time you need for a course you should bear in mind that there is normally homework after each class. It is usually possible for a student to be tested before the class starts to see whether they will be able to cope with it. Teaching tends to be traditional and may not suit people who require a modern, student-centred approach.

Students come from all over the world to study Turkish in Istanbul. There are usually students from the USA and Japan in every class, but you will also rub shoulders with students from Eastern Europe and the Middle East as well as many Western European countries.

Courses cost around €280 for four weeks. For a list of places to study Turkish in Turkey see Appendix XI.

CONVERSATION CLASSES

If you have already learnt some Turkish and want to practise, you might like to join a conversation group. Most language schools should be able to put you in touch with a conversation group, or you could try:

- *Turkish-American University Association:* Tel: 0212-247 5784, ucefoundation@superonline.com, TAUA, Rumeli Caddesi No: 60-62, Titiz Apt, Osmanbey, Istanbul

HIRING A PRIVATE TUTOR

Private tutors sometimes advertise in *Turkish Daily News* or at the language schools. Bear in mind that unless they are trained teachers they may not be able to teach in the structured way of a formal school. On the other hand they will be able to tailor what they teach to your particular needs, which is something the schools cannot. For most people it is probably best to think of hiring a private tutor as a way of practising what they already know rather than to learn from scratch.

STUDYING ON THE INTERNET

There are several sites on the Internet to help you learn Turkish.

- *www.practicalturkish.com/www.learningpracticalturkish.com*. Website of Learning Practical Turkish (LPT) which is based in Gümüldür, near Izmir. The company, run by an American man and his Turkish wife, also produces books to help you master Turkish.

- *www.turkish-center.com*. Tömer's online teaching site, offering a variety of basic Turkish courses.

- *www.turkishlanguage.co.uk*. Prepared by John Guise who spent several years working as an engineer in Manisa.

- *www.onlineturkish.com*. Seven-unit course for US$50.

MUDDLING THROUGH

Even if you don't think you can learn Turkish, or you will be in the country too short a time to justify the effort, it is still possible to muddle through by learning how to pronounce the few letters in the Turkish alphabet that don't appear in the English one. If you can at least say individual words correctly there is a fair chance that people will manage to understand you. Turkish has 21 consonants and 8 vowels but lacks the letters 'q', 'w' and 'x'. The unfamiliar letters are:

Cc	pronounced as English 'j' (e.g. *Caddesi* = Jadessi)
Çç	pronounced as English 'ch' (e.g. *çam* = cham)
Şş	pronounced as English 'sh' (e.g. *şapka* = shapka)
Ğğ	silent g (e.g. *doğan* = do-an)
Öö	pronounced as English 'ir' (e.g. *göz* = girz)
Üü	pronounced as English 'oo' (e.g. *dün* = doon)
Iı	pronounced as English 'uh' (e.g. *altın* = altuhn)

With the exception of the silent g (ğ), every letter of a word is pronounced in Turkish. So, for example, 'deve' is pronounced 'de-ve' rather than 'deev' as would be more logical in English.

Turkish plurals are indicated by 'ler' or 'lar' on the end of a noun. Don't confuse this with the 'si' ending which indicates a compound noun. For example a university in Turkish is 'üniversite' but if you are talking about a specific university it becomes ' üniversitesi', as in 'Ankara Üniversitesi'. If you are talking about more than one university it becomes 'üniversiteler'.

The infinitive of Turkish verbs ends in 'mek' or 'mak' ('etmek' - to be; 'almak' - to take). To conjugate a verb you remove the mek/mak ending and add the tense endings instead. If you can manage to learn to form the simple present, future and past tenses of verbs that will take you a long way.

The simple present has the following endings - iyorum, iyorsun, iyor, iyoruz, iyorsunuz, iyorlar, as in the verb 'bilmek' (to know):

Biliyorum - I know
Biliyorsun - You (sing.) know
Biliyor - He/She/It knows
Biliyoruz - We know
Biliyorsunuz - You (pl.) know
Biliyorlar - They know

The future has the following endings - eceğim, eceksin, ecek, eceğiz, eceksiniz, ecekler, as in the verb 'gelmek' (to come):

Geleceğim - I will come
Geleceksin - You (sing.) will come
Gelecek - He/She/It will come
Geleceğiz - We will come
Geleceksiniz - You (pl.) will come
Gelecekler - They will come

The past has the following endings - dim, din, di, dik, diniz, diler, as in the verb 'binmek' (to get in):

Bindim - I got in
Bindin - You (sing.) got in
Bindi - He/She/It got in
Bindik - We got in
Bindiniz - You (pl.) got in
Bindiler - They got in

As you will see, the verb forms include the personal pronouns which are not used separately as frequently as in English. Negatives are formed by inserting 'me' into the verb forms, as in 'bilmiyorum' (I don't know), 'gelmeyeceksin' (you will not come) and 'binmedi' (he/she/it did not get in).

All this is to grossly simplify things. Of course Turkish has many more tenses, and there is something called vowel harmony which makes things much more complex. There is also the wonderful *miş* tense which renders everything conveniently vague. But if you can make a start with the basics it will make your life in Turkey so much simpler and rewarding.

'TURKLISH'

'Turkish' (or Tarzan Turkish) is the name given to the broken English-Turkish spoken by many foreigners and some Turks. Usually it consists of a mixture of the two languages, as in *'açık tea'* (weak tea). More advanced examples of Turklish include such gems as 'friend*im*' (my friend) and 'gay *mi?*' (is he gay?), which neatly intermingle English vocabulary with Turkish grammatical forms.

DICTIONARIES *(SÖZLÜK)*

Redhouse dictionaries are to the Turkish language what Oxford dictionaries are to the English one. They come in a range of sizes, from minute versions that can be slipped into a money-belt to hefty volumes that could easily double as dumbbells.

Increasingly people are also using electronic dictionaries, some of which pronounce the words, others of which simply display them. To see what is available go to www.ectaco.co.uk which also offers Turkish-language packages for mobile phones and computers.

WHAT TO SAY	
book	*kitap*
cassette	*kaset*
class	*sınıf*
conversation	*konuşma*
course	*ders*
dictionary	*sözlük*
exam	*sınav*
graduation ceremony	*mezuniyet töreni*
homework	*ev ödevi*
language school	*dil okulu*
practise	*pratik yapmak*
tutor/private teacher	*özel öğretmen*

OTHER STUDY MATERIALS

- *201 Turkish Verbs,* Talat Sait Halman. Useful revision aid.
- *www.turkishlanguage.com.* Provides advice on installing Turkish fonts on your computer.
- *www.zargan.com.* Online Turkish dictionary.

CHAPTER 17

IMPORTING A CAR

Importing a car into Turkey is made difficult on purpose in an effort to protect the Turkish car industry. It is likely to become easier as the country moves to meet EU requirements over the next 10 years.

Bringing a Car into Turkey: If you come into Turkey on a tourist visa you can bring your car in and drive it for six months without problem. However, if you leave the country during that period you must either take the car with you or pay to have it garaged by the Customs department.

If you are coming to Turkey with a legal work permit you can bring in your car for as long as the permit lasts although you will have to leave a deposit with the Turkish Automobile and Touring Association (for contact details see Appendix XII). When your period of residency expires you will have to take the car out of the country again and your deposit will be refunded.

Unfortunately a lot of paperwork is required to bring a car into Turkey. You will need to show:

- Two copies of your work permit in your passport
- Two copies of your residence permit
- Bank guarantee from a local bank, the sum depending on the weight and model of the car
- Two copies of the original registration document for the car
- Two copies of the document registering the company you work for with the Chamber of Commerce in Turkey
- Two copies of the form confirming delivery of the car to the port warehouse
- Two copies of your driving licence translated into Turkish and notarised or approved by your Embassy
- An insurance policy for the car

- Two copies of the entry carnet issued by the Turkish Automobile and Touring Association
- A written undertaking in a form provided by Turkish Customs
- A health report from a Turkish hospital
- A report from the Justice Department confirming that you have no criminal record
- A report from the Ministry of Finance showing that your tax payments are up to date

Note that as well as all these copies Customs will also want to see the originals of all the documentation.

Your car will have to be reregistered with a number plate that carries the letters MA to MZ (e.g. 36 MZ 005; the letter 'M' stands for *misafir* (guest)). Because these plates used to be blue such reregistered cars are often called 'blue-plate' cars even though the plates are no longer actually blue for security reasons.

Even a foreigner cannot import duty-free a brand-new car that has not already been driven outside Turkey (i.e. you can't import a factory model). You will also have to register yourself and your spouse or next of kin as listed drivers. No one else is legally allowed to drive the car so if you plan to use a chauffeur you will also have to have them registered as a named driver.

Turkish nationals returning to the country can bring their car in with them but will be landed with hefty import duties depending on the age and weight of the car.

Taking a Car out of Turkey: When the time comes to leave you will be entitled to sell your car to another foreigner without any duty being levied. If you sell to a Turk, however, they will have to pay tax on the purchase. The result is that some of the best-value cars for sale belong to foreigners who want to offload them in a hurry.

BUYING A CAR

New Cars

If you want to buy a new car you will need to find a car showroom (*oto galeri*), usually on the outskirts of a big town. BMW, Chevrolet, Citroen, Fiat, Ford, Honda, Hyundai, Mazda, Mercedes, Nissan, Opel, Peugeot, Renault, Toyota, Volvo and VW vehicles are all on sale in Turkey now, and the price will be much the same as if you had bought the car elsewhere in Europe. If you choose a car that is made in Turkey (e.g. Renault) it will be easier and cheaper to find spare parts than if you opt for an imported model.

Second-Hand Cars (*İkinci El Arabaları*)

To find a second-hand car you usually have to look around for vehicles wearing a sign saying *'satılık'* (for sale) in their windows; ask a friend to help you find something; or hunt around for the nearest weekend car sale (*açık oto pazarı*). These sales take place on huge empty pieces of wasteland made available by the local authorities to enable would-be sellers to track down would-be buyers. However, the price of a second-hand car is likely to come as a shock since vehicles don't lose their value as rapidly as they do in the West; you may find yourself being asked for YTL3000 for a 20-year-old car that would be worth peanuts back home. The reason usually given for why you still see so many dreadful old bangers clogging up Turkey's roads is the cheap cost of labour which means that maintaining an old car isn't as expensive as in the West. However, recently things have started to change as more readily available credit has made it easier for people to buy new cars on the never-never. As a result second-hand cars have finally begun to fall in value.

Blue-Plate Cars: If you would like to buy a blue-plate car previously owned by another foreigner it's worth looking in the classified ads page of *Turkish Daily News* or *The New Anatolian,* in *Lale,* the magazine of the International Women of Istanbul group, or in local expat magazines such as Fethiye's *Land of Lights.*

The procedure for buying a blue-plate car is very long-winded. You start by finding a suitable vehicle and, perhaps, getting a mechanic to check it over for you to see that it is worth the asking price. Then you go to the Touring and Automobile Association of Turkey with a letter of credit from your bank and (if you are working) the appropriate forms signed by you and your employers. In return you will be given a Touring certificate for the car.

You then take the forms signed by your employers and yourself to the nearest Customs office to get another certificate. Then you go to the nearest Turkish Traffic Office to get a new number plate and registration document. The police will want to see your driving licence and residency permit. After that you get the car insured.

If you want to buy a blue-plate car it's worth looking at the following websites:

- www.araba.com
- www.blueplates.com
- www.motorplus.net/expats

Other Used Cars: If you want to buy a second-hand car from a Turk you can either ask around to find a bargain or try one of the many used car markets (*açık oto pazarı*). For a list of car dealers, second-hand car markets etc, see Appendix XII.

SELLING A CAR

If you want to sell your car before you leave Turkey you will need to have the sale registered with the Traffic Office and have the sale contract signed by a public notary.

To find a buyer, either place a notice in the window of the car or advertise in *Turkish Daily News, The New Anatolian* or one of the expat magazines. Alternatively you can try www.blueplates.com, www.motorplus.net/expats or www.araba.com.

DRIVING TESTS *(EHLİYET SINAVI)*

The Turkish driving test comes in three parts of which, arguably, the easiest is the practical driving part. Those wanting a licence have to be 18 and have to pass a medical and eyesight test before enrolling for the course. Then they sit a written test based on the Turkish version of the highway code (*Güvenli Sürüş Eğitimi Kitabı)* which is only published in Turkish. This involves learning about the internal combustion engine as well as about road signs and you need to get 70% to pass. Finally there is the actual driving test which is a doddle compared with, for example, the British version since you only need to drive for something like 400 metres, supervised by a school teacher registered with the Ministry of Education to assess your proficiency.

There are driving schools (*sürücü okulu*) all over Turkey and some decidedly overgrown practise circuits on the outskirts of large towns. Unfortunately there are still some drivers on the road who never took any formal lessons, hence the need to drive carefully and defensively at all times.

DRIVING LICENCES *(ŞOFÖR EHLİYETİ)*

A foreigner can drive in Turkey for six months on their domestic licence. After that the rules state that they must take the Turkish driving test and get a Turkish licence or at least have their overseas licence translated. To do this you have to go to your embassy and pay a fee for a translation and certificate of authentication. You take this to the local police who will reissue you with a Turkish licence for around YTL300. Hence the procedure tends to be offputtingly expensive.

In the past these requirements were rarely enforced. However, the police have cottoned on to the fact that they cannot endorse the foreign licence of a resident who infringes the traffic code, so now, at least on the coast, they seem to be trying to make people jump through the hoops to get a local licence. Elsewhere they still seem largely indifferent.

PEDESTRIANS *(YAYALAR)*

To be a pedestrian in Turkey is to find yourself the object of motorists' derision. Although things are slowly improving, official road crossing places are few and far between - and it would be a foolish person indeed who stepped onto one of the optimistically marked zebra crossings in Istanbul with any real expectation that the traffic would stop for them. However, in the last few years dropped kerbs suitable for baby buggies and wheelchairs have started to appear in most big cities, and some towns now have traffic lights which indicate how many seconds there are before red becomes green and vice versa. These lights also bleep when they are green which may be helpful for the visually impaired.

Some cities have pedestrian underpasses (*altgeçit*) but these are usually clogged up with street traders and their wares, and rarely incorporate ramps, lifts or escalators.

STAYING LEGAL

Vehicle Tax (*Taşıt Vergisi*): Vehicle tax becomes due twice a year, in January and July. The sum owed depends on the size and age of the car but tends to be between YTL360 and YTL550 a year. You pay at a bank where the clerk will work out what you owe. Although the police no longer routinely check that you have paid your road tax, if you don't do so and then want to sell the car you will have to pay all the missing tax plus interest on the sum owed.

Car Insurance *(Araba Sigortası)*: Every driver must have third-party accident insurance (*zorunlu trafik sigortası*). This costs around YTL120 a year and you will be liable to a heavy fine if you are caught without it. In addition you can also pay for *kasko*, a special insurance that covers fire and theft. Holders of *kasko* can also phone for assistance following a breakdown. This usually costs between YTL500 and YTL950 a year. As in other countries, discounts are available for drivers who don't make any claims on their insurance policies over the years.

Annual Car Tests: Every two years your car must be tested to ensure that all its lights are working and that no illegal alterations have been made to it. This *araç muayenesi* costs around YTL 90 and if you are caught without the paperwork to prove you have had it done the police are entitled to impound your car. Every year you must also have the car's exhaust system checked to see that it is in good working order. This *egzoz muayenesi* costs around YTL12 to YTL15 a year. Not all garages can carry out the tests; if you are having trouble finding one that does the traffic police should be able to point you in the right direction.

HIGHWAYS *(KARAYOLU)* & MOTORWAYS *(OTOYOL)*

Western Turkey has a fine network of highways and motorways which carry much lighter traffic than is usual in most Western countries. That means that driving can be more relaxing than you are used to. There are some accident black spots (the old Mt Bolu road linking Istanbul to Ankara is one of them although the problem should be reduced once the new Bolu Tunnel is completed) but on the whole the motorways are not as dangerous as more minor roads.

The worst problems occur on old two-lane roads that have to carry much more traffic than they were designed for. The problem is exacerbated when the road also has to carry a lot of ancient freight lorries that move slowly and block the roads, making overtaking difficult and dangerous. For that reason the busy road from Adana to the Cilician Gates at Polatlı can be nightmarish, especially in the dark.

Toll Roads *(Ücretli Yollar)*

Turkey's motorways are mostly toll roads. The tolls are not particularly high (usually a couple of lira) and there are several ways to pay them. The OGS *(Otomatik Geçiş Sistemi)* queue is for people who have pre-purchased a card from Ziraat Bankası or the post office; you hold this up (or stick it on your windshield) to be read by a camera and the toll is deducted from the amount stored on the card. If you have not already bought a card you need to join the KGS *(Kartlı Geçiş Sistemi)* queue; you take a ticket from the machine as you would in a car park and then pay what is owed when you leave the motorway.

ROAD RULES AND TRAFFIC SIGNS *(TRAFİK İŞARETLERİ)*

In Turkey you always drive on the right and give way to traffic coming from the right, even on a roundabout where extra care should be taken.

In general Turkey uses the same traffic signs as Western Europe. In built-up areas the maximum speed limit *(azami hız)* for cars is 50kph; in rural areas it is 90kph; and on motorways it is 120kph. Drivers and their passengers in the front and back of the car are required to wear seatbelts *(emniyet kemerleri)* and children under 10 are not supposed to sit in the front of the car - laws which are widely disregarded. Motorcyclists and their passengers are supposed to wear helmets and goggles although, once again, this rule is more observed in the breach than the observance. Drivers are also supposed to carry two warning triangles, a fire extinguisher and a first aid kit in their car in case of breakdown.

CAR REGISTRATION PLATES

You can easily tell where someone lives because the first two digits of their number plate *(plaka numarası)* indicate the city where the car was registered (e.g. 06 for Ankara, 34 for Istanbul and 35 for Izmir).

Drink-Driving (*Alkollü Araç Kullanmak*)

Car drivers are forbidden to drive with more than 50mg of alcohol per 100ml of blood which is generally interpreted as meaning that they shouldn't drive after drinking two bottles of beer, two glasses of wine or one glass of whisky/vodka/cognac/gin or rakı. Drivers of other vehicles are not supposed to drink any alcohol at all. Police are entitled to ask a driver to breathe into a breathalyser *(üfleme cihazı)* if they suspect that they have been drinking.

COST OF MOTORING

The price of petrol *(benzin)* has been on an upward trajectory for some time and now costs more than in the UK. Many people run their cars on liquid petroleum gas *(LPG)* which is cheaper than standard fuel. Otherwise you'll pay around YTL2 for a litre of normal petrol *(süper benzin)* or lead-free petrol *(kurşunsuz)*. Diesel *(motorin)* costs about YTL1.50 per litre.

Every driver is obliged to have third-party automobile insurance but private insurance is also readily available. Vehicle tax must be paid twice a year. The cost depends on the weight and make of the car. To tax and insure your car is likely to cost at least YTL480 a year. Road safety checks will cost around another YTL100 a year.

REPAIRS (*TAMİR*) AND SPARE PARTS (*YEDEK PARÇA*)

The outskirts of almost all big towns contain an industrial estate *(sanayi bölgesi)* where you can get simple repairs carried out. In particular you should be able to find a tyre repairer *(oto lastikçi)* there; Bridgestone, Goodyear and Michelin tyres are all on sale in Turkey. You can easily find spare parts for many European makes of car, particularly Renaults which are made in Turkey under licence to Tofaş.

For a list of help lines to contact for individual makes of car, see Appendix XII.

AT THE GARAGE *(TAMİRCİDE)*

accelerator	*gaz pedalı*	inside lamps	*iç lambalar*
air filter	*hava filtresi*	jack	*kriko*
antifreeze	*antifriz*	jump leads	*buji teli*
balancing steering rod	*rot balans*	manual car	*düz vites*
battery	*akü*	oil filter	*yağ filtresi*
bonnet	*motor kapağı*	oil gauge	*yağ göstergesi*
boot/trunk	*bagaj*	petrol can	*benzin bidonu*
brake cable	*fren kablosu*	points	*kesici platinler*
brake(s)	*fren(ler)*	points	*platin*
bumper/fender	*tampon*	radiator	*radiatör*
carburettor	*karbüratör*	rear lights	*arka lambalar*
clutch	*debriyaj*	rear mirror	*dikiz aynası*
disc brakes	*disk frenler*	roof rack	*üst bagaj yeri*
distributor	*distribütör*	seatbelt	*emniyet kemeri*
engine	*motor*	shock absorber	*amortisör*
exhaust pipe	*egzoz borusu*	spark plug	*buji*
fanbelt	*vantilatör kayışı*	speedometer	*hız göstergesi*
fuel gauge	*benzin göstergesi*	starter motor	*marş*
fuel pump	*benzin pompası*	steering wheel	*direksiyon*
gear lever	*vites kolu*	sunroof	*güneşlik*
gearbox	*vites kutusu/şanzıman*	tank	*depo*
handbrake	*el freni*	transmission	*vites*
hazard warning lights	*dörtlü flaşör*	tyre	*lastik*
headlamp(s)	*far(lar)*	wheel	*teker(lek)*
horn	*korna*	windscreen	*ön cam*
ignition	*kontak/ateşleme*	windscreen wipers	*silecekler*
indicator	*sinyal*		

My car has broken down	*Arabam bozuldu*
I have lost the keys	*Anahtarları kaybettim*
I've got a flat tyre	*Lastiğim patladı*
The engine keeps stalling	*Motor sık sık duruyor*

PETROL STATIONS *(BENZİN İSTASYONU)*

In Western Turkey petrol stations have become big business since the Petrol Ofisi state monopoly was broken up; Petrol Ofisi and Türk Petrol stations can now be found alongside those of BP, Shell, Total, and many other less well-known brands. All petrol stations sell normal petrol (*süper*), unleaded petrol (*kurşunsuz*) and dieşel (*motorin*) as well as liquid petroleum gas (*LPG/ otogaz*) although it is all very expensive. They also provide free air (*hava*) and water (*su*). In Turkey the norm is still for the petrol pumps to be manned - and you may well get your windscreen washed free into the bargain. Some petrol stations also have car-washing facilities (*oto yıkama yağlama)* to supplement the oil change.

Petrol stations are often attached to large shopping-cum-restaurant complexes complete with toilets, *mescit*s and hotels. In the west of Turkey these are often very impressive. However, the further east you travel, the ropier the service stations become.

WHAT DOES THIS SIGN *(İŞARET)* MEAN?

yol yapımı/çalışması	roadworks	*tek yön*	one way
dur	stop	*geç*	go
girilmez	no entry	*çıkmaz yol*	dead end
giriş	entrance	*çıkış*	exit
şehir merkezi	city centre	*araç çıkabilir*	vehicles exiting
askeri bölge	military zone	*yol tamiri*	road repairs
servis yolu	service drive	*dinlenme tesisleri*	rest facilities
yol ver	give way	*heyelan*	landslide
tırmanma şeridi	crawling lane	*tırmanma sağdan*	slow vehicles use right lane
ağır taşıtlar sağdan gidiniz	heavy vehicles use right lane	*yaya geçit(di)*	pedestrian crossing/ underpass
bozuk satıh	broken road surface	*tek yön*	one-way street
asfalt yapımı	roadworks	*iş makinesi çıkabilir*	work vehicles exiting
çevreyolu	ring road	*geçici yol*	detour

PARKING *(PARK)*

Finding somewhere to park in Turkey's big cities is as much of a problem as it is in London or New York and although you can sometimes get away with double-parking and switching on your hazard warning lights, at other times your car will be towed away as quickly as it would be elsewhere. Some but not all cities now have parking meters. Others have supervised car parks where you hand your keys to the attendant so that he can park the car and move it around as other cars arrive to make the best use of the available space.

If your car is towed away, you must go to the nearest centre to pay a fine and collect it.

DON'T PARK HERE!	
Park etme	No parking
Park yapılmaz	No parking
Park etmek yasaktır	No parking
Resmi araçları aittir/hariç	Reserved for official vehicles
Aracınız çekilir	Your vehicle will be towed away

Parking and Speeding Fines *(Park ve Hız Cezaları)*

If you are caught parking in the wrong place or speeding (and Turkey has radar speed traps) you will be issued with a penalty ticket that can be paid on the spot. Alternatively you can pay within one month over the Internet or in a bank. If you don't pay within the month the fine rises by increments of 5% until it reaches twice the original sum. On the other hand if you pay within 15 days the fine is sometimes reduced. If you are leaving Turkey soon after incurring the fine you can also pay it at the Customs office.

ROAD ACCIDENTS *(TRAFİK KAZASI)* AND BREAKDOWNS *(ARIZA)*

Turkey has an alarmingly high road accident rate, out of all proportion to the amount of traffic on the road. Some of the accidents are caused by vehicles – especially farm vehicles in rural areas – driving at night with no lights. Some are a legacy of the period when acquiring a driving licence in Turkey was more about paying money than studying driving technique. Some are the result of drunken driving. Others are the sort of freak accidents that happen anywhere.

To safeguard yourself, always drive defensively and don't even assume that everyone will stop at a red light. Avoid driving in the dark as much as possible. And bear in mind that there can be an obstacle on the road - a dead animal, fallen rocks, a pile of stones warning of an accident ahead - at any time.

If you suffer a mechanical breakdown, you should put some sort of warning in front and behind your vehicle to alert other motorists. Turkey does not have a national breakdown service (*araç kurtarma*) like the AA or RAC. If you have *kasko* insurance you can phone for help; otherwise you may have to wait until a good Samaritan stops and takes you to the nearest repairshop. Should you be involved in an accident you should never move your car until the police have arrived and made a report (*kaza raporu*) since their assessment of the accident scene will decide how blame for it is distributed.

Always make sure you have enough petrol for your journey. In most parts of Turkey there are adequate petrol stations but there are still some unexpected stretches of road in Central Anatolia where you will go a long way between fill-up points.

Driving in Winter: Although there is no real reason why you should be more at risk of an accident in winter, the fact remains that some foreigners are not used to driving in the sort of harsh conditions that are experienced during an Anatolian winter. If you plan to drive in icy conditions you should certainly put snow chains (*zincir*) on your wheels; if you live in an area with lengthy winters you should also consider investing in special snow tyres (*kar lastiği*) that grip the road better in icy conditions.

WHAT TO SAY			
car	*araba*	red	*kırmızı*
covered car park	*kapalı otopark*	ring road	*çevreyol*
crossroads	*dörtyol*	roundabout	*göbek*
fuel oil	*akaryakıt*	speed	*hız*
green	*yeşil*	speeding	*hızlı gitme*
junction	*kavşak*	to drive	*araba kullanmak/ sürmek*
long vehicle	*uzun araç*	traffic jam	*trafik sıkışıklığı*
lorry	*kamyon*	traffic lights	*trafik ışığı*
map	*harita*	traffic police	*trafik polisi*
mechanic	*mekanik*	vehicle registration document	*araç ruhsatı*
open-air car park	*açık otopark*	wide vehicle	*geniş araç*
yellow (the light the British call 'orange' which means proceed with caution)	*sarı*		
Can I see your licence please?	*Ehliyetinizi görebilir miyim lütfen?*		

CHAPTER 18

ALL ABOUT ANIMALS

The pets of choice in Turkey are not dogs and cats, but caged birds and fish. Although people are slowly starting to understand the pleasures of keeping furry animals, especially in the big urban centres, many Turks remain frightened of dogs. Religious Turks also claim that the Koran warns against canines as dirty animals on account of their omnivorous eating habits. Although Turks are more relaxed about cats, they rarely want them as house pets and are often terrified of swallowing their fur, believing it can make them ill.

When Turks do decide to keep dogs they often prefer pedigrees to homeless strays. At the time of writing huskies (*Sibirya köpeği*) had taken over from German shepherds (*Alman kurt köpeği)* as the pet canines of first choice although small fluffy dogs the size of cats were also increasingly popular.

Unfortunately Turkish streets are full of homeless dogs (*sokak köpeği*) and cats (*sokak kedisi*). Even foreigners who don't particularly want to keep a pet often end up doing so because a stray finds them when they are feeling vulnerable. However, taking on an animal brings with it many complications that would not arise in the West because of different attitudes to pet-keeping in Turkey, the cost of good veterinary care and the difficulty/expense of buying pet food.

A few pet shops in Turkey still sell animals like chimpanzees whose import is forbidden by the CITES convention. If you know that a pet shop is doing this you should, of course, try to avoid giving it your business.

IMPORTING A PET

You are allowed to import one cat (*kedi*), one dog (*köpek*), one bird (*kuş*) and 10 fish (*balık*) into Turkey although a dog or cat must have a Certificate of Origin and a Certificate of Health which is less than 15 days old. This must show that the animal has been vaccinated against rabies (*kuduz*) which is endemic in Turkey. All imported animals must be more than three months old.

EXPORTING A PET

Since Turkey is not yet part of the EU British citizens cannot bring a pet from Turkey into the UK without it going into quarantine. Some other countries take a more relaxed attitude to the importation of animals from Turkey. Note that you are not allowed to export a Van cat from Turkey without special permission.

BUYING A PET

There are so many homeless cats and dogs in Turkey that most people can find a pet without having to pay for it. However, if you do want to buy an animal there are pet shops in most of the big towns and coastal resorts. You could also try looking in the classified ads of local expat magazines such as Fethiye's *Land of Lights*.

Pet Shops: Most pet shops only sell fish and birds. Those that do sell dogs and cats often do so in conditions that would not be thought acceptable in the West. In wealthier parts of the big cities, however, there are decent pet shops which sell dogs, in particular, for extortionate prices.

Recently some people have been importing popular breeds of dogs such as huskies from neighbouring countries and then selling them with pedigree papers whose bona fides it is impossible to check. Be careful before agreeing to such an arrangement, especially as the price is likely to be high.

For a list of pet shops see Appendix XIII.

THE KANGAL

The kangal is unique to Turkey and used to be bred for use as a sheepdog. To this day you will still see these large, sturdy yellow-coloured dogs guarding flocks, especially in Eastern Turkey where they are often clad in ferocious spiked collars to protect them from wolves. Although pedigree kangals are expensive to buy there are many kangal-cross dogs among the street population and most are no fiercer than other dogs provided that they have been well treated.

Kangal puppies, with their huge feet, melting eyes and soft yellow fur, are particularly endearing. However, before taking one on you should consider how large the adult dog will become - they are not suitable pets for anyone living in an apartment and without access to a garden. It's also important to remember that a lot of Turks are terrified of dogs and that a kangal is likely to seem scarier than something smaller.

VETS (*VETERİNER*)

Except in the big cities and coastal resorts most vets earn their living from treating farm animals rather than domestic pets. Since they associate cat and dog-keeping with foreigners, they tend to charge premium prices for any-thing to do with treating such animals. What is more they may have very little experience of treating cats and dogs which means that accidents and fatali-ties can happen even during the course of such routine treatments as spaying and neutering. Rarely do they have facilities to care for convalescing animals. In cities such as Istanbul and Ankara most vets operate in the wealthier sub-urbs. Standards may be as high as at home but prices will be high as well.

For a list of vets see Appendix XIII. The website www.havhav.com has more names - look under Sağlık, then Vet Bilgi Bankası.

COST OF PET KEEPING

Because keeping cats and dogs as pets is still fairly unusual, everything to do with them is likely to be more expensive in Turkey than at home. A stand-ard tin of wet cat or dog food (*yaş mama*), for example, will cost more than €1.50 and that is always assuming you can find it. Dried cat or dog food (*kuru mama)* is easier to find but also expensive, as is cat litter (*kedi kumu*). If you live in a rural area and don't produce enough scraps to keep your pet going you may well have to resort to ordering ready-made food from Istanbul or Ankara and having it cargoed to your home. Some pet shops can organise this for you or try www.hepsiburada.com, www.estore.com.tr or www.arkadaspet.com for more competitive prices.

If pet food is hard to find, toys for cats and dogs are almost unobtainable, although you can buy cat baskets and dog beds from the market beside the Spice Bazaar in Istanbul. Cat flaps are particularly hard to find and when you do discover them they are likely to be of the expensive magnetic variety.

VACCINATIONS *(AŞI)*

Most vets, even in rural areas, will be able to vaccinate your dog or cat against the major diseases and issue an International Pet Passport which records the jabs so that you can take it out of the country when you want to leave Turkey.

NEUTERING AND SPAYING *(KISIRLAŞTIRMA)*

Traditionally Turks have not accepted the need to neuter/spay their ani-mals. Most still talk of 'depriving the animal of its sex life' even though they are not willing to take on the burden of caring for the ensuing offspring. Nor are they keen to take on unneutered female animals. The result is that most towns and villages are overrun with stray cats and dogs, few of whom make it to maturity.

As a foreign pet-owner you may well want to have an animal neutered or spayed regardless. However, you will need to be aware both that the operation (*ameliyat*) is likely to be more expensive than at home and that it entails some risk to the animal - outside the wealthier pet-keeping areas of the big towns vets may have had little experience of neutering/spaying small animals. The good news is that some vets in the coastal resorts can now do keyhole surgery on cats and dogs which reduces some of the trauma.

Older vets are usually very reluctant to neuter a male animal even though the operation is easier to perform and less risky than neutering a female. However, younger ones are coming round to the idea.

EUTHANASIA (*ÖTENAZİ*)

The idea of having a pet animal put to sleep because it is old or in pain is not normal in Turkey. Away from the big cities you may find that your vet has had little experience of carrying out euthanasia on a domestic pet although that doesn't mean that they will not be able to do it if you insist. You should not expect them to have any special facilities for burying or cremating your pet.

OFFICIAL KILLING

One way that the authorities deal with the problem of street dogs is to round them up and either shoot or poison them with strychnine. This is particularly likely to happen in tourist resorts at the end of the season when the restaurants that have kept them in food close for the winter. Sometimes this official killing is done discreetly and carefully but sometimes resident foreigners (and Turks) have found their own much-loved pets caught up in the cull. All this is almost certainly illegal under article 5199 of the Turkish Civil Code and some vets and foreigners have had success in changing the attitudes of local authorities. But it's a tough battle and all the more reason to argue for a policy of neutering and spaying.

KENNELS (*HAYVAN PANSİYONU*), PET-SITTERS (*HAYVAN BAKICISI*) AND PET TRAINERS (*HAYVAN ANTRENÖRİ*)

In the big cities there are some kennels where you can leave your dogs while you go on holiday. However, their prices are likely to be high. Most people make do with a network of animal-loving friends.

It is also possible to pay someone to look after your dog at home while you go on holiday. Once again you should expect to pay a lot for such a service.

There are a few specialised dog trainers in the big cities.

For a list of kennels, pet sitters and pet trainers see Appendix XIII.

WHAT TO SAY

bird	*kuş*	ginger (cat)	*sarı*
black and white (cat or dog)	*siyah beyaz*	kennel	*köpek kulübesi*
budgerigar	*muhabbet kuşu*	kitten	*kedi yavrusu*
cage	*kafes*	lead/leash	*tasma kayışı*
canary	*kanarya*	male	*erkek*
cat	*kedi*	'on heat;' ready to mate	*azgın/çiftleşmeye hazır*
cat basket	*kedi sepeti*	paw	*hayvan pençesi*
cat litter	*kedi kumu*	pedigree	*safkan*
cat/dog food	*kedi/köpek maması*	pet	*ev hayvanı*
claw	*pençe*	puppy	*köpek yavrusu*
collar	*tasma*	quarantine	*karantina*
dog	*köpek*	rabbit	*tavşan*
female	*dişi*	spotty (dog)	*benekli*
fish	*balık*	tabby (cat)	*tekir*
fish tank	*akvaryum*	tail	*kuyruk*
flea	*pire*	wild	*vahşi*
flea powder	*pire tozu*	worms	*kurtlar*
fur/fine hair	*tüy*		

CHAPTER 19

GETTING INVOLVED

For people who have been involved in politics, charity work or social activism at home coming to live in Turkey can appear to spell an end to such involvement. However, in reality there are plenty of organisations crying out for helpers. If you don't speak much Turkish you may have to stick to those organised by the expat community. If, however, you speak good Turkish you will find plenty of places where you can help out.

POLITICS (POLİTİKA)

Since 2002 politics have been greatly simplified by the effective death of most of the old political parties. The governing party is the AKP which has a religious bent, although in practise it has governed fairly pragmatically since sweeping to power. The only serious opposition is provided by the old Atatürkist CHP. There are a number of splinter left groups which are long on rhetoric if short on the sort of compromises needed to win power. There are also several right-wing nationalist parties, most prominently the MHP.

To find out what's going on in Turkey in order to be able to vote you will need to read the Turkish press or watch the television news channels. However, without fluent Turkish this can be a tall order. For information about newspapers see p. 354.

Voting Rights: Unless you have Turkish citizenship you will not be eligible to vote in Turkish elections, no matter how long you live in the country. If you do have citizenship you are obliged to vote in general elections that take place every five years if you are over 18.

Even if you are permanently resident in Turkey you may be able to register as an overseas voter in your home country. In the UK, for example, you can be registered as an overseas voter for up to 10 years.

ALPHABET SOUP - WHO'S WHO IN TURKISH POLITICS

AKP (AK Parti, Justice & Development Party - governing party, mildly Islamic, led by Prime Minister Recep Tayyip Erdoğan

CHP (Cumhuriyet Halk Partisi, Republican People's Party*)* – long-lived Kemalist secular party led by Deniz Baykal

MHP (Milliyetçi Hareket Partisi, Nationalist Action Party*)* – right-wing nationalist party led by Devlet Bahçeli

ANAP (Anavatan Partisi, Motherland Party*)-* centre-right party led by Erkan Mumcu

DYP (Doğru Yol Partisi, True Road Party*)* - centre-right party led by Mehmet Ağar

DSP (Demokratik Sol Parti, Democratic Left Party) – mildly left-wing party led by Zeki Sezer.

POLITICAL ACTIVISM

Before getting involved in politics you need to be aware that Turkish governments have a tendency to regard activists as traitors. The situation is slowly improving, not least because of pressure from the EU. However, you should be aware that the penalties for overstepping the mark can be severe. At the very least having a criminal conviction will make it impossible for you to obtain Turkish residency or citizenship later. It could also stop you buying property in the country.

Much political activism is focused on Eastern Turkey and the Kurdish question. Unless you are very sure what you are doing and (preferably) speak good Turkish, it is not wise to get involved in these areas. As the recent prosecution of famous novelist Orhan Pamuk showed, almost anyone who says the wrong thing is fair game as far as the authorities are concerned. The iniquitous Article 301 of the current Civil Code makes it an offence to deprecate Turkishness amongst other things – and it is written sufficiently broadly to catch almost anyone the authorities want caught.

For a list of political organisations, see Appendix XIV.

WHAT TO SAY			
candidate	*aday*	president	*cumhurbaşkanı*
election	*seçim*	prime minister	*başbakan*
member of parliament	*milletvekili*	vote	*oy*

ENVIRONMENTAL ACTIVISM

Concern for the environment has taken a back seat in Turkey as the country struggles to modernise. However, there are several national and international environmental organisations that you might want to contact; see Appendix XIV for details.

Animal Charities

Appendix XIV also has a list of organisations that try to help find homes for street dogs and cats.

SOCIAL ACTIVISM

If you are living in Turkey chances are that you need to find work that pays enough to live on. However, some women whose husbands are working and who have not been able to find appropriate work for themselves do voluntary work just as they might at home. Most of the churches in Istanbul have programmes to help the poor, refugees, street children etc and often they are crying out for help. Some, however, only want practising Christians on their teams or give priority when it comes to promotion to regular church-goers.

If you have been accustomed to giving to charity on a regular basis you may also want to consider giving money to Turkish charities. Alternatively you may want to get involved with their work.

SHOULD I GIVE TO THEM?

Like most other countries, Turkey has its fair share of beggars, many of them elderly or disabled people, lone women or homeless children. As well as those who simply ask for money there are also many people who sell paper tissues or loan people their scales in return for a handful of *kuruş*, especially in Istanbul. While it is probably true that Fagin types control some of the children behind the scenes, it takes a pretty hard heart to walk past a small child sitting alone on the pavement in the dark with just their tissues for company.

Everyone will have to make up their own mind as to whether to give to individuals. However, if you don't want to do that you can give money to organisations which do their best to help those in need instead. Some contact details are given in the text.

A useful source of information about voluntary work in Turkey is www.jobsabroad.com/Turkey. The site also has information for people seeking internships in the country. *Lale*, the magazine of the International Women of Istanbul (IWI) group, carries information for people who would like to volunteer in all sorts of ways. Regular projects seeking volunteers include:

- *Blue Angels:* Help out at old people's home in Bomonti-Şişli (Fransiz Fakirhanesi).
- *Breast Cancer Support Group:* Help Turkish women get access to mammograms, etc.
- *Ears to Hear:* Answer phone calls from IWI members with problems.
- *Green Angels:* Help at Kilyos School for the Blind.
- *Pink Angels:* Help run a three-times-weekly play group for terminally ill children in SSK Okmeydanı Hospital.
- *White Angels:* Help at Bakırköy Orphanage for half a day a week.
- *Mavi Kalem:* Help an educational project for children in Balat.

The German School, Ankara Charities Committee and British Women's and American Women's Groups in Ankara all need volunteers for charitable activities too.

For other possibilities, see under charities in Appendix XIV.

WHAT TO SAY			
association	*dernek/derneği*	support	*destek*
charity	*vakıf/vakfı*	volunteer	*gönüllü*
environment	*çevre*		

Local Agenda 21 (*Yerli Gündem 21*)

In some parts of Turkey local authorities have been trying to put into effect programmes on sustainable development to meet the requirements of the UN Conference on the Environment and Development held in Rio de Janeiro in 1992. To this end they have been consulting the different sections of their communities to come up with possible Local Agenda 21 initiatives which tend to focus on recycling, children's education etc. In areas with a large expat community meetings have sometimes been organised specifically to seek *yabancı* input, with interpreters provided. Elsewhere your Turkish will probably need to be pretty good if you want to be able to take part in the discussions.

OTHER PROJECTS

Appendıx XIV also lists a few miscellaneous projects that may be in need of helpers.

THE NATIONAL LOTTERY *(MİLLİ PİYANGO)*

   Whether you regard it as getting involved or not, you can hardly avoid Turkey's National Lottery whose ticket-sellers can be found virtually everywhere; the draw takes place on the 9th, 19th and 29th of every month. Besides the national lottery, the government lottery association organises several other games of chance (Sayısal Loto, Şans Topu, On Numara and Kazı Kazan [a scratch card]); you'll see them advertised in the windows of licensed sellers and sold from special kiosks. The New Year draw for the National Lottery has the biggest payout and even people who don't usually gamble buy tickets then. Unfortunately some tickets fall into the hands of the black market and prices begin to rise as the day of the draw gets closer, so make sure to buy yours early.

SUPPORT GROUPS *(DESTEK GRUPLARI)*

Most of these groups are run by private individuals and aim to bring together people with a common culture, background and language. Most organise social activities as well as offering help with all sorts of common problems. They also tend to arrange fairs for Christmas, Easter and other important Western occasions. Particularly when you first arrive in Turkey and may be feeling lost, contacting one of these groups may be helpful. Please remember, however, that as they are run by individuals the contact details may change. Also, please remember to ring at courteous times since you may be calling a private home.

For contact details, see Appendix XIV.

CULTURAL CENTRES *(KÜLTÜR MERKEZİ)* AND FRIENDSHIP ASSOCIATIONS

If you're feeling homesick, a cultural centre run by your own country can be a great place to head, especially if the ubiquitous English is not your native language. Cultural centres often show films in their original languages, keep a well-stocked library of books and magazines and run language courses, as well as giving lectures and organising other events that are likely to interest their nationals. They are also places where you can get some of your queries answered in your own language.

A list of cultural centres and friendship associations appears in Appendix XIV.

RELIGION *(DİN)*

Churches *(Kilise)*

Islam recognises the 'Peoples of the Book' (the Christians [*Hıristiyanlar*] and Jews [*Yahudiler*]) as worthy of respect, and in general Jews and Christians have been free to practise their religions in Turkey, provided they fulfilled whatever obligations were laid on them at that particular point in history. In the 1990s there was considerable ethnic tension in south-eastern Turkey and Christians belonging to the small Syrian Orthodox church found it increasingly hard to survive. However, if you want to attend a church service you are unlikely to have many problems – beyond working out when the building will be open.

In Istanbul most of the churches can be found on the northern side of the Golden Horn in Karaköy and Beyoğlu where most Westerners lived in the 19th century. There are also several working Orthodox churches in the heart of old Istanbul, especially in Fener, Balat and Kumkapı, as well as across the Bosphorus in Kadıköy, Moda and elsewhere.

For a list of churches in Turkey, see Appendix XV.

Synagogues (*Sinagog/Havra*)

Since the twin bomb attacks of 2003, synagogues, already tightly guarded, have been even more closely monitored. If you want to attend a service you will have to make prior arrangements.

For a list of synagogues in Turkey, see Appendix XV.

Converting to Islam

For a summary of the basic tenets of Islam, see box p. 33.

Converting to Islam is not difficult since it mainly consists of saying '*La ilahe ilallah ve Muhammedun Resülullah*' (There is no God but Allah and Muhammad is the Prophet of God) in the presence of an official witness from the local *Diyanet İşleri Başkanlığı* (Dept of Religious Affairs). Islam is a religion that welcomes converts and many Turks will suggest to their friends that they should become Muslims. Although it is not necessary for a foreign spouse to convert to Islam when they marry, some do so because they think it will make life easier for their children. Sometimes they come under pressure to convert from the Turkish spouse's parents. Some foreign men marrying Turkish women may find their new family expecting them to convert to Islam.

Turkish women generally pray at home except during Ramazan but most mosques have a separate area, usually at the back, set aside for them. If visiting a mosque, women should always cover their heads, arms and legs. Men, too, should refrain from wearing shorts. Everyone should remove their shoes before setting foot on the carpeted area of a mosque.

The Koran: Muslims believe that the Koran is the literal word of Allah as imparted to the Prophet Mohammed. Consequently all copies of the Koran should be treated with respect; families usually place them alone on a high shelf where no one will brush against them accidentally and they won't be sullied by contact with other books. Some Turks believe that only the Koran in Arabic has any value; until recently in a pre-literate society any paper with Arabic writing on it also had to be treated with great respect in case it had come from a Koran.

The Islamic Week: In Islamic tradition Friday is the day of rest and in Turkey even men who do not normally go to the mosque will visit for Friday midday prayers. On Thursday night every mosque will have its minarets lit up to remind people to be even more strictly observant of religious practice for the next 24 hours (these lights are also left on over important religious festivals for the same reason).

The Islamic Year: For day-to-day business Turkey follows the same Gregorian calendar as the West. However, when it comes to religious matters it follows the Islamic (*Hicri*) calendar which dates from 622 AD, the year in which the Prophet Mohammed moved to Mecca. Tracking the lunar year, this calendar has only 354 days, 11 fewer than the Gregorian one. The Islamic calendar has the following months which are used for calculating the dates of all religious holidays:

- Muharrem
- Sefer
- Rebiülevvel
- Rebiülahir
- Cemazilevvel
- Cemaziyel'ahır
- Receb
- Şaban
- Ramazan
- Şevval
- Zilkade
- Zilhicce

CHANGING DATES

In Turkey you will sometimes see dates (especially on mosques) prefixed by the letters 'AH'. This indicates that they are dates according to the Islamic (*Hicri*) calendar. To convert them to Gregorian (*Miladi*) calendar dates multiply by 0.97 and then add 622. So, for example the Hicri year 1254 would become 1838 in the Miladi one. It's not exact but it's near enough.

390 | A Handbook for Living in Turkey

The high points of the Islamic year are Eid ul-Adha (Kurban Bayramı in Turkish) and Ramadan (Ramazan in Turkish). Other important dates include:

- *Aşure Günü* (10 Muharrem): Some people fast for the day to commemorate several events including the birth of Adam, the emergence of Noah from the Ark after the Flood, and the day when Prophet İbrahim planned to sacrifice his son İsmael. Increasingly also occasion for making and sharing *aşure* pudding, a store-cupboard specialty said to incorporate up to 40 ingredients, including beans, sultanas and chickpeas.

- *Mevlit Kandili* (12 Rebiülevvel): Anniversary of birth of Prophet Mohammed, followed by *Kutlu Doğum Haftası*, week-long celebration of the event.

- *Regaip Kandili:* Night before first Friday in month of Receb, believed to be anniversary of conception of Prophet Mohammed.

- *Miraç Kandili* (27 Receb): Day Prophet Mohammed ascended to heaven with angel Cebrail (Gabriel). Religious people spend night in mosque reading Koran.

- *Berat Kandili* (14 Şaban): Day Prophet Mohammed used to begin preparations for fast. Religious people pray all night and then visit graves of relatives the next day. Many people believe that on this night angels decide what will happen to every human being during the course of the next year.

- *Kadir Gecesi* (27 Ramazan): Day Koran was given to Prophet Mohammed. Religious people spend whole night praying in mosque.

Hac and Umre: Every Muslim man and woman is supposed to go to Mecca (Mekke in Turkish) in Saudi Arabia at least once in their lifetime if they are able to. The most prestigious time to visit coincides with Kurban Bayramı, this being the time of the true Hac (Pilgrimage). Not everyone is able to travel then (which is just as well since so many Muslims converge on Mecca that there are often fatal accidents). If they travel at other times they are said to go on the Umre (Little Pilgrimage). Men and women who have visited Mecca are often given the honorific title 'hacı. This is then added to regular honorifics to create such interesting titles as Hacıbaba and Hacıanne.

Unless you convert to Islam you will not be able to visit Mecca since the town is closed to non-Muslims.

THE CALL TO PRAYER	
Five times a day the *ezan* (call to prayer) rings out across the land in Arabic. These are the words you hear:	And this is what they mean:
Allahu Akbar (four times)	God is the Most Great!
Ash-hadu an la ilaha illallah (twice)	I bear witness that there is no God but Allah.
Ash-hadu ana Muhammadur rasulullah (twice)	I bear witness that Muhammah is the Prophet of Allah.
Hayya alas salah (twice)	Come to prayer!
Hayya alal falah (twice)	Come to salvation!
Allahu Akbar (twice)	God is the Most Great!
La ilaha illallah (once)	There is no God but Allah!

WHO TO CONTACT

Diyanet İşleri Başkanlığı (Dept of Religious Affairs): Tel: 0312-295 7000, www.diyanet.gov.tr, Eskişehir Yolu 9km, Çankaya, Ankara. Responsible for supervising mosques, training *imams* etc.

Müftülük: Local offices of experts in Islamic law who are in charge of Islamic matters for each area.

WHAT TO SAY			
Bible	*İncil*	prayer leader	*imam*
call to prayer	*ezan*	prayers/worship	*namaz*
fountain for performing ritual ablution	*şadırvan*	prophet	*peygamber*
minaret	*minare*	ritual ablutions	*abdest*
mosque	*cami*	set of words and actions within a prayer	*rekat*
Muslim equivalent of chapel	*mescit*	man who calls people to prayer	*müezzin*
niche set in wall of mosque facing Mecca	*mihrab*	to pray	*dua etmek*

CHAPTER 20

THE TURKISH PAPERCHASE

It goes without saying that every foreigner who comes to Turkey must be in possession of a valid passport. In addition almost everyone has to buy a 'visa' on arrival at the port, airport or land border. This visa is a stamp that goes in your passport and is usually valid for multiple entries into Turkey within a one-month or three-month period, depending on your nationality. What you pay for this visa also depends on your nationality and tends to be reciprocal – if your country makes life tough for Turks, then chances are you will have to pay a steeper entry fee.

Turkey still suffers from dreadfully cumbersome bureaucratic procedures. Applying for any kind of official paperwork can be time-consuming and expensive - always allow more time than you think you will need to be on the safe side. Few government offices have officials who speak English, French or German so at least in the early days of your new life in Turkey you may need to take a friend along to act as a translator *(tercüman)*.

In general Turkey requires that foreigners be able to read all official paperwork in their own language which means that you will often have to pay a translator to comply with the law; if you have taken Turkish citizenship you are exempted from this requirement even if you can't speak Turkish. Bear in mind that even if you can read the documents they are often confusing and sometimes just plain wrong - occasionally you may have to ask for contracts to be altered or rewritten. Documents brought from abroad also often have to be 'legalised' which means getting the signatures on them counter-signed; embassies can usually explain the process involved. Within Turkey many documents also have to be notarised, a procedure which tends to bump up costs.

394 | A Handbook for Living in Turkey

The worst place to have to sort out your paperwork is Istanbul where you will be struggling to stand your ground in a flood of foreign students and people working illegally.

Application forms for most types of visa can be downloaded from Turkish embassy websites.

EXTENDING YOUR VISA

If you are intending to stay in Turkey you will probably need to extend your visa. In theory this can be done once at the nearest branch of the *Emniyet Müdürlüğü* (Security Police) – look for the *Yabancılar Bürosu* (Foreigners' Bureau) or something similar. However, the process is not as simple as getting a stamp at the border. Normally you will be obliged to visit innumerable different departments to get different officials to sign your paperwork, even though they barely look at it. Usually you will have to leave your passport for anything up to a week. The cost is also much greater than if you just bought a new visa at the border. On top of the cost of the visa extension itself you will also have to pay for up to six passport-sized photos and for a little blue booklet into which your permit will be stamped. Although some parts of the process are now computerised, other parts still involve clerks recording details in huge old-fashioned ledgers. You can only extend your visa once inside the country - the next time you must leave the country and come back in again.

The result of all this is that many foreigners prefer to leave the country every three months and then come back in again on a new visa. This is especially the case with people living in Istanbul who can easily take the train to the Greek border, people living in the Aegean coastal resorts who can hop across to one of the Greek islands and people living in Antalya who can take the ferry across to Northern Cyprus. It is much harder for people living in Kapadokya or further east for whom all these options require lengthy journeys.

In theory too many of these three-monthly visa-hops could attract the attention of officials who may demand that you get a residency permit or leave. However, this rarely seems to happen. Some people who take a train to the Greek border timed to arrive late at night and who then try to return on a train just after midnight are sometimes turned back by the border guards. The Bulgarian border authorities also have a bad reputation for hassling people they think are bending the rules.

FILLING OUT THAT FORM *(FORM DOLDURURKEN)*			
isim/ad	name	*boşanmış*	divorced
soyad	surname	*ziyaret sebebi*	reason for visit
adres	address	*iş*	work
doğum tarihi	date of birth	*turizm*	tourism
doğum yeri	place of birth	*akraba ziyareti*	visiting a relative
ikametgâh	place of residence	*meslek*	occupation
yaş	age	*din*	religion
cinsiyet	sex	*baba adı*	father's name
medeni hal	marital status	*milliyet*	nationality
bekâr	single	*imza*	signature
evli	married		

The Paperchase

It is impossible to say exactly what will happen when you come to extend your visa since each Emniyet Müdürlüğü is likely to have its own procedures. However, this is how it works in Nevşehir and you should anticipate something similar:

Step 1: Visit the Yabancılar Polisi at the Emniyet Müdürlüğü.

Step 2: Police prepare a *dilekçe* asking the Vali to allow you to extend your stay in the country. This may be headed '*Valilik Makamına*' ('to the Vali's office').

Step 3: Police give you the *dilekçe* and a '*hesap pusulası*' (Bill Slip).

Step 4: You go to the Valılık and get either the Vali himself or his secretarial staff to sign the *makam*. It may also have to be counter-signed in another office.

Step 5: You take the paperwork to the *Defterdarlık* (Accounts Department). There the details of your *hesap pusulası* will be recorded, probably in a large ledger.

Step 6: You go to the *Vezne* (Cashier's Office) to pay the *ikamet harcı* (residency fee). The *Vezne* may have two separate windows. If so, you hand over your *hesap pusulası* at one and it is then passed to the second window where you hand over payment for the visa. In return you will be given a *makbuz* (receipt).

Step 7: Return to the Emniyet Müdürlüğü and visit the *Evrak ve Arşiv* (papers and archives) department to collect yet another signature. You get this counter-signed by the manager (*müdür*) of the Emniyet Müdürlüğü.

Step 8: Leave your passport/residency booklet with the police, together with at least two passport photographs to support your application. You may also be asked for a photocopy of the most important pages of your passport and/or any pages showing exit stamps from Turkey during the period of your last visa.

If you're lucky all these departments will be in the same or adjacent buildings. If you're unlucky they will be scattered about town.

Usually the police can prepare your new visa in a couple of days but it is always wise to start the process a week or so ahead of the old visa's expiry date to guard against unforeseen hiccoughs. In the Muğla area in particular long delays are now common due to the sheer number of people moving into the area.

Overstaying Your Visa

If you overstay your visa you will be fined when you leave the country. The fine is usually the same as what you would have paid for the extension, so some people blithely overstay for up to three months and then pay the fine at the airport rather than deal with the bureaucracy involved in organising a legal extension. Others overstay for even longer. However, the authorities are unlikely to look favourably on people who do this and then want to apply for residency or citizenship. If you want to know how much you would be fined for an overstay phone the information desk at Atatürk airport (Tel: 0212-465 3000) and ask to be put through to the tourist police (ext. 4358).

When you arrive at the airport you should go first to the check-in desks. Once your baggage has been checked in, go to the Passport Police office near the cafes at the back of the terminal. There you will be given a paper saying how much you have to pay. Only after you are through security and in the departure lounge do you hand over the payment, which means that you cannot use this system as a way of getting out of dealing with the Istanbul Emniyet Müdürlüğü.

RESIDENCE PERMITS (*İKAMET TEZKERESİ/OTURMA İZNİ*)

If you want to live in Turkey for longer than six months it is possible to apply for a residency permit which will allow you to stay for at least a year without having to worry about renewal. To start the process you need to download an application form from the Internet, complete it and take it to the nearest Turkish embassy or consulate with your passport, several photographs and proof that you can support yourself financially. In theory it takes two months for the application to be processed; in practise if you can show that you have adequate resources (and it helps to have a house in Turkey) the permit may be issued in less than a week. You will be charged a processing fee for this first stage of your application.

Once the permit has been issued you will have a month in which to present yourself at the branch of the Emniyet Müdürlüğü nearest to where you live, They will then turn the provisional permit into a real one – a little blue booklet that fits inside your passport. You can also apply for the permit in Turkey in which case the procedure is virtually identical to that for extending your visa except that the police may also want to see a note from your local *muhtar*, confirming your address. The fee for an *ikamet* depends on your nationality but can be steep and rises every January; in 2006 a British citizen had to pay more than YTL460 for a one-year residency permit and YTL2,200 for a five-year one. Germans, Austrians, Belgians and Swedes pay considerably less.

Residency is usually granted for one year initially, then for three years, then for five years, although the local Emniyet Müdürlüğü can decide how long they want to give you. There is rarely much financial benefit attached to buying a longer period of residency and some people may feel that they are better off buying a year at a time and waiting to see if Turkey's negotiations with the EU eventually bring prices down for EU citizens. The EU generally takes the attitude that once people have been living in a country for five years they should be given the same rights as other residents, so this is an area of the law that may yet be updated.

Residency permits can in theory be issued in a couple of days. However, in Muğla province which covers Bodrum and Marmaris, delays of up to three months have become routine as the authorities struggle to cope with the surge in applications.

WHERE TO APPLY

Istanbul Emniyet Müdürlüğü: Tel: 0212-636 1722, Vatan Caddesi (Emniyet Metro stop), A Blok, Kat: 1. Operates a numbered queuing system. Arrive early to have any hope of getting a number.

Muğla Emniyet Müdürlüğü: Tel: 0252-214 1345.

APPLYING FOR A RESIDENCY PERMIT IN ISTANBUL

Step 1: Print out the application form from the website.

Step 2: Complete the form and take it to the first floor of the Emniyet Müdürlüğü with your passport and two photocopies of the front page and the page showing your last entry stamp for Turkey; five passport photos; bank statements showing that you can support yourself for a year without working (ideally you should be able to show savings of about YTL10,000); and around YTL600 in cash.

Step 3: Go back to the ground floor and look for a small window at the back marked 'Dilekçe'. Here you get a petition to apply for residency made out and hand over YTL9 for three copies all of which must be signed at the bottom.

Step 4: Go back upstairs to the information desk where a policeman speaking no English will check your paperwork and give you a queuing number.

Step 5: Take this number into the waiting room and look for a window showing a number close to yours.

Step 6: When your number comes up go to the desk where your paperwork will be stamped and the sum you need to pay written on the back.

Step 7: Go back downstairs to the cashier and pay for your residency permit.

Step 8: Go back upstairs with the receipt and your paperwork. Find another cashier, show your receipt and pay another YTL70 for the small blue booklet which acts as your residency permit. You will be given a receipt for the money and a date to come back and pick up the blue booklet.

Step 9: Return to pick up your booklet and that should be it. Until next year!

With thanks to Kate Drummond for talking me through this.

TURKISH CITIZENSHIP *(TÜRK VATANDAŞLIĞI)*

In June 2003 it became harder for many people to acquire Turkish citizenship. Until then any woman who married a Turk and asked immediately for citizenship was automatically awarded it (indeed at one time they were given it automatically). Now, however, wives must apply for citizenship at the time of marriage and then wait at least three years for it to be approved (this change was made to reduce the number of 'marriages' taking place solely to confer citizenship rights on a foreigner). A British wife must now wait five years before becoming eligible for citizenship.

Foreign men can also apply for citizenship if they are married to a Turkish woman. However, taking out Turkish citizenship exposes them to being called up for military service (see p. 226) so few younger men would want to apply.

Conditions for Being Granted Citizenship

To be eligible for Turkish citizenship you must fulfil the following criteria:

- Be an adult according to the laws of your own country
- Have lived in Turkey for five years without interruption (the calculation will not be affected if you leave Turkey for up to six months at a time)
- Have the intention to settle (as indicated by having bought property or married in the country)
- Be of good moral standing (i.e. with no criminal record)
- Be of good health (i.e. with no contagious diseases)
- Be able to provide for yourself and any dependents

However, if you are married to a Turk and have a child that is more than two or can prove that you have settled in the country with the intention of living here you may be allowed to apply for citizenship without waiting for the five years. This is also true of people who are perceived as bringing some worthwhile new invention or development into the country.

Applying for Citizenship: If a married partner wants to take out citizenship they need to take their *aile nüfus cüzdanı* together with their identity documents to the *Nüfus* department of the Valılık. Nowadays they will probably have to jump through some hoops before they can apply for their *kimlik* (ID) card although the Turkish language test was dropped recently; some applicants have been asked to recite the first two verses of the İstiklal Marşı (Independence March - the Turkish national anthem, see p. 578). The two partners in a marriage will be interviewed separately and asked questions about each other's families in an attempt to ensure that the marriage is genuine.

Kimlik **Cards:** Once you have become a citizen (*vatandaş*) you will be issued with a *kimlik* (also known as a *nüfus cüzdanı*) card. With that you will be able to work legally, apply for a Turkish credit card, vote in elections and buy property which is set aside for Turks: in short you will have all the rights of a native-born Turk. In the past it was sometimes difficult to put a non-Turkish name on a *kimlik* card; however, these days it is usually fine to put whatever name you want provided that you don't have more than two given names or a name incorporating characters that don't appear on a Turkish keyboard. There have also been problems attached to putting your true religious affiliation on the card; Jews and Christians (let alone atheists) have been advised to call themselves Muslims to avoid 'difficulties'. These days it is usually unproblematic to declare your actual religion on the cards although some people still succumb to pressure and deny their real beliefs. Recently a court case resulted in a ruling that people are not obliged to state their religion on their *kimlik*. The EU will almost certainly rule that religion must be removed from ID cards before Turkey can join it, so over the next few years it is likely that the problem will slowly disappear.

As well as the actual card number, a *kimlik* records the official number of the family to which you belong, your number within that family and the number of the ledger (*cilt*) in which your family details are recorded at the Nüfus department.

Once you have been issued with a *kimlik* you are expected to carry it with you at all times. If you lose the card you must report the loss immediately and go through a long-winded procedure to get a new one.

THIS CONCERNS YOU...

Even in fairly large cities Turkey tries to keep people abreast of the latest news by means of loudspeaker systems operating from the Belediye. Anything can be announced, from the names of those due for vaccination to requests for help in tracing a lost donkey. Unfortunately the announcements are only in Turkish – even if yours is good it can be hard to make out what is being said through the buzz and echo of the village tannoy.

duyuru	notice
ilan	announcement
Tadilât nedeni ile kapalı.	Closed for restoration.
Taşındık.	We have moved.
İnşaat sırasında çevremize verdiğimiz rahatsızlıktan dolayı özür dileriz..	Sorry for the inconvenience caused by our building work.

Marriages of Convenience: Since it is difficult to become a Turkish citizen without marrying a Turk some people who have wanted to set up businesses have gone through in-name-only marriages simply to get the right paperwork. As elsewhere in the world, there are people who are prepared to marry anyone in return for payment and provided you have a friend who is happy to do this, it might be a reasonable option. However, paying a stranger to marry you is obviously risky, not least because if anything goes wrong the authorities are unlikely to view your behaviour favourably. The current Civil Code gives the partners to a marriage equal rights to property acquired after the marriage, so anyone with a successful business would have to make sure that they had signed documents to safeguard their assets against future claims by the 'marriage' partner.

Turkish Citizenship for Children of Mixed Partnerships: Turkish law recognises all children with a Turkish mother or father as Turks, regardless of where they were born. The children of a foreign mother who is not married to their Turkish father will be regarded as citizens of the mother's country unless the courts have ruled that there is a clear link to the Turkish father. In that case they will be regarded as Turks too.

WHERE TO APPLY

Istanbul

Nüfus ve Vatandaşlık: Dizdariye Medresesi Sokak, Binbirdirek Mahallesi, Çemberlitaş

DUAL CITIZENSHIP (ÇİFT VATANDAŞLIK)

Under Turkish law anyone is entitled to have citizenship of more than one country. However, some countries don't permit dual citizenship, so before deciding whether you wish to take up Turkish citizenship you will need to check the rules of your own country, bearing in mind that holding only a Turkish passport may complicate obtaining visas to travel abroad.

Nationalities Permitted Dual Citizenship			
Australian	Yes	Japanese	No
Austrian	No	New Zealander	Yes
Canadian	Yes	Norwegian	No
Danish	No	South African	Yes
Dutch	No*	Spanish	Yes
French	Yes	Swedish	No
German	No	UK	Yes
Irish	Yes	USA	Yes
Italian	Yes		

* Exceptions made for people who 'need' to be dual citizens, perhaps because of business. Children of mixed Dutch and Turkish couples are also permitted dual nationalities.

FOREIGN CITIZENSHIP FOR BABIES

Where one or other of a couple is not Turkish they may want their baby to have dual citizenship. To obtain this for them you will need to take the foreign spouse's *kimlik*, birth certificate and passport, together with the Turkish spouse and the baby's *kimliks*, to the appropriate foreign embassy. You will also need to show your *aile nüfus cüzdanı* and *aile nüfus kayıt örneği* which MUST be presented with the baby's name at the top (to get the information presented in this order you will have to take the baby's *kimlik* to the Nüfus department). Increasingly embassies also lay down rigid rules about how the baby must appear in its photographs. For precise information for each nationality you will need to approach the relevant embassy (see p. 568).

All Turkish documentation will need to be officially translated, a procedure which is likely to cost around YTL80. In theory if you are taking the paperwork to the embassy in person the documents shouldn't have to be notarised. In practise, however, you may find that you still need to get them notarised, a procedure which can be quite expensive outside Istanbul (the *noter* levies a charge according to the number of pages and density of the information contained on them).

Children of mixed parentage are entitled to hold two passports, one Turkish and one foreign.

WORK PERMITS *(ÇALIŞMA İZNİ)*

If you are coming to Turkey with a job already waiting for you your employer should look after the paperwork required to get you a work permit (*çalışma izni*). If, however, you find a job while in Turkey you may have to leave the country to apply for a work permit and then come back in again. Since February 2002 it has been possible for people with residency permits to work for themselves without much difficulty (theoretically), although they do need to download an application form and send it to Ankara for approval (a process which can take months).

The law concerning work permits now has a reciprocity clause in it. This means that if a Turk can work in your country without a work permit, then you can work in Turkey without one. For the time being this is unlikely to be of much benefit to most Westerners. However, if Turkey does eventually join the EU then it could mean most Europeans being able to work here without a permit.

In the meantime most work permits are issued initially for one year. When they are extended the new permit is usually for three years, and then for six years. If you have been a resident of Turkey for eight years and have had a work permit for six of them you should then be able to get a permanent work permit.

Many people think the effort and uncertainty involved in applying for a permit not worth the hassle, and continue to leave Turkey every few months and return on a new tourist visa. Others simply vanish into the system. Provided you don't want to travel outside Turkey there is no particular reason why you would be discovered doing this. However, it is not something that can be recommended and in some areas the pressure of competition means that business rivals have informed on people they know to be working illegally.

Unfortunately, no matter what may be said in public, the reality is that some people are finding it harder than ever to get work permits. Even those who have had them in the past report difficulty in getting them extended.

Applying for a Work Permit: If you do want to apply for a work permit you will need to contact either a Turkish embassy abroad or the Ministry of Labour and Social Security. You will be given an application form that requires the following information:

- Your personal, family and educational details together with your passport details
- Name of the company you want to work for and the type of work it does
- Job title, proposed salary, length of contract and where you will work
- Head office address
- Whether it is a Turkish or foreign company together with details of its finances and export record (if appropriate)
- Date company was set up
- Details of its share capital
- Number of Turkish employees, with explanation as to why a Turk couldn't do the job you are applying for
- Details of your employment history
- Details of any previous work permit you held and information on where you worked
- Information about your residence and residency permit in Turkey
- Names of references

Together with the completed application form you will need to supply notarised copies of your passport, together with copies of any previous Turkish work permits and of your diplomas etc. Since wading through all this paperwork is a nightmare many legal firms are ready to do the work for you in return for a fee. You may find that the time saved more than justifies the cost.

Once the Ministry has approved your application they will forward it to the Directorate of Security for the Ministry of the Interior. If they, too, approve it they will send the work permit to your employer and notify the nearest Turkish consulate to your home that they can issue a work visa (*çalışma vizesi*).

You can apply for a work permit in your home country up to two months before you leave. The paperwork is supposed to be completed in 30 days but this is rather optimistic. Applying for a work visa will take another 45 days or so. You will also need to apply for residency (see above). Only when you have all three authorisations - work permit, work visa and residency permit - are you truly ready to go.

WHO TO CONTACT

Ministry of Labour & Social Security (Çalışma ve Sosyal Güvenlik Bakanlığı): Tel: 0312-212 9700, Fax: 0312-212 1963, www.calisma.gov.tr, İnönü Bulvarı No: 42, Emek Mevkii, Ankara

STUDENT VISAS *(ÖĞRENCİ VİZESİ)*

People who are coming to Turkey to study need a special student visa. They have to apply for this at the nearest Turkish embassy or consulate overseas at least two months before the start of term. As well as wanting to see your passport, a completed application form and several photos, the authorities will need proof of your student status in your own country as well as a letter confirming your place at the Turkish university. You will have to pay a non-refundable application fee.

Within one month of arriving in Turkey with the visa in your passport you will have to go to the Emniyet Müdürlüğü to apply for a normal residence permit (see above).

NOTARY PUBLIC *(NOTER)*

In Turkey the notary public plays a much bigger part in life than in some other Western countries, including the UK. A *noter* is rather like a legal clerk who prepares documents and confirms the legality of transactions on a fee-per-job basis. Whenever you are carrying out a legal transaction it is possible that you will have to have the documentation notarised. For example, if you are importing your belongings from overseas you may need to get a power-of-attorney *(vekâletname)* to allow the shipping company to act for you at the Customs office. That power-of-attorney will need to be notarised.

Research Visas: If you are coming to Turkey to do original research you need to apply for a research visa rather than a normal student one. These are harder to get and more problematic since you will need to explain what research you plan to do where, and will have to submit not just your notes but also your finished work to the Ministry of Education. Of course they have the right to refuse a visa to anyone whose research they don't like the sound of.

It is not normally possible to change your visa once you are in Turkey, so you cannot apply for a student visa and then switch to a research one without leaving the country and reapplying. If you are caught doing research without the right visa you can be fined and deported.

GETTING A TAX NUMBER *(VERGİ NUMARASI)*

Once you start work you will need a tax number. Even if you just want to open an interest-bearing bank account you will need such a number so that withholding tax *(stopaj)* can be applied to the interest.

To get a tax number you should visit the local *Maliye* (Finance Department). If you're lucky this will be in the same building as the Emniyet Müdürlüğü; if you're not it will be elsewhere in town.

Tax numbers are usually handed out by clerks inside the *Defterdarlık* (Accounts Department). Go there with photocopies of your passport and residency permit and look for the *Vergi Dairesi* (Tax Department) and then the *Sivil Yoklama Servisi* (Civil Test Service) section. It is likely that they will ask you to present a *dilekçe*, asking them to give you a tax number but if you look blank they will probably give in and write it for you. Then you will only need to sign it and get it counter-signed by the *Vergi Müdür Yardımcısı* (Tax Manager's Assistant) before you will be given a piece of paper the size of a business card with your number recorded on it.

THE *DİLEKÇE*

The *dilekçe* (petition) is a peculiarly unfortunate legacy of Ottoman times. Whenever you go to do anything official, be it applying for a visa extension or tax number, or asking for a new gas or electricity account, you must fill out one of these pointless pieces of paper which humbly requests that someone do the job they are paid to do! Where all the *dilekçes* end up and how many trees die to supply them are questions probably best not asked.

OFFICIAL RECEIPTS

Whenever you pay tax you should receive a tax receipt *(tahsilat makbuzu)* in return. If you pay for anything in the Belediye you should also receive a receipt for it. Occasionally a clerk will levy an unofficial charge for either reading or filling out paperwork for you. The sum involved is likely to be small. Whether you agree to pay it or not is entirely up to you.

WHO TO CONTACT

Acacia International Law Office: Tel: 0232-381 8319, www.acacia-int.com, 1719. Sokak No: 18, Kat: 2/3, Karşıyaka, Izmir, Turkey; 94 Bronsart Rd, London SW6 6AB, UK

Fethiye Translation & Consultation Office: Tel: 0252-612 3520, www.fethiye-translation.com, Postane arkası, Atatürk Caddesi No: 80

VISA-HOPPING

Luckily for those who want to leave the country and come back in again on a new visa Turkey has borders with lots of other countries. The visa-hop can seem a bind, especially if you have a demanding job and it has to be made in the depths of winter. However, if you plan carefully you should be able to make a holiday of it, or at least a pleasant overnight break from Turkish life. You can also use it as a chance to stock up on items that can't be found in Turkey (nutmeg, for example, or reasonably-priced cat food).

The easiest countries to use for visa-hopping are Greece and Northern Cyprus. However, if you want to make a holiday out of a necessity it's also possible to pop across to Bulgaria, Georgia, Syria or Iran. For the time being Iraq is not a realistic option (although some hardy souls are venturing across the Habur border into the Kurdish part of the country), but Ukraine is looking more promising now that EU citizens no longer need a visa to visit.

Greece (*Yunanistan*)

Relations between Turkey and Greece have warmed up considerably since 1999 when both countries suffered earthquakes and rescuers from each of them rushed to help the victims in the other. This is good news for Turkey residents who don't want the hassle of trying to extend their visa legally since there are many different border crossings with Greece for them to use.

Crossing from Istanbul: For people living in Istanbul the easiest options are to cut through Thrace by bus to cross the border near İpsala or to take the train to Uzunköprü and cross there.

Double-decker **buses** to Greece leave from Esenler otogar at 10am on Monday and Friday. They stop for lunch in Tekirdağ, then cross the border at İpsala/Kipi. The first stop is Alexandroupolis, a pleasant place to spend an evening before returning to Turkey the next day. You could continue on to Komotini, Xanthi or Kavala but only Kavala has cheap accommodation. Eventually the bus transits Thessaloniki before continuing south to Athens. If you want to stay in Thessaloniki you should be aware that the bus arrives there at 11pm.

Overnight sleeper **trains** to Thessaloniki (the Dostluk/Filia Express) leave from Sirkeci station at 8 pm daily. Alternatively you can travel during the day and change at Uzunköprü. All the trains pass through Alexandroupolis. Alternatively you can continue to Thessaloniki or even change there and continue to Athens. Sometimes the border guards look kindly on visa-hoppers (especially teachers) and let them go straight back to Istanbul on the same day with a new visa. However, it is safer to assume that you will have to stay away for at least one night.

It is also possible to cross into Greece by land at Kastanies, near Edirne, but this is probably only worth considering if you want to visit Edirne.

ALEXANDROUPOLIS

The town of Alexandropolis is an enjoyable place to spend a night in order to get a new visa. It sits on the seashore and has some attractive, rather upmarket shops as well as an excellent anthropology museum and a quaint old-fashioned cinema whose owners take film very seriously. There are plenty of bars and restaurants, and a bus station for connections to elsewhere in Greece.

Several reasonably cheap hotels are within walking distance of the railway station.

- *Erika: Tel*: 0243-5510-34115, Karaoli Dhimitriou 110
- *Lido:* Tel: 0243-5510-28808, Paleologou 15
- *Majestic:* Tel: 0243-5510-26444, Platia Eleftherias 7
- *Metropolis:* Tel: 0243-5510-26443, Athanasiou Dhiakou 11

Crossing Between Çanakkale and Izmir: For foreigners living along the North Aegean coast there are two ways to reach Greece by ferry: by crossing from Ayvalık to Lesbos (Midilli) or from Çeşme to Chios (Sakız). Both these ferry services run regularly between June and September. However, they reduce sharply in the autumn, and in winter there may be only one or two ferries a week. A new ferry service from Assos to Lesbos is on the drawing-board.

Crossing Between Kuşadası and Marmaris: For foreigners living along the South Aegean coast there are also several ways of reaching Greece by ferry: by crossing from Kuşadası to Samos, from Bodrum to Kos, from Bodrum to Rhodes, from Bodrum to Kalymnos, from Marmaris to Rhodes, or from Datça to Rhodes or Symi. All these ferries (with the exception of the Datça ones) are frequent in summer. However, they all reduce in frequency in autumn and in the winter you may only be able to cross on one or two days a week, depending on weather and demand.

VATHY ON SAMOS

Vathy (Samos Town) is everything that Kuşadası is not: low-key, underdeveloped and upmarket. It makes a great place to hang out for a night, with lots of pleasant cafes and restaurants overlooking the harbour and an excellent small museum. If you need to stock up on anything Greek there is also a small market although most of the produce is very touristy. For a better choice take a taxi up into the hills to the two supermarkets, Lidl and Bazaar, which stock such hard-to-find luxuries as condensed milk and couscous.

Cheap accommodation options include:

- *Hotel Artemis*: Tel: 0243-2730-27792, Themistokli Sofouli
- *Pension Avli*: Tel: 0243-2730-22939, Areos 2
- *Pension Ionia*: Tel: 0243-2730-28782, Manoli Kalomiri 5

Crossing From the Western Mediterranean

In high summer there are usually ferries from Fethiye to Rhodes. Otherwise the only possibility for foreigners living along the Western Mediterranean is to cross from Kaş to Kastellorizo (Meis). This crossing has an erratic timetable and can be disproportionately expensive considering how close the island is. So many Russian women had started to use it to cross on a monthly basis for new visas that the authorities deliberately tried to make it an inconvenient option for the visa-hop.

RHODES TOWN

Architecturally, Rhodes Town is one of the most beautiful cities in the Eastern Mediterranean, with a magnificent medieval walled city and good beaches. However, it's constantly overrun with tourists which can detract from its attraction and make it hard to find somewhere cheap to stay, especially in summer.

Pension-owners with rooms to let flock to meet the ferries. Otherwise you could try:

- *Apollo*: Tel: 0243-2410-63894, Omirou 28C
- *Youth Hostel:* Tel: 0243-2410-30491, Eryiou 12

For a list of companies selling ferry tickets for Greece, see Appendix XVI.

Northern Cyprus (*Güney Kıbrıs*)

For foreigners living along the Mediterranean it makes most sense to hop across to Northern Cyprus for a new visa. Northern Cyprus is an anomaly, the northern part of a segregated island which is recognised as a separate state by no country other than Turkey. The politics are complicated but if you need a new visa it simply means that Turkey will recognise that you have left the country and come back in again if you travel to Girne (Kyrenia) by ferry.

The main port for ferries to Girne is Taşucu, near Silifke. Akfer operates daily ferries and seabuses (catamarans) to Northern Cyprus. In theory it takes two hours to cross by seabus (in the morning) and four hours by ferry (at night). However, in winter the seabuses may not be able to set out because of high seas, while the ferry may take up to three times the scheduled time to arrive. (You don't spend all that time in transit. It is normal to board the boat two hours before it sails, which means that in winter you might board at midnight but not actually set sail until eight in the morning.)

The seabuses from Taşucu sail every day at 11.30am; the car ferries sail at least five times a week at midnight.The seabuses leave Girne daily at 9.30am, the car ferries at noon.

If you think you will want to visit Southern Cyprus at a later date, ask the authorities in Girne to stamp your entry visa for Northern Cyprus on a looseleaf piece of paper instead of in your passport. In theory once the stamp is in your passport the authorities could refuse you admission to Southern Cyprus. However, since the Republic joined the European Union in 2004 EU citizens have had the right to travel back and forth from north to south and vice versa.

Returning from Northern Cyprus you will need to disembark speedily unless you want to stand in a long line for your new visa. Try not to bring much baggage as you can't take it inside the catamaran with you. It will be piled up on deck with everybody else's luggage, making it hard to be on your way quickly.

In high summer there are also catamarans from Alanya to Girne.

GIRNE

Girne has an idyllic location centred on a harbour ringed with fish restaurants and overlooked by a massive castle. The town itself is small, with few specific attractions but there are regular dolmuşes to other parts of the north, including Lefkoşa (North Nicosia) and Gazimağusa (Famagusta). There are also several Indian restaurants which make a nice change if you've eaten nothing but Turkish food for months.

Possible cheap places to stay include:

- *Bingöl Guest House*: Tel: 0392-815-2749, Ziya Rızkı Caddesi No: 6A
- *New Bristol Hotel*: Tel: 0392-815-6570, Hürriyet Caddesi No: 114
- *Sidelya Hotel*: Tel: 0392-815-6051, Nasır Güneş Sokak No: 7

Three times a week there is also a ferry from Mersin to Gazimağusa (Famagusta) which might be more convenient for someone travelling from Adana. The ship is larger and more stable which means that it may be more comfortable in winter. Gazimağusa is an interesting town to visit. However, it has little accommodation, so you would probably have to travel to Girne to find a bed.

For a list of companies selling ferry tickets for Northern Cyprus, see Appendix XVI.

Bulgaria (*Bulgaristan*)

If you're living in Istanbul it is almost as easy to go to Bulgaria for a visa as it is to go to Greece. For some people this means a visit to the Bulgarian embassy or consulate although most EU citizens should now be able to enter the country without a visa.

You can get to Bulgaria either by train from Sirkeci station on the daily Bosfor Ekspresi at 11pm or by bus from Esenler otogar. Possible destinations include Plovdiv and the capital Sofya where there are now many hostels to choose from.

Georgia (*Gürcistan*)

Georgia doesn't make the most obvious destination for a visa-hop since few foreigners are settled along the eastern end of the Black Sea. However, if you have business to do in Trabzon this might be another option, especially as European and North American citizens no longer require visas. There are buses every evening from Trabzon otogar to Batumi in Northern Georgia, or direct to the capital, Tbilisi (Tiflis), although that is a very long journey to undertake in one go. The cheapest places to stay in Batumi are rooms in private houses. Failing that you could try:

- *Hotel Tanamgzavri/Sputnik:* Tel: 0995-760 63/66, Batumgora
- *L-Bakuri:* Tel: 0995-769 29/30, Chavchavadzis Kucha 121

You can also cross the border at Posof, near Ardahan, although this is rather off the beaten track.

Syria (*Suriye*)

Syria is also rather out of the way for a casual visa-hop. However, Aleppo in the north is a wonderful place to go for a weekend. Alternatively you can visit the beach resort of Lattakia from Antakya by changing bus several times.

ALEPPO *(HALEP)*

Aleppo has everything - a wonderfully atmospheric medieval *souk*, a huge castle, a marvellous *hamam* and some exquisite restaurants in what was once the old Armenian quarter. It's easy to get there from Antakya either by direct bus or by taking local transport to and from the border.

There are lots of clean, cheap places to stay in Aleppo but you might like to try:

- *Hotel Al-Jawaher:* Tel: 0963-223 9554, Bab-al-Faraj
- *Tourist Hotel:* Tel: 0963-221 6583, Sharia al-Dala
- *Baron Hotel:* Tel: 0963-221 0880, Sharia al-Baron

Getting to Aleppo from Antakya is not difficult, but unless you are from a country whose citizens don't need a visa to visit Syria the cost of getting one is a drawback. If you are British, for example, you have to pay the extortionate cost of a letter of introduction to the Syrian embassy on top of the already steep visa fee – the total comes to almost as much as the air fare to Damascus.

Iran (İran)

Iran is not only a long way from all the places where foreigners have settled but is also so reluctant to give visas to Westerners (except the Dutch) that it makes an unlikely visa-hop destination. However, the country is extremely interesting and makes a great place to combine a visa-hop with a proper holiday.

There are two border crossings from Turkey into Iran by bus: the more popular one is near Doğubeyazıt at Gürbulak/Bazargan whence you can travel by bus direct to Tabriz; the less popular one is near Van at Esendere/Sero whence you can travel to Orumiyeh. Tabriz is a more interesting town than Orumiyeh which is also less convenient for onward connections to the rest of the country. You can also travel to Iran by train from Istanbul's Haydarpaşa station every Wednesday night at 10.55pm although the journey to Tehran takes more than two days.

At the time of writing British and American citizens were likely to find it hard to obtain an Iranian visa; if you apply and are turned down your visa fee will not be returned to you. Women will not be given a visa unless they are wearing a headscarf in the photograph that accompanies their visa application. They will also be expected to dress in accordance with Iran's Islamic dress code from the moment they reach the border.

WHAT TO SAY			
acceptance signature	kabul imzası	official	memur
border	sınır	passport	pasaport
bribe	rüşvet	permit/licence	ruhsat
citizenship	vatandaşlık	residency permit	ikamet tezkeresi/oturma izni
Customs	gümrük	stamp tax	damga vergisi
document	belge	stamp/seal	damga
fee	ücret	tax certificate	vergi levhası
free	ücretsiz/bedava	tax paid	tahsil edilmiştir
ID card	kimlik	visa	vize
manager	müdür	work permit	çalışma izni

CHAPTER 21

OUT AND ABOUT

One of the great things about living in Turkey is that the public transport system is so efficient. There is almost nowhere in the country that cannot be reached by bus or dolmuş and increasingly the bigger towns are linked up by plane as well. Even within the towns you will find public transport readily available and at very reasonable prices. Although most foreigners still want to own a car there really is no need unless you are going to be doing a lot of travelling, especially to remote areas. The marginal cost of keeping a car, particularly when you consider the price of petrol, is likely to be very high.

INTERCITY TRAVEL *(ŞEHİRLERARASI ULAŞIM)*

Buses (*Otobüs*)

The intercity bus network is the backbone of the country's transport system. Big, comfortable buses equipped with reclining seats and host(ess) service (but not toilets) link up all the big population settlements, usually on a regular basis. Fares are still very reasonable, especially on routes where there is plenty of competition; at the time of writing there were only one-way fares, no returns, supersavers or other novelty fares. These days most towns have a flashy bus station (*otogar, terminal, garaj*), usually on the outskirts and linked to the centre by free *servis* minibus; only a few big towns (including Bursa, Konya and Safranbolu) lack these essential final links in the chain, leaving customers to make their own way from the bus station to the town centre. Buses stop every three or four hours at service stations (*dinlenme tesisleri)* where it is possible to buy snacks, hot meals, tea, coffee, and last-minute gifts.

Some of the bigger bus companies have their own terminals in Istanbul and Ankara and operate their own *servis* system into the town centre. This can make connections trickier than if you use bus services into and out of the main otogars. Boss, Ulusoy and Varan, in particular, offer upmarket bus services linking Istanbul with Ankara and Izmir. They advertise airline-quality service, with single seats, headsets, free newspapers etc.

For contact details for the main bus terminals, see Chapter 2. For a list of major bus companies, see Appendix XVI.

WHAT TO SAY			
aisle	*koridor*	exit	*çıkış*
bus	*otobüs*	host(ess) on bus	*muavin/yardımcı*
bus terminal	*otogar*	left luggage office	*emanet*
departure bay	*peron*	lost property office	*kayıp eşya bürosu*
discount	*indirim*	rest area	*dinlenme tesisleri*
driver	*kaptan/şoför bey*	ticket	*bilet*
duration of journey	*seyir süresi*	ticket office	*gişe*
emergency brake	*imdat freni*	timetable	*tarife*
emergency exit	*acil çıkış*	window seat	*cam/pencere kenarı*
emergency hammer	*imdat çekici*	How many hours to Istanbul?	*Istanbul'a kaç saat sürer?*
entrance	*giriş*	When does it leave?	*Ne zaman kalkar?*

Trains (*Tren*)

Unlike the bus network, Turkey's rail network is fairly poor. Trains are often elderly, dirty and lacking in even the most basic of facilities. They also take circuitous routes between towns which means that they are usually slower than buses. A few high-speed trains have recently been introduced on the busy Istanbul to Ankara route with premium fares to match their higher quality; a high-speed train from Ankara to Konya is also on its way. On all other routes, train fares are cheaper than bus fares. By paying extra you can sleep in a couchette or in a sleeper carriage on most of the longer overnight journeys.

Recently TCDD (www.tcdd.gov.tr) introduced monthly railcards for travel around Turkey. Otherwise, there are 20% discounts for return trips, for senior citizens, for students and for disabled passengers.

WHAT TO SAY			
1st/2nd class	*birinci/ikinci mevki*	sleeping compartment	*yataklı*
couchette	*kuşet*	ticket	*bilet*
discount	*indirim*	ticket office	*gişe*
full fare	*tam bilet*	timetable	*tarife*
no entry	*girilmez*	train	*tren*
platform	*peron*	train station	*istasyon*
railway terminal	*gar*		

Planes (*Uçak*)

It has never been easier or cheaper to fly between Turkish towns. The last few years have seen several private airlines (Atlasjet, Flyair, Onur Air, Pegasus, Sun Express) start up in competition with Turkish Airlines on domestic routes. They also operate on several completely new routes. Most offer cheap or flat fares, although on some of the carriers (especially THY) you need to book early to get a discount. Fares operate on a one-way basis with no reductions for round trips and no air passes available.

For contact details for domestic carriers, see Appendix XVI.

Ferries (*Feribot*)

Although the old ferry service between Istanbul and Trabzon has fallen victim to the competition from the cheap airlines there are still several ferry crossings that are useful for reducing car journey times. In particular the ferry services across the Sea of Marmara from Istanbul to Yalova and Bandırma (İDO, Tel: 444 4436, www.ido.com.tr) offer high standards of comfort while shaving many hours of driving from the journeys to Bursa or Izmir. Over summer weekends the seabuses from Sarayburnu and Erdek to and between the Marmara Islands (also operated by İDO) are equally welcome. The ferry between Eskihisar and Topçu can also be useful for cutting driving time inside eastern Istanbul.

The weekend ferry between Istanbul and Izmir has recently been reinstated to offer a journey more like a mini cruise.

Major Turkish Ferry Services

- Istanbul to Yalova

- Istanbul to Bandırma
- Istanbul to Izmir
- Istanbul to Marmara and Avşa
- Eskihisar to Topçular
- Gelibolu to Lapseki
- Eceabat to Çanakkale
- Çanakkale to Gökçeada
- Kabatepe to Gökçeada
- Yükyeri to Bozcaada
- Tatvan to Van
- Akıncılar to Çaylarbaşı (Kahta to Siverek)

For details of international ferry routes see Chapters 20 and 22.

WHAT TO SAY			
ferry	vapur/feribot	seabus	deniz otobüsü
harbour	liman/iskele	timetable	tarife

Dolmuşes

The dolmuş is an extremely handy form of transport that operates between smaller settlements. Originally dolmuşes were shared taxis that set out as soon as they filled up. These days intercity dolmuşes are almost always minibuses that operate to a set timetable whether or not they are full. Fares are usually a matter of a few lira.

IN-TOWN TRANSPORT OPTIONS (ŞEHİRİÇİ ULAŞIM)

Buses (Şehiriçi Otobüs)

Within towns the local authorities normally provide bus services. These are usually fairly frequent except late at night and fares are generally low.

WHAT TO SAY			
alighting only	indirme yeri	discount	indirim
back door	arka kapı	driver	kaptan/şoför bey
bus	otobüs	middle door	orta kapı
bus terminal	otogar, garaj, terminal	Don't get out via the front door	Önkapıdan inilmez
bus/dolmuş stop	durak	I want to get out	İnecek var
connection/transfer	aktarma	Where does it leave from?	Nereden kalkar?

Sometimes services start from the same bus terminal as intercity services but sometimes there is a separate inner-city bus terminal. Istanbul bus routes and schedules are listed on www.iett.gov.tr although this is not kept completely up-to-date. You can also phone 0800-211 6068 for advice on routes.

Trains (*Tren*)

If intercity train services are inadequate it is hardly surprising to discover that those inside towns are also pretty poor. **Istanbul** has a fairly extensive local rail service (*banliyö treni*) but it currently relies on trains that are dingy and poorly equipped. They run from Sirkeci to Halkalı along the Sea of Marmara on the European side of the city, and from Haydarpaşa to Gebze via Bostancı on the Asian side.

The good news is that 76km of this rail network is due to be upgraded as part of the ambitious Marmaray project, work on which has already begun (www.marmaray.com). This will see the trains taken from Yedikule to new underground stations at Yenikapı and Sirkeci, whence they will travel through tunnels under the Istanbul Strait to emerge at a new underground station in Üsküdar before continuing onto Söğütlüçeşme along the upgraded Asian-side railway line. The project is currently facing delays because of archaeological discoveries along the route of the tunnel. However, it should be up and running by 2010. Unfortunately, the city is likely to experience severe rail problems until it is completed.

Ankara also has a local train service that runs between Sincan in the west and Kayaş in the east. Local train services also trundle between Alsancak station and the airport in **Izmir**.

Ferries (*Vapur*)

If you live in Istanbul or Izmir you will find that the most pleasant way of getting about the city is by ferry. Inner-city ferries are cheap, regular and usually fairly comfortable, especially in **Istanbul**, where some are operated by the local authorities and others by private companies. Istanbul also has some enclosed, high-speed seabus services on the longer routes (e.g. to the Princes Islands). Note that some of these ferries only operate during commuting hours or at weekends and that there are separate summer and winter timetables.

Inner-City Ferry Routes – Istanbul

- Beşiktaş to Kadıköy

- Beşiktaş to Üsküdar
- Beşiktaş to Küçüksu
- Beykoz to Kadıköy
- Bostancı to Heybeliada, Büyükada (Princes' Islands) and Kartal
- Eminönü to Beşiktaş, Ortaköy, Kuzguncuk, Beylerbeyi, Çengelköy, Arnavutköy, Bebek, Kandilli, Anadolu Hisarı, Kanlıca, Emirgan, Çubuklu, İstinye, Paşabahçe, Beykoz, Yeniköy, Büyükdere, Sarıyer, Rumeli Kavağı and Anadolu Kavağı (Bosphorus)
- Eminönü to Beşiktaş, Kanlıca, Yeniköy, Sarıyer, Rumeli Kavağı and Anadolu Kavağı (Bosphorus tour)
- Eminönü to Bostancı
- Eminönü to Erenköy, Koçadere and Çınarcık
- Eminönü to Haydarpaşa and Kadıköy
- Eminönü to Karaköy and Beykoz
- Eminönü to Moda and Bostancı
- Eminönü to Üsküdar
- İstinye to Emirgan, Kanlıca, Anadolu Hisarı, Kandilli, Bebek, Arnavutköy, and Çengelköy
- Kabataş to Harem
- Kabataş to Karaköy and Eminönü
- Kabataş to Üsküdar
- Kadıköy to Bostancı
- Kanlıca to Arnavutköy via Anadolu Hisarı, Kandilli and Bebek
- Karaköy to Haydarpaşa and Kadıköy
- Karaköy to Üsküdar
- Sarıyer to Beykoz, İstinye, Beşiktaş, Üsküdar, Karaköy, Eminönü, Kadıköy and Bakırköy
- Sarıyer to Kadıköy
- Sarıyer to Rumeli Kavağı and Anadolu Kavağı
- Sirkeci to Kabataş, Kadıköy, Bostancı, the Princes' Islands, Yalova, and Çınarcık
- Sirkeci to Harem
- Sirkeci to Kadıköy, Kınalıada, Burguzada, Heybeliada and Büyükada (Princes' Islands)
- Üsküdar to Bakırköy
- Üsküdar to Eminönü, Kasımpaşa, Fener, Balat, Ayvansaray, Sütlüce and Eyüp (Golden Horn)

- Yenikapı to Kadıköy and Bostancı
- Yenikapı to Bakırköy

Inner-City Ferry Routes – Izmir

- Alsancak to Karşıyaka
- Konak to Pasaport and Alsancak
- Konak to Karşıyaka

BRIDGES OF SIGHS

At the time of writing Istanbul still had only two bridges – Fatih Sultan Mehmet Köprüsü and Boğaziçi Köprüsü (Bosphorus Bridge) – to convey cars from one side of the Bosphorus to the other. A third bridge is planned although there is, as yet, no agreement as to where it should be sited. If you live in Istanbul and need to commute to work across either bridge you will quickly discover their importance and learn to plan for the traffic – a journey from Kadıköy to Taksim, for example, that might take 15 minutes in the evening can take an hour or so during rush hours. Both bridges are toll roads; you must have an OGS or pre-paid KGS card (see p. 370) to use the Boğazici Köprüsü, although the Fatih Sultan Mehmet Köprüsü has a very limited number of toll booths that will take cash (the queues for these can be excruciatingly long).

Tram and Metro Services (*Tramvay-Metro*)

Increasingly the larger towns depend on tram and metro services to move people from place to place. **Istanbul** has the most comprehensive tram and metro network and this is still in the process of expansion. The *tramvay* runs from Zeytinburnu in the west through to Kabataş in the east, with a spur running north to Esenler. At Zeytinburnu the *tramvay* connects with the Metro which runs west to Atatürk International Airport via the main bus terminal at Otogar station and east to Aksaray. The tram is due to be extended from Kabataş to Beşiktaş. A second Metro line runs from Taksim to 4.Levent. A short stretch of tram also links Kadıköy to Moda. Finally, a historic tram trundles along İstiklal Caddesi for most of the day.

The **Ankara** Metro has two lines. The Ankaray runs from Dikimevi in the west to AŞTİ, the giant bus terminal in the east. The Metro runs from Kızılay in the town centre to Batıkent in the south-east. The two lines connect at Kızılay.

The **Izmir** Metro runs from Üçyol in the west to Bornova in the east.

The **Eskişehir** Metro runs from the bus terminal to the town centre.

Dolmuşes

Most of the bigger cities also have dolmuş services on popular routes. Usually these are minibuses which leave as and when they fill up although a few towns still depend either entirely on old-fashioned shared taxi-dolmuşes (e.g. Trabzon) or in part on them (e.g. Izmir and Bursa). Since taxi-dolmuşes only require five or six passengers to fill them they often run more frequently than the minibus services.

WHAT TO SAY			
a bit further ahead	*biraz ilerde*	full fare	*tam bilet*
alighting only	*indirme yeri*	I want to get out	*inecek var*
at the junction	*kavşakta*	minibus/shared taxi	*dolmuş*
bus/dolmuş stop	*durak*	short-hop fare	*indi bindi*
discount	*indirim*	ticket	*bilet*
driver	*kaptan/şoför bey*	wherever's convenient	*müsait bir yerde*

Funiculars (*Füniküler*)

In **Istanbul** a brand-new funicular links the tram and ferries at Kabataş with the Metro station at Taksim Square. Istanbul also has a historic funicular, the Tünel, that links Karaköy with the Galata end of İstiklal Caddesi. This operates continuously throughout the day although services finish early at 9pm.

Otherwise, the most important funicular service to know about is the one that runs from the outskirts of **Bursa** up to the ski slopes on Mt Uludağ. Out of season this operates a very limited service, and even in high summer strong winds can sometimes stop it running.

Taxis (*Taksi*)

Wherever you are in Turkey you are likely to be able to hire a taxi and in the big towns yellow cabs are to be seen everywhere. Legally, all taxis must be metered, although in rural areas if you are travelling a longish distance you may agree on a fare with the driver that may include waiting time at your destination. During the day the taxi meter should show the word '*gündüz*' to indicate that the daytime rate is being used; at night it should show '*gece*' to indicate that the (higher) night-time rate is operating. Generally speaking, taxi drivers are usually honest. However, if you are travelling a route popular with tourists you should keep a close eye on that meter to make sure that there is no fiddling.

WHAT TO SAY	
Please open/close the window	*camı açın/kapatın*
Please turn the meter on	*taksimetreyi çalıştırın*
Stop here please	*burada durun*
Straight on	*düz/doğru*
Turn left/right at the lights	*ışıklardan sola/sağa dönün*
Wait here	*burada bekleyin*

FARES FOR REGULAR PUBLIC TRANSPORT USERS

Within Istanbul, Ankara and Izmir it is possible for regular users of public transport to buy payment cards that not only give them a discount but also save them from having to queue for tickets. The most useful of these 'cards' is the Istanbul *akbil*. This extraordinary device is an electronic purse which can be used on all forms of inner-city transport: buses, trains, trams, ferries, funiculars and cable-cars; only the private dolmuşes remain outside the *akbil* system. The standard *akbil* is a plastic tag with a metal button set into it which you press into a machine at the front of every bus etc; the machine then deducts the fare (reduced to encourage usage) for the route. To buy an *akbil* (which you can attach to your key fob) you pay a small deposit plus however much money you think appropriate (usually YTL10 or YTL20 at a time); this is charged to the card and the balance reduces every time you use it – if you have to transfer between two modes of transport the first such transfer is free. An *akbil* can be recharged with more money at any Akbil Satış Noktası/Gişesi about town; some of these are staffed, others are simply machines.

Mavi Kart: As well as the normal *akbil* there is also a *Mavi Kart* (Blue Card) for which you pay a specific fee for a specific length of time: one day, one week, two weeks or one month. Students, teachers and people born before 1945 are eligible for a discounted *Mavi Kart*. To get your card made up look for a sign reading *'Mavi Kart Yapılır'* (normally near an Akbil Satış Noktası). You need a photograph for the card to ensure that only you can use it.

Izmir has a simpler system using rechargeable 'Kent' cards for bus journeys. In **Ankara** you can buy blocks of tickets which are valid on the Metro/Ankaray as well as on the buses.

Children under six normally travel free on the buses. There are also reduced prices for students (*öğrenci*). In Istanbul students, teachers and senior citizens (aged over 60) can obtain cards entitling them to discounts on public transport; disabled travellers, some civil servants and some ex-military personnel can get cards that allow them to travel free.

WHAT IT MEANS	
Sarı çizgiyi geçmeyiniz	Don't cross the yellow line
Lütfen cep telefonunuzu kapatınız	Please turn off your mobile phone
İnmek için düğmeye basınız	Press the button to get out
İnişler orta ve arka kapıdandır	Exit from the middle and back doors
Lütfen arkaya doğru ilerleyiniz	Please move to the back of the carriage
Yaşlılara çocuklu hanımlara ve gazilere yer veriniz	Give up your seat to the elderly, women with children, and veterans
Sigara içilmez	No smoking

CHAPTER 22

MAKING THE MOVE

There are many ways to get to Turkey from Western Europe. The quickest and cheapest method is to fly but sometimes you may want to turn a journey into an adventure and drive, or take the bus or train. Choosing how to get yourself to Turkey is likely to be less of a hassle than picking a removals company to transport your belongings. However, provided you make the right choice, bringing your worldly goods to the country needn't be too traumatic.

THE JOURNEY

For people living in Turkey access to cheap flights to and from their home country is an important consideration. From Europe the cheapest direct flights are usually from Germany, but those from the UK should begin to come down now that easyJet has started flights to Istanbul. Inevitably, flights from the USA and Australia/New Zealand are high.

For a list of scheduled airlines flying to and from Turkey see Appendix XVI. Conventional travel guidebooks will also have more information about the various options for flying to Turkey.

FROM THE UK
Direct Flights

Both British Airways (BA) and Turkish Airlines (THY) have daily flights from London Heathrow to Istanbul. Except in peak season these usually cost around £200 return, although THY has introduced some cheaper off-peak fares out of London Stansted. In summer (i.e. from April through October) there are also many charter flights to the main airports serving the tourist areas: Bodrum, Dalaman and Antalya. If seats are still available after the package holidays have been sold some may be offloaded on a seat-only basis for around £100 each way.

In 2006 the no-frills airline easyJet started flying into Istanbul's second, under-utilised airport, Sabiha Gökçen, way out on the Asian side of the city, with prices starting at £60 one way from London Luton airport.

Indirect Flights

To get a cheaper flight to Turkey from the UK you may have to buy an indirect flight on a scheduled airline and put up with the break of journey en route. Alternatively, you can fly to Cologne-Bonn from Gatwick, Stansted or Edinburgh on Germanwings (www.germanwings.com); from Manchester or Newcastle on Hapag-Lloyd Express (www.hlx.com); or from Gatwick or Nottingham on easyJet (www.easyJet.com) and then take an overnight flight on one of the cheaper German airlines (see below) to Turkey. The total cost is likely to be marginally less than flying direct from the UK. Sometimes it is also cheaper to fly on bmibaby (www.bmibaby.com) to Paris and from there to Istanbul on Onur Air.

Charter Airlines

Few of the charter companies operate flights to Turkey in winter. However, in 2005 Holidays 4U was offering weekly winter flights from Gatwick and Manchester to Dalaman. Other charter companies to try include:

- *Avro:* Tel: 0870-458 2841, www.avro.co.uk; Antalya, Dalaman
- *Cosmos:* Tel: 0870-443 5285, www.cosmos-holidays.co.uk; Bodrum, Dalaman, Antalya
- *Excel:* Tel: 0870-999 0069, www.xl.com; Bodrum, Dalaman, Antalya
- *First Choice:* Tel: 0870-850 3999, www.firstchoice.co.uk; Bodrum, Dalaman, Antalya
- *Holidays 4U:* Tel: 0870-444 2840, www.h4u.co.uk; Dalaman
- *My Travel:* Tel: 0870-241 5333, www.mytravel.com; Bodrum, Dalaman, Antalya
- *Thomas Cook:* Tel: 0870-750 5711, www.thomascook.com; Bodrum, Dalaman, Antalya

FROM GERMANY

Germany is Europe's main source of cheap flights to Turkey. There are daily scheduled flights to Istanbul and Ankara on Turkish Airlines and Lufthansa. In addition Germanwings (www.27-germanwings.com) flies from Cologne to Ankara and Izmir, while Air Berlin (www.airberlin.com) flies to Antalya. Both offer no-frills cheap flights.

FROM FRANCE

There are daily scheduled flights on Turkish Airlines and Air France to Istanbul and Ankara but it may be cheaper to fly on Onur Air.

FROM THE NETHERLANDS

There are daily scheduled flights on Turkish Airlines and KLM to Istanbul and Ankara. Cheaper flights on Pegasus are usually available via www.ticket-pot.com.

WHAT TO SAY			
aeroplane	uçak	international departures	dış hatlar
airport	havalimanı	one way	tek yön
arrival time	varış saati	passenger lounge	yolcu salonu
arrivals	geliş	return	gidiş-dönüş
boarding gate	çıkış kapısı	route	güzergâh
cost	ücret	small airport/airstrip	havaalanı
departure lounge	çıkış salonu	summer timetable	yaz tarifesi
departure time	kalkış saati	transfer	aktarma
departures	gidiş	winter timetable	kış tarifesi
domestic departures	iç hatlar		

OVERLAND TRAVEL

Unless you are prepared to travel by bus you are unlikely to be able to get to Turkey overland for less than the cost of the airfare. Indeed, if you travel by train or drive your own car it is likely to be much more expensive than flying. On the other hand the journey can be turned into an adventure and if you drive you will be able to transport some of your belongings at the same time.

By Train *(Trenle)*: It is no longer possible to travel directly to Turkey by train from Western Europe although there are daily trains from Budapest and Bucharest. Neither service is luxurious, so these journeys are for those in search of excitement. You can also travel by train from Athens to Istanbul, with one change in Thessaloniki (Salonica).

By Car *(Arabayla)*: If you want to drive to Turkey from Western Europe you could pick any route you want although most people opt for the two most direct routes; whichever way you choose it's a journey of around 3,000km from London to Istanbul so you will need to allow several days.

The most direct northern route follows the E5 through Belgium, Germany, Austria, Hungary, Romania and Bulgaria to Turkey. Alternatively, you can divert from Austria and travel south through Slovenia and along the coast of Serbia and Croatia, continuing through Albania to Greece (a tough journey) or east through Macedonia and Bulgaria. Alternatively you can drive south through France and Italy to Ancona or Brindisi and then take a ferry either to Greece or direct to Çeşme, near Izmir (a summer-only option). These journeys have become easier now that EU citizens are freed from the requirement to get visas for most of the countries along the way.

Making The Move

Once you've found a house, whether to rent or buy, you may want to move your personal effects to Turkey. To do this you must have a Turkish residency permit. The application form says that you must move your belongings no more than two months before and no more than six months after entering Turkey. What that means in effect is that if you have been resident in Turkey for some time you may have to leave the country and come back in again with a new residency permit in order to have a stamp in your passport that fits within the required time frame.

IN THE HOME COUNTRY

There are an increasing number of international removals firms operating out of the UK, although what appear at first glance to be different firms often turn out to be the same one operating under various names. If you don't have much to move, you can arrange to have it flown to Turkey. However, if you want to move bulky items such as furniture or heavy items such as books you will probably need to have them shipped over. The most popular entry port is Istanbul; indeed some international removals firms won't transport goods to any other ports. Unfortunately Istanbul port has a reputation for corruption; your goods will probably arrive there safely but you will then have trouble extricating them without handing over a series of unofficial payments.

An alternative is to use Izmir port (Alsancak Limanı) which is smaller and more manageable than Istanbul. This is perfectly convenient if you are moving to the Aegean, and no more inconvenient than Istanbul if you are moving to the Mediterranean, Ankara or Kapadokya. However, if you are moving to Istanbul it would be a pain.

It is obviously quicker to have your goods flown to Turkey. However, it is likely to be considerably more expensive. The price is calculated on a combination of volume and weight. Typically it may cost around £2.80 per kilo to fly your belongings from London to Istanbul.

International removals firms transport your belongings overseas in huge containers and usually charge by the square metre. If you are moving all the contents of a house you may have enough belongings to fill an entire container in which case your goods will be transported direct from your home (or storage unit) to the embarkation port. You can also opt to pay extra to have your contents shipped in a separate container. Otherwise the removals firm will consolidate your belongings into containers with those of other people (groupage). Quite often there will be a delay until space becomes available in a suitable ship. In the meantime your belongings will be stored in the removals firm's warehouse.

For a list of international removals companies, see Appendix XVII. A useful website that can help you by collecting multiple quotes for removal costs is www.reallymoving.com.

Insurance: Insuring your belongings is not compulsory and is fairly expensive relative to the cost of shipping (shop around for quotes - while one company may charge £175 to insure £3000-worth of goods from the UK, another will charge only £235 to insure £7000-worth). Some companies offer two levels of marine insurance, with the cheaper version excluding many potential risks. Tempting as it may be to forego the cost, if you don't insure your belongings and they are damaged or lost in transit, there will be nothing you can do about it. Insurers usually need time to come up with a quote and they will normally require you to supply a detailed inventory of what is being covered, as will the removals firm. If you are leaving the UK, you can check that your marine insurance company is registered with the Financial Services Agency (as it should be) by going to www.fsa.gov.uk.

Packaging: Reputable removals firms usually supply all the necessary packaging materials although you can minimise costs by doing some of the packing yourself. All boxes will need to have their contents listed on the outside, although, for example, 'books' will be adequate - you don't need to list all the titles. Normally you will have to be present when your belongings are being packed and loaded for removal.

Costs, Payment & Timing: If you are moving the entire contents of a small house in the UK to the Turkish coast you should expect to have to pay at least £3,000 and perhaps twice that. If, on the other hand, you are only moving your personal possessions (books, clothes etc), it should cost more like £1,250-1,500.

Most removals firms require full payment in advance of shipping. In return they offer an 'advanced payment guarantee' that your goods will be delivered to their destination even if the removals company goes into liquidation while they are in transit. The busiest times for removals firms tend to be Fridays, the school holiday periods and the end of each month. If you can move at other times you may be eligible for a cheaper rate.

You can save money by organising everything yourself: doing the packaging, hiring a van to drive to the port, renting space in a container privately etc. However, if you opt to do this you will have to handle Customs formalities on arrival without an intermediary. Unless you have a Turkish partner or speak fluent Turkish this is likely to involve a frustrating amount of rushing around different government departments without entirely understanding what is going on.

IN TURKEY

All reputable removals firms should have a destination partner who organises Customs clearance and the transfer of your belongings from the port to their final destination for you. Once your goods arrive in Turkey you may have to present yourself at Customs with your title deed, passport and residency permit (original documents required). However, sometimes it is sufficient to send your documents by courier to the agent handling your affairs at the port, handy if, for example, you live in Antalya and are importing your belongings through distant Izmir. If you do go to the harbour in person you should expect to do some hanging around. The Customs office will close for an hour for lunch, so take something with you to eat (and read). At the port city your agent will take you to a public notary (*noter*) so you can sign a power-of-attorney authorising them to act on your behalf. Unless your Turkish is excellent (and having a Turkish partner will not necessarily exempt you from this) you will also have to pay for a translator (*tercüman*) to tell you what the document says. Expect to pay around YTL40 to the *noter* and another YTL25 to the *tercüman*.

Some removals firms can only organise transport as far as the port but others offer a door-to-door removals service (*evden eve nakliyat*) which is likely to be a great deal more convenient. You may have to wait a few days after Customs clearance before onward transport can be organised. Expect to pay a small storage charge in the interim.

It will probably take around one month to six weeks for your belongings to be moved from a home in the UK to a new home in Turkey. This can be an expensive delay if you are depending on your UK belongings to furnish an empty property. Rather than waste money on hotel bills you could invest in an inflatable bed and primus stove to see you through the wait.

For more information about moving abroad go to www.gatewaysmoving.com.

For a list of Turkish removals companies, see Appendix XVII.

CUSTOMS *(GÜMRÜK)*

If you have Turkish residency you are allowed to import your belongings from home without paying duty on them. However, you can only import what the Customs officials regard as electrical goods compatible with the number of family members in the household. Tax of 15-17% of the sales value in Turkey will be levied on any excess electrical items.

You have to pay a charge of 15-17% of the Turkish sales value (*bandrol ücreti*) on ALL imported televisions, video/DVD recorders and stereos, even if these are old. This fee is a one-off payment levied on all such items in Turkey to cover payments to *TRT* and other entertainment companies. Once you have paid, the item will be stickered which means that in theory if you exported it from Turkey and then brought it back in again you would not have to pay the charge again. Unless your television etc are brand-new, it is probably wiser not to import such items since they are readily available in Turkey. You cannot easily change your mind about importing them once they arrive in the country. For example, if you say you don't want your television after all, you may be forced to abandon everything else that was packaged with it. Even Turks who are returning to Turkey have to pay the *bandrol* fee.

At the time of writing the following *bandrol* fees were being levied to import ONE television, radio etc (plus a flat €180 fee for any additional models):

€ (euro)

Television (screen upto 51cm)	55
(screen 51-67cm)	85
(screen 67-85cm)	100
(screen 85-116cm)	120
(screen 116cm+)	150
Portable radio	25
Video/video recorder/video camera/DVD recorder	180
Satellite receiver (Sky box)	180
TV and VCR	195
Walkman	10
Portable radio/turntable	36
Portable radio/cassette player	35
Portable radio/CD player	45
Auto radio/cassette player	35
Auto radio/CD player	45

Radio/cassette player	50
Radio/CD player	71
Radio/turntable	71
Radio/cassette/turntable	140
Radio/cassette/turntable/CD player	180
Radio/cassette/CD player	180

No one is allowed to import firearms, fireworks, foodstuffs (except dried or canned foods), narcotics, medicines (except with a doctor's prescription) or pornography. People who are coming to reside in Turkey without working are not normally allowed to import a car. People who are coming here to work may be able to do so but only if they can prove they have owned the car for more than six months and that it is less than three years old.

When you come to leave again you may need to prove that you had permission from a museum to export any antique carpets. It is also illegal to export any Turkish antiquities without a letter of permission from an appropriate museum. Archaeological artefacts cannot be exported under any circumstances except for short-term exhibitions which have been approved by the Ministry of Culture and Tourism. If you want to build up a private collection of antiquities inside Turkey you are supposed to get permission from the Ministry of Culture and Tourism first.

Separate regulations apply to:
* foreign diplomats
* Turkish diplomats
* foreign nationals temporarily residing in Turkey for work, research or education
* Turkish citizens returning from work abroad

'Gelin Hakkı' ('the Bride's Right'): Foreigners who are getting married to a Turk might like to know that they are allowed to import all their personal effects together with up to €3,000 of wedding presents (no one gift to be worth more than €300) for a period of up to two months before and six months after the wedding.

For more information phone Customs at Istanbul airport (Tel: 0212-663 6400/3298, www.gumruk.gov.tr). However, it will probably be easier to discuss the subject with an English-speaking shipping agent, ideally the one working with your removals firm.

WHO TO CONTACT

Undersecretariat for Customs: Tel: 0312-311 1251, Fax: 0312-310 2214, www.gumruk.gov.tr, Eski Maliye Bakanlığı Binası, Kat: 2, Hükümet Meydanı, Ulus, Ankara

RELOCATORS

Relocators specialise in helping people to settle into their new country. They can help you find somewhere to live, track down a nanny, research the best schools, help with the shopping, explain about insurance, line up a doctor etc. Most will even organise preview trips to help you make decisions about your move before the big day. If you have limited time to settle in and don't speak much Turkish you may find their services a real boon.

Most relocators also provide services for businesses in need of start-up assistance.

For a list of Turkish and international relocators, see Appendix XVII.

CARGO *(KARGO)* AND COURIER *(KURYE)* SERVICES

If you want to move a small item from one place to another in Turkey, it is quite common to put it on a bus in return for a small fee. Anything larger can be sent via a domestic cargo service; Aras Kargo, MNG Kargo and Yurtiçi Kargo are the three largest companies although none will carry uninsured fragile or valuable items. If you live somewhere remote they may deliver the item to their office in the nearest town rather than to your home.

The big international courier companies DHL, TNT and Fedex also operate throughout Turkey. In addition the post office offers a fast postal service (*Acele Posta Servisi, APS*). All these services seem reliable whether you want to move things around Turkey or send them abroad. *APS* is cheaper than the international courier services and usually fairly dependable.

WHO TO CONTACT

- *Aras Cargo:* Tel: 425 5555, www.arascargo.com
- *DHL:* Tel: 444 0040, www.dhl.com.tr
- *Fedex:* Tel: 440 0505, www.fedex.com/tr
- *MNG Kargo:* Tel: 444 0606, www.mngkargo.com.tr
- *TNT:* Tel: 444 0868, www.tnt.com
- *UPS:* Tel: 444 0033, www.ups.com.tr
- *Yurtiçi Kargo:* Tel: 444 9999, www.yurticikargo.com.tr

CHAPTER 23

LATER LIFE

For many people the idea of retiring to Turkey and its warmer climate is very appealing. This has become much easier now that you can withdraw your pension money from ATM machines all over the country and will no doubt become even easier if Turkey is admitted to the European Union.

Growing old in Turkey has some advantages over growing old elsewhere since Turkey is a society in which the elderly are still treated with respect. Although there are a few old people's homes, it is unusual for families to send their older members to live elsewhere. Instead they usually stay at home and are expected to help out with household tasks and childcare for as long as possible. However, there are few organised activities for elderly people even in the big cities.

As the currency has stabilised Turkey has started to introduce private pension facilities to back up very limited state provisions. There is nothing to stop foreign residents taking advantage of these too. However, it is important to remember that standards of healthcare in public facilities are not high, so unless you can afford good health insurance you could be storing up problems for the future. Western immigration is a new phenomenon for the Turkish Republic and there is no reason to think that the government has fully thought through the implications of a growing population of elderly foreigners who are used to high standards of healthcare. At the time of writing Turkey also lacked any facilities for cremation and had limited space for the burial of non-Muslims.

OLD AGE PENSIONS (EMEKLİLİK)

Foreigners in Turkey are sometimes surprised to be asked whether they are retired (emekli) when they are barely into their forties. This is because Turks who work for the government have always been able to retire and draw a small state pension after 25 years of service, regardless of age. However, with a rapidly growing population the government is facing the same problem of pension affordability as the rest of Europe and is taking several different approaches to resolving it.

State-Run Pension Programmes: There used to be three separate state-run pension schemes. Bağ-Kur (short for '*bağımsız kurumlar*') was for employers, the self-employed and independent professionals. SSK was for workers and employees. Emekli Sandık was for civil servants. However, at the time of writing these had just been merged and details of how the new pension schemes will function had yet to be worked out.

Until recently anyone who had paid into one of these three schemes for 25 years was able to retire on a small pension regardless of their age. People who had completed the qualifying period for a pension before 2003 can still retire at 48, but those who qualified after that must work on until 51 and it is likely that the retirement age will rise to at least 55 (the government has just accepted a proposal that will gradually raise the age of retirement to 65 over the next 20 years).

Private Pensions: Several banks and insurance companies have started to offer private pensions which anyone - even non-citizens - can pay into. These are very flexibly constructed and the money that you pay in is guaranteed by the government in an attempt to encourage people to save for their old age. How much you pay depends on your age, although at the moment there are no restrictions imposed because of lifestyle factors such as smoking and obesity that might effect how long you will live.

UK Pensions: Many people retiring to Turkey from the UK will have either a state or a private pension or both. At present UK state pensions are only subject to UK tax while private pensions from the UK are liable for Turkish but not British tax. The fact that you have moved abroad does not affect your eligibility for any pension you have paid for although you will have to arrange to have payments made in Turkey. Since most banks charge for every transfer or ATM transaction you may need to arrange to have your pension sent in lumps; for example, every three months. British state pensions are periodically updated in line with inflation and the fact that you are living in Turkey will not affect your right to these increases. However, you will not be eligible for other benefits including pension credit which tops up the smallest British incomes. You are also unlikely to be eligible for extra winter fuel payments. For more information contact:

- *The Pension Centre:* Tel: 0191-218 7777, www.thepensionservice.gov.uk; Tyneview Park, Benton, Newcastle-upon-Tyne NE98 1BA

- *Winter Fuel Payment Centre:* Tel: 08459-151515, www.thepensionservice. gov.uk; Southgate House, Cardiff Central, Royal Mail, Cardiff, CF911 1ZH

OLD PEOPLE'S HOMES *(HUZUREVİ)*

Although Turkey does have a few old people's homes, in general people still think that families should look after their elderly members and that there is something rather shameful about putting them in a home. Although Turks criticise Westerners for their 'heartless' treatment of the elderly, the reality is that few things are organised for the elderly in Turkey so that many old people lead very limited lives, virtually house-bound. Recently new nursing homes and semi-retirement/nursing home combinations have been built, especially by the Emekli Sandık for their pensioners. Some of these places are quite pleasant and there is no stigma attached to older individuals or couples moving into them. Turkey also has a few private nursing homes which offer top-class care, albeit at top-class prices. The Little Sisters of the Poor (a French nursing order) also run a nursing home in Istanbul for the elderly of all nationalities and faiths. While it is intended for the indigent old, in practise anyone who is willing to pay for their care or to turn over their pension income to the home is usually accepted and lovingly cared for by the nuns.

Home Care: Because wages are relatively low it is perfectly possible to employ people to come to your home to look after elderly relatives while you are at work (or to look after you when you can no longer do so yourself). However, more professional care is likely to be fairly expensive. One firm that provides care in the home is Eczacıbaşı Health Services (for contact details see under miscellaneous health contacts in Appendix VIII).

DEATH *(ÖLÜM)*

By the standards of Western Europe Turkey has a relatively low life expectancy rate: 68 years for men and 73 for women. This is probably in part because of greater poverty and in part because of heavy smoking, relatively poor healthcare and an epidemic of obesity.

When a death occurs a doctor must come to confirm it and issue a death certificate *(ölüm raporu)*; if the death occurs in a hospital, the hospital has responsibility for issuing the report. Following a suspicious death or one in which the cause is uncertain an autopsy *(otopsi)* must take place. Otherwise the family are free to remove the body as soon as the certificate has been issued.

Turkish hospitals are sometimes reluctant to concede that death has occurred and people can be kept on life-support machines long after hope is gone. As yet there is no such concept as a living will.

WHAT TO SAY TO THE BEREAVED

Although the Turkish for 'to die' is *ölmek*, this can seem very abrupt. Gentler alternatives include *hayatını kaybetmek* (to lose one's life), *vefat etmek* (to pass away) or *rahmetli olmak* (to pass away); if the person who has died was a foreigner it is more normal to say *toprağı bol olsun*, broadly meaning 'rest in peace'. *Rahmetli* means 'the deceased/the late', *rahmetli babam* roughly 'may God have mercy on my late father'.

FUNERALS *(CENAZE)* AND BURIAL *(GÖMME)*

When someone dies in Turkey their death, together with details of when the funeral will take place, is announced by the *müezzin* calling from the mosque. In Muslim tradition it is important to bury the body within a day or so of death, especially in summer. This can make it virtually impossible for relatives from other countries to attend the funeral.

In Turkish tradition, the dead body is taken to the mosque and washed, perfumed and wrapped naked in a white shroud; men wash a man's body, women wash a woman's. This task is generally carried out by family members in small towns or villages; alternatively the *imam* can be paid to do it. Some large city mosques have special body-preparation areas with body-washing facilities, usually discreetly tucked away in a back garden. Staff are on hand to do the washing and shrouding, but a close family member is expected to observe. While this service is provided free, a tip is much appreciated. The funeral service is held in the local mosque where the funeral prayer is recited. The body lies in a simple wooden coffin on a stone slab outside the mosque while friends, family and the community gather round to join in the prayer.

Bodies *(cenaze/ceset)* are buried in their shrouds *(kefen)* either without coffins or in simple wooden boxes. They are laid to rest lying slightly to the right side and facing Mecca. If there is a tombstone *(mezartaşı)* it goes at the head end of the grave as in the West. The *imam* comes and says prayers at the graveside. In traditional rural communities women still don't attend funerals; instead they stay at home and mourn with other women in their own houses. In the big cities women can attend funerals if they want to. If a foreigner wishes to go along too it is unlikely to cause problems.

In rural areas there is not normally a charge for a plot of land in the cemetery (*mezarlık*). However in urban areas people are expected to buy their own plot of land unless they want their family member to be buried in the paupers' part of the cemetery.

In the event of there being no body to bury (for example, after a plane crash) a piece of land will still be marked as a 'grave' so that relatives will have somewhere to go and pray. When an elderly or homeless person dies and there are no relatives to organise their funeral the Belediye will make the necessary arrangements.

VISITING THE BEREAVED (*TAZİYE ZİYARETİ*)

When people hear a death being announced from the mosque they rush to comfort the bereaved family. Visiting normally continues for several days and in rural areas it will be sexually segregated, with the men in one room and the women in another. It is perfectly acceptable for women to weep openly; indeed some women wail and throw themselves about in a way that most Westerners regard as over-the-top.

Sometimes an *imam* will visit to pray with the bereaved; where possible a woman schooled in the Koran will visit the women separately and pray with them.

Visitors offer the standard phrase '*başın(ız) sağ olsun*' (may your life be spared) as comfort to the bereaved. It is not customary to give gifts, although people sometimes give money to charity or plant a tree in the deceased's name.

Immediately after the funeral the bereaved family usually provides a meal for relatives, close friends and the *imam* who looked after the arrangements. Otherwise, neighbours usually provide food and other support for a few days.

SORTING OUT THE PAPERWORK

Following a death the family must take the death certificate (*ölüm raporu*) to the Nüfus department of the Valilık together with the dead person's *kimlik* card and their driving licence, if there is one. Their death is then registered and their licence and ID card cancelled. If the deceased held a gun license that, too, will have to be cancelled. All this has to be done immediately after the funeral with what, to Westerners, can seem like almost indecent haste.

WHAT HAPPENS WHEN A FOREIGNER DIES

Given the absence of cremation facilities and shortage of non-Muslim burial facilities it is important that all foreigners living in Turkey give some thought to what they would like to happen after they die and ensure that someone knows what those wishes are.

When a foreigner dies, someone has to contact their embassy or consulate which will know the procedure to be followed. Officials will normally arrange for a funeral director to call on the deceased's relatives or friends to decide what should be done with the body in terms of cleaning and dressing. They will be able to organise transport for the repatriation of the body, if this is required, and will help the survivors fill out the paperwork which will accompany it on its journey home.

If you don't have an insurance policy that covers the cost of having your body taken back to your native country you should bear in mind that this can be very expensive (in excess of €7,500). Since 9/11 some US airlines no longer will carry bodies which can complicate organising repatriation to the United States.

Burial/Cremation of Foreign Residents: Since cremation is looked upon with some disfavour by Muslims, Turkey currently has no facilities for it. Unless you have arranged to have your body repatriated and then cremated, you should assume that you will be buried when you die. However, it is possible that the EU will insist that cremation facilities are provided as part of membership negotiations with Turkey.

At present there are very few separate cemeteries for non-Muslims which means that unless you arrange to have your body repatriated it may be difficult to have it buried as you might have wished. At the moment most Westerners who die in Istanbul are buried in the two Feriköy cemeteries – one for Protestants and one for Roman Catholics (see Appendix XVIII for details). Those married to Muslims are occasionally permitted to be buried beside their spouses. There is also a Jewish cemetery in Levent. If you know that you are going to be living out the rest of your life in Turkey, it would make sense to buy a plot in one of these cemeteries to save your heirs from having to do so.

In areas where there is no separate cemetery for foreigners it is usually possible for non-Muslims to be buried in the main cemetery although they will probably be interred in an area apart from the other graves.

At the time of writing the Armutalan district authorities in Marmaris were looking for a piece of land suitable for between 250 and 300 non-Muslim burials.

REMEMBERING THE DEAD

On the 7th, 40th and 52nd day after a death the family may organise a *mevlüt* (prayer reading) or a *yasin* (a reading from the Koran) in memory of the dead. They may then distribute *helva* or *mevlüt şekeri* (a package of special candies) to everyone who attends the mosque or home service, or prepare a full meal for friends and relatives. Traditionally they also serve *şerbet,* a sweet drink made from sugary fruit flavoring and water, although increasingly this is being replaced with boxed or canned soft drinks. Most people also visit family graves on the first day of religious holidays. Some families also host annual *mevlüts* as a way of remembering their dead.

SUICIDE *(İNTİHAR)*

Islam may condemn suicide but of course it still happens in Turkey, as elsewhere. In the past the death of someone who committed suicide could not be announced from the mosque or their body buried in the usual cemetery. These days, however, many communities look more kindly on those who take their own lives and allow their bodies to be buried in the normal way.

INHERITANCE *(MİRAS)* AND MAKING A WILL *(VASİYETNAME)*

In Turkey if somebody dies intestate (i.e. without leaving a will) the law of succession sets out exactly what percentage of their assets should pass to their spouse and blood relatives (called 'parentals'). Although writing a will means that it is possible to dispose of some of one's assets according to personal preference, the Turkish state still dictates how some of the estate (the '*saklı pay*' [reserved portion]) must be shared out after death.

According to the new Civil Code both spouses now have a right to an equal share in all assets acquired after marriage; when one of them dies the other automatically inherits their share. On their death all the assets of the marriage are divided equally between the surviving children regardless of sex (an 'illegitimate' or adopted child will have the same right to a fixed share of the assets). Note that this only applies if the couple were married - the Turkish state does not recognise de facto partnerships.

If you are married to a Turk and living in Turkey, then Turkish law will apply to you which means that you do not have to make a will unless you want to.

Overseas assets owned by foreigners living abroad who are *not* married to a Turk can be disposed of in the normal way (i.e. by making a will in the country of origin). This also applies to property owned by foreigners in Turkey. So if you are *not* married to a Turk you can decide how you want to dispose of all your property and include that information in your normal will. If you *are* married to a Turk the law will dictate how you can dispose of some of the property you acquired as a couple after marriage, although you retain the right to dispose of property you already owned before it as you choose.

Some foreigners living in Turkey still want to make a will to cover their assets here. In this case they need to draw up a suitable draft and either show it or read it to a notary (*noter*). The notary will then prepare the will and arrange to have it translated into Turkish. You then sign the will in front of witnesses and the notary signs and stamps it. One copy will be kept in the notary's office. If you are living in a de facto relationship with a Turk and most of the assets are in *your* name, it is particularly important to ensure that you have drawn up a will that makes your intentions regarding your partner clear. If you die without a will the Turkish state will pursue your parents and/or children as your presumed heirs.

It is also possible to draw up your own will without witnesses. However, if you choose to do this and your legacies are contentious, this sort of will is more likely to be challenged than if it had been drawn up by a *noter*.

Note that Turkey makes a distinction between *moveable property* and *immoveable property*. If you own a house in Turkey that constitutes immoveable property. Your other assets are moveable property. If you are resident in Turkey your Turkish will can cover all your assets, whether moveable or immoveable. However, if you are *not* resident in Turkey your Turkish will should cover only your immoveable property in the country; the disposal of all your other assets, whether in Turkey or elsewhere, can be covered in a will made under the law of your country of origin.

Note also that anyone over the age of 15 is entitled to make a will in Turkey.

The heirs to an estate also inherit any outstanding debts although they can avoid this by completely renouncing their claim within a set period of time. If no heirs wish to accept an estate it will pass to the Turkish state. If there are any disagreements about the disposal of the estate they will be handled by the *Suhl Mahkemesi* (Peace Court) for the area in which the deceased last lived.

MORE INFORMATION

Introduction to Turkish Law (5th edition) by Tuğrul Ansay and Don Wallace Jnr (Turhan Kitabevi, 2006)

Inheritance (*Veraset Vergisi*) and Gift Tax (*İntikal Vergisi*)

Turkish **inheritance tax** rates are levied on a property's legal heirs but rates are very low (1-10%) and as the tax is paid by each of the heirs, how much each one pays can vary depending on their personal circumstances. The tax must be paid in twice-yearly instalments over a three-year period.

Gift tax rates are higher (10-30%) which means that if you want to leave your property to anyone other than immediate family they will have to pay considerably more tax on the acquisition.

WHAT TO SAY			
burial	*gömme*	retirement	*emeklilik*
burial plot	*kabristan*	shroud	*kefen*
death	*ölüm*	to bury	*gömmek*
funeral	*cenaze*	to die	*ölmek*
grave	*mezar*	to grieve	*yas tutmak*
heir	*mırasçı*	tomb	*türbe*
inheritance	*miras*	widow	*dul kadın*
retired person	*emekli*	widower	*dul erkek*

CHAPTER 24

WHEN THINGS GO WRONG

Hopefully, nothing will go wrong during your stay in Turkey. However, if it does it is helpful to understand how the legal system works and to know which police force you need to contact.

THE TURKISH LEGAL SYSTEM

Since the founding of the Turkish republic in 1923 there have been several constitutions. The one that currently underpins the law dates back to 1982 although it has been amended several times since then. The requirements of Turkey's application to join the European Union mean that the constitution (*Anayasa*) is being updated again even as this book goes to print.

Turkey has a number of different courts but resident foreigners are only likely to have to deal with the civil, administrative, financial and criminal versions (hopefully not the latter). The courts apply the Civil Code (*Medeni Kanun*) which consists of all the laws passed by parliament as well as supplementary ordinances, regulations and by-laws. They also take into account the most recent rulings of the Supreme Court of Appeal.

There is no jury system in Turkey; minor cases are decided by one judge (*hakim*) and more serious ones by three. There is no bail system and people accused of more serious crimes can be remanded into custody. Accused individuals should be brought before a court (*mahkeme*, usually housed inside the *Adliye Sarayı*, or Palace of Justice) within two to four days depending on the nature of the crime they are accused of (anyone accused of anything to do with state security will find their rights much diminished). Turkey has signed international conventions against torture and although it was still common in police stations even in the late 1990s it appears that more is now being done to ensure that accused people are not harmed while in custody. Turkey does not use corporal punishment and recently abolished the death penalty.

Criminal and civil offences are therefore punishable with fines (*ceza*) and/or imprisonment (*hapis*). For some minor traffic offences the police can issue a fixed-penalty fine on the spot but it is more normal for them to be imposed by a court. It goes without saying that the inside of a Turkish jail (*hapishane, cezaevi*), while not as bad as depicted in the infamous *Midnight Express,* is unlikely to prove attractive (most prisons now have two and three-person cells rather than dormitories). There is no system of community service as an alternative to imprisonment.

Juveniles: Under the Turkish legal system someone younger than 11 cannot be tried for a criminal offence unless it would incur a prison sentence of a year or more. Children between the ages of 11 and 15 should be tried in juvenile courts but as there are only a few of these in the country they often end up being tried in adult courts. Juveniles under 18 receive more lenient penalties and cannot be sentenced to life imprisonment. In theory they should be imprisoned in special juvenile prisons but there are very few of these, so most end up in adult jails.

Private International Law: Generally speaking, when there is the possibility of two national legal systems conflicting with each other, it is the law of the country where an action takes place that takes precedence. This means that any crimes committed in Turkey are subject to prosecution under Turkish law, even if they are carried out by a foreigner. However, in personal matters it is the law that relates to your nationality that is usually most important. This is why if an English person wants to marry a Turk they must still comply with the British law that requires the advance posting of banns. In theory this means that a British person can will their land in Turkey to whomsoever they choose in accordance with British law. In reality few property-owning foreigners have died in Turkey, so this has yet to be confirmed.

Going to Court: Whatever may be the case on paper it is worth saying that resorting to the Turkish courts is likely to prove a recipe for delays, disappointment and legal expense with no certainty about the outcome, even in what seem like the most cut and dried cases. Unless your Turkish is exceptionally good you are always going to be at a disadvantage when faced with the legal jargon. Nor are you likely to understand when and how the system is being subverted to someone else's benefit. Unless there is absolutely no alternative you should assume that going to court is unlikely to bring you much satisfaction.

THE POLICE (*POLİS*)

Within urban areas the blue-uniformed Turkish police force holds sway, along with the subsidiary traffic police (*trafik polisi*) who attempt to keep the traffic moving. In rural areas the conscripted gendarmerie (*jandarma*) usually keep an eye on daily life while the *trafik jandarma* take care of the traffic.

In the past the Turkish police force had a poor reputation, with corruption routine and torture commonplace in many police stations (*karakol*). These days, things have improved considerably and efforts are being made to stamp out the remaining corruption (*rüşvet*). However, this will probably take at least a generation to eradicate, as older policemen retire and younger, better educated ones with more modern ideas replace them.

If you live in Turkey you are most likely to come into contact with the police at road checks or after a traffic violation or road accident.

Zabıta: The *Zabıta* is a curiously Turkish phenomenon, a special policeman or city inspector, employed by the Belediye, whose job is to check that market traders are not cheating their customers. If you see anyone strange lurking around your neighbourhood, you should call the *zabıta*. Likewise if the paving stones near your house are broken or there are other problems of that nature they should be your first port of call.

EMERGENCY PHONE NUMBERS			
Fire	110	Police	155
Ambulance	112	Jandarma	156
International Operator	115	Coastguard	158
Istanbul Traffic Problems	116	Forest Fire Alarm	177
Telephone Repairs	121	Water Repairs	185
Wake-up Call	135	Electrical Repairs	186
Traffic Police	154	Natural Gas Leaks	187

MAKING A COMPLAINT (*ŞİKÂYET*)

Some companies, especially transport firms, have systems in place for customers to register complaints. However, unless you can write Turkish the comments you place in the boxes soliciting them are likely to go unheeded.

If you need to make a more serious complaint which involves calling in the police you will almost certainly be able to find someone who speaks English in any of the big resorts. In central Istanbul the Tourism Police employ English-speakers although they are more used to dealing with complaints about taxis and street hustlers than the sort of things residents may have to cope with (e.g. burglary). Elsewhere in the city English-speaking policemen (or women) are thin on the ground. The same is true in Ankara and Izmir.

If you do embark on making an official complaint you must expect to have to deal with a lot of seemingly pointless bureaucracy. No matter what the complaint the police will want to know to what level you were educated and the name of your father, regardless of whether he is still alive or not.

Shops vary in how much interest they take in disaffected customers. Some will happily replace items that don't work; others are inclined to turn a cold shoulder.

THEFT *(HIRSIZLIK)* AND BURGLARY *(EV/BİNA SOYMA)*

In general Turkey has a very low crime rate and there is less risk of suffering theft or burglary here than in most Western countries. However, there is always some risk and the Istanbul crime rate is rising rapidly as increased affluence, combined with the readier availability of items worth stealing, mean that would-be thieves find life easier. Mobile phones are particularly popular items for theft but even car crime is taking off in Istanbul.

If you have something stolen you must get a written report from the police to be able to claim for the loss against your insurance. In prime tourist areas the police are sometimes reluctant to write such reports because so many people lodge false claims to try and extort money from the insurance companies.

In rural areas not only is the risk of crime much smaller but you also have a better chance of recovering what was stolen because of neighbourly vigilance.

To protect yourself against theft always take the following precautions:

- Take out insurance (see p. 491) and make sure you have checked the small print for letout clauses
- Make sure you know how to cancel all your credit and debit cards.
- Press *#06# on your mobile phone and write the 15-digit IP number that appears in a safe place. Then if it is stolen you can contact the phone company and ask them to stop all calls to that number.
- Be aware of the latest scams. Recently groups of young women have been approaching mothers with pushchairs and trying to take the child out. While the mother is distracted one of the group makes a grab for her handbag.

- Consider installing a burglar alarm. Alternatively, get a dog – Turks are usually terrified of them!

Security: Although families used to take household security fairly casually you can buy most sorts of locks in Turkey; Kale Kilit, for example, produces Yale-style locks. You can also buy burglar alarms and car alarms fairly easily.

WHAT TO ASK FOR			
alarm	*alarm*	locksmith	*anahtarcı*
confidence	*güven*	padlock	*asma kilit*
key(s)	*anahtar(lar)*	security	*emniyet*
lock	*kilit*	to lock	*kilitmek*

Credit/ATM cards: Call the following numbers if you have problems with your cards:

- *American Express:* Tel: 0212-283 2201
- *Diners Club:* Tel: 444 0555
- *Visa/Mastercard:* Tel: 0212-225 0080

FRAUD *(DOLANDIRICILIK)* AND FAKE GOODS *(SAHTE/KORSAN)*

Many forged bank notes (*sahte parası*), especially fake YTL20 notes, are in circulation, so shopkeepers often want to check your notes before accepting them.

It goes without saying that there are also many fake goods on sale. Pirated CDs and DVDs are readily available, as are fake Levis, fake Louis Vuitton bags and fake pretty much anything else you care to mention.

PROPERTY PROBLEMS

With the boom in foreign land purchases it is inevitable that there has been a concomitant rise in problems arising from those sales. Since overcharging is a frequent occurrence it is worth noting that Turkish law does include an offence of 'unjust enrichment'. In theory if someone has charged you three or four times the true worth of a piece of property you could go to court to try and recover some of the money. In practise, however, especially with prices on an ever upward trajectory, you are unlikely to have much success except in cases of the most blatant robbery.

Infringements of Building Regulations: It is a laughable fact that almost anyone trying to build anything attractive or environmentally sensitive in Turkey is likely to end up in trouble with the powers-that-be, while builders of concrete monstrosities go unchallenged. However, it may come as a surprise to foreigners to discover that Turks can be sent to jail for breaches of the building regulations. This has been the fate of even quite high-profile restorers of old buildings – but although the odd foreigner has been threatened with a similar fate to date none has actually been imprisoned; you are more likely to be slapped with a fine. Ironically people are rarely required to demolish illegal structures, although this may eventually change.

INSULTING TURKISHNESS

Most of the offences that you can be charged with in Turkey will be familiar from home. However, the one that might catch you out, especially if you work in the media, is the crime of insulting Turkishness which is enshrined in the Turkish Civil Code as Article 301. What is meant by 'insulting Turkishness' is not always entirely clear but it can be used against anyone raising such thorny topics as the Armenian and Kurdish problems. Anything derogatory said against Atatürk or even Turkey itself is also potentially problematic and even such high-profile personalities as award-winning novelist Orhan Pamuk have fallen foul of this law. Some people have wound up in prison, and although so far they have all been Turks it is a risk every journalist needs to be aware of. This has the depressing affect of making many of them self-censor their work, since they know what will land them hot water.

You may think there is no risk to you if you are not a journalist but unfortunately Turks have been known to throw accusations of insulting Turkishness at foreigners during the course of quarrels. While the matter is usually resolved fairly quickly this can result in people being carted off to the police station for questioning even when they haven't actually done anything wrong. Be careful.

YOU ARE CHARGED WITH...	
Huzursuzluk yaratmak	Disturbing the peace
Uyuşturucu madde bulundurmak	Possession of illegal substances
Süresi geçmiş vize	Overstaying your visa
Trafik suçu	A traffic violation
İzinsiz çalışma	Working without a permit

WOMEN'S PROBLEMS

Although Turkey does have female police officers there is no guarantee that you will be able to see one, even if you are alleging rape.

Domestic Violence (*Aile İçi Şiddet*): It is a sad fact that domestic violence is still widespread in Turkey; it is likely that almost 50% of women experience some form of assault within their own homes. However, since 1998 the law has allowed anyone subject to domestic violence to apply to the courts for a protection order, with the threat of imprisonment if the offender doesn't observe its terms. Unfortunately there are almost no shelters outside the major cities to provide refuge for beaten women.

Sexual Harassment (*Cinsel Taciz*) Many foreigners new to Turkey are taken aback by the amount of low-level sexual harassment that they have to endure on the streets. The good news is that this almost always lessens as you grow more confident and learn to speak more Turkish. It is highly unlikely that you will continue to be publicly harassed once you have settled into a community. However, whenever you move away from that community you may find that the trouble starts all over again.

Obviously pretty young women are likely to face the worst problems although age and lack of looks are no cast-iron guarantee of being left in peace. The usual advice to women is to wear non-revealing clothes and avoid behaviour that might be interpreted as 'asking for it' which can mean anything from getting legless in the bars to smiling too winningly at a cab driver. However, the reality is that even if you are covered from head to toe there is still an outside chance that someone will recognise that you are a Western woman and interpret that as an invitation to offensive behaviour.

The Turkish Penal Code recognises verbal abuse as a crime, whether it manifests itself in improper sexual comments or written harassment. Verbal abuse carries a potential penalty of three months in prison. However, the offence would need to be very grave before it would be worth a woman's while attempting to get a case taken to court.

If you are being harassed you can always report it to the police/jandarma. However, they will probably be reluctant to press charges. In smaller communities a better bet may be to mention what is happening to a male friend who may be able to bring a halt to the problem with a few words in the right ear.

Sexual Abuse/Assault (*Cinsel Saldırı*): Turkish law attaches penalties to physical, rather than specifically sexual, abuse. This covers such unwelcome attentions as unwanted kissing and flashing. Those convicted of such offences can be sentenced to between six months and two years in jail.

Rape (*Tecavüz*): Rape is just as serious a crime in Turkey as elsewhere. Fortunately it is not particularly common since there are still strong social taboos against sexual assault (as opposed to sexual harassment). Should you be unlucky enough to be raped you need to know that the law allows for forcible vaginal tests if there is no other way to confirm the crime or if it is thought that the passage of time may result in the destruction of evidence.

Turkish law does not yet recognise rape in marriage as a crime, although several women's groups are working to have this changed.

DRUGS *(NARKOTİK)*

Ever since the hippy days of the 1960s Turkey has been known as a country where cannabis *(esrar)* is readily available. That is still the case, and those who want to can find supplies even in quite small communities. However, it is against the law to possess cannabis and the fact that you are a foreigner will not make any difference if you are caught.

Harder drugs are also available, especially, but not only, in the big cities. Nightclubbers in Istanbul are as likely to use heroin *(eroin)* or ecstasy as their counterparts in London or New York. You are not advised to copy them.

FIRE *(YANGIN)*

Fire is as big a risk in Turkey as anywhere else but although all large settlements have a fire service *(itfaiye)* it is not always especially efficient; in big cities traffic and narrow streets can make it hard for a fire tender to arrive quickly while in rural areas the tender may turn out not to be stocked up with water. Consequently you should think through your own fire safety precautions carefully. It is possible to buy fire extinguishers *(yangın söndürücü)* and sprinklers *(yangın tesisatı)* although you may have to go to a big town to find them. Smoke and fire alarms *(duman/yangın alarmı)* are virtually unheard of and *Turkish Daily News* once carried a funny story about a hotel with a wooden *yangın merdiveni* (fire escape)!

In summer forest fires are a serious risk all along the south coast and you will see many signs warning against throwing cigarette butts out carelessly. However, some of the fires are almost certainly set deliberately, either by vandals or by would-be property developers. Sadly, this has also been the case along the shores of the Bosphorus where many lovely old wooden mansions have fallen victim to suspicious fires.

FINDING A LAWYER *(AVUKAT)*

If you are buying a property in Turkey your estate agent will probably recommend a legal advisor although you are better off finding one for yourself to ensure impartiality. Sometimes a friend may be able to recommend a good lawyer. Otherwise, to find an English-speaking lawyer (*İngilizce konuşan avukat*) go to the websites of the British embassy (www.britishembassy.gov.uk) or the US Embassy (hhtp://ankara.usembassy.gov/list_of_attorneys.html). To find a French-speaking lawyer (*Fransızca konuşan avukat)* go to the website of the French Embassy (www.ambafrance-tr.org). To find a German-speaking lawyer (*Almanca konuşan avukat)* go to www.ankara.diplo.de/de/04/Informationen_fuer_Deutche.html. If you live in Kapadokya you will have difficulty finding anyone to give you legal advice in your own language.

WHO TO CONTACT

Turkish Bar Association (Türkiye Barolar Birliği - TBB): Tel: 0312-425 3100, www.barobirlik.org.tr, Karanfil Sokak No: 5/62, Kızılay, Ankara. Website lets you check whether your lawyer is registered with the TBB.

EARTHQUAKES *(DEPREM)*

It is an unfortunate fact that 90% of Turkey, including the popular southwest corner, lies in an active earthquake zone. Istanbul itself lies on the North Anatolian fault line which advertised its ability to kill on a massive scale as recently as 1999 when twin quakes hit İzmit/Kocaeli, Adapazarı/Sakarya and Düzce as well as other smaller communities with huge loss of life. Many deaths were attributed to the poor quality of new buildings which simply collapsed on their occupants. Most expert opinion takes it for granted that the next big earthquake will hit Istanbul, so it goes without saying that you should choose any house or apartment there with the utmost care. Some districts of Istanbul are thought to be at greater risk than others, so beware unexpectedly cheap prices which might suggest that the property is in a high-risk area.

As yet there is no way to predict an earthquake. This means that you may have very little warning of disaster. Ideally, therefore, you should have thought through a survival strategy ahead of a quake. The following suggestions might just help you escape the worst:

- Work out a potential escape route/meeting point and make sure your children understand it.
- Keep available a food and drink supply adequate for the three to five days it might take for rescue teams to reach you.
- Keep a torch (flashlight) and candles to hand in case of power cuts.
- Keep a whistle on hand to attract attention.

- Remove anything above your bed that could fall and crush you. Secure items like pictures and mirrors carefully if you don't want to move them.
- Keep shoes beside your bed to avoid cutting your feet on broken glass.
- Make sure you know how to turn off the electricity, gas and water supplies.
- Make sure you have extra supplies of medications readily available, together with instructions on how they should be used.
- Let your children's school know the names of people authorised to collect your offspring in the event that you cannot do so yourself.
- Give your family overseas a list of people who may want information about you. That way they can avoid making too many phone calls just when the emergency services most need the lines to be clear.

The latest information suggests that it is not a good idea to hide under a bed. Rather you should lie right beside a bed or other piece of furniture in the hope that it will protect you. You shouldn't stand in a doorway in case it collapses on you – it's better to stay near the outer walls of the house.

WHAT TO SAY

arrested	tutuklu	murderer	katil
bail/letter of guarantee	kefalet(name)	not guilty	suçsuz/masum
bribe	rüşvet	pickpocket	kapkaç
broken/out of order	bozuk	poison	zehir
compensation	tazminat	poisonous	zehirli
crime	suç	police officer	polis memuru
dangerous	tehlikeli	police station	karakol
dangerous material	tehlikeli madde	rights	haklar
fake/forged	sahte	thief	hırsız/yankesici
faulty	arızalı	to appeal	temyiz etmek
forbidden/prohibited	yasak(tır)	to complain	şikâyet etmek
forgery	sahtecilik	to kill	öldürmek
guilty	suçlu	to rob	soymak
innocent	masum	to steal	çalmak

law	yasa/kanun	to sue	dava açmak
murder	cinayet	trial	yargılama
Can I see the manager?		Müdürünüzle görüşebilir miyim?	
I've been mugged.		Saldırıya uğradım.	
I've been robbed.		Soyuldum.	
My purse/bag/mobile phone has been stolen.		Cüzdanım/çantam/cep telefonum çalındı.	
It's not my fault.		Hata/suç bende değil.	

APPENDICES

Note: Listings for Istanbul, Ankara and Izmir are given first, followed in alphabetical order by listings for other locations.

To avoid repetition, shopping mall and supermarket contact details are listed once in Appendix VII (Shopping) – you may need to cross-refer. Likewise hotel contacts are sometimes listed under Appendix III (Wedding Venues).

APPENDIX I:
ESTATE AGENTS, CONSTRUCTION COMPANIES, FLAT RENTAL AGENCIES AND TIMESHARE OPTIONS

ESTATE AGENTS AND CONSTRUCTION COMPANIES

Istanbul

Bluepoint: Tel: 0212-351 5198, www.bluepoint.com.tr, Zeytinoğlu Caddesi, Babil Sokak, Babil Apt, A Blok, Daire: 2, Akatlar.

Cengiz Emlak: Tel: 0212-270 0078, www.cengizemlakltd.com, Birlik Sokak, Manolya Apt No: 3, Daire: 4/5, 1.Levent

Century 21 Maxima Real Estate: Tel: 0212-352 1522, www.century21maxima.com, Nispetiye Caddesi, Arzu-2 Apt No: 25/12, Akatlar; Tel: 0212-245 8324, www.century21peran.com, Asmalımescit Mahallesi, Asmalımescit Sokak No: 7, Kat: 1, Daire: 3, Tünel, Beyoğlu

Colliers International: Tel: 0212-281 5166, Ali Kaya Sokak No: 4, Polat Plaza, B Blok, Levent

Evren: Tel: 0212-257 7184, www.evreninternational.com, Küçükbebek Caddesi No: 3/1

Hermes Real Estate Agency: Tel: 0212-292 1128, hermes@hermesturk.com, Tarık Zafer Tunaya Sokak No: 14, Gümüşsuyu

Mavi Ay: Tel: 0212-325 2056, www.maviayestate.com, İstinye Caddesi No: 110/1, İstinye

Premier: Tel: 0212-287 2797, www.premieremlak.com, Cevdetpaşa Caddesi No: 374, Bebek

Remax: Tel: 0212-232 4820, www.remax.com.tr/en, PK 647, Şişli; Tel: 0212-243 2222, www.remaxpera.com, Sıraselviler Caddesi No: 87/3, Beyoğlu

Royal RE Consulting Co: Tel: 0212-236 9580, www.royalestate.info, Süleyman Seba Caddesi No: 48, BJK Plaza, A Blok, Daire: 47, Maçka

Stewart International: Tel: 0232-284 7273, www.stewartaffiliates.com, Yapı Kredi Plaza, C Blok, Kat: 3/A, Levent

The Turkish Cottage: Tel: 0252-284 2824, www.theturkishcottage.com, Eski Karakol Sokak No: 12/C. Specialises in properties in Fener and Balat.

Turyap: Tel: 0212-327 4000, www.turyap.com.tr, Süleyman Seba Caddesi, Akaretler, BJK Plaza, A Blok B2-06, Beşiktaş

Ulus Real Estate: Tel: 0212-257 2141, Güzel Konutlar Sitesi, B Blok No: 1, Ulus

Viva: Tel: 0212-225 1945, www.vivaemlak.com; Abdi İpekçi Caddesi, Altın Sokak, Ahmet Kara İşhanı 2, Kat: 6, Nişantaşı

Ankara

Demos: Tel: 0312-447 5499, www.demos-ltd.com.tr, Uğur Mumcu Caddesi, Kırçiçeği Sokak No: 5/5, Gaziosmanpaşa

Deta: Tel: 0312-438 9917, Abdullah Cevet Sokak No: 28/1, Çankaya

Mavi Emlak: Tel: 0312-427 6043, Fax: 0312-427 8399, Attar Sokak No: 9/8, Gaziosmanpaşa

Remax: Tel: 0312-424 1124, www.remax-baskent.com, Esat Caddesi No: 70/13, Küçükesat, Çankaya

Izmir

Izmir Turizm İnşaat Ticaret: Tel: 0232-238 7878, www.izmirturizm.net, Mustafa Kemal Sahil Bulvarı No: 2, Narlıdere

Remax: Tel: 0232-464 0808, www.remaxtrio.com, Talatpaşa Bulvarı, Yayger Apt, Alsancak; Tel: 0232-250 0353, www.remax.com.tr/agora, İnönü Caddesi, Isıl Apt: 201/3, Hatay

Adana

Remax: Tel: 0322-232 0101, www.remax-as.com, Kenan Evren Bulvarı No: 111, Seyhan

Alanya

Costello: Tel: 0242-514 3565, www.costelloestates.com, Çevre Yolu Caddesi, Oba Beldesi, Yılmaz Apt: 2

Let's Go To Turkey: Tel: 0242-513 2064, www.letsgototurkey.com, Atatürk Sokak No: 90/1

M&C Professional Property Service: Tel: 0532-206 2928, www.mandcproperty.com, Hacıkadiroğlu Caddesi, Asta Residence, No: 9/43

Altınkum

Crystal Holiday Homes: Tel: 0256-813 1296, www.crystalhomesturkey.com, Vali Caddesi No: 99, Didim

Darius Homes: Tel: 0256-813 5358, www.dariushomes.com, Didyma Shopping Mall C/58-9

First Choice Turkish Homes: Tel: 0256-813 4646, www.1stchoiceturkishhomes.com, Didyma Shopping Mall C/70-1

Turkish Property Agents: Tel: 0256-813 8102, www.turkishpropertyagents.co.uk, Atatürk Bulvarı, Egemenlik Caddesi No: 1/1

Antalya

euroMedt Real Estate: Tel: 0242-715 2250, www.euromedt-turkey.com, Akdeniz Mahallesi, Turizm Caddesi, Dibektaşı Sokak No: 18/D, Belek

Turyap: Tel: 0242-323 6910, Barınkalar; Tel: 0242-311 6652, Burhanettin Onat Caddesi

Bodrum

Century 21: Tel: 0252-363 9466, www.century21halikarnas.com, Atatürk Bulvarı, Pamir İş Merkezi, B-1 Blok No: 4, Konacık, Bodrum; Tel: 0252-382 0200, Atatürk Meydanı, GMK Paşa Bulvarı No: 27/4, Turgutreis; Tel: 0252-385 3089, Yalıkavak İş Merkezi, Çökertme Caddesi No: 14, Yalıkavak

Cumberland Properties: Tel: 0252-317 1830, www.cumberland-properties.com, Oasis Shopping Mall

Euro Real Estate: Tel: 0252-385 3522, www.eurorealestate-bodrum.com, Atatürk Sokak No: 7, Yalıkavak

Mandalinci Properties: Tel: 0252-382 3069, Belediye Caddesi No: 1, Turgutreis

RMG Turkey: Tel: 0252-313 7511, www.rmgturkey.com, Caferpaşa Caddesi No: 7

Turyap: Tel: 0252-313 3700, bodrummerkez@turyap.com.tr

Bursa

Remax: Tel: 0224-247 8565, www.remax-prusa.com, Karaman Mahallesi, İzmir Yolu No: 82/1, Carrefour karşısı, Nilüfer

Dalyan & Around

Dalyan Property: Tel: 0252-284 4444, Fax: 0252-284 5181, Eski Karakol Sokak No: 11

Efsane Emlak: Tel: 0252-284 3239, www.efsaneemlak.com, Çavuşlar Mahallesi, Atatürk Caddesi No: 47/E

Lykia Homes: Tel: 0252-282 8282, www.lykiahomes.com, Cengiz Topel Caddesi No: 15, Ortaca

The Turkish Cottage: Tel: 0252-284 2824, www.theturkishcottage.com.

Datça

Turyap: Tel: 0252-712 9188, datca@turyap.com.tr

Fethiye & Around

Century 21 Lykia: Tel: 0252-612 0021, www.century21lykia.com, Atatürk Caddesi No: 8, Ticaret Odası altı, Fethiye

Ephesus Estate: Tel: 0252-612 7704, www.efesestate.com, Atatürk Caddesi No: 123, Fethiye

Falcon Estates: Tel: 0252-612 5344, ww.falconestates.net, Atatürk Caddesi No: 14/B, Fethiye

Golden Moon Estate: Tel: 0252-613 2200, www.goldenmoonestateagency.com, Köprübaşı Mevkii, Çalış

Hallmark Properties: Tel: 0252-612 3998, www.hallmarkproperties.co.uk, Fethiye. Specialises in wooden houses.

Harbour House Estates: Tel: 0252-614 7805, www.harbourhouses.com, Cumhuriyet Caddesi, Döğerli İş Merkezi, B Blok

Helt Estate: Tel: 0252-614 6377, www.heltfethiye.com, Mustafa Kemal Bulvarı No: 30, Fethiye

Ideal Properties: Tel: 0252-614 1816, www.ideal-property.co.uk, Hükümet Caddesi No: 6, PTT karşısı, Fethiye

Lycia Properties: Tel: 0252-612 9008, www.propertyinturkey.com, Atatürk Caddesi (opposite Gima)

Nicholas Homes: Tel: 0252-616 7455, www.nicholas-homes.com, St Nicholas Park Hotel, Hisarönü

Ozay Real Estate Agency: Tel: 0252-272 8030, www.ozayemlak.com, Köyceğiz

Real Home Estates: Tel: 0252-612 3428, www.real-home-estates.com, Atatürk Caddesi, Gima karşısı, Fethiye

Remax: Tel: 0252-612 5377, www.remax-avantaj.com, Cumhuriyet Mahallesi, Tütün Sokak No: 12

Seaside Real Estate Agency: Tel: 0252-622 1296, www.seasideestate.net, Çalış

Search Property Services: Tel: 0252-616 7930, Kavşak Dükkanları, Özyerler İş Merkezi No: 1, Hisarönü

Sunshine Properties: Tel: 0252-616 7455, wwww.sunshine-properties-turkey.co.uk. Resale arm of Nicholas Homes.

Taurean Properties: Tel: 0252-613 2377, www.calis-beach.co.uk, Çalış

Turkish Estate Agency: Tel: 0252-612 6010, www.turkishestateagency.co.uk, Yat Limanı karşısı No: 19/B, Fethiye

Turyap: Tel: 0252-614 8888, fethiye@turyap.com.tr

Kaş

Aura Estate, Projects & Consulting: Tel: 0242-836 2614, www.aura-estates.com, İbrahim Serin Caddesi No: 15/A. Specialises in wood and stone houses.

Eskidji: Tel: 0242-444 4545, www.eskidji.com, Atatürk Bulvarı, Şekerim Pasajı No: 13/D

Internasyonel Kaş Land Design Construction: Tel: 0242-836 1598, Çukurbağlı Caddesi No: 12/B

Lycian Real Estate: Tel: 0242-836 4217, www.kastourism.com, Hastane Caddesi, Özmen Apt. No: 1

Prima Emlak Estate Agency: Tel: 0242-836 2040, Liman Caddesi No: 16

Site Emlak: Tel: 0242-836 3083, Atatürk Bulvarı No: 8/B

Sun Estate Agency: Tel: 0242-836 1597, www.sunestate-tr.com, Bahçe Sokak No: 1/B

Theolite Real Estate & Construction Co: Tel: 0242-836 1436, www.turkishproperties.us, Ortaokul Sokak, Mustafa Tomruk Apt

Turkuaz Emlak: Tel: 0242-836 3620, www.turkuazemlak.com, Soğuk Çeşme karşısı No: 30/A

Kalkan

Black Lion: Tel: 0242-844 1345, www.2blacklions.com, Yalıboyu Mahallesi, 3. Sokak No: 7

Mavi Real Estate: Tel: 0242-844 1220, www.kalkanproperty.com, Yalıboyu Mahallesi

Köyceğiz

Melda Özden: Tel: 0252 262-5406, www.meldaozden.com,

Köyceğiz Real Estate: Tel: 0252-262 1304, www.koycegizrealestate.net

Kuşadası

Century 21: Tel: 0256-612 7917, www.century21-kusadasi.com, Barbaros Hayrettin Paşa Bulvarı No: 75

Kervan Real Estate: Tel: 0256-613 4270, www.kervanrealestate.com, Sağlık Caddesi No: 10

New Turkey Real Estate & Investment: Tel: 0256-614 5111, www.new-turkey.com, Barbaros Hayrettin Paşa Bulvarı No: 16

RealEstate: Tel: 0256-612 2068, www.realestate.com.tr, Adnan Menderes Bulvarı No: 30/A

TM Property: Tel: 0256-612 4044, www.tm.tr.com, Adnan Menderes Bulvarı, 7.Sokak No: 4, Kat:1

Turkish Gateway Property: Tel: 0256-614 8382, Adnan Menderes Bulvarı No: 36/D

Villa Turkey: Tel: 0256-612 2346, www.villaturkey.nl, Barbaros Hayrettin Paşa Bulvarı No: 8

Marmaris

Cartier Estate Agency: Tel: 0252-455 2979, www.icmelerestateagency.com, 69. Sokak No: 3, İçmeler

Kent Estate Agency: Tel: 0252-412 2247, www.kentestateagency.com, Kemal Elgin Bulvarı, Ketenci Otel karşısı

Red Tek Real Estate: Tel: 0252-413 0422, www.redtekrealestate.com, Sariana Mahallesi, 25.Sokak No: 2/5-8

Turyap: Tel: 0252-413 1601, marmaris@turyap.com.tr

Side

Mecitoğlu Homes: Tel: 0242-753 3910, www.homeinturkey.com, Kemer Mahallesi, Y. Sultan Selim Bulvarı, 1613 Sokak No: 3

Motif Homes: Tel: 0242-753 7175, www.turkishproperties4u.com, Kemer Mahallesi, Kazım Karabekir Caddesi No: 2

UK

All Turkey Real Estate: Tel 01538-398254, wwwturkeyrealestate.co.uk, 3 Campbell Ave, Leek, Staffs ST13 5RP

Buzz Estates: Tel: 0161-449 5228, www.buzzytravel.com/buzzestate.htm, 99 Moor End, Mellor, Stockport, Ches SK6 5PT. Ölüdeniz area.

Cumberland Properties: Tel: 0207-435 8113, www.cumberland-properties.com, 16 Alvanley Gardens, London NW6 1JD

EMP Eastern Mediterranean Properties Ltd: Tel: 0207-247 7407, www.emproperties. co.uk, 2nd Floor, 2-4 Great Eastern St, London EC2A 3NW

Forest Hill Houses/Selçuk Homes: Tel: 01772-816955, www.foresthillhouses.com, 2 Edward Close, Tarleton, Preston PR4 6NE

Gascoignes International: Tel: 01483-756633, www.gascoignesinternational.com, 5 Church Path, Woking GU21 6EJ

Headlands International: Tel: 01933-654000, www.headlands.co.uk, Station Rd, Nene Park, Irthlingborough, Northants NN9 5QF. Off-plan sales.

Lycia Properties: Tel: 08456-066569, www.lyciaproperties.com, 2 Coal Park Lane, Swanwick, Southampton, Hampshire SO31 7GW

McMahon Associates: Tel: 0292-022 6021, www.mcmahonassociates.co.uk, 98 Cowbridge Rd East, Cardiff CF11 9DX

Philip Clark Properties Ltd: Tel: 01622-719415, www.philipclarkproperties.co.uk, 9-10 Phoenix House, Forstal Rd, Aylesford ME20 7AD

Properties in Turkey: Tel: 0845-490 0272, www.propertiesinturkey.com, The Court, Rutland Ave, Matlock, Derbys DE4 3GQ

RMG Turkey: Tel: 0773-139 9407, 58 Earlswood St, London SE10 9ES

Turkish Holiday Homes: Tel: 0208-509 3691, www.turkishholidayhomes.com, 16 Foresters Drive, London E17 3PG

Turkish Property Agents: Tel: 0800-082 3823, www.turkishpropertyagents.co.uk, 319A Manchester Rd, Burnley, Lancs BB11 4HD

Turkish Property Centre: Tel: 0191-214 5533, www.theturkishpropertycentre.com, 5 Wingrove House, Ponteland Rd, Newcastle-upon-Tyne NE5 3DP

Ireland

Costello: Tel: 86-123 7874, www.costelloestates.com

Mozaik Property: Tel: 1800-946 324, www.mozaikproperty.com

Turkish Property Centre: Tel: 01-449 3218, www.theturkishpropertycentre.com, West Wing, Office 603, Adelaide Chambers, St Peters St, Dublin 8

Netherlands
Philip Clark Properties Ltd: Tel: 0223-610445, www.philipclarkproperties.com, Visstraat 26, 1781 CP, Den Helder

RENTAL AGENCIES

Many estate agents double as rental agencies. However, there are also some specialist flat-finding firms too. See p. 579 for a sample rental contract.

Istanbul
Flats in Istanbul: Tel: 0532-595 3498, www.flatsinistanbul.com, Kuloğlu Mahallesi, Enver Karababa Apt, Kocaağa Sokak No: 6, Beyoğlu

TIMESHARE

EvOtelEv: Tel 0212-339 0707, www.evturkbuku.com, Göltürkbükü, Bodrum Peninsula. Designer luxury, all sorts of health facilities and multiple swimming pools. One week per year for next 30 years from €20,000.

Orient Palace Resort: www.unifingroep.nl/www.turkeyrealestatedirect.co.uk. Apartments from €70,000. Use for six weeks in low season and anticipate 10% rental income for next 10 years.

APPENDIX II:
INTERIOR SUPPLIERS

ANTIQUE SHOPS

Istanbul
Anadolu Antik: Tel: 0212-251 5228, Turnacıbaşı Sokak No: 65, Çukurcuma
Antikarnas Istanbul: Tel: 0212-251 5928, Faik Paşa Yokuşu, Çukurcuma
Kato Export: Tel: 0212-526 4551, Halıcılar Caddesi No: 55, Grand Bazaar
Mecidiyeköy Antikacılar: Tomurcuk Sokak No: 1/7, Mecidiyeköy
Nejat Karpat: Tel: 0212-251 5228, Ağahamam Sokak No: 31, Çukurcuma
Oda Koleksiyon: Tel: 0212-245 5051, Çukurcuma
Old Bedesten: Grand Bazaar. Collection of antique shops at heart of bazaar.
Tombak II: Tel: 0212-244 3681, Faik Paşa Yokuşu No: 34/A, Çukurcuma
Yaman Antikhan: Tel: 0212-249 5188, Faik Paşa Yokuşu No: 41, Çukurcuma

Beyşehir
Ceylanlar: Tel: 0332-512 4384, Köprübaşı 6/A

Dalyan

The Turkish Village: Tel: 0252-284 2824, www.theturkishcottage.com, Eski Karakol Sokak No: 12/C

Fethiye

Antik Demirci: Tel: 0252-614 8385, Ölüdeniz Yolu üzeri

Kapadokya

Antik Dekorasyon: Tel: 0384-343 2032, H. Galip Efendi Caddesi No: 18, Ürgüp

Yöruk Halı Yıkama Art Collection: Tel: 0384-219 2808, Uçhisar. Good source of old dowry boxes (*sandıklar*)

Kaş

Turqueria: Tel: 0242-836 1631, www.turqueria.com, Uzun Çarşı No: 21

AUCTION HOUSES

Istanbul

Artium: Tel: 0212- 291 0131, Şakayık Aralığı Sokak No: 9, Teşvikiye

Bali Antik: Tel: 0212-233 3270, www.balimuzayede.com, Valikonağı Caddesi No: 93/1, Nişantaşı

BATHROOM FITTINGS

AHK Cam Lavaboda: Tel: 0212-249 3437, Meclis-i Mebusan Caddesi No: 14/B, Salıpazarı, Istanbul. Stunning range of modern glass sinks.

Duravit: www.duravit.com

BEDROOM FITTINGS

Linens: Tel: 0800-219 0108, www.linens.com.tr. Luxurious bedding, curtains and towels. Branches in all major towns.

Soley: www.soley.com.tr. Beds and bedding. Website lists outlets.

Yataş: Tel: 0216-451 4949, www.yatas.com.tr, Kartal Caddesi No: 31, Yakacık-Kartal, Istanbul. Beds and bedding. Website lists outlets.

Buldan's: Tel: 0252-614 4884, İnönü Bulvarı, Orman İşletmesi karşısı, 137. Sokak No: 10, Fethiye. Natural textiles.

ELECTRICAL GOODS SUPPLIERS

Arçelik: Tel: 0212-444 0888, www.arcelik.com.tr

Ariston: Tel: 0800-211 4042, www.ariston.com.tr

Beko: Tel: 0212-444 1404, www.beko.com.tr

Bosch: Tel: 0212-335 0673, www.bosch.com.tr

Electrolux: Tel: 0800-211 6032, www.electrolux.com.tr

Profilo: Tel: 444 7766, www.profilo.com.tr

Vestel: Tel: 0800-219 0112, www.vestel.com.tr

FABRIC SUPPLIERS
Istanbul
There are many inviting fabric shops along Halaskargazi Caddesi in Harbiye.
Beymen Home: Tel: 0212-282 0380, Akmerkez Shopping Mall
Ankara
Decorum: Tel: 0312-337 1199, Nenehatun Caddesi No: 123, Gaziosmanpaşa
Fethiye
Buldan's: Tel: 0252-614 4884, İnönü Bulvarı, Orman İşletmesi karşısı, 137.Sokak No: 10. Specialist in natural textiles.
Dolunay: Tel: 0252-614 8698, Çarşı Caddesi No: 268
Merkez Home Collection: Tel: 0252-612 9390, Tütün Sokak No: 27
Vizon Tekstil: Tel: 0252-612 6967, Çarşı Caddesi No: 238

FURNITURE
Istanbul
Mudo Concept: Tel: 0212-285 2390, Eski Büyükdere Caddesi, Ayazağa Yolu 28; Tel: 0216-302 3384, Bağdat Caddesi No: 320, Erenköy; Tel: 0216-339 7813, Tepe Nautilus Shopping Mall; Tel: 0212-275 4886, Profilo Shopping Mall
IKEA: Tel: 0216-528 0500, www.ikea.com.tr, Tepeüstü Mevkii, İnkilap Mahallesi, Ümraniye. 10am to 10pm daily.
Izmir
IKEA: Tel 0232-444 4532, Kazım Dirik Mahallesi, 371 Sokak 34, Bornova. 10am to 10pm daily.
Marmaris
Lara Home: Tel: 0252-413 2636, Yeniyol Caddesi, Engin Salman Apt No: 12
Fethiye
Light & Decoration Centre: Tel: 0252-646 7589, Çalıca Mahallesi, Narlı Caddesi No: 28/28
Önver: Tel: 0252-612 7575, 22 Metrelik Yol üzeri No: 32 (near Migros)

KITCHEN FURNITURE
Miele: Tel: 0800-211 7000, www.intemmutfak.com.tr
Istanbul
Aga Concept Shop: Tel: 0212-353 0410, Kanyon Shoppıng Mall
Merit: Tel: 0212-353 0738, Kanyon Shopping Mall; Tel 0212-282 1632, Akmerkez Shopping Mall
Fethiye
Mopa Mutfak Banyo: Tel: 0252-612 2882, Adnan Menderes Bulvarı No: 27/A

LIGHT FITTINGS

Fethiye

Light & Decoration Centre: Tel: 0252-646 7589, Çalıca Mahallesi, Narlı Caddesi No: 28/28

Önver: Tel: 0252-612 7575, 22 Metrelik Yol üzeri No: 32 (near Migros)

PICTURE FRAMERS

Istanbul

The Framing Gallery: Tel: 0212-251 2651, www.saber.com.tr, Galip Dede Caddesi, Tımarcı Sokak No: 5, Tünel

Levant Collection: Tel: 0212-293 6333, levant.kol@superonline.com, Meşrutiyet Caddesi No: 122, Beyoğlu

Kapadokya

Osmanlı Sanat Galerisi: Tel: 0384-341 2315, Atatürk Bulvarı 2, Ürgüp

STOVES

Istanbul

Hürpaş: Tel: 0212-233 3616, www.hurpas.com, Cumhuriyet Caddesi No: 187, Harbiye. Fireplaces and convection heating systems.

Uçaroğlu Antik: Tel: 0212-523 6891, Horhor Caddesi, Kırık Tulumba Sokak No: 13/173. Antique tiled stoves.

WALLPAPER STOCKISTS

Istanbul

Lot İngliz Duvar Kağıdı: Tel: 0212-225 7729, Valikonağı Caddesi No: 72, Nişantaşı; Tel: 0216-355 5464, Cemil Topuzlu Caddesi, Lalezar Sokak No: 12/2, Feneryolu

APPENDIX III:
WEDDING PREPARATIONS

BOAT HIRE

Istanbul

İncisu: Tel: 0216-418 5932, Söğütlü Çeşme Caddesi No: 70, Kat: 4, Kadıköy

Okyanus: Tel: 0216-330 3159, Dr Esat Işık Caddesi No: 59-61, Moda

The Sultan's Boats: Tel: 0212-296 5240, Cumhuriyet Caddesi No: 141, Kat: 3, Harbiye

CAKES

Istanbul

Cake Studio: Tel: 0216-541 4302, Kalamış Fener Caddesi, Kılıc Sokak No: 3/2, Fenerbahçe

Özel Tatlar: Tel: 0212-291 2321, Süleyman Nazif Sokak No: 34/1, Nişantaşı

DRESSES

Istanbul

Akay Maison de Couture: Tel: 0212-224 9485, Valikonağı Caddesi, Çiftçiler Apt No:12/1,
Nişantaşı

Beyaz Butik: Tel: 0212-296 6015, Rumeli Caddesi No: 85, Kat: 7, Nişantaşı

Esposa: Tel: 0212-248 3418, Maçka Caddesi No: 29, Kat: 2, Maçka

Lamedore: Tel: 0212-240 5030, Şakayik Sokak No: 39-2/4, Nişantaşı

Pronuptia: Tel: 0212-380 1210, Cevahir Shopping Mall

Very Important Bride: Tel: 0212-241 2075, Abdi İpekçi Caddesi No: 31/3, Nişantaşı

Weddies: Tel: 0212-224 6444, www.weddies.com, Valikonagı Caddesi, Marmara Apt
No: 16/1, Nişantaşı

FLOWERS

Istanbul

Necmi Rıza: Tel: 0212-219 4396, Kalıpçı Sokak No: 133/1, Teşvikiye

Woods: Tel: 0212-275 9194, Büyükdere Caddesi No: 84/A, Gayrettepe

HATS

Istanbul

Mod Kristin: Tel: 0212-244 2740, www.modkristin.com, İstiklal Caddesi, Elhamra Pasajı
No: 2, Beyoğlu

VENUES

Istanbul

Beylerbeyi Palace: Tel 0216-321 9320, Yalıboyu Caddesi, Üsküdar

Bosphorus Palace Hotel: Tel: 0216-422 0003, Yalıboyu Caddesi No: 64, Beylerbeyi

Binbirdirek Sarnıçı: Tel: 0212-518 1001, Binbirdirek Mahallesi, Sultanahmet

Çırağan Palace Kempinski Hotel: Tel: 0212-326 4646, Çırağan Caddesi No: 32,
Beşiktaş

Divan Catering: Tel 0212-315 5500, www.divanhoteli.com.tr, Kuruçeşme. Variety of
indoor and outdoor settings for wedding parties on shores of Bosphorus.

Esma Sultan Mansion: Tel: 0212-261 6923, Muallim Naci Caddesi, Yalı Çıkmazı Sokak
No: 20, Ortaköy

Four Seasons Hotel: Tel: 0212-638 8200, Tevkıfhane Sokak No: 1, Sultanahmet
Hilton Hotel: Tel: 0212-315 6000, Cumhuriyet Caddesi, Harbiye
Küçüksu Palace: Tel: 0216-332 3303, Küçüksu Caddesi, Beykoz
Marmara Pera: Tel: 0212-251 4696, www.themarmarahotels.com, Meşrutiyet Caddesi, Tepebaşı, Beyoğlu
Park Orman: Tel: 0212-328 2020, Büyükdere Caddesi, Fatih Çocuk Ormanı, Maslak
Polat Renaissance: Tel: 0212-414 1800, Sahil Caddesi No: 2, Yeşilyurt
Sait Halim Paşa Mansion: Tel: 0212-223 0566, Köybaşı Caddesi No: 117, Yeniköy
Yıldız Bahçe: Tel: 0212-236 5549, Yeni Teknik Üniversitesi, Barbaros Bulvarı, Beşiktaş

WEDDING PLANNERS

Istanbul

Beymen: Tel: 0212-282 0380, Akmerkez Shopping Mall. Branches in Suadiye and Nişantaşı (see p491). Sign up to Beymen's White List and they will help organise your wedding.
K&M: Tel: 0212-282 8600, 4.Gazeteciler Sitesi, Ülgen Sokak No: 4/4, Levent
Le Chic: Tel: 0216-330 9892, Bağdat Caddesi No: 62/2, Kızıltoprak

Selçuk

Turkish Weddings: www.turkishweddings.com. Sheryl Entwhistle will help you organise a wedding on the Aegean coast.

APPENDIX IV:
TURKISH SCHOOLS & UNIVERSITIES

Note that 'k12' indicates a school that offers education from kindergarten through to year 12.

INTERNATIONAL SCHOOLS
Istanbul

Alman Lisesi (German School): Tel: 0212-245 0794, www.almanlisesi.com, Şahkulu Bostane Sokak, Tünel. German-language teaching.
Bosphorus International Schools: Tel: 0212-226 3000, www.bipschools.net, Merkez Mahallesi, Valide Sultan Caddesi No: 2, Bahçeköy, Sarıyer. International pre-school and primary school with English-language teaching. Bilingual Turkish primary school. Also French classes.
British International School: Tel: 0212-257 3114, www.bis.k12.tr, Dilhayat Sokak No: 18, Etiler. Pre-school, primary and secondary. Follows British school curriculum. Teaching towards IB. Emphasis on languages.

Elementary & Primary Italian School: Tel: 0212-244 4225, Turnacıbaşı Sokak No: 30, Ağahamamı. Italian-language teaching.

Enka School: Tel: 0212-276 0545, www.enkaschools.com, Sadi Gülçelik Spor Sitesi, İstinye. Turkish and English-language teaching.

Eyüboğlu: Tel: 0216-522 1212, www.eyuboglu.k12.tr, Namık Kemal Mahallesi, Dr Rüstem Eyüboğlu Sokak No: 3, Ümraniye

Galatasaray Lisesi: Tel: 0212-249 1100, www.gsi.gsu.edu.tr, İstiklal Caddesi No: 263, Beyoğlu. Many classes in French. So oversubscribed that places allocated by lottery.

Istanbul International Community School ('American Community School'): Tel: 0212-857 8264, www.iics.k12.tr, Karaağaç Köyü, Hadımköy. Second campus in Rumeli Hisarı. English-language teaching. Three separate IB courses. Non-Turkish curriculum.

Istanbul Lisesi: Tel: 0212-514 1570, www.istanbullisesi.com, Türkocağı Caddesi No: 4, Cağaloğlu. Some German-language teaching.

İtalyan Lisesi: Tel: 0212-244 1301, www.liceoitaliano.net, Tom Tom Kaptan Sokak No: 13, Beyoğlu. Italian-language teaching.

Koç Özel Lisesi: Tel: 0216-585 6200, www.kocschool.k12.tr, Akfırat Deldesi, Tepeören, Çayırlar Mevkii, Tuzla. English and Turkish-language teaching. Most students are Turkish.

Lycee Francois St Benoit: Tel: 0212-244 1026, www.sbk12.tr, Kemeraltı Caddesi No: 35, Karaköy

Lycee Pierre Loti (Papillon): Tel: 0212-252 2558, www.pierreloti.k12.tr, Tom Tom Kaptan Sokak, Beyoğlu; Tel: 0212-299 9400, Kefeliköy Caddesi No: 6/1, Tarabya. Teaching in French aimed at French Baccalaureate so students can apply to French universities. Non-Turkish curriculum.

Lycee St Michel: Tel: 0212-248 1703, www.saintmichel.k12.tr, Abide-i Hurriyet Caddesi No: 21, Şişli. French-language teaching.

MEF International School: Tel: 0212-287 3871, www.mef.k12.tr, Ulus Mahallesi, Dereboyu Caddesi, Ortaköy. English-language teaching.

Notre Dame de Sion: Tel: 0212-240 6174, www.nds.k12.tr, Cumhuriyet Caddesi, Harbiye. French-language teaching.

Oesterreichisches St.Georgs-Kolleg (Avusturya Lisesi ve Ticaret Okulu): Tel: 0212-244 4255. Austrian school offering German-language teaching.

Robert College: Tel: 0212-359 2270, www.robcol.k12.tr, Kuruçeşme Caddesi, Bebek. Famous college, founded 1863, offering IB to non-Turkish foreign residents from grade 11.

St Joseph: Tel: 0216-414 5260, www.sj.k12.tr, Dr Esat Işık Caddesi No: 76-8, Kadıköy. French-language teaching.

Üsküdar American Academy (Üsküdar Amerikan Lisesi): Tel: 0216-310 6823, Fax: 0216-553 1818, Bağlarbaşı Sokak No: 1, Üsküdar.

Üsküdar Anadolu Lisesi: Tel: 0216-334 9321, Fax: 0216-553 1818, Yeni Ocak Sokak Nos: 1-5, Bağlarbaşı, Üsküdar. German-language teaching.

Yüzyıl Işıl Lisesi: Tel: 0212-226 2353, www.yuzyilisil.k12.tr, Valide Sultan Caddesi, Alay Yolu No: 2, Bahçeköy, Sarıyer. Teaches to IB.

Ankara

Bilkent International School: Tel: 0312- 266 4961, www.bupsbis.bilkent.edu,tr, East Campus, Ankara. Pre-school to secondary school. Teaches to IGCSE and IB.

German School (Alman Okulu/Ernst Reuter Okulu)*:* Tel: 0312-426 6382, www.dasan. de/ds_ankara/, Tunus Caddesi No: 56, Kavaklıdere. German-language teaching.

Lycee Charles de Gaulle: Tel: 0312-491 7225, www.lcdgankara.org, Paris Caddesi No: 70, Kavaklıdere

TED Ankara Koleji: Tel: 0312-536 9000, www.tedankara.k12.tr, İncek. Primary and secondary school.

Izmir

American Collegiate Institute: Tel: 0232-285 3401, www.aci.k12.tr, İnönü Caddesi No: 476, Göztepe

Izmir MEF International School: Tel: 0232-252 2052, www.international.mef.k12.tr/Izmir/, Akçay Caddesi No: 285, Gaziemir. English-language teaching. Emphasis on science.

Izmir Özel Türk Lisesi: Tel: 0232-244 0500, Mithatpaşa Caddesi No: 689, Balçova

Antalya

International Community College of Antalya: Tel: 0242-322 6285, Demircikara Mahallesi, Değirmenönü Caddesi, 1431 Sokak Nos: 2-3. English-language teaching for 3 to14-year-olds.

Bursa

TED Bursa Koleji: Tel: 224-549 2100, www.tedbursa.k12.tr

Marmaris

Kenan Evren Marmaris Koleji: Tel: 0252-419 1919, www.marmariskoleji.k12.tr, Kenan Evren Caddesi, Beldibi. Pre-school to high school with emphasis on English, sports and IT.

Tarsus

Tarsus American College: Tel: 0324-613 5402, www.tac.k12.tr. Follows Turkish and American curricula with emphasis on English-language teaching.

MONTESSORI SCHOOLS

Istanbul

Fenerbahçe Koleji; Tel: 0216-466 1907, Fax: 0216-466 6209, Uslu Caddesi, Yunus Sokak No: 1, Kayışdağı.

Erol Altaca Koleji: Tel: 0212-262 2222, Ferahevler, Tarabya

Bursa

Kırmızı Pabuçlar Çocuk Evi: Tel: 0224-236 6189, Karagöz Sokak, Pembegül Daire: 33, Çekirge

PLAY GROUPS

Istanbul

Gymboree: Tel: 0212-282 7666, www.gymboreeturkey.com, Meşeli Sokak No: 12, 4.Levent. US-oriented playgroup for pre-school children.

PRIVATE KINDERGARTENS

Istanbul

Atölye Pre-school: Tel: 0212-299 9325, www.atolyepre-school.com, Sümer Korusu Gülveren Sokak No: 5, Tarabya. Reggio Emilia approach to learning.

Bosphorus International Schools: Tel: 0212-277 8444, www.bipschools.net, Şirin Sokak No: 45, Reşitpaşa Emirgan. Second campus in Bahçeköy

Çakmalı Kindergarten: Tel: 0216-486 0955, www.cakmalicockevi.com, Nato Yolu, Ata 2 Sitesi, Ladin Caddesi No: 1, Çengelköy

Die Bunte: Tel: 0216-342 2144. German-speaking pupils aged two to six.

Eden's Garden International Pre-school: Tel: 0212-262 4302, www.edensgardenpre-school.com, Bağlar Caddesi No: 70, Yeniköy. Children aged two to six.

English Pre-school: Tel: 0212-229 3776, Şirin Sokak No: 32, Baltalimanı

Little Land International Pre-school: Tel: 0216-465 4197, www.littlelandschool.com, Otağtepe Caddesi, Kavaklı Sokak No: 15, Kavacık. Children in mixed age groups.

Pinocchio (The English International School of Istanbul - TEİS): Tel: 0212-280 8038 , www.teis.com.tr, Akağaç Sokak Nos: 6-8, 4.Levent

Sarı Papatya Çocuk Evi: Tel: 0216-326 6202, Cenap Şahabettin Sokak No: 12, Koşuyolu

Small Hands Academy: Tel: 0212-287 4785, www.small-hands.com, Ahular Sokak No: 18, Etiler; Tel: 0212-287 1568, Kaleağası Sokak No: 8, Rumelihisarı; Tel: 0216-411 9121, Hacı Mehmet Efendi Sokak No: 11/1, Selamiçeşme

Woods View International Pre-school: Tel: 0212-299 3906, woodsview@superonline. com, Kasımpatı Sokak No: 12, Sümer Korusu, Tarabya

Ankara

Early Success (Erken Başarı): Tel: 0312-2121 Reşit Galip Caddesi No: 102, Gaziosmanpaşa

English Pre-School: Tel: 0312-437 0028, Nenehatun Caddesi No: 62, Gaziosmanpaşa

First Name (İlkadım): Tel: 0312- 446 0486, Nenehatun Caddesi No: 73, Gaziosmanpaşa

My Share (Paylaşım): Tel: 0312-481 3366, Sinan Caddesi No: 120, Dikmen

New Little Ones (Yeni Ufuklar): Tel: 0312-490 1508, Rafet Canıtez Caddesi, Mustafa Fehmi Gerçeker Sokak No: 8, Oran

Rain (Yağmur): Tel: 0312-446 5156, Koza Sokak No: 111/3, Gaziosmanpaşa

Izmir

Izmir MEF International School: Tel: 0232-252 2052, www.international.mef.k12.tr Izmir/, Akçay Caddesi No: 285, Gaziemir

PRIVATE SCHOOLS
Antalya

Akdeniz Koleji: Tel: 0242-229 2020, www.akdenizkoleji.com, Arapsuyu

Antalya Koleji: Tel: 0242-238 2300, www.antalyakoleji.k12.tr, İl Jandarma, Alay Komutanlığı arkası

Kapadokya

Altınyıldız: Tel: 0384-214 1660, www.altinyildiz.k12.tr, Ürgüp Yolu, Nevşehir

Kardelen: Tel: 0384-219 2822, www.kardelen.k12.tr, Ürgüp Yolu 6km, Nevşehir

Lara: Tel: 0384-313 0309, www.larakoleji.k12.tr, Gülşehir Yolu 2km, Nevşehir. Most religious of Nevşehir schools.

SUMMER SCHOOLS
Bodrum

İsis Hotel Summer School: Tel: 0252-317 2140, Asarlık Mevkii, Gümbet

UNIVERSITIES
STATE UNIVERSITIES
Istanbul

Beykent Üniversitesi: Tel: 0212-872 6432, www.beykent.edu.tr, Beylikdüzü, Gürpınar E5 Karayolu Ayrımı, Beykent, Büyükçeşme

Galatasaray Üniversitesi: Tel: 0212-227 4480, www.gsu.edu.tr, Çırağan Caddesi No: 36, Ortaköy

Istanbul Teknik Üniversitesi: Tel: 0212-285 6611, www.itu.ed.tr, Ayazağa Kampüsü, Maslak

Istanbul Üniversitesi: Tel: 0212-440 0000, www.istanbul.edu.tr, Merkez Kampüsü, Beyazıt. Second campus in Eminönü.

Marmara Üniversitesi: Tel: 0216-338 2537, www.marun.edu.tr, Göztepe

Mimar Sinan Üniversitesi: Tel: 0212-252 1600, www.msu.edu.tr, Meclis-i Mebusa Caddesi No: 24, Fındıklı

Maltepe Üniversitesi: Tel: 0216-626 1050, www.maltepe.edu.tr, Marmara Eğitim Köyü

Yıldız Teknik Üniversitesi: Tel: 0212-258 7489, www.yildiz.edu.tr, Yıldız

Ankara

Ankara Üniversitesi: Tel: 0312-212 6040, www.ankara.edu.tr, Dögol Caddesi, Tandoğan

Gazi Üniversitesi: Tel: 0312-212 6840, www.gazi.edu.tr

Hacettepe Üniversitesi: Tel: 0312-305 1001, www.hacettepe.edu.tr, Sıhhıye

Orta Doğu Teknik Üniversitesi (Middle East Technical University - METU): Tel: 0312-210 2000, www.metu.edu.tr, İnönü Bulvarı

Izmir

Dokuz Eylül Üniversitesi: Tel: 0232-412 1212, www.deu.edu.tr, Cumhuriyet Bulvarı No: 144, Alsancak

Ege Üniversitesi: Tel: 0232-388 0110, www.ege.edu.tr, Bornova

Izmir Yüksek Teknoloji Üniversitesi: Tel: 0232-750 6000, www.iyle.edu.tr, Güzel-bahçeköyü, Urla

Izmir Ekonomi Üniversitesi: Tel: 0232-279 2525, www.izmirekonomi.deu.tr, Sakarya Caddesi No: 156, Balçova

Elsewhere in Turkey

Adana - Çukurova Üniversitesi: Tel: 0322-338 6350, www.cu.edu.tr, Balcalı

Afyon - Kocatepe Üniversitesi: Tel: 0272-228 1213, www.qku.edu.tr, Ahmet Necdet Sezer Kampüsü, Gazlıgöl Yolu

Antalya - Akdeniz Üniversitesi: Tel: 0242-227 4400, www.akdeniz.edu.tr, Dumlupınar Bulvarı

Aydın - Adnan Menderes Üniversitesi: Tel: 0256-214 6680, www.adu.edu.tr, Aytepe Mevkii

Balıkesir Üniversitesi: Tel: 0266-612 1400, www.balikesir.edu.tr

Bolu - Abant İzzet Baysal Üniversitesi: Tel: 0374-254 1000, www.ibu.edu.tr, Gölköy

Bursa - Uludağ Üniversitesi: Tel: 0224-442 8200, www.uludag.edu.tr

Çanakkale - Onsekiz Mart Üniversitesi: Tel: 0286-218 0018, www.comu.edu.tr

Denizli - Pamukkale Üniversitesi: Tel: 0258-212 5555, www.pamukkale.edu.tr, İncilipınar

Diyarbakır - Dicle Üniversitesi: Tel: 0412-248 8030, www.dicle.edu.tr

Edirne- Trakya Üniversitesi: Tel: 0284-214 4210, www.trakya.edu.tr, Karaağaç

Elazığ - Fırat Üniversitesi: Tel: 0424-237 0000, www.fırat.edu.tr

Erzurum - Atatürk Üniversitesi: Tel: 0442-231 1111, www.atauni.edu.tr

Eskişehir - Anadolu Üniversitesi: Tel: 0222-365 0580, www.anadolu.edu.tr, Yunusemre Kampüsü

Eskişehir - Osmangazi Üniversitesi: Tel: 0222-239 3750, www.ogu.edu.tr, Meşelik Kampüsü

Gaziantep Üniversitesi: Tel: 0342-360 1200, www.gantep.edu.tr, Şehitkamil

Isparta - Süleyman Demirel Üniversitesi: Tel: 0245-211 1000, www.sdu.edu.tr, Çünür

İçel - Mersin Üniversitesi: Tel: 0324-361 0001, www.mersin.edu.tr

Hatay - Mustafa Kemal Üniversitesi: Tel: 0326-221 3317, www.mku.edu.tr, Antakya

Kahramanmaraş - Sütçüimam Üniversitesi: Tel: 0344-219 1000, www.ksu.edu.tr, Avşar Kampüsü

Kars - Kafkas Üniversitesi: Tel: 0474-242-6800, www.kafkas.edu.tr, Paşaçayırı

Kayseri - Erciyes Üniversitesi: Tel: 0352-437 4901, www.erciyes.edu.tr

Kırıkkale - Kırıkkale Üniversitesi: Tel: 0318-357 3694, www.kku.edu.tr, Ankara Yolu 7km

Kocaeli Üniversitesi: Tel: 0262-303 1000, www.kou.com.tr, Umuttepe Yerleşkesi, Eski Istanbul Yolu 10km

Kocaeli Üniversitesi/Gebze Meslek Yüksekokulu: Tel: 0262-742 3290, www.kou.edu.tr, Emek Mahallesi, Bosna Caddesi, Çayırova

Konya - Selçuk Üniversitesi: Tel: 0332-241 0041, www.selcuk.edu.tr

Kütahya - Dumlupınar Üniversitesi: Tel: 0274-265 2031, www.dpu.edu.tr, Tavşanlı Yolu 10 km

Malatya - İnönü Üniversitesi: Tel: 0442-341 0010, www.inonu.edu.tr, Elazığ Yolu 15km

Manisa - Celal Bayar Üniversitesi: Tel: 0236-237 2886, www.bayar.edu.tr, İstasyon Mevkii

Muğla Üniversitesi: Tel: 0252-211 1000, www.mu.edu.tr, Kötekli

Niğde Üniversitesi: Tel: 0388-225 2148, www.nigde.edu.tr

Sakarya Üniversitesi: Tel: 0264-346 0090, Fax: 0264-346 0107, Esentepe

Samsun - Ondokuz Mayıs Üniversitesi: Tel: 0362-457 5870, www.omu.edu.tr

Sivas - Cumhuriyet Üniversitesi: Tel: 0346-219 1010, www.cumhuriyet.edu.tr

Şanlıurfa - Harran Üniversitesi: Tel: 0414-312 8143, www.harran.edu.tr, Yenişehir

Tokat - Gaziosmanpaşa Üniversitesi: Tel: 0356-252 1616, www.gop.edu.tr

Trabzon - Karadeniz Teknik Üniversitesi: Tel: 0462-377 3000, www.ktu.edu.tr

Van - Yüzüncü Yıl Üniversitesi: Tel: 0432-225 1024, www.yyu.edu.tr

Zonguldak - Karaelmas Üniversitesi: Tel: 0372-257 4010, www.karaelmas.edu.tr

PRIVATE UNIVERSITIES

Istanbul

Bahçeşehir Üniversitesi: Tel: 0212-169 1523, www.bahcesehir.edu.tr. Private university.

Bilgi Üniversitesi: Tel: 0212-311 5000, www.bilgi.edu.tr, İnönü Caddesi No: 28, Kuştepe. Private university.

Boğaziçi Üniversitesi: Tel: 0212-359 5400, www.boun.edu.tr, Bebek. Private university.

Doğuş Üniversitesi: Tel: 0216-327 1104, www.dogus.edu.tr, Kadıköy. Private university.

Fatih Üniversitesi: Tel: 0212-889 0810, www.fatih.edu.tr, Büyükçekmece. Private university.

Haliç Üniversitesi: Tel: 0212-621 3705, www.halic.edu.tr, Molla Gürani Caddesi Nos: 16-8, Fındıkzade. Private university.

Işık Üniversitesi: Tel: 0212-286 2960, www.isikun.edu.tr, Şile. Private university.

Istanbul Kültür Üniversitesi: Tel: 0212-639 3024, www.iku.edu.tr, E5 Karayolu üzeri, Şirinevler. Private university.

Kadir Has Üniversitesi: Tel: 0212-533 6532, www.khas.edu.tr, Cibali. Private university.

Koç Üniversitesi: Tel: 0212-338 1000, www.ku.edu.tr, Rumeli Fener Yolu, Sarıyer. Private university.

Sabancı Üniversitesi: Tel: 0216-483 9090, www.sabanciuniv.edu.tr, Tuzla. Private university.

Yeditepe Üniversitesi: Tel: 0216-578 0000, www.yeditepe.edu.tr, İnönü Mahallesi, Kayışdağı Caddesi, 26 Ağustos Yerleşimi. Private university.

Ankara

Atılım Üniversitesi: Tel: 0312-586 8000, www.atilim.edu.tr, Kızılcaşar Köyü, İncek, Gölbaşı. Private university.

Başkent Üniversitesi: Tel: 0312-212 8016, www.baskent.edu.tr, 1.Cadde No: 77, Bahçelievler. Private university.

Bilkent Üniversitesi: Tel: 0312-290 4000, www.bilkent.edu.tr, Bilkent. Private university.

Çağ Üniversitesi: Tel: 0324-651 4800, www.cag.edu.tr, Adana-Mersin Karayolu üzeri, Yenice. Private university.

Çankaya Üniversitesi: Tel: 0312-284 4500, www.cankaya.edu.tr, Öğretmenler Caddesi No: 14, Balgat. Private university.

Also:

Council of Higher Education (YÖK- Yükseköğretim Kurulu): Tel: 0312-298 7000, Fax: 0312-266 4759, www.yok.gov.tr, Bilkent, Ankara. Supervises higher education in Turkey.

Turkish International Prep Schools: Tel: 0212-351 9030, www.tippsonline.com, Zeytinoğlu Caddesi, Sedef Apt No: 28, Akatlar, Istanbul. Prepares students to study at American universities.

APPENDIX V:
USEFUL BUSINESS CONTACTS

BUSINESS ASSOCIATIONS

Istanbul

Association of Turkish Industrialists and Businessmen (TÜSİAD): Tel: 0212-249 1929, Fax: 0212-249 1350, www.tusiad.org.tr, Meşrutiyet Caddesi No: 74, Beyoğlu

Association of Turkish Travel Agencies (TÜRSAB): Tel: 0212-275 1361, www.tursab.org.tr, Aşık Kerem Sokak No: 55-1, Dikilitaş

Black Sea Business Co-operation: Tel: 0212-229 1114, Fax: 0212-229 0332, www.bsec-business.org, Müsir Fuad Paşa Yalısı, Eski Tersane, İstinye

Foreign Trade Association: Tel: 0212-272 6981, Fax: 0212-275 5136, www.turktrade.org.tr, Kore Şehitleri Caddesi, Arcıl Apt: 37/4, Zincirlikuyu

Independent Industrialists' and Businessmen's Association (MÜSİAD): Tel: 0212-213 6100, Mecidiye Caddesi No: 7/50, Mecidiyeköy

International Investors Association (Uluslararası Yatırımcılar Derneği - YASED): Tel: 0212-272 5094, Fax: 0212-274 6664, www.yased.org.tr, Barbaros Bulvarı, Morbasan Sokak, Koza İş Merkezi, B Blok, Kat: 1, Beşiktaş

Istanbul Export Associations: Tel: 0212-454 0500, Fax: 0212-454 0501, www.iib.org.tr, Dış Ticaret Kompleksi, C Blok, Yenibosna

Turkish-American Business Association (TABA): Tel: 0212-291 0916, www.amcham. org/Taba.asp, Büyükdere Caddesi No: 18/20, Kat: 7, Şişli

Turkish Hotel Association (TÜROB): Tel: 0212-275 0550, www.turob.org, Yıldız Posta Caddesi, Dedeman Ticaret Merkezi No: 52/1, Kat: 16, Beşiktaş

Tüyap: Tel: 0212-886 6843, Fax: 0212-886 6698, www.tuyap.com.tr, Tüyap Fair, Convention and Congress Centre, E5 Karayolu, Gürpınar Kavşağı, Beylikdüzü, Büyükçekmece. Organisers of Istanbul fairs.

Ankara

Ankara Chamber of Industry: Tel: 0312-417 1200, Fax: 0312-417 4370, www.aso.org.tr, Atatürk Bulvarı No: 193-4, Kavaklıdere

Association of Turkish Consulting Engineers & Architects: Tel: 0312-440 8970, Fax: 0312-440 8972, www.atcea.org.tr, Ahmet Rasim Sokak No: 35/2, Çankaya

Competition Authority: Tel: 0312-266 6969, Fax: 0312-266 7920, www.rekabet.gov.tr, Bilkent Plaza, B3 Blok, Bilkent

Confederation of Turkish Trade Unions (Türk-İş): Tel: 0312-433 3125, Fax: 0312-433 6809. www.turkis.org.tr, Bayındır Sokak No: 10, Yenişehir, Kızılay

European Commission: Tel: 0312-446 5511, www.deltur.cec.eu.int, Uğur Mumcu Caddesi No: 88/4, Gaziosmanpaşa

Export Promotion Centre: Tel: 0312-417 2223, Fax: 0312-417 2233, Mithatpaşa Caddesi No: 60, Kızılay

GAP Regional Development Administration: Tel: 0312-442 2324, Fax: 0312-440 1384, www.gap.gov.tr, Willie Brandt Sokak No: 5, Çankaya

Patent Institute: Tel: 0312-232 5425, www.turkpatent.gov.tr, Necatibey Caddesi No: 49

Privatization Administration: Tel: 0312-430 4560, Fax: 0312-435 9342, www.oib.gov.tr, Ziya Gökalp Caddesi No: 80, Kurtuluş

Small & Medium Industry Development Organisation: Tel: 0312-212 8141, Fax: 0312-212 2508, www.kosgeb.gov.tr, Tandoğan

State Institute for Statistics: Tel: 0312-417 6440, Fax: 0312-425 3387, www.di.e.gov.tr, Necatibey Caddesi No: 114, Bakanlıklar

State Planning Organisation: Tel: 0312-230 8720, Fax: 0312-230 9733, www.dpt.gov.tr, Necatibey Caddesi No: 110, Bakanlıklar

Technology Development Centre: Tel: 0312-210 1300, Fax: 0312-210 1309, www.tekmer.gov.tr, ODTÜ Kampüsü

Turkish-American Business Association (TABA): Tel: 0312-427 2548, Cinnah Caddesi No: 20, Kavaklıdere

Turkish Cooperative Association (Türk Kooperatifcilik Kurumu): Tel: 0312-431 6125, Fax: 0312-434 0646, www.koopkur.org.tr, Mithatpaşa Caddesi No: 38/A, Kızılay

Turkish Institute of Standards: Tel: 0312-417 0020, Fax: 0312-425 4399, www.tse.org.tr, Necatibey Caddesi No: 112, Bakanlıklar

Union of Chambers of Commerce, Industry, Maritime Trade & Commodity Exchanges: Tel: 0312-417 7700, Fax: 0312-418 3268, www.tobb.org.tr, Atatürk Bulvarı No: 149

World Bank: Tel: 0312-468 4527, Uğur Mumcu Caddesi No: 88, Kat: 2, Gaziosmanpaşa

Izmir

Aegean Exporters Unions: Tel: 0232-463 6950, Fax: 0232-421 6560, www.egebirlik.org.tr, 1375. Sokak No: 25/3, Alsancak

Aegean Industrialists & Businessmen's Association (ESİAD): Tel: 0232-483 8833, Fax: 0232-483 3525, www.esiad.org.tr, Heris Tower, Şehit Fethi Bey Caddesi 55, Kat: 8

CHAMBERS OF COMMERCE (TİCARET ODASI)

Antalya Chamber of Commerce: Tel: 0242-248 9900, Fax: 0242-242 6680, www.antaly-acci.org.tr, Kazım Özalp Caddesi, 2.Sokak No: 4

Bursa Chamber of Commerce: Tel: 0224-243 1500, Fax: 0224-242 8511, www.btso.org.tr, Organize Sanayi Bölgesi, Mavi Cadde, 2.Sokak No: 2, Nilüfer

International Chamber of Commerce: Tel: 0312-417 8733, Fax: 0312-417 1483, www.iccwbo.org, Atatürk Bulvarı No: 149, Bakanlıklar

Istanbul Chamber of Commerce: Tel: 0212-455 6000, Fax: 0212-513 1565, www.ito.org.tr, Reşadiye Caddesi, Sirkeci

Izmir Chamber of Commerce: Tel: 0232-441 7777, Fax: 0232-483 7853, Atatürk Caddesi No: 126, Pasaport

CONFERENCE AND EXHIBITION CENTRES

Most of the big four and five-star hotels in Istanbul, Ankara and Izmir have conference facilities.

Istanbul

CNR Expo: Tel: 0212-465 7474, Atatürk Havalimanı karşısı, Yeşilköy

Hilton Convention & Exhibition Centre: Tel: 0212-315 6600, Elmadağ

Grand Cevahir Hotel & Convention Centre: Tel: 0212-314 4242, Darülaceze Caddesi, Şişli

Lütfi Kırdar International Convention & Exhibition Centre: Tel: 0212-296 3055, www.icec,org, Harbiye. Twenty-six meeting rooms to hold up to 8,900 delegates. Anadolu Auditorium can seat 2,000 delegates.

CONFERENCE INTERPRETERS

Istanbul

UKT: Tel: 0216-418 6604, Fax: 0216-337 7924, Osmanağa Mahallesi, Nuşet Efendi Sokak No: 17, Kat: 4, Kadıköy. Simultaneous, consecutive and written translations.

CONSULTANCY AND RESEARCH SERVICES

Istanbul

IBS Research & Consultancy: Tel: 0212-252 2460, www.ibsresearch.com, İstiklal Caddesi, Turnacıbaşı Sokak No: 19, Neşe Han, Kat: 3, Beyoğlu

GOVERNMENT DEPARTMENTS

Ankara

General Directorate of Free Trade Zones (Dış Ticaret Müşteşarlığı): Tel: 0312-212 5890, Fax: 0312-212 8906, Emek

Ministry of Agriculture & Rural Affairs (TC Tarım ve Köyişleri Bakanlığı): Tel: 0312-424 0580, www.tarim.gov.tr, Milli Müdafaa Caddesi No: 20, Bahçelievler

Ministry of Education (TC Milli Eğitim Bakanlığı): Tel: 0312-424 0887, www.meb.gov.tr

Ministry of Energy & Natural Resources (TC Enerji ve Tabii Kaynaklar Bakanlığı): Tel: 0312-212 6420, Fax: 0312-222 9404, www.enerji.gov.tr, İnönü Bulvarı No: 27, Bahçelievler

Ministry of the Environment (TC Çevre Bakanlığı): Tel: 0312-417 6000, Fax: 0312-215 0094, www.cevreorman.gov.tr, Atatürk Bulvarı No: 153, Bakanlıklar

Ministry of Finance (TC Maliye Bakanlığı): Tel: 0312-419 1200, Fax: 0312-425 0058, www.maliye.gov.tr, İlkadım Caddesi, Dikmen

Ministry of Foreign Affairs (TC Dışişleri Bakanlığı): Tel: 0312-287 2555, Fax: 0312- 287 1683, www.mfa.gov.tr, Balgat

Ministry of Health (TC Sağlık Bakanlığı): Tel: 0312-435 6440, www.saglik.gov.tr

Ministry of Industry & Commerce (TC Sanayi ve Ticaret Bakanlığı): Tel: 0312-231 7280, Fax: 0312-286 5325, www.sanayi.gov.tr, Gazi Mustafa Kemal Bulvarı No: 128, Tandoğan Meydanı

Ministry of Justice (TC Adalet Bakanlığı): Tel: 0312-417 7770, www.adalet.gov.tr, Kızılay

Ministry of Public Works & Housing (TC Bayındırlık ve İskan Bakanlığı): Tel: 0312-410 1000, www.bayindirlik.gov.tr

Ministry of Tourism (TC Turizm Bakanlığı): Tel: 0312-212 8300, Fax: 0312-212 8391, www.turizm.gov.tr

Ministry of Transportation (TC Ulaştırma Bakanlığı): Tel: 0312-212 6730, Fax: 0312-212 4900, www.ulastirma.gov.tr

Undersecretariat General for European Union Affairs: Tel: 0312-285 7720, Fax: 0312-286 0408, www.abgs.gov.tr, Eskişehir Yolu 9km

Undersecretariat for Foreign Trade: Tel: 0312-212 8800, Fax: 0312-212 1622, www. foreigntrade.gov.tr, İnönü Bulvarı, Emek Mevkii

Undersecretariat of the Treasury: Tel: 0312-212 5000, Fax: 0312-212 8916, www.treasury.gov.tr, İnönü Bulvarı, Emek Mevkii

INTERNATIONAL ACCOUNTANTS

Istanbul

Accenture: Tel: 0212-280 8100, Fax: 0212-280 5100, İş Kuleleri, Kule 2, Kat: 5, 4.Levent

Deloitte & Touche: Tel: 0212-283 1585, www.deloitte.com, B Blok, Kat: 5, Yapı Kredi Plaza, Büyükdere Caddesi, Levent

Ernst & Young: Tel: 0212-315 3000, Fax: 0212-230 8291

PricewaterhouseCoopers: Tel: 0212-251 7454, B Blok, Kat: 9, BJK Plaza, Spor Caddesi No: 92, Akaretler

Ankara

Deloitte & Touche: Tel: 0312-427 6235, Fax: 0312-427 6202

Ernst & Young: Tel: 0312-447 2111, Fax: 0312-447 8291

PricewaterhouseCoopers: Tel: 0312-417 1137, Paris Caddesi No: 12/4, Kavaklıdere

INTERNATIONAL DEVELOPMENT CO-OPERATION ORGANISATIONS

German Agency for Technical Co-operation: Tel: 0312-447 4664, Fax: 0312-447 4663, www.gtz.de, Filistin Sokak No: 21/2, Gaziosmanpaşa, Ankara

Japan International Co-operation Agency: Tel: 0312-447 2530, Fax: 0312-447 2534, www.jica.go.jp, Uğur Mumcu Caddesi No: 88/6, B Blok, Gaziosmanpaşa, Ankara

Swiss Development Co-operation: Tel: 0262-332 2072, Fax: 0262-332 0256, www.sdc. admin/ch, Sefa Sirmen Bulvarı, İl Kriz Merkezi, Fuar İçi, Kocaeli

Turkish International Co-operation Agency: Tel: 0312-417 2790, Fax: 0312-417 2799, www.tika.gov.tr, Akay Caddesi No: 6, Küçükesat, Ankara

NON-GOVERNMENTAL ORGANISATIONS

Ankara

International Labour Organisation (ILO): Tel: 0312-428 5183, www.ilo.org, Atatürk Bulvarı No: 197, Kavaklıdere

UN Commission for Refugees (UNHCR): Tel: 0312-439 6615, Abidin Daver Sokak No: 17, Çankaya

UNICEF: Tel: 0312-290 3390, www.unicef.org, Tunalı Hilmi Caddesi No: 88/115, Kavaklıdere

UNESCO: Tel: 0312-426 5894, www.unesco.org.tr, Göreme Sokak No: 7, Kavaklıdere

UN Food & Agriculture Association (FAO): Tel: 0312-468 7513, www.fao.org, Atatürk Bulvarı No: 197, Kavaklıdere

UN Industrial Development Organisation: Tel: 0312-454 1100, www.un.org.tr, UN House, Birlik Mahallesi, 2.Cadde No: 11, Çankaya

World Health Organisation (WHO): Tel: 0312-428 4031, www.who.int, Birlik Mahallesi, 2.Cadde No: 11, Çankaya

TRADE CENTRES

Istanbul

World Trade Centre: Tel: 0212-663 0606, www.wtcistanbul.com, Çobançeşme Kavşağı, Atatürk Havalimanı

Ankara

World Trade Centre: Tel: 0312-468 8750, Tahran Caddesi No: 30, Kavaklıdere

APPENDIX VI:

TURKISH AND FOREIGN BANKS, FOREIGN EXCHANGE DEALERS AND INSURANCE COMPANIES

EXPAT INSURANCE SERVICES

AXA PPP Healthcare: Tel: 01892-612080, www.axappphealthcare.co.uk, Phillips House, Crescent Rd, Tunbridge Wells, Kent TN1 2PL, UK

BUPA: Tel: 01273-208181, www.bupa-intl.com, Russell House, Russell Mews, Brighton BN1 2NR, UK

ExpaCare Insurance Services: Tel: 01344 381650, www.expacare.net, 1 Crutched Friars, London EC3N 2PH, UK

FOREIGN BANKS

Istanbul

ABN-AMRO Bank: Tel: 0212-293 8802, www.abnamro.com, İnönü Caddesi No: 15, Taksim

American Express Bank: Tel: 0212-275 9526, Suite 23, Maya Centre No: 23, Kat: 15, Büyükdere Caddesi, Esentepe

Arab Turkish Bank: Tel: 0212-225 0500, www.arabturkbank.com, Valikonağı Caddesi No: 10, Nişantaşı

Banco di Roma: Tel: 0212-285 9310, Büyükdere Caddesi, Noramın İş Merkezi, Kat: 5, Maslak

Bank of New York: Tel: 0212-259 0466, BJK Plaza, B Blok, Akaretler, Beşiktaş

Banque National de Paris (BNP): Tel: 0212-282 5582, Büyükdere Caddesi No: 173, 1.Levent

Chase Manhattan Bank: Tel: 0212-236 8300, Emirhan Caddesi No: 145, Atakule A Blok, Kat: 11, Dikilitaş

Citibank: Tel: 0212-288 7700, www.citibank.com.tr, Büyükdere Caddesi No: 100, Esentepe

Commerzbank: Tel: 0212-280 5524, Büyükdere Caddesi No: 198, Yapı Kredi Plaza, B Blok, Kat: 7, Levent

Credit Lyonnais: Tel: 0212-251 6300, Haktan İş Hanı No: 45/4, Setüstü, Kabataş

Credit Suisse: Tel: 0212-351 8600, Yıldırım Oğuz Caddesi, Kat: 9, Maya Plaza, Akatlar

Deutsche Bank: Tel: 0212-317 0100, Eski Büyükdere Caddesi, Tekfen Towers No: 209/18, 4.Levent

Dresdner Bank: Tel: 0212-252 6684, İnönü Caddesi No: 70, Tumsah Han Kat:5, Daire: 12, Gümüşsuyu

HSBC: Tel: 444 0111, www.hsbc.com.tr, Ayazağa Mahallesi, Ahi Evren Caddesi, Dereboyu Sokak, Maslak

ING Bank: Tel: 0212-258 8770, Spor Caddesi, BJK Plaza, B Blok No: 92, Akaretler, Beşiktaş

Rabobank: Tel: 0212-326 7200, Spor Caddesi, Akaretler Sıraevler, Beşiktaş

Société Generale: Tel: 0212-282 1942, Nispetiye Caddesi, Akmerkez Shopping Mall, E-3 Blok, Etiler

Westdeutsche Landsbank: Tel: 0212-339 2500, Fax: 0212-283 0460, Ebulula Mardin Caddesi, Mayapark Kule 2, Akatlar

INTERNATIONAL FOREIGN EXCHANGE BROKERS

Abbey International: Tel: 01534-885100, www.abbeyinternational.com, PO Box 545, Abbey House, 19-21 Commercial St, St Helier, Jersey JE4 8XG

Currencies Direct: Tel: 0207-813 0332, www.currenciesdirect.com, Hanover House, 73/4 High Holborn, London WC1V 6LR

HIFX: Tel: 01753-859159, www.hifx.co.uk, Morgan House, Madeira Walk, Windsor SL4 1EP, UK; Tel: 001-415 678 2770, www.hifx.com, 250 Montgomery St, Suite 910, San Francisco, USA; Tel: 0061-2-9251 2626, www.hifx.com.au, Level 26, Maritime Trade Towers, 201 Kent St, Sydney, Australia; Tel: 0064-9-306 3707, www.hifx.co.nz, Level 15, Gen-I Tower, 66 Wyndham St, Auckland, New Zealand

TURKISH BANKS

Most bank websites have English versions.

Istanbul

Akbank: Tel: 0212-270 0044, www.akbank.com.tr, Sabancı Centre, 4.Levent

Denizbank: Tel: 444 0800, www.denizbank.com.tr, Levent Caddesi No: 17, 1.Levent

Dışbank: Tel: 444 0144, www.disbank.com.tr, Yıldız Posta Caddesi No: 54, Gayrettepe

Finansbank: Tel: 444 0900, www.finansbank.com.tr, Büyükdere Caddesi No: 129, Mecidiyeköy

Fortis: Tel: 0212-274 4280, www.fortis.com.tr, Yıldız Posta Caddesi No: 54, Gayrettepe

Garanti Bankası: Tel: 444 0333, www.garantibank.com, Büyükdere Caddesi No: 65, Maslak,

Halkbank: Tel: 444 0400, www.halkbank.com.tr, Mecidiyeköy

Koçbank: Tel: 0212-274 7777, www.kocbank.com.tr, Barbaros Bulvarı, Morbasan Sokak, Koza İş Merkezi C Blok, Balmumcu, Beşiktaş

MNG Bank: Tel: 444-0664, www.mngbank.com.tr, Cumhuriyet Caddesi No: 139, Elmadağ

Oyakbank: Tel: 444 0600, www.oyakbank.com.tr, Eski Büyükdere Caddesi, Ayazağa Köyyolu No: 6, Maslak

Şekerbank: Tel: 444-7878, www.sekerbank.com.tr, Büyükdere Caddesi No: 171, Metrocity İş Merkezi, A Blok, 1.Levent

T.C. Ziraat Bankası: Tel: 0212-285 0408, www.ziraat.com.tr, Eski Büyükdere Caddesi No: 43, Blok 4, 1.Levent

Türk Ekonomi Bankası (TEB): Tel: 444 0666, www.teb.com.tr, Meclis-i Mebusan Caddesi No: 35, Koçan, Fındıklı

Türk Ticaret Bankası: Tel: 0212-511 4040, www.turkbank.com.tr, Yalıköşkü Caddesi No: 36, Eminönü

Türkiye İş Bankası: Tel: 0212-316 0000, www.isbank.com.tr, İş Kuleleri, Büyükdere Caddesi, 4.Levent

Vakıfbank: Tel: 0212-316 7116, www.vakifbank.com.tr, Çamlık Caddesi, Çayır Çimen Sokak No: 2, 1.Levent

Yapı Kredi Bankası: Tel: 0212-281 6804, www.yapikredi.com.tr, D Blok, Yapı Kredi Plaza, Büyükdere Caddesi, Levent

Ankara

TC Merkez Bankası (Turkish Central Bank): Tel: 0312-310 3646, www.tcmb.gov.tr, İstiklal Caddesi No: 10, Ulus

APPENDIX VII:

SHOPPING MALLS, SUPERMARKETS & OTHER SHOPS

Time Out publishes an excellent *Alışveriş Rehberi* (Shopping Guide) but unfortunately only in Turkish. Otherwise, *The Guide,* in its various local guises, is great for keeping up on what new shops have opened.

CONSUMER'S ASSOCIATION

Association for the Protection of the Consumer (Tüketiciyi Koruma Derneği - TÜKOD-ER): Tel: 0216-349 8510, www.tukoder.org.tr, Osmanağa Mahallesi, Yoğurtçu Şükrü Sokak, Nüfus İdaresi üstü No: 53/2, Kadıköy, Istanbul

ART SUPPLIES

Mektup: Tel: 0212-244 1813, Yenicarşı Caddesi No: 26/A, Galatasaray, Istanbul

BEAUTY PRODUCTS
Istanbul
Body Shop: Tel: 0212-249 8437, www.shaya.com.tr, İstiklal Caddesi No: 109; Tel: 0212-282 0401, Akmerkez Shopping Mall; Tel: 0212-344 0442, Metrocity Shopping Mall; Tel: 0216-428 7571, Tepe Nautilus Shopping Mall

Debenham's: Tel: 0212-380 1198, Cevahir Shopping Mall

Defne: Tel: 0212-245 7593, Asmalı Mescit Mahallesi, Sofyalı Sokak No: 4/B, Tünel. Natural products including a range of soaps.

Douglas: Tel: 0212-353 0400, Kanyon Shopping Mall

Golden Rose: Tel: 0212-251 7662, İstiklal Caddesi No: 311, Mısır Apt, Beyoğlu

Transmed: Tel: 0212-281 1300, www.transmed.com.tr, Fulyalı Sokak No: 7, İç Levent

Ankara
Body Shop: Armada Shopping Mall; Karum Shopping Mall

Izmir
Body Shop: Konak Pier Shopping Mall; Alsancak

BICYCLES
Istanbul
Aslı: Tel: 0212-527 3563, Hamidiye Caddesi, Eski Duyunu Sokak No: 2/2, Sirkeci

Bahar Hırdavat: Tel: 0212-244 4715, Yüksek Kaldırım, Galip Dede Caddesi No: 181, Karaköy

Haşim İşcan Alt Geçidi: Unkapanı. Row of bike shops under arches of Aqueduct of Valens. Also bike parts and repairs.

Pedal Sportif: Tel: 0212-511 0154, Mimar Kemalettin Caddesi, Sirkeci

Taz Ticaret: Tel: 0216-337 4966, Altıyol, Yakuztürk Caddesi No: 33, Kadıköy

Ankara
Delta Bike: Tel: 0312-223 6027, 9.Sokak No: 4, Bahçelievler

Ürgüp
Yağmur: Tel: 0384-341 5878, Yeni Sanayı Sitesi, Tanriver İş Merkezi No: 25. Bikes, bike parts and repairs.

BOOKSHOPS

Istanbul

Ada: Tel: 0212-251 3878, İstiklal Caddesi No: 330, Beyoğlu

Arkeoloji ve Sanat Kitabevi: Tel: 0212-293 0378, Yeniçarşı Caddesi, Petek Han No: 32/A, Beyoğlu. Specialist archaeology and art bookshop.

Aypa: Tel: 0212-516 0100, Mimar Mehmet Ağa Caddesi No: 19

Bookstore: Tel: 0212-516 3366, Divanyolu Caddesi No: 11, Sultanahmet. Sells wide range of books on Turkey and Middle East in English.

Bookworm's LC: Tel: 0212-287 5155, Yaprak Sokak No: 11. Etiler. Good range of English-language books and puzzles for children.

D&R: Tel: 0212-244 5361, www.dr.com.tr, İstiklal Caddesi No: 131-33, Beyoğlu; Tel: 0216-467 5413, Erenköy; Tel: 0212-263 2914, Etiler; 0212-224 2415, Nişantaşı; Tel: 0216-387 8551, Kartal; Tel: 0212-216 4380, Profilo Shopping Mall; Tel: 0212-353 0870, Kanyon Shopping Mall; Tel: 0212-380 0583, Cevahir Shopping Mall

Dünya Aktüel Kitabevi: Tel: 0216-347 7906, Kadıköy; Tel: 0212-265 7103, Bebek; Tel: 0216-391 1880, Capital Shopping Mall; Tel: 0212-513 5079, Cağoğlu; Tel: 0212-233 0094, Hilton Hotel; Tel: 0212-259 0226, Swissotel The Bosphorus, Bayıldım Caddesi No: 2, Maçka

Galeri Kayseri: Tel: 0212-512 0456, Divan Yolu No: 58, Sultanahmet. Sells wide range of books on Turkey and Middle East in English.

Gözlem Kitabevi: Tel: 0212-292 5616, Karaköy Meydanı, Perçemli Sokak, Karaköy. Books on Jewish topics, including children's books in Turkish and Hebrew.

Greenhouse: Tel: 0216-449 3034, Caferağa Mahallesi, Dumlupınar Sokak No: 17, Kadıköy.

Homer Kitabevi: Tel: 0212-249 5902, www.homerbooks.com, Yeniçarşı Caddesi No: 28/A, Galatasaray, Beyoğlu.

Istanbul Kitapçısı: Tel: 0212-292 7692; İstiklal Caddesi No: 379, Beyoğlu. Specialises in books, guidebooks, maps and prints of Istanbul.

Kitap+evi: Tel: 0212-263 7676, Hamam Sokak, Bebek

Mavi Kum Kitap: Tel: 0212-251 4440, Cihangir Caddesi No: 13, Cihangir, Beyoğlu

Megavizyon: Tel: 0212-251 0323, İstiklal Caddesi No: 79-81, Beyoğlu

Mira Publishing: Tel 0212-245 5810, www.mirapublishing.com, Beyoğlu.

Pandora: Tel: 0212-230 0962, www.pandora.com.tr, Büyükparmakkapı Sokak No: 3, Beyoğlu.

Remzi Kitabevi: Tel: 0212-234 5475, www.remzi.com.tr, Rumeli Caddesi No: 44, Nişantaşı; Tel: 0212-282 2575, Akmerkez Shopping Mall; Tel: 0216-448 0373, Carrefour; Tel: 0212-352 3355, Mayadrom Shopping Mall; Tel: 0212-217 1225, Profilo Shopping Mall; Tel: 0216-361 9071, Bağdat Caddesi No: 452, Suadiye; Tel: 0212-234 5475, Rumeli Caddesi No: 44, Nişantaşı; Tel: 0212-520 0052, Selvili Mescit Sokak No: 3, Cağaloğlu; Tel: 0212-353 0500, Kanyon Shopping Mall

Robinson Crusoe: Tel: 0212-293 6968, İstiklal Caddesi No: 389, Beyoğlu

Urbanitas: Tel: 0212-251 3960, Gümüşsuyu Caddesi No: 25, Gümüşsuyu

Yapı Kitabevi: Tel: 0212-219 3939, www.yapikitabevi.com, Cumhuriyet Caddesi No: 329, Harbiye. Specialist architectural bookshop.

Ankara

D&R: Tel: 0312-541 1541, Migros Shopping Mall; Tel: 0312-431 0333, Bayındır Sokak No: 24, Kızılay

Remzi Kitabevi: Tel: 0312-219 1112, Armada Shopping Mall

Dünya Kitabevi: Tel: 0312-467 1633, Tunalı Hilmi Caddesi No: 82/A-2, Kavaklıdere

Turhan Kitabevi: Tel: 0312-418 8259; Yüksel Caddesi No: 8/32, Kızılay

Izmir

Artı Kitabevi: Tel: 0232-421 2632; Cumhuriyet Bulvarı No: 142/B

Deniz Kitabevi: Tel: 0232-464 4080, Kıbrısşehitleri Caddesi No: 104/A, Alsancak

D&R: Tel: 0232-464 1015, Cumhuriyet Bulvarı, Pulcuoğlu Apt No: 209, Alsancak; Tel: 0232-279 0700, Agora Shopping Mall; Tel: 0232-343 3232, Erzene Mahallesi, 80.Sokak No: 22, Bornova; Tel: 0212-324 0683, EGS Park Shopping Mall

Elma Book House and Activity Centre: Tel: 0232-421 6496, www.iwaizmir.com, Plevne Building No: 19/G, Alsancak

Remzi Kitabevi: Tel: 0232-489 5325, Konak Pier

Antalya

D&R: Tel: 0242-316 7041, Gima Shopping Mall; Tel: 0242-230 1207, Migros Shopping Mall; Tel: 0242-323 8368, White World City, Kat: 1, Demircikara Mahallesi

Remzi Kitabevi: Tel: 0242-323 4582, Lara Shopping Mall

Bodrum

D&R: Tel: 0252-313 7362, Milta Bodrum Marina

Bursa

D&R: Tel: 0224-225 2131, Zafer Plaza Shopping Mall

Fethiye

D&R: Tel: 0252-614 8360, Hillside Beach Club

Imagine: Tel: 0252-614 8465, Atatürk Caddesi No: 18

Kuşadası

D&R: Tel: 0256-612 2984, www.dr.com.tr, Kuşadası Limanı Shopping Mall

Kuydaş: Tel: 0256-614 1828; İsmet İnönü Bulvarı No: 8/B

Marmaris

D&R: Tel: 0252-413 5706, Gima Shopping Mall

Selçuk

Eser Kitabevi: Tel 0256-612 1765, Camekebir Mahallesi, Kemal Ankan Caddesi (Küçük Tansaş Sokağı), Gursoy Pasajı, Zemin Kat: No: 5

BOOKS IN FRENCH

Istanbul

Efy Kitabevi: Tel: 0212-251 4223, Yeniçarşı Caddesi, Ferat Sokak No: 33/1, Kat: 1, Beyoğlu; French Consulate, İstiklal Caddesi No: 8, Beyoğlu; Tel: 0212-251 0177, İstiklal Caddesi, Emin Nevruz Çıkmazı No: 18, Beyoğlu

BOOKS IN GERMAN

Istanbul

Türk-Alman Kitabevi: Tel: 0212-293 7731, www.tak.com.tr, İstiklal Caddesi No: 481, Beyoğlu; Tel: 0216-550 0292, Bahariye Caddesi, Nevzemin Sokak No: 6/2, Kadıköy

BOOK EXCHANGES

Istanbul

Natural Foreign Book Exchange: Tel: 0212-517 0384, Akbıyık Caddesi No: 31

Ebru: Şeyh Bender Sokak 18, Asmalımescit, Tünel. Free book exchange, open 5pm to 7pm Monday to Friday.

SECOND-HAND BOOKS

Istanbul

Sahhaf: Tel: 0212-528 8951, Ticarethane Sokak No: 67, Cağaloğlu

Antalya

Owl Bookshop: Barbaros Mahallesi, Akarçeşme Sokak No: 21, Kaleiçi. Open 10am to 1pm and 3pm to 7pm Monday to Saturday. One of Turkey's best second-hand bookshops.

Fethiye

Fethiye Sahaf: Tel: 0537-622 6000, Kordon Boyu, Cafe Geniş yanı

Göreme

Sultan Carpet Shop: Second-hand books in English and other foreign languages as well as some new *Lonely Planet* guidebooks.

CDs &TAPES

Istanbul

Harem: Tel: 0212-519 7950, Divan Yolu Caddesi No: 40, Sultanahmet. Turkish CDs and tapes.

Lale Plak: Galip Dede Caddesi No: 1, Beyoğlu. Turkish CDs and tapes.

Megavizyon: Tel: 0212-251 0323, İstiklal Caddesi No: 79-81, Beyoğlu. Sells Naxos classical music CDs.

www.kalan.com: Website selling wide range of old, new and hard-to-find Turkish music.

CHRISTMAS PRODUCTS

See also Greetings Cards below.

DECORATIONS

Istanbul

Hobby Dekorasyon: Tel: 0212-240 7575, Kurtuluş Caddesi No: 50, Pangaltı. Armenian-owned shop with great selection of imported Christmas decorations.

WRAPPING PAPER

Istanbul

Tahtakale (see box p. 288) is the best place to look for pretty, cheap wrapping paper and other packaging.

Deli Kızın Yeri: Tel: 0212-511 1914, www.delikiz.com, Halıcılar Caddesi No: 42, Grand Bazaar

Dinar Kırtasiye: Tel: 0212-225 3938, Şahin Sokak No: 13/B, Kurtuluş

Haşet Kitabevi: Tel: 0536-518 1512, Mühürdar Caddesi, Akmar Pasajı No: 71/2, Kadıköy

Nezih: Tel: 0216-414 3973, Mühürdar Caddesi No: 40, Kadıköy; Tel: 0212-282 1640, Akmerkez Shopping Mall; Tel: 0216-302 3201, Bağdat Caddesi No: 378, Şaşkınbakkal

UNESCO: Tel: 0212-252 5222, Yeniçarşı Caddesi No: 54/1, Galatasaray

Üniversite Kitabevi: Tel: 0216-347 7366, Mühürdar Caddesi No: 44, Kadıköy.

CLOTHES

FOREIGN LABELS

Istanbul

Benetton: Tel: 0212-230 8494, www.benetton.com.tr, Valikonağı Caddesi No: 28, Nişantaşı; Tel: 0212-293 4716, İstiklal Caddesi, Beyoğlu; Tel: 0212-282 0237, Akmerkez Shopping Mall

Burberry: Tel: 0216-445 5530, Bağdat Caddesi No: 495, Suadiye

Diesel: Tel: 0212-282 0752, Akmerkez Shopping Mall

Dorothy Perkins: Tel: 0212-380 0154, Cevahir Shopping Mall

Evans: Tel: 0212-344 0444, Metrocity Shopping Mall. Clothes for the larger woman.

Laura Ashley: Tel: 0212-227 6078, Teşvikiye Caddesi, İkbal İş Merkezi No: 103/2, Teşvikiye; Tel: 0216-363 7536, Bağdat Caddesi, Erenköy

Mango: Tel; 0212-282 2223, Akmerkez Shopping Mall; Tel; 0212-660 1333, Carousel Shopping Mall; Tel: 0216-651 3563, Capitol Shopping Mall; Tel: 0216-369 5811, Bağdat Caddesi, Şaşkinbakkal

Marks & Spencer: Tel: 0212-282 0602, Akmerkez Shopping Mall; Tel: 0212-344 0170, Metrocity Shopping Mall; Tel: 0212-219 6658, Abdi İpekçi Caddesi No: 2, Nişantaşı; Tel: 0216-360 8424, Bağdat Caddesi No: 401, Şaşkınbakkal; Tel: 0212-542 8360, Carousel Shopping Mall; Tel: 0212-356 2554, Profilo Shopping Mall; Tel: 0216-333 2648, Capitol Shopping Mall; Tel: 0212-679 4239, Olivium Outlet Centre

Next: Tel: 0212-353- 0616, Kanyon Shoppıng Mall

Peacocks: Tel: 0212-380 0221, Cevahir Shopping Mall

Polo Garage: Tel: 0212-280 8997, Harmancı Sokak, Polo Plaza No: 3, Levent; Tel: 0212-231 5182, Nişantaşı

Polo Ralph Lauren: Tel: 0212-282 0169, Akmerkez Shopping Mall

Quiksilver: Tel: 0212-661 2173, Galleria Shopping Mall; Tel: 0216-360 6393, Bağdat Caddesi No: 371/1, Erenköy; Tel: 0212-281 6972, Eski Büyükdere Caddesi No: 29, 4.Levent

River Island: Tel: 0212-380 1230, Cevahir Shopping Mall

Tommy Hilfiger: Tel: 0212-282 2626, Akmerkez Shopping Mall

Top Shop/Top Man: Tel: 0212-243 0177, İstiklal Caddesi, Beyoğlu; Tel 0212-380 0161, Cevahir Shopping Mall

Zara: Tel: 0212-228 1882, Akmerkez Shopping Mall; Tel: 0216-362 1303, Bağdat Caddesi No: 432, Suadiye

Ankara

Benetton: Tel: 0312-425 5716 Atatürk Bulvarı No: 135, Bakanlıklar; Tel: 0312-468 9465, Karum Shopping Mall; Tel: 0312-427 1027 Tunalı Hilmi Caddesi No: 108, Kavaklıdere; Tel: 0312-541 1327, Migros Shopping Mall

Burberry's: Tel: 0312-426 8390, Karum Shopping Mall; Tel: 0312-447 1178, Uğur Mumcu Caddesi No: 29, Gaziosmanpaşa

Calvin Klein: Tel: 0312-466 1071, Karum Shopping Mall

Laura Ashley: Tel: 0312-428 8432, İran Caddesi No: 2/A, Kavaklıdere

Lee Cooper: Tel: 0312-467 3645, Karum Shopping Mall

Levi's: Tel: 0312-468 5003, Karum Shopping Mall

Mango: Tel: 0312-467 6763, Tunal Hilmi Caddesi, Kavaklıdere; Tel: 0312-541 1980, Gimat Shopping Mall

Marks & Spencer: Tel: 0312-426 9938, Tunalı Hilmi Caddesi No: 103, Kavaklıdere; Tel: 0312-266 1762, Bilkent Shopping Mall

Polo: 0312-426 8234, Karum Shopping Mall

Polo Garage: Tel: 0312-541 1414, Migros Shopping Mall

Zara: Tel: 0312-419 8001, Atatürk Bulvarı No: 139; Tel: 0312-426 3926, Karum Shopping Mall

Izmir

Laura Ashley: Tel: 0232-324 3747, Carrefour Shopping Mall

Mango: Tel: 0232-421 5868, Mustafa Bey Caddesi

Marks & Spencer: Tel: 0232-386 5032, Kipa Shopping Mall; Tel: 0232-277 4495, Agora Shopping Mall; Tel: 0232-324 0311, Carrefour Ticaret Merkezi, Yalı Mahallesi, 6522. Sokak, Karşıyaka

Top Shop/Top Man: Tel 0232-464 6302, Alsancak

Zara: Tel: 0232-463 4477, Mustafabey Caddesi, Alsancak

Adana

Mango: Tel: 0322-256 5396, Carrefour

Marks & Spencer: Tel: 0322-271 0463, M1 Real Shopping Mall

Zara: Tel: 0322-271 0131, CC Tepe Shopping Mall

Alanya

Benetton: Tel: 0242-511 9084, Eczacılar Caddesi No: 8

Antalya

Adidas: Tel: 0242-230 1540, Migros Shopping Mall

Benetton: Tel: 0242-243 5331, Atatürk Caddesi No: 11/A; Tel: 0242-230 1051, Migros Shopping Mall

Mango: Tel: 0242-230 1212, Migros Shopping Mall

Laura Ashley: Tel: 0242-230 1521, Migros Shopping Mall

Marks & Spencer: Tel: 0242-316 7290, G-Mall Shopping Mall

Naf Naf: Tel: 0242-243 7998, Cumhuriyet Caddesi No: 35

Polo Garage: Tel: 0242-243 2196, Konyaaltı Caddesi No: 46; Tel: 0242-230 1369, Migros Shopping Mall

Puma-Quiksilver: Tel: 0242-238 1133, Beach Park, Gençlik Meydanı No: 56

Reebok: Tel: 0242-230 1405, Migros Shopping Mall

Tommy Hilfiger: Tel: 0242-230 1030, Migros Shopping Mall

Zara: Tel: 0242-230 1330, Migros Shopping Mall

Bodrum & Around

Diesel: Tel: 0252-313 2660, Milta Bodrum Marina

Emporio Armani: Tel: 0252-382 3654, D-Marin Turgutreis Marina

Hermes: Tel: 0252-316 3652, Kale Caddesi Nos: 46-48

Lacoste: Tel: 0252-316 1015, Kale Caddesi No: 20

Levi's: Tel: 0252-317 1199, Oasis Shopping Mall

Marks & Spencer: Tel: 0252-313 7640, Neyzen Tevfik Caddesi No: 204; Tel: 0252-317 1656 Oasis Shopping Mall

Polo Garage: Tel: 0252-317 0069, Oasis Shopping Mall

Reebok: Tel: 0252-382 8231, D-Marin Turgutreis Marina

Tommy Hilfiger: Tel: 0252-313 3741, Milta Bodrum Marina

Bursa

Evans: Tel: 0224-451 3200, Carrefour Shopping Mall

Mango: Tel: 0224-225 4400, Zafer Plaza Shopping Mall

Marks & Spencer: Tel: 0224-261 2464, Asmerkez Shopping Mall

Fethiye & Around

Quiksilver: Tel: 0252-612 6527

Kayseri

Mango: Armonium Shopping Mall, Esref Bitlis Bulvarı No: 12/A

Konya

Marks & Spencer: Tel: 0332-233 1909, Kulesite Shopping Mall

Marmaris

Quiksilver: Tel: 0252-413 1949, Kordon Caddesi No: 8

Side

Quiksilver: Tel: 0242-753 3106, Liman Caddesi

MATERNITY AND CHILDREN'S CLOTHES

Istanbul

Çilek: Tel 0212-211 6791, Profilo Shopping Mall; Tel: 0216-414 5584, Serasker Caddesi No: 95, Kadıköy

Chicco: Tel: 0212-224 6015, Nişantaşı; Tel: 0212-282 0704, Akmerkez Shopping Mall; Tel: 0216-380 5704, Bağdat Caddesi No: 418, Suadiye

Gebe: Tel: 0212-284 6383, İş Kuleleri, 4.Levent

Mom-To-Be: Tel: 0212-291 7474, Valıkonağı Caddesi, Akkavak Sokak No: 2/2, Nişantaşı; Tel 0216-386 8056, Kanyon Shopping Mall

Mothercare: Tel: 0212-233 3101, Rumeli Caddesi, Nişantaşı; Tel: 0216-302 9617, Kazım Özalp Sokak No: 26, Saşkınbakkal; Tel: 0212-570 4523, Carousel Shopping Mall; Tel: 0212-661 3965, Galleria Shopping Mall

Peros: Tel: 0212-232 2127, Rumeli Caddesi, Nişantaşı; also in Bağdat Caddesi, Etiler and Üsküdar.

Sesen: Tel: 022-296 8340, www.secen.com.tr, Rumeli Caddesi, Byrak Apt No: 33, Kat: 1, Nişantaşı

Studio Kids: Tel: 0212-240 4655, Şair Nigar Sokak No: 3-1, Nişantaşı. Warner Brothers-themed clothing for children.

Ankara

Çilek: Tel 0312-437 1250, Uğur Mumcu Caddesi No: 80/B, Köroğlu, Gaziosmanpaşa

Chicco: Tel: 0312-427 7220, Karum Shopping Mall

Mom-To-Be: Tel: 0312-428 6191, Tunalı Hilmi Caddesi, Binnaz Sokak 3/A, Kavaklıdere

Mothercare: Tel: 0312-428 8523, İran Caddesi No: 2/A, Kavaklıdere

Izmir

Çilek: Tel 0232-422 4212, Cumhuriyet Bulvarı No: 140/A, Alsancak

Mothercare: Tel: 0232-465 1636, 1386.Sokak 8/B, Alsancak; Tel: 0232-465 1636, Carrefour Shopping Mall, Karşıyaka

Adana

Çilek: Tel 0322-232 9986, Turgut Özal Bulvarı No: 145, Kemal Akdoğan Sitesi, A Blok, Seyhan

Mothercare: Tel: 0322-459 0924, Ramazanoğlu Caddesi, Nimet Sokak No: 13/3, Kurtuluş

Antalya

Çilek: Tel 0242-228 9816, Öğretmenevleri Mahallesi, Atatürk Bulvarı, Haci İbrahim Okur Apt, 899 Sokak No: 1/1, Konyaalti

Mothercare: Tel: 0242-230 1520, Migros Shopping Mall

Bodrum

Chicco: Tel: 0252-317 0085, Oasis Shopping Mall

Bursa

Çilek: Tel 0224-220 3636, Atatürk Caddesi No: 99/A

Mothercare: Tel: 0224-223 3206, Zafer Plaza Shopping Mall

TURKISH LABELS

Istanbul

Abbate: Tel: 0212-570 0971, Carousel Shopping Mall; Tel: 0216-651 1951, Capitol Shopping Mall; Tel: 0216-355 1672, Bağdat Caddesi, Bicener Pasajı No: 381/32-3, Şaşkınbakkal

Beymen: Tel: 0212-282 0380, Akmerkez Shopping Mall; Tel: 0216-467 1845, Bağdat Caddesi, Suadiye; Tel: 0212-343 0404, Abdi İpekçi Caddesi No: 23/1, Nişantaşı; Tel: 0212-559 3250, Galleria Shopping Mall

Collezione: Tel: 0212-292 4338, İstiklal Caddesi Nos: 73-5, Beyoğlu; Tel: 0212-245 7262, Odakule, İstiklal Caddesi 284-6, Beyoğlu; Tel: 0212-225 9168, Halaskargazi Caddesi 341, Şişli; Tel: 0212-560 4836, Galleria Shopping Mall; Tel: 0212-259 5758, Ortabahçe Caddesi, Sinan Paşa Mahallesi, Köşe Han No: 55/1, Beşiktaş

Gömlekci Hüseyin: Tel: 0212-233 8428, www.gomlekcihuseyin.com, Valikonagı Caddesi No: 70, Nişantaşı

Mavi Jeans: Tel: 0212-249 3758, www.mavijeans.com, İstiklal Caddesi No: 117, Beyoğlu; Tel: 0212-282 0424 Akmerkez Shopping Mall

Milimetric: Tel 0212-224 7850, www.milimetric.com, Metrocity Shopping Mall. Designer shirts and ties for men.

Vakko: Tel: 0212-224 3152, Abdi İpekçi Caddesi 38, Nişantaşı

Vakkorama: Tel: 0212-282 0695, www.vakkorama.com.tr, Akmerkez Shopping Mall; Tel: 0212-282 0965, Carousel Shopping Mall; Tel: 0212-661 5942, Galleria Shopping Mall; Tel: 0216-416 4204, Bağdat Caddesi No: 422, Suadiye

Zeki Triko: Tel: 0212-233 8279, www.zekitriko.com.tr, Akkavak Sokak No: 47/2, off Valikonağı Caddesi, Nişantaşı

Ankara

Abbate: Tel: 0312-419 8960, Atatürk Bulvarı No: 92/A, Kızılay

Beymen: 0312-468 1242, İran Caddesi No: 7, Kavaklıdere

Collezione: Tel: 0312-418 9180, Atatürk Bulvarı No: 80/2, Kızılay; Tel: 0312-541 1093, Migros Shopping Mall; Tel: 0312-419 6573, Meşrutiyet Caddesi No: 15/33, Çankaya; Tel: 0312-427 2350, Tunalı Hilmi Caddesi No: 111/143-5, Kavaklıdere

Mavi Jeans: Tel: 0312-419 8453, Atatürk Bulvarı, Ragıp Devres İş Hanı No: 74/B, Yenişehir

Vakko: Tel: 0312-468 3505, Karum Shopping Mall; Tel: 0312-427 1879, Tunalı Hilmi Caddesi, Odeka İş Merkezi No: 65/20, Kavaklıdere; Tel: 0312-541 1537, Migros Shopping Mall; Tel: 0312-266 6701, Bilkent Shopping Mall

Izmir

Abbate: Tel: 0232-464 4169, Alsancak

Collezione: Tel: 0232-464 9882, Kıbrısşehitleri Caddesi No: 47/A, Alsancak; Tel: 0232-343 4213, Fevzi Çakmak Caddesi No: 12/A, Bornova; Tel: 0232-425 6910, Fevzi Paşa Bulvarı No: 152/C, Çankaya; Tel: 0232-445 9070, Anafartalar Caddesi Nos: 59-61, Konak

Mavi Jeans: Tel: 0232-463 1539, 1382 Sokak No: 14/A, Alsancak

Vakko: Tel: 0232-421 6590, Plevne Bulvarı No: 17, Alsancak; Tel: 0232-324 4280, EGS Park Shopping Mall, 2040 Sokak No: 104/137 Kat: 1, Mavişehir

Adana

Collezione: Tel: 0322-363 4082, Çakmak Caddesi No: 109/1, Çakmak; Tel: 0322-271 0354, M1 Tepe Shopping Mall, Zencirli Bağlar Mevkii, Öğretmenler Bulvarı, Seyhan

Mavi Jeans: Tel: 0322-256 3106, Carrefour Shopping Mall, Kireçocağı Köyü Nos: B35-36

Vakko: Tel: 0322-453 3052, Kurtuluş Mahallesi, Mithat Saraçoğlu, Lütfiye Hanım Sokağı No: 7/A

Alanya

Beymen: Tel: 0242-513 1050, Atatürk Caddesi No: 22/A

Antalya

Vakkorama: Tel: 0242-230 1500, Migros Shopping Mall

Bodrum & Around

Abbate: Tel: 0252-317 0154, Oasis Shopping Mall

Beymen Club: Tel: 0252- 317 1425, Oasis Shopping Mall

Mavi Jeans: Tel: 0252-313 6217, Milta Bodrum Marina; Tel: 0252-382 8384, D-Marin Turgutreis Marina

Bursa

Abbate: Tel: 0224-452 6210, Carrefour Shopping Mall

Collezione: Tel: 0224, Hocatabip Mahallesi, Ünlü Caddesi No: 5, Heykel; Tel: 0224-220 3858, Altıparmak Caddesi No: 35/B, Altıparmak; Tel: 0224-451 3937, Carrefour Shopping Mall, Odunluk Mahallesi, Nilüfer

Vakko: Tel: 0224-233 3377, Çekirge Caddesi, İntam/101; Tel: 0224- 225 4395, Zafer Plaza Shopping Mall

COMPUTERS

Istanbul

Aidata: Tel: 0212-249 8149, www.aidata.com.tr, Ada Han, Kemeraltı Caddesi No: 87, Karaköy

Apple Center: Tel: 0212-353 0460, www.troyapplecenter.com, Kanyon Shopping Mall; Tel: 0212-232 7204, www.artiapplecenter.com, Abide-i Hürriyet Caddesi No: 168/B, Şişli

Arena Aş: Tel: 0212-364 6464, www.arena.com.tr, Istanbul Caddesi No: 90, Kemerburgaz. Compaq agent.

Bilkom: Tel: 0216-522 1400, www.bilkom.com.tr, Libadiye Caddesi, Yavuz Sokak No: 1, Daire: 1-4, Küçükçamlıca. Apple agent.

IBM: Tel: 0212-517 1000, www.ibm.com, Büyükdere Caddesi, Yapı Kredi Plaza, B Blok, Levent

Megavizyon: Tel: 0212-251 0323, İstiklal Caddesi No: 79-81, Beyoğlu. Apple product retailer.

Segment: Tel: 0212-266 6290, www.segment.com.tr, Dereboyu Caddesi No: 65, Mecidiyeköy. Sells English-language keyboards for around $4 each.

Tekno: Tel: 0212-444 0078, www.teknosa.com, Metrocity Shopping Mall, Büyükdere Caddesi, Levent; Osmanlı Sokak No: 13, Taksim, Tel: 0212- Kanyon Shopping Mall

Vatan: Tel: 0212-234 4800, www.vatanbilgisayar.com, Cumhuriyet Caddesi No: 75, Elmadağ; Tel: 0216-469 2454, Ankara Asfaltı, Yeşilvadi Sokak No: 1, Bostancı; Tel: 0212-665 5656, E5 Karayolu, Güney Yan Yol, Merkez Efendi Mahallesi, Tercüman Sitesi, Çarşı Binası, Topkapı. Hewlett Packard and Acer dealer.

Ankara

Arena Aş: Tel: 0312-472 7777, Çetin Emeç Bulvarı, 2.Cadde No: 36/A, Öveçler

Izmir

Arena Aş: Tel: 0232-441 8081, Gaziosmanpaşa Bulvarı, Süreyya Reyent İş Hanı No: 30/205-9, Çankaya

DUTY-FREE SHOPPING

Global Refund Turkey Office: Tel: 0212-232 1121, www.globalrefund.com; Ferah Sokak No: 19/A-1, Teşvikiye, İstanbul

Global Refund UK Office: Tel: 0208-222 0101, Fax: 0208-222 0102, 15 Galena Rd, London W6 0LT

CASH REFUND POINTS IN TURKEY

Ankara

Esenboğa Airport: Türkiye İş Bankası, open: 24/7

Antalya

Antalya Bayındır Airport: Cash Refund Office, open: 24/7; Post office, open: 24/7

Bodrum

Milas Airport: Türkiye İş Bankası, open: 9am to 12.30pm and 1.30pm to 5.30pm
Seaport: Cash Refund Office, open: 8am to 8pm

Dalaman

International Airport: Türkiye İş Bankası, open: 9am to 12.30pm and 1.30pm to 5.30pm

Dereköy

Border Crossing: Post office, open: 8am to 5.30pm

İpsala

Border Crossing: Post office, open: 8am to 5.30pm

Istanbul

Atatürk Airport: Türkiye İş Bankası, open: 24/7; Cash Refund Office, open: 24/7
Sahiba Gökçen Airport: Türkiye İş Bankası, open: 9am to 12.30pm and 1.30pm to 5.30pm Monday to Friday.
Karaköy Harbour: Türkiye İş Bankası, open: 9am to 12.30pm and 1.30pm to 5.30pm

Kapıkule

Border Crossing: Post office, open: 8am to 5.30pm

Kuşadası

Seaport: Türkiye İş Bankası, open: 9am to 12.30pm and 1.30pm to 5.30pm

Trabzon
Seaport: Karden Turizm, open: 9am to 12.30pm and 1.30pm to 5.30pm

ELECTRICAL GOODS
Istanbul
Doğubank İşhanı: Tel: 0212-526 4313, www.dogubank-ishani.gen.tr, Hamidiye Caddesi No: 30, Sirkeci, Istanbul. Busy multi-storey building selling all sorts of white goods, plus cameras, DVDs etc, for good prices. Bring cash and prepare to barter hard.

Izmir
Çankaya Elektronik Çarşısı: Smaller version of Istanbul's Doğubank. Surrounding streets also full of electrical shops.

DIY MATERIALS
Istanbul
Bauhaus: Tel: 0212-640 7141, www.bauhaus.com.tr, Altıntepe Mahallesi, Esenler Otogar karşısı, Bayrampaşa; Tel: 0216-578 7070, Eski Genoto Arsası, Kozyatağı, İçerenköy; Tel: 0212-852 4775, Haramidere Mahallesi, Tatilya yanı, Beylikdüzü. All in Istanbul. Open 8.30am to 10pm daily.

Koçtaş: Tel: 0212-315 9600, Cevahir Shopping Mall; Tel: 0212-454 6900, Fevzi Çakmak Mahallesi, Yıldırım Beyazıt Caddesi No: 1, Yenibosna, Bahçelievler; Tel: 0216-389 0000, Turgut Özal Bulvarı, Kartal Sahil Yolu, Kartal

Praktiker: Tel: 0212-602 0959, Koçman Caddesi 32, Bağcılar; Tel: 02126-451 0101, Kartal; Tel: 0216-451 0102, Ümraniye. Open 10am to 10pm daily. Range of power and other tools.

Ankara
Koçtaş: Tel: 0312-303 4500, Gazi Mahallesi, Konya Devlet Yolu üzeri No: 2, Ankamall, Akköprü

Fethiye
Arı Tool Hire: Tel: 0252-613 4636, Çalış. Everything from ladders to power tools for DIYers.

Izmir
Koçtaş: Tel: 0232-462 2021, 3.Sanayi Sitesi, 296.Sokak No: 1/B, Bornova; Tel: 0232-278 4042, Mithatpaşa Caddesi No: 1454, Balçova

Antalya
Koçtaş: Tel: 0242-310 9100, Aspendos Bulvarı No: 112

Bodrum
Koçtaş: Tel: 0252-363 8280, Beylik Kırlar Mevkii, Konacık

Fethiye

Akarsu: Tel: 0252-646 8948, Çalıca, Karaçulha. Ready-painted tanks for solar panels.

Kuşadası

Koçtaş: Tel: 0256-614 4200, Söke Yolu, Kadinlar Denizi Mahallesi, Süleyman Demirel Bulvarı No: 28

FACTORY OUTLET CENTRES

Istanbul

Aymerkez: Tel: 0212-863 0591, E5 Karayolu, Büyükçeşme

Ayyıldız Swimwear: Tel: 0212-295 4700, Uğur Sokak No: 2, Kağıthane

Benetton: Tel: 0212-589 9412, Gazi Mustafa Paşa Bulvarı, Bulvar Pasajı No: 37, Aksaray

Beymen Outlet (BSSD): Tel: 0212-552 3200, Merkez Mahallesi, Değirmenbahçe Caddesi No: 34/2, Yenibosna

Colony Outlet Centre: Tel: 0212-580 4575, E5 Londra Asfaltı, Bağlar Caddesi, Sefaköy

Diesel Outlet: Tel: 0216-573 0269, Bostancı Kavsağı, Kartal Sokak No: 5, Bostancı

DKNY Outlet: Tel: 0212-230 6686, Bostan Sokak No: 4/1, Teşvikiye

Lacoste: Tel: 0212 654 4980, Çınar Caddesi, Kavak Sokak No: 39, Yenibosna

LC Waikiki: Tel: 0212-551 5654, Olivium Outlet Centre

Levi's Outlet: Tel: 0216-573 0269, Kartal Sokak No: 5, Bostancı

Mudo Outlet Centre: Tel: Misr Çarşısı No: 63, Eminönü; Tel: 0216-348 5700, General Asım Gündüz Caddesi No: 29/17, Kadıköy; Tel: 0212-273 0617, Meliha Avni Sözen Caddesi, Bahçeler Sokak No: 10, Mecidiyeköy

Olivium Oulet Centre: Tel: 0212-547 7453, Prof. Muammer Aksoy Caddesi, Zeytinburnu

Tommy Hilfiger: Tel: 0212-653 4939, Kavak Sokak No: 23, Yenibosna

Vakko: Tel: 0212-481 6300, Londra Asfaltı, Çırpıcı Mevkii, Merter; Tel: 0212-522 8941, Sultanahmet Caddesi No: 24, Bahçekapı

Ankara

Boyner Outlet: Tel: 0312-419 6071, Atatürk Bulvarı No: 74/B, Kızılay

Izmir

Boyner Outlet: Tel: 0232-386 5800, Kipa Shopping Mall

Hugo Boss Outlet: Tel: 0232-252 0995, Akçay Caddesi, Havaalanı Yolu, Gaziemir

Park Bornova Outlet Centre: Tel: 0232-373 9215, Ankara Asfaltı No: 192, Bornova

İzmit/Kocaeli

Izmit Outlet Centre: Tel: 0262-225 3170, Sefa Sirmen Bulvarı (Eski Gölcük Yolu). Includes Vakko outlet (Tel: 0262-335 3561)

GARDEN SUPPLIERS

For addresses of Koçtaş, see DIY Materials above.

Istanbul

Bauhaus: Tel: 0212-640 7141, www.bauhaus.com.tr, Altıntepe Mahallesi, Esenler Otogar karşısı, Bayrampaşa; Tel: 0216-578 7070, Eski Genoto Arsası, Kozyatağı, İçerenköy; Tel: 0212-852 4775, Haramidere Mahallesi, Tatilya yanı, Beylikdüzü.

English Gardens: Tel: 0216-413 4872, www.englishgardens.com.tr, Dedeoğlu Caddesi, No: 158/A, Çubuklu, Beykoz

Garden Life: Tel: 0216-373 6756, www.gardenlife.com.tr, Bağdat Caddesi, No: 503/1, Suadiye

Mudo Bahçe: Tel: 0212-290 6395, Giz 2000 Plaza, Eski Büyükdere Caddesi, No: 7, Maslak

Mısır Çarşısı: In market on Yeni Cami side of Egyptian bazaar you can buy packets of seeds and tulip, daffodil, crocus, narcissus and hyacinth bulbs.

Ankara

Garden Life: Tel: 0312-441 4723, Turan Güneş Bulvarı No: 74/A, Çankaya

Ulusoy Seed Company: Tel: 0312-615 5173, Konya Yolu, Oğulbeyköyü Mevkii, Gölbaşı. Supplies grass seed.

Antalya

Garden Life: Tel: 0242-312 6590, Perge Bulvarı No: 99

Kervan Çeyiz: Tel: 0242-230 1080, Migros Shopping Mall

The Garden Store: Tel: 0242-323 9333, Sinanoğlu Caddesi No: 41/1-2

Bodrum

Bodrum Garden Homes: Tel: 0252-317 0916, Oasis Shopping Mall

Fethiye

Mopa Mutfak Banyo: Tel: 0252-612 2882, Adnan Menderes Bulvarı No: 27/A. Stocks garden furniture.

Su Mobilya: Tel: 0252-612 9903, Baha Şıkman Caddesi No: 171/1, Taşyaka

GREETINGS CARDS

Istanbul

Megavizyon: Tel: 0212-251 0323, İstiklal Caddesi No: 79-81, Beyoğlu. Sells Hallmark greetings cards in Turkish and English.

UNICEF: Tel: 0212-252 5222, www.unicefturk.org, Yeniçarşı Hayriye Caddesi No: 18/3, Galatasaray, Istanbul. Available from shop or website.

Üniversite Kitabevi: Tel: 0216-347 7366, Mühürdar Caddesi No: 44, Kadıköy

A Handbook for Living in Turkey

Ankara

UNICEF: Tel: 0312-290 3110, Bilkent Merkez Kampüsü Lojmanlar No: 20/2, Bilkent. Open Tuesday and Thursday from 11.30am to 4pm.

MARBLE FOUNTAINS

Istanbul

Kamayor Taş Atolyesi: Tel: 0212-293 7791, Kuledibi Şahkapısı Sokak No: 22, Galata, Beyoğlu. Made-to-measure modern marble fountains and other marble pieces.

Taşçı: Tel: 0212-249 6751, Çukurcuma Caddesi, Camii Sokak No: 15, Firuzağa, Beyoğlu. Old fountains and hamam basins.

MUSICAL INSTRUMENTS

Istanbul

Galip Dede Caddesi near the Tünel in Beyoğlu is almost entirely devoted to the sale of musical instruments.

A&N Müzik: Tel: 0216-343 5529, Selamiali Mahallesi, Cumhuriyet Caddesi, Kader Pasajı No: 26/23, Üsküdar. Hand-made *kemençes* (three-stringed violins).

Turkish Cymbals: Tel: 0212-292 1886, Galip Dede Caddesi No: 69, Beyoğlu. Hand-made cymbals.

Turkish Music House: Tel: 0542-824 2212, Mayköşkü Caddesi, Küçük Sokak No: 3/3, Sultanahmet

Burdur

Mehmet Bedel: Tel:0248-233 8976. Hand-made recorders *(kaval)* and flutes *(sipsi)*.

ORGANIC FOOD

City Farm: Tel: 0212-286 4785, Büyükdere Caddesi No: 57/1, Maslak; Tel: 0212-351 5375, Mayadrom Shopping Mall; Tel: 0216-465 5728 Mihrişad Valide Sultan Caddesi No: 48/A, Anadolu Hisarı. Organic breads, cheese, oils etc.

English Gardens: Tel: 0216-413 4872, www.englishgardens.com.tr, Dedeoğlu Caddesi, No: 158/A, Çubuklu, Beykoz. Organic vegetable boxes.

PET SHOPS

See Appendix XIII below.

PICTURES & PAINTINGS

Istanbul

İlhami Atalay: Tel: 0212-520 1083, Divan Yolu, İneili Çavuş Sokak No: 29, Sultanahmet

Nusret Çolpan: Tel: 0532-416 9311, www.minyatur.org

PRESENTS
Istanbul

Anemira: Tel: 0212-526 7493, Zenneciler Sokak No: 25, Kapalı Çarşı. Real, expensive Indian pashminas as well as the cheaper Chinese imitations.

Atrium: Tel: 0212-251 4302, Tünel Geçidi No: 7, Beyoğlu

Aznavur Pasajı: İstiklal Caddesi No: 212, Beyoğlu

Cocoon: Tel: 0212-638 3330, www.cocoontr.com, Arasta Bazaar No: 93, Sultanahmet; Tel: 0212-638 6271, Küçükayasofya Caddesi No: 13, Sultanahmet. Wonderful carpets and textiles. Also lovely art goods made from felt.

Dösim: Tel: 0212-513 3134, Topkapı Sarayı; Tel: 0212-512 6689, Ayasofya Girişi; Tel: 0212-526 6813, Şeyhülislam Hayri Efendi Caddesi No: 2/1, Eminönü

Eller: Tel: 0212-249 2364, İstiklal Caddesi, Postacılar Soak No: 12, Beyoğlu

Gale: Tel: 0212-225 6989, Kurtuluş Caddesi Nos: 45-47B, Şişli. Imported and local gift items, including choice of candles and candle-holders, and household goods.

Hediyenizvar: Tel: 0212-296 5731, Abdi İpekçi Caddesi No: 12/7, Nişantaşı. Specialises in wedding presents.

İpek: Tel: 0212-249 8207, İstiklal Caddesi No: 230/7-8, Beyoğlu. Gorgeous silk scarves.

Istanbul Handicrafts Centre: Tel: 0212-517 6782, Kabasakal Caddesi No: 7, Sultanahmet. Craft workshops in restored *medrese* offer interesting gift possibilities.

Istanbul Modern: Tel: 0212-353 0810, Kanyon Shopping Mall. Reproductions of items in Istanbul Modern art gallery.

İznik Vakfı: Tel: 0212-287 3243, info@iznik.com, Öksüz Çocuk Sokak No: 14, Kuruçeşme.

Karınca: Tel: 0212-353 0430, Kanyon Shopping Mall; Tel: 0212- 282 2014, Akmerkez Shopping Mall. Colourful array of household goods and novelty items.

Kız Teknik Öğretim Olgunlaşma Enstitüsü (Girls' Technical Training Finishing İnstitute): Tel: 0212-249 5752, İstiklal Caddesi No: 48, Beyoğlu. Hand-made embroidery and jewellery. Items made to measure.

Mon Markiz: Tel: 0212-251 7581, www.monmarkiz.com, İstiklal Caddesi No: 360, Beyoğlu. Hand-made chocolates and other luxury gift ideas.

Mudo Pera: Tel: 0212-251 8650, www.mudo.com.tr, İstiklal Caddesi No: 401, Beyoğlu. Also in Akmerkez, Carousel, Capitol and Carrefour Shopping Malls.

Ottomania: Tel: 0212-243 2157, Sofyalı Sokak Nos: 30-32, Tünel, Beyoğlu. Excellent selection of old prints and maps.

Paşabahçe: Tel: 0212-244 0544, www.pasabahce.com.tr, İstiklal Caddesi No: 314, Beyoğlu; Tel: 0212-276 1079, Büyükdere Caddesi, Maslak; Tel: 0212-233 5005, Teşvikiye Caddesi, Çevre Apt No: 117, Nişantaşı; Tel: 0216-386 1689, Bağdat Caddesi No: 392/7-8, Şaşkınbakkal; Tel: 0212-353 0734, Kanyon Shopping Mall

TShop: Tel: 0212-458 6365, www.tshop.com.tr, Yeni Çerçiler Caddesi No: 1/6,

Çemberlitaş; Tel: 0212-260 3240, Köyiçi Caddesi No: 53, Beşiktaş; Tel: 0212-261 4578, Ihlamurdere Caddesi No: 56/1, Beşiktaş. Wide range of cheap gifts, including toiletries, accessories, toys and small decorative items.

Turkişi: Tel: 0212-293 7861, İstiklal Caddesi No: 15, Taksim. Many of the items found in the Grand Bazaar but at fixed prices and with no hassle.

Ankara

Çeşni: Tel: 0312-426 5787, Tunalı Hilmi Caddesi, Ertuğ Pasajı No: 88/44, Kavaklıdere. Fine Turkish embroideries.

Dösim: Tel: 0312-309 4953, Mithatpaşa Caddesi No: 18.

İznik Foundation: Tel: 0312-466 2196, info@iznik.com, Kırlangıç Sokak No: 28, Gaziosmanpaşa.

Mudo: Tel: 0312-541 1128, Armada Shopping Mall

Paşabahçe: Tel: 0312-433 4671, Tunalı Hilmi Caddesi No: 97, Kavaklıdere.

Tourist Office Gift Shops: Tel: 0312-433 9981, Meşrutiyet Caddesi No: 11/B, Kızılay; Tel: 0312-433 9981, Gazi Mustafa Kemal Bulvarı No: 33, Maltepe.

Izmir

Dösim: Tel: 0232-483 0789, Cumhuriyet Bulvarı No: 115, Alsancak.

Paşabahçe: Tel: 0232-386 5544, Kipa Shopping Mall; Tel: 0232-483 4922, SSK Tesisleri, Milli Kütüphane Caddesi No: 14/A, Konak; Tel: 0232-278 5956, Agora Shopping Mall

Antalya

Mudo City: Tel: 0242-230 1430, Migros Shopping Mall

Dösim: Tel: 0242-238 5696, Antalya Museum, İçi Konyaaltı Caddesi No: 2

Paşabahçe: Tel: 0242-244 3364, Atatürk Caddesi No: 55/A

Adana

Dösim: Tel: 0322-359 5070, İl Kültür Müdürlüğü

Paşabahçe: Tel: 0322-454 3634, Atatürk Caddesi No: 2

Bodrum

Dösim: Tel: 0252-313 0792, Bodrum Castle

Mudo: Tel: 0252-316 3658, Milta Bodrum Marina; Tel: 0252-316 2271, Kale Caddesi 47; Tel: 0252-313 8398, Kıbrısşehitleri Caddesi No: 60

Paşabahçe: Tel: 0252-317 0399, Oasis Shopping Mall, Gümbet Kavşağı karşısı

Tepe Home: Tel: 0252-317 0856, Oasis Shopping Mall, Gümbet Kavşağı karşısı

Bursa

Paşabahçe: Tel: 0225 5746, Zafer Plaza Shopping Mall, Cemal Nadir Caddesi No: 181/122

Eskişehir

Savun: Tel: 0222-234 5920, www.savunmeerschaum.com, Yeni Mahallesi, 3.Dere Sokak No: 18. Meerschaum pipes and other gift items.

Fethiye & Around

Çitlembik: Tel: 0252-612 1644, Gürak İş Merkezi

Ertan Gift Shop: Tel: 0252-614 6333, Cumhuriyet Mahallesi, Turan Sokak No: 4

Silver Stone: Tel: 0252-612 0167, Cumhuriyet Caddesi No: 57, Fethiye. Traditional silver-backed mirrors.

Taner Maral: Tel: 0252-617 0713, Belcekız-Çarşı Caddesi No: 5, Ölüdeniz

Unique Anatolian Arts: Tel: 0252-616 6393, Hisarönü

Zafet Datça: Tel: 0252-612 9885, Çarşı Caddesi No: 9/C, Paspatur. Natural soaps, extra virgin olive oil, honey.

Kapadokya

Ebru Sanat Evi: Tel: 0384-341 3940, İmran Mahallesi, Dağıstanlı Sokak No: 12, Ürgüp. Pictures made from the marbling technique.

Kaş

A La Turka: Tel: 0242-836 4447, Uzun Çarşı No: 11

Turqueria: Tel: 0242-836 1631, www.turqueria.com, Uzun Çarşı No: 21

Konya

İkonium: Tel: 0332-350 2895, Pürügüklü Mahallesi, Bostangelebi Sokak No: 10, Karatay. Art felt works, including wall hangings, bags and hats.

Kuşadası

Mudo: Tel: 0256-614 5505, Kuşadası Marina

Marmaris

Canay: Tel: 0252-412 6229, Tepe Mahallesi, 43.Sokak No: 4/A

Paşabahçe: Tel: 0252-413 5320, Solaris Shopping Mall

SHOES

Istanbul

Adım: Tel: 0532-322 8785, İstiklal Caddesi No: 140/9, Halep Pasajı, Beyoğlu. Men's shoe sizes 45 to 55.

Beta Ayakkabı: Tel: 0212-380 0893, www.betashoes.com, Cevahir Shopping Mall; Tel: 0212-292 5786, İstiklal Caddesi No: 69/1, Beyoğlu; Tel: 0216-651 7455, Capitol Shopping Mall; Tel: 0212-230 3029, Tunaman Çarşısı, Şakayık Sokak No: 47/2, Nişantaşı

Candemir: Tel 0212-244 3379, Sıraselviler Caddesi No: 99, Taksim. Made to measure men's shoes.

Çayak: Tel: 0216-345 3993, Ahmet Mithat Efendi Caddesi No: 19/7, Fenerbahçe

Ceyo: Tel: 0212-282 0137, www.ceyo.com.tr, Akmerkez. Orthopedic shoes and sandals.

Coşkun Kundura: Tel: 0212-293 6376, Kurabiye Sokak No: 17/1, Beyoğlu. Made-to-measure shoes.

Divan Kundura: Tel: 0212-246 3765, Halaskargazi Caddesi No: 309/28, Osmanbey. Made-to-measure shoes.

Güvener: Tel: 0212-516 3966, www.guvenerkundura.net, Yeniçeriler Caddesi No: 11/B, Çemberlitaş. Stocks Clarks shoes for men.

Hotiç Shoes: Tel: 0212-679 0571, www.hotic.com.tr, Olivium Outlet Centre; Tel: 0212-295 9631, Ayazma Yolu, Demet İş Hanı, Kağıthane; Tel: 0212-282 0565, Akmerkez Shopping Mall

Nike: Tel: 0212-244 7575, İstiklal Caddesi 181-5, Beyoğlu; Tel: 0212-282 2612, Akmerkez Shopping Mall, Etiler; Tel: 0216-339 8690, Tepe Nautilus Shopping Mall

Sezgin Kundura: Tel: 0212-244 4123, Öğüt Sokak No: 6, Beyoğlu. Made-to-measure shoes.

Ankara

Bata: Tel: 0312-235 4754, Galeria Shopping Mall, 8.Cadde No: 53/83, Ümitköy

Beta Ayakkabı: Tel: 0312-541 1303, www.betashoes.com, Migros Shopping Mall

Hotiç: Tel: 0312-266 2583, Ankuva İş Merkezi No: 42, Bilkent; Tel: 0312-541 1291, Migros Shopping Mall; Tel: 0312-442 8228, Turan Güneş Bulvarı No: 28, Yıldız

Izmir

Beta Ayakkabı: Tel: 0232-465 2959, Kültür Mahallesi, Mustafa Bey Caddesi Nos: 9-9A, Alsancak

Hotiç: Tel: 0232-465 0599, Mustafa Bey Caddesi No: 11/A, Alsancak; Tel: 0232-324 4748, EGS Park Shopping Mall

Shoe City: Tel 0232-264 1296, Akçay Caddesi, Gaziemir. Sells Clark's shoes.

Adana

Hotiç: Tel: 0322-271 0421, M1 Shopping Mall

Antalya

Hotiç: Tel: 0242-230 1240, Migros Shopping Mall

Bodrum

Ali Güven: Tel 0252-313 2216, Çarşı İçi, Ziraat Bankası karşı. Sandal-maker to likes of Mick Jagger.

Bursa

Beta Ayakkabı: Tel: 0224-452 1228, Carrefour

Hotiç: Tel: 0224-220 6381, Atatürk Caddesi, Orhangazi Alt Geçidi No: 2

Fethiye

Lumberjack: Tel: 0252-612 5410, Cumhuriyet Caddesi, 37 Sokak No: 29

Gaziantep

Place to come to buy traditional leather shoes and slippers *(yemeniler)*.

Gaziantep Uslu Yemenici: Tel: 0348-814 6044, Odun Pazarı Caddesi No: 33
Yemenici: Tel:0342-230 2289, Şehitler Caddesi No: 24, Şahinbey

Konya

Hotiç: Tel: 0232-241 5651, Kulesite Shopping Mall

Kuşadası

Hotiç: Tel: 0256-613 0053, Liman İşletmeleri Caddesi, C Blok No: 3

SHOPPING MALLS *(ALIŞVERİŞ MERKEZLERİ, AVM)*

Istanbul

Akmerkez: Tel: 0212-282 0170, www.akmerkez.com.tr, Nispetiye Caddesi, Etiler. Accessorize, Arçelik, Benetton, Body Shop, Bosch, French Connection, Marks & Spencer, Migros, Mothercare, Nike, Remzi Kitabevi, Zara etc.

Atrium Shopping Mall: Tel: 0212-661 4833, Emlak Bankası Konutları, Ataköy

Capitol: Tel: 0216-651 3333, www.capitol.com.tr, Tophanelioğlu Caddesi, Altunizade, Üsküdar. Accessorize, Arçelik, Benetton, Body Shop, D&R Kitabevi, Marks & Spencer, Migros, Vakko etc.

Carousel Shopping Mall: Tel: 0212-570 8434, Halit Ziya Uşakligil Caddesi No: 1, Bakırköy. Benetton, Levi's, Marks & Spencer, Mothercare, Toys 'R' Us etc.

Carrefour Bayrampaşa: Tel: 0212-640 9900, Ferhatpaşa Çiftliği Mahallesi, Otogar yanı

Carrefour Harimdere: Tel: 0212-852 0606, E5 Karayolu, Eski Londra Asfaltı Mevkii, Yakuplu Köyü, Beylikdüzü

Carrefour Maltepe: Tel: 0216-515 1515, Cevizli Mahallesi, Tugay Yolu No: 73, Maltepe

Carrefour İçerenköy: Tel: 0216-448 0506, Eski Genoto Arsası, Hal Binası yanı

Carrefour (Ümraniye) Vega: Tel: 0216-525 1000, Küçüksu Caddesi No: 68, Ümraniye.

Carrefour: Tel: 0216-448 0505, E5 Karayolu yanı, Kozyatağı

Cevahir Shopping Mall: Tel: 0212-368 6900, www.istanbulcevahir.com, Büyükdere Caddesi No: 22, Şişli. Accessorize, Benetton, Body Shop, Debenhams, Dorothy Perkins, Evans, Migros, Miss Selfridge, Mothercare, Next, Peacocks, River Island, Topshop, Zara etc.

Fly Inn Shopping Mall: Tel: 0212-573 7575, Harman Sokak No: 48, Florya

G-Mall Shopping Mall: Tel: 0212-296 6890, Küçükçiftlik Parkı, Kadırgarlar Caddesi, Maçka

Galleria Shopping Mall: Tel: 0212-559 9560, Sahil Yolu, Ataköy.

Kanyon Shopping Mall: Tel: 0212-281 0800, www.kanyon.com.tr, Büyükdere Caddesi No: 185, Levent. Bally, Body Shop, D&R, Harvey Nichols, Macro, Mothercare, Next, Paşabahçe, Remzi Kitabevi, Vakko etc

M1-Tepe Shopping Mall: Tel: 0216-377 4800, Yalnız Selvi Caddesi, Soğanlık

Maltepe Park Shopping Mall: Tel: 0216-515 1212, Tugay Yolu No: 73, Maltepe

Mayadrom Shopping Mall: Tel: 0212-352 3122, www.mayadrom.com.tr, Yıldırım Göker Caddesi, Akatlar; Tel: 0212-352 3170, Tanburi Ali Efendi Sokak, Etiler.

Metrocity: Tel: 0212-344 0660, www.metrocity.com.tr, Büyükdere Caddesi No: 4, 1.Levent. Accessorize, Adidas, Benetton, Body Shop, Claire's, Dorothy Perkins, Evans, Levi's, Marks & Spencer, Migros, Mothercare, River Island, Top Shop, Zara etc.

Profilo Shopping Mall: Tel: 0212-216 4400, Cemal Sahir Caddesi Nos: 26-28, Mecidiyeköy

Tepe Nautilus Shopping Mall: Tel: 0216-339 3929, Fatih Caddesi No: 1, Acıbadem, Kadıköy. Accessorize, Adidas, Benetton, Body Shop, Carrefour, Lacoste, Mothercare, Nike, Zara etc.

Tower Shopping Mall: Tel: 0212-316 1015, İş Kuleleri, 4.Levent

Ankara

Ankuva Shopping Mall: Tel: 0312-266 0210, Bilkent Plaza, Bilkent

Arcadium Shopping Mall: Tel: 0312-241 1500, 8.Cadde No: 192, Çayyolu, Ümitköy

Armada Shopping Mall: Tel: 0312-295 6262, Atatürk Orman Çiftliği Mahallesi, Eskişehir Yolu 6, B Blok, Söğütözü.

Atakule: Tel: 0312-440 7701, Çankaya Caddesi, Çankaya

Bilkent Shopping Mall: Tel: 0312-266 0210, Bilkent. Marks & Spencer, Praktiker, Real supermarket, Tepe Home, Toys 'R' Us etc

Galleria Shopping Mall: Tel: 0312-235 0461, Eskişehir Yolu, 8.Cadde 97, Ümitköy

Gimat Shopping Mall: Tel: 0312-541 1980, Konya Devlet Yolu No: 2/B26, Akköprü

Karum: Tel: 0312-467 1547, www.karum.com.tr, İran Caddesi, Kavaklıdere

Mesa Plaza: Tel: 0312-240 5960, Ihlamur Cadde No: 2, Mesa Koru Sitesi, Çayyolu

Migros Shopping Mall: Tel: 0312-541 1212, Konya Devlet Yolu, İskitler.

Izmir

Agora Shopping Mall: Tel: 0232-277 2525, Mithatpaşa Caddesi No: 1444, Balçova

EGS Park Shopping Mall: 2040 Sokak No: 104, Mavişehir

Konak Pier: Tel: 0232-489 1004, Atatürk Caddesi 19, Konak. Body Shop

Adana

M1 Tepe: Tel: 0322-271 0117, Dr Sadi Ahmet Bulvarı, Zencerli Bağlar Mevkii

Antalya

G-Mall: Tel: 0242-316 7388, Şirinyalı, Özgürlük Yolu No: 5, Lara. D&R, Gima, Marks & Spencer, Sony etc.

Bodrum

Milta Bodrum Marina: Tel: 0252-316 1860, Neyzen Tevfik Caddesi No: 5

Oasis Shopping Mall: Tel: 0252-317 0002, Kıbrısşehitleri Caddesi

Bursa

Asmerkez Shopping Mall: Yeni Yalova Yolu
Zafer Plaza Shopping Mall: Tel: 0224-225 3900, Zafer Meydanı, Cemal Nadir Caddesi

Konya

Kulesite Shopping Mall: Feritpaşa Mahallesi, Kule Caddesi, Selçuklu
M1 Tepe Real: Şille Parsana Mahallesi, Dr Halil Ürün Caddesi, Yeni Otogar yanı No: 63, Selçuklu

Marmaris

Solaris Shopping Mall: Atatürk Caddesi No: 28

Mersin

Carrefour Shopping Mall: Limonluk Mahallesi, İsmet İnönü Bulvarı

SPECIALIST FOOD AND DRINK SHOPS

Istanbul

Antre Gourmet Shop: Tel: 0212-292 8972, Akarsu Caddesi No: 52, Cihangir

Bada Wine Shop: Tel: 0212-244 6860, Akyol Caddesi, Alçakdam Yokuşu No: 13, Cihangir

Çin Süper Marketi: Tel 0212-293 0536, Hariciye Konağı Sokak No: 5/A, Gümüşsuyu. Woks, oyster sauce, chili sauce, noodles, tinned lychees, water chestnuts, bamboo shoots, etc.

Coffee World: Tel: 0212-520 0204, Asmaaltı Caddesi, Kızılhan Sokak No: 18/1, Eminönü. Wide range of imported coffees.

KAV Şarap Butik: Tel: 0212-234 9120, Atiye Sokak 12/1, Teşvikiye

Kavaklıdere Wines: Tel: 0212-360 0540, 2. Kemer Mevkii, Kemerburgaz

Kolaylar: Tel: 0212-257 5705, 1.Cadde No: 124/1 Arnavutköy. Baby vegetables and unusual salad ingredients.

Kurukahveci Mehmet Efendi: Tel: 0212-511 4262, Tahmis Caddesi No: 66, Eminönü. Follow the smell of roasting coffee beans to find this tiny shop beside the Spice Bazaar.

La Cave Wine Shop: Tel: 0212-243 2405, www.lacavesa-rap.com, Sıraselviler Caddesi No: 207, Cihangir

Lazarı Kozmaoğlu Butcher Shop: Tel: 0212-235 7865, Dereboyu Caddesi, Katmerli Sokak No: 6/8, Kurtuluş. Pork products.

Manhattan Gourmet Shop: Tel: 0212-225 0047, Güzelbahçe Sokak No: 14, Nişantaşı. Hard to find foods, plus all sorts of coffees.

Memo's Tobacco & Wine Shop: Tel: 0212-352 3244, Mayadrom Shopping Mall

Milka Şarküteri ve Meze Çeşitleri: Tel: 0216-337 3531, Moda Caddesi No: 112, Kadıköy. Pork products, imported cheeses, sauces, chocolates etc.

Santral Şarküteri: Tel: 0212-263 6352, Cevdetpaşa Caddesi No: 57/D, Bebek. Expensive olive oils and other deli items.

Şütte: Tel: 0212-293 9292, Duduodaları Sokak No: 21, off Balık Pazarı; Tel: 0212-236 1899, Teşvikiye Caddesi No: 95/B, Teşvikiye. Delicatessen.

Vefa Bozacısı: Tel: 0212-519 4922, Vefa Katip Celebi Caddesi No: 102, Vefa. Original purveyor of *boza*, a drink made from *darı* wheat, water and sugar sprinkled with cinnamon.

Ankara

Agro-Food: Tel: 0312-468 0601, Arjantin Caddesi No: 21/C, Gaziosmanpaşa, Organic food specialist.

Dubonnet Wine House: Tel: 0312-427 5864, Bülten Sokak No: 21/6, Kavaklıdere

Kavaklıdere Wine House: Tel: 0312-467 5775, Tunus Caddesi No: 88/B, Kavaklıdere

Keyif: Tel: 0312-427 4449, Karum Shopping Mall; Tel: 0312-428 1657, Arjantin Caddesi No: 25, Gaziosmanpaşa

Sultan Market: Tel: 0312-446 6375, Uğur Mumcu Sokak No: 61/7, Gaziosmanpaşa. Ankara's branch of Şütte, amongst other stores.

Izmir

Çerkezköy Şarküteri: Tel: 0232-421 3862, 1379 Sokak No: 6, Alsancak

Bodrum

Bottega del Vino: Tel: 0532-213 7471, Milta Bodrum Marina. Imported wines.

Şütte: Tel: 0252-316 6061, Neyzen Tevfik Caddesi No: 196. Delicatessen

Safran Natural Foods: Tel: 0252-316 2746, Yeniçarşı, 1.Sokak No: 15. Olives and olive oils.

Fethiye & Around

Hobby Tobacco & Off-Licence: Tel: 0252 613 6664, Barış Manco Bulvarı No: 93/6, Çalış

Nazar Gıda: Tel: 0252-614 3322, Ölüdeniz Caddesi, Toptancı Sebze Hali karşısı, 2.Sokak No: 231. Heinz baked beans, Maxwell House coffee, pork sausages, Bisto gravy granules.

Porkland: Tel: 0252-616 7569, Hitit Sokak, Hisarönü. Pork products.

SPORTS EQUIPMENT
Istanbul

Adrenalin Tırmanış ve Doğa Sporları: Tel: 0212-260 6002, Ortabahçe Caddesi No: 19, Beşiktaş; Tel: 0216-386 7864, Ulaştırcı Sokak No: 10, Kozyatağı

Av Doğa: Tel: 0212-260 4978, Çırağan Caddesi No: 7, Beşiktaş

Marintek: Tel: 0216-349 1661, Bağdat Caddesi No: 30, Kızıltoprak

Sportpoint Extreme Shops: Tel: 0212-282 0436, Akmerkez Shopping Mall; Tel: 0212-661 4300, Galleria Shopping Mall

Sportive: Tel: 0212-282 0135, Akmerkez Shopping Mall

STATIONERY
Istanbul

There are lots of stationery shops off Ankara Caddesi in Cağaloğlu near the Iranian embassy.

Kıpçak: Tel: 0212-296 8472, Valikonaği Caddesi No: 66, Nişantaşı

Office 1 Superstore: Tel: 0212-230 3670, Yeni Maçka Caddesi No: 59/1, Teşvikiye; Tel: 0212-258 3949, Barbaros Bulvarı, Gürel Apt: 41/3, Beşiktaş; Tel: 0216-330 9061, Bağdat Caddesi No: 24/3, Kızıltoprak; Tel: 0212-284 4640, Üçyol Mevkii, Dereboyu Sokak No: 303, Kat: 1, Maslak; Tel: 0212-660 8617, Istanbul Caddesi, Ahmet Rasim Sokak No: 42/A, Bakırköy

Ankara

Office 1 Superstore: Tel: 0312-466 5780, Bülten Sokak No: 7/A, Kavaklıdere; Tel: 0312-219 1630, Armada Shopping Mall; Tel: 0312-385 1300, Bağdat Caddesi No: 390, Ostim

Izmir

Office 1 Superstore: Tel: 0232-324 4130, 6524 Sokak No: 1, Karşıyaka

SUPERMARKETS
Istanbul

Carrefour Hipermarket: Tel: 0216-448 0505, Eski Genoto Arsası, Hal Binası yanı, İçerenköy; Tel: 0216-458 3800, İnkilap Mahallesi, Küçüksu Caddesi No: 68, Ümraniye; Tel: 0212-640 9900, Ferhatpaşa Çiftliği, Altıntepsi Mahallesi, Esenler Otogar üstü, Bayrampaşa; Tel: 0216-515 1515, Cevizli Mahallesi, Tugay Yolu No: 73, Maltepe; Tel: 0216-544 4800, İbrahimağa Mahallesi. Dinlenç Sokak No: 18, Koşuyolu, Kadıköy; Tel: 0212-852 0626, E5 Karayolu, Londra Asfaltı, Haramidere Mevkii, Beylikdüzü

Gima: Tel: 444 1000, www.gima.com.tr, Sıraselviler Caddesi, Beyoğlu; Tel: 0212-664 1392, Olivium Outlet Centre

Macro: Tel: 0212-233 0570, Abdi İpekçi Caddesi No: 24, Nişantaşı; Tel: 0212-282 0310, Akmerkez Shopping Mall; Tel: 0212-257 1381, Muallim Naci Caddesi, Kuruçeşme

Metro Cash & Carry: Tel: 0212-478 7000, Koçman Caddesi, Güneşli; Tel: 0216-317 1274, Yavuzlar Caddesi, Yenisahra; Tel: 0216-317 1274, Kadıköy

Migros: Tel: 0212-246 6480, www.migros.com.tr, 19 Mayıs Caddesi No: 1, Şişli (MMM); Tel: 0212-285 4150, Büyükdere Caddesi No: 61, Maslak (MMM); Tel: 0216-418 1929, Damaga Sokak No: 23/15, Caferağa Mahallesi, Kadıköy; Tel: 0212-282 3369, Akasya Sokak No: 53, B Blok, Yeni Levent; Tel: 0212-661 4491, Galleria Shopping Mall (MMM); Tel 0212-380 0122, Cevahir Shopping Mall (MMM); Tel 0212-344 0030, Metrocity Shopping Mall (MMM)

REAL: Tel: 0216-309 1991, Kartal

Tansaş: Tel: 0212-325 0238, www.tansas.com.tr, Nispetiye Caddesi, Aydın Sokak No: 1,

Levent; Tel: 0216-348 5134, Caferağa Mahallesi, Neşet Ömer Sokak No: 5, Kadıköy; Tel: 0212-233 0570, Abdi İpekçi Caddesi, Ada Sokak No: 24-8, Nişantaşı; Tel: 0212-343 8927, Abide-i Hürriyet Caddesi No: 212, Şişli; Tel: 0212-260 8034, Barbaros Bulvarı, Halk Pazarı yanı No: 11, Beşiktaş

Yimpaş: Tel: 0216-443 7090, İnkilap Mahallesi, Alemdağ Caddesi No: 169/A, Ümraniye

Ankara

Beğendik: Tel: 0312-419 3232, www.begendik.com.tr, Dr. Mediha Eldem Sokak No: 72, Kocatepe, Kızılay

Carrefour: Tel: 0312-278 5200, Ankara Ticaret Merkezi B-46, Batıkent

Gima: Atatürk Bulvarı, Emek İşhanı, Kızılay; Hoşdere Caddesi No: 201/B, Çankaya; Istanbul Yolu 7km, Jandarma Kuruluşları karşısı, Batıkent; Armada Shopping Mall

Migros: Tel: 0312-231 8941, Celal Bayar Bulvarı, Tok Sokak No: 7, Maltepe (MMM); Tel: 0312-541 1043, Emniyet Sarayı yanı No: 1, Akköprü (MMM); Tel: 0312-446 4723, Uğur Mumcu Caddesi No: 66, Gaziosmanpaşa; Tel: 0312-232 6628, Gazi Mustafa Kemal Bulvarı No: 138, Tandoğan; Tel: 0312-241 5933, Arcadium, Koru Mahallesi, 8. Cadde No: 192, Çayyolu (MMM); Tel: 0312-240 9674, Koru Sitesi, Mesa Ticaret Merkezi, Eskişehir Yolu 16km; Tel: 0312-280 4944, Ayaş Yolu 20km, Eryaman

Tansaş: Tel: 0312-438 3656, Zübeyde Hanım Meydanı, Atakule, Çankaya; Tel: 0312-446 8949, Uğur Mumcu Caddesi No: 78/9, Gaziosmanpaşa; Tel: 0312-475 2851, Dikmen Caddesi No: 359, Keklikpınarı, Dikmen

Yimpaş: Tel: 0312-276 1061, Atatürk Mahallesi, Meltem Sokak No: 41, Sincan; Tel: 0312-310 9966, Sanayi Caddesi No: 5, Ulus

Real: Tel: 0312-266 0404, Bilkent Shopping Mall

Izmir

Carrefour: Tel: 0232-398 2100, 6524 Sokak No: 6, Şemikler Mahallesi, Mavişehir/ Karşıyaka

Kipa (Tesco): Tel: 0232-386 5050, www.kipa.com.tr, Havaalanı Yolu No: 40, Çiğli; Tel: 0232-373 3000, Bornova; Tel: 0232-252 3232, Gaziemir; Tel: 0232-277 3482, Balçova

Migros: Tel: 0232-422 1730, Belediye Katlı Otopark altı, Alsancak; Tel: 0232-259 2020, Mithatpaşa Caddesi 1460, Balçova (MMM); Tel: 0232-373 3530, Mustafa Kemal Caddesi No. 136, Bornova; Tel: 0232-350 1248, Şehitleri Bulvarı, Katlı Otopark altı, Bostanlı (MMM); Tel: 0232-324 4217, 2040 Sokak No: 104, Z11, Karşıyaka (MMM); Tel: 0232-482 2959, Vali Kazım Dirik Caddesi No: 11, Konak

Tansaş: Tel: 0232-463 8140, Talatpaşa Bulvarı No: 59/A, Alsancak; Tel: 0232-463 2629, Kıbrısşehitleri Caddesi, 1443 Sokak No: 131, Alsancak; Tel: 0232-362 5511, Yalı Mahallesi, 6640/4 Sokak No: 1, Atakent, Karşıyaka; Tel: 0232-259 8864, Akasya Ardıç Sokak 6/A, Balçova; Tel: 0232-446 2433, Anafartalar Caddesi No: 753, Basmane; Tel: 0232-342 0827, 80 Sokak 16, Bornova; Tel: 0232-330 2326, Şehitleri Bulvarı No: 41/A, Bostanlı; Tel: 0232-361 6191, 6653. Sokak No: 137, Pazar Yeri, Cumhuriyet

Yimpaş: Tel: 0232-253 5666, Akçay Caddesi No: 42, Gaziemir

Adana

Migros: Tel: 0322-235 9527, Toros Mahallesi, Kenan Evren Bulvarı 85; Tel: 0322-232 1415, Turgut Özal Bulvarı, Edip Özaltın Sitesi No: 110, Seyhan; Tel: 0322-611 4428, Burhaniye Mahallesi, Hükümet Caddesi No: 14, Ceyhan

Antalya

Gima: Tel: 0242-316 7038, Şirinyalı Mahallesi, Özgürlük Bulvarı No: 5, Dedeman Oteli karşısı, Lara; Çağlayan Mahallesi, Lara Fener Yolu, Astur Siteleri karşısı

Migros: Tel: 0242-230 1111, Meltem Mahallesi 155, 100.Yıl Bulvarı, (MMM)

Tansaş: Tel: 0242-312 0644, Metinkasapoğlu Caddesi, Metropol Çarşı C Blok; Tel: 0242-323 0150, Çağlayan Mahallesi, Fener Caddesi No: 14, Lara; Tel: 0242-225 9652, Gürsu Mahallesi, Atatürk Bulvarı, 10 Caddesi No: 25, B Blok, Kemer Yolu üzeri, Konyaaltı

Alanya

Migros: Tel: 0242-511 8210, Saray Mahallesi, Atatürk Caddesi No: 364

Tansaş: Tel: 0242-519 3578, Saray Mahallesi, Atatürk Caddesi, Gülen Sokak No: 12

Bodrum & Around

Gima: Tel: 0252-317 0140, Kıbrısşehitleri Caddesi, Bodrum; Neyzen Tevfik Caddesi No: 5, Bodrum Marina; Tel: 0252-382 5633, Mehmet Hilmi Caddesi, Zeyyat Mandalinci İlkokulu karşısı, Turgutreis; Tel: 0252-386 3168, Gökçebel Kalabak Mevkii, Yalıkavak

Kipa: Tel: 0252-311 1111, Ortakent Mahallesi, Kapuz Caddesi No: 2, Yahşi, Ortakent

Migros: Tel: 0252-316 0982, Turgutreis Caddesi No: 259, Elele Mevkii, Gümbet Kavşağı, (MMM); Tel: 0252-386 3704, Gökçebel Koyu, Koycivarı Mevkii, Yalıkavak; Tel: 0252-382 3920, Mehmet Hilmi Caddesi, Turgutreis; Tel: 0252-385 2112, Port Bodrum Yalıkavak Marina

Tansaş: Tel: 0252-313 4920, Santral Garaj üstü, Bodrum; Tel: 0252-382 5737, D-Marin Turgutreis Marina

Bursa

Carrefour: Odunluk Mahallesi, Izmir Yolu Caddesi 55, Nılüfer

Çeşme

Migros: Tel: 0232-712 6668, Atatürk Bulvarı No: 133

Denizli

Kipa (Tesco): Tel: 0258-371 7179, Izmir Asfaltı 5km, Gümüşler

Fethiye & Around

Gima: Atatürk Caddesi, Yeni Belediye altı

Migros: Tel: 0252-543 3593, İnönü Caddesi No: 4

Kayseri

Beğendik: Tel: 0352-222 6476, Cumhuriyet Meydanı; Tel: 0352-233 9158, Sivas Caddesi, Karagözlü Sokak Nos: 72-4

Migros: Tel: 0352-224 5558, Sivas Caddesi (MMM); Tel: 0352-222 9035, Cumhuriyet Meydanı, Hunat Camii yanı, Eski Hal Yeri

Kemer

Gima: Merkez Liman Caddesi, Yat Limanı

Migros: Tel: 0242-814 5520, Akdeniz Caddesi No: 88

Konya

Kipa (Tesco): Tel: 0332-257 0098, Akıncılar Mahallesi, Selçuklu

Marmaris

Gima: Karacan Point, Centre Siteler Mahallesi. Kemal Seyfettin Bulvarı No: 53

Migros: Tel: 0252-413 0315, Kenan Evren Bulvarı, Emniyet Müdürlüğü karşısı

Tansaş: Tel: 0252-413 9100, Ulusal Egemenlik Caddesi, Eski Dolmuş Durağı

Nevşehir

Beğendik: Tel: 0384-212 2244, Güzelyurt Mahallesi, Zübeyde Hanım Caddesi No: 88

Yimpaş: Tel: 0384-212 9605, Bedlik Mahallesi, Aksaray Caddesi No: 3

SWEETSHOPS

Istanbul

Ali Muhiddin Hacı Bekir: Tel: 0212-522 0666, Hamidiye Caddesi No: 83, Eminönü; Tel: 0212-244 2904, İstiklal Caddesi No: 127, Beyoğlu; Tel: 0216-336 1519, Kadıköy. Original Turkish delight shop.

Cafer Erol: Tel: 0216-337 1103, Yasa Caddesi No: 19/21, Kadıköy

Kahve Dünyası: Tel: 0212-293 1206, Meclis-i Mebusan Caddesi, Tütün Han No: 167, Kabataş

Koska: Tel: 0212-244 0919, www.koskahelvacisi.com.tr, İstiklal Caddesi No: 238, Beyoğlu

Lindt: Tel: 0212-231 0615, Milli Reasürans No: 53, Nişantaşı

Mabel: Tel 0212-225 2789, Valikonağı Caddesi 32/1, Nişantaşı

SWIMMING POOL CONTRACTORS

Istanbul

Arites: Tel: 0216-575 5000, www.arites.com.tr, Camlievler Köknar B1 Blok No: 33, İçerenköy, Kadıköy. Website shows variety of pool designs.

Fethiye

Istanpools: Tel: 0252-623 9783, 232 Sokak No: 14, Çiftlik

Mete Havuzculuk: Tel: 0252-612 5154, SSK Hastanesi karşısı

Şenel Kimya: Tel: 0252-612 5141, Taşyaka Mahallesi, Baha Şıkman Caddesi, Özkan Apt 121

Kaş
Şah Tek: Tel: 0242 836 2880, Çukurbağlı Caddesi No: 32/A

TOOLS
See DIY materials above.

TOY SHOPS
Istanbul
Ekincioğlu Ticaret: Tel: 0212-522 6220, Rüstem Paşa Mahallesi, Kalçın Sokak No: 5/7. Eminönü. Three floors of toys, including many jigsaws and wooden puzzles.

Elit Oyuncak: Tel: 0212-353 0906, Kanyon Shopping Mall

Gelar: Tel: 0212-280 8089, Birlik Sokak No: 9/20, 1.Levent. Wooden toys and imported educational toys.

Nest: Tel: 0212-231 5431, Mimar Kemal Öke Caddesi No: 23, Nişantaşı

Toys 'R' Us: Tel: 0212-543 5419, www.toysrus.com.tr, Carousel Shopping Mall; Tel: 0212-852 0030, Beylikdüzü Migros Shopping Mall; Tel: 0212-217 9615, Gayrettepe Express; Tel: 0212-352 5110, Mayadrom Shopping Mall; Tel: 0212-286 0016, Migros, Maslak; Tel: 0212-640 6272, Bayrampaşa Carrefour; Tel: 0212-852 8293, Haramidere Carrefour; Tel: 0212-574 0680, Florya Flyinn Express; Tel: 0216-332 0061, Gima, Anadolu Hisarı; Tel: 0216-388 8073, İdealtepe Express; Tel: 0216-442 3503, Maltepe ChampionSA Ticaret Merkezi

Ankara
Toys 'R' Us: Tel: 0312-266 0582, Bilkent Shopping Mall; Tel: 0312- 278 4991, Batıkent Carrefour

Izmir
Toys 'R' Us: Tel: 0232-279 2252, Balçova Migros; Tel: 0232-324 4888, Karşıyaka Carrefour

Adana
Toys 'R' Us: Tel: 0322-271 0571, M1 Tepe Real

Antalya
Toys 'R' Us: Tel: 0242-230 1443, Migros Shopping Mall

Bodrum
Bodrumdaki Oyuncakçı: Tel: 0252-317 3535, Oasis Shopping Mall

Bursa
Toys 'R' Us: Tel: 0224-452 1082, Carrefour Shopping Mall

Konya
Toys 'R' Us: Tel: 0332-265 1101, M1 Tepe Real

Marmaris

Toystoys: Tel: 0252-413 7782, Ulusak Egemenlik Caddesi No: 5 (Tansaş yanı)

Mersin

Toys 'R' Us: Tel: 0324-331 0550, Carrefour Shopping Mall

APPENDIX VIII:
TURKISH MEDICAL SERVICES

For a fuller list of medical facilities go to www.tiprehberi.com.

AMBULANCES

Istanbul

American Hospital: Tel: 0212-231 4050. Life support equipment on board.

International Hospital: Tel: 0212- 663 3000. Life support equipment on board.

Medline: Tel: 444 1212, www.medline.com.tr, Ahi Evren Caddesi, Ata Centre, K Blok, Ayazağa

International SOS: Tel: 0212-505 7272, www.internationalsos.com, Güzelbahçe Sokak, Tugrul Daire: 33-5/2, Nişantaşı

Ankara

Bayındır Hospital: Tel: 0312-287 9000, Atatürk Bulvarı No: 201, Kavaklıdere

Medline: Tel: 0312-459 4000, Uğur Mumcu Caddesi No: 99/7, Çankaya

Izmir

Medline: Tel: 0232-421 4500, 1375 Sokak No: 35, Alsancak

AIR AMBULANCES

Doruk Air: Tel: 0242-311 4316, www.dorukair.com.tr, Burhanettin Onat Caddesi No: 92/2, Antalya

International SOS Assistance: Tel: 0212-233 1131, www.internationalsos.com

Medline Ambulance Service: Tel: 444 1212, www.medline.com.tr, Ahi Evren Caddesi, Ata Centre, K Blok, Ayazağa

Redstar: Tel: 0216-588 0216, www.redstar-aviation.com, Sabiha Gökçen Havalimanı, Kurtköy, Pendik, Istanbul. US citizens only.

Stars Crescent: Tel: 0216-588 0885, www.starscrescent.com, Sabiha Gökçen Havalimanı, Kurtköy, Pendik, Istanbul

ALTERNATIVE HEALTH CENTRES
Istanbul
Akupunktur Tedavi Merkezi (Acupuncture Therapy Centre): Tel: 0212-283 6180, Akçam Sokak, No: 23/3, 4. Levent. Help with weight loss, quitting smoking, easing migraine.

Chiropractic Centre: Tel: 0216-341 9136, Paşakapısı Neyzenbaşı Halil Can Sokak No: 16/2, Üsküdar. Massage, reflexology and Reiki treatments.

Clinica: Tel: 0212-287 1595, Adnan Saygun Caddesi, Orkide Sokak No: 17/9, Daire:5, Ulus

Hay Clinic: Tel: 0212-283 1080, Levent. Homeopathy, Ayurvedic medicine and beauty services.

Mövenpick Wellness Centre: Tel: 0212-319 2929. Mövenpick Hotel, 4.Levent. Thai massage.

ReflexPoint: Tel: 0212-325 4519, www.reflekspoint.com, Ülgen Sokak No: 4. Gazeteciler Sitesi No: A13, 4. Levent. Relexology and Thai massage. Reduced prices in morning and early afternoon. Appointments only.

Ankara
Ankara Üniversitesi Tıp Fakültesi: Tel: 0312-319 2160, Cebeci. Acupuncture unit.

Izmir
Natur-Med Thermal Cure Centre: Tel: 0256-657 2280, www.naturmed.biz, Çınar Sokak Nos: 13-15, Davutlar. Acupuncture, ozone therapy etc. 15km from Kuşadası.

CHARITY HOSPITALS
Gaziantep
SEV Gaziantep American Hospital: Tel: 0342-220 0211, www.amerikan-hastanesi.com, Tepebaşı Mahallesi, Yüksek Sokak No: 3/A, Şahinbey

DENTISTS
Most of the dentists listed below speak English, French and/or German.

Istanbul
ADENT Dental Clinic: Tel: 0212-351 4667, www.adent.org, Zeytinoğlu Caddesi, Arzu Apt: 2, Daire: 15, Akatlar.

Vural Cankat: Tel: 0212-231 4050, www.amerikanhastanesi.com, İnönü Caddesi No: 11/1, Taksim

Catherine Feyzioğlu: Tel: 0212-233 0627, Abdi İpek Caddesi No: 12/5, Nişantaşı

Dentan: Tel: 0212-291 0303, www.dentan.com, Hakkı Yeten Sokak No: 10/2, Beşiktaş

Dent-Inn Clinic: Tel: 0212-263 1649, Çamlık Girişi No: 6, Etiler

Dentistanbul: Tel: 0212-327 4020, www.dentistanbul.com. Yıldız Caddesi No: 55, Beşiktaş. Dental hospital.

Dilek Ar: Tel: 0212-225 2824, Valikonağı Caddesi, Akkavak Sokak No: 15/4, Nişantaşı

German Hospital Dental Clinic: Tel: 0212-293 7979, Sıraselviler Caddesi No: 119, Taksim. Children's section.

Hakan Kaya: Tel: 0212-263 1649, Çamlık Girişi No: 6, Etiler

Prodent: Tel: 0212-230 4635, Valikonağı Caddesi No: 109/5, Nişantaşı

Reha Sezgin: Tel: 0212-240 3332, Halaskargazi Caddesi No: 48/9, Harbiye

Uğur Tan: Tel: 0212-230 7648, Halaskargazi Caddesi No: 289/8, Şişli

Ankara

Bayındır Hospital Dental Clinic; Tel: 0312-287 9000, Kızılırmak Mahallesi, 28 Sokak No: 2, Söğütözü

Izmir

Murat Gözübüyük: Tel: 0232-422 3769, Mustafabey Caddesi, Nos: 4-2, Alsancak

Antalya

Antalya Chamber of Dentists: Tel: 0242-237 5252. Keeps list of foreign-language-speaking dentists.

MATERNITY HOSPITALS

Istanbul

Cerrahpaşa Tıp Fakültesi Hastanesi (Medical School): Tel: 0212-588 4800, Kocamustafapaşa Caddesi, Cerrahpaşa

Istanbul Memorial Hospital: Tel: 0212-210 6666, Piyalepaşa Bulvarı, Şişli

Istanbul Tüpbebek ve Kadın Sağlılığı Merkezi: Tel: 0212-292 4919, www.istanbul-tupbebek.com.tr, Dershan Han No: 90/1, Gümüşsuyu Caddesi, Beyoğlu. Infertility clinic.

Jinepol Women's Illness & Maternity Centre: Tel: 0212-351 4571, Ground Floor, Kervan Apt, Nispetiye Caddesi No: 17, Etiler. English spoken.

Ankara

SSK Etlik Doğumevi: Tel: 0312-322 0180, Yeni Etlik Caddesi

Zübeyde Hanım Doğumevi: Tel: 0312-317 0606, Örnek Mahallesi, Telsizler

Izmir

Ege Üniversitesi Tıp Fakültesi Doğumevi: Bornova

Kadın Hastalıkları ve Doğum Hastanesi: Konak

SSK Tepecik Doğum Hastanesi: Yenişehir

Südekan Gynecologie & Maternity Clinic: Tel: 0232-421 6260, sudekan@efes.net.tr, Lozan Meydanı No: 35/2, Daire: 4, Alsancak

MISCELLANEOUS HEALTH CONTACTS

Alcoholics Anonymous: Tel: 0212-244 6933, Yüksek Kaldırım Caddesi No: 25, Kuledibi, Beyoğlu, Istanbul

Balıklı Kaplıca: Tel: 0346-457 3036, Kangal. Thermal resort renowned for tiny fish which nibble the skin of psoriasis sufferers with seemingly beneficial results.

Battle Against AIDS Association (AIDS Savaşım Derneği): Tel: 0212-231 7681, www. aidsdernegi.org.tr

Berkeman: Tel: 0212-246 3503, Rumeli Caddesi, Villa İşhanı, Nişantaşı, Istanbul. Orthopedic supplies. Pedicures.

Blood Bank: www.kanbankasi.gen.tr

Bodrum Special Needs Tourism Charity (Bodrum Sağlık Vakfı Engelli Turizmi): Tel: 0252-382 8586, Fax: 0252-382 8587, Bahçelievler Mevkii, Turgutreis, Bodrum Peninsula. Holidays for children with special needs under supervision of health experts including physiotherapists and psychotherapists.

Eczacıbaşı Health Services (Eczacıbaşı Sağlık Hizmetleri): Tel: 0212-317 2500, www. eczacibasisaglik.com, Büyükdere Caddesi, Ecza Sokak, Safher Han No: 6, Kat: 3, Levent, Istanbul. General health services including help at home.

Istanbul Health Centre: Tel: 0212-244 2594, Sahil Sihhıye, Karaköy. Pre-travel vaccinations.

Kifidis Orthopedics: Tel: 0212-240 8920, Valikonağı Caddesi, Akkavak Sokak No: 7, Nişantaşı, Istanbul

Marriage Guidance (Özel Sarıyer Eğitim Merkezi): Tel: 0212-271 4531, Maden Mahallesi, Hamitpaşa Çiftlik Bir Sokak No: 5, Sarıyer, Istanbul.

Medline Emergency Health Service: Tel: 0212-444 1212, www.medline.com.tr, Ahi Evren Caddesi, Ata Centre, B Blok Kat: 1, Istanbul

Poison Control Centre: Tel: 0800-314 7900

Scholl: Tel: 0216-391 8474, Capitol Shopping Mall. Orthopedic supplies. Pedicures.

Sigara Bırakma Merkezi: Tel 0212-254 5270, www.sigarabirakmamerkezi.com, Şehit Muhtar Sokak, Özerk İş Merkezi No: 17/5, Talimhane, Taksim. Private company offering help to stop smoking.

Support Association for the Physically Disabled (Bedensel Engellilerle Dayanışma Derneği): Tel: 0216-370 2626, www.bedd.org.tr, Dragos Yalı Mahallesi, Menekşe Sokak No: 6, Cevizli, Kartal; Tel: 0242-244 5898, Pamir Caddesi, 141. Sokak, Kırmıoğlu Apt No: 15. Website in Turkish only.

OPTICIANS & EYE HOSPITALS

Istanbul

Many opticians work together in *Gözlükçüler Çarşısı* in Nafızbey Pasaji in Eminönü.

Dünya Göz Hastanesi (World Eye Hospital): Tel: 0212-339 3999, www.dunyagoz.com,

Nispetiye Caddesi, Aydın Sokak No: 1, 1.Levent; Tel: 0212 444 4469, Ataköy; Tel: 0216-306 5888, Feneryolu; Tel: 0212-324 7373, Etiler; Tel: 0216-444 4463, Altunizade. Laser eye surgery at less than European prices.

Istanbul Göz Hastanesi: Tel: 0212-556 1313, www.igh.com.tr, İzzettin Çalışlar Caddesi, Neyyire Neyir Sokak No:3, Bahçelievler

Laser Taksim Private Eye Centre: Tel: 0212-248 8673, www.taksimgozmerkezi.com

Ankara

Lünet Optik: Tel: 0312-417 8161, Atatürk Bulvarı No: 72/A, Kızılay; Tel: 0312-417 5880, Kennedy Caddesi No: 56, Kavaklıdere

Izmir

Özel Batıgöz: Tel: 0232-489 0308, www.batigoz.com. Şair Eşref Bulvarı, 9 Sokak No: 137, Çankaya

Antalya

EMO Optik: Tel: 0242-230 1038, Migros Shopping Mall

Talya Göz: Tel: 0242-228 7878, www.talyagoz.com, Konyaaltı Öğretmenevleri Mahallesi, Atatürk Bulvarı No: 130

Fethiye & Around

Cem Optik: Tel: 0252-612 1157, Atatürk Caddesi No: 33

Star Optik: Tel: 0252-616 6400, Hisarönü

Kaş

Saydam Optik: Tel: 0242-836 3073, Merkez Mahallesi, İbrahim Serin Caddesi No: 14

PRIVATE HOSPITALS AND CLINICS

Istanbul

Acıbadem Hastanesi: Tel: 0212-414 4444, Halit Ziya Uşakligil Caddesi No: 1, Bakırköy; Tel: 0216-544 4444, Tekin Sokak No: 8, Acıbadem; Tel: 0216-414 4444, İnönü Caddesi, Okur Sokak No: 20, Kozyatağı

Alman Hastanesi: (German Hospital) Tel: 0212-293 2150, Sıraselviler Caddesi No: 119

American Hospital (Amerikan Hastanesi): Tel: 0212-311 2000, www.amerikanhastanesi.com.tr, Güzelbahçe Sokak No: 20, Nişantaşı

Avrasya Hospital: Tel: 0212-665 5050, 5.Telsiz Mahallesi, 101 Sokak No: 109, Akşemsettin, Zeytinburnu

Avrupa Florence Nightingale Hastanesi: Tel: 0212-212 8811, Mehmetçik Caddesi, Cahit Yalçın Sokak No: 1, Mecidiyeköy

Avustrya St George Hastanesi: Tel: 0212-243 2590, Bereketzade Medrese Sokak Nos: 5-7, Karaköy

Balıklı Rum Hastanesi: Tel: 0212-664 2190, Belgradkapı Yolu No: 2, Zeytinburnu. Greek

Orthodox hospital that accepts non-Orthodox patients. Cheaper than some other private hospitals.

Çağlayan Florence Nightingale Hastanesi: Tel: 0212-231 2021, Abide Hürriyet Caddesi No: 290, Çağlayan, Şişli

Intermed Check-up Centre: Tel: 0212-225 0660, Teşvikiye Caddesi, Bayar Apt No: 143, Nişantaşı

International Hospital: Tel: 0212-663 3000, www.internationalhospital.com.tr, Istanbul Caddesi No: 82, Yeşilköy

International Outpatient Clinic Etiler: Tel: 0212-280 4030, Nispetiye Caddesi No: 19, Levent

Istanbul Surgery Hospital: Tel: 0212-296 9450, Ferah Sokak No: 18, Nişantaşı

Italian Oncology & Rehabilitation Hospital: Tel: 0212-292 9000, www.italyahastanesi.com.tr, Defterdar Yokuşu No: 37, Tophane

Jewish Hospital: Tel: 0212-635 9280, Hisarönü Caddesi No: 46/48, Ayvansaray, Balat

Kadıköy Vatan Hastanesi: Tel: 0216-326 0655, www.kadikoyvatan.com.tr, Kurbağalıdere Caddesi No: 108, Hasanpaşa, Kadıköy

La Paix Hospital ('Lape'): Tel: 0212-246 1020, Büyükdere Caddesi Nos: 22-24, Şişli

Surp Agop Hospital: Tel 0212-230 1718, Yediykuyular Caddesi No: 6, Elmadağ. Armenian Catholic hospital that accepts non-Armenian patients. Cheaper than some other private hospitals.

Surp Pırgiç Hospital: Tel 0212-510 8052, www.surppirgic.com, Zakirbaşı Sokak No: 32, Kazlıçeşme. Armenian hospital that accepts non-Armenian patients. Cheaper than some other private hospitals.

Ankara

Başkent University Hospital: Tel: 0312-212 6868, Fevzi Çakmak Caddesi, 45 Sokak No: 10, Bahçelievler

Bayındır Hospital: Tel: 0312-428 0808, Atatürk Bulvarı No: 201, Kavaklıdere

City Hospital: Tel: 0312-466 3346, Büklüm Sokak No: 53, Kavaklıdere

Güven Hastanesi: Tel: 0312-468 7220, Paris Caddesi No: 5, Aşağı Ayrancı

Çankaya Hastanesi: Tel: 0312-426 1450, Bülten Sokak No: 44, Kavaklıdere

Izmir

Ege Sağlık Hastanesi: Tel: 0232-463 7700, 1399 Sokak, No: 25, Alsancak.

Kent Hastanesi: Tel: 0232-386 7070, 8229 Sokak, No: 30, Çiğli

Adana

Seyhan Hastanesi: Tel: 0322-458 6868, Baraj Yolu No: 1

Antalya

Antalya Hospital: Tel: 0242-335 0000, 325 Sokak, No: 8

Antalya International Hospital: Tel: 0242-311 1500, 931 Sokak, No: 6

Alanya

Can Hastanesi: Tel: 0242-512 3565, Eminpaşa Ganioğlu Çocuk Parkı Sokak

Hayat Hastanesi: Tel: 0242-512 4251, Şekerhane Mahallesi, Yayla Yolu

Bodrum

Karia Medical Centre: Tel: 0252-316 3635

Özel Bodrum Hospital: Tel: 0252-313 6566, Çeşmebaşı Mevkii, Marsmabeti Caddesi No: 41

Universal Hospital: Tel: 0252-319 1515, www.universalhospitalbodrum.com, Çevak Şakır Mahallesi, Gavaklı Şarnıç No: C/1

Bursa

Bursa Vatan Hastanesi: Tel: 0224-220 1040, www.bursavatan.com.tr, Fevzi Çakmak Caddesi No: 55

Fethiye

Letoon: Tel: 0252-646 9600, Pazaryeri Mahallesi, Tariş Sokak, Bölge Trafiği arkası, Patlangıç

Lokam Hekim Esnaf Hastanesi: Tel: 0252-612 6400, www.esnafhastanesi.com, Dolgu Sahası, 533 Sokak No: 6

Kalkan

Tuana Medical Centre: Tel: 0242-844 2244, Mentepe Mahallesi. Private clinic.

Kaş

Tuana Medical Centre: Tel: 0242-841 8456, Ova. Private clinic.

Kocaeli

Anadolu Sağlık Merkezi: Tel: 444 4276, Anadolu Caddesi No: 1, Bayramoğlu Çıkışı, Çayırova Mevkii, Gebze, Kocaeli. Works with John Hopkins Hospital in the USA.

Kuşadası

Meditürk Clinic: Tel: 0256-613 0606, Atatürk Bulvarı, Belvu Center No: 68/4A. Private clinic.

Özel Kuşadası Hastanesi: Tel: 0256-613 1616, Türkmen Mahallesi, Ant Sokak No: 1

Marmaris

Ahu Hetman Hospital: Tel: 0252-413 1415, www.ahuhetman.com, 67 Sokak No: 3

Side

Medicus Clinic: Tel: 0242-753 1111, www.medicus.com.tr, Fatih Caddesi No: 6. Outpatient services and clinic.

STATE HOSPITALS

Istanbul

Bakırköy Hastanesi: Tel: 0212-543 6565, Bakırköy

Çapa Hastanesi: Tel: 0212-534 0000, Millet Caddesi, Çapa

Cerrahpaşa Tip Fakültesi Hastanesi: Tel: 0212-588 4800, Kocamustafapaşa Caddesi, Cerrahpaşa

Haydarpaşa Siyami Ersek Kalp Hastanesi: Tel: 0215-349 9121, Haydarpaşa

Marmara Üniversitesi Hastanesi: Tel: 0216-327 1010, Tophanelioğlu Caddesi No: 13/15, Altunizade

Taksim İlkyardım Hastanesi: Tel: 0212-252 4300, Sıraselviler Caddesi, Taksim. Emergency and first-aid hospital in town centre.

Ankara

Ankara Üniversitesi Tıp Fakültesi: Tel: 0312-319 2160, Cebeci

Ankara Üniversitesi İbni Sina Hastanesi: Tel: 0312-310 3333, Dışkapı

Gazi Üniversitesi Tıp Fakültesi: Tel: 0312-202 4444, Beşevler

Hacettepe Üniversitesi Tıp Fakültesi: Tel: 0312-305 5000, Sıhhiye

Izmir

Alsancak Devlet Hastanesi: Tel: 0232-463 2121, Alsancak

Dokuz Eylül Hastanesi: Tel: 0232-412 2222, Balçova

Ege Üniversitesi Hastanesi: Tel: 0232-433 3333, Bornova

Karşıyaka Devlet Hastanesi: Tel: 0232-367 6767, Karşıyaka

Adana

Devlet Hastanesi: Tel: 0322-321 5752, Karataş Yolu üstü, Sanayi Çarşısı, Karşıyaka

Antalya

Antalya Devlet Hastanesi: Tel: 0242-238 5353, 100.Yıl Bulvarı, Soğuksu Caddesi

Alanya

Alanya Devlet Hastanesi: 0242-513 4842, Güller Pınarı Mahallesi

Bodrum

Bodrum Devlet Hastanesi: Tel: 0252-313 1420, Turgutreis Caddesi

Kaş

Kaş Devlet Hastanesi: Tel 0242-836 1185, Çukurbağ Yarımadası Yolu, Hastane Caddesi No: 37

Marmaris

Marmaris Devlet Hastanesi: Tel: 0252-412 1029

Selçuk

Selçuk Devlet Hastanesi: Tel: 0232-892 7036, Dr Sabri Yayla Bulvarı

APPENDIX IX:
RESTAURANTS

CHILD-FRIENDLY RESTAURANTS
Istanbul
Hippopotamus: Tel: 0212-345 0830, Park Plaza No: 22, Eski Büyükdere Caddesi, Maslak. French chain restaurant offering children's menu and crayons.

Princess Hotel Sports Bar: Tel: 0212-285 0900, Büyükdere Caddesi No: 49, Maslak. Bar with children's menu and play area.

TGI Fridays: Tel: 0212-257 7078, Nispetiye Caddesi No: 19, Etiler; Tel: 0216-356 8558, Bağdat Caddesi No: 445, Suadiye. Popular chain restaurant with children's menus and play area.

ETHNIC RESTAURANTS
Istanbul
Austrian
Schnitzel Restaurant: Tel: 0212-231 3161, Mega Residence Hotel, Eytam Caddesi No: 33, Maçka

Belgian
Belgo Bierodrome: Tel: 0212-248 0157, Abdi İpekçi Caddesi No: 48/2, Nişantaşı

Brazilian
Balcao Restaurant: Tel: 0212-265 6912, Muallim Naci Caddesi No: 130, Kuruçeşme

British
British Pub: Tel: 0212-244 4246, www.piratesbritishpub.com. İstiklal Caddesi, Bekar Sokak No: 16/1

The North Shield: Tel: 0212-245 2162, www.thenorthshield.com, İstiklal Caddesi Nos: 24-6, Beyoğlu; Tel: 0212-246 4846, Abdi İpekçi Caddesi No: 40/1-2, Nişantaşı; also in Ataşehir, Göztepe, Kalamış and Yeşilköy

Chinese
Dragon Restaurant: Tel: 0212-231 6200, Hilton Hotel

Little China: Tel: 0212-263 1715, Cevdetpaşa Caddesi No: 5, Bebek

Royal China: Tel: 0212-573 6774, Polat Renaissance Hotel

Sushico – Chinese in Town: Tel: 0216-372 7572, Bağdat Caddesi No: 466/2, Suadiye; Tel: 0212-243 8765, İstiklal Caddesi No: 445, Tünel, Beyoğlu; Tel: 0212-393 0973, Kanyon Shopping Mall

French

Fransiz Sokak, near İstiklal Caddesi, boasts a number of 'French' restaurants. However, not all of them offer truly French menus.

Citronelle: Tel: 0212-231 2121. Ceylan Intercontinental Hotel

La Maison: Tel: 0212-227 4263, Müvezzi Caddesi No: 63, Çırağan, Beşiktaş

Le Pain Quotidien: Tel: 0212-353 0676, Kanyon Shopping Mall

Paul: Tel: 0212-287 4249, Nispetiye Caddesi No: 29, Etiler; Tel: 0212-296 1100, Valikonağı Caddesi No: 36, Nişantaşı; Tel: 0212-327 4316, Muallim Naci Caddesi No: 6, Ortaköy. French-style patisserie.

Indian

Dubb: Tel: 0212-513 7308, İncili Çavuş Sokak No:10, Sultanahmet

Iranian

Café Pars Restaurant: Tel: 0212-292 1846, Meşrutiyet Caddesi, Baran Apt: 187, Tepebaşı

Italian

Cognato Spaghetti: Tel: 0212-249 7306, İstiklal Caddesi, Anadolu Pasajı İçi No: 201/8, Beyoğlu

Grissino: Tel: 0212-630 0151, Bağlar Mahallesi, Mimar Sinan Caddesi (S. Plaza) No: 86, Güneşli

Pacino Istanbul: Tel: 0212-573 0407, Halkalı Caddesi, Toplu Konut Sitesi No: 59/9, Yeşilköy

Paper Moon: Tel: 0212-282 1616, Ulus Caddesi, Akmerkez Residence Girişi, Ulus

Pidos: Tel: 0212- 249 4040, Dünya Sağlık Sokak No: 15, Ayazpaşa, Taksim

Pina Bistro: Tel: 0216-369 7510, Bağdat Caddesi No: 337, Erenköy

Spazio: Tel: 0212-236 3711, www.reina.com.tr, Muallim Naci Caddesi No: 44, Ortaköy

Japanese

Benihana: Tel: 0212-227 7171, Çırağan Palace Hotel; Tel: 0212-258 1625, Reina, Muallim Naci Caddesi No: 43/B, Ortaköy

Hai Sushi: Tel: 0212-231 4100, Divan Hotel

Maki Sushi: Tel: 0212-231 3524, Abdi İpekçi Caddesi, Milli Reasürans Çarşısı, No: 13, Tesvikiye

Mori: Tel: 0212-351 6465, Mayadrom Shopping Mall

Sushico: Tel: 0212-243 8765, İstiklal Caddesi No: 445, Beyoğlu; Tel: 0212-234 9880, Teşvikiye Caddesi No: 133/A, Nişantaşı; Tel: 0216-372 7572, Bağdat Caddesi No: 466/1, Suadiye, Kanyon Shopping Mall. Also Thai and Chinese dishes.

Sushi Home Store: Tel: 0212-282 0253, Akmerkez Shopping Mall

Tokyo: Tel: 0212-293 5858, İstiklal Caddesi, Meşelik Sokak No: 24, Beyoğlu

Udonya: Tel: 0212-256 9318, Point Hotel, Topçu Caddesi No: 2, Taksim

Wagamama: Tel: 0212-353 0474, www.wagamama.com.tr, Kanyon Shopping Mall

Korean

Mido: Tel: 0212-286 0515, Istanbul Princess Hotel, Büyükdere Caddesi No: 49, Üçyol Mevkii, Maslak

Tegik: Tel: 0212-254 6699, Receppaşa Caddesi No: 20, Taksim

Mexican

El Torito: Tel: 0212-257 0171, Nispetiye Caddesi No: 12, Etiler

Munchie's: Tel: 0212-352 4035, Mayadrom Shopping Mall

North American

Manhattan Café: Tel: 0212-234 3379, Güzelbahçe Sokak No: 8, Nişantaşı

New Yorker: Tel: 0212-287 5295, Cevdetpaşa Caddesi, Manolya Sokak No: 244, Bebek

Schlotsky's Deli: Tel: 0216-411 6262, Bağdat Caddesi, Akın Sokak No: 396, Şaşkınbakkal

Tribeca: Tel: 0212-223 9919, Kapalı Bakkal Sokak No: 5, Yeniköy

Russian

Rejans: Tel: 0212-243 4882, Olivio Geçidi No: 17, Beyoğlu

Swiss

Cafe Swiss: Tel: 0212-223 2777, Köybaşı Caddesi No: 237, Yeniköy

Marché Restaurant Mövenpick: Tel: 0212-316 5360, İş Kuleleri, Kule Çarşı, 4.Levent

Thai

Lokal Restaurant: Tel: 0212-245 5743, Müeyyet Sokak No: 9, Tünel. Mixture of cuisines but usually some Thai.

Pera Thai: Tel: 0212-245 5725, Meşrutiyet Caddesi No: 134, Beyoğlu

Ankara

British

The North Shield: Tel: 0312-466 1266, Güvenlik Caddesi No: 111, Aşağı Ayrancı

Chinese

Sushico – Chinese in Town: Tel: 0312-426 2526, Arjantin Caddesi, Attar Sokak No: 10, Gaziosmanpaşa

French

Paul: Tel: 0312- 426 5578, Arjantin Caddesi No: 15/A

Spanish

Tapa Tapa Tapas: Tel: 0312-428 3562, Tunalı Hilmi Caddesi No: 83

Izmir

British

The North Shield: Tel: 0232-483 0720, Konak Pier, Atatürk Caddesi

Fethiye & Around

British

Daphne's Fish and Chips Restaurant & Takeaway: Tel: 0252-616 9757, Kaya Yolu üzeri, Hisarönü

KOSHER RESTAURANTS

Istanbul

Carne Restaurant: Tel: 0212-260 8425, Muallim Naci Caddesi No: 41/10, Ortaköy

Levi: Tel: 0212-512 1196, Tahmis Kalçın Sokak, Çavuşbaşı Han No: 23/1, Eminönü. Lunch only.

Toda: Tel: 0216-357 0462, Ömerpaşa Sokak No: 63/1-2, Erenköy

NEW YEAR'S EVE DINNERS

Istanbul

Çırağan Palace Hotel Kempinski: Tel: 0212-326 4646, Çırağan Caddesi No: 84, Beşiktaş

Dedeman Hotel: Tel: 0212-274 8800, Yıldız Posta Caddesi No: 50, Esentepe

Hilton Istanbul: Tel: 0212-315 6000, Cumhuriyet Caddesi, Harbiye

Hilton Park: Tel: 0212-310 1200, Bayıldım Caddesi No: 12, Maçka

Hyatt Regency: Tel: 0212-368 1234, Taşkışla Caddesi No: 1, Elmadağ

The Marmara: Tel: 0212-251 4696, Taksim Square, Beyoğlu

The Marmara Pera: Tel: 0212-251 4646, Meşrutiyet Caddesi No: 155-57, Tepebaşı

Ritz-Carlton: Tel: 0212-334 4444, Askerocağı Caddesi No: 15, Elmadağ

Mövenpick Hotel: Tel: 0212-319 2929, Büyükdere Caddesi, 4.Levent

Polat Renaissance: Tel: 0212-414 1800, Sahilyolu, Yeşilköy

Taxim Hill Hotel: Tel: 0212-334 8500, Sıraselviler Caddesi No: 9, Beyoğlu

PROFESSIONAL CATERERS

Istanbul

Bakery'Z: Tel: 0212-257 4299, www.allsportscafe, Bıyıklı Mehmet Paşa Sokak No: 1/2, Etiler; Şakayık Sokak No: 49/1, Nişantaşı. Cakes to order with one day's notice.

Cumalı Tanıtım: Tel: 0212-291 0181, www.cumalitanitim.com, Şakayık Sokak No: 45-2, Teşvikiye. Full catering service plus cushions etc for hire.

Divan Catering: Tel: 0212-251 7150, www.divan.com.tr, Kuruçeşme Caddesi No: 36, Kuruçeşme. Worldwide cuisine.

Lokal Catering: Tel: 0212-245 5743, www.lokal-istanbul.com, Müeyyet Sokak No: 9, Tünel, Beyoğlu. Chinese catering as well as dishes using ostrich meat alongside more traditional fare.

Marmara Catering: Tel: 0212-251 4696, www.themarmaraistanbul.com, Taksim Square, Beyoğlu. Caters for groups of at least 50 people. Asian and Mexican dishes as well as traditional Turkish meals.

Nesil Davet: Tel: 0212-243 4080, www.nesildavet,com, Kardeşim Sokak No: 34, Karaköy. Hires out marquees for parties.

Roka Davet: Tel: 0212-325 4747, www.rokadavet.com, Ulubaş Caddesi No: 30/1, 4.Levent. Full catering service, plus tent hire, music, flowers etc.

Şans Catering: Tel: 0212-280 3838. www.sansrestaurant.com, Hacı Adil Caddesi No: 6, 1.Levent.

Sardunya Catering: Tel: 0212-266 4113, www.sardunyacatering.com, Vefa Bey Sokak No: 5/2, Gayrettepe. Specialises in traditional Turkish food.

Sushico-Chinese In Town Catering: Tel: 0212-234 9880, www.chineseintown.com, Teşvikiye Caddesi No: 133/A, Teşvikiye. Specialises in Asian food and can supply chopsticks, Chinese lanterns etc.

Tu Ta Bakery: Tel: 0212-244 5263, İstiklal Caddesi, Meşelik Sokak No: 22, Taksim, Beyoğlu; Tel: 0212-275 6619, Vefa Bey Sokak, Say Apt, Dükkan No: 9, Gayrettepe. Cakes made to whatever shape you want.

VEGETARIAN RESTAURANTS
Istanbul

Deep Restaurant: Tel: 0212-243 4483, Kurabiye Sokak No: 2, Beyoğlu

Kestane: Tel: 0212-265 6617, Cevdetpaşa Caddesi No: 97/A, Bebek

Nature & Peace: Tel: 0212- 252 8609, Büyükparmakkapı Sokak No: 21, Beyoğlu

Parsifal: Tel: 0212-245 2588, Kurabiye Sokak No: 13, Beyoğlu

Zencefil: Tel: 0212-243 8233, Kurabiye Sokak No: 8, Beyoğlu

Zerdeçal: Tel: 0216-414 8141, Halis Efendi Sokak No: 5/1, Caferağa, Kadıköy

Fethiye & Around
Our Place: Tel: 0252-616 6919, Hisarönü

APPENDIX X:
FUN AND GAMES

BABYSITTING SERVICES
Istanbul

Anıl Danışmanlık: Tel: 0212-293 4812, Sıraselviler Caddesi No: 84-86, Daire: 409, Taksim; Tel: 0216-348 3134, Serasker Caddesi, Dilber Pasajı No: 104/5, Kadıköy

BALLET *(BALE)* SCHOOLS

See Dance Classes below

BOWLING ALLEYS

Istanbul

Most bowling alleys are multi-purpose entertainment centres and popular places for children's parties.

Istanbul

Bab Bowling: Tel: 0212-251 1595, www.babbowling.com, Yeşilçam Sokak No: 24, Beyoğlu

Cosmic Bowling: Tel: 0212-286 1276, Maslak Üç Yol Mevkii, Büyükdere Caddesi

Galleria Bowling: Tel: 0212-661 3222, www.galleriabowling.com, Galleria Shopping Mall

Korukent Bowling: Tel: 0212-274 6663, www.korukentbowling.com, Korukent, Levent

Pin Bowling: Tel: 0216-385 3478, www.pinclubbowling.com, Bağdat Caddesi, Kazım Özalp Sokak No: 22

Prince Bowling: Tel: 0212-227 7100, Dereboyu Caddesi Nos: 36-8, Ortaköy

Time Out Bowling Centre: Tel: 0212-217 0993, www.timeoutbowling.com, Profilo Shopping Mall

Ankara

On: Tel: 0312-215 3400, Azerbeycan Caddesi No: 41, Bahçelievler

Roll House: Tel: 0312-266 1240, Ankuva Shopping Mall

Izmir

Planet Bowling: Tel: 0232-324 4569

EGS Park Bowling: Tel: 0232-343 7075, EGS Park Shopping Mall

Antalya

Dedeman Park Bowling: Tel: 0242-316 4400, Lara Yolu

Fethiye

Kumsal Bowling: Tel: 0252-617 0058, Belceğiz Mahallesi, 3.Sokak, Ölüdeniz

CINEMAS

Istanbul

Sultanahmet

Şafak Sinemaları: Tel: 0212-516 2660, Darüşşafaka Binası, Divan Yolu No: 134, Çemberlitaş

Beyoğlu

AFM Fitaş: Tel: 0212-251 2020, İstiklal Caddesi Nos: 24-26
Alkazar: Tel: 0212- 293 2466, İstiklal Caddesi No: 179
Atlas: Tel: 0212-252 8576, İstiklal Caddesi No: 209
Beyoğlu: Tel: 0212-251 3240, İstiklal Caddesi No: 140
Cine Majestic: Tel: 0212-244 9707, İstiklal Caddesi, Ayhan Işık Sokak No: 10,
Emek: Tel: 0212-293 8439, İstiklal Caddesi, Yeşilçam Sokak No: 5
Kafika: Tel: 0212-244 5167, Bolahenk Sokak No: 8, Cihangir (private café-cinema)
Sinepop: Tel: 0212-251 1176, İstiklal Caddesi, Yeşilçam Sokak No: 22
Tarık Zafer Tunaya Kültür Merkezı: Tel: 0212-293 1270, Şahkulu Bostanı Sokak No: 8,
   İstiklal Caddesi, Tünel,
Yeşilcam: Tel: 0212-249 8006, İstiklal Caddesi, İmam Adnan Sokak No: 10

Etiler

AFM Akmerkez: Tel: 0212-282 0505, www.afm.com.tr, Akmerkez Shopping Mall

Kadıköy

Atlantis: Tel: 0216-336 0622, Bahariye Caddesi No: 46
Kadıköy: Tel: 0216-337 7400, Bahariye Caddesi No: 25
Broadway: Tel: 0216-346 1481, Bahariye Caddesi No: 92
Rexx: Tel: 0216-336 0112, Sakızgülü Sokak No: 20-22

Ortaköy

AFM Princess: Tel: 0212-236 2072, Ortaköy Princess Hotel
Feriye: Tel: 0212-236 2864, www.umutsanat.com.tr, Çırağan Caddesi No: 124

Elsewhere in Istanbul

AFM Mayadrom: Tel: 0212-352 2351, Mayadrom Shopping Mall
AFM Teşvikiye: Tel: 0212-224 0505, Tesvikiye Caddesi, Milli Reasürans Shopping Mall
Biligi Cinema Centre: Tel: 0212-216 2315, İnönü Caddesi No: 28, Kuştepe, Şişli
Bonus Premium CineCity: Tel: 0216-315 1010, Hillside City Club Trio, Trio Konutları,
   Halk Caddesi No: 99, Kozyatağı
Capitol Spectrum 14: Tel: 0216-651 3343, Capitol Shopping Mall
Carousel: Tel: 0212-571 8380, Carousel Shopping Mall
Cinebonus G-Mall: Tel: 0212-232 4440, G-Mall Shopping Mall
Cine/Mall: Tel: 0212-323 5880, Yeni İstinye Caddesi, Maxi Centre, Kat: 3, İstinye
Cinemax Şaşkınbakkal: Tel: 0216-467 4467, Bağdat Caddesi No: 401/3
Cineplex Odeon: Tel: 0212-216 3790, Profilo Shopping Mall
Galleria Prestige: Tel: 0212-560 7266, Galleria Shopping Mall
Istanbul Megaplex: Tel: 0212-380 1515, Cevahir Shopping Mall

Istanbul Modern Sineması: Tel: 0212-334 7300, www.istanbulmodern.org, Meclis-i Mebusan Caddesi, Liman İşletmeleri Sahası, Antrepo No: 4, Karaköy. Foreign art films and documentaries.

Marks & Spencer Cinema: Tel: 0216-467 4468, Bağdat Caddesi No: 481, Şaşkınbakkal

Migros Beylikdüzü: Tel: 0212-852 0190, Migros Shopping Mall, Beylikdüzü

Moda: Tel: 0216-337 0128, Bahariye Caddesi, Halil Ethem Sokak No: 53, Moda

Movieplex Etiler: Tel: 0212-284 3005, Nispetiye Caddesi, Melodi Pasajı No: 14, Etiler

Movieplex Suadiye: Tel: 0216-467 6058, Suadiye Plaj Yolu No: 10

TIM Movie Theatre: Tel: 0212-286 6604, Büyükdere Caddesi, Debent Mevkii, Maslak

Ankara

Akün Sineması: Tel: 0312-427 7656, Atatürk Bulvarı No: 227, Kavaklıdere

Ankapol: Tel: 0312-419 3959, Kızılırmak Sokak No: 14, Kızılay

Ata On Tower: Tel: 0312-441 1414, Atakule, Çankaya

Batı: Tel: 0312-418 3028, Atatürk Bulvarı No: 151/1, Bakanlıklar

Büyülü Fener: Tel: 0312-212 9296, 7.Caddesi, 18.Sokak No: 22, Bahçelievler

Cinepol: Tel: 0312-235 4580, Ümitköy Galleria Shopping Mall

Cineplex-IMAX: Tel: 0312-541 1333, Migros Shopping Mall

Derya: Tel: 0312-229 9618, Necatibey Caddesi No: 57, Kızılay

Kavaklıdere: Tel: 0312-468 7193, Tunalı Hilmi Caddesi No: 105

Kızılırmak Sineması: Tel: 0312-425 5393, Kızılırmak Sokak, Kızılay

Koru: Tel: 0312-241 1100, Mesa Koru Sitesi, Ticaret Merkezi Nos: 5-6, Çayyolu

Megapol: Tel: 0312-419, Konur Sokak No: 33, Kızılay

Metropol: Tel: 0312-425 7479, Selanik Caddesi No: 76, Kızılay

Mithatpaşa: Tel: 0312- 431 8515, Mithatpaşa Caddesi No: 51/B, Kızılay

ON: Tel: 0312-215 3400, Azerbeycan Caddesi (3.Cadde) No: 41, Bahçelievler

Tepe Cinemaxx: Tel: 0312-266 1634, Bilkent Centre (Lower Ground Floor)

Izmir

AFM EGS: Tel: 0232-373 7320, Bornova

Batı Sinema: Tel: 0232-388 8923, Özkanlar 273 Sokak No: 1, Bornova

Cinecity Kipa Mavişehir: Tel: 0232-386 5888, Kipa Shopping Mall

Izmir: Tel: 0232-421 4261, Cumhuriyet Bulvari, 188 Sokak, Alsancak

Konak: Tel: 0232-483 2191

Mavişehir AFM EGS: Tel: 0232-324 4264, Mavişehir Shopping Mall

Metropol: Tel: 0232-251 0073

Parliament Cinema Club: Tel 0232-386 5888

Adana

M1 Tepe Real Shopping Mall: Tel: 0322-271 0260

Antalya

Megapol Sinemasi: Tel: 0242-237 0131, Meltem Mahallesi, Özlem Sitesi
Migros Cinebonus: Tel: 0242-230 1414, Migros Shopping Mall
Plaza: Tel: 0242-312 6296, Antalya 2000 Shopping Mall
Prestige: Tel: 0242-312 0543, Metin Kasapoğlu Caddesi, Metropol Çarşısı

Bodrum

Cinemarin: Tel: 0252-317 0001, Oasis Shopping Mall, Kıbrısşehitleri Caddesi
Karia Cinema: Tel: 0252-316 6272, Mindos Caddesi No: 15

Çeşme

Sinema Çeşme: Tel: 0232-712 0713, Migros Shopping Mall

Eskişehir

Sinema Anadolu: Tel: 0222-335 0580

Fethiye

Cinema Doruk: Tel: 0252-612 3000, Yat Limanı
Hayal Sineması: Tel: 0252-612 1314, İnönü Bulvarı No: 96

Kayseri

Kasseria Sineması: Tel: 0352-223 1153, Kasseria İş Merkezi, Sivas Caddesi,
Onay Sineması: Tel: 0352-222 1313, Serçeönü Mahallesi, Ahi Evran Caddesi No: 24

Mersin

Metro Sinemaları: Tel: 0324-331 0077, Hilton Hotel karşısı, Koluman Plaza altı

Nevşehir

Can Aile Sineması: Tel: 0384-213 1725

Selçuk

Selcuk Sineması: Above otogar.

OPEN-AIR CINEMAS

There is also an open-air cinema in Datça harbour.

Istanbul

Conrad Hotel: Tel: 0212-227 3000, www.afm.com.tr, Yıldız Caddesi
Kemer Golf and Country Club: Tel: 0212-239 7010, Kemerburgaz
Park Orman: Tel 0212-328 2000
Swissotel Sinema: Tel: 0212-326 1100, www.swissotel.com.tr, Swissotel

Bodrum

Port Bodrum Yalıkavak Marina: Tel: 0252-311 0600

Çeşme
Sole Mare Beach Club: Tel: 0232-712 2057

CLASSICAL MUSIC VENUES

Istanbul
Atatürk Cultural Centre (Atatürk Kültür Merkezi): Tel: 0212-251 5600, Taksim Square. Hosts State Opera, State Ballet, State Theatre and State Symphony Orchestra. Also used during Istanbul International Festival.

Akbank Cultural and Arts Centre: Tel: 0212-252 3500, İstiklal Caddesi Nos: 14-18, Beyoğlu

Aya İrini Church: Beautiful 6th-century building in grounds of Topkapı Palace. Hosts concerts during Istanbul International Festival.

Borusan Culture and Arts Centre: Tel: 0212-292 0655, İstiklal Caddesi No: 421, Beyoğlu

Cemal Reşit Rey (CRR) Konser Salonu: Tel: 0212-232 9830, www.crrks.org, Lütfü Kırdar Kongre Merkezi, Harbiye

Darphane-i Amire (Imperial Mint): Topkapı Palace. Hosts concerts during Istanbul International Festival.

Enka Auditorium: Tel: 0212-276 1540, İstinye

İş Towers Art and Culture Centre: Tel: 0212-316 1083, İş Bankası Kuleleri, 4.Levent

Lütfü Kırdar Convention and Exhibition Centre: Tel: 0212-296 3055, Harbiye

Nazım Hikmet Kültür Merkezi: Tel: 0216-414 2239, Osmanağa Mahallesi, Ali Suavi Sokak No: 7, Bahariye, Kadıköy

Tarik Zafer Tunaya Salonu: Tel: 0212-293 1270, Şahkulu Bostanı Sokak No: 8, Tünel, Beyoğlu

Yerebatan Sarnıcı: Tel: 0212-522 1259. Yerebatan Caddesi, Sultanahmet. Atmospheric venue for summer concerts in underground cistern.

Yıldız Palace Theatre: Tel: 0212-258 3080, Beşiktaş

Ankara
Bilkent University: Tel: 0312-266 4382, Bilkent. Home to Bilkent Symphony Orchestra

State Opera House: Tel: 0312-324 2210, Atatürk Bulvarı, Opera Meydanı, Ulus. Home to State Opera and Ballet companies.

Izmir
Izmir State Opera & Ballet: Tel: 0232-441 0173, Konak Meydanı

DANCE CLASSES

Istanbul
Akademi Istanbul: Tel: 0212-251 7484, İstiklal Caddesi, Bahçeli Hamam Sokak No: 3, Beyoğlu. Variety of classes in ballet, jazz dance, etc.

Baila Tango House: Tel: 0212-245 0717, İstiklal Caddesi, Balo Sokak No: 1, Beyoğlu. Tango specialists.

Boğaziçi Üniversitesi: Tel: 0212-287 0232, Hisarüstü. Latin American dance classes taught by Russians.

Dance Akademik: Tel: 0212-257 0154, Cevher Sokak No: 6, Etiler

Latinos en Salsa: Tel: 0212-351 4833, Akatlar Kültür Merkezi, Zeytinoğlu Caddesi No: 74, Akatlar, Istanbul. Latin dance classes.

Marmara Hotel: Tel: 0212-251 4696, Taksim Square. Latin American and oriental dance classes.

Mundo Latino: Tel: 0212-244 6359, İstiklal Caddesi, Galatasary İş Hanı No: 230, Kat: 2, Galatasaray, Beyoğlu. Salsa, tango etc.

Ankara

Latino Dance: Tel: 0312-467 4910, Tunus Caddesi No: 50/16, Kavaklıdere

Murphy's Dance (Bar) Course: Tel: 0312-468 2888, Hilton Hotel, Tahran Caddesi No: 12, Kavaklıdere

Turkish-American Association: Tel: 0312-426 2648, Cinnah Caddesi No: 20, Kavaklıdere

Ulusoy Ballet School: Tel: 0312-428 2119, Atatürk Bulvarı No: 243, İşbank Blokları B Blok, Kavaklıdere

DAY SPAS

Istanbul

Bosphorus Spa & Wellness Centre: Tel: 0212-326 1100, www.swissotel.com.tr, Swissotel

Camene Spa & Wellness Centre: Tel: 0212-313 5049, www.cameneclub.com, Point Hotel, Topçu Caddesi No: 2, Taksim

Chi'um Istanbul: Tel: 0212-287 1692, www.thelifeco.com, Mezarlık Çıkmazı Sokak 8, Kuruçeşme. Flotation tank, massage, yoga.

Çırağan Health Club: Tel: 0212-258 3377, Çırağan Palace Hotel

Hillside Day Spa; Tel: 0212-352 2333, Tepecik Yolu, Alkent, Etiler

Hilton Istanbul Health Club: Tel: 0212-315 6000, Hilton Hotel

Laveda Spa: Tel: 0212-334 4353, Ritz-Carlton Hotel

Leyla İnanır Spa Beauty Centre: Tel: 0212-219 1500, www.leylainanir.com.tr, Rumeli Caddesi No: 18/3, Nişantaşı

LS Natural Cosmetics: Tel: 0212-358 3192, www.is.com.tr, Cevdet Paşa Caddesi No: 31/A, Bebek

Maha D'Line: Tel: 0216-422 5967, Halk Caddesi, Sema Apt No: 60/3, Çengelköy

Mövenpick Wellness Centre: Tel: 0212-319 2929, Mövenpick Hotel

Plusmed: Tel: 0212-324 5097, Levent Caddesi, Mektep Sokak No: 30, 1.Levent

Sanda Day Spa: Tel: 0212-352 2333, Hillside City Club, Etiler

Spa Sefa: Tel: 0216-425 1950, www.sefaspa.com, Hacı Muhittin Sokak No: 34, Kanlıca

Yosun Dead Sea Spa: Tel: 0212-282 6500, www.deadseamagik.com, Levent Caddesi No: 34, 1.Levent

Adapazarı

Nua Wellness Spa: Tel: 0264-582 2100, www.richmondnus.com, Richmond Hotel, Sahilyolu, Sapanca

Antalya

Carpe Diem Spa: Tel: 0242-352 2626, www.concordehotel.com.tr, Concorde Resort and Spa, Lara Beach

Bodrum

Fuga Hotel: Tel: 0252-317 2360, www.fuga.com.tr, Asarlık Mevkii

The Marmara Bodrum: Tel: 0252-313 8130, Köybaşı Mevkii

Fethiye

Hillside Beach Club: Tel: 0252-614 8360, Kalemya Koyu

FOLK MUSIC VENUES

Istanbul

Şal: Tel: 0212-243 4196, Büyükparmakkapı Sokak No: 18/A, off İstiklal Caddesi, Beyoğlu. Small, unpretentious bar which encourages interest in folk traditions with live music nightly.

Türkü Bar: Tel: 0212-292 9281, İmam Adnan Sokak No: 9, off İstiklal Caddesi, Beyoğlu. Lively bar for traditional music and dancing.

FOOTBALL CLUBS

Istanbul

Beşiktaş: www.beskitas.org, İnönü Stadyumu, Beşiktaş ('the Black Eagles')

Fenerbahçe: www.fenerbahce.org, Şükrü Saracoğlu Stadyumu, Kadıköy ('the Canaries')

Galatasaray: www.galatasaray.org, Ali Sami Yeni Stadyumu, Mecidiyeköy ('Cim Bom')

Trabzon

Trabzonspor: www.trabzonspor.org.tr, Hüseyin Avni Aker Stadyumu

GOLF COURSES

Istanbul

Istanbul Golf Club: Tel: 0212-264 0742, 4.Levent. 9 holes.

Kemer Golf & Country Club: Tel: 0212-239 7010, Uzunkemer Mevkii, Göktürk Beldesi, Kemerburgaz. 9 and 18 holes.

Klassis Golf and Country Club: Tel: 0212-727 4050, Kargaburnun Mevkii, Silivri. 9 and 18 holes.

Belek (Antalya)

Antalya Golf Club: Tel: 0242-725 5970, www.antalyagolfclub.com.tr, Belek Tourism Centre, Serik. 18 holes.

National Golf Club: Tel: 0242-725 4620, www.nationalturkey.com, Belek Tourism Centre, Serik. 9 and 18 holes.

Nobilis Golf Club: Tel: 0242-710 0300, Acısu Mevkii, Belek. 9 and 18 holes.

Tat Golf Club: Tel: 0242-725 4080, Üçkumtepesi Mevkii, Bebek, Serik. 9 and 18 holes.

Adana

Hodja Golf Club: Tel: 0322-316 6249, İncirlik American Forces Base. 9 holes.

GO-KARTING

Istanbul

Gopis: Tel: 0212-501 8420, Çırpıcı Yedikule Yolu No: 10, Topkapı

GYMS

Istanbul

Akatlar Sports Complex: Tel: 0212-283 6600, 5.Gazeteciler Sitesi, Mayadrom yanı, Levent

Bali Sports Centre: Tel: 0216-680 0171, www.balisportcenter.com, Cumhuriyet Caddesi No: 99, Gürsel Plaza, Rüzgarlıbahçe, Kavacık, Beykoz

Cihangir Sports Centre: Tel: 0212-245 1255, Sıraselviler Caddesi No: 188 (above Dia), Cihangir, Beyoğlu

ENKA Sports Centre: Tel: 0212-276 5084, İstinye Yolu, İstinye

Flash Gym: Tel: 0212-249 5347, Aznavur Pasajı, Kat: 4, İstiklal Caddesi No: 202, Beyoğlu

Gymnasium: Tel: 0212-276 8865, Darüşşafaka Çetin Berkmen Tesisleri, Derbent Mevkii, Maslak

Hillside City Club: Tel: 0212-287 8585, www.hillside.com.tr, Tepecik Yolu, Alkent, Etiler

Hillside City Club-Trio: Tel: 0216-324 1111, Trio Konutları No: 9, Kozyatağı

Korukent Sports Centre: Tel: 0212-274 0668, A Blok, Koru Sokak, Korukent Sitesi, Levent

Marmara Gym: Tel: 0212-251 4696, info@themarmaraistanbul.com, Marmara Hotel, Taksim Square. Open 7am to 10pm daily. Fully-equipped modern gym with views over Taksim Square. Dance and yoga classes.

Mayadrom Sports Centre: Tel: 0212-352 3200, Otlukbeli Caddesi, Yol Sokak No: 16-17/28, Maya Residence, Etiler

Sports International: Tel: 0212-559 3333, Ataköy Marina Sahil Yolu; Tel: 0212-296 2515, Şişli

Unique: Tel: 0212-224 2609, Valikonağı Caddesi No: 30/8, Nişantaşı

Vakkorama Gym: Tel: 0212-251 1571, Osmanlı Sokak No: 13, Taksim. Open Monday to Friday 7.30am to 10pm, Saturday and Sunday 10am to 6pm. Upmarket gym equipment. Aerobics and other classes.

Ankara

Fitness Court: Tel: 0312-240 1161, Eskişehir Yolu 19km, Konutkent II, Çayyolu

Ute Gym: Tel: 0312- 466 1439, Tunalı Hilmi Caddesi, Kuğulu Han No: 123, Kavaklıdere

Fethiye

Colosseum: Tel: 0252-614 5354, www.colosseum.gen.tr, Esnaf Hastanesi karşısı, Dolgu Sahası, 533 Sokak

Selçuk

Zuhal Fitness; Tel: 0232-892 8880, 1039 Sokak. Yoga and aerobics as well.

HEALTH CENTRES

Istanbul

Ceylan Inter-Continental Health Club: Tel: 0212-231 2121, www.istanbul.interconti.net.tr, Ceylan Intercontinental Hotel. State-of-the-art gym. Aerobics and step classes.

Eresin Health Club: Tel: 0212-631 1212, www.eresin.com, Eresin Topkapı Hotel, Millet Caddesi No: 186, Topkapı

Mövenpick Club: Tel: 0212-319 2929, Mövenpick Hotel

Planet Health Club: Tel: 0212-257 2636, www.planethc.com, Muallim Naci Caddesi No: 170, Kuruçeşme

INDOOR PLAYGROUNDS

Istanbul

Play Barn: Tel: 0212-299 4803, Kirazlıbağ Sokak No: 4, Yeniköy; Tel: 0212-351 6486, Nispetiye Caddesi, Kervan Apt: 17/1, Etiler. For children up to 12. Private parties.

Party Kids: Tel: 0212-328 2000, www.partykids.com.tr, Park Orman

JAZZ MUSIC VENUES

Istanbul

Istanbul Jazz Centre: Tel: 0212-327 5050, www.istanbuljazz.com, Istanbul SAS Bosphorus Hotel

Babylon: Tel (0212) 292 73 68, Şeyhbender Sokak No. 3, Asmalımescit,

Nardis Jazz Club: Tel: 0212-244 6327, Kuledibi Caddesi No: 14, Galata

LIBRARIES

Istanbul

American Research Institute Library: Tel: 0212-257 8111, Üvez Sokak No: 5, Arnavutköy

Atatürk Library: Tel: 0212-249 5683, Mete Caddesi, Taksim, Beyoğlu

Dutch History & Archaeology Institute Library: Tel: 0212-293 9283, İstiklal Caddesi No: 393, Beyoğlu

French Library: Tel: 0212-334 8768, French Consulate, İstiklal Caddesi No: 8, Taksim

German Archaeology Institute Library: Tel: 0212-244 0714, Ayazpaşa Cami Sokak No: 48, Gümüşsuyu

Istanbul Modern Library: Tel: 0212-334 7300, www.istanbulmodern.org, Meclis-i Mebusan Caddesi, Liman İşletmeleri Sahası, Antrepo No: 4, Karaköy. Specialist arts library in basement of modern art gallery.

Süleymaniye Library: Tel: 0212-520 6460, Ayşekadın Hamam Sokak No: 35, Beyazıt. Specialist collection of books on Ottomans.

Topkapı Palace Library: Tel: 0212-512 0480 x125, Topkapı Palace, Sultanahmet. Specialist collection of hand-written books. Access by appointment only.

Women's Library: Tel: 0212-534 9550, Fener. Specialist collection of publications by and about women. Open 9am to 5.30pm Monday to Friday.

Ankara

American Research Institute in Turkey: Tel: 0312-427 2222, John F. Kennedy Caddesi No: 146/4, Gaziosmanpaşa

Bilkent University Main Campus Library: Tel: 0312-266 4472, library.bilkent.edu.tr, Bilkent. Open 9am to 11.30pm daily.

British Institute of Archaeology in Ankara: Tel: 0312-427 5487, Tahran Caddesi No: 24, Kavaklıdere. Open 9am to 5pm Wednesday and Friday, 9am to 9pm Tuesday and Thursday, and 9am to 2pm Saturday.

National Library (Milli Kütüphane): Tel: 0312-212 6200, İsmet İnönü Bulvarı, Bahçelievler

Izmir

British Council Library: Tel: 0232-295 0027, Izmir University of Economics, Sakarya Caddesi No: 156, Balçova

MARINAS

Istanbul

Ataköy Marina: Tel: 0212-560 4270, Sahilyolu, Ataköy

Atlantis Yachting Learning Centre: Tel: 0216-337 4911, Münir Nurettin Selçuk Caddesi No: 56, Kızıltoprak

Istanbul Sailing Club: Tel: 0216-348 7990, Fenerbahçe Burnu, Kadıköy

Setur Kalamış & Fenerbahçe Marina: Tel: 0216-346 2346, Münir Nurettin Selçuk Caddesi, Kalamış

Antalya
Kaleiçi Yacht Marina: Tel: 0242-248 4530
Setur Marina: Tel: 0242-259 1290

Ayvalık
Setur Marina: Tel: 0266-312 2696, Atatürk Bulvarı, Yat Limanı

Bodrum
D-Marin Turgutreis Marina: Tel: 0252-382 9200, www.dogusmarina.com.tr,

Milta Bodrum Marina: Tel: 0252-316 1860, www.miltabodrummarina.com, Neyzen Teyfik Caddesi

Port Atami: Tel: 0252-35 7416, Atami Hotel, Cennet Koyu, Gölköy

Port Bodrum Yalıkavak Marina: Tel: 0252-385 3860, www.portbodrum.com

Çeşme
Altınyunus Setur Marina: Tel: 0232-723 1434, Boyalık

Fethiye
Belediye Marina: Tel: 0252-614 3539

Finike
Setur Marina: Tel: 0242-855 5030

Kuşadası
Setur Marina: Tel: 0256-814 1490

Marmaris
Albatros Marina: Tel: 0252-412 2456, Adaköy Mevkii
Netsel Marina: Tel: 0252-412 2708

MUSIC LESSONS
Istanbul
Akademi: Tel: 0212-251 7484, Bahçeli Hamam Sokak No: 3, Beyoğlu

Baby Symphony: Tel: 0212-287 3631, Küçük Bebek Caddesi, Yeniyol Sokak No: 16/12, Bebek. Pre-school-age music lessons.

OPEN-AIR CINEMAS See Cinemas above.

PONY CLUBS See Stables, below.

POP MUSIC VENUES

Istanbul

Babylon: Tel: 0212- 292 7368, www.babylon-ist.com, Şehbender Sokak No: 3, Asmalımescit, Tünel. One of Istanbul's best live music venues with inspirational and varied programme.

Beşiktaş Cultural Centre: Tel: 0212-260 1156, Hasfırın Sokak No: 75, Beşiktaş

Binbirdirek Sarnıçı: Tel: 0212-517 8725, Öktem Sokak No: 4, Adliye Sarayı karşısı, Sultanahmet

Harbiye Open-Air Theatre: Tel: 0212-296 3630, behind Hilton Hotel

Roxy: Tel: 0212-245 6539, www.roxy.com.tr, Arslan Yatağı Sokak 3, off Sıraselviler Caddesi, Taksim. Popular live music venue with erratic programme.

Rumeli Hisarı: Tel: 0212-263 5305. Outdoor pop concerts by big-name stars every July and August.

RACECOURSES

Istanbul

Istanbul Veliefendi Racecourse: Tel: 0212-444 0855, Ekrem Kurt Bulvarı, Bakırköy

SKATING RINKS

Istanbul

Galleria Shopping Mall: Tel: 0212-560 8550, Galleria Shopping Mall

Park Orman Entertainment Centre: Tel: 0212-328 2000, www.parkorman.com.tr

Ankara

Belpa Ice-Skating Palace: Tel: 0312-222 2291, Bahçelievler

Izmir

Buca Hasanağa Park: Tel: 0232- 420 1953

SOLARIA

Istanbul

Sun Vital: Tel: 0212-241 5993, www.sunvital.com, Valikonağı Caddesi, Şair Nigar Sokak No: 1/2, Nişantaşı

Ankara

Dedeman Hotel: Tel: 0312-417 6200, Akay Caddesi, Büklüm Sokak No: 1

Izmir

Crowne Plaza Hotel: Tel: 0232-292 1300, www.cpizmir.com, İnciraltı Mevkii, 10 Sokak No: 67, Balçova

Hilton Hotel: Tel: 0232-497 6060, Gaziosmanpaşa Bulvarı

STABLES

Istanbul

Ferhat Bey Binicilik Club: Tel: 0216-429 5031, Şile Yolu, Alemdağ Mevkii

Galatasaray Binicilik Tesisleri: Tel: 0212-286 1889, Maslak

Istanbul Atlı Spor Club: Tel: 0212-276 2056, Maslak

Klassis Golf & Country Club: Tel: 0212-276 2056, Maslak

Saklıköy Country Club: Tel: 0216-434 5521, Beykoz

Samandıra Atlıspor Club: Tel: 0216-311 4333, Samandıra

Sipahi Ocağı Binicilik Club: Tel: 0212-276 2221, Maslak

Ankara

Ankara Atlı Spor Club: Tel: 0312-213 2192, Atatürk Orman Çiftliği

Pony Club: Tel: 0312-222 1285, Çiftlik Caddesi No: 22, Beştepe

Izmir

Atlı Spor Kulübü Buca: Tel: 0232-487 3195

Olga's Horse Farm: Tel: 0232-857 0271

Pony Club: Tel: 0535-735 3724, Uğur Mumcu Caddesi No: 126, Buca

Alanya

Bellis Horse Riding Club & Zoo: Tel: 0242-725 5727, Belek Tourism Centre, Serik

Antalya

Bagana Horse Club: Tel: 0242-425 2044, Düzlercami Mevkii, Yukarı Karaman Köyü

Bodrum

Farilya Atlı Spor: Tel: 0252-357 7977, Yukarı Göl Mevkii

Turgutreis Country Ranch: Tel: 0252-382 5654, Turgutreis-Bodrum road

Kapadokya

Akhal-Teke: Tel: 0384-511 5171, www.akhal-tekehorsecenter.com, Çamikebir Mahallesi, Kadı Sokak No: 1, Avanos

Kirkit Voyage: Tel: 0384-511 3259, www.kirkit.com, Atatürk Caddesi No: 50, Avanos

SWIMMING POOLS

Istanbul

Cemal Kamacı Okmeydanı Spor Kompleksi: Tel: 0212-238 4244, Şark Kahvesi Otobüs Durağı karşısı, Okmeydanı

Ceylan Intercontinental: Tel: 0212-231 2121, Asker Ocağı Caddesi No: 1, Taksim. Open 5.30am to 9pm daily. Outdoor pool.

Çırağan Palace Kempinski Hotel: Tel: 0212-258 3377. Open 8am to 7pm daily. Spectacular outdoor pool looking over the Bosphorus.

Conrad International: Tel: 0212-227 3000, Yıldız Caddesi, Beşiktaş. Open 6.30am to 10pm daily. Outdoor pool.

Crowne Plaza Hotel: Tel: 0212-560 8100, Sahil Yolu, Ataköy. 20% discount for women on weekdays.

Gaziosmanpaşa Hamza Yerlikaya Spor Kompleksi: Tel: 0212-594 6640, Eski Edirne Asfaltı üstü, Sultançiftliği Girişi, Gaziosmanpaşa

Hillside City Club: Tel: 0212-265 0950, www.hillside.com.tr, Tepecik Yolu, Alkent, Etiler

Hilton Hotel: Tel: 0212-315 6000

Hyatt Regency: Tel: 0212-225 7000, Taşkışla Caddesi, Taksim. Open 10am to 7pm daily. Outdoor pool.

Korukent Gym & Hobby Club: Tel: 0212-274 0668, Korul Sokak, Korukent Sitesi, A Blok, Levent. Open 9am to 10pm daily.

Marmara Hotel: Tel: 0212-251 4696, Taksim Square. Open 7am to 7pm daily. Daily, weekly and seasonal rates. Discounts for children aged 6 to12.

Park Orman: Tel: 0212-328 2020. Istanbul's largest swimming pool.

Polat Renaissance Hotel: Tel: 0212-414 1800. Olympic-sized pool with Marmara views.

Tuzla Kafkale Spor Kompleksi: Tel: 0216-446 7969, Kafkale Mevkii, Postane Mahallesi, Vatan Caddesi, Tuzla

Zeytinburnu Spor Kompleksi: Tel: 0212-582-9832, Telsiz Mahallesi, Prof. Muammer Aksoy Caddesi No: 15, Zeytinburnu Stadı yanı

Ankara

Healthy Life Club: Tel: 0312-467 6527, Bestekar Sokak No: 100-116/7, Kavaklıdere

Hilton Hotel: Tel: 0312-455 0000, Tahran Caddesi No: 12, Kavaklıdere

Sheraton Hotel: Tel: 0312-468 5454, Noktalı Sokak, Kavaklıdere

TENNIS CLUBS

Istanbul

Dalyan Tennis Club: Tel: 0216-336 2451, Atlı Han Sokak, Fenerbahçe

ENKA Tennis Club: Tel: 0212-276 5084, İstinye Yolu, İstinye

Hillside Tennis Club: Tel: 0212-257 7822, Tepecik Yolu, Alkent, Etiler

Kemer Country Tennis Club: Tel: 0212-239 7770, Kemerburgaz

Levent Tennis Club: Tel: 0212-279 2710, Akasyalı Sokak No: 3, 4.Levent

Maçka Tennis Club: Tel: 0212-326 1100, www.swissotel.com, Swissotel, Bayıldım Caddesi No: 2, Maçka

Raket Tennis Club: Tel: 0216-360 0115, Ogün Çıkmaz Sokak No: 14, Caddebostan

Taç Spor Tennis Club: Tel: 0216-576 9048, Prof. Dr. Hıfzı Özcan Caddesi No: 29, Küçükbakkalköy

TED Tennis Club: Tel: 0212-262 9080, Tarabya Caddesi, Tarabya

Yeşilyurt Sports Club: Tel: 0212-663 2840, Sahil Yolu Caddesi, Yeşilyurt

Ankara

Ankara Tennis Club: Tel: 0312-310 7174, 19 Mayıs Stadyumu, Ulus

Kavaklıdere Tennis Club: Tel: 0312-427 5092, İran Caddesi No: 1, Kavaklıdere

Izmir

Aegean University Club: Tel: 0232-388 1097

Egeli Tenis Veteran Derneği Tenis Kulübü: Tel: 0232-259 7576

Göztepe Spor Kulübü: Tel: 0232-247 7787

İZTİK Tennis Club: Tel: 0232-386 0616

Karşıyaka Tennis Club: Tel: 0232-381 3514

Antalya

Antalya Tennis İhtisas ve Spor Kulübü: Tel: 0242-238 5400, 100.Yıl Bulvarı

THEME PARKS

Istanbul

Tatilya: Tel: 0212-852 0505, www.tatilya.com, E5 Karayolu, Beylikdüzü Mevkii, Büyükçekmece. Undercover theme park 30km west of Istanbul. Children's cinema. Open noon to 8pm, Tuesday to Friday, 11am to 9pm Saturday and Sunday.

THERMAL RESORTS

Afyon

Oruçoğlu Termal Resort: Tel: 0272-251 5050, Kütahya Karayolu 14km

Bursa

Çelik Palas Termal: Tel: 224-233 3800, Çekirge Caddesi No: 79, Çekirge

Kervansaray Termal: Tel: 224-233 9300, Eski Kaplıca Sokak, Çekirge

Izmir

Balçova Agememnon Kaplıcası: Tel: 0232-259 0102, Vali Hüseyin Öğütçen Caddesi No: 2, Balçova

Termal Princess: Tel: 0232-238 5151, Ilıca Mahallesi, Zeytin Sokak No: 112, Narlıdere

Kangal

Balıklı Kaplıca Oteli: Tel: 0346-457 3036. Thermal resort renowned for tiny fish which nibble the skin of psoriasis sufferers with seemingly beneficial results.

Kütahya

Yoncalı Tütav Termal Otel and Treatment Centre: Tel: 0274-249 4212, Yoncalı

Pamukkale
Club Colossae: Tel: 0258-271 4156, Karahayıt
Pamukkale Richmond Hotel: Tel: 0258-271 4294, Karahayıt
Polat Hotel: Tel: 0258-271 4110, Karahayıt

Yalova
Yalova is within day-trip reach of Istanbul using the İDO high-speed ferries (see p. 415).
Turban Yalova Termal: Tel: 0226-675 7400, Termal

TURKISH COOKERY COURSES
Istanbul
Cookbook: Tel: 0212-219 1394, Valikonağı Caddesi, Güzelbahçe Sokak, Şenyuva Apartmanı No: 5/2, Nişantaşı
Istanbul Food Workshop: Tel: 0212-534 4788, www.istanbulfoodworkshop.com, Tahtaminare Mahallesi, Yıldırım Caddesi No: 111, Fener-Balat. Specialises in Ottoman cuisine.
Mutfaktayız: Tel: 0212-358 1825, mutfaktiyiz@mutfaktiyiz.com, Tepecik Yolu No: 28/2, Etiler
Sarnıç Hotel: Tel: 0212-518 2323; www.sarnichotel.com, Küçük Ayasofya Caddesi No: 25, Sultanahmet
Spazio Restaurant: Tel: 0212-368 1234, Hyatt Regency Hotel
Zanussi Culinary Arts Academy: Tel: 0212-352 2002, www.zmsa.com, Tepecik Yolu, Alkent Sitesi, F4 Blok Nos: 9-10, Etiler

Ankara
Turkish American Association: Tel: 0312-426 3727, www.taa.ankara.org.tr, Cinnah Caddesi No: 20, Çankaya.

WATER PARKS
Antalya
Aquapark: Tel: 0242-321 7939, www.depark.com.tr, Dedeman Hotel, Lara Yolu
Dolphinland/Aqualand: Tel: 0242-249 0900, www.beachpark.com.tr, Dumlupınar Bulvarı, Konyaaltı

Bodrum
Dedeman Aquapark: Tel: 0252-358 6205, Ortakent

Kemer
Aqua World Kemer: Tel: 0242-814 5823, Liman Caddesi No: 41

WATER SPORTS
Antalya
Medraft: Tel: 0242-312 5770, www.medraft.com, Yeşilbahçe Mahallesi, Portakal Çiçeği Bulvarı, Hüseyin Kuzu Sokak No: 14/3

YOGA
Istanbul
Ananda Yoga: Tel: 0212-230 1547, Sezai Selek Sokak No: 23/5, Nişantaşı

Caddebostan Yoga Centre: Tel: 0216-369 9404, Cemil Topuzlu Caddesi, Koru Palas Apt: 105/5, Caddebostan

Inner Balance - Centre for Healthy Living: Tel: 0216-372 3731, Ayşe Çavuş Caddesi, Çolak İsmail Sokak No: 52/4, Suadiye

Naya Retreats: Tel: 0216-382 4598, www.nayaretreats.com, Maden, Yılmaz Türk Caddesi No: 96, Büyükada

Open Body & Mind Studio: Tel: 0212-251 2435, www.studio-open.com, Yeniçarşı Cad. No: 66A Galatasaray, Beyoğlu

Yoga Academy: Tel: 0212-287 9998, Suna Sokak No: 31/2, Etiler

Yoga Sala: Tel: 0212-241 0067, Teşvikiye Caddesi, Celal Derviş Apt: 166/7, Nişantaşı

Ankara
Masala Yoga: Tel: 0312-426 8326, Kader Sokak No: 21/2, Gaziosmanpaşa

Sri Govinda Math Yoga: Tel: 0312-441 5857, Abdullah Cevdet Sokak No: 33/8, Çankaya

Yoga Centre: Tel: 0312-438 1292, Willy Brant Sokak No: 24/A, Çankaya

Bodrum
Fuga Hotel: Tel: 0252-317 2360, www.fuga.com.tr, Asarlık Mevkii

Health & Yoga Holidays/Yoga Turkey: Tel: 0252-357 7207, www.yogaturkey.co.uk, Gölköy

Yoga Retreats: Tel: 0252-357 7416, Atami Hotel, Cennet Koyu Caddesi, Gölköy

ZOOS
Istanbul
Bosphorus Zoo (Boğaziçi Hayvanat Bahçesi): Tel: 0262-653 8315, Tuzla Caddesi No: 15, Bayramoğlu, İzmit. 70-hectare zoo on Asian side of Bosphorus, 45km from Istanbul.

Ankara
Atatürk Orman Çiftliği: Tel: 0312- 211 0170, www.aoc.gov.tr, Gazi Mahallesi. Zoo, gardens and Atatürk house. Open 9am to noon and 1pm to 6pm daily.

APPENDIX XI:
TURKISH COURSES AND
ENGLISH LANGUAGE SCHOOLS

TURKISH COURSES OVERSEAS
UK

School of Oriental & African Studies (SOAS): Tel: 0207-898 4888, www.soas.ac.uk, Thornhaugh St, Russell Square, London WC1H 0XG. Evening class one day a week for a year.

Manchester University: Tel: 0161-306 6000, www.manchester.ac.uk, Oxford Rd, Manchester M13 9PL. Four-year Turkish studies course with compulsory language element.

France

It is possible to study Turkish at the universities of Lyon, Provence and Strasbourg or through CNED, the distance learning centre (www.cned.fr).

Elele: Tel: 01.43.57.76.28, www.elele.info, 20 rue de al Pierre Levée, Paris

INALCO (Institut National des Langues et Civilisations Orientales): Tel: 01.41.40.89.25, Centre Universitaire de Clichy, 106 quai de Clichy, Paris

Le Centre Culturel Anatolie: Tel: 01.42.80.04.74, www.ataturqui.e.asso.fr, 77 rue Lafayette, Paris

Lycée Buffon: Tel: 01.44.38.78.70, lyc-buffon.scola.ac-paris.fr, 16 Bd Pasteur, Paris

TURKISH COURSES IN TURKEY
Istanbul

Berlitz: Tel: 0212-293 7400, info@berlitz.com.tr, İstiklal Caddesi, Tütüncü Çıkmazı No: 1/1, Beyoğlu; Tel: 0216-362 884, suadiye@berlitz.com.tr, Bağdat Caddesi, Kılıcoğlu Apt: 489/6, Suadiye

Boğaziçi University: Tel: 0212-257 5039, www.boun.edu.tr, Language Centre, Bebek. Summer programme of intensive Turkish courses. More expensive than private language schools.

ED Foreign Language: Tel: 0212-287 9064, www.turkishlesson.com, Aydın Sokak, F Blok No: 12, Kat: 1, 1.Levent

International House: Tel: 0212-282 9064, www.ihturkey.com, Nispetiye Caddesi, Erdolen İşhanı No: 38/1, 1.Levent

Litera: Tel: 0212-291 3104, www.expatistanbul.com, Halaskargazi Caddesi, Ali Koçman Apt No: 335/8, Şişli

Taksim Dilmer: Tel: 0212-292 9696, www.dilmer.com, İnönü Caddesi, Prof Dr Tarık Zafer Tunaya Sokak No: 18, Taksim

Tömer: Tel: 0212-230 7083, www.tomer.ankara.edu.tr, Cumhuriyet Mahallesi, Abide-i Hürriyet Caddesi No: 43, Şişli. Affiliated to Ankara University.

Turkish Time: Tel: 0212-292 4775, www.turkishtime.com, Istanbul. Branches in Bağdat Caddesi, Bakırköy, Kadıköy, Şirinevler, Taksim and 2.Levent.

Ankara

Aktif Turkish Teaching Centre: Tel: 0312-418 7973, Atatürk Bulvarı No: 127, Kızılay

Tömer: Tel: 0312-435 9781, www.tomer.ankara.edu.tr, Ziya Gökalp Caddesi No: 18, Kızılay; Tel: 0312-468 7063, Tunalı Hilmi Caddesi No: 97, Kavaklıdere

Turkish American Association: Tel: 0312-426 3727, www.taa.ankara.org.tr, Cinnah Caddesi No: 20, Çankaya. Four-week courses for beginners.

Izmir

Tömer: Tel: 0232-464 0544, Kıbrısşehitleri Caddesi No: 55, Alsancak

Alanya

Tömer: Tel: 0242-513 4435, Atatürk Caddesi, ALTSO İş Merkezi No: 33

Antalya

Tömer: Tel: 0242-312 5013, Sinan Mahallesi, Cebesoy Caddesi No: 26, Doğu Garajı

Bursa

Tömer: Tel: 0224-250 7297, Ulubatlı Hasan Bulvarı No: 76

Fethiye

Akyalı Dil Kursu: Tel: 0252-614 7187, Antalya Yolu

Kayseri

Tömer: Tel: 0352-222 3043, Atatürk Bulvarı, Hastane Caddesi No: 30, Kümbet yanı

Samsun

Tömer: Tel: 0362-432 7095, 19 Mayıs Mahallesi, Osmaniye Caddesi No: 23

Trabzon

Tömer: Tel: 0462-326 8099, Ortahisar Mahallesi, Eski Türkevleri, Müftülüğü yanı, Ortahisar

ENGLISH LANGUAGE SCHOOLS IN TURKEY

Istanbul

Berlitz: See Turkish Courses in Turkey above. Operates strict teaching timetable. Training provided although some find it barely adequate preparation.

English Time: Tel: 0800-219 8044, www.englishtime.com. Schools in Bağdat Caddesi, Kadıköy and Şirinevler.

Gökdil: Tel: 0212-244 3424, www.gokdil.com.tr, İstiklal Caddesi No: 214, Beyoğlu. Branches in Aksaray, Bakırköy, Gaziosmanpaşa, Kadıköy, Mecidiyeköy and Üsküdar.

Interlang: Tel: 0212-543 5797, Istanbul Caddesi, Halkçı Sokak, Yalçınlar Han No: 4, Bakırköy. General English classes for adults.

Prestige School of American English: Tel: 0212-356 9175, www.prestige.gen.tr, Kervan Geçmez Caddesi, Musa Dayı Sokak, Kocabin İş Merkezi No: 2, Kat: 1, Mecidiyeköy. General and business English classes.

Turkish International Prep Schools: Tel: 0212-351 9039, Etiler. Helps prepare Turkish high-school students to study at US universities. Sometimes employs foreign English tutors.

Ankara

Best English: Tel: 0312-417 1819, www.bestenglish.com.tr, Bayındır (2.) Sokak No: 53, Kızılay

Bilkent University School of English Language: Tel: 0312-290 1712, teacher@bilkent.edu.tr, Bilkent University, Bilkent

English Club Language School: Tel: 0312-425 8528, Atatürk Bulvarı No: 64/1, Kızılay

Kent English: Tel: 0312-433 6016, Selanik Caddesi No: 7, Hamiyet İş Hanı, Kat: 3-4, Kızılay

Turkish American Association (TAA): Tel: 0312-426 2648, turkey.usembassy.gov/in_turkey.html, Cinnah Caddesi No: 20, Kavaklıdere

Izmir

Deren & Koray International Tourism & Education Centre: Tel: 0232-441 0436, 853 Sokak No: 29, Daire: 234, Kaptan Mustafa Paşa Vakıf Çarşısı, Konak

English West: Tel: 0232-425 9208, www.englishwest.com, Cumhuriyet Bulvarı No: 36, Kapanı İşhanı, Kat: 3, Konak

Izmir University of Economics: Tel: 0232-279 2525, www.ieu.edu.tr, Sakarya Caddesi No: 156, Balçova

The English Academy: Tel: 0232-446 2520, www.theenglishacademy.com.tr, 1374 Sokak No: 18, Kat: 4, Selvili İş Merkezi, Çankaya

Antalya

Best English: Tel: 0242-241 9091, 37 Sokak No: 12

APPENDIX XII:
AUTOMOBILE CONTACTS IN TURKEY

AUTOMOBILE CLUBS

Istanbul

Turkish Touring & Automobile Club: Tel: 0212-282 8140, 1.Oto Sanayi yanı, Çamlık Sokak, 4.Levent

Ankara

Touring Automobile Association: Tel: 0312-222 8723, Mareşal Fevzi Çakmak Caddesi No: 31/8, Beşevler

Antalya

Turkish Touring & Automobile Association: Tel: 0242-247 0699, 47 Sokak No: 5/4

'BLUE-PLATE' CAR DEALERS

Istanbul

Autoline: Tel: 0212-352 6161, www.autoline.com.tr, Nispetiye Caddesi, Petrol Sitesi No: 8/1, Etiler; Tel: 0212-281 4545, Nispetiye Caddesi, Nispetiye Daire: 18/B, Levent

Taurus Motors: Tel: 0212-320 4622, taxfree@taurus-motors.com, Perpa Taurus Merkezi, K13 Blok, No: 2291/2, Okmeydanı

SECOND-HAND CARS

Istanbul

Autocity: Tel: 0212-444 0156, Eski Londra Asfaltı, E5 Karayolu Yan Yol, Çobançeşme, Yenibosna

Autolink: Tel: 0216-473 9292, E5 üzeri, Esentepe Mahallesi, Erdoğan Sokak No: 7, Kartal

Beyaz Papyon: Tel: 0216-318 3206, Altunizade Millet Bahçesi, Üsküdar

DOD: Tel: 0216-572 0000, Fatih Caddesi No: 1, Kadıköy

Kartal Açık Oto Pazarı: Tel: 0216-459 0774, E5 Karayolu üzeri, Kartal Devlet Hastanesi yanı, Kartal

Otokoç: Tel: 0212-229 9555, İstinye Balabandere Mevkii, Yeniköy

Ankara

Otoborsa Otomobil Pazarı: Tel: 0312-334 9465, Bağdat Caddesi, Gimat Kavşağı

Izmir

Birleşik Car Market: Tel: 0232-278 7899, Ankara Asfaltı, Uslusluk Mevkii, Kutucak Köyü, Kemalpaşa

Adana

Yüreğir Açık Oto Pazarı: Mithat Özsan Bulvarı Kavşağı, ATO Ticaret Lisesi yanı, Balcalı Yolu

Bursa

Küçük Sanayi: Tel: 0224-441 7943, Küçük Sanayi Bölgesi, Nilüfer

Mersin

Açık Oto Pazarı: Tel: 0324-336 4180, İhsaniye Mahallesi, Zeytinlibahçe Caddesi,

SPECIALIST CAR DEALERS AND HELP LINES

Ford Euro Service: Tel: 0212-232 3673

Hyundai Assan Customer Service: Tel: 0216-581 0080

Mazda Auto Help-Line: Tel: 0800-211 4092

Peugeot Assistance: Tel: 0212- 292 2626, www.peugeot.com.tr

Renault Auto Help-Line: Tel: 0800-211 4100

Tofaş Auto Help-Line: Tel: 0800-211 4242

Toyota Help Line: Tel: 0800-211 6166

Izmir

Birmot: Tel: 0232-462 6000. Fiat dealer.

Cider: Tel: 0232-264 8484. Volvo dealer.

Egem: Tel: 0232-461 1000. Opel dealer.

Egemer: Tel: 0232-251 2111. Mercedes dealer.

Ege Oto: Tel: 0232-486 3770. Ford dealer.

Gönen: Tel: 0232-463 5075. Volkswagen dealer.

İrde: Tel: 0232-435 5048. Peugeot dealer.

Özgörkey: Tel: 0232-388 1990. BMW dealer.

Terakki: Tel: 0232-343 3838. Honda dealer.

Yükseliş: Tel: 0232-461 4600. Hyundai dealer.

APPENDIX XIII:

PET SHOPS, VETS ETC.

KENNELS

Vets can often put you in touch with a pet hotel.

Istanbul

Academy Dog Kennels: Tel: 0216-311 6999, Maltepe Büyükbakkalköy

Forest Kennel Club: Tel: 0212-223 7716, Hadımkoru Yolu 42, Fatih Ormanı, Maslak

International Kennels K-9 Academy: Tel: 0212-857 8016, Hazefen Havaalanı Yolu üzeri, Karaağaç Köyü, Büyükçekmece

Pako Sevgi ve Sağlık Merkezi: Tel: 0212-257 0069, 1.Cadde No: 53, Kuruçeşme

Topaz Kennels: Tel: 0216-479 9358, Kavacık Polonezköy Yol üzeri

United Kennels: Tel: 0212-239 7613, Başdere Caddesi No: 15, Kemerburgaz

Ankara

Akademi Dog Training Centre & Pet Hotel: Tel: 0312-442 6104, Yeşilkent Mahallesi 2.Cadde No: 13, Mühye Köyü, Yıldız

Izmir

Bafi K-9: Tel: 0232-768 3133, www.bafi-k-9.com.tr, Sıra Mahallesi, Küpalan Mevkii, İçmeler, Urla

Fethiye

Fethiye Pet Pension: Tel: 0252-612 4483, www.fethiyeveteriner.com, Muğla Yolu, 822. Sokak

PET SHOPS

Note that veterinary surgeries often sell pet food and other equipment for animals.

Istanbul

There is a pet market beside the Spice Baazar in Eminönü.

Anadolu Pet Ürünleri: Tel: 0216-346 3467, Şair Nefi Caddesi No: 24, Moda

Hedef İthalat: Tel: 0212-293 2332, Yeraltı Geçidi No: 21, Karaköy. Sells cat flaps.

Pet Market: Tel: 0216-385 0340, İskele Vaddesi No: 18/9, Caddebostan

Pet Market & Veteriner: Tel: 0216-384 5608, Vukela Caddesi No: 19/1, Bostancı

Petworld: Tel: 0212-282 0681, Akmerkez Shopping Mall

Rin-Tin-Tin Pet Shop: Tel: 0216-418 8067, Yusuf Kamil Paşa Sokak No: 13/A, Moda

Volkan Pet Market: Tel: 0212-268 1008, Aytar Caddesi No: 24/1, 1.Levent

Ankara

Pet Centre: Tel: 0312-431 1898, İnkilap Sokak No: 57/2, Kızılay

Pet's World: Tel: 0312-266 1505, Bilkent Centre No: 32, Bilkent; Tel: 0312-541 1560, Migros Shopping Mall

Izmir

Arkadaş Pet: Tel: 0232-324 3583, Karşıyaka Carrefour

Adana

Guppy Akvaryum & Pet Shop: Tel: 0322-233 7769, Güzelyalı Mahallesi, Turgut Özal Bulvarı, İncievler Sitesi No: 104/C, Seyhan

Bodrum & Around

Bora Veteriner Klinik & Pet Shop: Tel: 0252-385 2351, Şeyhülisav Ömer Lütfi Caddesi Nos: 2-3, Yalıkavak

Pet Garden: Tel: 0252-382 9258, Atatürk Caddesi No: 27/3

Pet World: Tel: 0252-317 1224, Oasis Shopping Mall, Bodrum; Tel: 0252-382 4977, D-Marin Turgutreis Marina

Fethiye & Around

Fethiye Pet Shop: Tel: 0252-612 4483, Köprübaşı Mevkii, Atatürk Caddesi No: 180/A, Fethiye

PET-SITTERS

Istanbul

Mustafa's Dog Grooming & Kennels: Tel: 02212-351 4116, Zeytinoğlu Caddesi, Yaşim Sokak No: 15, Akatlar

PET TRAINERS

Istanbul

International Kennels K-9 Academy: See Kennels above.

Ankara

Akademi Dog Training Centre & Pet Hotel: See Kennels above.

Izmir

Bafi K-9: See Kennels above.

Mimer Dog Training Club: Tel: 0232-463 0862, 1398 Sokak No: 8/A, Alsancak

VETS

Note that all reputable pet shops are required to work with a local vet and should be able to recommend somebody.

Istanbul

Animalia Hayvan Hastanesi: Tel: 0212-280 9277, Levent Caddesi No: 41, Levent

Artı Veteriner Kliniği: Tel: 0212-281 7354, Gazeteci Ümit Deniz Sokak No: 19, İç Levent

Atlantis Veteriner Hastanesi: Tel: 0216-330 3982, Tütüncü Mehmet Çıkmazı No: 18/1, Göztepe

Boğaziçi Veteriner Hastanesi: Tel: 0212-283 9033, Yeni Sülün Sokak No: 63, 1.Levent

Erenköy Veteriner Kliniği: Tel: 0216-385 1508, Köşe Apt No: 63/2, Taşmektep Sokak, Erenköy

Evcil Hayvan Kliniği: Tel: 0212-251 2464, Susam Sokak No: 34/A, Cihangir

Levent Veteriner Polikliniği: Tel: 0212-352 5715, Nispetiye Caddesi, Petrol Sitesi No: 6, D1 Blok, Levent

Ortaköy Veteriner Kliniği: Tel: 0212-236 2373, Dereboyu Caddesi, Lozan Sokak No: 12/A, Ortaköy

Pako: Tel: 0212-257 0069, 1.Cadde No: 53, Kuruçeşme, Beşiktaş
Pet's Veteriner Kliniği: Tel: 0216-347 0325, Rüştiye Sokak No: 4, Kızıltoprak
Ulus Veteriner Kliniği: Tel: 0212-287 1737, Güzel Konutlar Sitesi, C Blok, Daire: 2, 2.Ulus
Vet Station: Tel: 0212-263 1829, Yeniyol Sokak No: 16/1, Bebek

Ankara
Altis: Tel: 0312-426 9070, Bülten Sokak No: 20/1, Kavaklıdere
Pet Hospital: Tel: 0312-446 5065, Nenehatun Caddesi No: 117, Gaziosmanpaşa
Terapi: Tel: 0312-440 5553, Simon Bolivar Caddesi, Çankaya

Izmir
Peti Veteriner Polikliniği: Tel: 0232-239 2045, Narlıdere

Antalya
Antalya Veteriner Kliniği: Tel: 0242-247 1211, Teoman Paşa Caddesi, 138 Sokak No: 19/A
Işıklar Veteriner Kliniği: Tel: 0242-247 6288, Işıklar Caddesi No: 8/A
Lara Veteriner Kliniği: Tel: 0242-323 9484, Yeni Lara Caddesi No: 27/B

Bodrum & Around
Bora Veteriner Klinik & Pet Shop: Tel: 0252-385 2351, Şeyhülisav Ömer Lütfi Caddesi No: 2-3, Yalıkavak
Mehmet Akdemir: Tel: 0252-313 2127, Derviş Görgün Caddesi No: 8/F

Dalyan
Salih Gültekin: Tel: 0252-284 2472, Köyceğiz Caddesi No: 12, Çarşı İçi

Fethiye & Around
Kent Veteriner: Tel: 0252-614 7349, Mustafa Kemal Bulvarı, Migros karşısı.
Lara Veteriner: Tel: 0252-612 5916, SSK Hastanesi karşısı

Kayseri
Kayseri Bölgesi Veteriner Hekimler Odası: Tel: 0352-222 0753

ALSO USEFUL
Central Veterinary Control & Research Institute: Tel: 0312-326 0090, Fax: 0312-321 1755, www.etlik.gov.tr, Ahmet Defik Kolaylı Caddesi No: 23, Etlik, Ankara
Dog Information Association (Köpek Bilimleri Derniği): Tel: 0212-219 1221, www.kbd.org.tr. Organises annual Istanbul Dog Show in June.

APPENDIX XIV:

POLITICAL, ENVIRONMENTAL AND SOCIAL ORGANISATIONS, CHARITIES, CULTURAL CENTRES AND FRIENDSHIP SOCIETIES

ANIMAL CHARITIES

Istanbul

Environment and Street Animals Association (Çevre ve Sokak Hayvanları Derneği): Tel: 0212-227 7265, www.sokakhayvanlari.com, Çırağan Caddesi, Yıldız Parkı Girişi No: 1, Beşiktaş

Homeless Animals & Environmental Protection Foundation (Evsiz Hayvanları ve Doğayı Koruma Derneği): Tel: 0212-271 7717, www.evsizhayvanlar.org, Kocataş Mahallesi, Kılıçpınar Caddesi, Sarıyer

Marmaris

Kittycat Shelter: www.marmarisinfo.com/kittycat/

CHARITIES

Istanbul

Caritas: Tel: 0212-234 4564, www.caritas.org, Harbiye Çayırı Sokak No: 64, Elmadağ

Contemporary Living Support Association (Çağdaş Yaşamı Destekleme Derneği): Tel: 0212-252 4433, www.cydd.org.tr, Şimal Sokak No: 20, Şişhane. Works to spread and develop Atatürk's ideas, especially through schools.

Darüşşafaka: Tel: 0212-444 1863, www.darussafaka.org, Zümrütevler Mahallesi, Mercan Sokak No: 35, Maltepe/Başıbüyük. School for 900 gifted orphans.

Mother & Child Education Foundation (AÇEV- Anne Çocuk Eğitim Vakfı): Tel: 0212-213 4220, www.acev.org, Büyükdere Caddesi, Stad Han No: 85/1, Mecidiyeköy

Social Responsibility Education Association (SED - Sosyal Sorumluk Eğitim Derneği): Tel: 0212-267 3137, www.sed-tr.org

Street Children's Association (Sokak Çocukları Derneği): Tel: 0212-233 8723, Cumhuriyet Caddesi, Üftade Sokak, Latif Apt No: 10/3, Elmadağ

SOS Children's Villages Turkey: Tel: 0212-257 0911, Fax: 0212-257 3919, Garanti Mahallesi, Toprakkale Sokak, Ufuk A, Apt: 34, Daire: 9, Etiler. German-run project to help needy children.

Theodora Foundation (Thodora Çocuk Hizmetleri Vakfı): Tel: 0212-292 8414, www. theodora.org, İnönü Caddesi, Prof Dr Tarık Zafer Tunaya Sokak No: 16/3, Taksim. Sends trained 'clown' doctors to Çapa, Cerrahpaşa and Kartal hospitals to entertain sick children.

Turkish Education Foundation (TEV - Türk Eğitim Vakfı): Tel: 0212-217 5858, www. tev.org.tr, Büyükdere Caddesi, Kocabaş İş Hanı No: 111, Gayrettepe. Sends wreaths to weddings and funerals and uses profits from donations to finance educational scholarships for poor children.

Turkish Education Volunteers Foundation (TEGV- Türkiye Eğitim Gönüllüleri Vakfı): Tel: 0216-326 8696, www.tegv.org, Baba Nakkaş Sokak No: 8, Nakkaştepe. Works to improve education levels through education parks, mobile computer units and 'Firefly' mobile learning units.

Turkish Family Health & Planning Foundation (TAPV - Türkiye Aile Sağlığı ve Planlaması Vakfı): Tel: 0212-257 7941, www.tapv.org.tr, Güzel Konutlar Sitesi, A Blok, Daire: 3-4, Ulus/Etiler. Works to educate people about family planning, sexual health, women's health etc.

Turkish Foundation for Children in Need of Protection (Türkiye Korunmaya Muhtaç Çocuklara Vakfı): Tel: 0212-274 9545, Altan Erbulak Sokak, Hoşkalın Apt No: 4/5, Mecidiyeköy

Turkish Street Children's Charity (Türkiye Sokak Çocukları Vakfı): Tel: 0212-259 8991, Talimyeri Caddesi, Baraz Apt: 7/1, Daire: 5, Maçka, Beşiktaş

Youth Tour (Gençtur): Tel: 0212-249 2575, www.genctur.com, İstiklal Caddesi, Zambak Sokak No: 15/1, Taksim. Voluntary workcamps for young people over 18.

Ankara

Ankara International Charities Committee: Tel: 0312-442 6317, Portakal Çiçeği Sokak, Pak Sokak No:3, Vedi Apt: 50, Çankaya

Foundation for Children with Leukaemia (LÖSEV): Tel: 0312-447 0660, www.losev. org.tr, Reşit Galip Caddesi, İlk Adım Sokak No: 14, Gaziosmanpaşa. Runs Lösante Hospital for children with leukaemia. Aside from financial donations, also seeks toys etc.

Kızılay (Red Crescent): Tel: 0312-430 2300, www.kizilay.org.tr, Ataç Sokak No: 1/32, Yenişehir

Social Services & Child Protection (Sosyal Hizmetler ve Çocuk Esirgeme Kurumu): Tel: 0312-312 3366, www.shcek.gov.tr, Anafartalar Caddesi No: 70, Ulus

UNICEF: Tel: 0312-454 1000, Birlik Mahallesi, 2.Cadde No: 11, Çankaya

Fethiye

FETAV (Fethiye Tourism, Promotion, Education, Culture & Environment Foundation): Tel: 0252-612 3366, www.fetav.com, Hükümet Binası. Helps local children in need. Book exchange and second-hand clothes sales. Runs Starfish Centre at yanıklar Beach to provide therapy for children.

CULTURAL CENTRES AND FRIENDSHIP ASSOCIATIONS

Istanbul

Austrian Cultural Centre: Tel: 0212-223 7843, Köybaşı Caddesi No: 46, Yeniköy

British Community Council: www.bbcistanbul.org. Holds Christmas dinner with carols and stages Christmas pantomime.

Cervantes Institute: Tel: 0212-292 6536, Tarlabaşı Bulvarı, Zambak Sokak No: 33, Beyoğlu

French Cultural Centre: Tel: 0212-334 8740, İstiklal Caddesi No: 8, Beyoğlu

Goethe Institut: Tel: 0212-249 2009, Yeniçarşı Caddesi No: 52, Beyoğlu

Greek Cultural Centre: Tel: 0212-245 0596, Turnacıbaşı Sokak No: 32, Beyoğlu

Irish Centre: Tel: 0212-244 7970, www.theirishcentre.com, İstiklal Caddesi, Balo Sokak No: 26, Beyoğlu

Italian Cultural Institute: Tel: 0212-293 9848, www.iicist.org.tr, Meşrutiyet Caddesi No: 161, Tepebaşı

Japan Cultural Centre: Tel: 0212-293 3249, İstiklal Caddesi, Ana Çeşme Sokak No: 3, Taksim

Ankara

British Council: Tel: 0312-455 3600, İran Caddesi, Karum İş Merkezi No: 21, D Blok, Kat: 5

French Cultural Centre: Tel: 0312-431 1458, Ziya Gökalp Caddesi No: 15, Kızılay

German Cultural Centre: Tel: 0312-418 3124, Atatürk Bulvarı No: 131, Bakanlıklar

Italian Cultural Centre: Tel: 0312-446 5178, www.iic.org.tr, Mahatma Gandi Caddesi No: 32, Gaziosmanpaşa

Turkish-American Association: Tel: 0312-426 2648, Cinnah Caddesi No: 20, Çankaya

Turco-British Association: 0312-419 1844, www.tba.org.tr, Bestekar Sokak No: 32, Kavaklıdere

Turkish-Japanese Association/Japanese Cultural Centre: Tel: 0312-491 1748, Ferit Recai Ertuğrul Caddesi No: 2, Oran

US Community Centre: Tel: 0312-468 6110, Ahmet Mithat Sokak No: 33, Çankaya

Izmir

American Cultural Centre: Tel: 0232-464 2095

British Council: Tel: 0232-446 0131, PTT Pasaport

French Cultural Centre: Tel: 0232-463 ʿ979, www.frkultur.com. Cumhuriyet Bulvarı No: 152, Alsancak

German Cultural Centre: Tel: 0232-489 5687, Gaziosmanpaşa Bulvarı No: 13, Çankaya

Italian Cultural Centre (Carlo Goldoni): Tel: 0232-421 5242, www.italcons-Izmir.com/~ccgoldoni, 1443 Sokak No: 58, Alsancak

Turkish-American Association: Tel: 0232-464 2095, www.izmir-taa.org.tr, 1379 Sokak No: 39, Alsancak

Fethiye

British-Turkish Society: Tel: 0252-613 7017, www.britishturkish.org, Adnan Menderes Bulvarı, Muğla Yolu üzeri

UK

Anglo-Turkish Society: Tel: 0207-235 8148, Fax: 0207-056 2506, 43 Monrose Place, London SW1 7DT

Appendices | 553

British Turkish Society: Tel: 0113-245 1774, 14B Woodsley Rd, Leeds LS3 1DT

ENVIRONMENTAL ORGANISATIONS

Istanbul

Greenpeace: Tel: 0212- 292 7620, www.greenpeace.org/turkey/, Tarlabaşı Caddesi No: 60, Taksim

Turkish Foundation for Combating Soil Erosion, Reafforestation and the Protection of Natural Habitats (TEMA - Türkiye Erozyonla Mücadele Ağaçlandırma ve Doğal Varlıkları): Tel: 0212-283 7816, www.tema.org.tr, Çayır Çimen Sokak, A2 Blok, Daire:15, Emlak Kredi Blokları, Levent

Turkish Maritime Protection Organisation (Deniztemiz Turmepa): Tel: 0216-343 7893, www.turmepa.org.tr, Nakkaştepe Azizbey Sokak No: 1, Kuzguncuk

Worldwide Fund for Nature (WWF - Doğal Hayatı Koruma Derneği): Tel: 0212-528 2030, www.wwf.org.tr/www.dhkd.org, Büyük Postane Caddesi No: 43-5, Kat: 5-6, Bahçekapı

Ankara

Mediterranean Dolphin Research Group (Akdeniz Foku Araştırma Grubu): Tel: 0312-213 0834, www.afag.org, Kazakistan Caddesi No: 94/5, Emek

Antalya

Turkish Foundation for Combating Soil Erosion, Reafforestation and the Protection of Natural Habitats (TEMA - Türkiye Erozyonla Mücadele Ağaçlandırma ve Doğal Varlıkları): Tel: 0242-243 7252, 53. Sokak. Baykar Sanat No: 10/1

Turkish Maritime Protection Organisation (Deniztemiz Turmepa): Tel: 0242-259 1290, Setur Marina

MISCELLANEOUS PROJECTS

Istanbul

Foundation for Fine Arts and Cultural Heritage (KÜSAV): Tel 0212-262 3433, www.kusav.com, Köybaşı Caddesi Nos: 24-26, Yeniköy. Aims to increase interest in Turkey's artistic and cultural heritage.

Foundation for the Protection and Promotion of the Environmental and Cultural Heritage (Çekül Vakfı): Tel: 0212-249 6464, www.cekulvakfi.org.tr, Ekrem Tur Sokak No: 8, Beyoğlu

Tay Project: Tel: 0212-265 7858, info@tayproject.org, Hakan Apt No: 67/B, Kuruçeşme. Mapping Turkey's archaeological heritage.

POLITICAL ORGANISATIONS

Istanbul

Amnesty International (Uluslararası Af Örgütü): Tel: 0212-258 4367, www.amnesty-turkiye.org, Muradiye Bayır Sokak No: 50/1, Teşvikiye

Human Rights Association (İnsan Hakları Derneği): Tel: 0212-251 3526, www.ihd. org.tr, Çukurlu Çeşme Sokak, Bayman Apt No: 10/1, Taksim

Ankara
Human Rights Association (İnsan Hakları Derneği): Tel: 0312-466 4913, Tunalı Hilmi Caddesi No: 104, Kavaklıdere

Izmir
Human Rights Association (İnsan Hakları Derneği): Tel: 0232-445 4168, GOP Bulvarı, Kostak İşhanı, Kat: 2, Çankaya

SUPPORT GROUPS
Istanbul
American Women of Istanbul: Tel: 0212-357 2298, www.awi-istanbul.com. For Americans, Canadians and the spouses of Americans and Canadians.

Australians & New Zealanders: Tel: 0212-263 7631 or contact Sharon Croxford (sharon_croxford@yahoo.co.uk)

Communita Italiana: Tel: 0212-232 1351

Die Brüecke: Tel: 0212-262 1045, www.bruecke-istanbul.org

Dutch Group: Tel: 0212-359 2366

French Istanbul AKKA Association (La Passerelle): Tel: 0212-542 2034. Support group for French-speaking people.

Friends of India: Tel: 0212-269 1691

Global Life Centre (Küre Yaşam Merkezi): Tel: 0212-352 2490, www.kureistanbul.com, Maya Meridien Kat: 2, Akatlar, Etiler. Support group aiming to bring people together through art, drama, music, yoga etc.

International Women of Istanbul (IWI): www.iwi-tr.org, PK 11. Tarabya. Publishes *Lale*, a monthly magazine with information on courses, play groups, the IWI's Christmas Bazaar etc. Adverts for alternative medicine practitioners, Turkish tutors etc. Organises mother & baby groups, bridge groups, Scrabble groups, a photography club, book groups, and tennis and golf programmes. Telephone help line for personal problems. Lively social programme.

Istanbul Accueil: Tel: 0212-244 6560. Support group for French-speaking people.

Istanbul Blue Line: Tel: 0212-638 2626. General purpose support line with English-speaking staff.

Istanbul Friends of the American Research Institute in Turkey: Tel: 0212-257 8111, http://ccat.sas.upenn.edu/ARIT, Üvez Sokak No: 5, Arnavutköy. Offers back-up to Archaeological Research Institute. Organises lectures and tours of historic sites.

Las Chicas: Tel: 0212-262 8400. Support group for Spanish-speaking women in Istanbul.

Luso Brasileiro: Tel: 0212-669 4943. Support group for Portugese-speaking women in Istanbul.

Russian-speaking group: Tel: 0212-269 0895

South Africans: contact Sharon Croxford (sharon_croxford@yahoo.co.uk)

Swedish Women's Educational Association: Tel: 0216-467 4557, www.swea.org

Ankara

Ankara Women's Club: Tel: 0312-447 6319. Open to all foreign residents of Ankara.

Ankara Caledonian Society: Tel: 0312-447 6319. For Scottish residents of Ankara.

Ankara International Charities Committee: Tel: 0312-440 3020. Organises hospital and orphanage visits etc.

British Women's Group: Tel: 0312-447 1873. Meets on last Monday of month in Hilton Hotel at 10am.

La Passerelle; Tel: 0312-414 8068. Support group for French speakers.

Red Lion Club: Tel: 0312-466 1372, British Embassy, Şehit Ersan Caddesi. Primarily for Embassy staff but citizens of EU, US and Commonwealth countries can be associate members.

Turkish-American Women's Cultural and Charitable Society: Tel: 0312-490 0345. All sorts of charitable and social acitivities.

Izmir

International Women's Association of Izmir: www.iwaizmir.com, Elma Book House and Activity Centre, Plevne Building No: 19/G, Alsancak

La Passerelle: Tel: 0232-421 4234. Support group for French speakers.

APPENDIX XV:
CHURCHES AND SYNAGOGUES IN TURKEY

CHURCHES
Istanbul

A comprehensive list of churches appears on www.istanbulinfolink.com.

Armenian Orthodox churches

Armenian Patriarchate: Tel: 0212-517 0970, Şarapnel Sokak No: 3, Kumkapı

Surp Kevork: Tel: 0212-585 0193, Marmara Caddesi No: 79, Kocamustafapaşa

Surp Kirkor Lusavoric: Tel: 0212-292 5762, Sakızcılar Sokak No: 3, Karaköy

Üç Horan: Tel: 0212-244 1382, Balık Pazarı, Beyoğlu

Greek Orthodox churches

Aya Triada: Tel: 0212-244 1358, Meşelik Sokak No: 11/1, Taksim

St George Church: Tel: 0212-531 9670, Sadrazam Ali Paşa Caddesi, Fener

Protestant churches

Christ Church: Tel: 0212-251 5616, Serdar Ekrem Sokak No: 82, Tünel. Daily service 9am and 6pm. Sunday 10am.

Church of the Assumption: Tel: 0216-336 0322, Cem Sokak No: 5, Moda

St Helena's Chapel: Tel: 0212-244 4228, British Consulate, Galatasaray (not in use at time of writing)

Union Church of Istanbul: Tel: 0212-244 5212, Dutch Consulate, Postacılar Sokak No: 11, Beyoğlu. Sunday services 9.30am and 11am. Family carol service few weeks before Christmas.

Roman Catholic churches

Church of the Assumption: Tel: 0216-336 0322, Cem Sokak No: 5, Moda. Daily mass 6.30pm. Sunday mass 11.30am.

Church of Sts Peter & Paul: Tel: 0212-249 2385, Galata Kulesi Sokak No: 44, Kuledibi. Sunday mass 11am.

Santa Maria Draperis: Tel: 0212-244 0243, İstiklal Caddesi No: 429, Beyoğlu. Daily mass 8am (Italian). Saturday mass 6.30pm (Italian). Sunday mass 9am and 11.30am (Italian) and 6.30pm (Spanish).

St Anthony of Padua: Tel: 0212-244 0935, İstiklal Caddesi No: 225, Beyoğlu. Daily mass 8am (English) and 7pm (Turkish). Sunday mass 10am (English), 11am (Polish), 11.30am (Italian) and 7pm (Turkish).

St Espirit Cathedral: Tel: 0212-248 0910, Cumhuriyet Caddesi No: 205/B, Harbiye. Daily mass 6pm. Sunday 9am and 10.15am.

St Louis de France: Tel: 0212-244 1075, Postacılar Sokak No: 11, Beyoğlu, Mass Saturday 7 pm. Sunday 11 am.

Russian Orthodox churches

Andrievfskaya Church: Mumhane Caddesi No: 63, Karaköy

Russian on the Athos St Panteleimon Monastery: Hoca Tahsin Sokak No: 19, Kat: 6, Karaköy

Syrian Orthodox churches

Church of the Virgin Mary: Tel: 0212-238 5470, Karakurum Sokak No: 20, Tarlabaşı

Ankara

Anglican church

St Nicholas Church: Tel: 0312-468 6230, British Embassy Grounds, Şehit Ersan Caddesi, Çankaya. Sunday mass 9.45 am. Wednesday mass 7 pm. Thursday mass 7.45 am.

Baptist church

Ankara Baptist Church International: Tel: 0312-467 0808, Best Hotel, Atatürk Bulvarı No: 195, Kavaklıdere. Sunday mass 10am.

Catholic churches

Vatican Embassy Church: Tel: 0312-495 3505. English mass Sunday 9am. French mass Sunday 11am. Holy Day masses 7pm.

Old French Embassy Chapel: Tel: 0312-311 0118, Kardeşler Sokak No: 15, Ulus. Sunday mass 10.30am.

Izmir

St John the Evangelist: Tel: 0232-464 5753, Alsancak

St Mary Magdalene: Tel: 0232-464 5753, Bornova

Antalya

St Paul: Tel: 0242-247 6857, Yenikapı Sokak No: 24, Kaleiçi

SYNAGOGUES

Istanbul

Ashkenazi Synagogue: Tel: 0212-243 6909, Bankalar Caddesi No: 10, Karaköy

Balat Ahrida Synagogue: Tel: 0212-523 4729, Kürkçü Çeşme Sokak, Balat

Chief Rabbinate of Turkey: Tel: 0212-243 5166, Yemenici Sokak No: 23, Tünel

Ankara

Synagogue: Tel: 0312-311 6200, Birlik Sokak No: 8, Samanpazarı

APPENDIX XVI:
TRANSPORT COMPANIES

AIRPORT BUS SERVICE

Havaş (www.havas.com.tr) operates airport bus services in many towns.

SCHEDULED AIRLINES FLYING TO AND FROM TURKEY

Adria Airways: Tel: 0212-512 4231, Ordu Caddesi No: 206/1, Laleli

Aeroflot: Tel: 0212-296 6725, Cumhuriyet Caddesi No: 26, Elmadağ

Aerosvit-Ukranya Airlines: Tel: 0212-291 6693, Cumhuriyet Caddesi No: 95-9, Elmadağ

Air China: Tel: 0212-296 5342, Halaskargazı Caddesi, Yenipalas Apt 129/3, Harbiye

Air France: Tel: 0212-310 1919, www.airfrance.com, Emirhan Caddesi No: 145, Dikilitaş

Alia: Tel: 0212-230 4074, Cumhuriyet Caddesi No: 87, Elmadağ

Alitalia: Tel: 0212-315 1900, www.alitalia.com, Valikonağı Caddesi No: 73, Nişantaşı

American Airlines: Tel: 0212-219 8223, Halaskargazi Caddesi, Mısırlı Han No: 121, Harbiye

Asiana Airlines: Tel: 0212-334 2930, Mete Caddesi No: 24, Taksim

Austrian Airlines: Tel: 0212-293 6995, www.aua.com, İnönü Caddesi No: 26/7, Gümüşsuyu

Azerbaijan Airlines: Tel: 0212-245 1852, Rıhtım Caddesi No: 55, Karaköy

British Airways: Tel: 0212-234 1300, www.ba.com, Cumhuriyet Caddesi No: 10, Elmadağ

Cathay Pacific Airways: Tel: 0212-219 2123, www.cathaypacific.com, Cumhuriyet Caddesi No: 14/3, Elmadağ

Czech Airlines: Tel: 0212-230 4832, Cumhuriyet Caddesi No: 163, Elmadağ

Delta Airlines: Tel: 0212-310 2000, Teşvikiye Caddesi, İkbal İş Merkezi No: 103/4, Teşvikiye

easyJet: Tel: 0905-821 0905 (premıım rates apply), www.easyjet.com. Flights from Istanbul to London Luton and Basel-Mulhouse

Egyptair: Tel: 0212-231 1126, Halaskargazi Caddesi No: 202, Osmanbey

El Al: Tel: 0212-291 4516, www.elal.co.il, Rumeli Caddesi, Nişantaşı İş Merkezi No: 1, Nişantaşı

Emirates: Tel: 0212-334 8888, www.emirates.com, İnönü Caddesi No: 96, Gümüşsuyu

Georgian Airlines: Tel: 0212-253 1113, Cinnah Caddesi Nos: 161-6, Elmadağ

Gulf Air: Tel: 0212-231 3450, www.gulfairco.com, Cumhuriyet Caddesi No: 213, Harbiye

Iberia: Tel: 0212-368 8383, Mimar Kemal Öke Caddesi No: 9/1, Nişantaşı

Iranair: Tel: 0212-225 0255, Valikonağı Caddesi No: 17, Harbiye

JAL: Tel: 0212-233 0840, www.jal.co.jp, Cumhuriyet Caddesi No: 107, Elmadağ

Jata Yugoslav: Tel: 0212-293 2894, Mete Caddesi No: 14, Taksim

KLM: Tel: 0212-368 3333, www.klm.com, Valikonağı Caddesi No: 73/7, Nişantaşı

KHTY: Tel: 0212-274 6932, www.kthy.com, Büyükdere Caddesi No: 56/B, Mecidiyeköy

Kuwait Airlines: Tel: 0212-240 4081, Cumhuriyet Caddesi No: 169/2, Elmadağ

LOT: Tel: 0212-241 5749, www.lot.com, Cumhuriyet Caddesi No: 16, Elmadağ

Lufthansa: Tel: 0212-315 3434, www.lufthansa.com, Büyükdere Caddesi, Özsezen İş Merkezi, C Blok, Esentepe

Maersk Air: Tel: 0212-334 2940, Mete Caddesi No: 24/1, Taksim

Malaysian Airlines: Tel: 0212-230 7130, Valikonağı Caddesi No: 9, Nişantaşı

Malev: Tel: 0212-241 0909, www.malev.com.tr, Cumhuriyet Caddesi Nos: 141-47, Elmadağ

Middle East Airlines: Tel: 0212-248 2241, Cumhuriyet Caddesi No: 30, Elmadağ

Olympic Airways: Tel: 0212-247 3701, Cumhuriyet Caddesi No: 171/A, Elmadağ

Qantas: Tel: 0212-219 8223, www.qantas.com, Halaskargazi Caddesi No: 121, Harbiye

Qatar Airways: Tel: 0212-296 5888, Ceylan Intercontinental Hotel, Askerocağı Caddesi No: 1, Taksim

Royal Air Maroc: Tel: 0212-231 7121, Cumhuriyet Caddesi No: 87/2, Elmadağ

Saudi Arabian Airlines: Tel: 0212-213 0980, www.saudiairlines.com, Büyükdere Caddesi, Maya Centre No: 100-02, Esentepe

Singapore Airlines: Tel: 0212-232 3706, www.singaporeair.com, Halaskargazi Caddesi No: 113, Harbiye

Swiss International Airlines: Tel: 0212-319 1999, www.swiss.com, İş Towers, Tower 2, 4.Levent

Syrian Air: Tel: 0212-246 1781, Cumhuriyet Caddesi, Harbiye

Thai Airlines: Tel: 0212-334 2950, Mete Caddesi No: 24, Taksim

Tunisair: Tel: 0212-241 7096, Valikonağı Caddesi No: 8, Nişantaşı

Turkish Airlines: Tel: 0212-230 1817, www.thy.com, Cumhuriyet Caddesi Nos: 199-201, Harbiye

Turkmenistan Airlines: Tel: 0212-233 9306, Cumhuriyet Caddesi No: 171/1, Elmadağ

VASP Brazilian Airlines: Tel: 0212-293 4227, www.vasp.com.tr, Bankalar Caddesi No: 31-3, Karaköy

Izmir

Air France: Tel: 0232-425 9004, 1353 Sokak No: 205-6, Taner İşhanı No: 1, Kat: 2

Alitalia: Tel: 0232-421 7283, Atatürk Caddesi No: 328/A

Antalya

Sun Express: Tel: 0242-310 2727, www.sunexpress.com.tr, Mehmetçik Mahallesi, Aspendos Bulvarı, Aspendos İş Merkezi No: 63/1-2. Flies to Cologne, Frankfurt and Munich.

TURKISH DOMESTIC AIRLINES

Atlasjet: Tel: 444 3387, www.atlasjet.com. Flies to Istanbul, Ankara, Izmir, Adana, Adıyaman, Antalya, Bodrum, Dalaman, Denizli, Edremit, Erzincan, Isparta, Kahramanmaraş, Kars, Konya, Malatya, Mardin, Nevşehir, Siirt, Sivas, Tokat, Trabzon, Uşak, Şanlıurfa, Van and Northern Cyprus.

Flyair: Tel: 444 4359, www.flyair.com.tr. Flies to Istanbul, Ankara, Izmir, Antalya, Bodrum and Trabzon.

Onur Air: Tel: 444 6687, www.onurair.com.tr, Flies to Istanbul, Ankara, Izmir, Adana, Antalya, Bodrum, Dalaman, Diyarbakır, Erzurum, Gaziantep, Kayseri, Malatya, Samsun and Trabzon.

Pegasus: Tel: 444 0737, www.flypgs.com. Flies to Istanbul, Ankara, Adana, Antalya, Diyarbakır, Trabzon, Van and Northern Cyprus.

Sun Express: Tel: 444 0797, www.sunexpress.com.tr, Flies from Izmir to Adana, Antalya, Diyarbakır, Erzurum, Kayseri, Trabzon and Van, and from Antalya to Diyarbakır, Izmir and Kayseri.

Turkish Airlines (THY): Tel: 444 0849, www.thy.com. Flies to Istanbul, Ankara, Izmir, Adana, Adıyaman, Ağrı, Antalya, Batman, Bodrum, Dalaman, Denizli, Diyarbakır, Elazığ, Erzincan, Erzurum, Gaziantep, Kahramanmaraş, Kayseri, Konya, Malatya, Mardin, Muş, Şanlıurfa, Sivas, Trabzon, Van and Northern Cyprus.

MAJOR TURKISH BUS COMPANIES

Boss: Tel: 444 0880, www.bossturizm.com.tr

Kamil Koç: Tel: 444 0562, www.kamilkoc.com.tr

Metro: Tel: 444 3455, www.metroturizm.com.tr

Nilüfer: Tel: 444 0099, www.nilufer.com.tr

Pamukkale: Tel: 444 3535, www.pamukkaleturizm.com.tr

Ulusoy: Tel: 444 1888, www.ulusoy.com.tr

Varan: Tel: 444 8999, www.varan.com.tr

DOMESTIC FERRY BOOKINGS

Aegean Tour Travel: Tel: 0252-313 0722, www.aegeantourtravel.com, Neyzen Tevfik Caddesi No: 224A, Bodrum. Booking agent for Istanbul to Izmir ferry. Also for ferries from Italy to Turkey.

FERRY COMPANIES OPERATING BETWEEN EUROPE AND TURKEY

Marmara Lines: Tel: 0049-7031 866010, 07031 876568, www.marmaralines.com, Neckarestr 37, Sindelfingen, Germany; Tel: 0041-1-368 3111, Fax: 368 3119, Schaffhauserstr. 35, Switzerland. Brindisi & Ancona to Çeşme.

Turkish Maritime Lines: Tel: 0212-251 5000, www.tdi.com.tr, Rıhtım Caddesi, Merkez Han No: 4, Karaköy, Istanbul. Brindisi to Çeşme.

COMPANIES OFFERING FERRY TICKETS TO GREECE

Ayvalık

Jale Tours: Tel: 0266-312 2740, Gümrük Meydanı

Bodrum

Bodrum Express Lines: Tel: 0252-316 1087, www.bodrumexpresslines.com, Bodrum İskelesi

Bodrum Ferryboat Association: Tel: 0252-316 0882, www.bodrumferryboat.com, Bodrum İskelesi

D-Marin Ferryboat Services: Tel: 0252-382 9200, www.dogusmarina.com.tr, Turgutreis

Çeşme

Ertürk Travel Agency: Tel: 0232-712 6768, www.erturk.com.tr, Beyazıt Caddesi No: 6/7

Karavan: Tel: 0232-712 7230, karavances@superonline.com, Belediye Dükkanları No: 4

Datça

Knidos Yachting: Tel: 0252-712 9464

Kuşadası

Anker Travel: Tel: 0256-612 4598, www.ankertravel.com, İsmet İnönü No: 14

Ekol Travel Agency: Tel: 0256-614 5591, www.ekoltravel.com, Buyral Sokak No: 9/1

Meander Travel Agency: Tel: 0256-614 3859, www.meandertravel.com, Kıbrıs Caddesi No: 1/A

COMPANIES OFFERING FERRY TICKETS TO NORTHERN CYPRUS

Alanya

Akfer Denizcilik: Tel: 0242-512 8889, İskele Caddesi No: 86

Girne

Akfer Denizcilik: Tel: 0392-815 6002, Ramadan Cemil Meydanı No: 1

Mersin

Kıbrıs Denizcilik: Tel: 0324-223 9858, Mersin İskelesi

Taşucu

Akfer Denizcilik: Tel: 0324-741 4033, Taşucu İskelesi

COMPANIES OFFERING FERRY TICKETS TO UKRAINE

Istanbul

UKR Ferry: Tel: 0212-252 9720, Kemankes Caddesi, Karaköy

APPENDIX XVII:

TURKISH AND INTERNATIONAL REMOVALS COMPANIES, AND RELOCATORS

INTERNATIONAL REMOVALS COMPANIES ABROAD

UK

Anglo Pacific: Tel: 0208-965 1234, www.anglopacific.co.uk, Units 1-2 Bush Industrial Estate, Standard Rd, North Acton, London NW10 6DF; Tel: 0161-653 4455, Unit 4, Townley Park, Hanson St, Middleton, Manchester M24 2UF; Tel: 0141-764 1010; 26 Eastmuir St, Alnwick Industrial Estate, Shettleston, Glasgow G32 0HS

Atlantis Overseas Removals: Tel: 0113-278 9191, www.atlantisltd.co.uk, Atlantis House, Bennett Rd, Leeds West Yorkshire LS6 3HN; Tel: 0121-451 1588, 1607 Pershore Rd, Stirchley, Birmingham B30 2JF

British Association of Removers: Tel: 01923-699480, www.bar.co.uk, Tangent House, 62 Exchange Rd, Watford, Herts WD18 0TG. Keeps list of member firms; check before making decision on company to use.

Bishop's Move: Tel: 0800-616425, www.bishopsmove.co.uk, 102-4 Stewarts Rd, London SW8 4UF

Dolphin Movers: Tel: 0208-804 7700, www.dolphinmovers.com, 2 Haslemere Business Centre, Lincoln Way, Enfield, Middlesex EN1 1TE

EMS Hansard Ltd: Tel: 01304-241616, 27-29 Castle St, Dover CT16 1PT

First Move International: Tel: 0117-982 8123, www.shipit.co.uk, International House, Unit 5B Worthy Rd, Chittening Industrial Estate, Avonmouth

PSS: Tel: 0208-686 7733, www.pss.uk.com, 1-3 Pegasus Rd, Croydon, Surrey CR9 4PS

Germany

Schneider International: Tel: 49-711 780 2080, www.alliedintl.de, Raiffeiserstrasse 16, Stuttgart

France

All World Transport (AWT): Tel: 33.1.39.92.97.97, www.awt-relocation.com, 1 rue Le Nôtre/BP-804, Goussainville Cedex

TURKISH REMOVALS COMPANIES

Istanbul

Asya International Movers: Tel: 0212-243 6510, ist@asyanakliyat.com.tr, İnönü Caddesi Nos: 92-94, Taksim; Tel: 0212-216 3919, Büyükdere Caddesi No: 105/5, Gayrettepe

Bergen International Movers: Tel: 0212-275 1531, www.bergen.com.tr, Kore Şehitleri Caddesi, Yzb. Kaya Aldoğan Sokak No: 3/6, Zincirlikuyu

DTN International Movers: Tel: 0216-456 4375, Atatürk Mahallesi, Alemdaroğlu Sokak No: 12/1, Ataşehir B Kapısı, Kadıköy

Soyer: Tel: 0216-411 2720, soyer@soyer.com.tr, Cemil Topuzlu Caddesi No: 70, Arzum Apt, Kat:1/D, Göztepe

Sumerman International Moving: Tel: 0212-223 5818, www.sumerman.com, Menekşe Sokak, Ferahevler, Tarabya

Ankara

Asya International Movers: Tel: 0312-417 4184, ank@asyanakliyat.com.tr, Atatürk Bulvarı No: 127/2, Bakanlıklar

Izmir

Asya International Movers: Tel: 0232-465 0784, izm@asyanakliyat.com.tr, Şehit Nevres Bulvar No: 1/1, Alsancak

Soyer: Tel: 0232-425 7772, Ragıp Şamlı İş Merkezi, Şair Eşref Bulvarı No: 6/603, Çankaya

Adana

Asya International Movers: Tel: 0322-332 7302, and@asyanakliyat.com.tr, Ceyhan Yolu 12km, İncirlik

Soyer: Tel: 0322-332 9353, 322 9427, Adana Ceyhan Karayolu 12km, İncirlik

OVERSEAS RELOCATORS

Australia

Crown Relocations: Tel: 61-2-8787 0400, www.crownworldwide.com, 288 Woodpark Rd, Smithfield, Sydney

Canada

Crown Relocations: Tel: 1-905-332 4332, www.crownworldwide.com, 1375 Artisans Court, Burlington, Ontario L7L 57Z

France

Crown Relocations: Tel: 33.1.45.73.66.00, www.crownworldwide.com, 15 ave de Président Salvador Allende, Vitry-sur-Seine

Germany

Crown Relocations: Tel: 49-69 1539 4000, www.crownworldwide.com, Wolf Heidenheimstr. 12, Frankfurt

Ireland

Crown Relocations: Tel: 353-1-885 0171, www.crownworldwide.com, Unit 15, Northwest Business Park, Ballycoolin, Dublin

Netherlands

Crown Relocations: Tel: 31-20-653 5003, www.crownworldwide.com, Fokkeweg 211, 1438 BG Oude Meer, Amsterdam

New Zealand

Crown Relocations: Tel: 64-9-415 8683, www.crownworldwide.com, 200 Bush Rd, Albany, Auckland

UK

Crown Relocations: Tel: 0208-839 8000, www.crownworldwide.com, 19 Stonefield Way, South Ruislip, Middx HA4 0BJ

Robinsons: Tel: 0208-208 8484, www.robinsons-intl.com, The Gateway, Priestley Way, Staples Corner, London NW2 7AJ

USA

Crown Relocations: Tel: 001-714 898 0961, www.crownworldwide.com, 5252 Argosy Drive, Huntington Beach, California

TURKISH RELOCATORS

Istanbul

Bedel Relocation & Tourism: Tel: 0212-356 3640, www.bedelrelocation.com, Büyükdere Caddesi No: 105/5, Gayrettepe. Part of Asya International Movers.

Crown Relocations: Tel: 0212-347 4410, www.crownrelo.com.tr, Mevlut Pehlivan Sokak, A Blok Daire: 6, Mecidiyeköy

Istanbul Support Team (IST): Tel: 0212-223 7790, www.sumerman.com, Menekşe Sokak, Ferahevler, Tarabya. Part of Sumerman International.

Istanbul Danışmanlık: Tel: 0212-213 5855, istrelocation@superonline.com, Kore Şehitleri Caddesi, Yzb. Kaya Aldoğan Sokak No: 15/2A, Zincirlikuyu

Lameta Real Estate & Relocation: Tel: 0532-421 1339, www.lameta.com.tr

Litera: Tel: 0212-291 3104, www.expatistanbul.com, Halaskargazi Caddesi, Ali Koçman Apt No: 335/8, Şişli

Professional Relocation Services (PRS): Tel: 0212-351 3344, www.relocation-turkey.com

Solutions Consultancy International Ltd.: Tel: 0212-327 1272, www.solutions-int.com, Hüsrev Gerede Cad., Ful Palas No: 39/1 Daire:2, Teşvikiye

YKC/Bosphorus Relocation: Tel: 0212-352 6162, www.expatsturkey.com, Zeytinoğlu Caddesi, Sarı Konaklar İş Merkezi 8, A Blok, Daire:2, Akatlar

APPENDIX XVIII:
CEMETERIES AND UNDERTAKERS

FOREIGN CEMETERIES
Istanbul
Tayyarea Fehmi Sokak No: 3/1, Pangaltı

UNDERTAKERS (CENAZE LEVAZIMATÇISI)
Istanbul
Roman Catholics should phone 0212-248 0797 for assistance. Protestants should try 0212-219 2283.

Angelidis: Tel: 0212-244 1852, Asmalımescit, Emir Nevhiz Sokak No: 18, Beyoğlu

Berç Kaç: Tel: 212-252 8555/0216-351 4233 (winter/summer), İstiklal Caddesi No: 164, Tokatlıyan İş Hanı, Beyoğlu

Collaro: Tel: 0212-245 4145, Balıkpazarı, Duduodalar Sokak No: 4, Beyoğlu

Manuk Çapan: Tel: 0212-293 9901/0216-381 4179 (winter/summer), Ana Çeşme Sokak
No: 4/2, Taksim

APPENDIX XIX:
INTERNET CAFES AND USEFUL WEBSITES

If you can't get a phone line connected to your house, you won't need to worry about not having access to the web as Turkey has Internet cafes on almost every street corner.

In the past the government has waged sporadic war on them, fearing that adults would read separatist propaganda while children might be exposed to pornography. In the more relaxed atmosphere currently prevailing in Turkey it's hard to see the café owners being bothered again. However, sensitive souls should bear in mind that Internet cafes with a largely local clientele tend to be used only by game-playing boys and men in search of porn. It's not pleasant to be assailed with hard-core images as you try to check your emails, so stick to 'touristy' Internet cafes wherever possible.

WIRELESS INTERNET ACCESS

It would be unrealistic to expect Turkey to have wireless Internet access on tap everywhere. However, such is the speed of change that there are already many venues in Istanbul (especially the big shopping malls) that are geared up for those with laptops and no wires.

LOGGING ON			
password	*şifre/parola*	forward	*ileri*
user name	*kullanıcı adı*	erase	*sil*
home page	*anasayfa*	link/connection	*bağlan(tı)*
site map	*site haritası*	log on	*oturum açmak*
contacts/ communications	*iletişim*	log off	*oturum kapatmak*
information	*bilgi*	to click on	*tıkırdamak*
FAQs	*sık sorulan sorular*	to download	*yüklemek*
search	*ara*	left click	*sola tıkla*
useful sites	*faydalı siteler*	right click	*sağa tıkla*
back	*geri*	memory card	*hafıza kartı*
pages from Turkey (restrict your Google searches by getting rid of the pages about Thanksgiving turkeys!)	*Türkiye'den sayfalar*		

RECOMMENDED WEBSITES

Expat Sites

- www.calis-beach.co.uk/forum. Information exchange for Çalış residents.
- www.expatfocus.com. Information for expats living in Turkey, with several discussion forums.
- www.expatindex.com. Expatriate resource centre aimed at British people.
- www.expatinturkey.com. Forum for expats to exchange information, with a section for selling cars, electrical goods etc.
- www.mymerhaba.com. Excellent source of information of interest to expats in English and French.

TRAVEL SITES:

- www.hemenbilet.com. Website of SDC travel agency, with cheap tickets
- www.neredennereye.com. Public transport information.
- www.turkeytravelplanner.com. Aladdin's cave of information on all aspects of travel to Turkey created by Tom Brosnahan, original author of *Lonely Planet Turkey*.
- www.ido.com.tr. Istanbul Deniz Otobüsleri (Istanbul seabus company) ferry timetables.
- www.tcdd.gov.tr. Website of Turkish Railways with timetables and booking facility. In Turkish only.
- www.turkishportal.com. Cheap deals on flights between the USA and Turkey.

General Sites:

- www.atu.com.tr. Shop for duty-free goods from the airport and let someone bring your shopping to you.
- www.ebay.com. Source hard-to-find-in-Turkey items.
- www.istanbul.com. Official city guide with information about festivals, concerts etc.
- www.meteor.gov.tr. Turkish state meteorological service with weather forecasts in English.
- www.ttrehber.gov.tr. Türk Telekom Yellow Pages-style website
- www.turkishpress.com/turkishpress. Summary of news from a range of newspapers.
- www.ykc.com.tr. Private 'Yellow Pages' for Turkey.

LAYOUT OF TURKISH KEYBOARD

If you are using a Turkish keyboard it is possible to change it so that the letters are in the same position as on a more familiar Western one. However, when you do this the punctuation will all end up in a different place. The only way to get to grips with this is to work your way along the keys finding out where the comma, full stop etc have moved to.

APPENDIX XX:
TOUR OPERATORS FEATURING TURKEY

Turkey

Fez Travel: Tel: 0212-516 9024, www.fezbus.com, Akbıyık Caddesi No: 15, Sultanahmet, Istanbul. Operates hop-on, hop-off bus service round Turkey plus more conventional tours. Employs 'offsiders' as group escorts. Some vacancies every year but not well paid.

Pacha International: Tel: 0212-264 0300, www.pachaint.com, Yeni Sülün Caddesi, Figen Sokak No: 5, Levent, Istanbul

UK

Anatolian Sky: Tel: 08708-504040, www.anatolian-sky.co.uk, 81 Warwick Rd, Solihull, West Midlands B92 7HP

Elixir Holidays: Tel: 0207-722 2288, www.elixirholidays.com, 51 Charlbert St, St John's Wood, London NW8 6JN

Exodus: Tel: 0870-240 5550, www.exodus.co.uk, Grange Mills, Weir Rd, London SW12 0NE

Explore: Tel: 01252-760020, www.exploreworldwide.com/worldwide/tourleaders, 1 Frederick St, Aldershot, Hants GU11 1LQ

First Choice: Tel: 0870-750 1204, www.firstchoice4jobs.co.uk, HR Direct, Jetset House, Lowfield Heath, Crawley, West Sussex RH11 0PQ

Imaginative Traveller: Tel: 0800-316 2717, www.imaginative-traveller.com, 1 Betts Avenue, Martlesham Heath, Suffolk IP5 7RH

Intrepid: Tel: 0207-554 6170, www.intrepidtravel.com, 76 Upper St, Islington, London N1 0NU

My Travel: Tel: 0870-238 7701, www.mytravelcareers.co.uk, Holiday House, Sandbrook Park, Sandbrook Way, Rochdale OL11 1SA

Savile: Tel: 0207-242 8488, www.saviletours.com, 8 Southampton Park, London WC1A 2EA

Sunvil: Tel: 0208-568 4499, www.sunvil.co.uk, Sunvil House, Upper Square, Old Isleworth, Middlesex TW7 7BJ

Tapestry: Tel: 0208-235 7500, www.tapestryholidays.com, The Glassmills, 322B King St, London W6 0AX

Thomson/Tui: Fax: 0207-387 8733, www.thomson.co.uk, Human Resources Overseas, Thomson Holidays Ltd, Greater London House, Hampstead Rd, London NW1 7SD

Australia

Intrepid: Tel: 1300-360 887, Fax: www.intrepidtravel.com, 11 Spring St, Fitzroy, Victoria

Peregrine Adventures: Tel: 1300-854 444, www.peregrine-adventures.com, 258 Lonsdale St, Melbourne

APPENDIX XXI:

FOREIGN EMBASSIES (*ELÇİLİKLER*) AND CONSULATES (*KONSOLOSLUKLAR*) IN TURKEY

REGISTERING WITH YOUR EMBASSY/CONSULATE

Foreigners who are living in Turkey are normally advised to register their contact details with their Embassy or Consulate. The intention behind this is that in the event of an emergency (terrorism, earthquake etc) the authorities will be able to get in touch with their citizens and advise them on what to do. Embassies and consulates vary in how helpful they are in such circumstances - the New Zealand Embassy has a particularly good record for looking after the interests of its citizens but others are less proactive.

It is up to you whether you choose to follow this advice. Some expats prefer to keep the authorities as far away as possible from their lives. But it's worth remembering that the embassies and consulates often stock up-to-date newspapers and have useful information about reliable doctors, dentists, lawyers and other services.

Visiting Your Embassy/Consulate: Unfortunately world events have conspired to make embassies and consulates far less accessible than they used to be. You should expect to have to submit to stringent security checks before you will be allowed in - be sure to have your ID with you - and some embassies (including the UK one) will no longer allow you to take any bags inside the building. You will have to park some distance away from the UK and other embassies. In many cases you will not be allowed in without an appointment and anyone you bring with you will be expected to wait outside.

Phoning Your Embassy/Consulate: If the idea of visiting your embassy is offputting, it is not always much easier trying to get in touch by phone. Most embassies and consulates have automated telephone systems that result in long holds - one has 22 options to select from and none of them is 'speak to an operator'!

WHAT IT MEANS	
consul-general	*başkonsolos*
ambassador	*elçi*
honorary consul	*fahri konsol*
representative	*temsilci*

Afghanistan (*Afganistan*)

Embassy: Tel: 0312-442 2523, Cinnah Caddesi No: 88, Çankaya, Ankara

Albania (*Arnavutluk*)

Embassy: Tel: 0312-441 6103, Ebuziya Tevfik Sokak No: 17, Çankaya, Ankara; **Consulate:** Tel: 0212-244 3256, Deniz Apt: 6, Gümüşsuyu Caddesi No: 30, Beyoğlu, Istanbul

Algeria (Cezayir)
Embassy: Tel: 0312-468 7719, Şehit Ersan Caddesi No: 42, Çankaya, Ankara

Argentina (Arjantin)
Embassy: Tel: 0312-446 2062, Uğur Mumcu Caddesi No: 60/1, Gaziosmanpaşa, Ankara

Australia (Avustralya)
Embassy: Tel 0312-459 9550, www.embaustralia.org.tr, Uğur Mumcu Caddesi No: 88, MNG Building, Kat: 7, Gaziosmanpaşa, Ankara; *Consulate:* Tel: 0212-243 1333, Asker Ocaği Caddesi No: 15, Elmadağ, Şişli, Istanbul

Austria (Avusturya)
Embassy: Tel: 0312-419 0431, Atatürk Bulvarı No: 189, Kavaklıdere, Ankara; *Consulate:* Tel: 0212-262 9315, Köybaşı Caddesi No: 45, Yeniköy, Istanbul; *Consulate:* Tel: 0232-425 4564, Şehit Fethi Bey Caddesi No: 41/705, Pasaport, Izmir; *Honorary Consulate:* Tel: 0242-345 1800, Namık Kemal Bulvarı No: 82, Antalya

Azerbaijan (Azerbaycan)
Embassy: Tel: 0312-491 1681, Cemal Nadir Sokak No: 20, Çankaya, Ankara; *Consulate:* Tel: 0212-293 2123, Sümbül Sokak No: 17, 1.Levent, Istanbul

Bangladesh (Bangladeş)
Embassy: Tel: 0312 -439 2750, Cinnah Caddesi No: 78/7-10, Çankaya, Ankara

Belarus (Belarus)
Embassy: Tel: 0312-446 3042, Reşit Galip Caddesi, Han Sokak No: 13/2, Gaziosmanpaşa, Ankara

Belgium (Belçika)
Embassy: Tel: 0312-446 8247, Mahatma Gandi Caddesi No: 55, Gaziosmanpaşa, Ankara; *Consulate:* Tel: 0212- 243 3300, Sıraselviler Caddesi No: 73, Taksim, Istanbul; *Honorary Consulate:* Tel: 0232-483 7073, 1374 Sokak No: 18, Kat: 4, Selvili İş Merkezi, Pasaport, Izmir; *Honorary Consulate:* Tel: 0242-244 6853, Işıklar Caddesi No: 21/1, Antalya

Bosnia & Herzegovina (Bosna Hersek)
Embassy: Tel: 0312-427 3602, Turan Emeksiz Sokak Nos: 3-9, Park Sitesi, B Blok, Gaziosmanpaşa, Ankara; *Consulate:* Tel: 0212-245 1616, Beyaz Karanfil Sokak No: 45, 3.Levent, Istanbul

Brazil (Brezilya)
Embassy: Tel: 0312-448 1840, Reşit Galip Caddesi, İlk Adım Sokak No: 1, Gaziosmanpaşa, Ankara; *Honorary Consulate:* Tel: 0212-252 8772, Bankalar Caddesi Nos: 31-33, İstanbul

Bulgaria (Bulgaristan)

Embassy: Tel: 0312-426 2071, Fax: 0312-427 3178, Atatürk Bulvarı No: 124, Kavaklıdere, Ankara; **Consulate:** Tel: 0212-281 0114, Fax: 0212-264 1011, Zincirlikuyu Caddesi No: 44, Ulus, Levent, Istanbul ; **Consulate:** Tel/Fax: 0284-225 1069, Talat Paşa Caddesi No: 31, Edirne

Canada (Kanada)

Embassy: Tel: 0312-409 2700, Fax: 0312-409 2810, Cinnah Caddesi No: 58, Cankaya, Ankara; **Consulate:** Tel: 0212-272 5174, Fax: 0212-272 3437, Büyükdere Caddesi No:107/3, Bengun Han, Kat: 3, Gayrettepe, Istanbul

Chile (Şili)

Embassy: Tel: 0312-447 3418, Reşit Galip Caddesi, Hirfanlı Sokak No:14/1-3, Gaziosmanpaşa, Ankara; **Honorary Consulate:** Tel: 0212-272 5790, Bestekar Şevki Bey Sokak No: 30, Balmumcu, Istanbul

China (Çin)

Embassy: Tel: 0312-436 0628, Gölgeli Sokak No: 34, Gaziosmanpaşa, Ankara; **Consulate:** Tel: 0212-299 2631, Memduh Paşa Yalısı, Mısırlı Caddesi No: 6/8, Kireçburnu, Istanbul

Colombia (Kolombya)

Honorary Consulate: Tel: 0212-279 9828, Aytar Caddesi No:20/17, Levent, Istanbul

Croatia (Hirvatistan)

Embassy: Tel: 0312-446 9460, Kelebek Sokak No: 15/A, Gaziosmanpaşa, Ankara

Cuba (Küba)

Embassy: Tel: 0312-442 8970, Solen Sokak No: 8, Çankaya, Ankara

Czech Republic (Çek Cumhuriyeti)

Embassy: Tel: 0312-405 6139, Kaptanpaşa Sokak No: 15, Gaziosmanpaşa, Ankara; **Consulate:** Tel: 0212-230 9597, Abdi İpekçi No: 71, Maçka, Istanbul; **Honorary Consulate:** Tel: 0232-371 5150, Manas Bulvarı No: 72, Salhane, Izmir

Denmark (Danimarka)

Embassy: Tel: 0312-4446 6141, Mahatma Gandi Caddesi No: 74, Gaziosmanpaşa, Ankara; **Consulate:** Tel: 0212-359 1900, Bilezik Sokak No: 2, Fındıklı, Istanbul; **Honorary Consulate:** Tel: 0242-241 1069, Konyaaltı Caddesi No: 19/A, Antalya; **Honorary Consulate:** Tel: 0232-489 5401, Akdeniz Caddesi No:1/702, Pasaport, Izmir

Egypt (Mısır)

Embassy: Tel: 0312-426 1026, Atatürk Bulvarı No: 126, Kavaklıdere, Ankara; **Consulate:** Tel: 0212-263 6038, Konaklar Mahallesi, Akasyalı Sokak No: 26, 4.Levent, Istanbul

Estonia (Estonya)
Consulate: Tel: 0212-211-3480, Kosehıttler Caddesi No: 39, Zincirlikuyu, Istanbul

Finland (Finlandiya)
Embassy: Tel: 0312-426 1930, Kader Sokak No: 44, Gaziosmanpaşa, Ankara; *Consulate:* Tel: 0212-283 5737, Yeni Cami Sokak No: 5, Seyrantepe, Istanbul; *Honorary Consulate:* Tel: 0232-259 8845, 814 Sokak No: 30, Balçova, Izmir

France (Fransa)
Embassy: Tel: 0312-455 4545, Paris Caddesi No: 70, Kavaklıdere, Ankara; *Consulate:* Tel: 0212-334 8730, İstiklal Caddesi No: 8, Taksim, Istanbul; *Honorary Consulate:* Tel: 0232-421 4234, Cumhuriyet Bulvari No: 153, Alsancak, Izmir

Georgia (Gürcistan)
Embassy: Tel: 0312-442 6508, Hilal Mahallesi, 7.Cadde No: 31, Yıldız, Çankaya, Ankara; *Consulate:* Tel: 0462-326 2226, Fax: 0462-326 2296, Gazipaşa Caddesi No: 20, Trabzon

Germany (Almanya)
Embassy: Tel: 0312-455 5100, Atatürk Bulvarı No: 114, Kavaklıdere, Ankara; *Consulate:* Tel: 0212-455 5100, İnönü Caddesi No: 16/18, Taksim, Istanbul; *Consulate:* Tel: 0232-421 6995, Atatürk Caddesi No: 260, Alsancak, Izmir; *Honorary Consulate:* Tel: 0242-322 9466, Yeşilbahçe Mahallesi, 1447 Sokak No: 5/14, Antalya

Greece (Yunanistan)
Embassy: Tel: 0312-436 8860, Fax: 0312-446 3191, Ziya Ül-Rahman (Karagöz) Caddesi Nos: 9-11, Gaziosmanpaşa, Ankara; *Consulate:* Tel: 0212-245 0596, Turnacıbaşı Sokak No: 32, Galatasaray, Istanbul; *Consulate:* Tel: 0232-421 6992, Atatürk Caddesi No: 262, Alsancak, Izmir; *Consulate:* Tel: 0284-235 5804, Fax: 0284-235 5808, Koca Sinan Mahallesi, 2.Sokak No: 13, Edirne

Hungary (Macaristan)
Embassy: Tel: 0312-442 2273, Sancak M Kahire Caddesi No: 30, Çankaya, Ankara; *Consulate:* Tel: 0212-225 5501, Prof. Dr. Müfide Küley Sokak No: 35, Teşvikiye, Istanbul; *Honorary Consulate:* Tel: 0232-421 2861, Atatürk Bulvarı, Tereste Apt: 222/5, Alsancak, Izmir

India (Hindistan)
Embassy: Tel: 0312-438 2195, Cinnah Caddesi No: 77/A, Çankaya, Ankara; *Consulate:* Tel: 0212-296 2131, Cumhuriyet Caddesi No: 18, Elmadağ, Istanbul; *Honorary Consulate:* Tel: 0232-461 4660, Anadolu Caddesi No: 39, Alsancak, Izmir

Indonesia (Endonezya)
Embassy: Tel: 0312-438 2190, Abdullah Cevdet Sokak No: 10, Çankaya, Ankara

Iran (İran)
Embassy: Tel: 0312-468 2821, Fax: 0312-468 2823, Tahran Caddesi No: 10, Kavaklıdere, Ankara; *Consulate:* Tel: 0212-513 8230, Fax: 0212-511 5219, Ankara Caddesi No: 1/2, Çağaloğlu, Istanbul; *Consulate:* Tel: 0442-315 4883, Fax: 0442-316 1182, off Atatürk Bulvarı, Erzurum

Iraq (Irak)
Embassy: Tel: 0312-468 7421, Turan Emeksiz Sokak No: 11, Gaziosmanpaşa, Ankara

Ireland (İrlanda)
Embassy: Tel: 0312-446 6172, Uğur Mumcu Caddesi, MNG Binası, B Blok, Kat: 3, Gaziosmanpaşa, Ankara; *Honorary Consulate:* Tel: 0212-259 6979, Acısu Sokak No: 5/4, Maçka, Istanbul

Israel (İsrail)
Embassy: Tel: 0312-446 3605, Mahatma Gandi Caddesi No: 85, Gaziosmanpaşa, Ankara; *Consulate:* Tel: 0212-317 6500, Büyükdere Caddesi, Yapı Kredi Plaza C Blok, Kat: 7, 4.Levent, Istanbul

Italy (İtalya)
Embassy: Tel: 0312-426 5460, Atatürk Bulvarı No: 118, Kavaklıdere, Ankara; *Consulate:* Tel: 0212-243 1024, Fax: 0212-252 5879, Tom Tom Kaptan Sokak No: 15, Beyoğlu, Istanbul; *Honorary Consulate:* Tel: 0232-463 6676, Cumhuriyet Meydanı, Cumhuriyet Apt: 12/3, Alsancak, Izmir

Japan (Japonya)
Embassy: Tel: 0312-446 0500, Refik Galip Caddesi No: 81, Gaziosmanpaşa, Ankara; *Consulate:* Tel: 0212-317 4600, Büyükdere Caddesi, Tekfen Kule, Kat: 10, 4.Levent, Istanbul

Jordan (Ürdün)
Embassy: Tel: 0312-440 2054, Mesnevi Dede Korkut Sokak No: 18, Çankaya, Ankara

Kazakhstan (Kazakistan)
Embassy: Tel: 0312-491 9100, Oran Sitesi, Kılıç Ali Sokak, Çankaya, Ankara

Korea (Kore)
Embassy: Tel: 0312-468 4821, Alaçam Sokak No: 5, Çankaya, Ankara

Kuwait (Kuveyt)
Embassy: Tel: 0312-445 0576, Reşit Galip Caddesi, Kelebek Sokak No: 110, Gaziosmanpaşa, Ankara

Kyrgyzstan (Kırgızistan)
Embassy: Tel: 0312-491 3506, Turan Güneş Bulvarı, 15.Cadde No: 23, Yıldız, Ankara

Lebanon (Lübnan)
Embassy: Tel: 0312-446 7485, Kizkulesi Sokak No: 44, Gaziosmanpaşa, Ankara;
Consulate: Tel: 0212-236 1365, Teşvikiye Caddesi No: 134/1, Teşvikiye, İstanbul

Libya (Libya)
Embassy: Tel: 0312-438 1110, Cinnah Caddesi No: 60, Çankaya, Ankara; **Consulate:** Tel:
0212-251 8100, Miralay Şefik Bey Sokak No: 3, Gümüşsuyu, İstanbul

Lithuania (Litvanya)
Embassy: Tel: 0312-447 0766, Mahatma Gandi Caddesi No: 17/8-9, Gaziosmanpaşa,
Ankara

Luxembourg (Lüksemburg)
Honorary Consulate: Tel: 0232-480 7073, 1374 Sokak No: 18, Kat: 4, Selvili İş Merkezi,
Pasaport, İzmir

Macedonia (Makedonya)
Embassy: Tel: 0312-446 9204, Filistin Sokak No: 30/2, Gaziosmanpaşa, Ankara; **Con-
sulate:** Tel 0212-251 2233, Üçler Apt, Kat: 3, Gümüşsuyu Caddesi No: 20, Beyoğlu,
İstanbul

Malaysia (Malezya)
Embassy: Tel: 0312-446 3547, Mahatma Gandi Caddesi No: 58, Gaziosmanpaşa, Ankara

Mexico (Meksika)
Embassy: Tel: 0312-442 3003, Kırkpınar Sokak No: 18/6, Çankaya, Ankara; **Consulate:**
Tel: 0212-227 3500, Teşvikiye Caddesi No: 107/2, Teşvikiye, İstanbul

Moldova (Moldova)
Embassy: Tel: 0312-446 5527, Kaptanpaşa Sokak No: 49, Gaziosmanpaşa, Ankara

Monaco (Monako)
Consulate: Tel: 0212-263 3989, Cevdetpaşa Caddesi No: 164/17, Bebek, İstanbul

Mongolia (Moğolistan)
Embassy: Tel: 0312-446 7977, Kaza Sokak No: 109/1, Gaziosmanpaşa, Ankara

Morocco (Fas)
Embassy: Tel: 0312-437 6020, Rabat Sokak No: 11, Gaziosmanpaşa, Ankara

Netherlands (Hollanda)
Embassy: Tel: 0312-409 1800, Fax: 0312-409 1898, Turan Güneş Bulvarı, 7.Cadde 3,
Yıldız, Ankara; **Consulate:** Tel: 0212-393 2121, İstiklal Caddesi No: 393, Tünel, İstan-
bul; **Honorary Consulate:** Tel: 0232-463 4960, H. Ziya Bulvarı No: 42, Kat: 6, Kayha
İşhanı, Alsancak, İzmir

New Zealand (Yeni Zelanda)
Embassy: Tel: 0312-467 9056, Fax: 0312-467 9013, Kat: 4, İran Caddesi No: 13, Kavaklıdere, Ankara; **Consulate:** Tel: 0212-244 0272, Fax: 0212-251 4004, İnönü Caddesi No: 92/3, Istanbul

Northern Cyprus (Kuzey Kıbrıs/KKTC)
Embassy: Tel: 0312-446 0185, Fax: 0312 446 5238, Rabat Sokak No: 20, Gaziosmanpaşa, Ankara; **Consulate:** Tel: 0212-227 3490, Fax: 0212-227 3493, Emirhan Caddesi, Yeni Gelin Sokak No: 24, Balmumcu, Istanbul; **Consulate:** Tel: 0324-237 2482, corner of Silifke & Atatürk caddesis, Mersin

Norway (Norveç)
Embassy: Tel: 0312-447 8690, Kırkpınar Sokak No: 20, Gaziosmanpaşa, Ankara; **Honorary Consulate:** Tel: 0212-249 9753, Bilezik Sokak No: 2, Fındıklı, Istanbul; **Honorary Consulate:** Tel: 0242-259 0083, Akdeniz Caddesi No: 528/11, Antalya; **Honorary Consulate:** Tel: 0232-421 9280, 1378 Sokak No: 4/1, Kordon İşhanı, Kat: 2/201, Alsancak, Izmir

Oman (Oman)
Embassy: Tel: 0312-447 0630, Mahatma Gandi Caddesi No: 63, Gaziosmanpaşa, Ankara

Pakistan (Pakistan)
Embassy: Tel: 0312-427 1419, İran Caddesi No: 37, Gaziosmanpaşa, Ankara; **Consulate:** Tel: 0212-233 5801, Abide-i Hürriyet Caddesi No: 11, Şişli, Istanbul

Palestine (Filistin)
Embassy: Tel: 0312-426 0823, Filistin Sokak No: 45, Gaziosmanpaşa, Ankara

Peru (Peru)
Consulate: Tel: 0212-279 0750, Soğut Sokak, Meltem Apt: A/14, Levent, Istanbul

Philippines (Filipinler)
Embassy: Tel: 0312-446 5831, Mahatma Gandi Caddesi No: 56, Gaziosmanpaşa, Ankara

Poland (Polonya)
Embassy: Tel: 0312-467 5619, Atatürk Bulvarı No: 241, Kavaklıdere, Ankara; **Consulate:** Tel: 0212-290 6630, Giz 2000 Plaza, Ayazağa, Maslak, Istanbul

Portugal (Portekiz)
Embassy: Tel: 0312-446 1890, Kuleli Sokak No: 26, Gaziosmanpaşa, Ankara; **Honorary Consulate:** Tel: 0212-251 9118, Meclisi Mebusan Caddesi No: 157, Kat: 5, Fındıklı, Istanbul

Qatar (Katar)
Embassy: Tel: 0312-490 7224, Baku Sokak No: 6, Oran, Ankara

Romania (Romanya)
Embassy: Tel: 0312-446 3706, Bukres Sokak No: 4, Çankaya, Ankara; *Consulate:* Tel: 0212-292 4125, Sıraselviler Caddesi No: 55, Taksim, Istanbul; *Honorary Consulate:* Tel: 0232-464 1557, Kemelpaşa Caddesi No: 12, Pınarbaşı, Izmir

Russia (Rusya)
Embassy: Tel: 0312-439 2122, Karyağdı Sokak No: 5, Çankaya, Ankara

Saudi Arabia (Suudi Arabistan)
Embassy: Tel: 0312-468 5540, Turan Emeksiz Sokak No: 6, Gaziosmanpaşa, Ankara; *Consulate:* Tel: 0212-281 9140, Akasyalı Sokak No: 6, 4.Levent, Istanbul

Serbia (Sırbistan)
Embassy: Tel: 0312-426 0236, Paris Caddesi No: 47, Kavaklıdere, Ankara; Tel: 0212-248 1004, Valikonağı Caddesi No: 96/A, Nişantaşı, Istanbul

Singapore (Singapur)
Consulate: Tel: 0216-358 0133, Kazım Özalp Sokak, Ethem Bey Apt, Kat: 3, Şaşkınbakkal, Istanbul

Slovak Republic (Slovak Cumhuriyeti)
Embassy: Tel: 0312-467 5075, Atatürk Bulvarı No: 245, Kavaklıdere, Ankara; *Consulate:* Tel: 0212-317 9431, Akasya Sokak No: 1, 1.Levent, Istanbul

Slovenia (Slovenya)
Embassy: Tel: 0312-446 5904, Küpe Sokak No: 1/3, Gaziosmanpaşa, Ankara

South Africa (Güney Afrika)
Embassy: Tel: 0312-446 4056, Filistin Sokak No: 27, Gaziosmanpaşa, Ankara; *Honorary Consulate:* Tel: 0232-376 8445, Atatürk Organize Sanayı Bölgesi, 1008 Sokak No:1, Cigili, Izmir

Spain (İspanya)
Embassy: Tel: 0312-438 0392, Abdullah Cevdet Sokak No: 8, Çankaya, Ankara; *Consulate:* Tel: 0212-270 2465, Karanfil Aralığı Sokak No: 9, 1.Levent, Istanbul; *Honorary Consulate:* Tel: 0242-241 7770, Konyaaltı Caddesi No: 24, Kat: 7, Antalya; *Honorary Consulate:* Tel: 0232-489 7936, Cumhuriyet Bulvarı No: 109/703 Bulvar İşhanı, Alsancak, Izmir

Sudan (Sudan)
Embassy: Tel: 0312-441 3884, Sancak Mahallesi, 12.Cadde No: 16, Çankaya, Ankara

Sweden (İsveç)
Embassy: Tel: 0312-455 4100, Katip Celebi Sokak No: 11-17, Kavaklıdere, Ankara; *Consulate:* Tel: 0212-243 5770, İstiklal Caddesi No: 497, Tünel, Istanbul; *Honorary Consulate:* Tel: 0242-312 4660, Metin Kasapoğlu Caddesi No: 42, Antalya; *Honorary Consulate:* Tel: 0232-422 0138, 1378 Sokak No: 4/1, Kat: 2/201, Kordon İşhanı, Alsancak, Izmir

Switzerland (İsviçre)
Embassy: Tel: 0312-467 5555, Atatürk Bulvarı No: 247, Kavaklıdere, Ankara; *Consulate:* Tel: 0212-283 1282, Büyükdere Caddesi No: 173, Levent, Istanbul; *Honorary Consulate:* Tel: 0242-243 1500, Işıklar Caddesi No: 57/B, Antalya; *Honorary Consulate:* Tel: 0232-421 4239, 1380 Sokak No: 2/1, Kat: 4/6, Alsancak, Izmir

Syria (Suriye)
Embassy: Tel: 0312-440 9657, Fax: 0312-438 5609, Sedat Simavi Sokak No: 40, Çankaya, Ankara; *Consulate:* Tel: 0212-232 6721, Fax: 0212-230 2215, Maçka Caddesi No: 59/5, Teşvikiye, Istanbul

Tajikistan (Tacikistan)
Embassy: Tel: 0312-446 1602, Çayhane Caddesi No: 24, Gaziosmanpaşa, Ankara

Thailand (Tayland)
Embassy: Tel: 0312-467 3409, Çankaya Caddesi, Kader Sokak No: 45/3-4, Gaziosmanpaşa, Ankara

Tunisia (Tunus)
Embassy: Tel: 0312-437 7812, Kuleli Sokak No: 12, Gaziosmanpaşa, Ankara

Turkmenistan (Türkmenistan)
Embassy: Tel: 0312-441 7122, Koza Sokak No: 28, Çankaya, Ankara

Ukraine (Ukranya)
Embassy: Tel: 0312-441 5899, Sancak Mahallesi, 206 Sokak No: 17, Çankaya, Ankara

United Arab Emirates (Birleşik Arap Emirlikleri)
Embassy: Tel: 0312-440 1414, Turan Güneş Bulvarı, 15.Cadde No: 290, Sokak 3, Çankaya, Ankara; *Consulate:* Tel: 0212-279 6349, Alt Zeren Sokak, 1.Levent, Istanbul

United Kingdom (Birleşik Krallığı/Büyük Britanya – İngiltere, İskoçya, Gal ve Kuzey İrlanda)
Embassy: ; Tel: 0312-455 3344, Fax: 0312-468 3214, Şehit Ersan Caddesi No: 46/A, Çankaya, Ankara; *Consulate-General:* Tel: 0212-334 6400, Fax: 0212-334 6407, cons-istanbul@fco.gov.uk, Mesrutiyet Caddesi No: 34, Tepebaşı, Beyoğlu, Istanbul

Honorary Consulates: Tel: 0242-244 5313, Gençlik Mahallesi, 1314 Sokak No: 6/8, Antalya; Tel: 0252-317 0093, Kıbrısşehitleri Caddesi No: 401/B, Konacık Mahallesi, Bodrum; Tel: 0252-614 6302, Fax: 0252-614 8494, Atatürk Caddesi No: 8, Fethiye; Tel: 0326-613 0363, Marasel Çakmak Caddesi No: 28/D, İskenderun; Tel: 0232-463 5151, 1442 Sokak No: 49, Alsancak, Izmir; Tel: 0412-6486, Fax: 0412-412 5077, Yeşil Marmaris Travel Agency & Yacht Management Building, Barbaros Caddesi No: 249, Marmaris; Tel: 0324-327 8687, Catoni Maritime Agency, Çakmak Caddesi, 124 Sokak, Tece İş Merkezi, A Blok, Kat: 4, Mersin

United States (Amerika Birleşik Devletleri/ABD)
Embassy: Tel: 0312-455 5555; Fax: 0312-467 0019, Atatürk Bulvarı No: 110, Kavaklıdere, Ankara; **Consulate:** Tel: 0212-335 9000, Fax: 0212-323 2037, Şehit Halil İbrahim Caddesi No: 23, İstinye, Istanbul; **Consulate:** Tel: 0232-441 0072, Kazım Diri Caddesi No: 13/8, Atabey İş Merkezi, Pasaport, Izmir

Uzbekistan (Özbekistan)
Embassy: Tel: 0312-441 3872, Sancak Mahallesi, 211 Sokak No: 3, Yıldız, Çankaya, Ankara

Vatican (Vatikan)
Embassy: Tel: 0312-495 3514, Birlik Mahallesi, 3.Cadde No: 37, Çankaya, Ankara

Venezuela (Venezuella)
Embassy: Tel: 0312-447 8131, Koza Sokak No: 2, Gaziosmanpaşa, Ankara

Vietnam (Vietnam)
Embassy: Tel: 0312-440 2054, Mesnevi Dede Korkut Sokak No: 18, Çankaya, Ankara; Tel: 0212-274 6908, İtri Sokak No: 3/1, Balmumcu, Beşiktaş, Istanbul

Yemen (Yemen)
Embassy: Tel: 0312-446 2637, Fethiye Sokak No: 2, Gaziosmanpaşa, Ankara

TURKISH EMBASSIES AND CONSULATES ABROAD

Australia: Tel: 02-6296 0227; Fax: 02-6239 6592, 60 Mugga Way, Red Hill, ACT 2603
Belgium: Tel: 032-2514 2978, 4 rue Montoyer 1000, Brussels
Canada: Tel: 0613-789 4044; Fax: 0613-789 3442, 197 Wurtemburg St, Ottawa, Ontario KIN 8L9
France: Tel: 33.1.45.24.52.24, Fax: 33.1.45.20.41.91. 16 avenue de Lamballe, Paris 75116
Germany: Tel: 49 30 27 58 50, Fax: 49 30 27 59 09 15, www.tcberlinbe.de, Rungestr. 9, Berlin
Ireland: Tel: 0668 5240, 11 Clyde Road, Ballsbridge, Dublin 4

Italy: Tel: 06-446 9932, Via Palestro 28

Netherlands: Tel: 31-70-360 4912, Jan Evertstraat 15, Den Haag 2514 BS

New Zealand: Tel: 04-472 1290, Fax: 04-472 1277, 15-17 Murphy St, Level 8, Wellington

Spain: Tel: 34-91 319 8064, Fax: 34-91 308 6602, www.tcmadridbe.org/, Rafael Calvo 18, Madrid 28010

UK: Tel: 020-7393 0202; Fax: 020-7393 0066, 43 Belgrave Square, London SW1X 8PA; *Consulate:* Tel: 0207-589 0949, www.turkishconsulate.org.uk, Rutland Lodge, Rutland Gardens, Knightsbridge, London SW7 1BW

USA: Tel: 0202-659 8200; Fax: 0202-659 0744, 1714 Massachusetts Ave NW, Washington, DC 20036

İstiklal Marşı (Independence March)

The Turkish National Anthem was written by Mehmet Akif Ersoy in 1921 and is sung to music composed by Osman Zeki Üngör. It plays a much bigger part in Turkish life than, for example, the British national anthem does and it is still quite normal for people to stop dead in the street if they hear it playing. Most people stand to attention with their hands by their side in respectful silence. If you apply for citizenship you may be required to recite the first two verses of the national anthem.

Korkma, sönmez bu şafaklarda yüzen al sancak;
Sönmeden yurdumum üstünde tüten en son ocak.
O benim milletimin yıldızıdır parlayacak;
O benimdir, o benim milletimindir ancak.

Çatma, kurban olayım çehreni ey nazlı hilal!
Kahraman ırkıma bir gül! Ne bu şiddet bu celal?
Sana olmaz dökülen kanlarımız sonar helal,
Hakkıdır, Hakk'a tapan, milletimin istiklal!

* * *

Never fear! For the crimson flag that proudly waves in these dawns shall never fade
Before the last fiery hearth that is ablaze within my nation burns out.
For it is the star of my nation, and it will forever shine;
It is mine; and solely belongs to my valiant nation.

Frown not, I beseech you, oh thou coy crescent,
But smile upon my heroic race! Why the anger, why the rage?
Our blood we shed for you will not be worthy otherwise;
For freedom is the absolute right of my God-worshipping nation.

Translation of standard Turkish rental contract by Çitlembik Publications

RENTAL CONTRACT

Apartment			
District			
Name of Street and Number of House			
Kind of Property Leased			
Name and Surname of Owner			
Turkish Republic Identity Number of Owner		Tax Number	
Residential Address of Owner			
Name and Surname of Renter			
Turkish Republic Identity Number of Renter		Tax Number	
Residential Address of Renter			
Business Address of Renter			
Rental Payment per Month			
Rental Payment per Year			
Method of Rent Payment			
Period of Rental Agreement			
Beginning of Rental Agreement			
State of rental property			
Use to which the rental property will be put			

Declaration of list of fixtures that have been transferred together with the rental property

According to tax laws:

Merchants, professionals and farmers, will deduct the percentage indicated by the law from their rent payments related to their commercial, professional or agricultural business, and deposit it at the tax office.

Translation of standard Turkish rental contract by Çitlembik Publications

1- The Renter is obliged to use the rental property as if it were his own property, not to cause its deterioration or loss of features, advantages, fame and reputation, and to treat well those living in it, if there are such persons.

2- If the rental property is rented by the Renter partially or in its entirety to a third person and as a result of this its internal subdivisions or ways of utilisation change, or it is damaged or changed in any way, the owner will have the right to rescind the rental contract, but also to make an official request for the ensuing damages, and the Renter will be obliged to compensate for the damage without a court judgement. The fact that the damage has been caused by a third person does not influence the right of the owner to request damages from the first Renter.

3- If the rental property has to be repaired and the third person claims responsibility for it, then the Renter will have to notify the owner. If he does not notify him, he will be responsible for damages.
The Renter is obliged to permit the carrying out of essential repairs. If repairs like changing door hinges, changing window panes, locks and padlocks, or painting work has to be done for the ordinary use of the rental property, the Renter will be able to carry these out without authorisation from the owner, but compensation for their related costs cannot be requested from the owner.

4- The owner is required to pay any taxes and repair expenses, while the cleaning and repair expenses necessary for day to day life have to be paid by the Renter. On this particular point, tradition will be the reference point.

5- The Renter has to relinquish the rental property to the owner in the same conditions in which he received it and according to traditions.
The Renter has to give back also all the fixtures and equipment in the property at the end of the contract period. If the accessories and indivisible parts of the object of the rental and of its fixtures and equipment are lost, or if their value is decreased more than would be expected from normal use, then the Renter will have to compensate their value and if the owner so wishes he will have to put everything back as it was.

6- The Renter will not be responsible for the decreases and changes that have occurred in the object of the lease and the fixtures, if he has used it in accordance with the use established by the rental contract. What is important is that the Renter should have received the rental property in good condition.

7- The Renter cannot prevent people interested in the object of the lease from coming to view the property and to analyze its features, during the last month of the contract.

8- If the rental property is not evacuated, even though the rental contract has expired, the Renter will compensate the owner for damages.

9- Things that are not of a nature that can cause great problems to the health of the Renter or those living with him or to workers, cannot constitute a reason for the Renter to withhold restitution, to annul the contract or to reduce the rent to be paid even if these things appeared after the signing of the contract.

10- All expenses for decorations carried out by the Renter inside and outside the lease object, will be covered in their entirety by the Renter, and at the end of the contract the Renter will have no right to compensation and will have to relinquish the property in its redecorated shape.

11- After having obtained the written authorisation of the owner, the Renter will be able to add systems for water, natural gas and electricity, and if the building does not have a common antenna for TV, to install a private one, but will have to cover all expenses. The cost of this equipment, and the opening costs of a phone if it is among the fixtures, will be covered by the Renter.

Translation of standard Turkish rental contract by Çitlembik Publications

SPECIAL CONDITIONS

1- The Renter accepts and undertakes to follow the flat ownership law in its entirety.

2- The Renter cannot transfer the lease object either partially or in its entirety.

3- The Renter cannot change the property rented without notifying and getting authorisation from the owner.

4- The Renter undertakes to pay the rent in advance every month within the first ..... days of the corresponding month.

5- The Renter accepts and undertakes as of now to increase the rent payment by ...... % at the end of the contract.

6- The Renter will pay for electricity, water, natural gas, heating, expenses concerning the building and the Environmental Cleaning Tax.

7- The Renter will follow in their entirety the instructions given by the management of the building.

8- The Renter agrees to let the owner know with at least a month's advance notice his intention of evacuating the property.

9- The Renter has paid as an advance .... to the owner.

10- The Renter has given as a deposit .... to the owner.

11- The Renter cannot request interest payment or any other benefit for the advance and deposit he has paid to the owner.

12- The Renter cannot deduct repair expenses from the advance and deposit he has paid to the owner.

13- When the Renter evacuates the rented property the owner will deduct from the deposit all the damages wrought by the Renter and all unpaid electricity, water, natural gas and phone bills. The Renter accepts and agrees at the beginning of the contract that he will pay for the difference, if this deposit is not enough to cover these expenses.

14- All expenses and debts from before the beginning of the contract will be covered by the owner.

15- All expenses and debts occurring after the beginning of the contract will be covered by the Renter.

16- The tax related to the object of lease will be paid by the Renter.

17- If the rent is not paid for two consecutive months during the same period, all the rent payments beginning from the month for which rent is not paid become urgent and the Renter accepts in advance that this situation may lead to forced evacuation of the property.

18- The guarantee of the guarantor being in common and consecutive, the guarantor agrees with his signature that the guarantee established during the first rent period will continue.

19- This contract is for .... years. If one of the parties does not notify the other party in writing at least one month before the end of the contract, the contract will be considered to have been automatically extended.

20- The addresses of the parties written in the contract will be considered their official residences. If a change of address is not communicated in writing to the other party, all communications sent to the address in the contract will be considered valid.

This contract is made up of ...... articles, has been compiled in ..... copies, and been given to the interested parties. In case of conflict, the courts and plaintiffs of .... are authorised to deal with it. The owner, Renter and guarantor of the Renter, the signatures of which have been indicated below, have read all the articles of the contract and have signed the contract without having been subjected to any kind of pressure.

GUARANTOR   RENTER   OWNER

Translation of standard Turkish rental contract by Çitlembik Publications

PAYMENTS MADE TO THE OWNER

NTL	Nkr.	Date	Payer	Payee